WRITERS' AND ARTISTS'
YEARBOOK 1987

Writers' & Artists' Yearbook 1987

EIGHTIETH YEAR OF ISSUE

A Directory for writers, artists, playwrights, writers for film, radio and television, photographers and composers

A & C BLACK · LONDON

© 1987 A. & C. BLACK (PUBLISHERS) LTD.
35 BEDFORD ROW, LONDON WC1R 4JH

All rights reserved. No part of this publication may be reproduced, stored in a retrieval system, or transmitted, in any form or by any means, electronic, mechanical, photocopying, recording or otherwise, without the prior permission of A. & C. Black (Publishers) Ltd.

A. & C. Black (Publishers) Ltd has used its best efforts in collecting and preparing material for inclusion in the *Writers' and Artists' Yearbook 1987*. It does not assume, and hereby disclaims any liability to any party for any loss or damage caused by errors or omissions in the *Writers' and Artists' Yearbook 1987,* whether such errors or ommissions result from negligence, accident or any other cause.

Distributed in the United States by
Writer's Digest Books
9933 Alliance Road
Cincinnati 45242
Ohio

British Library Cataloguing in Publication Data

Writers' and artists' yearbook. — 1987
1. Authorship — Periodicals
808'.02'05   PN101
ISBN 0-7136-2836-7

REPRODUCED, PRINTED AND BOUND IN GREAT BRITAIN BY
HAZELL WATSON & VINEY LTD,
MEMBER OF THE BPCC GROUP.
AYLESBURY, BUCKS

CONTENTS

newspapers and magazines

Writing for newspapers, magazines etc. 11
Journals:
   United Kingdom journals and magazines 13
   United Kingdom magazine publishers 85
   African journals and magazines 87
   Australian journals and magazines 89
   Canadian journals and magazines 95
   Indian journals and magazines 97
   Irish journals and magazines 99
   New Zealand journals and magazines 103
   South African journals and magazines 105
   Writing for US journals 108
Syndicates, news and press agencies 109
Poetry Publishing Today: *John Medlin* 116

book publishers

Writing books 122
Publishers:
   United Kingdom publishers 122
   Australian publishers 173
   Canadian publishers 176
   Indian publishers and agents 178
   Irish publishers 182
   New Zealand publishers 184
   Other Commonwealth publishers 186
   South African publishers 188
   United States publishers 190
Book packagers 199 *(cont'd)*

Book clubs   203
International Standard Book Numbering
     (ISBN)   205
Vanity publishing   207

theatre, tv radio, agents

Marketing a play: *Julia Jones*   208
Markets for plays:
  London theatres   212
  Provincial theatres   214
  Touring companies   216
Publishers specialising in the publication of
     plays   217
Markets for screenplays: *Jean McConnell*   218
Screenplays for films: *Jean McConnell*   220
Writing for television: *Bill Craig*   223
Broadcasting:
  BBC national radio and tv   226
  BBC local radio stations   230
  Independent broadcasting   232
  Independent tv   232
  Independent local radio   234
  Australian radio and tv   237
  Canadian radio and tv   238
  Indian radio and tv   238
  Irish radio and tv   238
  New Zealand radio and tv   239
  South African radio and tv   239
  United States broadcasting   240
Literary agents:
  United Kingdom   241
  United States   254
  Others   259
Agents specialising in plays, films, tv and
   radio   263
Character merchandising   264

art, music
prizes, clubs

Opportunities for freelance artists: *Camilla Bryden-Brown* 265
Artists' and designers' Code of Professional Conduct 269
Markets for artists 271
Art agents and commercial art studios 271
Firms prepared to consider drawings, designs and verses for cards etc. 273
Markets for photographers 275
Firms prepared to consider photographs for calendars, greetings cards etc 275
The freelance photographer and agent: *Bruce Coleman* 277
Photographic agencies and picture libraries 278
Picture research: *Judith Harries* 292
Music publishers:
  United Kingdom 298
  US and others 302
Mechanical Copyright Protection Society Ltd 304
Performing Right Society Ltd 304
Literary prizes 306
Societies and clubs 326

copyright
tax, services

British copyright: *E. P. Skone James* 357
US copyright: *Gavin McFarlane* 376
Subsidiary rights: *E. P. Skone James* 384
Libel and criminal liability in libel: *James Evans* and *Antony Whitaker* 388
Income Tax for writers and artists: *Peter Vaines* 395
Social Security contributions: *J. Philip Hardman* 405
Social Security benefits: *K. D. Bartlett* 413
Publishers' agreements 420   *(cont'd)*

Florence Agreement   421
Net Book Agreement   422
Society of Authors   423
Writers' Guild of Great Britain   426
Authors' Lending and Copyright Society Ltd   429
Public Lending Right in the UK:
   John Sumsion   431
Books, research and reference sources for writers:
   Margaret Payne   449
Journalists' calendar 1987   438
Preparation of typescripts   457
Word processing: A beginner's guide for authors:
   Louis Alexander   462
Correcting proofs   470
Editorial, literary and production services   481
Indexing   490
Translation   490
Government offices and public services   492
Journals:
   recent changes   498
   ceased publication   498
   classified index   499
Press-cutting agencies   510

Index   512

preface

This year, as in every previous year, the *Writers' and Artists' Yearbook* has been thoroughly revised and updated. The market sections, giving details of journals and publishers, have been checked by referring each entry to the relevant editor or publishing house. All addresses, requirements, rates of payment and other details were therefore up-to-date at the time of going to press. Similarly, all the many other features of the book have been carefully revised — for the benefit of contributors to newspapers or magazines, of writers of books, of freelance artists, designers and photographers, and of those whose aim is to find a market in the theatre or films, radio or television. As well as the many existing detailed articles in the *Yearbook,* this edition includes a new article on books, research and reference sources for writers, by Margaret Payne A.L.A.

From time to time we receive comments on the fact that some of the firms listed do not appear to offer a significant market to the writer and artist. Our difficulty here is that although the directory sections are first and foremost market sections, the *Yearbook* is also used as a general reference book. We must, therefore, take some account of this when considering new entries.

Vanity publishing Every edition of the *Yearbook* in recent years has contained a strong warning that the author who pays for the publication of his work is almost invariably making an expensive mistake. It has been suggested that several distinguished poets have found it necessary to underwrite their first books in order to establish themselves, and in this respect the cautionary note on "vanity publishing" on page 207 has been mildly modified; but unhappily there is still ample evidence that an emphatic general warning is necessary.

It should be repeated, too, that the publishers of the *Yearbook* cannot provide an advisory service, and that to rely on an out-of-date edition is to invite inevitable difficulties and disappointments.

newspapers and magazines

WRITING FOR NEWSPAPERS, MAGAZINES, ETC.

More than six hundred journals are included in the British Journals section of the *Yearbook,* almost all of them offering opportunities to the writer. Some 200 leading Commonwealth and South African journals are also included, and while some of these have little space for freelance contributions, many of them will always consider outstanding work. Many journals do not appear in our lists because the market they offer for the freelance writer is either too small or too specialised, or both. It is impossible to include all such publications in the *Yearbook,* for the benefit of only a small proportion of its purchasers, without substantially increasing its price. Those who wish to offer contributions to technical, specialist or local journals are likely to know their names and can ascertain their addresses; before submitting a manuscript to any such periodical they are advised to write a preliminary letter to its editor.

Magazine editors frequently complain to us about the unsuitability of many manuscripts submitted to them. Not only are the manuscripts unsuitable, but no postage is sent for their return. In their own interests, writers and others are advised to *enclose postage for the return of unsuitable material.*

Before submitting manuscripts, writers should study carefully the editorial requirements of a magazine; not only for the subjects dealt with, but for the approach, treatment, style and length. Obvious though these comments may be to the practised writer, the beginner would be spared much disappointment if he studied markets more carefully (though he must not expect editors to send him free specimen copies of their magazines). An article or short story suitable for *Woman's Own* is unlikely to appeal to the readers of *The New Statesman.* The importance of studying the market cannot be over-emphasised. It is an editor's job to know what his readers want, and to see that they get it. Thus freelance contributions must be tailored to fit a specific market; subject, theme, treatment, length, etc., must meet the editor's requirements.

A number of magazines and newspapers will accept letters to the editor, paragraphs for gossip columns, and brief filler paragraphs, and will pay for these sums up to £15. For a list of these journals see the Classified Indexes at the end of the *Yearbook.* These Indexes provide only a rough guide to markets and must be used with discrimination. For list of recent journal mergers, changes of title, and terminations, also see end of the *Yearbook.*

A list of British magazine publishers, with their addresses, follows the section on **United Kingdom Journals.**

Writers and artists, and others, are advised not to accept from editors less than a fair price for their work, and to ascertain exactly what rights they are being asked to dispose of when an offer is made.

It has always been our aim to obtain and publish the rates of payment offered for contributions by journals and magazines. Certain journals of the highest standard and reputation are reluctant, for reasons that are understandable, to state a standard rate of payment, since the value of a contrbution may be dependent not upon length but upon the standing of the writer or of the information he has to give. Many journals when giving a rate of payment indicate that it is the "minimum rate", others, in spite of efforts to extract more precise information from them, prefer to state "usual terms" or "by arrangement".

The Society of Authors makes the following additional suggestions when submitting freelance contributions to periodicals.

General points:
1. Keep copies of all material and correspondence and a note of telephone conversations.
2. Confirm any oral arrangements (whether made on the telephone or face-to-face) in writing immediately.
3. Make clear to the editor, in the letter accompanying your MSS or on its cover sheet, what rights you are offering. As a rule, offer only First British Serial Rights.
4. Enclose a stamped addressed envelope for the return of your manuscript.
5. Don't wait for more than five weeks before you ask for a decision or the return of your manuscript, but don't start making enquiries until the editor has had it for a fortnight—unless, of course, it is highly topical material.
6. When your piece is accepted make sure that there is a letter (either from the editor or sent to him) confirming the rate of payment and the probable date of publication. Aim for payment on acceptance even though most magazines will insist on paying on publication. As publication is sometimes considerably delayed, make it clear that you wish to be paid by a specified date even if your article has not been published by then.
7. If you are asked to rewrite your piece as a condition of acceptance, ensure that the request is confirmed in writing and that you will be paid even if the material is not used.

Commissioned articles:
1. Agree the fee or rate of payment at the outset, specify the rights offered, and ask for payment on delivery.
2. If payment is to be made on publication, make it clear that your fee will become due in any event if the article has not been published by a specified date.

Writing for markets outside the UK The lists of overseas journals contain only a selection of those journals which offer some market for the freelance. To print, and to keep up-to-date, a complete list for each English-speaking country would increase the extent and cost of the *Yearbook* quite disproportionately to the value of such enlargement. For the overseas market for stories and articles is small and editors often prefer their fiction to have a local setting.

The larger newspapers and magazines buy many of their stories, as the smaller papers buy general articles, through one or other of the well-known syndicates, and a writer may be well advised to send printed copies of stories he has had published at home to an agent for syndication overseas.

Most of the big newspapers depend for news on their own staffs and the press agencies. The most important papers have permanent representatives in Britain who keep them supplied, not only with news of especial interest to the country concerned, but also with regular summaries of British news and with articles on events of particular importance. While many overseas journals have a London office, it is usual for MSS from freelance contributors to be submitted to the headquarters editorial office overseas.

Would-be contributors to Indian magazines must be prepared for disappointment and not infrequently to hear no more of MSS submitted to publications in that country.

When sending MSS abroad it is important to remember to enclose International Reply Coupons; these can be exchanged in any foreign country for stamps representing the minimum postage payable on a letter sent from that country to this country.

UNITED KINGDOM

A la Carte (1984), Monica Tyson, IPC Magazines, King's Reach Tower, Stamford Street, London SE1 9LS. *T.* 01-261 5615.
£1.75 Bi-M. Articles on food, drink and entertaining. Recipes and food ideas. *Payment:* advantageous rates but only a very high quality of work accepted. *Illustrations:* colour photographs.

Aberdeen Evening Express, Harry L. Roulston, Lang Stracht, Aberdeen, AB9 8AF *T.* (0224) 690222.
18p. D. Lively evening paper reading. *Payment:* by arrangement. *Illustrations:* mainly half-tone.

(Aberdeen) The Press and Journal (1748), Peter Watson, Lang Stracht, Aberdeen, AB9 8AF *T.* (0224) 690222. London Office: Pemberton House (Third Floor), East Harding Street, EC4A 3AS *T.* 01-353 9131.
22p. D. Contributions of Scottish interest. *Payment:* by arrangement. *Illustrations:* half-tone.

Accountancy (1889), Geoffrey Holmes, 40 Bernard Street, London, WC1N 1LD *T.* 01-628 7060.
£1.70. M. Articles on accounting, taxation, financial, legal and other subjects likely to be of professional interest to accountants in practice or industry, and to top management generally. *Payment:* £78 per page. *Illustrations:* half-tone and colour. Cartoons.

Accountant's Magazine, The (1897), official journal of The Institute of Chartered Accountants of Scotland, Winifred N. Elliott, M.A., 27 Queen Street, Edinburgh, EH2 1LA *T.* 031-225 5673. *Telex:* 727530. *Fax:* 031-225 3813.
£1.70 (£17.00 p.a.). M. Articles on accounting, auditing, company law, finance, taxation, topical subjects, management, investment. *Length:* 1000-2500 words. *Payment:* by arrangement. *Illustrations:* line, half-tone, colour.

Achievement, World Trade House, 145 High Street, Sevenoaks, Kent, TN13 1XJ *T.* (0732) 458144.
£1.25. M. Lively articles relating to British business achievements in international project management. *Illustrations:* first-class photographs. *Payment:* by arrangement.

Administrative Accountant (incorporating **Book-keepers Journal**) (1920), Derek Bradley, The Institute of Administrative Accountants, Burford House, 44 London Road, Sevenoaks, Kent TN13 1AJ *T.* 01-657 1247.
£6.00 post paid. Bi-M. Articles on accounting and general business practice. *Length:* 1000-2000 words. *Payment:* by arrangement. *Illustrations:* offset litho.

Administrator (1971), official journal of The Institute of Chartered Secretaries and Administrators, A. Bartleman, Salisbury Publishing Services Ltd., Salisbury Square House, 8 Salisbury Square, London EC4X 8AP *T*. 01-353 1000.
£1.50. M. (£15.75 p.a. post free). Practical and topical articles 750-1600 words (occasionally longer) on law, finance, and personnel-orientated problems and development affecting company secretaries and other senior administrators in business, nationalised industries, local and central government and other institutions in Britain and overseas. Articles on management theory are generally *not* required: most articles commissioned from leading administrators. *Payment:* by arrangement. *Illustrations:* line and half-tone, only by special commission.

Aeromodeller (1935), Geoff Clarke, Argus Specialist Ltd., P.O. Box 35, Hemel Hempstead, Hertfordshire. *T*. (0442) 41221.
£1.85. M. Articles and news concerning model aircraft and radio control of model aircraft. Suitable articles and first-class photographs by outside contributors are always considered. *Length:* 750-2000 words, or by arrangement. *Illustrations:* photographs and line drawings to scale.

Aeroplane Monthly (1973), Richard T. Riding, Business Press International Ltd., Quadrant House, The Quadrant, Sutton, Surrey SM2 5AS *T*. 01-661 3855. *Telex:* 892084.
£1.20. M. Articles relating to historical aviation. *Length:* up to 3000 words. *Illustrations:* half-tone, line, colour. *Payment:* £30 per 1000 words; photographs £5.00 minimum; colour £35 minimum.

African Business (1978), Linda Van Buren, P.O. Box 261, Carlton House, 69 Great Queen Street, London WC2B 5BN *T*. 01-404 4333.
£1.00 M. Articles on business, economic and financial topics of interest to businessmen, ministers, officials concerned with African affairs. *Length:* 400 to 600 words; shorter coverage 100 to 400 words. *Payment:* £50 per 1000 words. *Illustrations:* line, half-tone.

Agenda, William Cookson and Peter Dale, 5 Cranbourne Court, Albert Bridge Road, London, SW11 4PE *T*. 01-228 0700.
£12.00 p.a. (£15 for Libraries and Institutions). Q. Poetry and criticism. *Payment:* £15.00 per poem or per page of poetry. *Illustrations:* half-tone. Contributors should study the journal before submitting MSS with S.A.E.

Air Pictorial, Unit 1, Pontiac Works, Fernbank Road, Ascot, Berks, SL5 8JH *T*. (0344) 884222.
85p. M. Journal with wide aviation coverage. Many articles commissioned, and the Editor is glad to consider competent articles exploring fresh ground or presenting an individual point of view on technical matters. *Payment:* £15.00 per 1000 words. *Illustrations:* half-tones and line; new photographs of unusual or rare aircraft considered.

Albion (1977), Roger Burford Mason, 26 West Hill, Hitchin, Hertfordshire.
£5.00 p.a. 3 p.a. Devoted to the work of the private presses worldwide and to every aspect of the history and practice of letterpress printing and the arts of the book. Contributions always welcome by discussion with the editor. *Payment:* by arrangement. *Illustrations:* line, half-tone.

Amateur Gardening (1884), P. Wood, Westover House, West Quay Road, Poole, Dorset, BH15 1JG *T*. (0202) 671191.
48p. W. Articles up to 700 words about any aspect of gardening. *Payment:* by arrangement. *Illustrations:* half-tone, colour.

UNITED KINGDOM

Amateur Photographer (1884), Barry Monk, Prospect House, 9 – 15 Ewell Road, Cheam, Surrey SM3 8BZ *T.* 01-661 4300.
70p. W. Original articles of pictorial or technical interest, preferably illustrated with either photographs or diagrams. Good instructional features especially sought. *Length preferred:* (unillustrated) 400 to 800 words: articles up to 1500 words; (illustrated) 2 to 4 pages. *Payment:* monthly, at rates according to usage. Illustrations unaccompanied by text will be considered for covers or feature illustrations; please indicate if we can hold on file.

Amateur Stage (1946), Roy Stacey, 1 Hawthorndene Road, Hayes, Bromley, BR2 7DZ *T.* 01-462 6461.
80p. M. Articles on all aspects of the amateur theatre, preferably practical and factual. *Length:* 600-2000 words. *Payment:* minimum of £3.00 per 1000 words. *Illustrations:* photographs and line drawings, *payment* for which varies.

Ambit (1959), Dr. Martin Bax, 17 Priory Gardens, Highgate, London, N6 5QY *T.* 01-340 3566.
£2.00 Q. Poems, short stories, criticism. *Payment:* by arrangement. *Illustrations:* line and half-tone.

Angler's Mail, Roy Westwood (IPC Magazines Ltd.), King's Reach Tower, Stamford Street, London, SE1 9LS *T.* 01-261 5778.
45p. W. Features and news items about sea, coarse and game fishing. *Length:* 650 to 800 words. *Payment:* by arrangement. *Illustrations:* half-tones, colour, line and wash drawings. (Web offset litho printing).

Angling Times (1953), Allan Haines, EMAP, Bretton Court, Bretton, Peterborough, PE3 8DZ *T.* Peterborough (0733) 266222.
38p. W. Articles, pictures, news stories, on all forms of angling. *Illustrations:* colour, half-tone, line.

Anglo-Welsh Review, The (1949), Greg. Hill, College of Further Education, Llanbadarn Fawr, Aberystwyth, Dyfed, SY23 3BP *Publisher:* H. G. Walters (Publishers) Ltd., Knowling Mead, Tenby, Dyfed, SA70 8EE.
£8.50 p.a. Three times a year. Short stories, poetry and articles on literature, the arts, history, having some relation to Wales. Reviews of books with a Welsh connection. *Payment:* by arrangement.

Animal World, Elizabeth Winson, RSPCA, Causeway, Horsham, Sussex, RH12 1HG *T.* Horsham (0403) 64181.
30p. Q. Fiction and factual articles concerning animals and animal welfare. *Length:* 350-1000 words. All MS. must be typewritten. *Readership:* young people between 5 and 17. *Payment:* according to value. *Illustrations:* mainly colour transparencies and black and white photographs.

Annabel (D. C. Thomson & Co., Ltd.), 80 Kingsway East, Dundee, DD4 8SL, and 185 Fleet Street, London EC4A 2HS.
60p. M. Colour gravure monthly for the modern woman with wide interests. Personal experience stories, biographical stories of well-known personalities, family and parenthood topics, fashion, cookery, knitting, fiction. Art *illustrations* and photographs in full colour and black-and-white. *Payment:* on acceptance.

Antique Collector (1930), David Coombs, National Magazine House, 72 Broadwick Street, London W1V 2BP *T.* 01-439 7144.
£1.50. M. Authoritative and fully illustrated information for those interested in extending their knowledge and enjoyment of all aspects of antiques and art. *Illustrations:* fine black and white and colour photographs.

Antique Dealer & Collectors Guide, The, Philip Bartlam, IPC Magazines Ltd., Kings Reach Tower, Stamford Street, London SE1 9LS *T.* 01-261 6894.
£1.50. M. Articles on antique collecting and art. *Length:* up to 2000 words. *Payment:* £68 per 1000 words. *Illustrations:* line, half-tone and colour.

Antiques (1963), Tony Keniston, Old Rectory, Hopton Castle, Craven Arms, Salop, SY7 0QJ *T.* (05474) 356 and 464.
10p. Q. Articles on antiques and of interest to antique dealers and serious collectors. *Length:* 300 to 600 words. *Payment:* £2.00 per 100 words published. *Illustrations:* line and half-tone.

Antiquity, Glyn Daniel, St. John's College, Cambridge CB2 1TP *T.* (0223) 61629 and 356082. Publisher: Heffers Printers Ltd., King's Hedges Road, Cambridge CB4 2PQ *T.* Cambridge 351571.
£5.00. 3 p.a. (£12.00 p.a.). General articles on archaeology of all parts of the world. *Length:* 2000 to 5000 words. *Payment:* 25 free offprints supplied. *Illustrations:* half-tones and line blocks.

Apollo (1925) (Apollo Magazine Ltd.), Editorial: Denys Sutton, 22 Davies Street, London W1Y 1LH *T.* 01-629 3061.
£3.00. M. Knowledgeable articles of about 2500 words on art, ceramics, furniture, armour, glass, sculpture, and any subject connected with art and collecting. *Payment:* by arrangement. *Illustrations:* colour and half-tone.

Aquarist and Pondkeeper, The (1924), John Dawes (The Buckley Press Ltd.), 58 Fleet Street, London EC4Y 1JU *T.* 01-583 4060.
95p. M. Illustrated authoritative articles by professional and amateur biologists, naturalists and aquarium hobbyists on all matters concerning life in and near water. *Length:* about 1500 words. *Payment:* by arrangement. *Illustrations:* photographs, line, colour.

Architects' Journal, The (1895), Peter Carolin, R.I.B.A., 9 Queen Anne's Gate, London SW1H 9BY *T.* 01-222 4333.
£1.00. W. Articles (mainly technical) on architecture, planning and building accepted only with prior agreement of synopsis. *Payment:* by arrangement. *Illustrations:* photographs and drawings.

Architectural Design (1930), Dr. Andreas C. Papadakis, 42 Leinster Gardens, London W2 3AN *T.* 01-402 2141. *Telex:* 896928 Academ G. Subscriptions: 7-8 Holland Street, London W8 *T.* 01-937 6996.
£45.00 p.a. 6 double issues, plus 10 issues of *Art & Design.* International magazine comprising an extensively illustrated thematic profile presenting architecture and critical interpretations of architectural history, theory and practice. *Payment:* by arrangement. *Illustrations:* drawings and photographs, colour, half-tone, line.

Architectural Review (1896), Peter Davey, 9 Queen Anne's Gate, Westminster, London SW1H 9BY *T.* 01-222 4333.
£4.25. M. Contains articles (up to 3000 words in length) on architecture and the allied arts. Must be thoroughly qualified writers. *Payment:* by arrangement. *Illustrations:* photographs, drawings, etc.

Argo (incorporating **Delta**) (1979), Hilary Davies and David Constantine, Old Fire Station, 40 George Street, Oxford OX1 2AQ.
£1.50. (£5.00 p.a.) 3 p.a. Poetry, short stories, translations of poetry, extracts from unpublished novels. S.a.e. essential. No unsolicited reviews. *Payment:* £3.00 per contributor. *Illustrations:* line, half-tone.

Art & Artists (1966), Bernard Denvir, 43b Gloucester Road, Croydon CR0 2DH *T.* 01-689 4258 *Telex:* 298133.
90p. M. Articles on all aspects of the visual arts. *Payment:* by arrangement. *Illustrations:* line, half-tone, colour.

Art & Craft (1946), Eileen Lowcock, Scholastic Publications (Magazines) Ltd., Marlborough House, Holly Walk, Leamington Spa, Warwickshire CV32 4LS *T.* (0926 81) 3910. *Telex:* 312138 Spls G.
£1.10. M. Articles to offer fresh, creative ideas of a practical nature, based on sound art practice, for the infant/junior school teacher and parents. Articles by experts on traditional crafts. *Illustrations:* colour and black-and-white photographs, line drawings. *Payment:* by arrangement.

Art & Design (1985), Dr Andreas C. Papadakis, A. D. Editions Ltd., 42 Leinster Gardens, London W2 3AN *T.* 01-402 2141. *Telex:* 896928 Academ G
£1.95 10 p.a. Feature articles, exhibition reviews/previews, book reviews, product news. *Payment*: by arrangement. *Illustrations*: line, half-tone, colour.

Art Book Review (1982), Eric Shanes, 7 Cumberland Road, London, W3 6EX *T.* 01-992 7985.
£2.50 Q. Articles on art history; book reviews. *Payment:* £5.00 per 100 words. *Illustrations:* colour and half-tone.

Art Magazine, The, Tony Peto, Cricket House, 423 Fulham Road, London SW10 9TX.
90p. Q. Articles, interviews, news shorts, technical features about all aspects of the arts. *Length:* up to 1500 words. *Payment:* by arrangement. *Illustrations:* line, half-tone, colour.

Artist, The (1931), Sally Bulgin, 102 High Street, Tenterden, Kent, TN30 6HT *T.* (05806) 3673.
80p. M. Instructional, technical and topical articles relating to every branch of the fine arts. Articles commissioned are from artists of highest repute. *Length:* 1500 to 2000 words. *Payment:* by arrangement. *Illustrations:* must relate to articles. Line, half-tone, colour, original art work.

Arts Review (1949), Starcity Ltd., 16 St. James Gardens, London W11 4RE *T.* 01-603 7530 and 8533.
£1.40. (£28.00 p.a.) F. Art criticism and reviews. Commissioned work only. *Illustrations:* half-tone and line; colour.

Author, The (1890), Derek Parker, 84 Drayton Gardens, London SW10 9SB *T.* 01-373 6642. *T.A.* Auctoritas, London.
£2.00. Q. Organ of The Society of Authors. Commissioned articles from 1000 to 2000 words on any subject connected with the legal, commercial, or technical side of authorship. *Payment:* by arrangement. (Little scope for the freelance writer: a preliminary letter is advisable.)

Autocar (1895), Matthew Carter, Haymarket Publishing Ltd, 38-42 Hampton Road, Teddington, Middlesex TW11 0JE *T.* 01-977 8787. *Telex:* 8952440.
60p. W. All aspects of cars, motoring and motor industries. Articles, general, practical, competition and technical. *Payment:* varies; mid-month following publication. *Illustrations:* tone, line (litho) and colour. Press day news: Friday.

Back Street Heroes (1983), Steven Myatt, P.O. Box 28, Altrincham, Cheshire, WA15 8SH *T.* 061-928 3480.
£1.20. M. Custom motorcycle features plus informed lifestyle pieces. Biker fiction. *Payment:* by arrangement. *Illustrations:* half-tone, colour. Cartoons.

Balance (1935), Beth Noakes, The British Diabetic Association, 10 Queen Anne Street, London W1M 0BD *T.* 01-323 1531.
60p. Bi-M. Articles on diabetes or related topics. *Length:* 1000-2000 words. *Payment:* £45.00 per 1000 words. *Illustrations:* line, half-tone, colour.

Ballroom Dancing Times (1956), Alex Moore, Editorial Adviser, Mary Clarke, Executive Editor, Clerkenwell House, 45-47 Clerkenwell Green, London EC1R 0BE *T.* 01-250 3006.
50p. M. Dealing with ballroom dancing from every aspect, but chiefly from the serious competitive, teaching and medal test angles. Well informed freelance articles are occasionally used, but only after preliminary arrangements. *Payment:* by arrangement. *Illustrations:* web offset; action photographs preferred.

Banker, The (1926), Colin Jones, 102-8 Clerkenwell Road, London EC1M 5SA *T.* 01-251 9321-7. *Telex:* 23700 Finbi G.
£3.25. M. Articles on economic policy, finance and banking technology, home and overseas, 1500 to 3000 words. Outside contributions are accepted on banking and general economic subjects. *Payment:* by arrangement. *Illustrations:* half-tones of people, charts, tables.

Banking World (1983), Peter Jay, Maxwell House, 74 Worship Street, London EC2A 2EN *T.* 01-377 4824. *Telex:* 888804.
£2.00. M. Commissioned articles on developments in retail banking world wide. *Length:* 200-2000 words. *Payment:* by arrangement. *Illustrations:* line, half-tone.

Baptist Times (1855), Geoffrey Locks, 4 Southampton Row, London WC1B 4AB *T.* 01-405 5516.
25p. W. Religious or social affairs matter, 800 words. *Payment:* by arrangement. *Illustrations:* half-tone.

BBC Wildlife Magazine, Rosamund Kidman Cox, Broadcasting House, Whiteladies Road, Bristol BS8 2LR *T.* (0272) 732211.
£1.10 M. Popular but scientifically accurate articles about wildlife and conservation (national and international), some linked by subject to BBC tv and radio programmes. Two news sections for short, topical biological and environmental stories. *Length:* 1,000-2,000 words. *Payment:* £100 per article. *Illustrations:* top-quality colour and black-and-white photographs.

Beano, The (D. C. Thomson & Co., Ltd.), Courier Place, Dundee, DD1 9QJ, and 185 Fleet Street, London EC4A 2HS.
16p. W. Picture paper for young folk. Comic strip series, 12-22 pictures. *Payment:* on acceptance.

Beano Library (D. C. Thomson & Co. Ltd.), Courier Place, Dundee, DD1 9QJ and 185 Fleet Street, London EC4A 2HS.
24p. 2 per month. Extra-long comic adventure stories featuring well-known characters from the weekly Beano publication.

Bedfordshire Magazine (1947), Betty Chambers, 50 Shefford Road, Meppershall, Shefford, SG17 5LL *T.* Hitchin (0462) 813363.
90p. Q. Articles of Bedfordshire interest, especially history and biography. *Length:* up to 1500 words. *Payment:* £1.05 per 1000 words. *Illustrations:* line and half-tone.

Beezer, The (D. C. Thomson & Co., Ltd.), Courier Place, Dundee DD1 9QJ, and 185 Fleet Street, London EC4A 2HS.

20p. W. Picture paper for children. Stories told in pictures in 14-20 panels per instalment. Also comic strips in series, 6-15 pictures each number. Interest drawings—history, geography, general—suitable for full colour reproduction. *Payment:* on acceptance.

Birmingham Evening Mail (1870), N. K. Whetstone, Colmore Circus, Birmingham B4 6AY *T.* 021-236 3366. *Telex:* 337552. London Office: 19-21 Tudor Street, EC4Y 0DJ *T.* 01-353 0811.
15p. D. Ind. Features of topical Midland interest considered. *Length:* 400-800 words.

Birmingham Post, The, N. K. Whetstone, P.O. Box 18, 28 Colmore Circus, Birmingham B4 6AY *T.* 021-236 3366.
18p. D. Authoritative and well-written articles of industrial, political or general interest are considered, especially if they have relevance to the Midlands. *Length:* up to 1000 words. *Payment:* by arrangement.

Blue Jeans (D. C. Thomson & Co., Ltd.), Courier Place, Dundee DD1 9QJ *T.* 23131; and 185 Fleet Street, London EC4A 2HS *T.* 01-242 5086.
26p. W. Colour gravure magazine for teenage girls. Photo love stories. True experience text stories up to 3000 words. Pop features and pin-ups. General teen interest features. Fashion and beauty. *Illustrations:* pop and boy/girl transparencies and black and whites, photo story photography, humorous illustrations. *Payment:* on acceptance.

Blue Jeans Photo Novels (D. C. Thomson & Co., Ltd.), Courier Place, Dundee DD1 9QJ *T.* (0382) 23131, and 185 Fleet Street, London EC4A 2HS.
24p. Four per month. Teenage stories in photo story form. Approx 120 frames. Scripts required. *Payment:* on acceptance.

Boards (1982), Jeremy Evans, 196 Eastern Esplanade, Southend-on-Sea, Essex SS1 3AB *T.* (0702) 582245.
£1.20. 9 p.a. (Monthly during summer, bi-monthly during winter). Articles, photographs and reports on all aspects of windsurfing and boardsailing. *Payment:* by arrangement. *Illustrations:* line, half-tone, colour.

Bolton Evening News (1867), L. Gent, Mealhouse Lane, Bolton, Greater Manchester BL1 1DE *T.* Bolton (0204) 22345. *T.A.* Newspapers, Bolton.
18p. D. and W. Articles, particularly those with South Lancashire appeal. *Length:* up to 700 words. *Illustrations:* photographs; considered at usual rates. *Payment:* on 15th of month following date of publication.

Book Collector, The (1952) (incorporating **Bibliographical Notes and Queries**), Editorial Board: Nicolas Barker (Editor), A. Bell, J. Commander, T. Hofmann, D. McKitterick, Stephen Weissman, The Collector Ltd., 90 Great Russell Street, London WC1B 3PS *T.* 01-637 3029.
£18.00 p.a. ($35.00), postage extra. Q. Articles, biographical and bibliographical, on the collection and study of printed books and MSS. *Payment:* by arrangement.

Book News From Wales—see **Llais Llyfrau.**

Books & Bookmen (1955), Carolyn Hart, 43 Museum Street, London WC1 *T.* 01-404 0304.
£1.20. M. Book reviews and interviews; articles on publishing; special features. Most material commissioned. Please contact before submission. *Payment:* by arrangement. *Illustrations:* line, half-tone.

Bookseller, The (1858), Louis Baum (J. Whitaker and Sons Ltd.), 12 Dyott Street, London WC1A 1DF *T.* 01-836 8911.

£43.00 p.a. W. The journal of the publishing and bookselling trades. While outside contributions are always welcomed, most of the journal's contents are commissioned. *Length:* about 1000 to 1500 words. *Payment:* by arrangement.

Brewing & Distilling International (1865), Bruce Stevens, 52 Glenhouse Road, Eltham, London SE9 1JQ *T.* 01-859 4300. *Telex:* 885375 Abta G.
M. Devoted to the interests of brewers, maltsters, hop growers, barley growers, distillers, soft drinks manufacturers, bottlers and allied traders, circulating in 73 countries. Contributions (average 1000 words) accepted are technical and marketing articles written by authors with a special knowledge of the subjects dealt with. *Illustrations:* line drawings, photographs. *Payment:* by arrangement.

Bridge International (1926), Alan Hiron, 30 Fleet Street, London EC4Y 1AH. *T.* 01-353 9093. *Telex:* 8814338.
£1.30 (£16.95 p.a.). M. Articles on bridge. *Payment:* £25 per page. *Illustrations:* line, half-tone.

Bristol Evening Post (1932), B. Jones, Temple Way, Bristol BS99 7HD *T.* Bristol 20080.
16p. D. Articles up to 600 words with strong West-country interest. *Payment:* at recognised rates.

British Chess Magazine (1881), B. Cafferty, 9 Market Street, St. Leonards-on-Sea, East Sussex TN38 0DQ *T.* Hastings 424009.
£1.30p. Annual subscription £15.60 post free. M.

British Deaf News, The (1955), British Deaf Association, 38 Victoria Place, Carlisle CA1 1HU *T.* Carlisle (0228) 48844 (Voice). 28719 (Vistel).
25p. M. (£4.70 p.a.) Articles, news items, letters dealing with deafness. *Payment:* by arrangement. *Illustrations:* line and half-tone.

British Esperantist, The (Journal of the Esperanto Association of Britain) (1905), W. Auld, 140 Holland Park Avenue, London W11 4UF *T.* 01-727 7821.
80p. (£5.00 p.a.). M. Articles in Esperanto, by arrangement, on the applications of the International Language, Esperanto, to education, commerce, travel, international affairs, scouting, radio, television, literature, linguistics, etc. *Illustrations:* photos by arrangement. *Payment:* by arrangement.

British Journal of Photography, The (1854), G. W. Crawley, 28 Great James Street, London WC1N 3HL *T.* 01 404 4202.
45p. W. Articles on professional, commercial and press photography, and on the more advanced aspects of amateur, technical, industrial, medical, scientific and colour photography. *Payment:* by arrangement. *Illustrations:* in line, half-tone, colour.

British Journal of Special Education, Official Journal of the National Council for Special Education. Margaret Peter, 12 Hollycroft Avenue, London, NW3 7QL *T.* 01-794 7109.
£12.00 p.a. (£18.00 Inland Institutions). Q. Articles by specialists on the education of the physically, mentally and emotionally handicapped, including the medical, therapeutic and sociological aspects of special education. *Length:* about 2000 to 3000 words. *Payment:* by arrangement. *Illustrations:* half-tone and line.

British Medical Journal (1840), Stephen Lock, M.A., M.B., F.R.C.P., British Medical Association House, Tavistock Square, London WC1H 9JR *T.* 01-387 4499.
£2.55. W. Medical and related articles.

British Printer (1888), Andrew Parker, 76 Oxford Street, London W1N 9FD *T.* 01-434 2233.
£22.00 p.a. M. Articles on technical and aesthetic aspects of printing processes and graphic reproduction. *Payment:* by arrangement. *Illustrations:* offset litho from photographs, line drawings and diagrams.

British-Soviet Friendship (formerly **Russia To-day**) (1927), 36 St. John's Square, London EC1V 4JH *T.* 01-253 4161.
30p. M. An illustrated magazine on British-Soviet relations. Good photographs and well-informed news items and articles up to 900 words (on Soviet Union and British-Soviet relations). *Payment:* for articles and photographs only by special arrangement.

British Weekly & Christian Record (Interdenominational Weekly) (1969), 11 Carteret Street, London SW1H 9DJ.
25p. W. Emphasis on news features for Evangelical Free Church market. Mostly commissioned feature articles. *Length:* 1000 words maximum. *Payment:* £10.00 per 1000. *Illustrations:* photographs and line drawings.

Broadcast, Peter Monteith, 100 Avenue Road, London NW3 3TP *T.* 01-935 6611. *Telex:* 299973 Aether G.
75p. (£48.00 p.a.). W. News and authoritative articles designed for all concerned with the British broadcast and non-broadcast industries, and with programmes and advertising on television, radio, video, cable, satellite, business. *Payment:* by arrangement.

Brownie, The, Official Magazine of The Girl Guides Association, Mrs. J. V. Rush, 17-19 Buckingham Palace Road, London SW1W 0PT *T.* 01-834 6242.
18p. W. Short articles for Brownies (girls 7-10 years). Serials with Brownie background (300-500 words per instalment). Puzzles, Line Drawings, "Things to make", etc. *Payment:* £25.35 per 1000 words. *Illustrations:* line and half-tone.

Budgerigar World (1982), Gerald S. Binks, Tanglewood, Knowle Grove, Virginia Water, Surrey GU25 4JB *T.* Wentworth (09904) 3250.
£1.50. M. Articles and short stories about budgerigars. *Payment:* by arrangement. *Illustrations:* half-tone, colour.

Building (1842), Graham Rimmer, Builder House, 1-3 Pemberton Row, London EC4P 4HL *T.* 01-353 2300. *Telex:* 28212 Builder G.
80p. W. A magazine covering the entire professional, industrial and manufacturing aspects of the building industry. Articles on architecture and techniques at home and abroad considered, also news and photographs. *Payment:* by arrangement.

Building Societies Gazette, The (1869), Christine Whelan, Franey & Co., Ltd., 7 Swallow Place, London W1R 7AA *T.* 01-409 3322.
£1.75. (£22.75 p.a. pre-paid). M. Articles on matters of interest to building societies, financial rather than on house construction. *Length:* up to 1500 words. *Average payment:* £90.00 per 1000 words. *Illustrations:* line and half-tone.

Built Environment, Professor Peter Hall, Alexandrine Press, P.O.Box 15, 51 Cornmarket Street, Oxford OX1 3EB *T.* (0865) 724627.
£7.00. Q. (£22.00 p.a.). Articles about architecture, planning and the environment. *Length:* 1000 to 5000 words. *Payment:* by arrangement. *Illustrations:* photographs and line. A preliminary letter is advisable.

Bulletin of Hispanic Studies (1923), Department of Hispanic Studies, The University, P.O. Box 147, Liverpool L69 3BX *T.* 051-709 6022, ext. 3056. Published by the Liverpool University Press, P.O. Box 147, Liverpool L69 3BX.
£28.00 p.a. (institutions); £16 p.a. (individual). Q. Specialist articles on the languages and literatures of Spain, Portugal and Latin America, written in English, Spanish, Portuguese, Catalan or French. *No payment.*

Bunty (D. C. Thomson & Co. Ltd.), Courier Place, Dundee, DD1 9QJ, and 185 Fleet Street, London, EC4A 2HS.
20p. W. Picture-story paper for young girls of school age. Vividly told stories in picture-serial form, 16-18 frames in each 2 page instalment; 23-24 frames in each 3-page instalment. Comic strips and features. *Payment:* on acceptance. Special encouragement to promising scriptwriters and artists.

Bunty Library (D. C. Thomson & Co. Ltd.), Courier Place, Dundee, DD1 9QJ, and 185 Fleet Street, London, EC4A 2HS.
24p. M. Stories told in pictures for schoolgirls; 64 pages (about 140 line drawings). Ballet, school, adventure, theatre, sport. Scripts considered; promising artists and script-writers encouraged. *Payment:* on acceptance.

Burlington Magazine (1903), Neil MacGregor, Elm House, 10-16 Elm Street, London, WC1X 0BP *T.* 01-278 2345. *T.A.* Rariora, London, WC1.
£5.75. M. Deals with the history and criticism of art. Average *length* of article, 500 to 3000 words. The Editor can use only articles by those who have special knowledge of the subjects treated and cannot accept MSS compiled from works of reference. Book and exhibition reviews and an illustrated monthly Calendar section. No verse. *Illustrations:* almost invariably made from photographs.

Buses (1949), Stephen Morris, Coombelands House, Addlestone, Weybridge, Surrey KT15 1HY *T.* (0932) 58511.
£1.00. M. Articles of interest to both road passenger transport operators and bus enthusiasts. *Illustrations:* half-tone, line maps. *Payment:* on application. Preliminary inquiry essential.

Business Magazine (1986), Nigel Adam, 234 Kings Road, London SW3 5UA *T.* 01-351 7351. *Telex:* 914549 Intmag G.
£2.00 M. Business and finance articles. *Payment:* £200 per 1000 words. *Illustrations:* photographs, graphics, colour.

Business Credit and Hire Purchase Journal, Quaintance & Co. (Publishers) Ltd., 46 Bridge Street, Godalming, Surrey GU7 1HH *T.* (04868) 27333.
£25.00 p.a. Bi-M. Articles on any aspect of Credit, preferably by contributors with practical or professional experience. *Length:* 1500 to 2500 words. *Payment:* by arrangement. *Illustrations:* half-tone or line.

Business Scotland (1947), Ian Peebles, Peebles Publishing Group, 2 Park Gardens, Glasgow, G3 7YE *T.* 041-331 1933.
Controlled circulation. M. Articles and news items relevant to finance, business and industry in Scotland.

Buster (1960), King's Reach Tower, Stamford Street, London, SE1 9LS *T.* 01-261 5000.
24p. W. Juvenile comic. Comedy characters in picture strips. For boys and girls ages 6 to 12. Full colour, and black and white.

UNITED KINGDOM

Busy Bees' News, P.D.S.A. House, South Street, Dorking, Surrey, RH4 2LB *T.* (0306) 888291.
25p. Bi-M. (£2.40 p.a.). Short stories (max. *length* 700 words) and factual articles (max. *length* 700) about animals suitable for children; also puzzles, poetry and cartoons. *Payment:* by arrangement, on acceptance. *Illustrations:* line and half-tone, black and white.

Butterfly News (1985), Simon Regan, Lodmoor Country Park, Greenhill, Weymouth, Dorset DT4 7SX *T.* (0305) 776300.
25p. Bi-M. Hard news stories about butterflies, insects, conservation. *Payment:* £25 to £50 per 1000 words. *Illustrations:* black-and-white, colour.

Cage and Aviary Birds (1902), Brian Byles, Prospect House, 9-15 Ewell Road, Cheam, Surrey, SM3 8BZ *T.* 01-661 4300.
50p. W. Practical articles on aviculture. First-hand knowledge only. *Payment:* by arrangement. *Illustrations:* line and photographs.

Campaign, Christine Barker, 22 Lancaster Gate, London, W2 3LY *T.* 01-402 4200.
80p. W. News and articles covering the whole of the mass communications field, particularly advertising in all its forms, marketing, newspapers and publishing, public relations, television and printing. Features should not exceed 2000 words. News items also welcome. Press day, Wednesday. *Payment:* by arrangement.

Camper, Mike Scott, Haymarket Publishing Ltd., 38-42 Hampton Road, Teddington, Middlesex, TW11 0JE *T.* 01-977 8787.
95p. M. Practical articles, touring features, site reports and general interest articles with a lightweight or family camping bias by arrangement with editor. *Payment:* by arrangement. *Illustrations:* line, half-tone, colour. *Preliminary letter* essential.

Camping & Trailer (1961), Philip Pond, Link House, Dingwall Avenue, Croydon, CR9 2TA *T.* 01-686 2599. *Telex:* 947709 Linkho G.
95p. M. Articles based on real camping experiences, all aspects, illustrated with photographs; also camp site reports. Practical articles welcomed. *Length:* 1600 words average. *Payment:* by arrangement. *Illustrations:* line, half-tone.

Candour (1953), R. de Bounevialle, Forest House, Liss Forest, Hants, GU33 7DD *T.* (0730) 892109.
50p. M. Politico-economic articles with a national and Commonwealth appeal. *Length:* 1200-1500 words. *Payment:* £5 per 1000 words.

Car (1962), Steve Cropley, 97 Earls Court Road, London W8 6QH *T.* 01-370 0333.
£1.00. M. Top-grade journalistic features on car driving, car people and cars. *Length:* 1000-2500 words. *Payment:* £125 per 1000 words minimum. *Illustrations:* black-and-white and colour photographs to professional standard.

Car Mechanics, Dave Walker, Audit House, Field End Road, Eastcote, Ruislip, Middlesex HA4 9LT.
99p. M. Practical articles on car maintenance and repair for the non-technical motorist with limited facilities. *Length:* Average 1500 words of hard fact. *Payment:* £40.00 per 1000 words; pictures £4.00 each (minimum). *Illustrations:* line and half-tone. *Preliminary letter outlining the article is necessary.*

Caravan Magazine, (1933), Barry Williams, Link House, Dingwall Avenue, Croydon, CR9 2TA *T.* 01-686 2599. *Telex:* 947709 Linkho G.
95p. M. Lively articles based on real experience of touring caravanning, especially if well illustrated by photographs. General countryside or motoring material not wanted. *Payment:* by arrangement.

Cat World (1981), Grace McHattie, Scan House, Southwick Street, Southwick, Brighton, BN4 4TE *T.* (0273) 595944.
£1.00 M. Bright, lively articles on any aspect of cat ownership. Articles on breeds of cats and veterinary articles by acknowledged experts only. No unsolicited fiction. *Payment:* by arrangement. *Illustrations:* mono, colour.

Catholic Gazette (1910), Fr. Kevin O'Connell, 114 West Heath Road, London, NW3 7TX *T.* 01-458 3316.
40p. M. Articles concerned with evangelisation and the Christian life. *Length:* up to 2500 words. *Payment:* by arrangement. *Illustrations:* line, half-tone; cartoons.

Catholic Herald, The, Terence Sheehy, Herald House, Lambs Passage, Bunhill Row, London EC1Y 8TQ *T.* 01-588 3101-5.
30p. W. An independent newspaper covering national and international affairs from a Catholic Christian viewpoint as well as Church news. Articles 600 to 1100 words. *Payment:* by arrangement. *Illustrations:* Photographs of Catholic and Christian interest.

Catholic Pictorial (1961), Norman Cresswell, Media House, Stafford Street, Liverpool, L3 8LX *T.* 051-207 6846.
30p. W. News and photo features (maximum 1000 words plus illustration) *strictly* of Lancashire Catholic interest only. Has a strongly social editorial and is a trenchant tabloid. *Payment:* £1 per 100 words. News: on merit.

Celebrity, D. C. Thomson & Co. Ltd., 80 Kingsway East, Dundee DD4 8SL and 185 Fleet Street, London EC4A 2HS.
30p. W. Colour gravure weekly for men and women in 20-40 age group. Lively profiles of around 1200 words on television, film and stage personalities. Fashion, sport, general interest features (1000-1200 words) and Fillers (up to 500 words), single-frame cartoons and cartoon strips. *Illustrations:* photographs; colour and mono. *Payment:* on acceptance.

Cencrastus (1979), Geoff Parker, 34 Queen Street, Edinburgh EX2 1JX *T.* 031-226 5605.
£1.50 Q. Essays, short stories, poetry. *Payment:* by arrangement. *Illustrations:* line, half-tone. Preliminary study of magazine essential.

Certified Accountant, Richard Garlick, Chapter Three Publications Ltd., 8A Hythe Street, Dartford, Kent. *T.* 28584.
£1.20. M. Articles of accounting and financial interest.

Chapman (1970), Joy Hendry, 35 East Claremont Street, Edinburgh EH7 4HT *T.* 031-556 5863.
£1.50. Q. Poetry, short stories, articles on Scottish culture. *Payment:* £6.00 per page. *Illustrations:* line, half-tone.

Cheshire Life (1934), Julie Spencer, (OPL Magazines Ltd.), The Custom House, Watergate Street, Chester CH1 2LF *T.* (0244) 45226.
80p. M. Articles of county interest only. No fiction. *Length:* 800-1500 words. *Payment:* £13.00 per 1000 words minimum. *Illustrations:* line and half-tone, 4-colour positives for cover. Photographs of news value and definite Cheshire interest.

UNITED KINGDOM

Child Education (1924), Gill Wilton, Scholastic Publications Ltd., Marlborough House, Holly Walk, Leamington Spa, Warwickshire CV32 4LS *T.* Southam (0926 81) 3910. *Telex:* 312138 Spls G.
£1.00. M. For teachers, pre-school staff, nursery nurses and parents concerned with children aged 3-8. Articles by specialists on practical teaching ideas and methods, child development, education news. *Length:* 800 to 1200 words. *Payment:* by arrangement. Profusely illustrated with photographs and line drawings; also large pictures in full colour. Also **Child Education Special** (1978). Janet Parsons. £1.00. Bi-M.

China Quarterly, The, Brian Hook, Contemporary China Institute, School of Oriental and African Studies, Malet Street, London, WC1E 7HP *T.* 01-637 2388.
£4.50 Q. (£17.50 p.a.). Articles on Contemporary China. *Length:* 8000 words approx. *Payment:* on specially commissioned articles only.

Christian Herald (1866), 59 Lyndhurst Road, Worthing, West Sussex. BN11 2DB *T.* (0903) 204221.
25p. W. Bright, general interest articles, well *illustrated* if possible. *Length:* 1000 words. *Payment:* ££20-£24. Pleasant short stories. *Length:* 1600 words. *Payment:* £20. The paper is evangelical and aimed at families and middle of the road church-goers.

Church of England Newspaper (1828), 11 Carteret Street, London SW1H 9DJ.
25p. W. The newspaper contains Anglican news and articles relating the Christian faith to everyday life. Study of paper desirable. Evangelical basis; mostly commissioned articles. *Length:* 1000 words maximum. *Payment:* £15.00 per 1000. *Illustrations:* photographs and line drawings.

Church News (1948), Canon Rhodes, College Gate House, Bury St. Edmunds, Suffolk, IP33 1NN *T.* (0284) 3530.
£3.25 p.a. M. An Illustrated Church magazine inset. Articles of popular Church interest (500 to 800 words); occasional short stories and verse. *Illustrations:* photographs and line drawings of religious and ecclesiastical subjects. *Payment:* by arrangement.

Church Times (1863), B. H. M. Palmer, 7 Portugal Street, London, WC2A 2HP *T.* 01-405 0844.
22p. W. Articles on ecclesiastical and social topics are considered. Usual *length:* 750 to 1500 words. No verse or fiction. *Payment:* £20.00 per 1000 words minimum. *Illustrations:* news photographs.

Civil Engineering (incorporating **Public Works Review**) (1906), Colin Degerlund, Morgan-Grampian (Construction Press) Ltd., 30 Calderwood Street, London, SE18 6QH *T.* 01-855 7777.
Controlled circulation and subscription £21.00 p.a. M. Contains in-depth reviews and technical articles of current interest to Civil Engineers. *Length:* 1000-3000 words. *Payment:* by arrangement. *Illustrations:* line drawings and photographs germane to article. *A preliminary letter is essential.*

Classical Music (1976), Robert Maycock, 239-241 Shaftesbury Avenue, London, WC2H 8EH *T.* 01-836 2383.
£1.00. Fortnightly. News, opinion, features on classical music and general arts matters; few reviews (commissioned only). *Payment:* £50 per 1000 words. *Illustrations:* half-tone, colour covers.

Clergy Review, The, Revd. B. W. Bickers, M.A., Ushaw College, Durham DH7 9RH *T.* (0385) 732202.
£16.25 p.a. M. A journal of information, dialogue and research for Catholics of the English-speaking countries. *Length* and *payment* by arrangement.

Climber (1962), Walt Unsworth, Harmony Hall, Milnthorpe, Cumbria.
£1.10. M. Articles on all aspects of mountaineering and hill walking in Great Britain and abroad and on related subjects. *Length:* 1500 to 3000 words, preferably illustrated. *Payment:* according to merit. *Illustrations:* colour, half-tone, line. Study of magazine essential.

Clocks (1978), Argus Specialist Publications Ltd., P.O. Box 35, Wolsey House, Wolsey Road, Hemel Hempstead, Herts *T.* (0442) 41221.
£2.25. M. Articles on antique clocks and their makers, clock repair and restoration, and in general anything of interest to knowledgeable horologists. Sundials, barometers and associated scientific instruments are minority interests of Clocks readers. *Length:* 1500-3000 words. *Payment:* £30 per 1000 words, £5 per black and white photograph, £8 per colour print/transparency. *Illustrations:* line, half-tone, colour.

Club Secretary (1953), Simon Jack, UTP House, 33-35 Bowling Green Lane, London, EC1R 0DA *T.* 01-837 1212.
£18.00 p.a. M. Features, news, drink news, catering news, legal and financial advice as a guide to the successful management of clubs. *Payment:* by arrangement. *Illustrations:* line and half-tone.

Coin & Medal News (1964), John W. Mussell, Token Publishing Ltd., Crossways Road, Grayshott, Hindhead, Surrey GU26 6HF *T.* (0428) 737242.
90p. M. Articles of high standard on coins, tokens, paper money and medals. *Length:* up to 2000 words. *Payment:* by arrangement.

Coin Monthly (1966), Penny Phillips, Sovereign House, Brentwood, Essex, CM14 4SE *T.* (0277) 219876.
£1.10. M. Articles on all aspects of numismatics. *Length:* 1500 to 2000 words. *Payment:* £10.00 per 1000 words. *Illustrations:* half-tone.

Commando (D. C. Thomson & Co. Ltd.), Albert Square, Dundee, DD1 9QJ *T.* (0382) 23131 and 185 Fleet Street, London, EC4A 2HS.
24p. Eight each month. Fictional war stories of World War II told in pictures. Scripts should be of about 135 pictures. Synopsis required as an opener. Send for details. New writers encouraged. *Payment:* on acceptance.

Commerce International, Ron Grace, Queensway House, Redhill, Surrey, RH1 1QS *T.* (0737) 68611.
£36.00 p.a. (£41.00 p.a. overseas). M. Authoritative outside contributions are accepted on commercial and industrial subjects. *Payment:* by arrangement. *Illustrations:* half-tone, line.

Commercial Motor (1905), Allan Winn, Transport Press, Quadrant House, The Quadrant, Sutton, Surrey, SM2 5AS *T.* 01-661 3302.
75p. W. *Payment:* varies for articles (technical and road transport only), maximum length 2000 words, drawings and photographs.

Community Care (1974), Terry Philpot, Surrey House, 1 Throwley Way, Sutton, Surrey, SM1 4QQ *T.* 01-643 8040.
65p. W. Articles of professional interest to local authority and voluntary body social workers, managers, teachers and students. *Length:* 1200 to 2000 words. *Payment:* at current rates. *Illustrations:* half-tone and line.

Company (1978), Maggie Goodman, National Magazine House, 72 Broadwick Street, London, W1V 2BP *T.* 01-439 7144.
80p. M. Short stories, articles on a wide variety of subjects. Most articles commissioned. *Payment:* usual magazine rate.

Company Law Digest (1979), Tolley Publishing Co. Ltd., 17 Scarbrook Road, Croydon CR0 1SQ *T.* 01-686 9141.
£35.00 p.a. Q. Articles dealing with company law. *Length:* 1000 words plus. *Payment:* by arrangement. *No illustrations.*

Computing (1973) Graham Cunningham, 32-34 Broadwick Street, London W1A 2HG *T.* 01-439 4242.
40p. W. Features and news items on the computer industry and on applications and implications of computers and microelectronics. *Length:* up to 1500 words. *Payment:* £94 per 1000 words. *Illustrations:* half-tone, line.

Contemporary Review (incorporating the **Fortnightly**) (1866), Editor: Rosalind Wade, O.B.E. Literary Review: A. G. de Montmorency. Editorial Advisers: Professor Paul Wilkinson and Professor Esmond Wright. Music Correspondent: David Fingleton, 61 Carey Street, London, WC2A 2JG *T.* 01-242 3215.
£1.10. M. Independent, but slightly left of centre. A review dealing with all questions of the day, chiefly politics, theology, history, literature, travel, poetry, the arts. A great part of the matter is commissioned, but there is scope for free-lance specialists. Articles submitted should be typewritten and should be about 2000 to 3000 words. If refused, articles are returned, *if stamped envelope is enclosed. Payment:* £5.00 per 1000 words, 2 complimentary copies. Intending contributors should study journal before submitting MSS.

Contributors' Bulletin see **Freelance Press Services** in **Editorial, Literary and Production Services.**

Control & Instrumentation (1958), Brian J. Tinham, B.Sc., M.INST.M.C. (Morgan-Grampian (Process Press) Ltd.), 30 Calderwood Street, Woolwich, London, SE18 6QH *T.* 01-855 7777.
£29.00 p.a. M. Authoritative main feature articles on measurement, automation, control systems, instrumentation, and data processing. Also export, business and engineering news. *Payment:* according to value. *Length of articles:* 750 words for highly technical pieces. 1000 to 2500 words main features. *Illustrations:* half-tone and photographs and drawings of equipment using automatic techniques, control engineering personalities.

Cosmetic World News (1949), M. A. Murray-Pearce, Caroline Marcuse, Kim Richards, 130 Wigmore Street, London, W1H 0AT *T.* 01-486 6757-8. *Telex:* 817133.
£48.00 p.a. M. International news magazine of perfumery, cosmetics and toiletries industry. World-wide reports, photo-news stories, articles (500-1000 words) on essential oils and new cosmetic raw materials, and exclusive information on industry's companies and personalities welcomed. *Payment:* by arrangement. Minimum 5p. per word. *Illustrations:* black-and-white photographs or colour separations.

Cosmopolitan (1972), Linda Kelsey, National Magazine House, 72 Broadwick Street, London, W1V 2BP *T.* 01-439 7144.
80p. M. Short stories, articles. Commissioned material only. *Payment:* by arrangement.

Country, The Magazine of the Country Gentlemen's Association (1901), Jeanne Griffiths, Telepress Ltd., London House, 243-253 Lower Mortlake Road, Richmond, Surrey TW9 2LL.
£14.00 p.a. M. Practical and authoritative articles of general country interest. From 1000 to 2000 words. *Payment:* by arrangement.

Country Life (1897), Marcus Binney, O.B.E., King's Reach Tower, Stamford Street, London, SE1 9LS *T.* 01-261 7058.
£1.10. W. An illustrated journal, chiefly concerned with British country life, social history, architecture and the fine arts, natural history, agriculture, gardening and sport. *Length of articles:* about 900, 1350 or 1800 words; short poems are also considered. *Payment:* according to merit. Press day, Thursday. *Illustrations:* mainly photographs.

Country Living (1985), Deirdre McSharry, 72 Broadwick Street, London W1V 2BP *T.* 01-439 7144.
£1.00. M. Well written features or news items on all aspects of country living. *Payment:* by arrangement. *Illustrations:* line, half-tone, colour.

Countryman, The (1927), Christopher Hall. Editorial Office: Sheep Street, Burford, Oxford, OX8 4LH *T.* Burford (099 382) 2258.
£1.00. Q. Every department of rural life and progress except field sports. Party politics and sentimentalising about the country barred. Copy must be trustworthy, well-written, brisk, cogent and light in hand. Articles up to 1500 words. Good paragraphs and notes, first-class poetry, and skilful sketches of life and character from personal knowledge and experience. Dependable natural history based on writer's own observation. Really good matter from old unpublished letters and MSS. *Payment:* £40.00 per 1000 words and upwards according to merit. *Illustrations:* black-and-white photographs and drawings, but all must be exclusive and out of the ordinary, and bear close scrutiny. Humour welcomed if genuine.

Country Quest, Brian Barratt, Centenary Buildings, King Street, Wrexham, Clwyd, LL11 1PN *T.* (0978) 355151.
80p. M. Illustrated articles on matters relating to countryside of Wales and border counties. *Length:* 500 to 1500 words. No fiction. *Payment:* by arrangement. *Illustrations:* half-tone and line.

Country-Side (1905), R. Freethy, Thorneyholme Hall, Roughlee, Burnley, Lancashire BB12 9LH *T.* (0282) 66568.
£7.00 p.a. Q. Official organ of the British Naturalists' Association (B.N.A.), the national body for naturalists. Original observations on wild life and its protection, and on natural history generally, but not on killing for sport. *Payment:* not usually made. *Illustrations:* photographs, drawings. *Preliminary letter* or study of magazine advisable.

Courier and Advertiser, The (1816 and 1801), (D. C. Thomson & Co. Ltd.), 7 Bank Street, Dundee, DD1 9HU *T.* Dundee 23131. *Telex:* DCThom 76380; and 185 Fleet Street, London, EC4A 2HS *T.* 01-242 5086.
18p. D. Independent.

Coventry Evening Telegraph, Geoffrey Elliott, Corporation Street, Coventry, CV1 1FP *T.* Coventry (0203) 25588. London Office: Clan House, 19-21 Tudor Street, EC4Y 0DJ.
16p. D. Illustrated articles of topical interest, those with a Warwickshire interest particularly acceptable. *Maximum length:* 600 words.

Creative Camera (1964), Peter Turner, CC Publishing, c/o Battersea Arts Centre, Old Town Hall, Lavender Hill, London SW11 5TF *T.* 01-924 3017.
£1.75. M. Illustrated articles and pictures dealing with creative photography, sociology of, history of and criticism of photographs. Book and Exhibition reviews. Arts Council supported. *Payment:* by arrangement. *Illustrations:* black-and-white; colour.

Creative Photography, Barry Hunter, EMAP, Bushfield House, Orton Centre, Peterborough, PE2 0UW *T.* (0733) 237111.
£1.50. M. Interested primarily in photographer's personal portfolio material (amateur or pro), plus well illustrated articles on photographic techniques. *Payment:* upwards of £25 per published page, colour or mono. *Illustrations:* print, slide, line, half-tone.

Cricketer International, The (1921), Christopher Martin-Jenkins, 29 Cavendish Road, Redhill, Surrey, RH1 4AH *T.* (0737) 72221.
95p. M. Articles on cricket at any level. *Payment:* £40 per 1000 words. *Illustrations:* line, half-tone, colour.

Criminologist, The (1966), Nigel Morland, 87 London Street, Chertsey, Surrey KT16 8AN *T.* (093 28) 62933.
Controlled circulation. £1.50 post free or £6.00 p.a. Q. Specialised material designed for an expert and professional readership. Covers nationally and internationally criminology, the police, forensic science, the law, penology, sociology and law enforcement. Articles, up to 2000 words, by those familiar with the journal's style and requirements are welcomed. *A preliminary letter* with a brief résumé is preferable. *Payment:* is wholly governed by the nature and quality of manuscripts. *Illustrations:* line and photographs.

Critical Quarterly (1959), Editorial Board: J. R. Banks, C. B. Cox, W. Hutchings, D. J. Palmer, The University, Manchester, M13 9PL *T.* 061-273 3333.
£5.00. Q. Literary criticism, poems. *Length:* 2000-8000 words. *Payment:* by arrangement. Interested contributors should study magazine before submitting MSS.

CTN (Confectioner, Tobacconist, Newsagent), Michael Eaton, Consumer Industries Press Ltd., Quadrant House, The Quadrant, Sutton, Surrey, SM2 5AS *T.* 01-661 3500.
45p. W. (£40.00 p.a.). Trade news and brief articles illustrated when possible with photographs or line drawings. Must be of live interest to retail confectioner-tobacconists and newsagents. *Length:* Articles 600-800 words. *Payment:* news lineage rates, minimum of £6.50 per 100 words, articles at negotiated rates.

Cue – Technical Theatre Review (1979), James Twynam, Twynam Publishing Ltd., Kitemore House, Faringdon, Oxon SN7 8HR *T.* (0367) 21141.
£1.75 (£10.50 p.a.) Bi-M. Technical and general interest articles on theatre architecture, theatre management, stage design, lighting and sound. *Length:* 2000-3000 words, usually illustrated. *Payment:* £40 per 1000 words. *Illustrations:* line, half-tone, colour.

Cumbria (1951), W. R. Mitchell, Dalesman Publishing Company Ltd., Clapham, via Lancaster, LA2 8EB *T.* Clapham (046 85) 225.
40p. M. Articles of genuine rural interest concerning Lakeland. Short *length* preferred. *Payment:* according to merit. *Illustrations:* line drawings and first-class photographs.

Current Crime (1973), Nigel Morland, 87 London Street, Chertsey, Surrey. *T.* (093 28) 62933.
£2.00. Q. Comprises brief reviews of new crime novels; awards an annual Silver Cup for the Best British Crime Novel of the year. Works closely with the Crime Writers' Association in promoting crime books. Occasional articles. *Length:* up to 400 words. The magazine should be studied before submissions; send SAE for a voucher copy.

Custom Car (1970), Link House, Dingwall Avenue, Croydon, CR9 2TA *T.* 01-686 2599. *Telex:* 947709 Linkho G.
£1.00. *Payment:* by arrangement. *Length:* by arrangement.

Cycling (1891), Martin Ayres, Prospect House, 9-15 Ewell Road, Cheam, Surrey, SM3 8BZ *T.* 01-661 4300.
60p. W. Racing, touring, technical, articles not exceeding 2100 words. Topical photographs with a cycling interest also considered. *Payment:* by arrangement.

Daily Express, Nicholas Lloyd, 121 Fleet Street, London, EC4P 4JT *T.* 01-353 8000; Great Ancoats Street, Manchester, M60 4HB *T.* 061-236 2112.
20p. D. Exclusive news: striking photographs. Leader page articles, 600 words; facts preferred to opinions. *Payment:* according to value.

Daily Mail (1896) (Now incorporating **News Chronicle** and **Daily Sketch**), Sir David English, Northcliffe House, London, EC4Y 0JA *T.* 01-353 6000.
20p. D. Highest payments for good, exclusive news. Leader page articles, 500-800 words average. Ideas for these welcomed. Exclusive news photographs always wanted.

Daily Mirror (1903), R. Stott, Holborn Circus, London, EC1P 1DQ *T.* 01-353 0246.
18p. D. Top payment for exclusive news and news pictures. Few articles from free-lances used, but ideas bought. Send only a synopsis. 'Unusual' pictures and those giving a new angle on the news are welcomed.

Daily Record, B. Vickers, Anderston Quay, Glasgow *T.* 041-248 7000. *Telex:* 778277. London: 33 Holborn, EC1P 1DQ *T.* 01-353 0246.
20p. D. Web off-set with full colour facilities. Topical articles of from 300 to 700 words. Exclusive stories of Scottish interest and exclusive photographs.

Daily Telegraph, The (1855), Max Hastings, 135 Fleet Street, London, EC4P 4BL *T.* 01-353 4242.
23p. D. Independent.

Dairy Farmer, David Shead, Wharfedale Road, Ipswich, IP1 4LG *T.* Ipswich (0473) 43011.
Controlled circulation. M. Authoritative articles dealing in practical, lively style with dairy farming. Topical controversial articles invited. Well-written, illustrated accounts of new ideas being tried on dairy farms are especially wanted. *Length:* up to 2500 words. *Payment:* by arrangement. *Illustrations:* half-tone or line.

Dairy Industries International (1936), Pauline Russell, 33-35 Bowling Green Lane, London, EC1R 0DA *T.* 01-837 1212.
£33.00 post free. M. Covers the entire field of milk processing, the manufacture of products from liquid milk, and ice cream. Articles relating to dairy plant, butter and cheese making, ice cream making, new product developments and marketing, etc. *Payment:* by arrangement. *Illustrations:* glossy prints and indian ink diagrams.

Dalesman, The (1939), W. R. Mitchell, Dalesman Publishing Company Ltd., Clapham, via Lancaster, LA2 8EB *T.* Clapham (046 851) 225.
40p. M. Articles and stories of genuine rural interest concerning Yorkshire; but no fiction. Short *length* preferred. *Payment:* according to merit. *Illustrations:* line drawings and first-class photographs preferably featuring people.

Dance & Dancers (1950), John Percival, 43b Gloucester Road, Croydon, CR0 2DH *T.* 01-689 3979. *Telex:* 298133.
90p. M. Specialist features, reviews on modern/classical dance, dancers. *Length:* up to 2000 words. *Payment:* by arrangement. *Illustrations:* line, half-tone; colour covers.

Dancing Times (1910), Editor: Mary Clarke, Editorial Adviser: Ivor Guest, Clerkenwell House, 45-47 Clerkenwell Green, London, EC1R 0BE *T.* 01-250 3006.
90p. M. Dealing with ballet and stage dancing, both from general, historical, critical and technical angles. Well informed free-lance articles are occasionally used, but only after preliminary arrangements. *Payment:* by arrangement. *Illustrations:* web offset, occasional line, action photographs always preferred.

Dandy, The (D. C. Thomson & Co. Ltd.), Courier Place, Dundee, DD1 9QJ, and 185 Fleet Street, London, EC4A 2HS.
16p. W. Comic strips for boys and girls. 10-12 pictures per single page story, and 18-20 pictures per 2 page story. Promising artists encouraged. *Payment:* on acceptance.

Dandy Library (D. C. Thomson & Co. Ltd.), Courier Place, Dundee, DD1 9QJ and 185 Fleet Street, London, EC4A 2HS.
24p. 2 per month. Extra-long comic adventure stories featuring well-known characters from the weekly Dandy publication. 'Guest appearances' by characters from weeklies Topper and Beezer publications.

Darts World (1972), Tony Wood, World Magazines Limited, 2 Park Lane, Croydon, Surrey, CR9 1HA *T.* 01-681 2837.
70p. M. Articles and stories with darts theme. *Payment:* £30 to £40 per 1000 words. *Illustrations:* half-tone. Cartoons.

Data Processing (1959), Butterworth Scientific Ltd., P.O. Box 63, Westbury House, Bury Street, Guildford, Surrey, GU2 5BH *T.* (0483) 31261. *Telex:* 859556 Scitec G.
£9.00. 10 issues p.a. (£82.00 p.a., $148.00 in US and Canada). Papers on software design and development and the application of information processing in large organizations, especially multinationals. *Length:* 2500 to 3000 words. *Payment:* by arrangement. *Illustrations:* half-tone and line.

Day by Day (1963), Patrick Richards, Woolacombe House, 141 Woolacombe Road, Blackheath, London, SE3 8QP *T.* 01-856 6249. Published by The Loverseed Press.
43p. M. Articles and news on non-violence and social justice. Reviews of art, books, films, plays, musicals, and opera. Cricket reports. Occasional poems and very occasional short stories in keeping with editorial viewpoint. *Payment:* £2 per 1000 words. No *illustrations* required.

Debbie Library (D. C. Thomson & Co. Ltd.), Courier Place, Dundee, DD1 9QJ, and 185 Fleet Street, London, EC4A 2HS.
24p. M. Stories told in pictures, for schoolgirls; 64 pages (about 140 line drawings). Adventure, animal, mystery, school, sport. Scripts considered; promising script-writers and artists encouraged. *Payment:* on acceptance.

Dental Update (1973), Professor C. E. Renson (Consultant Editor), Sue Kay (Managing), Update-Siebert Publications Ltd., Friary Court, 13-21 High Street, Guildford, Surrey, GU1 3DX *T.* (0483) 502125. *Telex:* 859500 Ref S/054.
£16.00 p.a. 10 p.a. Clinical articles, clinical quizzes. *Payment:* £50-£100 per 1000 words. *Illustrations:* line, colour.

Derbyshire Life and Countryside (1931), Lodge Lane, Derby, DE1 3HE *T.* Derby 47087-8-9.
60p. M. Articles, preferably illustrated, about Derbyshire life, people, and history. *Length:* 1200-1600 words. Short stories set in Derbyshire accepted,

but verse not used. *Payment:* according to nature and quality of contribution. *Illustrations:* photographs of Derbyshire subjects.

Design (1949), Steve Braidwood, Design Council, 28 Haymarket, London, SW1Y 4SU *T.* 01-839 8000.
£2.00. M. Articles on industrial design; case-histories of new products. *Payment:* by arrangement. *Illustrations:* line, half-tone and drawings.

Designers' Journal (1985), Lance Knobel, 9 Queen Anne's Gate, London SW1H 9BY *T.* 01-222 4333.
£2.00. Bi-M. Articles on new developments in interior design, new products, technical innovation and practice guidance. *Payment:* by arrangement. *Illustrations:* photographs, drawings.

Devon Life (1965), Jan Beart-Albrecht, Queen's House, Little Queen Street, Exeter, Devon EX4 3LJ *T.* (0392) 216766.
£1.00. M. Articles and stories about nature, people, life in Devon. *Length:* 1000 words. *Payment:* by arrangement. *Illustrations:* line, photos.

Dickensian, The, Andrew Sanders, B.A., M.LITT., PH.D., Birkbeck College, Malet Street, London, WC1E 7HX.
£9.50 p.a. 3 times a year. Published by The Dickens Fellowship. Welcomes articles on all aspects of Dickens' life, works and character. *No payment.*

Digests with one or two exceptions are not included since they seldom use original material, but reprint articles previously published elsewhere and extracts from books. But see **The Reader's Digest.**

Dirt Bike Rider (1981), Peter Donaldson, Bushfield House, Orton Centre, Peterborough PE2 0UW *T.* (0733) 237111.
£1.00. M. Features, track tests, coverage on all aspects of off road motorcycling. *Length:* up to 1000 words. *Payment:* £60 per 1000 words. *Illustrations:* colour, half-tone.

Diver (1953), Bernard Eaton, 40 Grays Inn Road, London, WC1X 8LR *T.* 01-405 0224.
£1.00. M. Articles on sub aqua diving and underwater developments. *Length:* 1500 to 2000 words. *Payment:* by arrangement. *Illustrations:* line and half-tone, colour.

DIY Today (1983), David Nunn, Sovereign House, Brentwood, Essex CM14 4SE *T.* (0277) 219876.
99p. M. Articles on DIY subjects. *Length:* 1500 words with illustrations. *Payment:* £25.00 per 1000 words. *Illustrations:* line, half-tone.

Do It Yourself (1957), John McGowan, Link House, Dingwall Avenue, Croydon, CR9 2TA *T.* 01-686 2599. *Telex:* 947709 Linkho G.
90p. M. Authorative articles on every aspect of do-it-yourself in the house, garden, workshop and garage. Leaflet describing style, requirements, available on request. *Payment:* by arrangement. *Length:* up to 1000 words unless negotiated. Press 3 months ahead.

Dog & Country (1897), Edward Askwith, Gilbertson & Page Ltd., Corry's, Roestock Lane, Colney Heath, St. Albans, Herts, AL4 0QW *T.* Bowman's Green (0727) 22614.
60p. M. (£8.00 p.a.). Informative articles of from 300 to 1000 words on angling, shooting, dogs, conservation, and natural history. *Payment:* by arrangement. *Illustrations:* camera-ready art work, monochrome only.

Dorset—the county magazine (1967), Rodney Legg and Colin Graham, Knock-na-cre, Milborne Port, Sherborne, Dorset, DT9 5HJ *T.* (0963) 32583.

85p. M. A campaigning regional magazine specialising in reports on threats to the environment. Subject matter exclusively about Dorset. Major historical features also used with *payment* by arrangement depending on *length* (preferably over 3000 words) and *illustrations*. £2 each paid for black-and-white photographs put on file and later used separately in the magazine. £15 paid for striking 2¼" square (or larger) colour transparencies of Dorset for front cover use. Line drawings not used except with features. Deals exclusively with controversial stories from both the present and the past; *no* short stories or poetry.

Downside Review, The, Dom Daniel Rees, Downside Abbey, Stratton on the Fosse, nr. Bath, Somerset. *T.* Stratton-on-the-Fosse (0761) 232 720.
£3.50. Q. (£14.00 p.a.). Articles and book reviews on theology, metaphysics, mysticism and modernism and monastic history. *Payment:* by arrangement.

Drama (1919), Christopher Edwards, Clare Colvin, 9 Fitzroy Square, London, W1P 6AE *T.* 01-387 2666.
£1.95. Q. The longest established theatre magazine in this country carrying reviews and articles on theatre at home and abroad, including the history of theatre, views of new playwrights, the avant-garde, experimental, fringe and young people's theatre. Articles, 1000 to 3000 words. *Payment:* by arrangement. *Illustrations:* photographs.

Drapers Record (1887), Cliff Waller, International Thomson Publishing Ltd., 100 Avenue Road, London NW3 3TP *T.* 01-935 6611. *Telex:* 299973 ITP LM G.
80p. W. Matter should be of special interest to the retail and wholesale fashion and textile trade. *Length* of articles from 500 to 1000 words. *Payment:* by arrangement. *Illustrations:* drawings or photographs.

Dundee Evening Telegraph and Post (D. C. Thomson & Co. Ltd.), Bank Street, Dundee, DD1 9HU *T.* Dundee 23131. *Telex:* DCThom 76380; and 185 Fleet Street, London, EC4A 2HS *T.* 01-353 2586.
16p. D.

Early Music (1973), Nicholas Kenyon, Oxford University Press, Ely House, 37 Dover Street, London W1X 4AH *T.* 01-493 9376.
£5.75 (£21.00 p.a.). Q. Lively, informative and scholarly articles on aspects of medieval, renaissance, baroque and classical music. *Payment:* £20 per 1000 words. *Illustrations:* line, half-tone; colour on cover.

Eastern Daily Press (1870), J. A. Downing, Prospect House, Rouen Road, Norwich, NR1 1RE *T.* Norwich (0603) 628311; London Office: Temple Chambers, Temple Avenue, EC4Y 0DT *T.* 01-583 0379.
21p. D. Independent. Limited market for articles of East Anglian interest not exceeding 900 words.

Eastern Evening News (1882), Lawrence Sear, EEN, Prospect House, Rouen Road, Norwich, NR1 1RE *T.* Norwich (0603) 628311; London Office: Temple Chambers, Temple Avenue, EC4Y 0DT *T.* 01-583 0379.
16p. D. Independent.

Ecologist, The, Edward Goldsmith, Worthyvale Manor Farm, Camelford, Cornwall, PL32 9TT *T.* (0840) 212711.
£2.00. 6 issues p.a. Articles and news stories on economic, social and environmental affairs from an ecological standpoint. *Length:* 1000 to 3000 words. *Payment:* by arrangement. *Illustrations:* line and half-tone. Magazine should be studied for level and approach.

Economic Journal (1891), John D. Hey, Department of Economics, University of York, York, YO1 5DD *T.* (0904) 413551.
£47.50 p.a. (Free to members). Q. The organ of the Royal Economic Society. The kind of matter required is economic theory, applied economics and the development of economic thinking in relation to current problems. *Payment:* none. Statistical and economic diagrams. Reviews of new books and other publications.

Economica (1921. New Series, 1934), Editors: Dr. F. A. Cowell, J. E. H. Davidson, D. de Meza, London School of Economics and Political Science, Houghton Street, London, WC2A 2AE *T.* 01-242 3388, ext. 249.
£19.50 p.a. (U.K.), £26.00 or $47.00 (Overseas). Individuals: £11.00 (U.K.), £11.00 or $20.00 (Overseas). Q. A learned journal covering the fields of economics, economic history, and statistics.

Economist, The (1843), 25 St. James's Street, London, SW1A 1HG *T.* 01-839 7000.
£1.20. W. Articles staff-written.

Edinburgh Evening News, Ian A. Nimmo, 20 North Bridge, Edinburgh EH1 1YT *T.* 031-225 2468.
17p. D. Independent. Features on current affairs, preferably in relation to our circulation area. Women's talking points, local historical articles; subjects of general interest.

Edinburgh Review (1969), Peter Kravitz, 48 Pleasance, Edinburgh EH8 9TJ *T.* 031-558 1117.
£2.95 Q. (£10 p.a.) Fiction, clearly written articles on Scottish and international cultural and philosophical ideas. *Payment:* by arrangement.

Education (1903), George Low, 5 Bentinck Street, London, W1M 5RN *T.* 01-935 0121.
95p. W. Special articles on educational administration, all branches of education; technical education; universities; school building; playing fields; environmental studies; physical education; school equipment; school meals and health; teaching aids. *Length:* 1000 to 1500 words. *Payment:* by arrangement. *Illustrations:* photographs and drawings.

Education and Training (1959), Derek Bradley, A.B.E. Publications, 14 Worple Road, London, SW19 4DD *T.* 01-657 1247.
£1.20. M. Authoritative articles of 1000-2000 words on all aspects of further education, commercial and industrial training. *Payment:* by arrangement. *Illustrations:* offset litho.

Electrical Review (1872), T. C. J. Cogle, B.SC.(ENG.), M.I.C.E., F.I.E.E., Electrical-Electronics Press Ltd., Quadrant House, Sutton, Surrey, SM2 5AS *T.* 01-661 3113. *Telex:* 892084 Bisprs-G.
80p. W. Articles on electrical engineering and international trade; outside contributions considered. Electrical news welcomed. *Illustrations:* photographs and drawings.

Electrical Times, The (1891), G. A. Jack, Quadrant House, The Quadrant, Sutton, Surrey, SM2 5AS *T.* 01-661 3138. *Telex:* 892084 Bisprs G (EEP).
90p. M. Technical articles about 1000 to 1500 words, with illustrations as necessary. *Payment:* by arrangement. *Illustrations:* line, half-tone.

Elle (UK) (1985), Sally Brampton, Rex House, 4-12 Lower Regent Street, London SW1Y 4PE *T.* 01-930 9050.

£1.00 M. Commissioned material only. *Payment:* by arrangement. *Illustrations:* colour.

Embroidery, The Embroiderers' Guild, P.O.Box 42B East Molesey, Surrey, KT8 9BB *T.* 01-943 1229.
£1.25. Q. (£6.50 p.a.). Articles on historical and contemporary embroidery by curators and artists. Exhibition and book reviews. Saleroom report. Diary of events. *Payment:* by arrangement. *Illustrations:* line, half-tone, colour.

Encounter (1953), Melvin J. Lasky and Richard Mayne, 43-44 Great Windmill Street, London W1V 7PA *T.* 01-434 3063.
£1.50. 10 p.a. Reportage, stories, poems. *Length:* 3000-5000 words. *Payment:* £10 per 1000. Interested contributors should study magazine before submitting MSS; s.a.e. essential for return if unsuitable.

Engineer, The (1856), John Pullin, 30 Calderwood Street, London, SE18 6QH *T.* 01-855 7777.
£1.50. W. (£50.00 p.a.). Outside contributions paid for if accepted.

Engineering (1866), Graham Cooper, Design Council, 28 Haymarket, London, SW1Y 4SU *T.* 01-839 8000.
£2.00. M. Contributions considered on all aspects of engineering, particularly design. *Payment:* by arrangement. Photographs and drawings used.

Engineering Materials and Design, Rex Narraway, C.ENG., M.I.MECH.E., Industrial Press, Quadrant House, The Quadrant, Sutton, Surrey, SM2 5AS *T.* 01-661 3174.
Controlled circulation. Technical articles on engineering design and on materials and components. *Payment:* by arrangement. *Length:* from 1000 words. *Illustrations:* line and half-tone.

English Historical Review (1886), Dr. P. H. Williams, Dr. R. J. W. Evans, Longman Group, 6th. Floor, Westgate House, The High, Harlow, Essex, CM20 1NE *T.* (0279) 442061.
£29.00 p.a. Q. High-class scholarly articles (such as are usually found in quarterlies), documents, and reviews or short notices of books. Contributions are not accepted unless they supply original information and should be sent direct to Dr. P. H. Williams, Editor, E.H.R., New College, Oxford, OX1 3BN. Books for review should be sent to Dr. R. J. W. Evans, Editor, E.H.R., Brasenose College, Oxford, OX1 4AJ. *No payment.*

Entertainment & Arts Management (1973), John Offord, John Offord Publications Ltd., 12 The Avenue, Eastbourne, East Sussex, BN21 2YA *T.* (0323) 645871.
£1.50 M. Articles by specialists on the policies, practices, production and state of the arts and entertainment with emphasis upon their administration and management. *Length:* 1,000-2,000 words. *Payment:* by arrangement. *Illustrations:* line and half-tone.

Entomologist's Monthly Magazine (1864), K. G. V. Smith, Gem Publishing Co., Brightwood, Bell Lane, Brightwell cum Sotwell, Wallingford, Oxon, OX10 0QD *T.* (0491) 33882.
£20.00 p.a. 3 times p.a. Articles on all entomological subjects, foreign and British. *No payment.*

Envoi (1957), Anne Lewis-Smith, Pen Ffordd, Newport, Dyfed SA42 0QT *T.* (0239) 820285.
£5 p.a. 3 p.a. New poetry and reviews. Poetry Competitions. Editorial panel of 30 who criticise each poem sent in (with SAE) at no charge.

Essex Countryside (1952), Meg Davis-Berry, Essex Countryside Ltd., The Laurels, High Street, Barley, Royston, Herts SG8 3JA *T.* (076 384) 677.
60p. M. Articles of county interest. *Length:* approximately 1000 words. *Illustrations:* half-tone and line.

European Plastics News (1929), Tim Tunbridge, Quadrant House, The Quadrant, Sutton, Surrey, SM2 5AS *T.* 01-661 3292. *Telex:* 892084.
£3.50. £40.00 p.a. M. Technical articles dealing with plastics and allied subjects. *Length:* depending on subject. *Payment:* by arrangement. *Illustrations:* half-tone blocks 120 screen, line.

European Racehorse, The, Richard Onslow, 19 Clarges Street, London, W1Y 7PG *T.* 01-493 7353.
£5.50. March, June, July, September, November. Preliminary letter essential. Articles on breeding of racehorses and ancillary subjects by recognised experts.

Evangelical Quarterly (1929), Prof. I. H. Marshall, Department of New Testament Exegesis, King's College, Aberdeen, AB9 2UB. Published from Paternoster House, 3 Mount Radford Crescent, Exeter, Devon, EX2 4JW *T.* Exeter 50631.
£1.95. Q. An international review of Bible and theology in defence of the historic Christian faith. Articles on the defence or exposition of Biblical theology as exhibited in the great Reformed Confessions. *No payment.*

Evening Chronicle (Newcastle), Graeme Stanton, Newcastle Chronicle and Journal Ltd., Thomson House, Groat Market, Newcastle upon Tyne, NE99 1BO *T.* (0632) 327500. London: Thomson Regional Newspapers, Pemberton House, East Harding Street, EC4A 3AS *T.* 01-353 9131.
18p. D. News, photographs and features covering almost every subject which are of interest to readers in Tyne Wear, Northumberland and Durham. *Payment:* according to value.

Evening Post, 395 High Street, Chatham, Kent, ME4 4PG *T.* Medway (0634) 48354.
14p. Monday to Friday. Local news covering the Medway towns, Gravesend, Dartford, Swale and Maidstone. Also national news. Paper with emphasis on news and sport, plus regular feature pages. *Illustrations:* line and half-tone.

Evening Post (Reading) (1965), Trevor Wade, 8 Tessa Road, Reading, RG1 8NS *T.* Reading (0734) 55833.
16p. D. Topical articles based on current news. *Length:* 800 to 1200 words. *Payment:* based on lineage rates. *Illustrations:* half-tone.

Everyday Electronics (1971), Mike Kenward, Wimborne Publishing Ltd., 6 Church Street, Wimborne, Dorset, BH21 1JH *T.* (0202) 881749.
£1.10 M. Constructional and theoretical articles aimed at the student and hobbyist. *Length:* 1000-5500 words. *Payment:* £55-£90 per 1000 words depending on type of article. *Illustrations:* line and half-tone.

Everywoman (1985), Barbara Rogers, 34a Islington Green, London N1 8DU *T.* 01-359 5496.
75p. M. Short stories up to 1200 words. Features, especially news features. Study of magazine essential, submit outline in first instance. *Payment:* by arrangement. *Illustrations:* line, half-tone; cartoons.

Exchange and Mart (1868), Link House, 25 West Street, Poole, Dorset, BH15 1LL *T.* Poole (0202) 671171. *Telex:* 417109.
45p. W. No editorial matter used.

Face, The (1980), Nick Logan, The Old Laundry, Ossington Buildings, Moxon Street, London W1 *T.* 01-935 8232.

90p. M. Articles on music, fashion, films, popular youth culture. *Payment:* £60.00 per 1000 words. *Illustrations:* half-tone, colour.

Faith and Freedom: A Journal of Progressive Religion (1947), Manchester College, Oxford. Editor: Peter B. Godfrey, B.A., 62 Hastings Road, Sheffield S7 2GU *T.* (0742) 363797.
£5.00 p.a., 3 issues (April, July, Oct.). Articles on philosophy and religions from free, non-dogmatic point of view, 3000 to 5000 words. No *Payment*.

Family Circle, 3rd Floor, 38 Hans Crescent, London SW1X 0LZ *T.* 01-589 2000.
49p. M. Practical, medical and human interest material. *Length:* minimum 650 words. *Payment:* NUJ rates or above.

Family Law (1971), Miles McColl, Elizabeth Walsh, P.O. Box 260, 15 Pembroke Road, Bristol BS99 7DX *T.* (0272) 732861. *Telex:* 449119.
£37.50 p.a. M. Articles dealing with all aspects of the Law as it affects the Family, written from a legal or sociological point of view. *Length:* 1000 words plus. *Payment:* £11.00 per 1000 words, or by arrangement. No *illustrations*.

Farmers Weekly (1934), Gary Noble, The Farmers Publishing Group, Carew House, Wallington, Surrey SM6 0DX *T.* 01-661 3500.
60p. W. Articles on agriculture from freelance contributors will be accepted subject to negotiation.

Farming News (1983), Marcus Oliver, 30 Calderwood Street, London SE18 6QH *T.* 01-855 7777. *Telex:* 896238.
60p. W. (£40 p.a.) News, business, technical and leisure articles; crosswords, features. *Payment:* NUJ freelance rates. *Illustrations:* half-tone, colour; cartoons.

Fashion Forecast (1946), Suzanne Turower, 33 Bedford Place, London WC1B 5JX *T.* 01-637 2211. *Telex:* 8954884.
£10.00 in U.K. and Europe, £16.00 airmail. Twice p.a. (March, September). Factual articles on fashions and accessories with forecast trend. *Length;* 800 to 1000 words. *Illustrations:* half-tone and line.

Fashion Weekly (1959), Roy Kent, 6 & 7 Cambridge Gate, London, NW1 4JR *T.* 01-486 0155.
50p. W. (£26.00 p.a.). Business and product paper for clothing retailers. *Payment:* by arrangement. *Illustrations:* line and half-tone.

Fiction Magazine (1982) Judy Cooke, 12-13 Clerkenwell Green, London EC1R 0DP *T.* 01-250 1504.
£1.50. 10 p.a. £9.50 p.a. Short stories, essays, reviews, interviews. *Length:* up to 8000 words. *Payment:* by arrangement. *Illustrations:* line, half-tone; cartoons.

Field, The (1853), (incorporating **Land and Water** and **The County Gentleman**), Carmelite House, Carmelite Street, London EC4Y 0JA *T.* 01-353 6000. *T.A.* Field Newspaper, London.
£1.00. W. Specific and informed comment on the British countryside and country pursuits, including natural history, field sports, gardening and farming. Overseas subjects considered but opportunities for such articles are limited. No fiction or children's material. Articles, *length* 800-1200 words, by outside contributors considered, and occasional openings for brief news items.*Payment:* on merit. *Illustrations:* photographs, some colour if sufficiently high standard.

Films & Filming, John Russell Taylor, 43b Gloucester Road, Croydon, CR0 2DH *T.* 01-689 4104. *Telex:* 298133.

£1.25. M. Articles on serious cinema, preferably with illustrations. *Payment:* by arrangement. *Illustrations:* line, half-tone.

Filtration & Separation (1964), R. Feather, 38 Mount Pleasant, London WC1X 0AP *T.* 01-833 0392. *Telex:* 261177.
£4.50. Bi-M. Articles on the design, contruction and application of filtration and separation equipment and dust control and air cleaning equipment for all industrial purposes; articles on filtration and separation and dust control and air cleaning operations and techniques in all industries. *Payment:* by arrangement. *Illustrations:* line and half-tone.

Financial Times (1888), G. Owen, Bracken House, 10 Cannon Street, London, EC4P 4BY *T.* 01-248 8000.
35p. D.

Financial Weekly (1979), Tom Lloyd, 14 Greville Street, London EC1. *T.* 01-405 2622.
95p. W. Financial, industrial and commercial features. Interviews and profiles. *Payment:* £100 per 1000 words. *Illustrations:* line, half-tone and colour.

Fine Art Trade Guild Journal, The, 192 Ebury Street, London, SW1W 8UP *T.* 01-730 3220.
Distributed to members only; 75p extra copies. Bi-M. For the promotion and improvement of all aspects of the Fine Art Trade. *Length* of articles 2000 words with good illustrations. *No payment.*

Fitness (1984), Laura Swaffield, Cover Publications Ltd., The Northern and Shell Building, P.O. Box 381, Millharbour, London E14 9TW *T.* 01-987 5090. *Telex:* 24676 Norshl G.
£1.20. M. Articles on all aspects of fitness. *Payment:* by arrangement. *Illustrations:* line, half-tone, colour; cartoons.

Flight International (1909), D. Mason, Quadrant House, The Quadrant, Sutton, Surrey, SM2 5AS *T.* 01-661 3321. *Telex:* 892084 Bisprs G.
85p. W. Deals with aviation in all its branches. Articles operational and technical, illustrated by photographs, engineering cutaway drawings, also news, paragraphs, reports of lectures, etc. *Payment:* varies; cheques month following publication. *Illustrations:* tone, line, two- and four-colour. News press day: Monday.

Football Picture Story Library, D. C. Thomson & Co. Ltd., Courier Place, Dundee DD1 9QJ and 185 Fleet Street, London EC4A 2HS.
26p. Two each month. Football stories for boys told in pictures.

Forensic Photography, incorporating **Medico-Legal Photography** (1972), Nigel Morland, 87 London Street, Chertsey, Surrey KT16 8AN *T.* (093 28) 62933.
£10.00 p.a. Q. Though this journal goes only to subscribers and is not sold through retail channels, the editor is always interested in articles (illustrated or not) concerned with photographic techniques slanted to the professional and concerned with any aspect of the journal's title. *Payment:* by arrangement. *Illustrations:* line or half-tone.

Freelance Writing & Photography (1965), Arthur Waite, 5-9 Bexley Square, Salford, Manchester, M3 6DB *T.* 061-832 5079.
£5.50 p.a. Q. Articles and market news of interest to the freelance writer. *Length:* 500 to 1200 words. *Payment:* £10.00 per 1000 words. *Illustrations:* line and half-tone. Guide-lines for contributors available.

Friend, The (1843), David Firth, Drayton House, 30 Gordon Street, London, WC1H 0BQ *T.* 01-387 7549. Publishing: Headley Brothers Ltd., Ashford, Kent.
38p. W. A Quaker weekly paper. Matter of interest to the Society of Friends, devotional or general, considered from outside contributors. No fiction. 1200 words maximum length. No *payment*.

Fruit Trades' Journal (1895), David Shapley, 430 Market Towers, New Covent Garden, Nine Elms Lane, London, SW8 5NN *T.* 01-720 8822 and 622 6677. *Telex:* 915149 Frtjnl G.
70p. W. Articles dealing with above trades on the marketing aspects of production but particularly importing and distributing sides; articles should average 500-700 words. *Payment:* by arrangement. *Illustrations:* half-tone or line artwork.

Gambit (1963), John Calder, Tony Dunn, (John Calder (Publishers) Ltd.), 18 Brewer Street, London, W1R 4AS *T.* 01-734 3786.
£3.00. 2 p.a. Plays by contemporary writers, neglected authors, translations of foreign works. Full length and short. Also articles and interviews on theatre, opera. Reviews. *Payment:* by arrangement. *Illustrated*.

Garden News (1958), Pam Deschamps, Bushfield House, Orton Centre, Peterborough, PE2 0UW *T.* Peterborough (0733) 237111.
38p. W. Gardening news and human features on gardeners and their methods of success. *Payment:* £25.00 per 1000 words. Higher rate for good short pieces and suited to our style. *Illustrations:* line, half-tone and colour.

Gas World (1884), Roger Pechey (Benn Publications Ltd.), Sovereign Way, Tonbridge, Kent TN9 1RW *T.* (0732) 364422. *Telex:* 95162 Benton G.
£3.85. M. (£35.00 p.a.). Full news coverage and technical articles on all aspects of engineering and management in the gas industry. *Length:* up to 1800 words. Pictures and news items of topical interest are paid for at standard rates. *Payment:* by arrangement.

Gay News (1972), Ian Dunmore, 1 Campden Hill Road, London W8 7DU *T.* 01-995 3335.
60p. F. Short stories up to 3000 words; articles up to 3000 words. S.A.E. essential. *Payment:* by arrangement.

Gay Times (1982), John Marshall, 283 Camden High Street, London NW1 7BX *T.* 01-482 2576.
£1.00. M. Full news and review coverage of all aspects of homosexual life. Short stories and feature articles. *Length:* up to 3000 words. *Payment:* by arrangement. *Illustrations:* line and half-tone; cartoons.

Gemmological Newsletter (1969), Michael O'Donoghue, 7 Hillingdon Avenue, Sevenoaks, Kent, TN13 3RB *T.* (0732) 453503.
£6.50 p.a. 30 p.a. (Oct-July). Articles about minerals, gemstones, man-made crystals, lapidary and jewellery making. *Length:* up to 800 to 1000 words. *Payment:* by arrangement. *Illustrations:* line and half-tone.

General Practitioners, Journal of the Royal College of (founded as the Journal of the College of General Practitioners in 1954), Dr. E. G. Buckley, F.R.C.G.P., 8 Queen Street, Edinburgh EH2 1JE *T.* 031-225 7629.
£60.00 p.a. (£65 outside UK). M. Articles relevant to general medical practice. *No payment*. *Illustrations:* half-tone and colour.

Geographical Journal (1893), B. H. Farmer, Royal Geographical Society, Kensington Gore, London, SW7 2AR *T.* 01-589 5466.
£10.00 (post free). 3 times a year (£28.00 p.a.). Papers read before the Royal

Geographical Society and papers on all aspects of geography or exploration. *Length:* max. 3500 words. *Payment:* for reviews. *Illustrations:* photographs, maps and diagrams.

Geographical Magazine, The, Iain Bain, 1 Kensington Gore, London, SW7 2AR *T.* 01-584 4436.
£1.20. M. Informative, readable, well-illustrated, authentic articles, from 1500 to 2000 words in length, dealing with people and their environment in all parts of the world; modern geography in all its aspects; kindred subjects such as hydrology, meteorology, communications, civil engineering, space, etc.; man's control of the environment in which he lives, works and plays; travel, exploration, research; plant and animal life in their relationship with mankind. A *preliminary* letter is recommended. *Payment:* from £50.00 per 1000 words. *Illustrations:* of highly technical and artistic quality. Photographs unaccompanied by articles may be considered. *Payment:* colour, from £12.00 upwards, covers by negotiation; black and white, from £5.00 upwards, depending on size of reproduction.

Geological Magazine (1864), Mr. W. B. Harland, Dr. C. P. Hughes, Dr. R. S. J. Sparks, Cambridge University Press, The Edinburgh Building, Shaftesbury Road, Cambridge, CB2 2RU *T.* (0223) 312493.
£68.00 p.a. Bi-M. (January etc.). Original articles on general and stratigraphical geology, petrology, palaeontology, mineralogy, etc., containing the results of independent research by experts and amateurs. Also reviews and notices of current geological literature, correspondence on geological subjects—illustrated. *Length:* variable. *No payment* made.

Gifts International, Vhairi Cotter (Benn Publications plc.), Sovereign Way, Tonbridge, Kent, TN9 1RW *T.* (0732) 364422.
£22.00 p.a., £30.00 p.a. overseas. M. News of gift industry—products, trends, shops. *Articles:* retailing, exporting, importing, manufacturing, crafts (U.K. and abroad). *Payment:* by agreement. *Illustrations:* products, news, personal photographs.

Girl, Holborn Publishing Group, IPC Magazines Ltd., Commonwealth House, 1-19 New Oxford Street, London WC1A 1NG *T.* 01-829 7777.
30p. W. A photo-story and feature magazine for pre-teen girls. Does have some drawn script. Good writers required for photo-story scripts with good visual ideas and exciting story lines.

Girl About Town Magazine (1973), Louisa Saunders, 141-3 Drury Lane, Covent Garden, London, WC2B 5TS *T.* 01-836 4433.
Free. W. Articles of general interest related to London. *Length:* about 1000 words. *Payment:* by arrangement. *Illustrations:* line, half-tone, colour.

Glasgow Evening Times (1876), George McKechnie, 195 Albion Street, Glasgow, G1 1QP *T.* 041-552 6255; London Office: 1 Jerome Street, London, E1 6NJ *T.* 01-377 0890.
20p. D.

Glasgow Herald (1783), Arnold Kemp, 195 Albion Street, Glasgow, G1 1QP *T.* 041-552 6255; London: 1 Jerome Street, E1 6NJ *T.* 01-377 0890.
25p. D. Independent. Articles up to 1000 words.

Gloucestershire and Avon Life, John Hudson, 10 The Plain, Thornbury, Bristol, BS12 2AG *T.* Thornbury, (0454) 413173. *Publisher:* Opax Publishing Ltd.
60p. M. Articles of interest to the counties concerned based on first-hand experience dealing with the life, work, customs and matters affecting welfare

of town and country. *Length:* articles 500 to 1500 words. *Payment:* by arrangement. Photographs also by arrangement. *Illustrations:* preference given to articles accompanied by good photographs.

Golf Illustrated (1890), Bill Robertson, 47 Dartford Road, Sevenoaks, Kent TN13 3TE *T.* (0732) 451861. *Telex:* 95509.
75p. (£23.00 p.a.) Fortnightly. Articles on golf and of interest to golfers. *Payment:* by arrangement. *Illustrations:* photographs of golfers and golf courses.

Golf Monthly (1911), Malcolm Campbell, 1 Park Circus, Glasgow, G3 6AS *T.* 041-332 2828.
£1.20. M. Original articles on golf considered (not reports). *Payment:* by arrangement. *Illustrations:* half-tone, colour.

Golf World (1962), Peter Haslam, Advance House, 37 Millharbour, Isle of Dogs, London E14 9TX *T.* 01-538 1031.
£1.20. M. Expert golf instructional articles, 500-3000 words; general interest articles, personality features 500-3000 words. Little fiction. *Payment:* by negotiation. *Illustrations:* line, half-tone, colour.

Good Housekeeping (1922), Charlotte Lessing, National Magazine House, 72 Broadwick Street, London, W1V 2BP *T.* 01-439 7144.
85p. M. Articles of 1000-2500 words from qualified writers are invited on topics of interest to intelligent women. Domestic subjects covered by staff writers. Short stories and humorous articles also used. *Payment:* good magazine standards. *Illustrations:* mainly commissioned.

Gramophone, Christopher Pollard, 177-179 Kenton Road, Harrow, Middx., HA3 0HA *T.* 01-907 4476.
95p. M. Outside contributions are occasionally used. Features on recording artists, technical articles, and articles about gramophone needs. 1000 to 1500 words preferred. *Payment:* by arrangement. *Illustrations:* line and half-tone.

Granta (1889; new series 1979), Bill Buford, 44a Hobson Street, Cambridge, CB1 1NL *T.* (0223) 315290. Published in association with Penguin Books U.K., Ltd.
£3.95. Q. Original fiction and cultural journalism. *Length:* determined by content. *Payment:* by arrangement. *Illustrations:* line and half-tone.

Great Outdoors, The (1978), Roger Smith, Ravenseft House, 302 St. Vincent Street, Glasgow, G2 5NL *T.* 041-221 7000.
£1.10. (£14.00 p.a.). M. Articles on walking or camping in specific areas, or about walking generally, preferably illustrated. *Length:* 1500-2000 words. *Payment:* by arrangement. *Illustrations:* line, half-tone and colour.

Grocer, The (1861), A. de Angeli, 5-7 Southwark Street, London, SE1 1RQ *T.* 01-407 6981.
15p. W. This journal is devoted entirely to the trade. Contributions accepted are articles or news or illustrations of general interest to the grocery and provision trades. *Payment:* by arrangement.

Grower, The (1923), Peter Rogers, 50 Doughty Street, London, WC1N 2LP *T.* 01-405 0364.
65p. W. News and practical articles on commercial horticulture, preferably illustrated. *Payment:* by arrangement. *Illustrations:* photographs, line drawings.

Guardian, The (1821), 119 Farringdon Road, London, EC1 *T.* 01-278 2332 and 164 Deansgate, Manchester, M60 2RR *T.* 061-832 7200.
25p. D. Independent. The paper takes few articles from outside contributors

except on its specialist pages. Articles should not normally exceed 1200 words in length. *Payment:* from £96.00 per 1000 words. *Illustrations:* news and features photographs.

Guiding, Official Organ of the Girl Guides Association, Mrs. J. V. Rush, 17-19 Buckingham Palace Road, London, SW1W 0PT *T.* 01-834 6242.
50p. M. Short articles of interest to adult youth leaders, 500-1500 words, mostly by experts in the wide range of training subjects. Cartoons about Guide Movement. *Payment:* £25.35 per 1000 words. *Illustrations:* line and half-tone.

Hampshire—The County Magazine, Dennis Stevens, 74 Bedford Place, Southampton, SO1 2DF *T.* Southampton (0703) 223591 and 333457.
40p. M. Factual articles concerning all aspects of Hampshire and Hampshire life, past and present. *Length:* 500-1500 words. *Payment:* £10 per 1000 words. *Illustrations:* photographs and line drawings.

Handicapped Living (1982) Charles Lloyd, Stanley House, 9 West Street, Epsom, Surrey KT18 7RL *T.* 41411.
70p. M. Factual and informative articles. *Length:* up to 1200 words. *Payment:* by arrangement. *Illustrations:* line, half-tone.

Harpers & Queen (1929), Willie Landels, National Magazine House, 72 Broadwick Street, London, W1V 2BP *T.* 01-439 7144.
£1.80. M. Features, fashion, beauty, art, theatre, films, travel, interior decoration, mainly commissioned. *Illustrations:* line, wash, full colour and two- and three-colour, and photographs.

Health & Efficiency International (1900), Kate Sturdy, 2nd Floor, 67-73 Worship Street, London, EC2A 2DU *T.* 01-377 5122.
£1.20. M. Articles on nudist/naturist/health matters. Naturist travel features. *Length:* from 1000 to 1500 words. *Payment:* £35 per 1000 words. *Illustrations:* line, half-tone, colour transparencies, colour prints.

Health Educational Journal (1943), Public Affairs Division, Health Education Council, 78 New Oxford Street, London, WC1A 1AH *T.* 01-631 0930.
£3.00 p.a. Q. Matter on mental and physical health, health education and social well-being; reports of surveys of people's knowledge of health: educational method and material; nutrition; educational psychology and preventive psychiatry. Book reviews. *Length:* 1500 to 3000 words. *No payment. Illustrations:* camera ready artwork.

Heredity: An International Journal of Genetics (1947), L. M. Cook, Department of Zoology, University of Manchester, Manchester M13 9PL.
£60.00 (two volumes each of three parts yearly). Research and review articles in genetics of 1000 to 15,000 words with summary and bibliography. Book reviews and abstracts of conferences. *No payment. Illustrations:* line, half-tone and colour.

Here's Health, 30 Station Approach, West Byfleet, Surrey. *T.* Byfleet 49123.
85p. M. Articles on nutrition; dieting; slimming; health foods; beauty care; natural food cookery; natural health and healing therapies; pollution; organic gardening; alternative medicine. *Length:* 750-1800 words. *Payment:* on publication. Preliminary letter essential.

Hertfordshire Countryside (1946), Charles Fleet, Beaumonde Publications Ltd., 4 Mill Bridge, Hertford, Herts. SG14 1PY *T.* (0992) 553571.
60p. M. Articles of county interest, 1500 words. *Illustrations:* line and half-tone.

Heythrop Journal, The (1960), Rev. Dr. Joseph A. Munitiz, Heythrop College, University of London, 11 Cavendish Square, London, W1M 0AN *T.* 01-580 6941.
£3.50 including postage. Q. (£12.00 p.a., U.S.A. $30.00). Articles (5000-8000) in: philosophy, theology speculative and positive, scripture, canon law, church relations, moral and pastoral psychology, of general interest but of technical merit. *Payment:* Authors receive 24 offprints.

Hi-Fi News & Record Review (1956), John Atkinson, Link House, Dingwall Avenue, Croydon, CR9 2TA *T.* 01-686 2599. *Telex:* 947709 Linkho G.
£1.20 M. Articles on all aspects of high quality sound recording and reproduction; also extensive record review section and supporting musical feature articles. Audio matter is essentially technical, but should be presented in a manner suitable for music lovers interested in the nature of sound. *Payment:* by arrangement. *Length:* 2000 to 3000 words. *Illustrations:* line and/or half-tone; cartoons.

History (1916), Professor W. A. Speck, M.A., D.PHIL. Editorial: School of History, The University of Leeds, Leeds LS2 9JT *T.* (0532) 431751 (ext. 6365). Business: 59A Kennington Park Road, London, SE11 4JH *T.* 01-735 3901.
£8.50 for Historical Ass. Members; £17.00 p.a. non-members. 3 p.a. Published by the Historical Association. Historical articles and reviews by experts. *Length:* usually up to 8000 words. *No payment. Illustrations:* only exceptionally.

History Today (1951), Gordon Marsden, 83-84 Berwick Street, London W1V 3PJ *T.* 01-439 8315.
£1.40p. M. History in the widest sense—political, economic, social, biography, relating past to present; World history as well as British. *Length:* about 3500 words. *Payment:* by agreement. *Illustrations:* from prints and original photographs. Please do not send original material until publication is agreed.

Home and Country (1919), Penny Kitchen, 39 Eccleston Street, London, SW1W 9NT *T.* 01-730 0307.
32p. M. A good deal of the material published relates to the activities of the National Federation of Women's Institutes, whose official journal it is, but articles of general interest to women, particularly country women, of 800 to 1000 words are considered. *Payment:* by arrangement. *Illustrations:* photographs and drawings.

Home and Family (1954), Eryl Jackson, The Mothers' Union, The Mary Sumner House, 24 Tufton Street, London, SW1P 3RB *T.* 01-222 5533.
25p. Q. Short articles related to Christian family life. *Payment:* approx. £5.00 per 1000 words. *Illustrations:* line and half-tone.

Home Science (1964), Arthur J. Fearon, Church Lane, Dagenham, Essex, RM10 9UL. A. J. Fearon & Associates. *T.* 01-592 2033.
25p. M. Articles on home, food, nutrition, cooking, hygiene, textiles, grooming, home management, furnishing, domestic appliances, laundry. *Length:* 1000 words. *Payment:* by arrangement. *Illustrations:* line, half-tone, colour.

Home Words (1870) P.O. Box 44, Guildford, Surrey, GU1 1XL *T.* (0483) 33944. M. An illustrated C. of E. magazine inset. Articles of popular Christian interest (400 to 800 words) with relevant photographs.

Homes and Gardens (1919), Jenny Greene, King's Reach Tower, Stamford Street, London, SE1 9LS *T.* 01-261 6099.
£1.00. M. Articles of general interest to intelligent women and men. *Length:*

articles, 900-3000 words. *Payment:* generous, but exceptional work required. *Illustrations:* all types.

Hoot, D. C. Thomson & Co. Ltd., Courier Place, Dundee DD1 9QJ and 185 Fleet Street, London EC4A 2HS.
20p. Picture strip comic for children. Single page sets, 9-12 pictures. *Payment:* on acceptance.

Horse and Hound, M. A. Clayton, King's Reach Tower, Stamford Street, London, SE1 9LS *T.* 01-261 6315.
70p. W. Special articles, news items, photographs, on all matters appertaining to horses, hunting.

Horse & Pony (1980), Lesley Eccles, EMAP Pursuit Publications, Bretton Court, Bretton, Peterborough, PE3 8DZ *T.* (0733) 264666.
65p. Fortnightly. All material relevant to young people with equestrian interests. *Payment:* on value to publication rather than length. *Illustrations:* colour, black and white, with a strong story line.

Horse and Rider (1959), Kate O'Sullivan, 104 Ash Road, Sutton, Surrey, SM3 9LD *T.* 01-641 4911.
75p. M. A sophisticated magazine covering all forms of equestrian activity at home and abroad. Good writing and technical accuracy essential. *Length:* 1000 to 1600 words. *Payment:* by arrangement. *Illustrations:* photographs and drawings, the latter usually commissioned.

Horticulture Week, J. Deen, 38-42 Hampton Road, Teddington, Middlesex, TW11 0JE *T.* 01-977 8787.
60p. W. (£35.00 p.a.). A practical horticultural journal for the nursery trade, landscape industry and public parks staff. Outside contributions considered and, if accepted, paid for. *Length:* 500 to 1500 words. No fiction. *Payment:* by arrangement. *Illustrations:* in half-tone and line.

Hospitality (1980), Julian Demetriadi, M.H.C.I.M.A., 35 Albemarle Street, London W1X 3FB *T.* 01-629 4320. Official magazine of the Hotel Catering & Institutional Management Association.
£1.25. M. Articles for a management readership on food, accommodation services and related topics in hotels, restaurants, educational establishments, the health service, industrial situations, educational and other institutions. *Illustrations:* photographs, line. *Payment:* by arrangement.

House & Garden, Robert Harling, Vogue House, Hanover Square, London, W1R 0AD *T.* 01-499 9080. *Telex:* 27338 Volon G.
£1.20. M. Articles (always commissioned), on subjects relating to domestic architecture, interior decorating, furnishing, gardening, household equipment.

House Builder, Phillip Cooke, 82 New Cavendish Street, London, W1M 8AD *T.* 01-580 5588.
£1.50. M. A technical journal for those engaged in house and flat construction and the development of housing estates. The Official Journal of the House-Builders Federation, National House Building Council and New Homes Marketing Board. Articles on design, construction, and equipment of dwellings, estate planning and development, and technical aspects of house-building. *Length:* articles 500 words and upwards, preferably with illustrations. *Preliminary letter* advisable. *Payment:* by arrangement. *Illustrations:* photographs, plans, constructional details.

Ideal Home (1920), Terence Whelan, King's Reach Tower, Stamford Street, London, SE1 9LS *T.* 01-261 6474.

95p. M. Specialised home subjects magazine, and articles usually commissioned. Contributors advised to study editorial content before submitting material. *Payment:* according to material. *Illustrations:* usually commissioned.

Illustrated London News (1842), James Bishop, 20 Upper Ground, London SE1 9PF *T.* 01-928 6969.
£1.30. M. A news monthly dealing chiefly with current and cultural affairs of British and international interest. Stories for the Christmas number are usually accepted only from authors of established repute. Interesting articles dealing with politics, social issues, science, art, archaeology, ethnology, travel, exploration, are particularly acceptable. *Payment:* for *illustrations* at the usual rates, or by special arrangement; special prices for exclusive material. Photographs (especially exclusive).

Impact of Science on Society (1950), Unesco, Place de Fontenoy, Paris, 75700. *T.* 33(1) 568-4147 *T.A.* Unesco, Paris.
96p. Q. Articles and original studies on the social, political, economic, cultural aspects of science and technology. A *preliminary letter* to the Editor is requested. *Length:* 4500 words. *Payment:* up to £200 on acceptance. *Illustrations:* photographs, tables, graphs and drawings. Intending contributors are advised to study the magazine.

In Britain (1930), Bryn Frank, The British Tourist Authority, Thames Tower, Black's Road, London W6 9EL *T.* 01-846 9000.
95p. M. (£12.75 p.a.). Features magazine about events and places in Britain. Short pieces (maximum 150 words) sometimes accepted.

Index on Censorship (1972), George Theiner, 39c Highbury Place, London N5 1QP. *T.* 01-359 0161.
£1.40 (£14.00 p.a.). 10 p.a. Articles up to 5000 words dealing with political censorship, book reviews 750-1500 words. *Payment:* Articles £42 per 1000 words, book reviews £21.

Indexer, The (1958), Journal of the Society of Indexers, American Society of Indexers, Australian Society of Indexers, and Indexing & Abstracting Society of Canada. Hazel Bell, 139 The Ryde, Hatfield, Herts, AL9 5DP *T.* Hatfield (070-72) 65201.
Free to members (subscription £7.50 p.a. from Journal Subscriptions Officer, 16 Coleridge Close, Hitchin, Herts SG4 0QX). 2 p.a. Articles of interest to professional indexers, authors, publishers, documentalists. *Payment:* by arrangement.

Industrial Participation (1884), D. Wallace Bell, 85 Tooley Street, London SE1 2QZ *T.* 01-403 6018.
£6.00 p.a. post free. Q. Journal of the Industrial Participation Association. Articles on participation and involvement in industry, employee shareholding, joint consultation, the sharing of information, labour-management relations, workers participation, and kindred industrial subjects from the operational angle, with emphasis on the practice of particular enterprises, usually written by a member of the team involved, whether manager or workers, and with a strong factual background. *Length:* up to 3500 words. *Payment:* £10 per 1000 words.

Industrial Society (1918), Denise Granatt, The Industrial Society, Peter Runge House, 3 Carlton House Terrace, London, SW1Y 5DG *T.* 01-839 4300.
£10.00 p.a., £15.00 p.a. overseas. Q. Articles, news items, photographs on developments in industry and commerce in five inter-related areas: effective leadership, productive management-union relations and participation, practical

communication, relevant conditions of employment and working environment and the development of young employees. *Length:* 1000-2000 words. *Payment:* £25 per 1000 words or by negotiation. *Illustrations:* half-tones and line drawings.

Information & Library Manager (1981), ELM Publications, Seaton House, Kings Ripton, Cambridgeshire PE17 2NJ *T.* (04873) 238.
£19.50 p.a. Q. Information and library professional articles. *Illustrations:* line. *Payment:* from £10.00 per 1000 words.

Inquirer, The (1842), Rev. Frank Walker, B.A., 1-6 Essex Street, London, WC2R 2HY *T.* 01-240 2384.
15p. Fortnightly. A journal of news and comment for Unitarians. Articles 700 to 1100 words of general religious, social, cultural, and international interest. Religious articles should be liberal and progressive in tone.

Insurance Brokers' Monthly (1950), Brian Susman, 7 Stourbridge Road, Lye, Stourbridge, West Midlands, DY9 7DG *T.* Lye (038 482) 5228.
80p. M. Articles of technical and non-technical interest to insurance brokers and others engaged in the insurance industry. Occasional articles of general interest to the City, on finance, etc. *Length:* 1000 to 1500 words. *Payment:* from £12.50 per 1000 words on last day of month following publication. Authoritative material written under true name and qualification receives highest payment. *Illustrations:* line and half-tone, 100-120 screen. Cartoons with strong insurance interest.

InterMedia (1970), Andrew H. Waller, International Institute of Communications, Tavistock House South, Tavistock Square, London, WC1H 9LF *T.* 01-388 0671. *Telex:* 24578 IIC LDN. *Fax:* 01-380 0623.
£25.00 p.a. 5 issues p.a.; Institutions: £45 p.a. International journal concerned with policies, events, trends and research in the field of communications. *Preliminary letter* essential. *Payment:* by arrangement. *Illustrations:* black-and-white line.

International Affairs (1922), Royal Institute of International Affairs, Chatham House, St James's Square, London, SW1Y 4LE *T.* 01-930 2233.
£5.00. Q. (£20.00 p.a.; $42.00 p.a. U.S.A., £25.00 p.a. elsewhere). Serious long-term articles on international affairs. *Length:* average 7000 words. *Illustrations:* none. *Payment:* by arrangement. *A preliminary letter is advisable.*

International Broadcast Engineer, David Kirk, Queensway House, 2 Queensway, Redhill, Surrey RH1 1QS *T.* (0737) 68611.
£31.00 p.a. Bi-M. An independent journal devoted to the design, manufacture and operation of professional television and radio broadcast equipment. Circulates to over 144 countries and international aspect is stressed. Preliminary letter essential. *Illustrations:* line and half-tone. *Payment:* by arrangement.

International Construction, A. J. Peterson, Surrey House, 1 Throwley Way, Sutton, Surrey, SM1 4QQ *T.* 01-643 8040. *Telex:* 892084.
M. Articles dealing with new techniques of construction, applications of construction equipment and use of construction materials in any part of the world. *Length:* maximum 1000 words plus illustrations. *Payment:* from £60.00 per 1000 words, plus illustrations. *Illustrations:* half-tone, line, colour. Some two-colour line illustrations can be used.

Inverness Courier (1817), Miss Eveline Barron, O.B.E., M.A., P.O. Box 13, 9-11 Bank Lane, Inverness, IV1 1QW *T.* (0463) 233059.
12p. Bi-W. Short articles (no stories or verses) of Highland interest. *Payment:* by arrangement. No *illustrations.*

Investors Chronicle, Gillian O'Connor, Greystoke Place, Fetter Lane, London, EC4A 1ND *T.* 01-405 6969.
£1.00. W. The leading British journal for investment and personal finance. Occasional outside contributions are accepted. *Payment:* by negotiation.

Iron (1973), Peter Mortimer, 5 Marden Terrace, Cullercoats, North Shields, Tyne & Wear NE30 4PD *T.* Tyneside (091) 2531901.
£1.25p. 3 p.a. Poems; short stories up to 7000 words. *Payment:* £10.00 per page. *Illustrations:* line, half-tone.

Jackie (D. C. Thomson & Co. Ltd.), Courier Place, Dundee, DD1 9QJ *T.* 23131; and 185 Fleet Street, London, EC4A 2HS *T.* 01-242 5086.
24p. W. Colour gravure magazine for teenage girls. Complete photo love stories. Type stories up to 2000 words dealing with young romance. Pop features and pin-ups. General features of teen interest—emotional, astrological, humorous. Fashion and beauty advice. *Illustrations:* transparencies, colour illustrations for type stories. *Payment:* on acceptance.

Jazz Journal International (1948), Eddie Cook (Publisher and Editor-in-Chief), Jazz Journal Ltd., 35 Great Russell Street, London WC1B 3PP *T.* 01-580 7244 and 6976.
£1.20. M. Articles on jazz. Record reviews. *Payment:* by arrangement. *Illustrations:* photographs; line drawings of jazz subjects.

Jewish Chronicle (1841), Geoffrey Paul, 25 Furnival Street, London, EC4A 1JT *T.* 01-405 9252.
20p. W. Authentic and exclusive news stories and articles of Jewish interest from 500 to 1500 words are considered. There are weekly children's, women's and teenage sections. *Payment:* by arrangement. *Illustrations:* of Jewish interest, either topical or feature.

Jewish Telegraph (1950), Paul Harris, Telegraph House, 11 Park Hill, Bury Old Road, Prestwich, Manchester, M25 8HH *T.* 061-740 9321, 389 Street Lane, Leeds LS1Y 6HQ *T.* (0532) 695044, 2a Westgate Road, Wavertree, Liverpool L15 5BA *T.* 051-734 3911.
14p. W. Non-fiction articles of Jewish interest, especially humour. Exclusive Jewish news stories and pictures, international, national and local. *Length:* 1000-1500 words. *Payment:* by arrangement. *Illustrations:* half-tone and line.

Journal, The, Phillip Crawley, Thomson House, Groat Market, Newcastle upon Tyne, NE1 1ED *T.* Newcastle (0632) 327500. London Office: Pemberton House, 3rd Floor, East Harding Street, EC4A 3AS *T.* 01-353 9131.
18p. D. Independent.

Journalist, Bernie Corbett, N.U.J., Acorn House, 314 Gray's Inn Road, London, WC1X 8DP *T.* 01-278 7916.
30p. (£7.50 p.a., £10 p.a. abroad) M. Official organ of the National Union of Journalists. Relating to journalism, trade unionism and general conditions in the newspaper industry. Mainly contributed by members, and outside written contributions not paid.

Judy (D. C. Thomson & Co. Ltd.), Courier Place, Dundee, DD1 9QJ, and 185 Fleet Street, London, EC4A 2HS.
20p. W. Picture-story paper for schoolgirls. Stories in pictures (mainly line drawings) as serials or series, 8-9 frames per page. Also interesting features written to appeal to girls of school age. *Payment:* on acceptance. Encouragement to young artists and writers of promise.

Judy Library (D. C. Thomson & Co. Ltd.), Courier Place, Dundee, DD1 9QJ, and 185 Fleet Street, London, EC4A 2HS.
24p. M. Stories told in pictures, for schoolgirls; 64 pages (about 140 line drawings). Ballet, school, adventure, theatre, sport. Scripts considered; promising artists and script-writers encouraged. *Payment:* on acceptance.

Junior Bookshelf, Marsh Hall, Thurstonland, Huddersfield, HD4 6XB *T.* Huddersfield (0484) 21467.
£1.10. Six issues p.a. (£5.60 inland, £6.50 overseas p.a.). Articles on children's books and authors. *Length:* about 1200 to 1500 words.

Junior Education (1977), Terry Saunders, Scholastic Publications Ltd., Marlborough House, Holly Walk, Leamington Spa, Warwickshire CV32 4LS *T.* (0926 81) 3910. *Telex:* 312138 Spls G.
£1.00. M. For teachers, educationalists and students concerned with children aged 7-12. Articles by specialists on practical teaching ideas and methods, the politics and philosophy of education. *Length:* 800 to 1200 words. *Payment:* by arrangement. Profusely *illustrated* with photographs and line drawings; also large pictures and photographs in full colour. Also **Junior Education Special** (1982), Janet Parsons, £1.00 Bi-M.

Just Seventeen (1983), Beverly Hillier, 52-55 Carnaby Street, London, W1V 1PF *T.* 01-437 8050.
45p. W. Articles of interest to girls aged between 12 and 20. Fashion, beauty, fitness articles. Short stories up to 1500 words. Quizzes. *Payment:* £75 per 1,000 words. *Illustrations:* line, half-tone, colour; cartoons.

Justice of the Peace (1837), N. A. McKittrick, LLB, Bryan Gibson, BA, Little London, Chichester, Sussex, PO19 1PG *T.* (0243) 775552.
£1.50 W. Articles on magisterial law and associated subjects including children and young persons, criminology, medico-legal matters, penology, police, probation (length preferred, under 1400 words). Short reports of conferences, meetings, etc. Rate of *payment:* articles minimum £5.50 per column except when otherwise commissioned. *Preliminary letter welcomed although not essential.*

Karate and Oriental Arts Magazine (1966), Paul H. Crompton, 638 Fulham Road, London, SW6 5RT *T.* 01-736 2551.
95p. Bi-M. Accounts of eastern dancing, body development, body training systems: yoga, karate, fencing, etc. Photographs of men and women with brief notes on same. *Payment:* £20.00 per 1000 words. *Illustrations:* half-tones, line.

Kent (The Journal of the Men of Kent and Kentish Men), Clifford W. Russell, F.R.S.A., 193 White Horse Hill, Chislehurst, Kent, BR7 6DH *T.* 01-857 7509.
Free to members. Q. Articles referring to County of Kent. *Length:* maximum 500 to 600 words. *Payment:* modest, by arrangement. *Illustrations:* photographs and line.

Kent Life (1962), Rod Cooper, Basted, Borough Green, Sevenoaks, Kent TN15 8PW *T.* (0732) 884564.
85p. M. All articles must have a Kent connection. *Length:* 500 to 1200 words; sharp black-and-white pictures with articles; colour transparencies (minimum 2¼ in. square) also considered for front cover and the occasional inside colour feature. *Illustrations:* half-tone or line-drawings. *Payment:* by arrangement.

Kent Messenger, Messenger House, New Hythe Lane, Larkfield, Kent, ME20 6SG *T.* Maidstone (0622) 77880. London Office: Suite 511 International Press Centre, 76 Shoe Lane, London, EC4A 3JB.

27p. Friday. Articles of special interest to Kent particularly Maidstone and Mid-Kent areas. *Payment:* state price. *Illustrations:* line and half-tone.

Labour Weekly (1971), Donald H. Ross, 150 Walworth Road, London, SE17 1JT *T.* 01-703 0833.
40p. W. Political articles. *Payment:* £6.50 per 100 words. *Illustrations:* half-tone.

Lady, The (1885), Joan L. Grahame, 39 and 40 Bedford Street, Strand, London, WC2E 9ER *T.* 01-836 8705.
43p. W. British and foreign travel, countryside, human-interest, animals, cookery, historic-interest and commemorative articles (a preliminary letter is advisable for articles dealing with anniversaries). *Length:* 800-1500 words. Viewpoint: 800 words. *Payment:* by arrangement, averaging £36.00 per 1000 words for first British Serial Rights only, plus varying *payments* for *illustrations* (drawings, mono photographs).

Lancashire Evening Post, C. S. Kendall, 127 Fishergate, Preston, PR1 2DN *T.* (0772) 54841.
17p. D. Topical articles on all subjects. Area of interest Wigan to Lake District and coast. 600 to 900 words. *Payment:* by arrangement. *Illustrations:* half-tones and line blocks.

Lancashire Evening Telegraph (1886), Peter Butterfield, New Telegraph House, High Street, Blackburn, Lancashire, BB1 1HT *T.* (0254) 63588.
17p. D.

Lancashire Life, Howard Reynolds, (OPL Magazines Ltd), Opax House, Primrose Hill, London Road, Preston, Lancashire PR1 4BX *T.* (0772) 50022.
80p. M. Quality features and photographic material of national and regional interest. *Payment:* by negotiation.

Lancashire Magazine, The (1977), Winston Halstead, Barclays Bank Chambers, Sowerby Bridge, Yorkshire HX6 2DX *T.* Halifax (0422) 839643 and 839633.
50p. Bi-M. Articles about people, life and character of all parts of Lancashire. *Length:* 1500 words. *Payment:* £20 approx. per published page. *Illustrations:* line and half-tone.

Lancet (1823), I. Munro, M.B., 7 Adam Street, Adelphi, London, WC2N 6AD *T.* 01-836 6942.
£2.75. W. Mainly from medical profession.

Land & Liberty (1894), Fred Harrison, 177 Vauxhall Bridge Road, London, SW1V 1EU *T.* 01-834 4266.
80p. (£5.00 p.a.) Bi-M. Articles on land economics, land taxation, land prices, land speculation as they relate to housing, the economy, production, politics. *Length:* up to 3000 words. *Payment:* by arrangement. *Illustrations:* half-tone. Study of journal essential.

Language Monthly (1983), Geoffrey Kingscott, 5 East Circus Street, Nottingham, NG1 5AH *T.* (0602) 411087.
£1.20 M. News and informative articles on any aspect of language or translation. *Payment:* NUJ rates. *Illustrations:* half-tone; cartoons.

Legion, The, magazine of The Royal British Legion, D. A. Bosley, Maidstone Press Centre, Bank Street, Maidstone, Kent ME14 1PZ *T.* (0622) 674177.
40p. Bi-M. Authoritative articles preferably with ex-Service interest (Army, Air or Naval), also vignettes, features concerning British Legion. *Length:* not more than 1000 words. *Payment:* by arrangement. *Illustrations:* transparencies, line, half-tone.

Leisure Manager, The (1985), official journal of The Institute of Leisure and

Amenity Management, Hilary Sanders, Victoria House, 25 High Street, Over, Cambridgeshire CB4 5NB *T.* (0954) 30940.
£25.00 p.a. M. Articles on amenity, leisure, parks, entertainment, recreation and sports management. *Payment:* by arrangement. *Illustrations:* line, half-tone.

Leisure Painter (1966), Irene Briers, 102 High Street, Tenterden, Kent, TN30 6HT *T.* Tenterden (05806) 3315.
85p. M. Instructional articles on painting and fine arts. *Payment:* £25 per 1200 words. *Illustrations:* line, half-tone, colour, original artwork.

Liberal News, Paul Sample, 1 Whitehall Place, London, SW1A 2HE *T.* 01-839 4092.
30p. W. (£15.00 p.a.). W. The official newspaper of the Liberal Party. News, political and social features. No *payment.*

Library, The (1889), M. J. Jannetta, British Library, Humanities & Social Sciences, Collection Development, Great Russell Street, London WC1B 3DG *T.* 01-636 1544. Oxford University Press for the Bibliographical Society.
£8.00. (£22.00 p.a.) Q. Articles up to 15,000 words as well as shorter Notes, embodying original research on subjects connected with bibliography. No *payment. Illustrations:* half-tone and line.

Library Review (1927), Holmes McDougall Bookselling, 30 Clydeholm Road, Clydeside Industrial Estate, Glasgow G14 0BJ. *T.* 041-954 2271.
£26.00 p.a. Q. Concerned with information transfer, conservation and exploitation. Papers of 2500-5000 words considered. Line *illustrations.* Publication of contributions accepted, after referring, is regarded as conferring distinction to which *payment* is irrelevant.

Life and Work: Record of the Church of Scotland, 121 George Street, Edinburgh, EH2 4YN *T.* 031-225 5722.
23p. M. Articles and news not exceeding 1200 words. *Illustrations:* photographs and line. Seldom uses poems or stories. Study the magazine. *Payment:* up to £30.00 per 1000 words, or by arrangement.

Linguist, The, The Institute of Linguists, 24A Highbury Grove, London, N5 2EA *T.* 01-359 7445.
£3.50. Q. (£12.00 p.a.). Articles of interest to professional linguists in translating, interpreting and teaching fields. Articles usually contributed, but *payment* by arrangement. All contributors have special knowledge of the subjects with which they deal. *Length:* 3000-3500 words. *Illustrations:* line.

Listener, The, Russell Twisk, BBC Enterprises, 35 Marylebone High Street, London, W1M 4AA *T.* 01-927 4457.
80p. W. Articles based on, or relating to BBC and Independent television and radio broadcasts. General articles on broadcasting. Poems, book reviews and reviews of the arts. The vast majority of articles are commissioned. *Payment:* at market rates. *Illustrations:* colour, half-tone and line.

Literary Review, The (1979), Auberon Waugh, 51 Beak Street, London, W1R 3LF *T.* 01-437 9392.
95p. M. Reviews, articles of cultural interest, interviews, profiles, short stories. *Length:* Stories 2000 words maximum, articles and reviews 800-1500 words. *Payment:* £25.00 per 1000 words. *Illustrations:* line. Material mostly commissioned.

Litmus (1983), Laurie Smith, The City Lit, Stukeley Street, Drury Lane, London WC2B 5LJ *T.* 01-242 9872.
£1.25 3 p.a. Poems which show awareness of late 20th century sensibility. Critical articles by commission only. *Payment:* by arrangement. *Illustrations:* line.

(Liverpool) Daily Post (1855), Jim Mansell, P.O. Box 48, Old Hall Street, Liverpool, L69 3EB *T*. 051-227 2000. London: Wine Office Court, 146 Fleet Street, London, EC4A 2BU *T*. 01-353 7656.
18p. D. Independent. Takes articles of general interest and topical features of special interest to North West England and North Wales. *Payment:* month following publication: according to value. News and feature photographs used. No verse or fiction.

Liverpool Echo, Chris Oakley, P.O. Box 48, Old Hall Street, Liverpool, L69 3EB *T*. 051-227 2000.
16p. D. Articles of up to 600-800 words of local or topical interest. *Payment:* according to merit; special rates for exceptional material. Independent. This newspaper is connected with, but independent of the **Liverpool Daily Post**. Articles not interchangeable.

Living Magazine (1967), Dena Vane, 38 Hans Crescent, London, SW1X 0LZ *T*. 01-589 2000.
60p. M. General interest and human interest features; law, money, health, leisure, home, food, fashion and beauty. *Payment:* by arrangement.

Llais Llyfrau/Book News From Wales (1964), D. Geraint Lewis, Welsh Books Council, Castell Brychan, Aberystwyth, Dyfed, SY23 2JB *T*. (0970) 4151.
£2.00 p.a. Q. Articles in Welsh and English on authors and their books, Welsh publishing; reviews and book lists. Mainly commissioned. *Payment:* by arrangement.

Local Council Review, The (The Official Journal of the National Association of Local Councils), Mrs. Valerie Shepard, B.A., M.A.I.E., 18 Stone Park Drive, Forest Row, East Sussex RH18 5DG *T*. (034 282) 3042.
£2.80 p.a. post free. Q. Articles on the law and practice of local government in relation to parishes and communities. *Length:* 400-1000 words. *Illustrations:* black and white photographs, drawings.

Local Government Chronicle (1855), Crispin Derby, 122 Minories, London, EC3N 1NT *T*. 01-623 2530. *Telex:* 945828.
80p. W. Articles relating to financial, legal and administrative work of the local government officer. *Payment:* by arrangement. *Illustrations:* half-tone, cartoons.

Local Government Review (until 1971, part of **Justice of the Peace**, 1837). Barry Rose, Little London, Chichester, West Sussex, PO19 1PG *T*. (0243) 775552.
£1.00. W. Articles on local government law and practice, including administration, finance, environmental health, town and country planning, rating and valuation (*length* preferred, 1200-1400 words). Short reports of Conferences, Meetings, etc. Rates of *payment:* articles minimum £4.00 per column except where otherwise commissioned. *Preliminary letter welcomed although not essential.*

Local Historian, The (formerly **The Amateur Historian**), (1952). Dr. K. Tiller, Oxford University, Department for External Studies, Rewley House, 1 Wellington Square, Oxford OX1 2JA *T*. (0865) 52901. British Association for Local History, The Mill Managers House, Cromford Mill, Derbyshire, DE4 3RQ.
£2.20p. Q. (£8.50 p.a. post free). Articles, popular in style but based on knowledge of research, covering methods of research, sources and background material helpful to regional, local and family historians—histories of particular places, people or incidents *not* wanted. *Length:* maximum 4000 words. *Payment:* none. *Illustrations:* line and photographs.

London Magazine: A Review of the Arts (1953), Alan Ross, 30 Thurloe Place, London, SW7 2HQ *T.* 01-589 0618.
£1.50. M. (£12.50 p.a.). Poems, stories, literary memoirs, critical articles, features on art, photography, sport, theatre, cinema, music, architecture, events, reports from abroad, drawings. Self-addressed envelope necessary. *Payment:* by arrangement.

London Review of Books (1979), Karl Miller, Tavistock House South, Tavistock Square, London WC1H 9JZ *T.* 01-388 6751.
95p. Bi-M. Features, essays, short stories, poems. *Payment:* by arrangement. *Illustrations:* line and half-tone.

London Traveletter (1984), Clark C. Siewert, Siewert Publications Ltd., Box 662, London, W10 6EQ *T.* 01-960 2424.
£25.00 p.a. 11 p.a. Articles on travel, discoveries and unusual places to visit or stay at in Britain. *Length:* 500 to 1000 words. *Payment:* £90 per 1000 words. No *illustrations*.

Look Now (1972), Adèle-Marie Cherreson, 25 Newman Street, London, W1P 3PE *T.* 01-631 3939.
75p. M. Fashion and beauty, features and articles, personality interviews slanted towards young women between the ages of 18-25. *Payment:* by arrangement. *Illustrations:* line.

Loving (1970), Gerry Fallon, IPC Magazines Ltd., King's Reach Tower, Stamford Street, London, SE1 9LS *T.* 01-261 6510.
30p. W. First person real-life stories with strong love content for teenage and early twenties readership. Do not accept un-commissioned features material, but will look at short stories. *Length:* 1000 to 4000 words. *Payment:* by arrangement.

Mail on Sunday (1982), Stewart Steven, Northcliffe House, London EC4Y 0JA *T.* 01-353 6000.
40p. W. Articles. *Payment:* by arrangement. *Illustrations:* line and half-tone. Includes colour supplement.

Making Better Movies (1985), Tony Rose, Henry Greenwood & Co. Ltd., 28 Great James Street, London WC1N 3HL *T.* 01-404 4202.
£1.25 M. Articles on narrow gauge cinematography. *Length:* 1000 to 3000 words. *Payment:* £20 per printed page. *Illustrations:* line, half-tone, colour.

Manchester Evening News, Michael Unger, 164 Deansgate, Manchester, M60 2RD *T.* 061-832 7200.
18p. D. Feature articles of up to 1000 words, topical or general interest and illustrated where appropriate, should be addressed to the Features Editor. *Payment:* on acceptance.

Mandy (D. C. Thomson & Co. Ltd.), Courier Place, Dundee, DD1 9QJ, and 185 Fleet Street, London, EC4A 2HS.
20p. W. Picture-story paper for schoolgirls. Serials and series in line drawings. 2 and 3 page instalments, 8-9 frames per page. Editorial co-operation offered to promising scriptwriters. *Payment:* on acceptance.

Mandy Library (D. C. Thomson & Co. Ltd.), Courier Place, Dundee, DD1 9QJ, and 185 Fleet Street, London, EC4A 2HS.
24p. M. Stories told in pictures, for schoolgirls; 64 pages (about 140 line drawings). Adventure, animal, mystery, school, sport. Scripts considered; promising script-writers and artists encouraged. *Payment:* on acceptance.

Manx Life (1971), Robert Kelly, 11 Myrtle Street, Douglas, Isle of Man. *T.* Douglas (0624) 20562.

UNITED KINGDOM

60p. M. Factual articles on historical or topical aspects of the social, commercial, agricultural or cultural activities and interests of the Isle of Man. *Payment:* £20.00 per 1000 words on publication. *Illustrations:* black and white, half-tone and line.

Market Newsletter (1965), John Tracy, Focus House, 497 Green Lanes, London, N13 4BP *T.* 01-882 3315.
£25.00 p.a. M. Current information on editorial requirements of interest to writers and photographers.

Masonic Square (1975), B. P. Hutton, Terminal House, Shepperton, Middlesex, TW17 8AS *T.* Walton-on-Thames (0932) 228950.
95p. Q. (£4.00 p.a.). Biographies, history, symbolism, news items all relevant to Freemasonry or affiliated subjects. *Length:* 1000 to 1500 words. *Illustrations:* black and white, line and half-tone.

Mayfair (1966), Kenneth H. Bound, 95A Chancery Lane, London, WC2A 1DZ *T.* 01-242 1593.
£1.20. M. Masculine interest features of 3000 to 4000 words, humorous articles and well written reader-identifying short stories. Particularly receptive to well-researched and highly-anecdotal features on historical events or characters. *Payment:* £50.00 per 1000 words or by arrangement. *Illustrations:* only commissioned.

Media Reporter, The (1976), James Brennan, 3 College Place, Derby. *T.* (0332) 368295 and 551884. Bouverie Publishing Co., 244-249 Temple Chambers, Temple Avenue, London EC4Y 0DT *T.* 01-583 6463.
£1.50 (£6.80 p.a.). Q. Articles on media practice and ethics (press, radio, television). *Payment:* by arrangement. *Illustrations:* half-tone.

Melody Maker, Allan Jones, IPC Magazines Ltd., Berkshire House, 168-173 High Holborn, London, WC1V 7AU *T.* 01-379 3581.
45p. W. Technical, entertaining and informative articles on rock and pop music. *Payment:* by arrangement. *Illustrations:* half-tone and line.

Men Only (published by Paul Raymond: 1971), Nevile Player, 2 Archer Street, London, W1V 7HE *T.* 01-734 9191.
£1.20. M. Erotic fiction. Humour. Glamour photography. *Payment:* by arrangement.

Methodist Recorder (1861), Michael Taylor, 122 Golden Lane, London, EC1Y 0TL *T.* 01-251 8414.
25p. W. Britain's No. 1 Free Church newspaper; ecumenically involved. Limited opportunities for freelance contributors. *A preliminary letter* is advised.

Middle East Construction, A. R. Davis, Quadrant House, The Quadrant, Sutton, Surrey, SM2 5AS *T.* 01-661 3500 *Telex:* 892084 Bisprs G.
12 issues p.a. Articles dealing with the design and construction of buildings and civil engineering projects throughout the Arab world and Iran. *Length:* maximum 1500 words plus illustrations. *Payment:* by agreement. *Illustrations:* colour, half-tone and line. Some two-colour line illustrations can be used.

Military Modelling, Kenneth M. Jones, Argus Specialist Publications Ltd., P.O. Box 35, Hemel Hempstead, Herts. *T.* (0442) 41221.
£1.10. M. Articles on military modelling. *Length:* up to 2500 words. *Payment:* by arrangement. *Illustrations:* line, half-tone, colour.

Millennium—Journal of International Studies (1971), J. K. Barling, S. Economides, London School of Economics and Political Science, Houghton Street, London, WC2A 2AE *T.* 01-405 7686 ext. 2407-8.

£4.35. 3 times a year (£11.00 p.a.). Serious articles on International Studies; original research work published, as well as topical articles on all aspects of international affairs. *Length:* 4500-8000 words (in triplicate with abstract). No *payment*. No *illustrations*.

Mind (1876), Dr Simon Blackburn, Pembroke College, Oxford OX1 1DW.
£4.00. Q. A review of philosophy intended for those who have studied and thought on this subject. Articles from about 5000 words. Shorter discussion notes. Critical notices and reviews. No *payment*.

Mobile & Holiday Homes (1960), Anne Webb, Link House, Dingwall Avenue, Croydon CR9 2TA. *T.* 01-686 2599. *Telex:* 947709 Linkho G.
90p. M. Informative articles on residential mobile homes and holiday static caravans—personal experience articles, site features, news items. No preliminary letter. *Payment:* by arrangement. *Illustrations:* photographs, half-tone and line.

Model Boats (1964), John L. Cundell, Argus Specialist Publications Ltd., P.O. Box 35, Hemel Hempstead, Herts. *T.* (0442) 41221.
£1.20. M. Articles, drawings, plans, sketches of model boats. *Payment:* £25 per page; plans £80. *Illustrations:* line, half-tone.

Model Engineer (1898), Ted Jolliffe, Argus Specialist Publications Ltd., P.O. Box 35, Hemel Hempstead, Herts. *T.* (0442) 41221.
90p. Detailed description of the construction of models, small workshop equipment, machine tools and small electrical and mechanical devices; articles on small power engineering, mechanics, electricity, workshop methods and experiments. *Payment:* up to £25 per page. *Illustrations:* half-tone and line drawings.

Model Railway Constructor (1934), Chris Leigh, Coombelands House, Addlestone, Weybridge, Surrey KT15 1HY *T.* (0932) 58511.
90p. M. Short or medium length feature articles on relevant subjects; photo features. *Illustrations:* line and half-tone.

Modern Churchman (1911), The Modern Churchmen's Union, The School House, Leysters, Leominster, Hereford, HR6 0HS. *T.* (056 887) 271.
£1.30. Q. Covers contemporary and pastoral theology, ethics, politics, current affairs. *Length:* 1500 to 3500 words. Contributions voluntary.

Modern Language Review (1905), Modern Humanities Research Association, King's College, Strand, London, WC2R 2LS.
£34.50 p.a. (U.K.), £41.50 overseas; $78.00 (U.S.A.). Q. Contains articles and reviews of a scholarly or specialist character on English, Romance,Germanic, and Slavonic languages and literatures. No *payment* is made, but offprints are given.

Modern Languages (Journal of the Modern Language Association) (1905), Dr. I. Hilton, Penarbronydd Cottage, Tregarth, Nr. Bangor, North Wales, LL57 4AE *T.* (0248) 600040.
£2.50 (£10.00 p.a.). Q. All aspects of modern language study, linguistic, pedagogic, and literary. *No payment*.

Modus, Geoffrey Thompson, Official Journal of the National Association of Teachers of Home Economics Ltd., Hamilton House, Mabledon Place, London, WC1H 9BJ *T.* 01-387 1441.
£1.85. 8 p.a. (£14.80 p.a.). Articles on the teaching of home economics, including needlecrafts, nutrition, and social and technical background information for teachers. *Length:* up to 1500 words. *Payment:* by arrangement. *Illustrations:* line and half-tone. Most articles for teachers and educationists.

Month, The (1864), Hugh Kay, 114 Mount Street, London, W1Y 6AH *T.* 01-491 7596.
85p. M. A Christian review of theology, social, political and economic affairs, with literary section, edited by the Jesuit Fathers. *Length:* 3000 to 3500 words. *Payment:* by arrangement.

Morning Star (formerly **Daily Worker**, 1930), Tony Chater (The Morning Star Co-operative Society Ltd.), 75 Farringdon Road, London, EC1M 3JX *T.* 01-405 9242. *Telex:* 28749. *T.A.* Morsta Telex, London.
30p. D. Articles of general interest. *Illustrations:* photos, cartoons and drawings.

Mother (1936), Tessa Hilton, 12-18 Paul Street, London EC2A 4JS *T.* 01-247 8233.
65p. M. Articles on subjects of interest to parents of young children. *Length:* 1500 words. *Payment:* by arrangement. *Illustrations:* photographs and sketches.

Motor (1902), Howard Walker, Prospect House, 9-15 Ewell Road, Cheam, Surrey, SM3 8BZ *T.* 01-661 4300.
65p. W. Offers scope for topical and technical motoring articles and photographs. Colour photographs considered. *Payment:* varies.

Motor Boat & Yachting (1904), Alex McMullen (Business Press International Ltd.), Quadrant House, Sutton, Surrey, SM2 5AS *T.* 01-661 3098.
£1.35. M. General interest as well as specialist motor boating material welcomed. Features up to 2000 words considered on all aspects sea-going and inland waterways. *Payment:* varies. *Illustrations:* photographs and line. Colour photographs considered.

Motor Cycle News (1955), Jim Lindsay, P.O. Box 11, Huxloe Place, High Street, Kettering, Northants, NN16 8SS *T.* (0536) 81651. *Telex:* 3215710 MCN G.
48p. W. Features (up to 1000 words), photographs and news stories of interest to motor cyclists.

Motorcaravan and Motorhome Monthly (1966 as Motor Caravan and Camping), John Hunt, 20 Barons Walk, Lewes, Sussex, BN7 1EX *T.* (0273) 476668.
90p. M. Articles including motorcaravan travel and D.I.Y. *Payment:* from £10 per printed page. *Illustrations:* line, half-tone, colourprint.

Municipal Review and AMA News (1930), a journal of urban affairs published by the Association of Metropolitan Authorities. Peter Smith, 35 Great Smith Street, London, SW1P 3BJ *T.* 01-222 8100.
£6.00 p.a. including postage. (£12.00 overseas.) M. (10 issues p.a.). Articles on the current urban local government scene.

Museums Journal, The (1901), Steve Caplin, The Museums Association, 34 Bloomsbury Way, London, WC1A 2SF *T.* 01-404 4767.
£7.00. Q. to non-members (£25.00 p.a.). Articles on museum and art gallery policy, administration, research, architecture and display, notes on technical developments and conservation, book reviews. *Length:* 1000 to 4000 words. *Payment:* none; contributions voluntary. *Illustrations:* half-tone, line, occasional colour.

Music and Letters (1920), Editorial: Dr. Edward Olleson, Dr. Nigel Fortune, c/o Faculty of Music, St. Aldate's, Oxford, OX1 1DB. For other matters: Journals Production, Oxford University Press, Walton Street, Oxford OX2 6DP.
£5.50. Q. Scholarly articles, 2000-5000 words, on musical subjects, neither merely topical nor purely descriptive. Technical, historical, and research matter preferred. *Payment:* no payment. *Illustrations:* music quotations and plates.

Music & Musicians (1952), Robert Matthew-Walker, 43b Gloucester Road, Croydon, CR0 2DH *T.* 01-689 4116. *Telex:* 298133.
£1.20. M. Long and short features, previews, reviews about music and musicians. *Payment:* by arrangement.

Music Review, The (1940), A. F. Leighton Thomas, Glyneithin, Burry Port, Dyfed, SA16 0TA. Other matters: Heffers Printers Ltd., King's Hedges Road, Cambridge, CB4 2PQ.
£12.50 Q. (£39.00 p.a.). Articles from 1500 to 8000 words dealing with any aspect of standard or classical music (no jazz). *Payment:* small, by arrangement.

Music Week (1959), David Dalton, Morgan-Grampian plc, Greater London House, Hampstead Road, London NW1 7QZ *T.* 01-387 6611.
£1.50. W. (£45.00 p.a.). News and features on all aspects of producing, manufacturing, marketing and retailing music. *Payment:* NUJ rates.

Musical Opinion (1877), Charles Myers, 3-11 Spring Road, Bournemouth, Dorset, BH1 4QA *T.* (0202) 23397.
90p. M. Musical articles, 500 to 2000 words of general musical interest, opera, organ and church music matters. Record, book, music reviews. *Payment:* on publication. No verse. *Illustrations:* photographs.

Musical Times (1844), Stanley Sadie, 8 Lower James Street, London, W1R 4DN *T.* 01-734 8080.
£1.00. M. Musical articles, reviews, 150 to 2500 words. *Payment:* by arrangement. *Illustrations:* photographs and music. Intending contributors are advised to study recent numbers of the journal.

My Weekly (1910) (D. C. Thomson & Co. Ltd.), 80 Kingsway East, Dundee, DD4 8SL, and 185 Fleet Street, London, EC4A 2HS.
22p. W. Serials, from 30,000 to 80,000 words, suitable for family reading. Short complete stories of 1500 to 5000 words with humorous, romantic or strong emotional theme. Articles on prominent people and on all subjects of feminine interest. All contributions should make their appeal to the modern woman. *No preliminary letter* required. *Payment:* on acceptance. *Illustrations:* colour and black and white.

My Weekly Story Library, D. C. Thomson & Co. Ltd., Courier Place, Dundee, DD1 9QJ *T.* Dundee 23131.
24p. 4 per month. 35,000 to 37,500-word romantic stories aimed at the post-teenage market. *Payment:* by arrangement; competitive for the market. No *illustrations.*

National Builder (1921), Michael Harnett, 82 New Cavendish Street, London, W1M 8AD *T.* 01-580 5588. *T.A.* Natbuild, Westcent, London.
£1.00. M. The official journal of the Building Employers Confederation. Articles on building and constructional methods, management techniques, materials and machinery used in building. Articles, 1000-3000 words, preferably with *illustrations. Preliminary letter* advisable. *Payment:* by arrangement.

Natural World (1981), The Magazine of the Royal Society for Nature Conservation, Linda Bennett, 20 Upper Ground, London SE1 9PF *T.* 01-928 6969.
Membership subscription. 3 p.a. Short articles on nature conservation; contributors normally have special knowledge of subjects on which they write. *Length:* up to 2000 words. *Payment:* by arrangement. *Illustrations:* line, half-tone, colour.

UNITED KINGDOM

Naturalist (1875), M. R. D. Seaward, M.SC., PH.D., D.SC., The University, Bradford, BD7 1DP *T.* (0274) 733466, ext. 8540.
£10.00 p.a. Q. Original papers on British Natural History subjects of all kinds relating to this country to include various aspects of geology, archaeology and environmental science; length immaterial. *No payment. Illustrations:* photographs and line drawings.

Nature (1869), John Maddox (Macmillan Journals Ltd.), Little Essex Street, London, WC2R 3LF *T.* 01-836 6633. *Telex:* 262024.
£1.90. W. Devoted to scientific matters and to their bearing upon public affairs. All contributors of articles have specialised knowledge of the subjects with which they deal. *Illustrations:* half-tone and line.

Nautical Magazine (1832), L. Ingram-Brown, F.INST.S.M.M., M.B.I.M., M.R.I.N., Brown, Son & Ferguson Ltd., 4-10 Darnley Street, Glasgow, G41 2SD *T.* 041-429 1234. *T.A.* Skipper, Glasgow.
£16.56 p.a. including postage; 3 years £49.00. M. Articles relating to nautical and shipping profession, from 1500 to 2000 words, also translations. *Payment:* by arrangement. No *illustrations*.

Navy International, Anthony J. Watts, Hunters Moon, Hogspudding Lane, Newdigate, Nr. Dorking, Surrey, RH5 5DS *T.* (0306) 77442.
£21.00 p.a. M. Geo-political, strategic and technical articles on current world naval affairs. *Length:* 1500-4000 words. *Payment:* £50 per 1000 words. *Illustrations* used.

New Beacon (1930) (as **Beacon,** 1917), Donald Bell, R.N.I.B., Braille House, 338-346 Goswell Road, London, EC1V 7JE *T.* 01-837 9921.
50p. M. (£5.65 p.a.). Authoritative articles on all aspects of blind welfare. *Length:* from 800 words. Also original contributions in prose and verse by blind authors. *Payment:* £15.00 per 1000 words; verse by arrangement. *Illustrations:* half-tone. Also Braille edition (£2.85 p.a.).

New Blackfriars (1920), The English Dominicans (Rev. John Orme Mills, O.P.), Blackfriars, Oxford, OX1 3LY *T.* Oxford (0865) 57607.
95p net. M. (£10.00 p.a.) A critical review, surveying the field of theology, philosophy, sociology and the arts, from the standpoint of Christian principles and their application to the problems of the modern world. Incorporates *Life of the Spirit. Length:* 2500 to 4500 words. *Payment:* by arrangement.

New Health (1983), Deirdre McQuillan, 38-42 Hampton Road, Teddington, Middlesex, TW11 0JE *T.* 01-977 8787.
£1.00. M. Features on health, food, fitness, personalities, fashion, beauty. *Payment:* NUJ rates. *Illustrations:* line, half-tone, colour; cartoons.

New Hi-Fi Sound (1983), Neville Farmer, Haymarket Publishing Ltd., 38-42 Hampton Road, Teddington, Middlesex TW11 0JE *T.* 01-977 8787.
£1.00. M. Articles by professional contributors on audio equipment and related subjects by arrangement with editor. *Payment:* by arrangement. *Illustrations:* line, half-tone and colour transparencies. *Preliminary letter* essential.

New Library World, (1898), NLW Journals Ltd., Seaton House, Kings Ripton, Cambridgeshire PE17 2NJ *T.* (04873) 238.
£24.00 p.a., personal subs. £9.00. M. Professional and bibliographical articles. *Illustrations. Payment:* from £15.00 per 1000 words.

New Musical Express, Ian Pye, 4th Floor, Commonwealth House, 1-19 New Oxford Street, London WC1A 1NG *T.* 01-404 0700.

45p. W. Authoritative articles and news stories on the world's rock and movie personalities. *Length:* by arrangement. *Payment:* by arrangement. *Illustrations:* action photos with strong news-angle of recording personalities. *Preliminary letter or phone call* desirable.

New Scientist, Michael Kenward, Commonwealth House, New Oxford Street, London WC1A 1NG *T.* 01-404 0700. *T.A.* Newscient, London WC1.
£1.10. W. Authoritative articles of topical importance on all aspects of science and technology are considered. *Length:* 1000 to 3000 words. Preliminary letter or telephone call is desirable. Short items from specialists also considered for *Science, Comment, This Week,* and *Technology.* Intending contributors should study recent copies of the magazine. *Payment:* varies but average £100 per 1000 words. *Illustrations:* line and half-tone, colour.

New Society, David Lipsey, 5 Sherwood Street, London, W1V 7RA *T.* 01-439 2831.
85p. W. Social science, social policy, documentary reportage, the arts, book reviews.

New Statesman (1913), John Lloyd, 14-16 Farringdon Lane, London EC1R 3AU *T.* 01-253 2003. *Telex:* 28449.
90p. W. Interested in news and analysis of current political and social issues at home and overseas, plus book reviews and coverage of the arts, seen from the perspective of the British Left. *Length:* strictly according to the value of the piece. *Payment:* basic £68 per 1000 words; news £78.50 per 1000 words.

New Theatre Quarterly (1985; as **Theatre Quarterly** 1971), Clive Barker, Simon Trussler, Great Robhurst, Woodchurch, Ashford, Kent TN26 3TB.
£5.00 (individual subs. £10.00 p.a.) Q. Articles, documentation, reference material covering all aspects of live theatre. An informed, factual and serious approach essential. Preliminary discussion and synopsis desirable. *Payment:* by arrangement. *Illustrations:* line, half-tone.

New World, United Nations Association, 3 Whitehall Court, London, SW1A 2EL *T.* 01-930 2931.
30p. 6 p.a.

News of the World (1843), David Montgomery, 1 Virginia Street, London, E1 9BH *T.* 01-481 4100.
28p. W.

Nikki (1985), (D. C. Thomson & Co. Ltd.), 2 Albert Square, Dundee, DD1 9QJ *T.* (0382) 23131. London Office: 185 Fleet Street, EC4A 2HS *T.* 01-242 5086/8.
22p. W. Picture stories and features for schoolgirls 7-12 years.

19 (1968), Deirdre Vine, King's Reach Tower, Stamford Street, London, SE1 9LS *T.* 01-261 6360.
75p. M. A glossy fashion and general interest magazine for young women aged 16 to 19 including beauty, music and social features of strong contemporary interest.

Nottingham Evening Post (1878), Forman Street, Nottingham, NG1 4AB *T.* Nottingham (0602) 475521.
19p. D.

Numismatic Chronicle (1839), c/o Dr. A. M. Burnett, Department of Coins and Medals, British Museum, London WC1B 3BG.
£24 per annual volume. The Journal of the Royal Numismatic Society. Articles on coins and medals. Memoirs relating to coins and medals are unpaid, and contributions should reach a high standard of quality.

Nursery World, Sue Hubberstey, 24-25 Cowcross Street, London EC1M 9OQ *T.* 01-253 1691.
45p. Fortnightly. For all grades of nursery and child care staff, nannies, foster mothers and all concerned with the care of expectant mothers, babies and young children. Authoritative and informative articles, 750-1500 words, and photographs, on all aspects of child welfare, from 0-7 years, in the U.K. Practical ideas and leisure crafts. *No* short stories. *Payment:* by arrangement. *Illustrations:* line and half-tone.

Nursing Times (1905), Niall Dickson, Macmillan Journals Ltd., 4 Little Essex Street, London, WC2R 3LF *T.* 01-836 1776.
50p. W. Articles of clinical interest, nursing education and nursing policy. Illustrated articles not longer than 2000 words. Contributions from other than health professionals rarely accepted. Press day, Friday.

Observer, The (1791), Donald Trelford, 8 St. Andrew's Hill, London, EC4V 5JA *T.* 01-236 0202. *T.A.* Observer, London, EC4.
50p. W. Independent. Some articles and illustrations commissioned.

Observer Colour Magazine, The (1964), J. Foley, 8 St. Andrew's Hill, London, EC4V 5JA *T.* 01-236 0202. *T.A.* Observer, London, EC4.
Free with newspaper. W. Articles on all subjects. *Illustrations:* also accepted. *Payment:* by arrangement.

Opera, Harold Rosenthal, O.B.E., 6 Woodland Rise, London, N10 3UH *T.* 01-883 4415; Seymour Press Ltd., 334 Brixton Road, London, SW9 7AG.
£1.20. 13 issues a year. Articles on general subjects appertaining to opera; reviews; criticisms. *Length:* up to 2000 words. *Payment:* by arrangement. *Illustrations:* photographs and drawings.

Options (1982), Sally O'Sullivan, 25 Newman Street, London, W1P 3HA *T.* 01-631 3939.
£1.00. M. Articles only of 1000 to 3000 words. Mostly commissioned. *Payment:* by arrangement.

Orbis (1968), Mike Shields, 199 The Long Shoot, Nuneaton, Warks, CV11 6JQ *T.* (0203) 327440.
£10.00 p.a. Q. Poetry, short stories (up to 1000 words), literary essays and criticism, letters. *Payment:* by arrangement. *Illustrations:* line.

Organ, The (1921), D. Carrington, 3-11 Spring Road, Bournemouth, Dorset, BH1 4QA *T.* (0202) 23397.
£2.00. Q. Articles, 4000 to 5000 words, relating to the organ, historical, technical, and artistic. Reviews of music, records. *Payment:* small. *Illustrations:* half-tone and line.

Other Poetry (1978), Evangeline Paterson, 2 Stoneygate Avenue, Leicester LE2 3HE *T.* (0533) 703159.
£1.50. 3 p.a. Poetry. *Payment:* token £2 per poem.

Outposts Poetry Quarterly (1943), Howard Sergeant, M.B.E. (Outposts Publications), 72 Burwood Road, Walton-on-Thames, Surrey, KT12 4AL *T.* 240712.
£1.25. Q. Poems, essays and critical articles on poets and their work. Poetry competitions. *Payment:* by arrangement.

Over 21 (1972), Pat Roberts, Spotlight Publications Ltd., Greater London House, Hampstead Road, London NW1 7QZ *T.* 01-387 6611.
75p. M. Features of interest to independent women. *Length:* 800 to 2000 words. Fiction, strong, 4000 to 5000 words. *Payment:* by arrangement.

Parents (1976), Wendy Rose-Neil, 116 Newgate Street, London, EC1A 7AE *T.* 01-726 6999.
70p. M. Articles on pregnancy, childbirth, general family health, child upbringing and marital relations. Preliminary letter essential. *Payment:* £65 per 1000 words. *Illustrations:* Black-and-white half-tones or colour.

Parents Voice (1950), Alan Leighton, Royal Society for Mentally Handicapped Children and Adults, 123 Golden Lane, London, EC1Y 0RT *T.* 01-253 9433.
£4.40 p.a. Q. Journal of MENCAP. Contributions on the subject of mental handicap considered. No *payment. Illustrations:* photographs.

Parks & Sports Grounds (1935), 61 London Road, Staines, Middlesex, TW18 4BN *T.* Staines 61326.
£18.00 p.a. M. Articles on the design, construction, maintenance and management of parks, sports grounds, golf courses, open spaces and amenity areas. Any aspect of outdoor recreation. *Length:* 750-2000 words. *Payment:* from £30.00 per 1000 words. *Illustrations:* line, half-tone. Cartoons.

Patches (D. C. Thomson & Co. Ltd.), Courier Place, Dundee, DD1 9QJ, and 185 Fleet Street, London, EC4A 2HS.
26p. W. Photo stories and true experience text stories. Pop, fashion, beauty and features. Transparencies and black-and-white shots. Humorous and realistic *illustrations*. Scripts required: *payment:* on acceptance.

Peace News for nonviolent revolution (1936), 8 Elm Avenue, Nottingham NG3 4GF *T.* (0602) 503587 and 5 Caledonian Road, London, N1 9DX *T.* 01-837 9795.
50p. Fortnightly. Political articles based on nonviolence in every aspect of human life. *Payment:* none. *Illustrations:* line, half-tone.

Penthouse Magazine, The International Magazine for Men (1965), Sightline Publications Ltd., The Northern & Shell Building, P.O. Box 381, Mill Harbour, London E14 9TW *T.* 01-987 5090.
£1.95. M. Serious articles on motoring and general subjects, investigations, light features, star interviews, humour 3000 words. *Payment:* by arrangement. *Illustrations:* colour, black and white, but by commission only.

People's Friend (1869), (D. C. Thomson & Co. Ltd.), 80 Kingsway East, Dundee, DD4 8SL, and 185 Fleet Street, London, EC4A 2HS.
22p. W. An illustrated weekly appealing to women of all ages and devoted to their personal and home interests. Serial and complete stories of strong romantic and emotional appeal—serials of 60,000-70,000 words, completes of 1500-3500 words. Stories for children considered. Knitting, fashions and cookery are especially featured. *Illustrations:* colour and black and white. No *preliminary letter* is required. *Payment:* on acceptance.

Pepper Street (1985), (D. C. Thomson & Co. Ltd.), 2 Albert Square, Dundee, DD1 9QJ *T.* (0382) 23131. *Telex:* 76380. London Office: 185 Fleet Street, EC4A 2HS *T.* 01-242 5086/8.
25p. W. The read-with-mum weekly for younger children.

Performance Car (1967), Jesse Crosse, AGB, Specialist Publications Ltd., Audit House, Field End Road, Eastcote, Ruislip, Middx. HA4 9LT *T.* 01-868 4499.
£1.15. M. Articles, 2000 to 3000 words on all aspects of cars. *Payment:* by arrangement. *Illustrations:* half-tone, colour.

Personal Computer World (1977), Peter Jackson, 32-34 Broadwick Street, London W1A 2HG *T.* 01-439 4242. *Telex:* 23918 VNU G.
£1.10 M. Articles about computers. *Length:* 2000-5000 words. Reviews. *Payment:* £85.00 per 1000 words. *Illustrations:* line, half-tone.

Personnel Management, Journal of the Institute of Personnel Management, Susanne Lawrence, Personnel Publications Ltd., 1 Hills Place, London, W1R 1AG *T.* 01-734 1773.
£2.70. M. (£30.00 p.a.). Features and news items on recruitment and selection, training; wage and salary administration; industrial psychology; industrial relations; labour law; welfare schemes, working practices and new practical ideas in personnel management in industry and commerce. *Length:* up to 3000 words. *Payment:* by arrangement. *Illustrations:* Photographers and illustrators should contact Art Editor.

Pharmaceutical Journal, The (1841), R. Blyth, F.P.S., 1 Lambeth High Street, London, SE1 7JN *T.* 01-735 9141. *T.A.* and *Cables:* Pharmakon, London, SE1.
80p. W. The official journal of the Pharmaceutical Society of Great Britain. Articles of 1000 words on any aspect of pharmacy may be submitted. *Payment:* by arrangement. *Illustrations:* litho.

Photoplay, Movies & Video, Lisa Dewson, 1 Golden Square, London W1R 3AB *T.* 01-437 0626.
£1.25. M. Features on the film, video and TV scene. Stamped addressed envelope to be enclosed for return of MS. if not suitable. *Payment:* by arrangement.

Physiotherapy, Journal of the Chartered Society of, Jill Whitehouse, 14 Bedford Row, London, WC1R 4ED *T.* 01-242 1941.
£1.67. M. Articles on physiotherapy and related subjects, technical items and news regarding activities of members of the Society. Contributions welcomed from physiotherapists and doctors. *Length:* 2000 words (average). *Payment:* £10 per published page for technical and medical articles. *Illustrations:* photographs and line.

Pig Farming, M. C. Looker, Farming Press Ltd., Wharfedale Road, Ipswich, IP1 4LG *T.* Ipswich (0473) 43011.
55p. M. Practical, well-illustrated articles on all aspects of pig production required, particularly those dealing with new ideas in pig management, feeding and housing. *Length:* 1000 to 2000 words. *Payment:* by arrangement. *Illustrations:* colour, half-tone or line.

Pilot (1968), James Gilbert, 88 Burlington Road, New Malden, Surrey, KT4 3NT *T.* 01-949 3462.
85p. M. Feature articles on general aviation. *Payment:* £80 to £150 per article on acceptance. *Illustrations:* line, half-tone; also some colour.

Pippin, D. J. Hooper, 159-161 Camden High Street, London, NW1 7JY *T.* 01-482 3202.
24p. W. Picture strips, including some licensed content. (Artwork and scripts.) *Payment:* by arrangement, when commissioned.

Plays and Players, Robert Gore Langton, 43b Gloucester Road, Croydon CR0 2DH *T.* 01-689 3602. *Telex:* 298133.
90p. M. Articles and photos on world theatre. *Payment:* by arrangement. *Illustrations:* line, photographs.

PN Review, formerly **Poetry Nation** (1973), Michael Schmidt, Michael Freeman, 208 Corn Exchange Buildings, Manchester M4 3BQ *T.* 061-834 8730.
£2.50 (£11.50 p.a.). Q. Poems, essays, reviews, fiction, translations. *Payment:* by arrangement.

Poetry Durham (1982), Michael O'Neill, Gareth Reeves, Department of English, University of Durham, Elvet Riverside, New Elvet, Durham DH1 3JT *T.* (0385) 64466.

£3.00 p.a. 3 p.a. Poems. *Payment:* £10.00 per poem.

Poetry Nottingham (1941), Howard Atkinson, 21 Duncombe Close, Nottingham NG3 3PH *T.* (0602) 584207.
£1.25. Q. Poems. *Length:* not more than 50 lines. No *payment*, complimentary copy of magazine. *Illustrations:* line.

Poetry Now (1984), Ravi Mirchandani, Scotswood, South Park, Sevenoaks, Kent, TN13 1EL.
£1.95 Q. Poetry and related articles. *Payment:* by arrangement.

Poetry Review, 21 Earls Court Square, London, SW5 9DE *T.* 01-373 7861-2.
£10.00 p.a. (Institutions, schools and libraries £13.00 p.a.) Q. Poems, features and reviews. Send no more than six poems with s.a.e. Preliminary study of the magazine is essential. *Payment:* £10-£15 per poem.

Poetry Wales (1965), Cary Archard, 56 Parcau Avenue, Bridgend, Mid-Glamorgan. *T.* Bridgend (0656) 3480.
£1.25 (£6 p.a. inc. postage). Q. Poems mainly in English and mainly by Welsh people or resident: other contributors (and Welsh poetry) also published. Articles on Welsh, Anglo-Welsh, British and international poetry. Special features; reviews on poetry and wider matters. *Payment:* by arrangement.

Police Journal (1928), R. W. Stone, Little London, Chichester, West Sussex, PO19 1PG *T.* 775552.
£30.00 p.a. Q. Articles of technical or professional interest to the Police Service. *Payment:* by arrangement. *Illustrations:* half-tone.

Political Quarterly, The (1930), Basil Blackwell Ltd., 108 Cowley Road, Oxford OX4 1JF *T.* (0865) 722146. Editors: Colin Crouch and Rudolf Klein. Literary Editor: James Cornford. Books for review to be sent to: James Cornford, Nuffield Lodge, Regents Park, London, NW1 4RS.
£4.50. Q. £18.00 p.a. (Students £15.00). A journal devoted to topical aspects of national and international politics and public administration; it takes a progressive, but not a party, point of view. *Average payment:* £7.50 per 1000 words. *Average length:* 4000 words.

Pony (1949), Nancy Roberts, 104 Ash Road, Sutton, Surrey, SM3 9LD *T.* 01-641 4911.
70p. M. Articles and short stories with a horsy theme likely to be of interest to young readers between the ages of 10 and 18. Technical accuracy and good writing essential. *Length:* up to 1600 words. *Payment:* by arrangement. *Illustrations:* drawings (commissioned) and interesting photographs.

Popular Caravan (1982), Rick Haden, Sovereign House, Brentwood, Essex, CM14 4SE *T.* (0277) 219876.
99p. M. Articles on all aspects of caravanning. *Length:* 400 to 2000 words. *Payment:* £20.00 per 1000 words. *Illustrations:* half-tone.

Popular Crafts (1980), Sue Sharp, Argus Specialist Publications, 1 Golden Square, London W1R 3AB *T.* 01-437 0626.
£1.25p. M. Factual articles on crafts in general; silvercraft, lapidary, pottery, weaving, embroidery and features on crafts people and exhibitions. *Payment:* by arrangement. *Illustrations:* transparencies and half-tones.

Port of London, Port of London Authority, Leslie Ford House, Tilbury Docks, Tilbury, Essex RM18 7EH T. (037 52) 75477. *Telex:* 99267.
£1.00. Q. The magazine of the Port of London Authority. Articles up to 2500 words considered, semi-technical, historical or having bearing on trade and commerce of London essential. *Preliminary letter* essential. *Payment:* £50 per 1000 words. *Illustrations:* half-tone, line, colour.

Post, The (1920), A. Slater, UCW House, Crescent Lane, Clapham, London, SW4 9RN *T.* 01-622 9977. *T.A.* Postact, London, SW4. *Telex:* 913585.
Free to members. M. The journal of the Union of Communication Workers. Articles on postal, telephone and telegraph workers in the UK and abroad and on other questions of interest to a Trade Union readership. *Length:* 1000 words or less. *Payment:* by arrangement. *Illustrations:* line and half-tone occasionally.

Poultry World, John Farrant, The Farmers Publishing Group, Carew House, Wallington, Surrey SM6 0DX *T.* 01-661 3500.
£1.00. M. Articles on commercial poultry breeding, production, marketing and packaging. News of international poultry interest. *Payment:* by arrangement. Line and photographic illustrations.

Power Farming, Stephen Howe, The Farmers Publishing Group, Carew House, Wallington, Surrey SM6 0DX *T.* 01-661 3500.
£1.10. M. Articles concerning all aspects of farm equipment, its use and management. General engineering in its application to machinery maintenance. *Length:* up to 1500 words. Short practical workshop hints welcomed. *Payment:* by arrangement. *Illustrations:* photographs, drawings.

Powys Review, The (1977), Belinda Humfrey, Dept. of English, Saint David's University College, Lampeter, Dyfed, SA48 7ED *T.* (0570) 422351 and 422018.
£2.50. Twice yearly. Articles and reviews on the writings of John Cowper Powys, T. F. Powys and Llewelyn Powys, and on related subjects and literature, especially of the period 1890-1960. *Payment:* £4.00 per 750 words. *Illustrations:* line, photographs.

PR Week (1984), Geoffrey Lace, 100 Fleet Street, London, EC4Y 1DE *T.* 01-353 9804.
£40.00 p.a. W. News and features on public relations. *Length:* approx. 800 words. *Payment:* £100 per 1,000 words. *Illustrations:* half-tone.

Practical Boat Owner (1967), George Taylor, Westover House, West Quay Road, Poole, Dorset, BH15 1JG *T.* (0202) 671191.
£1.00. M. Articles of up to 2000 words in length, about practical matters concerning the boating enthusiast. *Payment:* by negotiation. *Illustrations:* photographs or drawings.

Practical Computing, Glyn Moody, Room L307, Quadrant House, The Quadrant, Sutton, Surrey SM2 5AS *T.* 01-661 3633.
£1.25. M. Articles on business and professional microcomputing. *Length:* 1000 to 2500 words. *Payment:* from £50 per page. *Illustrations:* line.

Practical Electronics (1964), Mike Kenward, Westover House, West Quay Road, Poole, Dorset, BH15 1JG *T.* (0202) 671191.
£1.00. M. Constructional and theoretical articles. *Length:* 1000-5500 words. *Payment:* £55-£90 per 1000 words depending upon type of article. *Illustrations:* line and half-tone.

Practical Fishkeeping (1966), Nick Fletcher, EMAP National Publications, Bretton Court, Bretton, Peterborough, PE3 8DZ *T.* Peterborough (0733) 264666.
95p. M. Practical experiences in fishkeeping and informative interviews with people of special standing in this field. *Payment:* by arrangement. *Illustrations:* line, half-tone, occasional colour.

Practical Gardening (1959), M. Wyatt, Bushfield House, Orton Centre, Peterborough, PE2 0UW *T.* (0733) 237111.
95p. M. 500 to 1000 words on practical gardening subjects. *Payment:* from £50 per 1000 words. *Illustrations:* line, half-tone, colour.

Practical Householder (1955), Diane Carr, Cambridge House, 373 Euston Road, London NW1 3AR *T.* 01-388 3171.
85p. M. Articles about 1500 words in length, about practical matters concerning home improvement. *Payment:* according to subject. *Illustrations:* line and half-tone.

Practical Model Railways (1983), Quentin Williamson, Sovereign House, Brentwood, Essex, CM14 4SE *T.* (0277) 219876.
£1.20. M. Illustrated articles about railway model-making. *Length:* up to 3,000 words. *Payment:* £15 per 1,000 words. *Illustrations:* line, half-tone, colour.

Practical Motorist (1934), Denis Rea, Unit 8, Forest Close, Ebblake Industrial Estate, Verwood, Wimborne, Dorset BH21 6DQ *T.* (0202) 823581.
£1.00. M. Practical articles on upkeep, servicing and repair of all makes of cars, also practical hints and tips. *Payment:* according to merit. *Illustrations:* black and white, transparencies and line drawings.

Practical Photography (1959), Dominic Boland, EMAP, Bushfield House, Orton Centre, Peterborough, PE2 0UW *T.* (0733) 237111.
£1.10. M. Features on any aspect of photography with practical bias. *Payment:* from £50 per 1000 words. *Illustrations:* line, half-tone, colour. *Payment:* from £8 black and white or colour.

Practical Wireless (1932), G. Arnold, PW Publishing Ltd., Enefco House, The Quay, Poole, Dorset, BH15 1PP *T.* (0202) 678558.
48p. M. Articles on the practical aspects of domestic and amateur radio and communications. Constructional projects. *Illustrations:* photographs, line drawings and wash half-tone for offset litho. *Payment:* from £40 to £50 per 1000 words, plus extra for illustrations.

Practical Woodworking, Alan Mitchell, King's Reach Tower, Stamford Street, London, SE1 9LS *T.* 01-261 6602.
£1.10. M. Articles of a practical nature covering any aspect of woodworking. Articles on tools, joints or timber technology. *Illustrations*.

Practitioner, The (1868), R. M. F. Lawry, Morgan-Grampian (Professional Press) Ltd., 30 Calderwood Street, London, SE18 6QH *T.* 01-855 7777.
£2.50. M. (£24.00 p.a., Overseas $55).

Prediction (1936), Jo Logan, Link House, Dingwall Avenue, Croydon, CR9 2TA *T.* 01-686 2599. *Telex:* 947709 Linkho G.
85p. M. Articles on all occult subjects. *Length:* 2000 words maximum. *Payment:* by arrangement. *Illustrations:* Litho; full-colour cover.

Preparatory Schools Review, IAPS, 138 Kensington Church Street, London W8 4BN *T.* 01-727 2316.
£4.50 p.a. 3 p.a. The organ of the Incorporated Association of Preparatory Schools. Articles dealing with the education and activities of children in the Association's schools, or of general educational interest. *Length:* 700 to 3000 words. Half-tone and line *illustrations* optional. *Payment:* by arrangement.

Printing World (1878), Roy Coxhead (Benn Publications Ltd.), Benn House, Sovereign Way, Tonbridge, Kent TN9 1RW *T.* (0732) 364422.
£1.20. W. (£41.00 p.a.). Commercial, technical, financial and labour news covering all aspects of the printing industry in the UK and abroad. Outside contributions. *Payment:* by arrangement. *Illustrations:* half-tone, line, colour.

Private Eye (1962), Ian Hyslop, 6 Carlisle Street, London, W1V 5RG *T.* 01-437 4017.
45p. F. Satire. *Payment:* by arrangement. *Illustrations:* black and white, line.

Progress (1881), Ann Lee, Royal National Institute for the Blind, Braille House, 338-346 Goswell Road, London, EC1V 7JE *T.* 01-837 9921.
£2.85. M. A magazine in braille type for the blind.

Proteus (1985), Mike Kenward, Wimborne Publishing Ltd., 6 Church Street, Wimborne, Dorset BH21 1JH *T.* (0202) 881749.
80p. Bi-M. A complete fantasy adventure game in each issue. *Length:* 15,000 words. *Payment:* £40 per 1000 words, negotiable. *Illustrations:* line and colour fantasy artwork.

Publishing News (1979), Fred Newman, 43 Museum Street, London, WC1A 1LY *T.* 01-404 0304.
80p. W. Articles and news items on books and publishers. *Payment:* £40 to £50 per 1000 words. *Illustrations:* half-tone.

Pulse, Howard Griffiths, Morgan-Grampian (Professional Press) Ltd., Morgan-Grampian House, 30 Calderwood Street, Woolwich, London, SE18 6QH *T.* 01-855 7777.
£48.00 p.a. W. Articles and photographs of direct interest to G.P.s. Purely clinical material can only be accepted from medically-qualified authors. *Length:* up to 750 words. *Payment:* £75 average. *Illustrations:* black and white, and colour photographs.

Punch (1841), Alan Coren, 23-27 Tudor Street, London, EC4Y 0HR *T.* 01-583 9199.
80p. W. Most articles are commissioned, but unsolicited contributions are still encouraged, although fiction is no longer published. Maximum article *length:* 1000 words; minimum *payment:* £100.00; topical material preferred. Cartoons may also be submitted, *payment* by arrangement, and all submissions *must* be accompanied by a s.a.e.

Purchasing (founded 1966 as **Industrial Purchasing News**), Anthony Barry, Morgan-Grampian Ltd, 30 Calderwood Street, Woolwich, London, SE18 6QH *T.* 01-855 7777.
£30.00 p.a. M. Accepts features (1000-2500 words) on developments in manufacturing industry or purchasing management policies and practices; also news items up to 400 words. *Payment:* by arrangement. *Illustrations:* photographs, line drawings, cartoons.

Quaker Monthly (1921), Meg Chignell, Quaker Home Service, Friends House, Euston Road, London, NW1 2BJ *T.* 01-387 3601.
37p. M. (£6.75 p.a.). Articles, poems, reviews, expanding the Quaker approach to the spiritual life. Writers should be members or attenders of a Quaker meeting. *Illustrations:* line, half-tone. No *payment*.

Quarterly Journal of Medicine (1907), *Publisher:* Oxford University Press, Walton Street, Oxford OX2 6DP. *Executive Editor:* Dr. J. M. Holt, John Radcliffe Hospital, Oxford, OX3 9DU *T.* (0865) 817348.
£9.00. M. (£60 p.a., overseas £70 p.a.). Devoted to the publication of original papers and critical reviews dealing with clinical medicine. *No payment.*

Radio Control Models and Electronics (1960), David Boddington, Argus Specialist Publications Ltd., P.O. Box 35, Hemel Hempstead, Herts. *T.* (0442) 41221.
£1.00. M. Well illustrated articles on topics related to radio control. *Payment:* £30.00 per published page. *Illustrations:* line, half-tone. Cartoons.

Radio Times (The Journal of the BBC), Brian Gearing, BBC Enterprises, 35 Marylebone High Street, London, W1M 4AA *T.* 01-580 5577.

32p. W. Articles support and enlarge BBC Television and Radio programmes, and are, therefore, on every subject broadcast. *Length:* from 600 to 2500 words. *Payment:* by arrangement. *Illustrations:* in colour and black and white; photographs, graphic designs, or drawings.

Railway Gazette International, Richard Hope, Business Press International Ltd., Quadrant House, The Quadrant, Sutton, Surrey, SM2 5AS *T.* 01-661 3740.
£2.00. M. Deals with management, engineering, operation and finance of railways world wide. Articles of practical interest on these subjects are considered and paid for if accepted. Illustrated articles, of 1000 to 3000 words, are preferred. A *preliminary letter* is desirable.

Railway Magazine (1897), Prospect House, 9-15 Ewell Road, Cheam, Surrey, SM3 8BZ *T.* 01-661 4480.
95p. M. An illustrated magazine dealing with all railway subjects; not fiction. Articles from 1500 to 2000 words accompanied by photographs. A *preliminary letter* is desirable. No verse. *Payment:* by arrangement. *Illustrations:* colour transparencies, half-tone and line.

Railway World (founded as **Railways** 1939), Michael Harris, Coombelands House, Addlestone, Weybridge, Surrey KT15 1HY *T.* (0932) 58511.
90p. M. Articles on railway and allied matters. *Length:* 500 to 3000 words. *Payment:* by arrangement. *Illustrations:* line, half-tone and colour.

Reader's Digest, Michael Randolph (The Reader's Digest Association Ltd.), 25 Berkeley Square, London, W1X 6AB *T.* 01-629 8144.
£1.05. M. Original anecdotes—£100 for up to 300 words—are required for humorous features.

Red Letter (D. C. Thomson & Co. Ltd.), Courier Place, Dundee, DD1 9QJ, and 185 Fleet Street, London, EC4A 2HS.
20p. W. Serials of strong emotion; romantic, with movement and incident. First instalment 5000 words. Short stories 1000 to 4000 words. Real-life series. Articles of interest to girls and women. *Payment:* on acceptance. *Illustrations;* line or wash.

Red Tape (1911), C. J. Bush, Civil and Public Services Association, 215 Balham High Road, London, SW17 7BN *T.* 01-672 1299.
3p. 2 per month. Well-written articles on Civil Service, trade union and general subjects considered. *Length:* 750 to 1400 words. Also photographs and humorous drawings of interest to Civil Servants. *Illustrations:* line and half-tone.

Reform (1972), Norman Hart, 86 Tavistock Place, London, WC1H 9RT *T.* 01-837 7661.
40p. Monthly published by United Reformed Church. Articles of religious or social comment. *Length:* 600-1000 words. *Illustrations:* full colour, half-tone and line subjects. *Payment:* by arrangement.

Report (Journal of the Assistant Masters and Mistresses Association), Peter Smith, 7 Northumberland Street, London WC2N 5DA *T.* 01-930 6441.
35p. 8 times a year. Features, articles, comment, news about primary, secondary and further education. *Payment:* £60 per 1000 words (minimum). Cartoons, illustrations, photographs.

Retail Attraction, Managing Editor: Piers G. Harding, AGB Business Publications Ltd., Audit House, Field End Road, Eastcote, Ruislip, Middlesex HA4 9XE *T.* 01-868 4499.

£24.00 p.a. post free. Bi-M. (£4.00 per copy.) Reviews, retail business orientated articles, features and news, preferably illustrated, of shop and store premises design, display, planning, construction and fitting, services and lighting. *Length:* 750-1250 words (or longer by arrangement), or short paragraphs; features by arrangement. *Payment:* by arrangement. *Illustrations:* photographs, plans and sketches.

Rialto, The (1984), Michael Mackmin, Jenny Roberts, John Wakeman, 32 Grosvenor Road, Norwich, Norfolk NR2 2PZ *T.* (0603) 666455.
£1.90 3 p.a. (£5.00 p.a.). Poetry. *Illustrations:* line. No *payment* at present. S.A.E. essential.

Round Table, The (1910), The Commonwealth Journal of International Affairs, Peter Lyon, Institute of Commonwealth Studies, University of London, 27-28 Russell Square, London WC1B 5DS *T.* 01-580 5876.
£39 p.a. Q. Appropriate articles. *Payment:* £10 per 1000 words. No *illustrations*.

Running Magazine (1979), Andrew Etchells, 57-61 Mortimer Street, London, W1N 7TD *T.* 01-637 4383.
£1.20. M. Articles on jogging, running and fitness. *Payment:* by arrangement. *Illustrations:* line, half-tone, colour.

RUSI Journal (Journal of the Royal United Services Institute for Defence Studies), Dr. Brian Holden Reid, Whitehall, London, SW1A 2ET *T.* 01-930 5854.
£5.50. Q. Articles from 2000 to 5000 words on strategy, tactics, logistics and defence technology; military sociology and the economics of defence; moral ethics, disarmament and the behavioural sciences; current affairs affecting defence, and military history. *Illustrations:* maps or diagrams in each issue. *Payment:* £12.50 per printed page.

Safety Education (1966; founded 1937 as **Child Safety**; 1940 became **Safety Training**), Deborah Williams, Royal Society for the Prevention of Accidents, Cannon House, The Priory Queensway, Birmingham, B4 6BS *T.* 021-233 2461.
£3.15 p.a. 3 p.a. Articles on every aspect of safety for children and in particular articles on the teaching of road, home, water and leisure safety by means of established subjects on the school curriculum. All ages. *Illustrations:* line, half-tone and colour.

Sandwell Evening Mail (1975), Roger Monkman, Shaftesbury House, 402 High Street, West Bromwich. *T.* 021-553 7221. London office: Clan House, 19-21 Tudor Street, London, EC4Y 0DJ *T.* 01-353 0811.
15p. D. Independent. Features of topical West Midland interest considered. *Length:* 400-800 words.

Scale Models International, Kelvin Barber, Argus Specialist Publications Ltd., P.O. Box 35, Hemel Hempstead, Herts. *T.* (0442) 41221.
£1.20. M. Articles on scale models. *Length:* up to 2500 words. *Payment:* £20 per page. *Illustrations:* line, half-tone, colour.

School Librarian (1937), Joan Murphy, The School Library Association, Liden Library, Barrington Close, Liden, Swindon, Wilts. SN3 6HF *T.* (0793) 617838.
£20.00 p.a. post free. Q. Official journal of the School Library Assoc. (free to members). Articles and critiques on children's books and authors, and authors of books likely to be read by up to 18-year-old sixth-formers; administration and organisation of school libraries, and library user education. *Length:* 3200 words maximum. *Payment:* by arrangement.

Science Progress, Professor J. M. Ziman, F.R.S., Professor P. J. B. Slater, Professor Patricia H. Clarke, F.R.S., (Blackwell Scientific Publications, Ltd.), Osney Mead, Oxford, OX2 0EL *T.* Oxford (0865) 40201.

£9.00. Q. (£35.00 p.a.). Articles of 5000 to 10,000 words suitably illustrated on scientific subjects, written so as to be intelligible to workers in other branches of science. *Payment:* £1.50 per printed page. *Illustrations:* line and half-tone.

Scootering (1985), Mike Roberts, P.O. Box 69, Altrincham, Cheshire WA15 8SJ *T.* 061-941 3296.
£1.20. M. Custom, racing and vintage scooter features, plus related lifestyle pieces. *Payment:* by arrangement. *Illustrations:* half-tone, colour.

Scorpion, The, (1981) Michael E. Walker, BCM 5766, London, WC1N 3XX.
£1.50. 3 p.a. Each issue deals with a particular subject related to problems of culture. A magazine in defence of European culture. *Preliminary letter essential. Payment:* £10-£20 per 1,000 words. *Illustrations:* line, half-tone.

Scots Magazine, The (1739) (D. C. Thomson & Co. Ltd.), Bank Street, Dundee, DD1 9HU *T.* Dundee 23131.
55p. M. Articles on all subjects of Scottish interest. Short stories, poetry, but must be Scottish. *Payment:* varies according to quality. *Illustrations:* colour and black and white photographs, and drawings.

Scotsman (1817), Chris Baur, 20 North Bridge, Edinburgh, EH1 1YT *T.* 031-225 2468.
25p. D. Independent. Considers articles, 1000-1200 words on political, economic and general themes, which add substantially to current information. Prepared to commission topical and controversial series from proved authorities. *Illustrations:* outstanding news pictures.

Scottish Educational Journal, 46 Moray Place, Edinburgh, EH3 6BH *T.* 031-225 6244.
30p. 10 p.a. Published by the Educational Institute of Scotland.

Scottish Farmer, The (1893), Angus MacDonald, Ravenseft House, 302-4 St. Vincent Street, Glasgow, G2 5NL *T.* 041-221 7000.
60p. W. Articles on agricultural subjects. *Length:* 1000-1500 words. *Payment:* by arrangement. *Illustrations:* line and half-tone.

Scottish Field (1903), Roderick Martine (Holmes-McDougall Ltd.), Ravenseft House, 302 St. Vincent Street, Glasgow, G2 5NL *T.* 041-221 7000.
£1.00. M. (£13.00 p.a.) Will consider all material with a Scottish link and good photographs. *Payment:* good average rates.

Scottish Historical Review (Company of Scottish History, Ltd.), Prof. I. B. Cowan. Distributed by Pergamon Journals Ltd, Headington Hill Hall, Oxford OX3 0BW *T.* (0865) 64881.
£12.00 p.a. (£14.40 through booksellers). Twice-yearly. Contributions to the advancement of knowledge in any aspect of Scottish history. *Length:* up to 8000 words. *Payment:* none; contributors are given offprints. *Illustrations:* line and half-tone.

Scottish Home and Country (1924), Monica Sharon, 42A Heriot Row, Edinburgh, EH3 6ES *T.* 031-225 1934.
35p. M. Articles on crafts, cookery, travel, personal experience, village histories, country customs, DIY, antiques, farming; humorous rural stories. *Illustrations:* half-tone. *Length:* up to 1200 words. *Payment:* by arrangement.

Scouting, David Easton, The Scout Association, Baden-Powell House, Queens Gate, London, SW7 5JS *T.* 01-584 7030.
90p. M. The National Magazine of The Scout Association. Ideas, news, views, features and programme resources for Leaders and Supporters. Training

material, accounts of Scouting events and articles of general interest with Scouting connections. *Illustrations:* photographs—action shots preferred rather than static posed shots for use with articles or as fillers or cover potential. *Payment:* on publication by arrangement.

Screen International, Editor-in-Chief: Peter Noble; Editor: Terry Ilott; News Editor: Alex Sutherland, 6-7 Great Chapel Street, London, W1V 3AG *T.* 01-734 9452 and 437 5741. Published by King Publications Ltd.
£1.10. W. International news and features on every aspect of films, television and associated media. *Length:* variable. *Payment:* by arrangement.

Sea Angler (1973), Melvyn Russ, EMAP Pursuit Publishing Ltd., Bretton Court, Bretton, Peterborough, PE3 8DZ *T.* (0733) 264666.
80p. M. Topical articles on all aspects of sea-fishing around the British Isles. *Payment:* by arrangement. *Illustrations:* line, half-tone and colour.

Sea Breezes (1919), Craig J. M. Carter, 202 Cotton Exchange Building, Old Hall Street, Liverpool, L3 9LA *T.* 051-236 3935.
£1.10. M. Short factual articles, on the sea, seamen and merchant and naval ships, preferably illustrated. *Payment:* by arrangement. *Illustrations:* half-tone, line.

Secrets (D. C. Thomson & Co. Ltd.), Courier Place, Dundee, DD1 9QJ, and 185 Fleet Street, London, EC4A 2HS.
20p. W. Complete stories of 1500 to 4000 words, with mainly romantic interest to appeal to women of most ages. Serials, 5000-word instalments. *No preliminary letter* required. *Payment:* on acceptance.

Secrets Story Library (D. C. Thomson & Co. Ltd.), Courier Place, Dundee, DD1 9QJ, and 185 Fleet Street, London, EC4A 2HS.
24p. M. 64 pages. Exciting and romantic stories in text.

Selling Today, the official journal of the United Commercial Travellers' Association Section of ASTMS. R. Tomlinson, Bexton Lane, Knutsford, Cheshire, WA16 9DA *T.* Knutsford (0565) 4136-7.
M. Professional and Trade Union guidance in selling and the various fields of salesmanship. No *payment.*

She (1955), Eric Bailey, National Magazine House, 72 Broadwick Street, London, W1V 2BP *T.* 01-439 7144.
75p. M. Articles 1000 to 2500 words on all subjects except fashion and beauty; controversial, factual, medical, relating to women but not traditionally "feminine". First person experiences. Picture features welcome. *Payment:* NUJ freelance rates. *Illustrations:* photos; cartoons.

Ship & Boat International, Richard White, Metal Bulletin plc, 16 Lower Marsh, London SE1 7RJ *T.* 01-633 0525. *Telex:* 917706 Metbul G.
£33.00 p.a. M. Technical articles on the design, construction and operation of all types of specialised small ships and workboats. *Length:* 500-1500 words. *Payment:* by arrangement. *Illustrations:* line and half-tone, photographs and diagrams.

Ships Monthly (1966), Robert Shopland, Waterway Productions Ltd., Kottingham House, Dale Street, Burton-on-Trent, DE14 3TD *T.* (0283) 64290.
£1.10. M. Illustrated articles of maritime interest—both mercantile and naval, preferably of 20th century ships. Well-researched, factual material only. No short stories or poetry. 'Notes for Contributors' available. *Payment:* by arrangement. *Illustrations:* half-tone and line, colour on cover and inside front cover only.

Shooting Times and Country Magazine (1882), Derek Bingham, (Burlington Publishing Co. Ltd.), 10 Sheet Street, Windsor, Berkshire, SL4 1BG *T.* Windsor (0753) 856061.
65p. W. Articles on field sports, natural history and the countryside not exceeding 1200 words. *Payment:* by arrangement. *Illustrations:* photographs and drawings.

Short Wave Magazine, The (1937), Paul Essery, G3KFE, 34 High Street, Welwyn, Herts, AL6 9EQ *T.* (04-3871) 5206-7.
£1.35. M. (£16.00 p.a.). Technical and semi-technical articles, 500 to 20,000 words, dealing with design, construction and operation of radio amateur short wave receiving and transmitting equipment. *Payment:* £36.00 per page. *Illustrations:* line and half-tone.

Sight and Sound (1932), Penelope Houston (Published by the British Film Institute), 127 Charing Cross Road, London, WC2H 0EA *T.* 01-437 4355.
£1.55. Q. Topical and critical articles on the cinema of any country. Highly specialised articles only occasionally. 1000 to 5000 words. *Payment:* by arrangement. *Illustrations:* relevant photographs.

Sign, The (1905), A. R. Mowbray & Co. Ltd., Saint Thomas House, Becket Street, Oxford, OX1 1SJ *T.* Oxford (0865) 242507.
3p. M. Leading national inset for C. of E. parish magazines. Unusual b & w. photos, drawings considered. *Payment:* by arrangement. Items should bear the author's name and address; return postage essential.

Signal, Approaches to Children's Books (1970), Nancy Chambers, Lockwood, Station Road, South Woodchester, Stroud, Gloucestershire, GL5 5EQ *T.* Amberley 2208.
£2.10 Three p.a. (£6.30 p.a.). Articles on any aspect of children's books or the children's book world. *Length:* no limit but average 2500-3000 words. *Payment:* £2 per printed page. *Illustrations:* line occasionally.

Signature (1953), Erica Brown, Margam House, 26 St. James's Square, London SW1Y 4JY *T.* 01-839 7301.
£1.50 10 p.a. Articles on travel, food and wine. *Payment:* by arrangement. No unsolicited manuscripts accepted.

Singles Magazine (1977), John Patterson, 23 Abingdon Road, London, W8 6AH *T.* 01-938 1011.
75p. M. Articles of interest to single people. *Length:* up to 2000 words. *Payment:* by arrangement. *Illustrations:* line and half-tone.

Ski Magazine, Ocean Publications Ltd., 34 Buckingham Palace Road, London SW1W 0RE. *T.* 01-828 4551.
£1.00. 6 p.a. (September Annual £1.50). Articles, instructive and informative on all aspects of skiing and resorts in all parts of the world. Winter travel articles, news items. *Length:* 1000 words, illustrations preferred. *Payment:* by arrangement. *Illustrations:* black and white photographs and colour transparencies.

Slimmer Magazine (1972), Judith Wills, Tolland, Lydeard St. Lawrence, Taunton TA4 3PS *T.* (0984) 23014.
75p. Bi-M. Articles of interest to people interested in health, nutrition, slimming. *Length:* 500 to 1500 words. *Payment:* £10 per 100 words (s.a.e. essential).

Snooker Scene (1971), Clive Everton, Cavalier House, 202 Hagley Road, Edgbaston, Birmingham B16 9PQ *T.* 021-454 2931.
80p. M. News and articles about snooker. *Payment:* by arrangement. *Illustrations:* photographs.

Sociological Review, Managing Editors: John Eggleston, Ronald Frankenberg, Gordon Fyfe, University of Keele, Keele, Staffs ST5 5BG *T.* Newcastle under Lyme (0782) 621111 Ext. 371.
£27.50 p.a. (Institutions £40.00 p.a.) including Monograph. Q. Articles of 8000 to 10,000 words treating social subjects in a scientific way. No *payment* is made. *Illustrations:* line.

Solicitors' Journal, The (1857), 21-27 Lambs's Conduit Street, London WC1N 3NJ *T.* 01-242 2548.
80p. W. Articles, preferably by practising solicitors on subjects of practical interest. *Length:* up to 2000 words.

South, The Third World Magazine (1980), Andrew Graham-Yooll, New Zealand House (13th Floor), 80 Haymarket, London SW1 4TS *T.* 01-930 8411.
95p. M. News—economic, political, commodity, business relating to the Third World. *Payment:* approx. £70.00 to £100 per 1000 words. *Illustrations:* half-tone; some colour.

Spaceflight (1956), Prof. G. V. Groves, 27-29 South Lambeth Road, London, SW8 1SZ *T.* 01-735 3160. Published by The British Interplanetary Society. Free to members. £2.00 to non-members. M. Articles up to 2500 words dealing with topics of astronomy, space and astronautics. *Illustrations:* line and half-tone. *Payment:* none.

Spare Rib, 27 Clerkenwell Close, London, EC1R 0AT *T.* 01-253 9792.
80p. M. (£10.50 p.a.). Women's Liberation features, news, fiction, cartoons. *Illustrations:* black and white with second colour drawings; black-and-white photographs.

Spectator, The (1828), Charles Moore, 56 Doughty Street, London, WC1N 2LL *T.* 01-405 1706.
90p. W. Articles of a suitable character will always be considered. The rate of *payment* depends upon the nature and length of the article.

Speech and Drama (1951), Kenneth Pickering, Society of Teachers of Speech and Drama, 211B Old Dover Road, Canterbury, Kent, CT1 3ER.
£3.50 p.a. Two issues yearly. Specialist articles only. *Length:* from 3000 words. Covers the field of speech and drama in education. Preliminary letter essential. *Payment:* none. No *illustrations.*

Spiritualist Gazette (1972), Tom Johanson, S.A.G.B. Ltd., 33 Belgrave Square, London, SW1X 8QB *T.* 01-235 3351.
£4.30 p.a. M. Spiritualism, healing, life after death and allied subjects. No *payment.*

Spoken English (1968), Jocelyn Bell, English Speaking Board (International), 32A Roe Lane, Southport, Merseyside, PR9 9DZ *T.* Southport (0704) 44452.
£6.00 p.a., 3 times p.a. Articles on all aspects of oral English and drama at all levels of education and of a serious nature. Overseas as well as U.K. *Length:* from 1000 words. *Payment:* by arrangement.

Sport and Leisure (1949), Chris Middleton, The Sports Council, 16 Upper Woburn Place, London, WC1H 0QP *T.* 01-388 1277.
70p. 6 p.a. Articles on various sports, physical education, sports politics, the leisure boom, sponsorship, buildings, equipment and outdoor activities. *Length:* 500-1500 words. *Payment:* £50.00 per 1000 words. *Illustrated.* Sports photographers encouraged; black and white photographs.

Sporting Cars International (1982), Nigel Fryatt, Link House, Dingwall Avenue, Croydon CR9 2TA *T.* 01-686 2599.
£1.10. M. Motoring articles, to be negotiated with editor. *Payment:* by arrangement. *Illustrations:* transparencies and black and white.

Sporting Life, The, Monty Court, (Odhams Newspapers Ltd.), Alexander House, 81-89 Farringdon Road, London EC1M 3LH *T.* 01-831 2102. *Telex:* 263403. *Fax:* 01-831 7423.
25p. D.

Sports Car Monthly (1981), Ian Ward, CW Editorial Ltd., 538 Ipswich Road, Slough, Berks SL1 4EQ *T.* (0753) 820161.
£1.10. M. Articles on all aspects of sports cars. *Length:* 1500 to 2500 words. *Payment:* by arrangement. *Illustrations:* line, half-tone.

Stage and Television Today, The (1880), Peter Hepple, Stage House, 47 Bermondsey Street, London, SE1 3XT *T.* 01-403 1818.
30p. W. Original and interesting articles on professional stage and television topics may be sent for the Editor's consideration, 500-800 words. *Illustrations:* line and half-tone.

Stamp Lover (1908), Publisher: National Philatelic Society, The London International Stamp Centre, 27 King Street, London, WC2E 8JD *T.* 01-836 6294 and 240 7349. Editor: Arthur Blair, F.R.P.S.L.
60p. Q. Original articles on stamps and postal history. *Payment:* by arrangement. *Illustrations:* photographs, half-tone and line.

Stamp Magazine (1934), Richard West, Link House, Dingwall Avenue, Croydon, CR9 2TA *T.* 01-686 2599. *Telex:* 947709 Linkho G.
£1.00. M. Informative articles and exclusive news items on stamp collecting and postal history. *No preliminary letter. Payment:* by arrangement. *Illustrations:* photographs, half-tone and line.

Stamp Monthly, John Holman, Stanley Gibbons Publications Ltd., 5 Parkside, Ringwood, Hants BH24 3SH *T.* (04254) 2363.
£1.00 M. (£17.40 p.a.). Articles on philatelic topics. Previous reference to the editor advisable. *Length:* 500 to 2500 words. *Payment:* by arrangement, £17.00 per 1000 words and up. *Illustrations:* photographs.

Stamp News (1981), Irwin Margolis, Stamp News Ltd., 6 London Street, London W2 1HR *T.* 01-724 0168.
60p. 2 per month. Articles of high standard on stamps, postal history, postal stationery and postcards. *Length:* up to 1000 words. *Payment:* £25 per 1000 words published.

Stamps and Foreign Stamps (1979), Ray Edwards, EMAP National Publications, Bushfield House, Orton Centre, Peterborough PE2 0UW.
£1.00. M. Stamps, postal history, and anything of interest to philatelists. *Payment:* £13.50 per 1000 words. *Illustrations:* line, half-tone.

Stand Magazine (1952), Jon Silkin, Lorna Tracy, Michael Blackburn, John Wardle, 179 Wingrove Road, Newcastle on Tyne, NE4 9DA *T.* (091) 273 3280 and 2812614.
£1.60. Q. (£6.00 p.a.). Poetry, short stories, drama, translations, literary criticism, music. *Payment:* £30.00 per 1000 words of prose; £30.00 per poem. S.A.E. for return.

Standard, The (1827), Louis Kirby, P.O.Box 136, 118-121 Fleet Street, London EC4P 4JT *T.* 01-353 8000. *Telex:* 21909.
20p. D. Independent. Articles of general interest considered, 1500 words or shorter; also news, pictures and ideas.

Star, The (1978), Lloyd Turner, Great Ancoats Street, Manchester, M60 4HB *T.* 061-236 9575.

18p. D. Major interviews with big-star personalities; short features (particularly directed at women); series based on people rather than things; picture features. *Payment:* Short features: £50-£75; full page £200-£250; double page £400-£600. *Illustrations:* line, half-tone; cartoons.

Star, The (1887), M. Corner, York Street, Sheffield, S1 1PU *T.* 78585. London: 23-27 Tudor Street, EC4 *T.* 01-583 9199.
17p. D. Well-written articles of local character. *Length:* about 800 words. *Payment:* according to value. *Illustrations:* topical photographs, line drawings, graphics.

Star Love Stories (D. C. Thomson & Co. Ltd.), Albert Square, Dundee, DD1 9QJ *T.* (0382) 23131, and 185 Fleet Street, London, EC4A 2HS.
24p. 2 each month. Romantic and emotional stories told in pictures. Scripts should be about 135 pictures. New writers encouraged. Synopsis required as an opener. Send for details. *Payment:* on acceptance.

Starblazer Library (D. C. Thomson & Co. Ltd.), Courier Place, Dundee, DD1 9QJ, and 185 Fleet Street, London, EC4A 2HS.
24p. M. 64 pages. Fantasy fiction picture story adventure for boys.

Street Machine (1979) Clive Househam, AGB Specialist Publications Ltd., Audit House, Field End Road, Eastcote, Ruislip, Middlesex HA4 9LT *T.* 01-868 4499.
£1.00. M. Articles on all cars and bodywork, 2000 to 3000 words. *Payment:* by arrangement. *Illustrations:* line, half-tone, colour.

Studies in Comparative Religion, Perennial Books Ltd., Pates Manor, Bedfont, Middlesex, TW14 8JP *T.* 01-890 2790.
£3.95. Q. Comparative religion, metaphysics, traditional studies, eastern religions, mysticism, holy places, etc. *Length:* 2000-4000 words.

Studio International (1893), Michael Spens, Tower House, Southampton Street, London, WC2E 7LS *T.* 01-379 6005.
£5.00. Q. An international magazine dealing with the contemporary fine arts. *Remarks:* only *illustrated* articles and notes accepted. A *preliminary letter* is desirable. *Payment:* by arrangement. *Illustrations:* reproductions of paintings, sculpture, drawings, engravings, applied art.

Studio Sound (1959), Keith Spencer-Allen, Link House, Dingwall Avenue, Croydon, CR9 2TA *T.* 01-686 2599. *Telex:* 947709 Linkho G.
£1.50. M. Articles on all aspects of professional sound recording. Technical and operational features on the functional aspects of studio equipment: general features on studio affairs. *Length:* widely variable. *Payment:* by arrangement. *Illustrations:* line and half-tone.

Sun, The (1969), Editorial Director: Peter Stephens; Editor: Kelvin MacKenzie, News Group Newspapers Ltd., Virginia Street, London E1 9BH *T.* 01-481 4100. *T.A.* Sunnews, London. *Telex:* 262135 Sunews.
18p. D.

Sunday Express (1918), Robin Esser, Fleet Street, London, EC4P 4JT *T.* 01-353 8000.
35p. W. Exclusive news stories, photographs, personality profiles and features of controversial or lively interest. *Length:* 800 to 1000 words. *Payment:* Top rates.

Sunday Express Magazine, Ron Hall, 3rd Floor, Newspaper House, 8-16 Great New Street, London, EC4A 3AJ *T.* 01-353 8000.
Free with newspaper. W. General interest features. *Length:* 1500 words. *Payment:* from £150 per 1000 words. *Illustrations:* colour, half-tone, art work.

Sunday Magazine (1981), Eve Pollard, 18 Ogle Street, London, W1P 7LG *T.* 01-636 5010.
Free with News of the World. W. Features by commission only. *Payment:* by arrangement.

Sunday Mail, Endell J. Laird, Anderston Quay, Glasgow, G3 8DA *T.* 041-242 3353. London Office: 33 Holborn Circus, EC1P 1DQ.
26p. W. Exclusive stories and pictures (in colour if possible) of national and Scottish interest. *Payment:* above average.

Sunday Mercury, J. Bradbury, Colmore Circus, Birmingham, B4 6AZ *T.* 021-236 3366.
26p. W. News specials or features of Midland interest. Any black-and-white *illustrations*. Special rates for special matter.

Sunday Mirror, M. Molloy, 33 Holborn, London, EC1P 1DQ *T.* 01-353 0246.
25p. W. Concentrates on human interest news features, social documentaries, dramatic news and feature photographs. Ideas, as well as articles, bought. *Payment:* high, especially for exclusives.

Sunday People, Ernest Burrington, Orbit House, 9 New Fetter Lane, London, EC4A 1AR *T.* 01-822 3400.
28p. W. A Sunday paper for all classes of readers. Features, single articles and series, considered. Pictures should be supplied with contributions if possible. Features should be of deep human interest, whether the subject is serious or light-hearted. The first investigative newspaper, the People is particularly noted for its exposures of social evils, criminal activities, financial and other rackets and bureaucratic malpractices, in the public interest. Very strong sports following. Exclusive news and news-feature stories also considered. Rates of *payment* high, even for tips that lead to published news stories.

Sunday Post (D. C. Thomson & Co. Ltd.), 144 Port Dundas Road, Glasgow, G4 0HZ, Courier Place, Dundee, DD1 9QJ, and 185 Fleet Street, London, EC4A 2HS *T.* (Glasgow) 041-332 9933; (Dundee) (0382) 23131; (London) 01-353 2586-8.
26p. W. Human interest, topical, domestic, and humorous articles and exclusive news; and short stories up to 2000 words. *Illustrations:* humorous drawings. *Payment:* on acceptance.

Sunday Sun, The (1919), Jim Buglass, Thomson House, Groat Market, Newcastle, NE1 1ED *T.* Newcastle 327500.
28p. W. Immediate topicality and human sidelights on current problems are the keynote of the Sun's requirements. Particularly welcomed are special features of family appeal and news stories of special interest to the North of England. Photographs used to illustrate articles. *Length:* 500 to 1200 words. *Payment:* normal lineage rates, or by arrangement. *Illustrations:* photographs and line.

Sunday Telegraph, Peregrine Worsthorne, 135 Fleet Street, London, EC4P 4BL *T.* 01-353 4242.
35p. W.

Sunday Times, The (1822), Andrew Neil, 1 Pennington Street, London E1 9XW *T.* 01-481 4100.
50p. W. Special articles by authoritative writers on politics, literature, art, drama, music, finance and science, and topical matters. Top payment for exclusive features. *Illustrations:* first-class photographs of topical interest and pictorial merit very welcome; also topical drawings.

UNITED KINGDOM

Sunday Times Magazine, Genevieve Cooper, 1 Pennington Street, London, E1 9XN *T.* 01-481 4100 *T.A.* Sunday Times, London, E1.
Free with paper. W. Articles and pictures. *Payment:* £150 per 1000 words. *Illustrations:* colour photographs; *payment* £150 per page.

Surrey Life, Rod Cooper, Basted, Borough Green, Sevenoaks, Kent TN15 8PW *T.* (0732) 884564.
85p. All articles must have a Surrey connection. *Length:* 500 to 1200 words; sharp black-and-white pictures with articles; colour transparencies (minimum 2¼ in. square) also considered for front cover and the occasional inside colour feature. *Illustrations:* half-tone or line drawings. *Payment:* by arrangement.

Sussex Life Rod Cooper, Basted, Borough Green, Sevenoaks, Kent TN15 8PW *T.* (0732) 884564.
85p. M. All articles must have a Sussex connection. *Length:* 500 to 1200 words; sharp black-and-white pictures with articles; colour transparencies (minimum 2¼ in. square) also considered for front cover and the occasional inside colour feature. *Illustrations:* half-tone or line drawings. *Payment:* by arrangement.

Suzy (1982), (D. C. Thomson & Co. Ltd.), 2 Albert Square, Dundee, DD1 9QJ *T.* (0382) 23131. London Office: 185 Fleet Street, EC4A 2HS *T.* 01-242 5086/8.
28p. W. Picture story and photo feature magazine for girls.

Tablet, The (1840), John Wilkins, 48 Great Peter Street, London, SW1P 2HB *T.* 01-222 7462.
70p. W. The senior Catholic weekly. Religion, philosophy, politics, society, the arts. Freelance work welcomed. Articles should not exceed 1500 words. *Payment:* by arrangement.

Tatler, The (1709), Mark Boxer, Vogue House, Hanover Square, London, W1R 0AD *T.* 01-499 9080.
£1.50. 10 issues p.a. Smart society magazine favouring sharp articles, profiles, fashion and the arts. *Illustrations:* colour, black and white, but all arranged by the journal.

Teacher, The (1872), Alan Slingsby, Hamilton House, Mabledon Place, London, WC1H 9BS *T.* 01-388 1952.
10p. W. The newspaper of the National Union of Teachers; News of current educational events. Articles mostly commissioned. No unsolicited MSS will be considered. *Illustrations:* photographs and cartoons.

Telegraph Sunday Magazine (formerly **The Daily Telegraph Magazine**) (1964), Felicity Lawrence, 135 Fleet Street, London, EC4P 4BL *T.* 01-353 4242. *T.A.* Teleweek London.
Free with the paper. W. Short profiles (about 1600 words), articles of topical interest. *Payment:* £150 per 1000 words minimum. *Illustrations:* all types. *Payment for Illustrations:* dependent on the feature requirements. *Photographs* £150 colour page, £120 black and white minimum. *Preliminary study of the magazine essential.*

Television (1950), IPC Magazines Ltd., King's Reach Tower, Stamford Street, London, SE1 9LS *T.* 01-261 5752.
£1.20. M. Articles on the technical aspects of domestic tv and video equipment, especially servicing; long-distance television; constructional projects; satellite tv; video recording; teletext and viewdata; test equipment. *Illustrations:* photographs and line drawings for litho. *Payment:* by arrangement.

Tempo, Calum MacDonald (Boosey & Hawkes, Music Publishers, Ltd.), 295 Regent Street, London, W1R 8JH *T.* 01-580 2060.

£1.20p. Q. (£6.00 p.a.). Authoritative articles about 2000 to 4000 words on contemporary music. *Payment:* by arrangement. *Illustrations:* music type, occasional photographic or musical supplements.

Tennis (1979), Catherine J. Bell, 34 Buckingham Palace Road, London SW1W 0RE *T.* 01-828 4551.
£1.20. 8 p.a. Articles on any aspect of tennis. *Payment:* by arrangement. *Illustrations:* half-tone.

Tennis World, Henry Wancke, Dennis Fairey Publishing Ltd, Chilton House, 184 High Street, Berkhamsted, Herts, HP4 3AP *T.* (04427) 74947.
£1.20. 10 times p.a. Tournament reports, topical features, personality profiles, instructional articles. *Length:* 600 to 1500 words. *Payment:* by arrangement. *Illustrations:* colour, black and white, line.

Theology (1920), Peter Coleman, Diocesan House, Palace Gate, Exeter EX1 1HX *T.* (0392) 73509.
£1.60. Bi-M. Articles and reviews on theology, ethics, Church and Society. *Length:* up to 3500 words. *Payment:* by arrangement.

Third Way (1977), Tim Dean, 37 Elm Road, New Malden, Surrey KT3 3HB *T.* 01-942 9761.
90p. 12 issues p.a. Aims to present a biblical perspective on a wide range of current issues, e.g. sociology, politics, education, economics, industry, and the arts. *Payment:* for articles: on publication.

35mm Photography (1945), Nigel Skelsey, Argus Specialist Publications, 1 Golden Square, London W1R 3AB *T.* 01-437 0626.
£1.00. M. Illustrated articles of 900 to 1400 words on all aspects of photography, pictorial and technical, and how-to-do-it articles, slanted towards the serious amateur and young professional. *Payment:* by arrangement. *Illustrations:* line, half-tone and colour.

This England (1968), Roy Faiers, P.O. Box 52, Cheltenham, Gloucestershire, GL50 1HT *T.* (0242) 577775.
£1.80. Q. Articles on towns, villages, traditions, customs, legends, crafts of England; stories of people. *Length:* 250 to 2000 words. *Payment:* £15 per page and pro rata. *Illustrations:* line, half-tone, colour.

Thoroughbred & Classic Cars, Tony Dron, Prospect House, 9-15 Ewell Road, Cheam, Surrey, SM3 8BZ *T.* 01-661 4300. *Telex:* 892084 Bisprs G.
£1.20. M. Specialist articles on older cars. *Length:* from 1000 to 4000 words (subject to prior contract). *Payment:* by negotiation. *Illustrations:* half-tone and colour.

Times, The (1785), Charles Wilson, 1 Pennington Street, London E1 9XN *T.* 01-481 4100. *Telex:* 925088.
23p. D. Independent. Outside contributions considered from (1) experts in subjects of current interest: (2) writers who can make first-hand experience or reflection come readably alive. Best *length:* up to 1200 words. *No preliminary letter* is required.

Times Educational Supplement, The, Stuart Maclure, Priory House, St. John's Lane, London, EC1M 4BX *T.* 01-253 3000. *Telex:* 264971.
55p. W. Articles on education written with special knowledge or experience. News items. Books, arts and equipment reviews. *Illustrations:* suitable photographs and drawings of educational interest.

Times Educational Supplement Scotland (1965), Willis Pickard, 56 Hanover Street, Edinburgh, EH2 2DZ *T.* 031-225 6393.

55p. W. Articles on education, preferably 1100 words, written with special knowledge or experience. News items about Scottish educational affairs. *Illustrations:* line and half-tone.

Times Higher Education Supplement (1971), Peter Scott, Priory House, St. John's Lane, London, EC1M 4BX *T.* 01-253 3000. *Telex:* 264971.
60p. W. Articles on higher education written with special knowledge or experience or articles dealing with academic topics. News items. *Illustrations:* suitable photographs and drawings of educational interest.

Times Literary Supplement, The, Jeremy Treglown, Priory House, St. John's Lane, London, EC1M 4BX *T.* 01-253 3000. *Telex:* 264971.
80p. W. General articles of literary interest are welcomed.

Today (1986), Brian MacArthur, 70 Vauxhall Bridge Road, London SW1V 2RP *T.* 01-630 1300. *Telex:* 919925. *Fax:* 01-630 6839 Group 2/3.
20p; 30p Sunday. D. Feature-type articles. *Length:* 300 to 3000 words. *Payment:* by arrangement. *Illustrations:* line, half-tone, colour.

Today (1955), Ian Cory, 37 Elm Road, New Malden, Surrey KT3 3HB *T.* 01-942 9761.
85p. M. Aimed at everyone with leadership responsibility at any level in their local church. Major features designed to present a non-party view of biblical Christianity and to provide practical help for leaders. Emphasis on issues and current affairs as well as news and down-to-earth advice.

Today's Guide, Official Monthly of the Girl Guides Association, Mrs. J. V. Rush, 17-19 Buckingham Palace Road, London, SW1W 0PT *T.* 01-834 6242.
40p. M. Articles of interest to Guides (aged 10-15) and general interest topics. Serials and short stories with Guiding background (800 words per instalments). Cartoons. *Payment:* £25.35 per 1000 words. *Illustrations:* line, and half-tone.

Together (1956), Church House Publishing, Church House, Dean's Yard, London, SW1P 3NZ *T.* 01-222 9011. Editor: Mrs. Pamela Egan, Church of England Board of Education, Church House, Dean's Yard, London, SW1P 3NZ.
50p. 9 issues p.a. Short, practical or topical articles dealing with all forms of children's Christian education or concerned with the development and psychology of children. *Illustrations:* half-tone and line. *Length:* up to 1200 words. *Payment:* by arrangement.

Topper, The (D. C. Thomson & Co. Ltd.), Courier Place, Dundee, DD1 9QJ, and 185 Fleet Street, London, EC4A 2HS.
20p. W. All-picture paper for children. Comic strip series, in sets of 6-20 pictures each. Picture stories of 8-16 pictures per instalment. Special encouragement to promising writers and artists. *Payment:* on acceptance.

Town and Country Planning (Journal of the Town and Country Planning Association), 17 Carlton House Terrace, London, SW1Y 5AS *T.* 01-930 8903-5.
£38.50. M. Informative articles on town and country planning, regional planning, land use, new towns, green belts, countryside preservation, industrial, business and social life in great and small towns, environment in general and community development. *Length:* 1000 words. *Payment:* none. *Illustrations:* photographs and drawings.

Townswoman, Hazel Thompson, 2 Cromwell Place, London, SW7 2JG *T.* 01-581 5581.

25p. M. Official journal of the National Union of Townswomen's Guilds. Lively, informative general articles and reports on work of Townswomen's Guilds. *Length:* 600-800 words. Priority to T.G. members. *Illustrations:* half-tone, line, colour.

Toy Trader, Turret-Wheatland Ltd., Penn House, Penn Place, Rickmansworth, Herts, WD3 1SN.
£16.30 p.a. M. A trade journal specialising in anything to do with games and toys circulating to manufacturers and retailers. *Length:* by negotiation. *Payment:* by negotiation.

Traveller, The (1970), Wexas Ltd., 45 Brompton Road, London SW3 1DE. *T.* 01-581 4130 *T.A.* Wexas London SW3.
£17.58 p.a. 3 p.a. Features on independent travel of all kinds but specialising in long-haul and off beat destinations with first class photographs. Articles giving useful tips on particular aspects of travel, country reports providing an insight and factual information of use to other travellers. Articles not strictly on travel but of related interest also welcomed. *Length:* 1000 to 2000 words. Rates of *payment* and leaflet giving full details of requirements available; SAE required. *Illustrations:* line, half-tone, colour; maps.

Treasure Hunting (1977), Rita Smith, Sovereign House, Brentwood, Essex, CM14 4SE *T.* (0277) 219876.
£1.10. M. Stories of interesting finds. Articles on all aspects of treasure hunting with or without a detector. *Payment:* £15.00 per 1000 words. *Illustrations:* half-tone, colour.

Trefoil, The, Jean Rush, Official Journal of the Trefoil Guild, C.H.Q., The Girl Guides Association, 17-19 Buckingham Palace Road, London, SW1W 0PT *T.* 01-828 7610.
25p. Q. Articles on the activities of The Guild and of Guiding in the UK and overseas and on the work of voluntary organisations. *Length:* not more than 1400 words. Photographs. No fiction. No *payment*.

Tribune, Nigel Williamson, 308 Gray's Inn Road, London WC1X 8DY *T.* 01-278 0911.
50p. W. Political, literary, with Socialist outlook. Informative articles (about 800 words), short political notes (250-300 words). *Payment:* by arrangement. *Illustrations:* cartoons and photographs.

Trout and Salmon (1955), John Wilshaw, EMAP, Bretton Court, Bretton Centre, Peterborough PE3 8DZ *T.* (0733) 264666. *Telex:* 32157.
£1.10. M. Articles of good quality with strong trout or salmon angling interest. *Length:* 400 to 1500 words, accompanied if possible by photographs. *Payment:* by arrangement. *Illustrations:* line, half-tone, four colour cover.

True Romances, Isobel Irvine, 12-18 Paul Street, London, EC2A 4JS *T.* 01-247 8233.
75p. M. First-person stories with strong love interest. *Length:* 1500 to 5000 words. *Payment:* by arrangement, on acceptance.

True Story, Sally Parsons, 12-18 Paul Street, London, EC2A 4JS *T.* 01-247 8233.
75p. M. First-person stories with strong love interest. *Length:* 1500 to 5000 words. *Payment:* by arrangement, on acceptance.

TVTimes, Anthony Peagam, 247 Tottenham Court Road, London, W1P 0AU *T.* 01-323 3222.
32p. W. Features with an affinity to ITV and Channel Four programmes and personalities and television generally. *Length:* from 500 words or by arrangement. *Photographs:* only those of outstanding quality. *Payment:* by arrangement.

Twinkle (D. C. Thomson & Co. Ltd.), Albert Square, Dundee, DD1 9QJ, and 185 Fleet Street, London, EC4A 2HS.
22p. W. Picture stories, features and comic strips, specially for little girls. Drawings in line or colour for gravure. *Payment:* on acceptance. Special encouragement to promising writers and artists.

Unesco Courier, The (1948), E. Glissant, Unesco, P.O.Box 5738, 7 Place de Fontenoy, Paris 75700. *T.* 577 16 10. *T.A.* Unesco, Paris.
£5.25 p.a. Monthly in 27 language editions. Illustrated feature articles in the fields of science, culture, education and communication; promotion of international understanding; human rights; first-hand accounts of ways of life in other lands. *Length:* 2000 words. *Illustrations:* colour and black-and-white photographs, drawings, graphs, maps.

Universe, The (1860), Rowanne Pasco, 33-39 Bowling Green Lane, London, EC1R 0AB *T.* 01-278 7321. *T.A.* Unicredo London.
30p. W. A newspaper and review for Catholics. News stories, features and photographs on all aspects of Catholic life required. MSS should not be submitted without stamped envelope. *Payment:* by arrangement.

Universities Quarterly: Culture, Education & Society (1946), Professor Boris Ford, Basil Blackwell Ltd., 108 Cowley Road, Oxford OX4 1JF *T.* (0865) 722146.
Q. Articles on educational, cultural and general topics that will be of interest to those engaged in higher education. *Length:* 2000 to 5000 words. No *payment:* 6 copies of issue.

Use of English, The, Roger Knight, School of Education, 21 University Road, Leicester LE1 7HF *Publishers:* Scottish Academic Press Ltd., 33 Montgomery Street, Edinburgh, EH7 5JX *T.* 031-556-2796.
£2.20. 3 issues p.a. (£7.50 p.a. institutions; £5.95 p.a. individuals). For teachers in all fields of English in Great Britain and overseas. *Length:* usually up to 3500 words. No *payment.*

Vegetarian, The, Bronwen Humphreys, Parkdale, Dunham Road, Altrincham, Cheshire, WA14 4QG *T.* 061-928 0793.
65p. Bi-M. Articles on animal welfare, nutrition, world food problems, vegetarian and alternative lifestyles. Interviews with vegetarian celebrities. *Payment:* by arrangement. *Illustrations:* photographs and line drawings of foods, crops, relevant events, nature studies; colour for cover.

Verse (1984), Robert Crawford, David Kinloch, Henry Hart, St. Hugh's College, Oxford OX2 6LE *T.* (0865) 57341 ext. 67.
£1.50 3 p.a. Poems in English, Scots, or translation; critical pieces on contemporary poetry.

Victor (D. C. Thomson & Co. Ltd.), Courier Place, Dundee, DD1 9QJ, and 185 Fleet Street, London, EC4A 2HS.
20p. W. Vigorous, well-drawn stories in pictures (line drawings) for boys and young men. War, adventure, Western, sport. Instalments 2, 3, or 4 pages; 8 to 10 frames per page. *Payment:* on acceptance.

Video Week (1983), Steve Hurst, Morgan-Grampian plc, Greater London House, Hampstead Road, London NW1 7QZ *T.* 01-387 6611. *Telex:* 299485 Music G.
£1.00. (Controlled circulation.) W. News and features on all aspects of producing, manufacturing, marketing and retailing video software programmes; also cable and satellite TV, video games and computer software. *Payment:* NUJ rates.

Vogue, Anna Wintour, Vogue House, Hanover Square, London, W1R 0AD *T.* 01-499 9080. *Telex:* 27338 Volon G.

£1.80. M. Fashion, beauty, health, decorating, art, theatre, films, literature, music, travel, food and wine. Articles from 1000 words.

Voice of the Arab World, William Morris, 15a Lowndes Street, London, SW1X 9EY *T.* 01-235 5966.
60p. (£15.00 p.a.). M. Articles on Arabs, Arab world. *Length:* 500 to 1500 words. *Payment:* by arrangement. *Illustrations:* half-tone.

Voluntary Action (1979), Catherine Dawson (Acting Editor), 26 Bedford Square, London, WC1B 3HU *T.* 01-636 4066.
85p W. (£42 p.a.) Published weekly in **New Society.** Articles of interest to a wide range of charities, voluntary organisations and community projects. *Length:* 500-950 words. *Payment:* by arrangement. *Illustrations:* photographs.

War Cry (1879), Published by The Salvation Army. Major Robert Street, 101 Queen Victoria Street, London, EC4P 4EP *T.* 01-236 5222.
12p. W. (£16.25 p.a. UK). Voluntary contributions, mostly by Salvationists. Puzzles. *Illustrations:* Line and photographs.

Warlord (D. C. Thomson & Co. Ltd.), Courier Place, Dundee, DD1 9QJ and 185 Fleet Street, London, EC4A 2HS.
20p. W. Picture stories in line for boys. Subject: War. Instalments, 2-4 pages, 8-10 frames per page, also special war features. *Payment:* on acceptance.

Warwickshire and Worcestershire Life (including **West Midlands**), D. J. N. Green, 27 Waterloo Place, Leamington Spa, Warwickshire, CV32 5LF *T.* (0926) 22003 and 22372. A member of the Opax Publishing Group.
65p. M. Articles of interest in the counties concerned based on first-hand experience dealing with work, customs and matters affecting urban and rural welfare. *Length:* 500 to 1500 words. *Payment:* by arrangement. Photographs also by arrangement. *Illustrations:* preference given to articles accompanied by good photographs relating to subject.

Waterways World (1972), Hugh Potter, Waterway Productions Ltd., Kottingham House, Dale Street, Burton-on-Trent, Staffordshire, DE14 3TD *T.* (0283) 64290 and 42721.
£1.10. Feature articles on all aspects of inland waterways in Britain and abroad, including historical material. Factual and technical articles preferred. No short stories or poetry. *Payment:* by arrangement. *Illustrations:* black and white photographs, colour, line.

Weekend, Bill Ridley, New Carmelite House, London, EC4Y 0JA *T.* 01-353 6000.
30p. W. Factual articles appealing to men and women, true-life dramas, show business (500 to 1000 words). *Payment:* by arrangement. *Illustrations:* mono and colour action photographs, glamour, cartoons.

Weekly News, The (D. C. Thomson & Co. Ltd.), Courier Place, Dundee, DD1 9QJ *T.* 23131; 139 Chapel Street, Manchester, M3 6AA *T.* 061-834 2831-7; 144 Port Dundas Road, Glasgow, G4 0HZ *T.* 041-332 9933; and 185 Fleet Street, London, EC4A 2HS *T.* 01-242 5086.
20p. W. Real-life dramas of around 2000 words told in the first person. Non-fiction series with lively themes or about interesting people. Keynote throughout is strong human interest. Joke sketches. *Payment:* on acceptance.

WES Journal formerly **PNEU Journal** (1890), Hugh Boulter, M.A., World-wide Education Service, Strode House, 44-50 Osnaburgh Street, London, NW1 3NN *T.* 01-387 9228. *Telex:* 922488 PNE 118.

£6.00 p.a. 3 times p.a. Journal of the World-wide Education Service. Articles on education, psychology, teaching methods and children's activities within the age-range 3-16. Feature articles preferably related to children or parents whose children have been taught with the help of WES. *Length:* 1000-2000 words. *Payment:* by arrangement.

West Africa, K. Whiteman, Graybourne House, 52-54 Gray's Inn Road, London WC1X 8LT *T.* 01-831 7654.
70p. W. A weekly summary of West African news, with articles on political, economic and commercial matters, and on all matters of general interest affecting West Africa. Also book reviews. Covers Ghana, Nigeria, Sierra Leone, The Gambia, French-speaking African States, former Portuguese West Africa, Liberia and Zaire. Articles about 1200 words. *Payment:* as arranged. *Illustrations:* half-tone.

Western Mail (1869), John Rees, Thomson House, Cardiff, CF1 1WR *T.* 33022. London Office: Pemberton House, East Harding Street, London EC4A 3AS *T.* 01-353 9131.
22p. D. Independent. Articles of political, industrial, literary or general and Welsh interest are considered. *Payment:* according to value. Special fees for exclusive news. Topical general news and feature pictures.

Western Morning News, The (1860), Colin Davison, Leicester Harmsworth House, Plymouth, PL1 1RE *T.* 266626.
20p. D. Articles of 600 to 900 words, plus illustrations, considered on West Country subjects.

Which Computer? (1978), Lynne McTaggart, Abbot's Court, 34 Farringdon Lane, London EC1R 3AU *T.* 01-251 6222.
£1.50 M. Will consider proposals for equipment reviews and general features about business computing. *Payment:* £100 per 1000 words. *Illustrations:* line, half-tone, colour. *Preliminary letter essential.*

Wisden Cricket Monthly (1979), David Frith, 6 Beech Lane, Guildford, Surrey, GU2 5ES *T.* (0483) 32573.
95p. M. Cricket articles of general interest. *Length:* 1000 maximum. *Payment:* by arrangement. *Illustrations:* half-tone, colour.

(Wolverhampton) Express and Star (1874), Keith Parker, Queen Street, Wolverhampton, WV1 3BU *T.* (0902) 22351. London: Chronicle House, 72-78 Fleet Street, London, EC4P 4BE.
17p. D. Open to consider topical contributions up to 750 words with or without illustrations. *Payment:* by arrangement.

Woman (1937), Richard Barber, King's Reach Tower, Stamford Street, London, SE1 9LS *T.* 01-261 6452.
33p. W. Practical articles of varying length on all subjects of interest to women. Short stories of 2500 to 4000 words, serials and serialisation of book material. *Payment:* by arrangement. *Illustrations:* colour transparencies, photographs, sketches.

Woman and Home (1926), Sue Dobson, King's Reach Tower, Stamford Street, London, SE1 9LS *T.* 01-261 5423.
75p. M. Centres on the personal and home interests of the lively-minded woman with or without career and family. Articles dealing with leisure pursuits, crafts, gardening, dressmaking and fashion, needlework and knitting. Things to make and buy for the home. Features on people and places. Fiction: serial stories 3 to 6 instalments, and complete stories from 2000 to 7000 words in *length,* of strong romantic interest. *Illustrations:* photographs and sketches for full-colour and mono reproduction.

Woman Journalist, The, Organ of the Society of Women Writers and Journalists (1894), Jocelyn Glegg, 300 Hills Road, Cambridge CB2 2QG.
Free to members. 3 p.a. Short articles of interest to professional writers, but no *payment* is made.

Woman's Journal (1927), Laurie Purden, King's Reach Tower, Stamford Street, London, SE1 9LS *T*. 01-261 6622.
£1.00. M. A magazine devoted to the looks and lives of intelligent woman. Contents include short stories of literary merit (3000 words maximum); interviews and articles (1000-2000 words) dealing in depth with topical subjects and personalities; fashion, beauty and health, food and design. *Illustrations:* full colour, line and wash, first-rate photographs.

Woman's Own, Bridget Rowe, King's Reach Tower, Stamford Street, London, SE1 9LS *T*. 01-261 5474.
33p. W. Appealing to modern women of all ages, all classes, predominantly in the 20-35 age group. No unsolicited fiction accepted except for annual short story competition. Good, original feature ideas welcome from show business to human interest and sociological issues. *Illustrations:* in full colour and mono. Original knitting, crochet, craft designs, interior decorating and furnishing ideas, fashion. Please address work to relevant department editor.

Woman's Realm (1958), Judith Hall, King's Reach Tower, Stamford Street, London, SE1 9LS *T*. 01-261 6033.
27p. W. Lively general interest weekly magazine specialising in service to women with growing families. Articles on personalities, topical subjects, cookery, fashion, beauty, home. Short stories of 1000 to 4000 words; serials of 25,000-60,000 words. *Payment:* by arrangement. *Illustrations:* four-colour and two-colour drawings; photographs in colour and monotone.

Woman's Story Magazine (1956), Gill Pilcher, 12-18 Paul Street, London, EC2A 4JS *T*. 01-247 8233.
75p. M. Short stories with realistic characterisation and strong woman-interest plot. *Length:* 1500-5000 words. *Payment:* by arrangement, on acceptance.

Woman's Weekly (1911), Brenda McDougall, King's Reach Tower, Stamford Street, London, SE1 9LS *T*. 01-261 6131.
30p. W. A lively, family-interest magazine. Two serials, averaging 6000 words each instalment, and one short story of 2500 to 4000 words of strong romantic interest. Important biographies, and memoirs of celebrities. Personality features with photographs. *Payment:* by arrangement. *Illustrations:* full colour and mono fiction illustrations, small sketches and photographs.

Woman's World (1977), Kerry Mackenzie, 25 Newman Street, London, W1P 3HA *T*. 01-631 3939.
80p. M. A wide-ranging magazine for women, covering all aspects of a woman's world and her interests today. Personal profiles, viewpoints and opinions on topical and contemporary subjects, cartoons, humorous and thought-provoking articles on man-woman and family relationships; fashion, beauty, cookery, home, competitions; short stories. *Illustrations:* full colour, line and wash, photographs.

Women's Review (1985), Helen Carr, Nicci Gerrard, Deborah Philips, Unit 1, 1-4 Christina Street, London EC2 *T*. 01-739 4906.
£1.00. M. Short stories, articles, 1500 to 2000 words; reviews 300-600 words. *Payment:* £45.00 per 1000 words. *Illustrations:* black-and-white, half tone; cartoons.

Woodworker, Aidan Walker, Argus Specialist Publications, 1 Golden Square, London W1R 3AB *T*. 01-437 0626.

£1.10. M. For the craft and professional woodworker. *Payment:* by arrangement. Practical illustrated articles on cabinet work, carpentry, wood polishing, wood turning, wood carving, rural crafts, craft history, antique and period furniture; also wooden toys and models; timber procurement, conditioning, seasoning; tool, machinery and equipment reviews. *Illustrations:* line drawings and photographs.

Work Study, F. Conyers (Sawell Publications, Ltd.), 127 Stanstead Road, London, SE23 1JE *T.* 01-699 6792. *T.A.* Sawells, London.
£1.75 including postage. M. (£10.50 p.a. post £4.00). Authoritative articles about all aspects of Work Study, i.e. Motion and Time study, methods, engineering, process control, scientific management, incentive schemes, and business efficiency. *Length:* 1000 to 4000 words. *Payment:* by arrangement. *Illustrations:* half-tone and line.

Working Woman (1984), Pandora Wodehouse, 40 Fleet Street, London EC4Y 1BT *T.* 01-583 2990.
£1.25 M. Articles of interest to women who work; fiction. *Length:* 1500-2000 words. *Payment:* by arrangement. *Illustrations:* line, half-tone, colour.

World Bowls (1954), *Publisher:* G. K. Browne, P.O. Box 17, East Horsley, Surrey KT24 5JU *T.* (0372) 59319.
80p. M. Unusual features, fiction and news about all codes of bowling. *Payment:* by arrangement. *Illustrations:* half-tone, colour.

World Development, Pergamon Press Ltd., Headington Hill Hall, Oxford, OX3 0BW *T.* Oxford (0865) 64881.
$260.00 p.a. M. The multi-disciplinary international journal devoted to the study and promotion of world development.

World Fishing (1952), Nortide Ltd., Nortide House, Stone Street, Faversham, Kent ME13 8PG *T.* (0795) 536536.
£27 p.a. M. The International Journal of commercial fishing. Technical and management emphasis on catching, processing farming and marketing of fish and related products. Fishery operations and vessels covered world wide. *Length:* 20,000 to 30,000 words. *Payment:* by arrangement. *Illustrations:* Photographs and diagrams for litho reproduction.

World Outlook, The Baptist Men's Movement, 93 Gloucester Place, London, W1H 4AA *T.* 01-935 1482.
£2.00 p.a. Q. Articles on world questions from a Christian standpoint. *Length:* from 700 to 1000 words. *Illustrations.*

World Today, The (1945), Christopher Cviic, The Royal Institute of International Affairs, Chatham House, 10 St. James's Square, London, SW1Y 4LE *T.* 01-930 2233. *T.A.* Areopagus, London.
£1.50. M. Objective and factual articles on current questions of international affairs. *Length:* about 3500 words. *Payment:* £25 each article.

World's Children, The (1920), the magazine of The Save the Children Fund, Sharon Welch, (Editorial Director), Mary Datchelor House, 17 Grove Lane, London, SE5 8RD *T.* 01-703 5400.
£2.00 p.a. Q. Articles on child welfare in all its aspects throughout the world, 500 words. *Payment:* by arrangement. Photographs for cover and article illustration.

Writers' Monthly (1984), Raymond Lamont-Brown, M.A., The Writer Ltd., P.O. Box 34, St. Andrews, Fife, KY16 9RH. London Office: *T.* 01-888 1242.
£2.50 M. Articles and features of interest to the freelance writer. *Payment:* by arrangement. *Illustrations:* half-tone.

Writing (1959), Sean Dorman, Barbara Horsfall, 4 Union Place, Fowey, Cornwall, PL23 1BY.
65p. 2 p.a. Articles 250 to 350 words, on all subjects of interest to authors and journalists. Verse of 8 to 24 lines. *Payment:* £3 per article or poem.

Writing Women (1981), Eileen Aird, Linda Anderson, Cynthia Fuller, 10 Mistletoe Road, Newcastle upon Tyne NE2 2DX.
£1.50. 3 p.a. Poems, short stories, critical articles. *Payment:* £5.00 per poem or per 1000 words.

Y Faner (Banner and Times of Wales), (1843), County Press, Bala, Gwynedd, LL23 7PG *T.* (0678) 520262.
35p. W. National weekly news review in Welsh; articles of economic, literary and political interest. Non-party. *Length:* 1000 words. *Payment:* minimum £7 per article. *Illustrations:* line and photographs.

Yachting Monthly (1906), Andrew Bray, Room 2209, King's Reach Tower, Stamford Street, London, SE1 9LS *T.* 01-261 6040.
£1.30p. Technical articles, up to 2250 words, on all aspects of seamanship, navigation, the handling of sailing craft, and their design, construction and equipment. Well-written narrative accounts, up to 3000 words, of cruises in yachts. *Payment:* quoted on acceptance. *Illustrations:* black-and-white, colour transparencies, line or wash drawings.

Yachting World (1894), Dick Johnson, Business Press International Ltd., Quadrant House, The Quadrant, Sutton, Surrey, SM2 5AS *T.* 01-661 3864.
£1.35. M. Practical articles of an original nature, dealing with sailing and boats, 1500 to 2000 words. *Payment:* varies. *Illustrations:* black and white prints and colour transparencies, or drawings.

Yachts and Yachting (1947), Peter Cook, 196 Eastern Esplanade, Southend-on-Sea, Essex, SS1 3AB *T.* (0702) 582245.
95p. F. Short articles which should be technically correct. *Payment:* by arrangement. *Illustrations:* line and half-tone; occasional colour.

Yorkshire Evening Press (1882), 18p. **Sports Press,** 18p. Richard Wooldridge, (York and County Press), 15 Coney Street, York, YO1 1YN *T.* York 53051. London Office: Newspaper House, 8-16 Great New Street, EC4 *T.* 01-353 1030. Articles of Yorkshire or general interest, humour, personal experience of current affairs. *Length:* 500-1500 words. *Payment:* by arrangement. *Illustrations:* half-tone and line.

Yorkshire Gazette and Herald Series, N. Railton, 15 Coney Street, York, YO1 1YN *T.* (0904) 53051.
14p. W. Stories and pictures of local interest. *Payment:* varies. *Illustrations:* half-tone and line.

Yorkshire Life (1947), Maurice Colbeck, Lencett House, 45 Boroughgate, Otley, LS21 1AG *T.* Otley (0943) 464901. A publication of Opax Publishing Ltd.
65p. M. Topics of Yorkshire interest, with or without photographs. Humour and topical subjects treated from a Yorkshire angle especially required. *Length:* 200-500 words and 800 to 1500 words. *Payment:* varies. *Illustrations:* Colour, tone or line. Transparencies for cover.

Yorkshire Post (1754), John Edwards, Wellington Street, Leeds, LS1 1RF *T.* 432701. London Office: 23-27 Tudor Street, EC4. *T.* 01-583 9199.
23p. D. Conservative. Authoritative and well-written articles elucidating new topics or on topical subjects of general, literary or industrial interests are

preferred. *Length:* 800 words. *Payment:* by arrangement. Contributions to *People*, a column about personalities in the news, are welcomed. *Illustrations:* photographs and frequent pocket cartoons (single column width), topical wherever possible.

Yorkshire Riding Magazine (1964), Winston Halstead, Barclays Bank Chambers, Sowerby Bridge, Yorkshire HX6 2DX *T.* (0422) 839633 and 839643.
50p. Bi-M. Articles exclusively about people, life and character of the three Ridings of Yorkshire. *Length:* up to 1500 words. *Payment:* approx. £20.00 per published page. *Illustrations:* line and half-tone.

Young Soldier, The (1881), Major Connie Croly, The Salvation Army's children's newspaper; 101 Queen Victoria Street, London, EC4P 4EP *T.* 01-236 5222, Ext. 201.
12p. W. Stories, pictures, cartoon strips, puzzles etc., often on Christian themes. *Payment:* usual. *Illustrations:* half-tone, line and two-colour line.

Your Computer (1981), Gary Evans, 79-80 Petty France, London SW1H 9ED *T.* 01-222 9090.
£1.00. M. Articles and news about computers. *Payment:* £75 per printed page. *Illustrations:* line, half-tone, colour.

Your Model Railway (1971), Dave Lowery, Argus Specialist Publications Ltd., P.O. Box 35, Hemel Hempstead, Herts. *T.* (0442) 41221.
£1.10. M. Descriptive articles on model railways and prototype railways suitable for modelling. Articles covering all aspects of construction, planning, electrical wiring, experimental model railway engineering, and operation of model layouts. *Payment:* by arrangement. *Illustrations:* photographs, line.

UNITED KINGDOM MAGAZINE PUBLISHERS

The publishers included here are those who issue journals listed in the earlier pages of this *Yearbook*. For a fuller list of journal and magazine publishers, with the titles they publish, see *Willing's Press Guide*.

Academic Press Inc. (London) Ltd., 24-28 Oval Road, London, NW1 7DX *T.* 01-267 4466. *Telex:* 25775 Acpres G.

Argus Specialist Publications Ltd., P.O. Box 35, Hemel Hempstead, Herts. HP2 4SS *T.* (0442) 41221.

Allan (Ian), Ltd., Coombelands House, Addlestone, Weybridge, Surrey KT15 1HY *T.* (0932) 58511. *Telex:* 929806 Iallan G.

Architectural Press Ltd., The (1902), 9 Queen Anne's Gate, London, SW1H 9BY *T.* 01-222 4333. *T.A.* Buildable, London, SW1. *Telex:* 8953505 Archip G.

Baillière Tindall (1826), (a division of **Holt Saunders Ltd.**), 1 St. Anne's Road, Eastbourne, East Sussex BN21 3UN *T.* (0323) 638221. *T.A.* Volumists, Eastbourne. *Telex:* 877503 Volmst.

Benn Publications Ltd. (1977), Sovereign Way, Tonbridge, Kent, TN9 1RW *T.* (0732) 364422. *Telex:* 95132 Benton G. *Directors:* Brian Downing (Chairman), James Lear (Managing), Ian Baker, Iain Laughland, Christopher Leonard-Morgan, Malcolm Lowe, John Brazier.

Blackwell (Basil) Ltd. (1922), 108 Cowley Road, Oxford, OX4 1JF *T.* (0865) 722146. *Telex:* 837022 Oxbook G. *Directors:* Nigel Blackwell (Chairman), David Martin (Managing), Sir John Brown, Julian Blackwell, Ray Addicott, Terry Collins, John Davey, Norman Drake, Michael Hay, Michael Holmes, Christopher Kerr (USA), James Nash, René Olivieri (USA), Per Saugman.

Blackwell Scientific Publications, Ltd. (1939), Osney Mead, Oxford, OX2 0EL, 8 John Street, London, WC1N 2ES, 23 Ainslie Place, Edinburgh, EH3 6AJ, 107 Barry Street, Carlton, Victoria, Australia 3053, 52 Beacon Street, Boston, Massachusetts 02108, USA, 667 Lytton Avenue, Palo Alto, California 94301, USA. *T.* Oxford: (0865) 240201, London: 01-404 4101, Edinburgh: 031-226 7232. *Telex:* 83355 Medbok G. *Cables:* Research, Oxford. *Directors:* Per Saugman, Keith Bowker, Nigel Palmer, Peter Pleasance, John Robson, Robert Campbell, Nigel Blackwell, Peter Saugman, Oluf Møller.

Business Press International Ltd., Quadrant House, The Quadrant, Sutton, Surrey SM2 5AS *T.* 01-661 3500.

Cambridge University Press (1534), The Edinburgh Building, Shaftesbury Road, Cambridge, CB2 2RU *T.* (0223) 312393. *T.A.* Unipress, Cambridge. *Telex:* 817256 Cupcam. *Publishing Director* (Journals): Dennis B. Forbes M.A.

Cass (Frank) & Co., Ltd. (1958), 11 Gainsborough Road, London, E11 1RS *T.* 01-530 4226. *T.A.* Simfay, London. *Telex:* 897719 Cass G. *Directors:* Frank Cass (Managing), A. E. Cass, M. P. Zaidner.

Condé Nast Publications, Ltd. The (1916), Vogue House, Hanover Square, London, W1R 0AD *T.* 01-499 9080. *T.A.* Volon, London. *Telex:* 27338 Volon G. *Directors:* Daniel Salem (Chairman), Bernard H. Leser (Managing), R. S. Hill, W. G. Stanford, P. F. Osborne (Secretary), B. M. O'Connell, M. J. M. Garvin, D. J. Montgomery, M. Boxer, C. Bourne.

EMAP Pursuit Publishing Ltd., Bretton Court, Bretton, Peterborough, PE3 8DZ *T.* Peterborough (0733) 264666.

Harmsworth Press, Ltd., The, Carmelite House, Carmelite Street, London, EC4Y 0JA *T.* 01-353 6000.

IPC Magazines Ltd., King's Reach Tower, Stamford Street, London, SE1 9LS *T.* 01-261 5000.

Link House Magazines Ltd., Dingwall Avenue, Croydon, CR9 2TA *T.* 01-686 2599. *Telex:* 947709 Linkho G. *Directors:* C. D. Jakes (Chairman), P. J. Cosgrove (Managing), D. G. Shuard, A. P. Swinburne, C. K. Gamm, A. F. Shanks.

Longman Group UK Ltd, Professional and Business Communications Division, 21-27 Lamb's Conduit Street, London WC1N 3NJ *T.* 01-242 2548.

Macmillan Journals Ltd., 4 Little Essex Street, London, WC2R 3LF *T.* 01-836 6633. *Telex:* 262024 Macmil G. *Chairman:* N. G. Byam Shaw; *Directors:* R. Barker (Managing), Miss E. Hughes, J. Barnes, M. Barnard, G. R. Todd.

Marketing Publications Ltd, 22 Lancaster Gate, London, W2 3LY *T.* 01-402 4200.

Mirror Group Newspapers Ltd., Holborn Circus, London, EC1P 1DQ *T.* 01-353 0246.

Morgan-Grampian plc, 30 Calderwood Street, London, SE18 6QH *T.* 01-855 7777.

National Magazine Co., Ltd., The, National Magazine House, 72 Broadwick Street, London, W1V 2BP *T.* 01-439 7144.

Numismatic Publishing Company, Sovereign House, Brentwood, Essex, CM14 4SE *T.* (0277) 219876.

Opax Publishing Ltd (OPL Magazines Division), Opax House, Primrose Hill, London Road, Preston, Lancashire PR1 4BX *T.* (0772) 50022.

Pergamon Press Ltd., (1948), Headington Hill Hall, Oxford, OX3 0BW *T.* Oxford (0865) 64881. *T.A.* Pergapress, Oxford. *Telex:* 83177.

Polystyle Publications Limited, 159-161 Camden High Street, London NW1 7JY *T.* 01-482 3202. Children's books and periodicals.

Royal National Institute for the Blind, The (1868), Braille House, 338-346 Goswell Road, London, EC1V 7JE *T.* 01-837 9921. *T.A.* Pharnib, London. *Director of Publications:* Donald Bell.

Sawell Publications, Ltd., 127 Stanstead Road, London, SE23 *T.* 01-699 6792.

Scholastic Publications (Magazines) Ltd., Marlborough House, Holly Walk, Leamington Spa, Warwickshire CV32 4LS *T.* (0926 81) 3910. *Telex:* 312138 Spls G.

Scout Association, The, Baden-Powell House, Queen's Gate, London SW7 5JS *T.* 01-584 7030. *T.A.* Scouting. *General Editor:* David Easton.

Scripture Union (1867), Scripture Union House, 130 City Road, London, EC1V 2NJ *T.* 01-250 1966. Christian Publishers and Booksellers.

Taylor & Francis, Ltd., 4 John Street, London, WC1N 2ET *T.* 01-405 2237-9.

Thomson-Leng Publications, Dundee, DD1 9QJ *T.* 23131. *T.A.* Courier, Dundee. *Telex:* 76380. London: 185 Fleet Street, London, EC4A 2HS *T.* 01-242 5086. *T.A.* Courier, London, EC4.

Times Newspapers Ltd., Virginia Street, London E1 9BH *T.* 01-481 4100. *Telex:* 925088.

United Society for the Propagation of the Gospel, 15 Tufton Street, London, SW1P 3QQ *T.* 01-222 4222.

United Trade Press Ltd., UTP House, 33-35 Bowling Green Lane, London, EC1R 0DA *T.* 01-837 1212. *Telex:* 299049 Utpres G.

Whitaker (J.) & Sons, Ltd., 12 Dyott Street, London, WC1A 1DF *T.* 01-836 8911. *Telex:* 987117 Sbdata. *Directors:* R. F. Baum, J. W. Coates, F.L.A., A. C. E. Musk, C.V.O., David Whitaker, Sally Whitaker.

Whitehall Press Ltd., Earl House, Maidstone, Kent, ME14 1PE *T.* Maidstone (0622) 59841. *Telex:* 965204 Whpres G.

Wright (John) (1825), Techno House, Redcliffe Way, Bristol BS1 6NX *T.* (0272) 290691. *Managing Director:* A. Pearce, *Editorial Director:* D. J. Kingham.

AFRICA

KENYA

Daily Nation, Group Managing Editor: George Mbugguss; Managing Editor: J. Kadhi, P.O. Box 49010, Nairobi. *T.* 337691.
K Sh 2.50. D. News, features, etc. Pictures.

East African Agricultural & Forestry Journal (1935), J.O. Mugah, P.O. Box 57811, Nairobi. *T.* Karuri 32880.
£18.00 p.a. Q. Papers on agriculture, forestry and applied sciences. *Length:* 100 to 125 pages.

East African Medical Journal (1923), M. L. Oduori, M.B., ChB., D.C.H., M.R.C.P., P.O. Box 41632, Nairobi. *T.* 724711, 724617.
£45.00 p.a. M. Medical articles, preferably on tropical medicine, case reports, etc. *Illustrations:* Photographs.

Standard, The, P.O. Box 30080, Nairobi. *T.* 540280. *Telex:* 22204.
K.Sh. 2.50 daily; K.Sh. 3.00 Sunday. D. News and topical articles of East African interest.

Swara (1978), the Magazine of the East African Wild Life Society, Shereen Karmali, P.O. Box 20110, Nairobi, Kenya. *T.* 27047.
£15.00 p.a. 6 p.a. Articles on wild life and natural beauty of East Africa. *Payment:* by arrangement. *Illustrations:* Photographs, colour and black and white; line drawings occasionally.

NIGERIA

Monthly Life (1984) West African Book Publishers Ltd., Ilupeju Industrial Estate, P.O. Box 3445, Lagos, Nigeria. *T.* 900760-4 *Telex:* 26144 Presac NG. UK: Magazine Production Ltd., 13 Southgate Street, Winchester, Hampshire, SO23 9DZ. *T.* (0962) 60444 *T.A.* Hambleside, Winchester. *Telex:* 477357.
N1.50 M. Features, human interest stories, short stories with a West African setting. *Illustrations:* line drawings, cartoons, colour and black & white photographs—West African subjects. *Payment:* by arrangement.

SUDAN

Sudanow, Fath el Rahman Mahjoub, Ministry of Culture and Information, P.O. Box 2651, Khartoum. *T.* 77913.
£S1.50 M. News stories, business stories, book reviews, travelogues—all about the Sudan. *Payment:* £S20 per column. *Illustrations:* line, half-tone.

TANZANIA

Daily News, The, Ulli Mwambulukutu, P.O. Box 9033, Dar es Salaam. *T.* 25318.
2½p. D.

Sunday News, Box 9033, Dar es Salaam. *T.* 29881.
4p. W.

UGANDA

Eastern Africa Journal of Rural Development, Department of Agricultural Economics, Makerere University, P.O. Box 7062, Kampala.

Uganda Times, P.O. Box 20081, Kampala. *T.* 34403.
40 cents. D. News, topical features, news pictures.

ZIMBABWE

Chronicle, The (1894), Geoff Nyarota, P.O. Box 585, Bulawayo. *T.* 65471.
15c. D. (not Sunday). Topical articles.

Farmer, The, Modern Farming Publications (1928), Myfanwy van Hoffen, Agriculture House, Moffat Street, P.O. Box 1622, Harare. *T.* 708245-6. $31 p.a. Fortnightly Illustrated. Official journal of the Commercial Farmers Union. Articles on all aspects of agriculture. *Payment:* by arrangement.

Herald, The (1891), T. A. G. Sithole, P.O. Box 396, Harare. *T.* 795771 *T.A.* Manherald, Harare.
12c. D. Topical articles of news value. *Payment:* varies, depends on length, content and news value. *Illustrations:* bromides, colour.

Hotel & Catering Gazette, P.O. Box 66070, Kopje, Harare. *T.* 705911.
Free. Controlled circ. M. Articles dealing with hotel and catering management. *Payment:* $20.00 per 1000 words.

Mahogany, Gill Beach, P.O. Box UA589, Harare. *T.* Harare 705411. *Telex:* 4748 ZW.

70c. F. Articles concerning events and personalities; standard women's magazine formula. Average *length:* 1500 words. *Payment:* by arrangement. *Illustrations:* line, half-tone, colour.

Manica Post, The L. M. Hatugari, P.O. Box 960, Mutare. *T.* 61212.
12c. W. Non-fiction articles only. *Length:* up to 500 words. *Payment:* by arrangement. *Illustrations:* half-tone.

Prize Africa (1973), Tinos Calfinos Guvi, P.O. Box UA189, Harare. *T.* 705411. *Telex:* 4748ZW.
41c. M. Political reports, features and biographies, love, crime, thriller short stories. *Payment:* Short story (approx. 2000 words) $30, two-part serial (maximum) $50. *Illustrations:* line, half-tone, colour.

Sunday Mail, The (1935), H. E. Muradzikwa, P.O. Box 396, Harare. *T.* 795771. *T.A.* Manherald, Harare.
15c. W. Topical articles of news value. *Payment:* varies, depends on length, content and news value. *Illustrations:* bromides, colour.

Sunday News, The (1930), Alex B. Mahlangu, P.O. Box 585, Bulawayo. *T.* 65471.
14c. W. Topical articles.

AUSTRALIA

Newspapers are listed under the towns in which they are published.

(Adelaide) Advertiser (1858), Ian Meikle, 121 King William Street, Adelaide 5000. London: 1 Maltravers Street, WC2R 3DZ *T.* 01-836 5161. *Telex:* 21989.
25c., Sat. 30c. D. The only morning daily in S. Australia. Descriptive and news background material, 400-800 words, preferably with pictures.

(Adelaide) News, The (South Australia) (1923), R. G. Holden, 112 North Terrace, Adelaide. *T.* 51-0351.
25c. D. One feature page open for topical articles. *Length:* preferably 600-750. *Payment:* by arrangement. *Illustrated* articles preferred.

(Adelaide) Sunday Mail (1912), R. Jory, 116 North Terrace, Adelaide, 5000. *T.* 51-0351.
60c. W. Limited scope for free-lance writers.

Australasian Dirt Bike, G. Eldridge, P.O. Box 696, Brookvale, Sydney, N.S.W. 2100 *T.* 02-938 4155.
$2.95. M. Tests and reports of off-road bikes and equipment, news and features of interest to off-road enthusiasts. *Payment:* by arrangement.

Australasian Sporting Shooter, Mark Maccallum, Yaffa Publising Group, 432-6 Elizabeth Street, Surry Hills, N.S.W. 2010. *T.* 02-699 7861. *Telex:* AA 121887.
$2.50. All aspects of game shooting, collecting, antiques, archery (associated with hunting), pistol shooting, clay target shooting, reloading, ballistics and articles of a technical nature. *Payment:* by arrangement.

Australian, The, Les Hollings, G.P.O. Box 4245, Sydney, N.S.W. 2000. *T.* 288 3000.
30c. Will consider topical articles from free-lance writers. *Length:* up to 1500 words. *Payment:* by arrangement.

Australian Angler's Fishing World, Ron Calcutt, Page Publications Pty. Ltd., 432-6 Elizabeth Street, Surry Hills, N.S.W. 2010. *T.* 699 7861. *Telex:* AA 21887.
$2.00. M. All aspects of rock, surf, stream, deep sea and game fishing, with comprehensive sections on gear, equipment and boats. *Payment:* by arrangement.

Australian Financial Review, The, Editor-in-chief: P. P. McGuinness, Editor: A. N. Maiden, Sydney. London: 12 Norwich Street, London, EC4A 1BH *T.* 01-353-9321. New York: Suite 802, 1500 Broadway, N.Y. 10036. *T.* 212-398 9494.
60c. D. (except Saturday & Sunday). Investment business and economic news and reviews; government and politics, production, banking, commercial, and Stock Exchange statistics; company analysis. General features in Friday *Weekend Review* supplement.

Australian Flying, Peter Ricketts, Page Publications Pty. Ltd., 432-6 Elizabeth Street, Surry Hills, N.S.W. 2010. *T.* 699 7861. *Telex:* AA 21887.
$2.20. 6 times p.a. Appeals to light and medium aircraft owners, as well as those directly and indirectly associated with the aircraft industry. *Payment:* by arrangement.

Australian Home Beautiful, The (1913), A. J. Hitchin, 61 Flinders Lane, Melbourne. London: 1 Maltravers Street, WC2R 3DZ.
$2.00. M. Deals with home building, interior decoration, furnishing, gardening, cookery, etc. Short articles with accompanying photographs with Australian slant accepted. *Preliminary* letter advisable. *Payment:* higher than Australian average.

Australian House and Garden (1948), Beryl Clarke Marchi, 168 Castlereagh Street, Sydney, New South Wales 2000. *T.A.* Conpres.
$2.50. M. Factual articles dealing with interior decorating, home design, homemaker themes and activities. *Payment:* by arrangement. *Illustrations:* line, half-tone, colour. Preliminary letter essential.

Australian Journal of Politics and History, The, J. A. Moses, Department of History, University of Queensland Press, St. Lucia, Queensland 4067. *T.* 377 2265.
$36.00; US $40.00, UK £24.00 p.a. inc. postage. 3 a year. Australian, Commonwealth, Asian, S.W. Pacific, and international articles. Special feature: regular surveys of Australian Foreign Policy and State and Commonwealth politics. *Length:* 8000 words max. No *payment*. Necessary line *illustrations* only.

Australian Mining, Peter Barrett, Thomson Publications Australia, 47 Chippen Street, Chippendale, N.S.W. 2008. *T.* 699-2411. *Postal Address:* P.O. Box 65, Chippendale, N.S.W. 2008.
$30.00 p.a. in Australia; $50 p.a. overseas.

Australian Outdoors Specials, Federal Publishing Co., 140 Joynton Avenue, Waterloo, 2017. N.S.W. *T.* Sydney 02-663 9999. *T.A.* Fedpub A74488.
$2.50. Articles of 1000-3000 words on adventure sports, bushwalking, bushcraft, hunting and shooting, outdoor personalities, travel. *Payment:* By arrangement. *Illustrations:* colour, half-tone and line.

Australian Outlook, Dr. Richard Higgott, School of Social Inquiry, Murdoch University, Murdoch, Western Australia 6150 *T.* (09) 332 2518.
$15.00 p.a. in Australia and New Zealand; $18.00 p.a. in other countries. 3 times p.a. Scholarly articles on international affairs. *Length:* 4000 to 7000 words. No *payment*.

Australian Quarterly, The (1929), Elaine Thompson and Hugh Pritchard, Australian Institute of Political Science, 2nd Floor, 149 Castlereagh Street, Sydney, N.S.W. 2000. *T.* 264 8923.
$16.00 p.a.; $24.00 overseas. Q. Articles of high standard on politics, law, economics, social issues, etc. *Length:* 3500 words preferred. No *payment*.

Australian Women's Weekly, The (Australian Consolidated Press, Ltd.), 54 Park Street, Sydney, N.S.W. 2000.

$1.80 M. Short stories and features. *Length:* short stories, 1000 to 3000 words. Features 1000 to 2500 words plus colour or black-and-white photographs. *Payment:* according to length and merit. *Fiction illustrations:* sketches by own artists and freelances.

(Brisbane) Courier Mail, D. Smith, (Queensland Newspapers Pty. Ltd.), Campbell Street, Bowen Hills, Brisbane 4006.
30c. D. Occasional topical special articles required, 1000 words.

(Brisbane) Sunday Mail, N. F. Wiseman, G.P.O. Box No. 130, Brisbane, Queensland, 4001. London: 1 Maltravers Street, WC2R 3DZ.
50c. W. Anything of general interest. Up to 1500 words. *Illustrations:* line, photographs, black and white, and colour. *Payment:* by arrangement. Rejected MSS. returned if postage enclosed.

(Brisbane) Telegraph (1872), D. W. Flaherty, Campbell Street, Bowen Hills, Brisbane 4006.
25c. D.

Catholic Weekly, R. F. Robinson (Catholic Press Newspaper Co., Ltd.), Freeman House, 397 Riley Street, Surry Hills 2010, N.S.W. *T.* 2114499.
60c. W. Christian newspaper and review magazine of general interest. *Length:* up to 1000 words. *Payment:* standard rates. *Illustrations:* half-tone.

Cleo (1972), Lisa Wilkinson, 54 Park Street, Sydney 2000, N.S.W. *T.* 268-0666. *T.A.* Packpress, Sydney.
$2.40. M. Short stories, articles up to 3000 words, longer fiction up to 10,000 words, short quizzes. *Payment:* Articles $120 per 1000 words; fiction by arrangement. *Illustrations:* colour, half-tone, cartoons.

Countryman, The, George A. Boylen, Newspaper House, St. George's Terrace, Perth 6000. *T.* 321-0161. *T.A.* Westralian Perth. London: Maltravers Street, London, WC2R 3DZ..
40c. W. Agriculture, farming or country interest features and service columns. *Payment:* standard rates. *Illustrations:* line and half-tone.

Current Affairs Bulletin (1942), Dr. J. Angel, Centre for Continuing Education, University of Sydney, Sydney 2006, N.S.W. *T.* Sydney 692-2583. *T.A.* Univsyd.
$1.80. $24.00 p.a. ($37.00 overseas). M. Authoritative well-documented articles on all national and international affairs: politics, science, ecology, economics, literature, business and social questions. *Length:* 2000-5000 words. *Payment:* by arrangement. *Illustrations:* line, half-tone.

Daily Sun, R. M. Richards (Daily Sun-Sunday Sun Newspapers Pty. Ltd.), 367 Brunswick Street, Fortitude Valley, Brisbane 4006. *T.* 07-253 3333. London Office: 8 Bouverie Street, Fleet Street, London EC4Y 8HJ.
25c. D.

Dolly (1970), Deborah Bibby, 57 Regent Street, Chippendale, New South Wales 2008. *T.* 699-3622.
$2.00. M. Features on fashion, make-up, personalities, and how to cope with growing up, etc. Fiction, including serials, mainly romantic boy-girl stories. *Length:* not less than 1750 words. *Payment:* by arrangement.

Electronics Australia (incorporating **Radio, Television and Hobbies**) (1939), L. Simpson, Box 227, Waterloo, N.S.W. 2017. London: 12 Norwich Street, London EC4A 1BH. *T.* 01-353 9321.
$2.95 M. Articles on technical television and radio, hi-fi, popular electronics, microcomputers and avionics. *Length:* up to 3000 words. *Payment:* by arrangement. *Illustrations:* line, half-tone.

Geo, Australasia's Geographical Magazine (1979), Alfredo Roces, 176 South Creek Road, Dee Why West, New South Wales 2099. *T.* 981-0462.
$4.50. Q. Non-fiction articles on wild life and natural history. *Length:* 1500 to 4000 words. *Payment:* $500 to $1,200 by arrangement. *Illustrations:* photographs, colour transparencies.

Historical Studies (formerly **Historical Studies-Australia and New Zealand**), Stuart Macintyre, Melbourne University, Parkville, Victoria 3052.
$30.00 p.a., $35.00 p.a. overseas. Twice yearly. *Length:* 8000 words maximum. No *payment.* Tables and maps.

Labor News, Harry Hurrell, F.I.A., 51-65 Bathurst Street, Sydney, 2000, New South Wales. *T.* 264 2877.
Bi-M. Official Journal Federated Ironworkers' Association of Australia.

(Launceston) Examiner, Michael Courtney, Box 99A, P.O. Launceston, Tasmania, 7250. *T.* 315111. *T.A.* Examiner, Launceston, Tasmania. *Telex:* 58511.
25c. D.

(Launceston) Sunday Examiner, The, Box 99A, P.O. Launceston, Tasmania, 7250. *T.* 315111.
20c. W.

(Melbourne) Age, C. Burns (David Syme & Co., Ltd.), 250 Spencer Street, Melbourne, Victoria 3000. *T.* 600421. London: 20-22 Bedford Row, London, WC1R 4EB.
40c., (Sat. 50c.) D. Independent liberal morning daily. Room occasionally for outside matter. An illustrated weekend magazine and literary review is published on Saturday. Accepts occasional freelance material.

(Melbourne) Australasian Post, The Herald and Weekly Times Ltd., 44-74 Flinders Street, Melbourne 3000. London: 1 Maltravers Street, London, WC2R 3DZ *T.* 01-836 4743.
80c. W. Opening for casual contributions of topical factual illustrated articles. All contributions must have Australian interest. Male appeal. *Payment:* average $100 per 500 words plus $30 (minimum) per picture.

(Melbourne) Herald, Pat Hinton, 44-74 Flinders Street, Melbourne. *T.* 63-0211. London: 1 Maltravers Street, London, WC2R 3DZ.
40c. D. Evening broadsheet with greatest evening circulation in Australia. Articles with or without illustrations. *Length:* up to 750 words. *Payment:* on merit. *Illustrations:* half-tone and line.

(Melbourne) Sun News Pictorial (1922), R. Cronin, 44-74 Flinders Street, Melbourne, 3000.
40c. D. Freelance articles with or without illustrations. *Payment:* on merit.

Modern Boating (1965), 140 Joynton Avenue, Waterloo, N.S.W. 2017. *T.* (02) 663 9999. *Telex:* AA 74488.
$3.25. M. Articles on all types of boats and boating. *Payment:* $80-$150 per 1000 words. *Illustrations:* half-tone and colour.

National Times, The, Jefferson Penberthy, Sydney. London: 12 Norwich Street, London EC4A 1BH. *T.* 01-353 9321. New York: 1501 Broadway, New York 10036. *T.* 536-6835.
80c. W. Foreign affairs, government and politics, production, banking, commercial, entertainment, the arts, sport, good living, books, education, science.

New Idea, The (1902), Mrs. D. Boling, 32 Walsh Street, Melbourne, 3001. *T.* 328 0241.
60c. W. General interest woman's magazine; news stories, features, fashion, services, short stories of general interest to women of all ages. *Length:* stories, 1500 to 4000 words: articles, 1200 to 2000 words. *Payment:* on acceptance. Minimum $70.00 per 1000 words.

New Poetry, Robert Adamson, James Taylor, Debra Adamson, Box N110, Grosvenor Street P.O., Sydney 2000, N.S.W.
$16.00 p.a. Q. Poetry, articles and reviews. *Payment:* minimum poems $10.00, reviews $15.00, leading articles $50.00.

Newcastle Herald, The (1858), J. A. Allan, P.O. Box 510G, 28-30 Bolton Street, Newcastle, 2300, N.S.W. *T.* 049-263-222.
40c. D (Monday to Saturday). Travel articles up to 800 words. *Payment:* up to $50 per 1000 words.

Overland, S. Murray-Smith, P.O. Box 249, Mt. Eliza, Victoria 3930. *T.* 03-787 1545.
$4.00. Q. Literary and general. Australian material preferred. *Payment:* by arrangement. *Illustrations:* line and half-tone.

People Magazine (National weekly news-pictorial), D. Naylor, 57 Regent Street, Sydney, N.S.W. *T.* 699-3622. London: 12 Norwich Street, London EC4A 1BH.
90c. W. Mainly people stories, but good documentary subjects needed. Photographs depicting exciting happenings, candid camera pictures of events affecting Australians, glamour and show business, modern-living features, and complete series of any subject such as unusual occupations, rites, customs. *Payment:* highest Australian scale.

(Perth) Daily News (1840), I. L. Hummerston, Newspaper House, St. George's Terrace, Perth, 6000. *T.* 321-0161. London: 1 Maltravers Street, London WC2R 3DZ.
25c. D. (Evening). Accepts special articles on subjects of outstanding interest. *Payment:* according to merit. *Illustrations:* half-tone, line.

(Perth) Sunday Times (1897), 34 Stirling Street, Perth, 6000, Western Australia. *T.* 326-8326.
50c. W. Topical articles to 800 words. *Payment:* on acceptance.

(Perth) West Australian, The (1833), D. B. Smith, Newspaper House, 125 St. George's Terrace, Perth, 6000. *T.* 321-0161. *T.A.* Westralian, Perth. London: 1 Maltravers Street, London WC2R 3DZ *T.* 01-836 5161.
25c. D. Articles and sketches about people and events in Australia and abroad. *Length:* 300-700 words. *Payment:* Award rates or better. *Illustrations:* line or half-tone.

Poetry Australia (1964), Grace Perry, South Head Press, Market Place, Berrima, 2577 N.S.W. *T.* 048-771421.
$27 p.a. Q. Previous unpublished new poetry, and criticism. *Payment:* $5 to $40 per poem depending on length.

Quadrant, Peter Coleman, 404 Kent Street, Sydney 2000. *Postal Address:* Box C344, Clarence Street P.O., Sydney, 2000, New South Wales. *T.* 264-8152.
$3.50. M. Articles, short stories, verse, etc. *Prose length:* 2000-5000 words. *Payment:* minimum $10 per 1000 words, verse $15 minimum.

Racing Car (1961), Stewart Wilson, P.O. Box 518, Neutral Bay, NSW 2089. *T.* 02-908-4422. *T.A.* Racing Car News.
$3.95. Q. Stories on racing cars and personalities. *Length:* up to 3000 words. *Payment:* from $120 per 1000 words. *Illustrations:* full colour.

Reader's Digest (Australian and New Zealand editions), Denis Wallis, 26-32 Waterloo Street, Surry Hills, N.S.W., 2010. *T.* 699-0111 *T.A.* Readigest, Sydney.
$1.90. M. Articles on Australia and New Zealand subjects of all kinds. *Length:* 2500 to 3000 words. *Payment:* $500-$2500 per article. Brief filler paragraphs, $25 to $100. *Illustrations:* half-tone, colour.

Sports Car World (1956), Bob Murray, (Australian Consolidated Press), 168 Castlereagh Street, Sydney, 2000, N.S.W. *T.* (02) 268 0666.
$3.50. Bi-M. Articles up to 2500 words on subjects allied to the high performance car, classic car, motor sport, etc. *Payment:* by arrangement. *Illustrations:* colour, and black and white photography and artwork.

Sunday Sun, R. M. Richards (Daily Sun-Sunday Sun Newspapers Pty. Ltd.), 367 Brunswick Street, Fortitude Valley, Brisbane, 4006. *T.* 07-253 3333. London Office: 8 Bouverie Street, Fleet Street, London, EC4Y 8HJ.
40c. W.

Sun-Herald, The (Sunday edition of **The Sydney Morning Herald** and the **Sun**), Peter Smark, P.O. Box 506, Sydney, 2001. London: 12 Norwich Street, London EC4A 1BH. *T.* 01-353 9321.
60c. W. Topical articles to 1000 words; sections on politics, social issues, show business, finance and fashion. *Payment:* as for *The Sydney Morning Herald*.

(Sydney) Bulletin (1880), Trevor Kennedy, 54 Park Street, Sydney, N.S.W. *T.* 268-0666. London: Australian Consolidated Press, 112 Westbourne Park Road, W2 *T.* 01-229 3916. New York: Australian Consolidated Press, Anne Rosengren, Suite 2003, 90 Park Avenue, New York, N.Y. 10016. *T.* 212-685 9570.
$1.70. W. Concerned mainly with reporting Australia to Australians, or the world from an Australian aspect. *Payment:* by arrangement.

(Sydney) Daily Mirror (1941), 2 Holt Street, Sydney, 2010, N.S.W. *T.* 02-288 3000.
30c. D. Accept modernly written feature articles and series of Australian or world interest. *Length:* 1000 to 2000 words. *Payment:* according to merit and length.

(Sydney) Daily Telegraph (News Limited), L. Hoffman, 2 Holt Street, Surry Hills, 2010, N.S.W. *T.* 02-288 3000.
30c. D.

Sydney Morning Herald, The (1831), C. J. Anderson, P.O. Box 506, Sydney 2001. London: 12 Norwich Street, London, EC4A 1BH *T.* 01-353 9321.
40c. D. Saturday edition has pages of literary criticism and also magazine articles. Topical articles 600 to 4000 words. *Payment:* varies, but minimum $80.00 per 1000 words. All types of *illustrations*.

(Sydney) Sun (1910), G. R. Ford, Jones Street, Broadway, Sydney. *T.* 282 2822. London: 12 Norwich Street, London EC4A 1BH. *T.* 01-353 9321.
30c. D. Topical articles, 900 to 1500 words, particularly on international subjects. *Payment:* from $40 according to length and quality. *Illustrations:* line or half-tone; colour.

Weekend News, J. R. Davies, Newspaper House, 125 St. George's Terrace, Perth 6000, Western Australia. *T.* 321-0161. *T.A.* Westralian, Perth.
25c. W. Articles, radio and television stories, non-fiction serials. Highly technical articles not required. *Payment:* standard rates. *Illustrations:* line, half-tone. London: 1 Maltravers Street, WC2R 3DZ.

What's On Video (1983), Peter Barrett, P.O. Box 12, Rockdale, N.S.W. 2216. *T.* 587 7165.
$26 p.a. M. Star interviews, linked with video movies. *Length:* upto 1000 words. *Payment:* AJA freelance rates. *Illustrations:* half-tone.

Woman's Day, Henry Plociennik, 55-59 Regent Street, Chippendale, 2008 *T.* 699-3622.
$1.10. W. National women's magazine; news, show business, fiction, fashion, general articles, cookery, home economy.

CANADA

Newspapers are listed under the towns in which they are published.

Atlantic Advocate, The, H. P. Wood, P.O. Box 3370, Fredericton, New Brunswick, E3B 5A2 *T.* 452 6671.
$1.95. M. Non-fiction and short stories, focus must be on Atlantic Provinces. *Length:* up to 1500 words. *Payment:* up to 8 cents per word. *Illustrations:* line and half-tone.

Beaver, Christopher Dafoe, (Hudson's Bay Co.), Hudson Bay House, Winnipeg, Manitoba R3C 2R1.
$18.00 p.a., foreign $24.00 p.a. Bi-M. Articles, historical and modern in the sphere of Hudson's Bay Company's activities and Canadian history. *Length:* 1500 to 3000 words, with illustrations. *Payment:* on acceptance, about 10 cents a word. *Illustrations:* photographs or drawings. Black and white and colour.

Broadcaster (1942), Colin Wright, 7 Labatt Avenue, Toronto, M5A 3P2 *T.* 416-363-6111.
$3.00 ($20.00 p.a.). M. Articles pertaining to broadcasting. *Length:* 500 to 1500 words. *Payment:* minimum $100.

Canadian Author and Bookman, 24 Ryerson Avenue, Toronto, Ontario, M5T 2P3.
$12.50 p.a. $17.00 p.a. overseas. Q. Published by Canadian Authors Association. Interested in an international view on writing techniques, profiles, interviews, freelance opportunities for Canadian writers. *Query only. Payment:* 1 cent per word.

Canadian Aviation (1928), Hugh Whittington (Maclean-Hunter, Ltd.), 777 Bay Street, Toronto, Ontario, M5W 1A7 *T.* 416-596-5789. London: Maclean-Hunter Ltd., 76 Oxford Street, W1N 9FD.
$35 (Gt. Britain) p.a. M. Stories with a Canadian angle, on civil or military aviation. *Payment:* $250 to $700. *Photographs:* from $25.

Canadian Forum, The, John Hutcheson, 70 The Esplanade, Toronto, Ontario, M5E 1R2 *T.* 416-364-2431.
$2.00, $18.00. p.a. 10 issues p.a. Articles on public affairs and the arts. *Length:* up to 2500 words. *Payment:* $100 per article. *Illustrations:* line and photographs.

Canadian Interiors, Dean Shalden, The Maclean Hunter Building, 777 Bay Street, Toronto, M5W 1A7 *T.* 416-596-5976. *T.A.* Macpub.
$28.00 p.a. 8 issues p.a. Articles on all aspects of interior design; also technical and business articles. *Payment:* $100-$400 per article. *Illustrations:* half-tone and colour.

Canadian Literature (1959), W. H. New, 2029 West Mall, University of British Columbia, Vancouver, B.C., V6T 1W5 *T.* 604-228-2780.

$7.50. Q. Articles on Canadian writers and writing in English and French. *Length:* up to 5000 words. *Payment:* $5.00 per printed page.

Chatelaine, 777 Bay Street, Toronto, M5W 1A7 *T.* 416-596-5425.
$1.75. M. Articles with woman's slant used; Canadian angle preferred; interested in first short stories with serials, romance, marriage, adventure, children. *Payment:* on acceptance; from $1000. *Illustrations:* by leading artists in Canada and the U.S.

Dalhousie Review, The, Dr. Alan Kennedy, Dalhousie University Press Ltd., Sir James Dunn Building, Suite 314, Halifax, N.S., B3H 3J5 *T.* 902-424-2541.
$3.00 (plus $2.33 postage). Q. ($10.00 p.a. or $24.00 for 3 years). Articles on literary, political, historical, educational and social topics; fiction; verse. *Length:* prose, normally not more than 5000 words; verse, up to 300 words. *Payment:* $1 per printed page; from $3 per poem. Contributors receive one copy of issue and 25 offprints of their work. Usually not more than one story and about 10 or 12 poems in any one issue.

Fiddlehead, The (1945), Michael Taylor, Room 317, Old Arts Building, University of New Brunswick, P.O. Box 4400, Fredericton, N.B., E3B 5A3 *T.* 506-454-3591.
$4.25. Q. Reviews, poetry, short stories. *Payment:* $12.00 per printed page (approx.). *Illustrations:* line and photographs.

Hamilton Spectator, The (1846), Publisher, Gordon Bullock, 44 Frid Street, Hamilton, L8N 3G3 *T.* 416-526-3333.
30 cents. Monday to Friday; 75 cents Saturday. Articles of general interest, political analysis and background; interviews, stories of Canadians abroad. *Length:* 800 maximum. *Payment:* rate varies.

Journal of Canadian Studies, Michael Peterman, Trent University, Peterborough, Ontario, K9J 7B8.
$16.00 p.a. (Institutions: $30.00 p.a.). Q. Major academic review of Canadian studies. Articles of general as well as scholarly interest on history, politics, literature, society, arts. *Length:* 2000-10,000 words.

Maclean's Magazine, Kevin Doyle, Maclean Hunter Building, 777 Bay Street, 7th Floor, Toronto, M5W 1A7. London: 76 Oxford Street, W1N 9FD.
$1.25. W. News magazine articles of interest to Canadian readers, 500 to 3000 words. *Payment:* by arrangement. *Illustrations:* on assignment.

Malahat Review, The (1967), Constance Rooke, University of Victoria, P.O. Box 1700, Victoria, British Columbia, V8W 2Y2 *T.* 604-721 8524.
$15.00 p.a.; Overseas $20.00 p.a. Q. Short stories, poetry, short plays, reviews, some graphics and critical essays. *Payment:* Prose: $35.00 per 1000 words; Poetry: $15.00 per page or per poem. *Illustrations:* half-tone.

Performing Arts in Canada Magazine (1961), Emslie T. Dick, 2nd Floor, 52 Avenue Road, Toronto, Ontario, M5R 2G2 *T.* 416-921-2601 and 5188.
$6.00 p.a., $12.00 p.a. outside Canada. Q. Feature articles on Canadian theatre, music and dance artists and organizations; technical articles on scenery, lighting, make-up, film, costumes, etc. *Length:* 1500 to 2000 words. *Payment:* $150 to $250, one month after publication. *Illustrations:* black-and-white photographs, line.

Quebec Chronicle Telegraph (1764), Bob Dawson (Quebec Chronicle-Telegraph Inc.), 980 Holland Avenue, Quebec City, Quebec, G1S 3T1 *T.* 418-527-2591.
35 cents. W. Covers local events within English community in Quebec City. Some feature articles.

Quill & Quire (1935), Susan Walker, 56 The Esplanade, Suite 213, Toronto, Ontario, M5E 1A7 *T.* 416-364-3333.

$45.00 p.a. (in the UK). 17 issues p.a. Articles of interest about the Canadian Book trade. *Payment:* from $100. *Illustrations:* line, half-tone.

Reader's Digest, Alexander Farrell, 215 Redfern Avenue, Montreal, Quebec, H3Z 2V9 *T.* 514-934-0751.
$1.69. M. Original articles on all subjects of broad general appeal, thoroughly researched and professionally written. Outline or query recommended. *Length:* 3000 words approx. *Payment:* from $2300.00 Also previously published material. *Illustrations:* colour, half-tone, line.

(Toronto) Globe and Mail, The (1844), A. Roy Megarry, Publisher; Norman Webster, Editor-in-Chief, 444 Front Street West, Toronto, Ontario, M5V 2S9. London: 164-167 Temple Chambers (2nd Floor), Temple Avenue, London, EC4Y 0EA *T.* 01-353-5795.
25c. Mon-Fri; 75c. Sat. D.

Toronto Life (1967), Marq de Villiers, 59 Front Street East, Toronto, Ontario, M5E 1B3 *T.* 416-364-3333.
$2.50. M. Articles, profiles on Toronto and Torontonians. *Illustrations:* line, half-tone, colour.

Toronto Star (1892), One Yonge Street, Toronto, M5E 1E6 *T.* 367-2000. *L.A.:* Suite 238A, The Times Building, 200 Gray's Inn Road, London WC1X 8EZ *T.* 01-833 0791.
25 cents. D. (£1.00 Saturday, 50 cents Sunday.)

(Vancouver) Province (1898), Robert McMurray, 2250 Granville Street, Vancouver, V6H 3G2 *T.* 732-2484.
35 cents. M.-F. 60 cents Sunday.

Vancouver Sun, Bruce Larsen, Editor; Frank Rutter, Editor of Editorial Pages; Bruce Hutchison, Editor Emeritus, 2250 Granville Street, Vancouver, V6H 3G2, B.C. *T.* 732-2111. London: Southam News, 8 Bouverie Street, 4th Floor, London, EC4Y 8AX *T.* 01-583 7322.
35 cents. D. Fri, Sat. 60 cents (not Sunday). Rates depending on arrangements. Very little outside contribution.

Wascana Review (1966), Joan Givner, c/o English Department, University of Regina, Regina, Sask., S4S 0A2.
$2.50 per issue. Semi-annual ($5.50 p.a.; $13 for 3 years). Criticism, short stories, poetry, reviews. *Length:* prose, not more than 6000 words; verse, up to 100 lines. *Payment:* $3 per page for prose; $10 per printed page for verse; $3.00 per page for reviews. Contributors also receive two free copies of the issue. Manuscripts from freelance writers welcome.

Winnipeg Free Press (1872), John Dafoe, 300 Carlton Street, Winnipeg, Manitoba, R3C 3C1 *T.* 943-9331.
25 cents, £1.00 Saturday. D. Some freelance articles. *Payment:* $50 to $100.

INDIA

Newspapers are listed under the towns in which they are published.

Aryan Path (1930), Sophia Wadia, Theosophy Hall, 40 New Marine Lines, Bombay, 400 020 *T.* 292173. London: 62 Queen's Gardens, Lancaster Gate, W2 3AH *T.* 01-723 0688.
45p. Alternate months (£2.20 p.a.). An international review of philosophy, mysticism, comparative religion, psychical research, Indian culture and the brotherhood of humanity. Articles 1200 to 2500 words. *Payment:* on acceptance and by arrangement.

NEWSPAPERS AND MAGAZINES

Asian Literary Market Review (1975), Kunnuparampil P. Punnoose, Kunnuparampil Buildings, Kurichy 686549, Kottayan District. *T.* 04826-470.
US$10 p.a. Q. Articles on books, authors, publishing, promotion and distribution. *Payment:* RS.100 per 1000 words. *Illustrations:* line, half-tone.

(Bombay) Eve's Weekly, Mrs. Gulshan Ewing, Eve's Weekly Ltd., J. K. Somani Building, Bombay, Samachar Marg, Bombay 400023. *T.* 271444.
Rs.4.00. W. Articles and features on a wide variety of topics with special emphasis on women's issues, and reflecting a feminist point of view. Also social news, fashion, health, child development, handicrafts, etc. *Illustrations:* pictures, sketches, artwork.

(Bombay) Illustrated Weekly of India, The, Pritish Nandy, Bombay. U.K.: 26 Station Approach, Sudbury, Wembley, Middlesex, HA0 2LA *T.* 01-903 9696.
Rs. 3.00. W. First-class photo features and illustrated articles dealing with topical matters by authoritative writers only, for educated Indian public of modern outlook. *Length:* articles from 800-5000 words; fiction up to 2000 words; serials, 60,000 words. *Payment:* on publication. First reproduction rights India, Pakistan, Burma and Ceylon required.

(Bombay) The Indian Express (Daily) (Proprietors: Indian Express Newspapers (Bombay), Private, Ltd.), Express Towers, Nariman Point, Bombay, 400 021. Editor-in-Chief: S. Mulgaokar; General Manager: N. M. Dugar. Also Delhi, Madras, Madurai, Vijayawada, Ahmedabad, Bangalore and Cochin. London Correspondent: B. K. Tiwari, 92 Hamilton Terrace, St. John's Wood, London, NW8. *T.* 01-289 3133.
35 paise. D. For editorial page articles of current political interest. *Length:* from about 1000-2000. *Payment:* average £2 per 750 words.

(Calcutta) Capital (1888), J. M. Kaul, 19 R.N. Mookerjee Road, Calcutta 700 001 *T.* 235825.
Rs. 125 p.a. W. India's premier business weekly. Newsy articles related to Indian industrial and world trade developments; also national/international political, economic, financial, commodity and management trends. *Payment·* by arrangement.

(Calcutta) Statesman, Amalendu Das Gupta, Statesman House, Chowringhee Square, Calcutta 700 001. *T.* 27-1000-9, 27-1515. For Northern India a separate edition is published daily from Statesman House, New Delhi.
80 paise. D. Published simultaneously in Calcutta and Delhi. Circulates widely in India, and generally respected for its reliable news and independent policy. Articles mainly commissioned. *Payment:* by arrangement. *Illustrations:* photographs or line drawings according to merit. **The Statesman Weekly** (Rs. 2.75). A digest of Indian news and views, market trends and quotations.

Chandrabhaga (1979), Jayanta Mahapatra, Tinkonia Bagicha, Cuttack 753 001, Orissa. *T.* 20566.
Rs. 25.00. Twice p.a. Poetry, short stories, essays, literary translations; bias on creative writing in English on Indian themes. *Length:* 4000 words. *Payment:* one copy of magazine. No *illustrations.* S.A.E. with submissions essential.

Christian Writer & Publisher (1983), Kunnuparampil P. Punnoose, Kunnuparampil Buildings, Kurichy 686549, Kottayam District.
US $2.50 Q. Inspirational and how-to articles on writing, publishing, bookselling. *Payment:* Rs 100 per 1000 words. *Illustrations: line, half-tone.*

Commerce (1910), Commerce Publications Ltd., Vadilal Dagli, Post Box No. 11017, Bombay 400 020. *T.* 202-4505.

Rs. 4.00. W. (Rs. 200 p.a.). Special articles from 1000 to 1500 words, on economic, commercial, financial, and industrial topics with special reference to India and the East generally; matters connected with Indian firms and companies domiciled in the United Kingdom. *Payment:* £4.00 per column (approximately 350 words).

Current Events, (1955), Dev Dutt, 15 Rajpur Road, Dehra Dun, 248 001. *T.* 23792, 23187.
Rs. 10.00 Q. Review of national and international affairs.

(Lucknow) National Herald (1938), Hari Jai Singh (Associated Journals, Ltd.), 1 Bisheshwar Nath Road, Lucknow. *T.* Lucknow 49832.
60 paise (65 paise on Sunday). D. Articles, maps and illustrations of all kinds.

(Madras) Hindu, The, 859 and 860 Mount Road, madras. 600 002. Proprietors: Kasturi & Sons, Ltd. London: 26 Beaumont Avenue, Wembley, Middlesex, HA0 3BZ. Washington: Apartment 1531, The Irene, 4701 Willard Avenue, Chevy Chase, Maryland 20015. Tokyo: 31-10 Jingumae 6-Chome, Shibuya-Ku. Branches at Bombay, Calcutta, New Delhi, Bangalore, Hyderabad, Madurai, Tiruchirapalli, Coimbatore, Trivandrum and Cochin.
70 paise. (75 paise Sunday.) D. Printed in English, having the widest and most influential circulation among the reading public in India. Accepts contributions on Indian affairs and international topics. *Payment:* by arrangement. *Illustrations:* photographs.

(New Delhi) Indian Express (1953), B. G. Verghese, Bahadur Shah Zafar Marg, New Delhi 110002. *T.* 276094.
80 paise. D. Articles of about 1200 words in length. *Payment:* Rs. 300 per article. *Illustrations:* line, half-tone.

(New Delhi) National Herald (1968), Anser Kidwai (Associated Journals, Ltd.), Herald House, Bahadurshah Zafa Marg, New Delhi, 110002. *T.* New Delhi 3319839.
80 paise. D. Articles, maps and illustrations of all kinds.

Onlooker, The (1939), Rajat Sharma, 215 Free Press Journal Marg, Nariman Point, Bombay 400 021. *T.* 234143. *T.A.* Newsads.
Rs. 3.00. Fortnightly News Magazine. News features, photo features and subjects of human interest with a news slant. *Length:* 1000-1500 words. *Payment:* £10 per article. *Illustrations:* photographs and drawings.

Times of India, The, Girilal Jain, Bombay, Delhi and Ahmedabad. U.K.: 26 Station Approach, Sudbury, Wembley, Middlesex, HA0 2LA *T.* 01-903 9696. *Telex:* 8951317.
70 paise. D. Topical articles and photographs likely to be of particular interest in India and to Indian readers. *Length:* preferred, 1000-1500 words. *Payment:* Rs. 150 to Rs. 400 per article. Action photographs and line drawings.

THE REPUBLIC OF IRELAND AND NORTHERN IRELAND

Africa - St. Patrick's Missions, Rev. Thomas C. Randles, St. Patrick's, Kiltegan, Co. Wicklow. *T.* (0508) 73233.
25p. (£4.00 p.a.) 9 times p.a. Articles of general interest. *Length:* upto 1,500 words. *Payment:* £25 per article. *Illustrations:* All kinds.

Aspect Magazine (1982), John O'Neill, P.O. Box 15, New Road, Greystones, Co. Wicklow. *T.* 01-875514.
75p. M. Hard business stories relevant to Irish readers. *Length:* up to 1000 words. *Payment:* by arrangement. *Illustrations:* half-tone.

(Belfast) News Letter (1737), Sam Butler, 51-59 Donegall Street, Belfast, BT1 2GB *T.* (0232) 244441.
20p. D. Unionist.

Books Ireland (1976), Bernard Share, Goslingtown, Kilkenny. *T.* Kilkenny (056) 65964.
80p. £8.50 p.a. (M. except January and August). Reviews of Irish interest and Irish-author books, articles of interest to librarians, booksellers and readers. *Length:* 800 to 1400 words. *Payment:* £20 per 1000 words.

Caritas (1934), Bernardine Edwards, O.H., St. Augustine's, Carysfort Avenue, Blackrock, Co. Dublin. *T.* 885518.
Q. A magazine of Christian concern. Articles and features on mental and physical health concerning family and community well-being. Scripts of 1200 to 1500 words on children and youth, personal and case histories, biographies, religious and general interest. Poems not normally accepted. *Payment:* £15 to £60. Photos, illustrations and appropriate cartoons paid for separately.

Church of Ireland Gazette (1885, New Series 1963), Rev. Canon C. W. M. Cooper, 48 Bachelor's Walk, Lisburn, Co. Antrim, BT28 1XN *T.* Lisburn (08462) 75743.
15p. W. Church news, articles of religious and general interest. *Length:* 600 to 1000 words. *Payment:* according to length and interest.

Commercial Transport (1970), Bridget Gavin, Rathcoole, Co. Dublin. *T.* 589211.
£1.00 M. Articles relating to transport on land, sea and air. *Payment:* £35 to £50 per 1000 words. *Illustrations:* line, half-tone, colour.

Cyphers (1975), Leland Bardwell, Pearse Hutchinson, Eiléan Ní Chuilleanáin, Macdara Woods, 3 Selskar Terrace, Dublin 6 *T.* 978866.
£1.20. 2 to 3 p.a. Poems, fiction, articles on literary subjects, translations. *Payment:* £7 per page (verse), £5 per page (prose).

East Cork News, Peter Doyle, Industrial Estate, Waterford. *T.* (051) 74951.
35p. W. News articles. *Payment:* by arrangement. *Illustrations:* line and half-tone (web offset).

Evening Herald, Dublin, Michael Brophy, Middle Abbey Street, Dublin 1 *T.* 731331.
30p. D. Articles. *Payment:* by arrangement. *Illustrations:* line, half-tone.

Evening Press (1954), Sean Ward, Burgh Quay, Dublin 2. *T.* 713333.
30p. D. News items, articles. *Payment:* NUJ rates.

Fortnight. An Independent Review for Northern Ireland (1970), Leslie Van Slyke, 7 Lower Crescent, Belfast BT7 1NR *T.* (0232) 232353.
50p. M. Current affairs analysis, profiles, literary criticism, short stories (up to 2500 words), poetry, opinion pieces, humorous pieces. *Payment:* £10 to £30 per article. *Illustrations:* line, half-tone. Cartoons.

Furrow, The (1950), Rev. Ronan Drury, St. Patrick's College, Maynooth, Co. Kildare. *T.* 286215.
£1.20. M. Religious, pastoral, theological, social articles. *Length:* 4000 words. *Payment:* average £10 per page (450 words). *Illustrations:* line or half-tone.

Honest Ulsterman, The, Frank Ormsby, Robert Johnstone, 70 Eglantine Avenue, Belfast, BT9 6DY *T.* (0232) 668 231.
£1.00. 3 p.a. Poetry, short stories, critical articles. *Payment:* by arrangement.

Hotel and Catering Review, Frank Corr, Jemma Publications Ltd., 22 Brookfield Avenue, Blackrock, Co. Dublin. *T.* Dublin 886946. *Telex:* 90169.
£15 p.a. M. Short news and trade news pieces. *Length:* approx. 200 words. Features. *Payment:* £50 per 1000 words. *Illustrations:* half-tone and cartoons.

Image (1974), Geraldine Niland, 22 Crofton Road, Dun Laoghaire, Co. Dublin. *T.* 01-808415.
80p. M. Short stories of a high literary standard and of interest to women. *Length:* up to 3000 words. Interviews with actors, writers, etc. Human interest stories. *Payment:* by arrangement.

In Dublin (1976), John Waters, 40 Lower Ormond Quay, Dublin 1 *T.* 726622.
75p. Fortnightly. Articles, short stories, reviews, current affairs, arts and entertainment. *Length:* 200-5000 words. *Payment:* £50 per 1000 words. *Illustrations:* line, half-tone; cartoons.

Ireland of the Welcomes, Baggot Street Bridge, Dublin, 2. *T.* Dublin 765871.
95p. Bi-M. Irish items with cultural, sporting or topographical background designed to arouse interest in Irish holidays. No fiction. *Length:* 1200 to 1800 words. *Payment:* by arrangement. *Illustrations:* scenic and topical. Preliminary letter preferred. Mostly commissioned.

Ireland's Own (1902), John McDonnell, North Main Street, Wexford. *T.* 053-22155.
28p. W. Short stories (1500 to 2000 words); romances in particular, but with an Irish background; articles of interest to Irish readers at home and abroad (1000 to 3000 words); general and literary articles (1000 to 2500 words). Special issues for Christmas and St. Patrick's Day. Jokes, funny stories, riddles, always welcome. Suggestions for new features considered. *Payment:* varies according to quality, originality and length. Serials of novel length, preliminary letter advisable, enclosing synopsis and S.A.E., payment by arrangement. *Illustrations:* no restriction (web off-set).

Irish Business (1975), Frank FitzGibbon, 126 Lower Baggot Street, Dublin 2. *T.* 608264.
£1.10. (£13.00 p.a.) M. Topical articles on finance, banking, economics. *Length:* 900 to 1500 words. *Payment:* by arrangement. *Illustrations:* line, half-tone.

Irish Independent, Vincent Doyle, Independent House, 90 Middle Abbey Street, Dublin 1. *T.* 731666.
45p. D. Special articles on topical or general subjects. *Length:* 700 to 1000 words. *Payment:* Editor's estimate of value.

Irish Journal of Medical Science (1st series 1832, 6th series January 1926, Volume 155, 1986), Royal Academy of Medicine, 6 Kildare Street, Dublin 2. *T.* 767650.
£3.00. M. (Subscription Great Britain and Ireland £36.00 post free; overseas £42.00 post free). Official Organ of the Royal Academy of Medicine in Ireland. Original contributions in medicine, surgery, midwifery, public health, etc.; reviews of professional books, reports of medical societies, etc. *Illustrations:* half-tone, line and colour.

Irish Medical Times, Dr. John O'Connell, 15 Harcourt Street, Dublin 2 *T.* 757461.
70p. W. Medical articles, also humorous articles with medical slant. *Length:* 850-1000 words. *Payment:* £40 per 1000 words. *Illustrations:* line and half-tone.

Irish News and Belfast Morning News, The, (1855), J. J. Fitzpatrick, Managing Editor, 113-117 Donegall Street, Belfast BT1 2GE *T.* 242614.
15p. D. Articles of historical and topical interest. *Payment:* by arrangement.

Irish Press, The, T. P. Coogan, Burgh Quay, Dublin 2. *T.* 713333.
45p. D. Topical articles about 1200 words. *Payment:* by arrangement. *Illustrations:* topical photographs.

Irish Times, Douglas Gageby, 11-15 D'Olier Street, Dublin 2. *T.* Dublin 792022. *Telex:* 93639.

55p. D. Mainly staff-written. Specialist contributions (800 to max. 2000 words) by commission on basis of ideas submitted, *payment* at editor's valuation. *Illustrations:* photographs and line drawings.

IT Magazine, Noelle Campbell-Sharp, The Village Centre, Ballybrack Village, Co. Dublin. *T.* 826411.
£1.00. M. (£14.50 p.a.). Fashion and social magazine; beauty, interiors, health books, wine and cookery, art, theatre, cinema, television, music, motoring, knitting and special monthly interviews. *Length:* 700 to 2500 words. *Payment:* by arrangement. *Illustrations:* half-tone.

Nationalist and Munster Advertiser, The, (1890), Brendan Long, Queen Street, Clonmel, Co. Tipperary. *T.* 052-22211.
40p. W. Requirements by arrangement. *Payment:* £18 per 1000 words. *Illustrations:* line, half-tone.

Poetry Ireland (1982), Terence Brown, 44 Upper Mount Street, Dublin 2.
£1.50 Q. Poetry, short lyric and sections from long poems. *Payment:* by arrangement.

Portadown Times & Craigavon News (1859), David Armstrong, 38a High Street, Portadown, BT62 1HY *T.* (0762) 336111.
30p. W. Articles and crosswords. *Payment:* N.U.J. rates.

Reality (1936), Rev. K. H. Donlon, Redemptorist Publications, Orwell Road, Rathgar, Dublin 6. *T.* Dublin 961488 and 961688.
40p. M. Illustrated magazine for christian living. Articles on all aspects of modern life, including family, youth, religion, leisure. Illustrated articles black/white photos only. Short stories. *Length:* 1000-1500 words. *Payment:* by arrangement; average £20.00 per 1000 words.

Songwriter, The (1967), James D. Liddane, International Songwriters Association Ltd., Limerick City. *T.* 061 28837.
Available to members only as part of membership fee. 4 times a year. Articles on song writing and interviews with music publishers and recording company executives. *Length:* 400-5000 words. *Payment:* from £40 per page and by arrangement. *Illustrations:* photographs.

Studies An Irish quarterly review (1912), Rev. Brian Lennon, S.J., 35 Lower Leeson Street, Dublin 2. *T.* 766785.
£3.75. Q. A general review of social comment, literature, history, the arts. Articles written by specialists for the general reader. Critical book reviews. *Length:* 5000 words. Token *payment. Preliminary letter.*

Sunday Independent, Aengus Fanning, Independent House, 90 Middle Abbey Street, Dublin, 1. *T.* 731333.
30p. W. Special articles. *Length:* according to subject. *Payment:* at Editor's valuation; good. *Illustrations:* topical or general interest.

Sunday News, (1965), Ken Reid, 51-67 Donegall Street, Belfast, BT1 2GB *T.* (0232) 244441.
28p. W. General topical articles of 500 words. *Payment:* by arrangement. *Illustrations:* line and half-tone.

Sunday Press, The, Vincent Jennings, Tara House, Tara Street, Dublin, 2. *T.* Dublin 713333. *T.A.* Sceala, Dublin.
50p. W. Articles of general interest. *Length:* 1000 words. *Illustrations:* line and half-tone.

Theatre Ireland Magazine (1982), Paul Hadfield, Lynda Henderson, 29 Main Street, Castlerock, Co. Derry BT51 4RA *T.* (0265) 848130.

£1.50. Q. Articles, photographs, practical information, reference material on all aspects of live theatre, international as well as of Irish interest. *Length:* 1000 to 3000 words. *Payment:* by arrangement. *Illustrations:* colour and black and white. Also **Theatre Ireland Yearbook** (£7.00 annually).

Waterford News & Star, Peter Doyle, Industrial Estate, Waterford. *T.* (051) 74951.
50p. W. News articles. *Payment:* by arrangement. *Illustrations:* line and half-tone (web-offset).

Woman's Way (1963), Celine Naughton, J. S. Publications, 126 Lower Baggot Street, Dublin 2. *T.* 608264.
55p. W. Short stories, light romance, career, holiday, 2000 to 3000 words. *Payment:* £30.00 to £50.00. Articles of interest to women. *Illustrations:* half-tone, line and colour.

Word, The (1936), Rev. Brother Paul Hurley, S.V.D. (The World Press, Hadzor, Droitwich), Divine Word Missionaries, Maynooth, Co. Kildare. *T.* Dublin 286391.
30p. M. A Catholic illustrated magazine for the family. Illustrated articles of general interest up to 1000 words and good picture features. *Payment:* by arrangement. *Illustrations:* photographs and large colour transparencies.

NEW ZEALAND

Newspapers are listed under the towns in which they are published.

(Auckland) New Zealand Herald (1863), P. J. Scherer, P.O. Box 32, Auckland. *T.* 795-050. London: Ludgate House, 107 Fleet Street, EC4. *T.* 01-353 2686.
35c. D. Topical and informative articles 800 to 1100 words. *Minimum payment:* $30-$100. *Illustrations:* Half-tone blocks (65 screen).

Auckland Star (1870), Warwick Spicer (Auckland Star Ltd.), P.O. Box 3697, Auckland. *T.* 797-626.
35c. Monday to Friday.

(Christchurch) Press, The, E. B. Lock, P.O. Box 1005, Christchurch. London: 107 Fleet Street, EC4A 2AN *T.* 01-353 2686.
35c. D. Articles of general interest not more than 1000 words. *Payment:* by arrangement. Extra for photographs and line drawings.

(Christchurch) Star, The (1868), R. A. Swinard, (New Zealand Newspapers, Ltd.), Kilmore Street, Christchurch. *T.* 797-100.
30c. D. Topical articles.

(Dunedin) Otago Daily Times (1861), R. K. Eunson, P.O. Box 181, Dunedin. London: 107 Fleet Street, EC4A 2AN *T.* 01-353 2686.
35c. D. Any articles of general interest up to 1000 words, but preference is given to New Zealand writers. Topical illustrations and personalities. *Payment:* current New Zealand rates.

Gisborne Herald, The (1874), Iain Gillies, P.O. Box 1143, 64 Gladstone Road, Gisborne. *T.* 82099. *T.A.* Herald, Gisborne.
12c. D. Topical features of local interest. *Length:* 1000 to 1500 words. *Payment:* by arrangement. *Illustrations:* bromides.

Hawke's Bay Herald Tribune (result of merger between Hawke's Bay Herald (1857), Hastings Standard (1896) and Hawke's Bay Tribune (1910)), J. E. Morgan, Karamu Road, Hastings. *T.* 85-155. *Telex:* H.B.News 21394.
45c. D. Limited requirements. *Payment:* $6 to $30 for articles, $6 to $10 for photographs. *Illustrations:* web off-set.

(Invercargill) Southland Times, The (1862), P. M. Muller, P.O. Box 805, Invercargill. *T.* 81-909. *T.A.* Times, Invercargill. *Telex:* NZ 5254.
35c. D. Articles of up to 1500 words on topics of Southland interest. *Payment:* by arrangement. *Illustrations:* colour, line and half-tone.

Islands, Robin Dudding, 4 Sealy Road, Torbay, Auckland 10. *T.* 4039007.
$10. Q. ($30 p.a.; overseas: $15 single issue, $36 p.a.). Short stories, verse criticism, reviews. No limits to *length*. Most critical work commissioned or prior letter preferred. *Payment:* about $1200 divided among contributors to a single issue. *Illustrations:* usually commissioned.

Landfall (1947), David Dowling, The Caxton Press, P.O. Box 25-088, Christchurch. *T.* 68516.
$24.00 p.a. ($30.00 p.a. overseas). Q. Literary and general material by N.Z. writers considered of any length. Illustrates the work of N.Z. painters, sculptors, architects, photographers. *Payment:* by arrangement.

Management, Neil Prentice (Profile Publishing), Box 5544, Auckland. *T.* 769 178.
$3.00. M. Articles on management efficiency, profiles on important management figures, topics of general interest to the top businessman. A New Zealand angle or application preferred. *Length:* 2000 words. *Payment:* by arrangement. *Illustrations:* photographs, line drawings.

(Napier) Daily Telegraph, The (1871), K. R. Hawker, P.O. Box 343, Napier. *T.* 54488.
35c. D. Limited market for features. *Payment:* $20 upwards per 1000 words; $10 a picture. *Illustrations:* line and half-tone.

Nelson Evening Mail, The, R. S. Neville, P.O. Box 244, 15 Bridge Street, Nelson. *T.* 87-079.
30c. D. Features, articles on New Zealand subjects. *Length:* 500-1000 words. *Payment:* up to $50 per 1000 words. *Illustrations:* half-tone, colour.

(New Plymouth) Daily News, The (1857), D. Garcia, P.O. Box 444, New Plymouth. *T.* 80559.
35c. D. Articles preferably with a Taranaki connection. *Payment:* by negotiation. *Illustrations:* half-tone.

New Zealand Farmer, Neil Rennie, P.O. Box 56-064, 360 Dominion Road, Auckland.
$1.50. F. Authoritative, simply-written articles on new developments in livestock husbandry, grassland farming, cropping, farm machinery, marketing, agrionics, biotechnology. *Length:* 1000 to 1800 words. *Payment:* according to merit.

New Zealand Gardener, Deslandes Ltd., Private Bag, Petone. *T.* 687-179.
$1.75. M. Topical articles on gardening and gardeners, new plants and methods of cultivation, new products of horticultural interest, home workshop projects for the home and garden. Authoritative articles by specialists but general interest articles by freelance writers. *Payment:* $50 per 1000 words. *Illustrations:* $10 per print on publication; $15 per colour slide, $50 for cover shots.

New Zealand Listener, The (1939), David Beatson, P.O. Box 3140, Wellington. *T.* 721-777.
75c. W. Topical features of New Zealand and international interest: also features related to television and radio programmes. *Length:* up to 2500 words. *Illustrations:* colour and black and white. *Payment:* from $160.00 per 1000 words, or by arrangement.

New Zealand Motorcycle News, David Hall, P.O. Box 1717, 66 Abel Smith Street, Wellington. *T.* 849-566.

$1.00. F. Circulation New Zealand. New Zealand's only motorcycle publication. Contains reports, interviews, road tests, new products and developments, technical drawings. *Payment:* minimum $25.00. Special rates for exclusive stories. $5-$10 photos published.

New Zealand Woman's Weekly (1932), Michal McKay, (New Zealand Newspapers, Ltd.), P.O. Box 56-064, Auckland 3. *T.* 688-177.
90c. W. Pictorial features. Illustrated articles of general, family, world interest, particularly with a New Zealand slant. *Length:* articles 750-1750. *Payment:* acceptance fee, remainder on publication. *Illustrations:* black-and-white, colour.

N.Z. Engineering (1946), L. W. McEldowney, B.A., Engineering Publications Co. Ltd., P.O. Box 12241, Wellington.
$1.50. M. Articles of interest to New Zealand engineers, not necessarily technical. Preliminary letter essential. *Payment:* by arrangement.

N.Z. Truth (News Media Ownership Ltd.), A. F. Hitchens, Glenside Crescent, Auckland, P.O. Box 1074. *T.* 794780.
£1.00. W. Bold investigative reporting, exposés. *Length:* 500-1000 words, preferably accompanied by photographs. *Payment:* about $50 per 500 words, extra for photographs.

Sea Spray (1945), David Pardon, P.O. Box 56-064, 360 Dominion Road, Auckland. *T.* 688-177.
$2.00. M. Feature material and photographs on pleasure boating concerning New Zealanders, power or sail. Technical and how-to articles. *Payment:* $100 per 1000 words. *Illustrations:* line, half-tone.

Sunday Star (1986), Warwick Spicer, (Auckland Star Ltd.), P.O. Box 3697, Auckland. *T.* 797-626.
80c. Sunday.

Timaru Herald, The, M. J. Vance, P.O. Box 46, Bank Street, Timaru. *T.* 44-129.
35c. D. Topical articles. *Payment:* by arrangement. *Illustrations:* screened bromides.

(Wellington) Evening Post, The (1865), D. R. Churchill, P.O. Box 3740, Willis Street, Wellington. *T.* 729-009. *London Office:* N.Z. Associated Press, 107 Fleet Street, EC4A 2AN *T.* 01-353 2686.
10c. D. General topical articles, 600 words. *Payment:* N.Z. current rates or by arrangement. News illustrations.

SOUTH AFRICA

Newspapers are listed under the towns in which they are published.

Argus South African Newspapers.
The Argus, Cape Town, 40c. D.; **Weekend Argus** (Sat.), 40c.; **The Star,** Johannesburg, 40c. D.; **The Sunday Star,** Johannesburg, R1; **The Daily News,** Durban, 40c. D.; **Sunday Tribune,** Durban, R1.; **The Diamond Fields Advertiser,** Kimberley, 30c. D. Accepts articles of general and South African interest. *Payment:* for contributions accepted for publication is made in accordance with an Editor's estimate of the value of the manuscript. Contributions should be addressed to the Foreign Editor, Argus South African Newspapers Ltd., 32-33 Hatton Garden, London, EC1N 8DL *T.* 01-831 0882, and not direct.

Bethlehem Express (1904), T. C. Roffe, 10 Muller Street, Bethlehem 9700 *T.* 35611.
20c. W. English and Afrikaans.

Bona, Republican Press (Pty) Ltd., P.O. Box 32083, Mobeni 4060, Natal. *T.* Durban 422041. *T.A.* Keur Durban. UK: Suite 437-439 High Holborn House, 52-54 High Holborn, London WC1V 6RB *T.* 01-831 2965.
70c. M. Articles on fashion, cookery, sport, music of interest to black people. *Length:* up to 3000 words. *Payment:* by arrangement. *Illustrations:* line, half-tone, colour.

(Cape Town) Cape Times, The (1876), A. H. Heard, 77 Burg Street, Cape Town. *T.* 24-2233. *Postal address:* P.O. Box 11, Cape Town 8000. London Editor: Stanley Uys, 135 Fleet Street, EC4. *T.* 01-353 4473.
30c. D. Contributions must be suitable for daily newspaper and must not exceed a column (about 1000 words). *Illustrations:* photographs of outstanding South African interest.

Car (1957), David Trebett, P.O. Box 180, Howard Place, 7450. *T.* 53-1391. *T.A.* Confrere.
R1.70. M. New car announcements with pictures and full colour features of motoring interest. *Payment:* by arrangement. *Illustrations:* half-tone and colour.

(Durban) Natal Mercury (1852), J. O. McMillan, Natal Newspapers (Pty.) Ltd., Devonshire Place, Durban, 4001. *T.* 319331.
40c. D.(except Sunday). Serious background news and inside details of world events. *Length:* 700 to 900 words. *Illustrations:* photographs of general interest.

Fair Lady, Dene Smuts (National Magazines), P.O. Box 1802, Cape Town 8000. *T.* 254878. *T.A.* Ladyfair. London: *T.* 01-353-3166.
R1.20. F. Articles and stories for women including showbiz, travel, humour. *Length:* articles up to 2000 words, short stories approx. 3000 words; short novels and serialisation of book material. *Payment:* on quality rather than length—by arrangement.

Farmer's Weekly (1911), L. Mundell, P.O. Box 32083, Mobeni 4060, Natal. *T.* Durban 422041. U.K.: Suite 437-439 High Holborn House, 52-54 High Holborn, London WC1V 6RB *T.* 01-831 2965.
R1.25. W. Articles, generally illustrated, up to 1000 words in length dealing with all aspects of practical farming and research with particular reference to conditions in Southern Africa. *Payment:* according to merit. *Illustrations:* continuous-tone, full colour and line. Includes women's section which accepts articles suitably illustrated, on subjects of interest to women. *Payment:* according to merit.

Femina (incorporating **Darling**), Pat Garlick, Republican Press (Pty.) Ltd., Box 32083, Mobeni 4060, Natal. *T.* Durban 422041 *T.A.* Keur, Durban. UK: Suite 437-439 High Holborn House, 52-54 High Holborn, London WC1V 6RB *T.* 01-831 2965.
R1.00. M. Show business articles, romantic fiction, women's general interest. *Length:* 1500 words. *Payment:* by arrangement. *Illustrations:* half-tone, line, colour.

Garden and Home, Margaret Wasserfall, Republican Press (Pty.) Ltd., P.O. Box 32083, Mobeni 4060, Natal. *T.* Durban 422041. *T.A.* Keur, Durban. U.K.: Suite 437-439 High Holborn House, 52-54 High Holborn, London WC1V 6RB *T.* 01-831 2965.
R1.80. M. Well illustrated articles on gardening, suitable for Southern Hemisphere. Articles for home section on furnishings, flower arrangement, food. *Payment:* by arrangement. *Illustrations:* half-tone and colour.

(Johannesburg) Sunday Times, Tertius Myburgh, P.O. Box 1090, Johannesburg 2000. *T.* 710-2600. London: South African Morning Newspapers Ltd., 135 Fleet Street, EC4. *T.* 01-353 4473.

R1.00. Every Sunday. Illustrated articles of political or human interest, from a South African angle if possible. Maximum 1000 words long and two or three photographs. Shorter essays, stories, and articles of a light nature from 500 to 750 words. *Payment:* average rate £30.00 a column. *Illustrations:* photographic (colour or black and white) and line.

Living and Loving (1970), June Vigor, Republican Press (Pty.) Ltd., P.O. Box 32083, Mobeni 4060, Natal. *T.* Durban 422041. *T.A.* Keur Durban. U.K.: Suite 437-439 High Holborn House, 52-54 High Holborn, London WC1V 6RB *T.* 01-831 2965.
R1.00. M. Romantic fiction, 1500 to 4000 words. Articles dealing with first person experiences; baby, family and marriage, medical articles up to 3000 words. *Payment:* by merit.

Natal Witness (1846), R. S. Steyn, 244 Longmarket Street, Pietermaritzburg, Natal 3201. *T.* Maritzburg 0331-42011. London: 85 Fleet Street, EC4Y 1ED. 20c. D. Accepts topical articles. *Length:* 500 to 1000 words. *Payment:* Average of R30 per 1000 words. *Illustrations:* press photos R10.00 each. All material should be submitted direct to the Editor in Pietermaritzburg.

Personality, M. Fisher, Republican Press (Pty.) Ltd., P.O. Box 32083, Mobeni 4060, Natal. *T.* Durban 422041. *T.A.* Keur, Durban. U.K.: Suite 437-439 High Holborn House, 52-54 High Holborn, London WC1V 6RB *T.* 01-831 2965.
R1.10. W. Illustrated. Primarily an entertainment-oriented magazine but also a market for articles about people and places, preferably with South African angle. Strong news features and/or photojournalism. 1000-4000 words, with b/w and colour photographs. Short stories 1500-5000 words. *Illustrations:* usually commissioned. *Payment:* by arrangement.

(Port Elizabeth) Eastern Province Herald, P.O. Box 1117, Port Elizabeth 6000. *T.* 523470. London: 135 Fleet Street, London, EC4. *T.* 01-353 4473.
25c. D. Contributions from 700 to 1500 words considered. *Payment:* £6.00 per 700 words minimum. *Illustrations:* topical photographs.

Scope, C. Backeberg, Republican Press (Pty.) Ltd., P.O. Box 32083, Mobeni 4060, Natal. *T.* Durban 422041. *T.A.* 624422 Durban. U.K.: Suite 437-439 High Holborn House, 52-54 High Holborn, London WC1V 6RB *T.* 01-831 2965.
R1.10. F. Strong news features, well illustrated, about people and places in all parts of the world. *Length:* up to 4000 words. Short stories 1500 to 5000 words, serials from 20,000 words. *Illustrations:* half-tone, colour.

South African Yachting, Power Waterski & Sail (1957), Neil Rusch, P.O. Box 3473, Cape Town 8000. *T.* 467472. *T.A.* Fairlead. *Telex:* 52-7826 SA.
R2.50. M. Articles on yachting, boating or allied subjects. *Payment:* R4.00 per 100 words. *Illustrations:* half-tone and line. Colour covers.

Southern Cross, P.O. Box 2372, 8000 Cape Town. *T.* 455007. *T.A.* Catholic. 40c. W. The national English language Catholic weekly. Catholic news reports, world and South African. 1000-word articles, cartoons of Catholic interest acceptable from freelance contributors. *Payment:* 30c. per column cm. for all copy used. *Illustrations:* photographs, R2.50 per column width.

World Airnews, Tom Chalmers, P.O. Box 35082, Northway 4065. *T.* (031) 52-6551.
R2.00. M. Aviation news and features with an African angle. *Payment:* £75 per 1000 words. *Illustrations:* photographs, £25 each (conditional).

Your Family, Angela Waller-Paton, Republican Press (Pty.) Ltd., P.O. Box 32083, Mobeni 4060, Natal. *T.* Durban 422041. *T.A.* Keur, Durban. U.K.: Suite 437-439 High Holborn House, 52-54 High Holborn, London WC1V 6RB *T.* 01-831 2965.

R1.00. M. Cookery, knitting, crochet and homecrafts. Short fiction, family drama, happy ending. *Payment:* by arrangement. *Illustrations:* continuous tone, colour and line.

UNITED STATES

Because of the difficulties in providing an up-to-date list of US journals, the *Yearbook* does not contain a detailed list; instead we refer readers who are particularly interested in the US market to *Writer's Market*, an annual guidebook giving editorial requirements and other details of over 4,000 U.S. markets for freelance writing, published by **Writers Digest Books**, 9933 Alliance Road, Cincinnati, Ohio 45242. *The Writer's Handbook* is a substantial volume published by **The Writer Inc**, 120 Boylston Street, Boston, Mass. 02116 ($25.00 plus $5.00 handling and postage). It contains 100 chapters, each written by an authority in his field, giving practical instruction on a wide variety of aspects of freelance writing and including details of 2200 markets, payment rates and addresses. Also publishes books on writing fiction, non-fiction, poetry, articles, plays, etc.
The Writer Inc. also publish a monthly magazine *The Writer* ($25 per year) which contains articles of instruction on all writing fields, lists of markets for manuscripts and special features of interest to freelance writers everywhere.
Writer's Digest Books also publish the monthly magazine *Writer's Digest* ($25 per year) and the annual directories, *Fiction Writer's Market*, *Poet's Market*, and many other books on creating and selling writing.
Further details may be obtained from:
Freelance Press Services, 5-9 Bexley Square, Salford, Manchester M3 6DB *T.* 061-832 5079.
Poplar Press Ltd., Studio 6, Kingsley House, Avonmore Place, London W14 8RY *T.* 01-602 7341.

SUBMISSION OF MSS

When submitting MSS. to US journals send your covering letter with the MS. together with any illustrations, stamped return envelope or international postage coupon. Make clear what rights are being offered for sale for some editors like to purchase MSS. outright, thus securing world copyright, i.e. the traditional British market as well as the US market. MSS. should be sent direct to the US office of the journal and not to any London office.

In many cases it is far better to send a preliminary letter giving a rough outline of your article or story. Enclose International Reply Coupons for reply. Most magazines will send a leaflet giving guidance to authors.

SYNDICATES, NEWS AND PRESS AGENCIES

In their own interests writers and others are strongly advised to make preliminary enquiries before submitting MSS., and to ascertain terms of work. Commission varies. The details given in the following entries should be noted carefully in respect of syndication, as many news and press agencies do not syndicate articles.

Advance Features, Kerry House, 34A High Street, East Grinstead, Sussex, RH19 3AS *T.* (0342) 28562. *Managing Editor:* Peter Norman. Supplies text and visual services to the regional press in Britain and newspapers overseas. Editorial for advertising supplements on consumer and commercial themes. Instructional graphic panels on a variety of subjects. Text services (weekly); D.I.Y., answers (teenagers and pensioners), property, video, paperbacks. Legal and business articles for the specialist press. Daily and weekly cartoons for the regional press (not single cartoons).

Ameuropress, Las Heras 3894, Buenos Aires 1425, Argentina. *T.* 72-8258. *Cables:* Ameuropres. *Director:* José Gregorio Ríos. Illustrated features to newspapers and magazines world-wide. Specialising in Latin American subjects including travel, human interest stories, hobbies, science, animal features. Regularly supplying women's material including cookery, beauty, fashion, interior decorating, glamour. Also stock colour library for advertising, calendars and illustrations. Undertakes assignments for Latin American subjects.

Aries Press Features, P.O. Box 14235, Lyttelton 0140, Transvaal, South Africa. *T.* Pretoria 629103. *Director:* Major J. W. Lamb. Well written features suitable for newspaper reading for world-wide syndication. *Payment:* by arrangement.

Associated Press (The), Ltd. (News Department), The Associated Press House, 12 Norwich Street, London, EC4A 1BP. *T.* 01-353 1515. *T.A.* Associated Londonpsy.

Associated Press, The (of America), London Office: The Associated Press House, 12 Norwich Street, London, EC4A 1BP. *T.* 01-353 1515.

Australasian News & Press Services (D. J. Varney & Associates 1964), Box T 1834, G.P.O., Perth, W. Australia, 6001. *T.* 293-1455. Australian correspondents and representatives for the international media. Services provided: features and news for colour photo magazines. Articles for consumer, trade, technical and professional journals. Trade news summaries and newsletters. Full range of professional public relations and market research services available including film, television and stage writing, production and talent services.

Australian Associated Press (1935), Jane Eyre, (*Chief Correspondent, London,*) 85 Fleet Street, London, EC4Y 1EH *T.* 01-353 0153-4. *T.A.* Austpress, London. *Telex:* 24661. News service to the Australian, New Zealand and Pacific Island press, radio and television.

Ayrshire Press Agency Ltd. (1956), 42 Main Street, Kilwinning, Ayrshire, KA13 6AQ *T.* (0294) 52530. Supplies photo news features to daily and weekly papers. Assignments undertaken by own staff photographers. Representatives of the national and provincial press.

Bar-David Ltd. 1 Hashahar Street, P.O. Box 1104, Tel Aviv 61010, Israel. *T.* 656 184-5-6. *Cables:* Davidbarco. *Telex:* 33721 Brvid Il.

BIPS—Bernsen's International Press Service, Ltd., 9 Paradise Close, Eastbourne, East Sussex BN20 8BT *T.* (0323) 28760. Theo C. Bernsen, Managing Director-Editor; Emile L. Habets, Manager, London Editor. Specialise in photo-features, both black and white and colour. Want human interest, oddity, gimmicky, popular mechanical, scientific, medical, etc., material suitable for marketing through own branches (London, San Francisco, Paris, Hamburg,

Milan, Stockholm, Amsterdam (for Benelux), Helsinki) in many countries. Give full information, well researched. Willing to syndicate, but prefer to assign free-lances either on BIPS' ideas or photographer's ideas. Buy outright and pay on acceptance. Query with picture story ideas. Syndicate written features, preferably illustrated.

Bulls Presstjänst AB, Birger Jarlsgatan 58, Box 5603, 114 86 Stockholm, Sweden. *T.* 23 40 20. *Telex:* 19 482. *Cables:* Pressbull. **Bulls Pressedienst GmbH,** Eysseneckstrasse 50, 6000 Frankfurt am Main 1, Western Germany. *T.* 59 04 18. *Telex:* 412117. *Cables:* Pressbull. **Bulls Pressetjeneste A/S,** Rädhusgaten 28, Oslo, Norway. *T.* 20 56 01. *Telex:* 71439. *Cables:* Bullpress. **Bulls Pressetjeneste A/S,** Vesterbrogade 14B, 1620 Copenhagen V, Denmark. *T.* 21 37 27. *Telex:* 19385. *Cables:* Pressbull. *Market:* Newspapers, magazines and weeklies in Sweden, Denmark, Norway, Finland, Iceland, Germany, Austria and German-speaking Switzerland. *Syndicates:* dramatic and human interest picture stories; topical and well-illustrated background articles and series; photographic features dealing with science, people, personalities, glamour; condensations and serialisations of best-selling fiction and non-fiction, cartoons, comic strips.

Camellion International (1980), Reunion House, 27-35 Jackson Road, Clacton-on-Sea, Essex CO15 1JA *T.* (0255) 475636. *Telex:* 8951182 Gecoms G. *Directors:* A. Shove, Mrs J. Shove, A. Powell. Press/news agency for freelance journalists and photo-journalists. (Will consider news material and written matter.) *Commission:* 10% standard; 25% exclusive.

Camera Press, Ltd., Russell Court, Coram Street, London, WC1H 0NB *T.* 01-837 4488, 0606, 1300 and 9393. *Telex:* 21654. *Managing Director:* Jon Blau. Syndicates picture stories, portraits, illustrated short stories, and cartoons to the Press of 45 countries. *Terms:* 50-50 per cent commission.

Canadian Press, The (1919), Paul Koring (Chief Correspondent), The Associated Press House, 12 Norwich Street, London, EC4A 1EJ *T.* 01-353 6355. London Bureau of the national news agency of Canada.

Capital Press Service, 2 Long Cottage, Church Street, Leatherhead, Surrey, KT22 8EJ *T.* (0372) 377451. *Directors:* M. Stone, E. W. Stone. *News Editor:* Nicholas Miller. Stories of trade, commerce and industry for trade papers in this country and abroad, and diary paragraphs for the National press. Interested in tobacco, air-cargo affairs and business travel for U.K., U.S. and German journals.

Caters News Agency, Ltd., 191 Corporation Street, Birmingham, B4 6RP *T.* 021-236 9001. *T.A.* Copy, Birmingham. *Joint Managing Directors:* J. Barnwell and T. A. Stone. Collection of news and pictures throughout Midlands. Representatives of Overseas, National and Provincial Press.

Central Press Features, Hulton House, 161 Fleet Street, London, EC4A 2AR *T.* 01-353 7131. *T.A.* Features, London, EC4. Supplies every type of feature to newspapers and other publications in 50 countries. Included in over 100 daily and weekly services are columns on international affairs, politics, sports, medicine, law, finance, computers, video, motoring, science, women's and children's features, strips, crosswords, cartoons and regular 6-12 article illustrated series of international human interest; also editorial material for advertising features.

Compass News Features (1984), 16 Boulevard Royal, 2449 Luxembourg, *T.* (352) 274-94. *Telex:* 3187 Compa Lu. *General Manager:* Claude Hippeau; *Managing Editor:* Gerard Loughran. News features and graphics agency specializing in subjects relating to the developing world.

SYNDICATES, NEWS AND PRESS AGENCIES

Crabtree (J. W.) and Son (1919), 36 Sunbridge Road, Bradford, BD1 2AA *T.* 732937 (Office); 637312 (Home). News, general, trade and sport; information and research for features undertaken.

Daily Telegraph Syndication, 135 Fleet Street, London, EC4P 4BL *T.* 01-353 4242, exts. 3681, 3683. *Telex:* London 22874 Telesyndic. *Cables:* Telesyndic London. News, features, cartoon-strips, photography, book serialisation. World-wide distribution and representation. (See also **Daily Telegraph Colour Library** and **Peterborough Literary Agency.**)

Europa-Press, Sveavägen 47, 4th Floor, Box 6410, S-113 82, Stockholm, Sweden. *T.* 34 94 35. *Cables:* Europress. *Telex:* 12359 Eupress S. *Managing Director:* Sven Berlin. Market: Newspapers, magazines and weeklies in Sweden, Denmark, Norway and Finland. Syndicates: High quality features of international appeal such as topical articles, photo-features, black and white and colour, women's features, short stories, serial novels, non-fiction stories and serials with strong human interest, crime articles, popular science, cartoons, comic strips.

Europress Features (UK), 18 St. Chads Road, Didsbury, near Manchester, M20 9WH *T.* 061-445 2945. Representation of newspapers and magazines in Europe, Australia, United States. Syndication of top-flight features with exclusive illustrations—human interest stories—showbusiness personalities. 30-35% commission on sales of material successfully accepted; 40% on exclusive illustrations.

Exchange Telegraph Co., Ltd., The, Extel House, East Harding Street, London, EC4P 4HB. *T.* 01-353 1080. Alan B. Brooker (*Chairman*), Kenneth C. S. Young (*Managing Director*), Philip W. Arkless (*Secretary*).

Features International, Tolland, Lydeard St. Lawrence, Taunton, TA4 3PS *T.* (0984) 23014. *Cables:* Deadline, Taunton. *Editorial Director:* Anthony Sharrock. Syndicates features and picture stories to magazines and newspapers throughout the world. The agency produces a wide range of material—mainly from freelance sources—including topical articles, women's features, weekly columns, popular photo-features, series by international celebrities, glamour and pin-up photographs. Distributes directly to all English-language countries, and to major European magazines. Agents throughout the Common Market countries, Scandinavia, Japan, the Americas and Eastern Europe. Buys copy outright and welcomes story ideas. Average commission rate for picture material: 40-50%. SAE essential.

Gemini News Service, 40-43 Fleet Street, London, EC4Y 1BT *T.* 01-353 2567/8. *Cables:* Gemininews. Derek Ingram (*Editor*). Elizabeth Pritchard (*General Manager*). Network of correspondents and specialist writers all over the world. Some opening for freelance. Specialists in news-features of international, topical and development interest. Preferred *length* 1000-1200 words.

Global Syndication & Literary Agency, Limited, *President:* A. D. Fowler, 323 N. Euclid, Fullerton, California 92632, U.S.A. Always in need of cartoons, comic strips, non-fiction articles of interest to women, juvenile activity drawings, celebrity interviews.

Graphic Syndication (1981), 2 Angel Meadows, Odiham, Hampshire RG25 1AR *T.* (025671) 3004. *Manager:* M. Flanagan. Cartoon strips and single frames supplied to newspapers and magazines in Britain and overseas. *Terms:* 50%.

India-International News Service, *Head Office:* Jute House, 12 India Exchange Place, Calcutta, 700001. *T.* 22-9563, 22-6572, 45-0009. *T.A.* Zeitgeist. *Proprietor:* Ing H. Kothari, B.SC., D.W.P.(LOND), F.I.MECH.E., F.I.E., F.B.I.M.,

F.INST.D. 'Calcutta Letters' and Air Mail news service from Calcutta. Specialists in industrial and technical news. Public relations and publicity consultants.

Inter-Prensa, S.R.L., P.O. Box 4052, 1000 Capital Federal, Argentina. *T.* 30-1633. *Cables:* Interprensa Baires. Picture stories, fashion photos, comics. 40% commission.

International Fashion Press Agency, Mumford House, Mottram Road, Alderley Edge, Cheshire SK9 7JF *T.* (0625) 583537; London: 17 Bridle Lane, London W1R 3HL *T.* 01-437 3220. *Directors:* P. Bentham (Managing), P. Dyson, L. C. Bentham, J. Nicholls, N. Warren. Monitors and photographs international fashion collections. Supplies illustrated features, regular columns and pages to press on: fashion, health and beauty, personality profiles. Copywriting, photography and artwork for advertising and marketing literature.

International Feature Service, 104 rue de Laeken, 1000 Brussels, Belgium. *T.* 217-03-42. *Managing Director:* Max S. Kleiter. Feature articles, serial rights, tests, cartoons, comic strips and illustrations. Handles English TV-features and books; also production of articles for merchandising.

International Press Agency (Pty) Ltd., The (1934), P.O. Box 67, Howard Place 7450, South Africa. *Managing Editor:* Mrs. U. A. Barnett, PH.D. *London Office:* Mrs. S. Power, P.O. Box 149A, Surbiton, Surrey KT6 5JH. *T.* 01-398 7723. South African agent for many leading British, American and Continental Press firms for the syndication of comic strips, cartoons, jokes, feature articles, short stories, serials, press photos for the South African market.

Irish International News Service, *Editor:* Barry J. Hardy, P.C., 12 Greenlea Park, Terenure, Dublin 6. *T.* 906183. News, sport, book reviews, TV, radio, photographic department; also equipment for TV films, etc.

London Express News and Feature Services, 121-128 Fleet Street, London, EC4P 4JT *T.* 01-353 8000. Strips, features, cartoons, photographs, book serialisations and rights, merchandising, etc.

London News Service. 68, Exmouth Market, London, EC1R 4RA. *T.* 01-278 5661. Worldwide Syndication of features and photographs. *Editor:* Neil McCarthy.

Magazine Production Ltd (1984), 13 Southgate Street, Winchester, Hampshire SO23 9DZ *T.* (0962) 60444 *T.A.* Hambleside, Winchester. *Telex:* 477357. *Directors:* D. R. Yellop, R. A. Jeffery, D. K. Sleap. Requirements: features, short stories, line illustrations, cartoons, colour and black and white photographs mainly for West African market. *Payment:* by arrangement.

Maharaja Features Private Ltd., 5/226 Sion Road East, Bombay, 22, India. *T.* 484776. *Managing Editor:* K. R. Padmanabhan. Syndicates feature and pictorial material to newspapers and magazines in India and abroad. Specialists in well-researched articles on India by eminent authorities for publication in prestige journals throughout the world. Also topical features 1000-1500 words. *Illustrations:* Monochrome prints and colour transparencies.

New Zealand Associated Press, 107 Fleet Street, London, EC4A 2AN *T.* 01-353 2686.

New Zealand Press Association, 85 Fleet Street, London EC4P 4AJ *T.* 01-353 7040.

News Blitz International, Via Cimabue 5, 00196 Rome. *T.* 36.00.620, 36.19.014, 36.01.489. *President:* Vinicio Congiu. *Sales Manager:* Gianni Piccione. *Graphic Dept:* Giovanni A. Congiu. *Literary* and *Television Depts:* Giovanni A. Congiu. Syndicates cartoons, comic strips, humorous books with drawings, general books, feature and pictorial material, especially high-quality nudes, throughout the world and Italy. Television: importation and dubbing TV series, documentaries, educational films and video for schools. Material from freelance sources required. Average rates of commission 60-40% monthly report of sales, payments on receipt of invoice.

North West News & Sports Agency, Ltd. (1956), 148 Meols Parade, Meols, Wirral L47 6AN *T.* 051-632 5261. News and sports coverage, Birkenhead, Bebington, Wallasey and Wirral.

Northpix, 75a Bold Street, Liverpool L1 4EZ. *T.* 051-708 6044. North West and North Wales areas, news, sport, features. 24 hour wire service.

Orion Press, 55 1-Chome, Kanda-Jimbocho, Chiyoda-ku, Tokyo, 101. *T.* (03) 295-1402. *T.A.* Orionserv, Tokyo. *Telex:* J24447 Orionprs. International press service.

P.A. Features (the Feature Service of the Press Association, Ltd.), 85 Fleet Street, London, EC4P 4BE *T.* 01-353 7440. Terry Timblick (*Editor*). World-wide syndication to newspapers, magazines and trade journals of regular text and strip services.

Palach Press Ltd., Press and Literary agency, (1976), P.O. Box 222, London, WC2H 9RP *T.* 01-609 0152. *Directors:* Jan Kavan, Dr. Trevor Roberts. Czechoslovakia: current affairs, news items, political, economic and cultural information not covered by the official government agency. Also make available opposition documents, literary works by banned authors. Film and news items for TV. Publishes: *Palach Press Bulletin* and *Summary of Available Documents*.

Perera, Chandra S., Cinetra, 437 Pethiyagoda, Kelaniya, Sri Lanka. *T.* 521885. *Cables:* Telecinex, Colombo. Press and TV news, news films on Sri Lanka and Maldives, colour and black-and-white photo news and features, photographic and film coverages, screen plays and scripts for TV and films, Press clippings.

Pixfeatures (Mr. P. G. Wickman), 5 Latimer Road, Barnet, Hertfordshire. *T.* 01-449 9946 and 01-441 6246. Specialises in sale of picture features and news to European and South African press.

Press Association Ltd., The (1868), I. H. N. Yates (*General Manager*), C. Webb (*Editor-in-Chief*), R. C. Henry (*Financial Controller*) 85 Fleet Street, London, EC4P 4BE *T.* 01-353 7440. *T.A.* Press Association, London. Home News Agency: Teleprinter and viewdata news, photographs, features. Distributes world agencies' news in British Isles outside London.

Rann, Christopher, & Associates Pty. Ltd. (1977), *Proprietors:* C. F. Rann, J. M. Jose, 182 Melbourne Street, North Adelaide, South Australia, 5006. *T.* 08-267 2299. Former BBC, Guardian and CBS News foreign correspondents offering full range of professional PR, press releases, special newsletters, commercial intelligence, media monitoring. Major clients in Australia, Britain and Germany. Welcomes approaches from organisations requiring PR representation or press release distribution.

Reportage Bureau RBL. Philip Laszlo Kalevankatu 14 C, 00100 Helsinki-10, Finland. *T.* (9)0-640 522. *Cables:* Reportage Helsinki. *Telex:* 123949 rbl sf.

Republican Press (London), Suite 437-439 High Holborn House, 52-54 High Holborn, London WC1V 6RB *T.* 01-831 2965. *Telex:* 264461 Litalc G.

Reuters Limited, 85 Fleet Street, London, EC4P 4AJ *T.* 01-250 1122. *Telex:* 23222.

Rippon, Anton, Press Services, 45 Overdale Road, Derby DE3 6AU *T.* (0332) 769753. News, sport, feature and photo coverage of East Midlands.

St. Albans Crown Court News Agency, 134 Marsh Road, Luton, LU3 2NL *T.* (0582) 572222. *Telex:* 826634.

Sandesa News Agency, 23 Canal Row, Colombo 1, Sri Lanka. *Director:* Gamini Navaratne, B.SC.(ECON)LOND. Supplies—news, features, photographs and press cuttings to local and overseas newspapers and agencies.

Singer Communications Inc. (formerly **BP Singer Features, Inc.**). *Chairman:* Kurt Singer, 3164 Tyler Avenue, Anaheim, California, 92801. *T.* 714-527 5650. Use 25 features every week which are distributed to publications in 35 countries. Current needs for reprint rights (no originals): Profiles of famous people—1-3 parts; Men's fiction; Women's fiction (high standard only); Adventure features (which are not blood-dripping or over-sexed); Westerns—short stories and books; books published by reputable publishers. 'We accept only previously published material.' Interested in books for serial and book rights. World-wide syndication of cartoons, strips and interviews with celebrities.

Skye Agencies, Calum Mackenzie Neish, Portnalong, Isle of Skye. *T.* Portnalong (047 872) 272. *Telex:* 75317 Skpres G. News, features and picture agency for the Inner Hebrides and adjacent mainland (Skye and Lochalsh District).

Solo Syndication & Literary Agency Ltd. (1976), 8 Bouverie Street, London EC4Y 8BB *T.* 01-583 9372. *Telex:* 858623. *Chairman:* Don Short. World-wide syndication of newspaper features, photos, strips and book serialisations. Professional journalists only. *Commission:* 50/50. Agency represents the international syndication of the London Daily Mail group *The Sun,* London, the Guinness Book of Records strip cartoon, Guinnes Books, the Melbourne Herald group and *New Idea* magazine, Australia, the *Johannesburg Star* and Argus South African newspaper titles.

Southern Media Services, P.O. Box 140, Springwood NSW 2777, Australia *T.* (047) 514967. *Proprietors:* Nic van Oudtshoorn, Daphne van Oudtshoorn. Illustrated features (colour and black and white) to newspapers and magazines in Australasia and many parts of the world. Also stock colour library. Assignments (news and feature stories, photographs) accepted at moderate rates. Syndicates freelance features and photo features in Australia and abroad, but query before submitting. Commission 50% or by arrangement.

Swedish Features, Sweden, Ralåmbsvägen 17, S–105 15 Stockholm, Sweden. *T.* 8-738 10 00. *Telex:* 17480. *Managing Director:* Gustaf von Sydow. *Market:* Newspapers, magazines and weeklies in Sweden, Norway, Denmark and Finland, West Germany. *Syndicates:* High quality features of international appeal such as topical articles, photo-features, black and white and colour, women's features, short stories, serial novels, non-fiction stories and serials with strong human interest, popular science, cartoons, comic strips and TV features and TV personalities.

Syndication International, Ltd., 9 New Fetter Lane, London, EC4A 1AR *T.* 01-822 3823. Strips, features, news and feature photography, magazine articles and merchandising, etc.

Tass Agency, Room 205 (2nd FLoor), Communications House, 12-16 Gough Square, London, EC4A 3JH. General news service to USSR. *T.* 01-353 9831; economic and commercial news service to USSR. *T.* 01-353 2661. *Telex:* 24201.

Tauber, Peter, Press Agency (1950), 94 East End Road, London, N3 2SX *T.* 01-346 4165. *T.A.* Tauberpres N3. Regular syndication of exclusive interviews and human interest features to national newspapers and magazines in the U.K., U.S.A., Canada, Australia, South Africa, Japan and all countries of Western Europe. *Commission* 25%.

SYNDICATES, NEWS AND PRESS AGENCIES

TransAtlantic News Service, 7100 Hillside Avenue, Suite 304, Hollywood, California 90046. *T.* 213-874-1284. News and photo agency serving the British and Foreign press. Staffed by former Fleet Street reporters, TANS supplies entertainment news, features and columns from Hollywood, and topical news in general from California. Covers all Hollywood events and undertakes commissions and assignments in all fields. Candid photos of stars at major Hollywood events a speciality.

United Press International (UK), Ltd., News Division, 8 Bouverie Street, London, EC4Y 8BB *T.* 01-353 2282 and 5832.

Universal News Services Ltd., Communications House, Gough Square, Fleet Street, London, EC4P 4DP *T.* 01-353 5200. *Managing Director:* Alfred Geiringer.

World-Wide News Bureau, 309 Varick Street, Jersey City, N.J. 07302. *T.* 201-333 4660. *Editor/Manager:* Arejas Vitkauskas. Publishers' news of forthcoming or published books on any subjects. Buys old books on Communist defectors, spies, memoirs, diaries, factual fiction.

Yaffa Newspaper Service of New Zealand, P.O. Box 509, 31-35 Dixon Street, Wellington 1, New Zealand. *T.* 845-505 (after hours: 793-531). *T.A.* and *Cables:* Yaffaz, Wellington. *Telex:* NZ3859 Seek Yaffa.

Yaffa Syndicate Pty, Ltd., 432-6 Elizabeth Street, Surry Hills, Sydney, N.S.W. 2010. *Postal Address:* Box 606, G.P.O. Sydney, N.S.W. 2001. *T.* 699 7861. *Telex:* AA 121887 Yaffa.
Largest and oldest established Australian syndicate and literary agency.

POETRY PUBLISHING TODAY

JOHN MEDLIN
Publications Officer of The Poetry Society

Suddenly, poetry is popular. Hardly a market-leader, agreed, but nevertheless there has been a definite revival of interest in poets and poetry. The media take more notice of them, a brave handful of publishers maintain, and even extend, their poetry lists, and poets themselves have become more professional in gaining publicity and selling their books.

Publishers have taken the opportunity to effect a large-scale clear-out of old ways of publishing and promoting poetry. The days of the gentleman publisher content to subsidise a poetry list which makes no attempt to keep itself are gone. This gives new opportunities to aspiring poets as well as posing new problems. Certainly more poetry is being written, read and bought. And yet publishers are warier than ever of bringing out new books by new poets; many poetry magazines have closed in recent years and the small press scene is somnolent. The answer to this paradox is that much of this increased interest is centred on a handful of 'star' poets – Seamus Heaney, James Fenton, Craig Raine, Ted Hughes etc. – and it is *their* books which publishers are pushing, and it is *they* who get invited to give readings, interviews, appear on TV etc. There is, of course, a spin-off for less-established poets and newcomers, but the way to the top is as tough as ever.

MARKETS FOR POETRY

'Many are called but few are chosen . . .' No words could be more apt to the position of the aspiring poet. Whilst it is true that in recent years a few, a very few, poets have been plucked from obscurity and given the *cachet* of publication in book form by a reputable major firm, it is also true that many more now-established poets have had to serve a long and morale-sapping apprenticeship before finally achieving book publication. It is simply too expensive for publishers to take a chance on an unknown talent. So the first rule for the newcomer is to forget the publishers and establish a track record in the magazines.

MAGAZINES

Easier said than done. Many magazines were started in the heady days of the last poetry boom in the late sixties and early seventies. They are now set in their ways, often with a *coterie* of regular contributors which it is difficult to break into. Also, they are often one-man-bands. Their editors are now getting tired or developing new interests, and so they are folding. The handful that are left find conditions increasingly difficult. Worries about funding; printing, paper and postage costs; the difficulty of publicity without a budget; the sheer unrelenting slog of producing regular issues – perhaps it's surprising that so many magazines survive! There is an up-to-date list of the more well-established magazines at the end of this article. Poets can be fairly confident that having sent them their work it will be read, accepted or returned with reasonable efficiency.

The magazines and papers which publishers probably take most seriously when considering a poet's track record are *Agenda*, *Ambit*, *Encounter*, *Listener*, *Literary Review*, *London Magazine*, *London Review of Books*, *New Statesman*, *Observer*, *PN Review*, *Poetry Review*, *Stand* and the *Times Literary Supplement*. Some of these publish relatively few poems, but if you are serious about getting published these are the ones you will want to get to accept you.

Payment varies widely – certainly no one is going to get rich through publishing his poetry in magazines. The smaller magazines may well be able to afford no more than free copies in payment; the larger ones might pay between £10-£20 per poem. Payment is normally for one appearance only, copyright remains with the author and he is free to re-use the poem in anthologies or a subsequent book, although it is usual to include an acknowledgement of the place of first publication. Some poets send their work to so many places at once that the same poem ends up being used by more than one magazine. Nothing infuriates an editor more than finding that he has used work which has already appeared elsewhere, and he will be unlikely to look favourably at you again. Therefore, keep track of your poems and make sure that each one is on offer to only one magazine at a time.

It is astonishing how many people do not take the trouble to present themselves to their potential markets in a professional way, submitting ill-prepared, even handwritten mss, without the courtesy of enclosing return postage. In submitting work the following straightforward rules should always be observed:

1. *Study your market*. Familiarise yourself with magazines you intend to submit work to. The biggest problem for most editors is the mass of unsuitable material they have to plough through. It is pointless submitting a short, inspirational poem which might be acceptable to a traditional women's magazine to, say, the *Times Literary Supplement* or *New Statesman*.

2. Type your poems one to a page using double-spacing and with your name and address also typed on each page. *Handwritten mss are not acceptable to editors*.

3. Only send about six poems in each submission. If you send your life's work it will probably be returned unread. There are, after all, only 24 hours in an editor's day, just like yours.

4. Always keep copies of your poems: mss *do* go astray either in the post or in the best-run of offices.

5. Keep your covering letter short and to the point. Your views on poetry, politics, morals or your life history are irrelevant. If an editor wants to know more about you, he will ask.

6. *Always* include a suitably-sized, stamped, self-addressed envelope for return of unwanted work. If you submit to overseas publications you should enclose sufficient international reply coupons – UK stamps, money or cheques for small amounts are of no use to an overseas publication. Postage costs are a major factor in running a magazine: *if you don't enclose sufficient postage your mss are unlikely to be returned*.

7. Allow the editor plenty of time to make his decision on your work. He is as overworked as you are: it is not unusual for a reply to take 2 to 3 months. If you feel you must jog his memory, write only the briefest of letters. Getting published involves bags of patience.

8. If an editor rejects your work don't bombard him with abusive letters demanding explanations. They'll only end up in his rubbish bin and waste your time. If your poems are returned by one magazine get them off smartly to another.

No less a figure than Craig Raine recently wrote in the Poetry Book Society *Bulletin* of the number of rejection slips he garnered in long years of trying before finally getting a poem published. *Don't feel self-pity*. There are far too many poets chasing all too few publishing opportunities. So get on with it or get out of it.

SMALL PRESSES

Small presses produce everything from cyclostyled and stapled pamphlets to properly bound books. They are traditionally the places where poets make their names preliminary to the final step of publication by one of the major publishing houses. It is possible to get your work accepted by a small press without first going through the discipline of magazine publication: after all, small press editors are in business to back their judgements – sometimes getting it right, sometimes disastrously wrong. But it is increasingly unlikely that a small press will take a complete unknown onto its list. As with poetry magazines, this is largely to do with fatigue and financial problems.

It is extremely difficult to recover the costs of producing a small press book or pamphlet, even if the entire print run were to be sold – which is very rare. Hence, if the enthusiasm of a small press owner/editor wanes and if his sources of funding dry up (since these sources are mainly from public funds, they are drying up very quickly) he is left in the unenviable position of facing a major financial risk if he takes a new book on board. Not surprisingly, many small presses are in semi-hibernation, content to sell from their backlists as best they can. If a small press *is* able to publish further volumes they are more likely to be follow-up collections by authors already on the list rather than new work accepted from an unknown.

There are, of course, exceptions to the above, and the trick for the aspiring poet is to be persistent enough, and to know his market well enough, so that when an owner/editor feels just a little more hopeful or has some spare cash, *his* mss comes tumbling through the editor's letter box the same day!

For information on small presses it is worth contacting the Association of Little Presses, 89A Petherton Road, London N5 2QT. *Always* enclose a large SAE. A comprehensive, regularly updated Address List of Small Presses and Little Magazines in the UK and Ireland is published by Oriel Bookshop, 53 Charles Street, Cardiff CF1 4ED price 75p (by post £1.00).

MAJOR TRADE PUBLISHERS

Compared to the situation of ten or fifteen years ago, the outlook for poetry publishing measured by the number of major publishers who maintain poetry lists, as opposed to keeping the odd title or two in print, is bleak. The market is dominated by three or four large firms, with two or three independents following on. Faber alone accounts for over 21% of total poetry sales in the UK (although much of this is due to its exceptionally strong backlist).

However, all is not lost. Those companies which have maintained their poetry lists – especially Faber, Oxford University Press, Secker & Warburg and Chatto & Windus – are experiencing a new growth in sales and are prepared to put at least *some* time and money into encouraging this. Small independent firms such as Carcanet and Bloodaxe have grown enormously over the past few years from the smallest of small press beginnings. They are still very dependent on Arts Council or Regional Arts Association funding and the situation may change dramatically for the worse in the next few years. Nevertheless it is encouraging that some trade publishers in the UK are still committed to working hard for poetry.

The drawback for new or unknown poets is that, because of the need to recoup their investment of time and money, publishers are extremely wary of taking on board anyone who does not have a track record in the reputable magazines or, increasingly, can not show that he knows how to publicise himself effectively, especially through readings. After all, it's such activity *after* publication which may well account for most of the sales: so publishers these days take a close look at their poets from the marketing angle.

A very effective 'half-way house' in recent years has been the *Poetry Introduction* series published by Faber. This brings together in a single volume five or six poets not previously published in book form. Many of them have gone on to full solo collections with various firms. Chatto & Windus introduced their own version of the idea—*New Chatto Poets* in 1986.

OTHER PUBLISHERS

There has also been a major growth recently in what is known as 'alternative publishing'. Indeed, it is the alternative publishers who have taken over much of the small presses' traditional role. The two main areas of growth have been in Black publishing and feminist publishing.

A number of firms and co-operatives now exist to publish Black poetry, and work of the highest quality, such as that of Linton Kwesi Johnson, has emerged. Several bookshops in London and other large cities specialize in Black writing and a visit to one of them, such as the New Beacon Bookshop, 76 Stroud Green Road, London N4 3EN, is well worthwhile to get names and addresses of current publishers and magazines. Many bookshops will provide booklists on receipt of a SAE.

The boom in feminist writing has produced several well-established publishers, chief of which is Virago, now with a total turnover of over £1 million p.a. It introduced its own poetry list in 1984. Shops such as Sisterwrite, 190 Upper Street, London N1 or Virago's own shop (Virago Bookshop, 34 Southampton Street, London WC2) are mines of information on current feminist publishing firms and magazines.

Street poetry and cabaret poetry are less well-served by publishing houses. Much material tends to be available only in small, often self-published, pamphlets or fanzines. Some publishers have dipped a toe in the water though – Faber with its *Hard Lines* anthologies, Pluto Press with its *Apples & Snakes* anthology.

There may not be a lot of money around in these new areas of publishing but there is undeniably a lot of excitement and commitment. Obviously, poets whose work falls into these areas will be better off approaching one of these specialist publishers rather than trying to convert the major trade publishers who are more cautious and inhibited in their ideas.

VANITY PUBLISHING

Attention is drawn to the separate article on vanity publishing. Perhaps it is worth saying here that, apart from the damage to his pocket, a poet will severely damage his reputation, or his chances of one, if his work appears from a vanity press. If, after every effort on your part, only a vanity publisher is prepared to accept your poems you would be better advised, both for your peace of mind and your bank balance, to give up trying to get published rather than undergo the inevitable frustrations and disappointments of dealing with the vanity press.

OTHER MARKETS AND ORGANISATIONS

Poetry competitions have been a feature of the poetry world for some years although they have now lost some of their initial impact. There is, though, still a lot of publicity and money to be won. Apart from anything else it is tremendously encouraging to find that a judge has chose *your* poem out of thousands of jostling hopefuls. Competitions come in every size from small, such as one organised by a local writers group, to national, such as the Poetry Society's prestigious annual National Poetry Competition which awards over £4,500 in prizes each year. Many of its winners have been snapped up by major publishers. Details of the smaller competitions are often available from your local or Regional Arts Association, or your local library. The major competitions advertise, and distribute their entry forms, nationally.

The development of local radio – both BBC and Independent – has been a boon to poets. Obviously, newcomers are not going to gain easy access to the flagship arts programmes of the BBC national networks; but local radio through its arts and special interest programmes offers ground worth cultivating by poets.

Again, local and Regional Arts Associations often publish their own news-sheets or magazines. They will sometimes print poems and/or carry reviews of new poetry books. They should be able to provide details of poetry groups and readings in your area. If they cannot, try your local library. The library is an information resource often ignored by poets. It will normally have details of poetry groups and workshops in your neighbourhood; will often have entry forms for the larger poetry competitions and, through its poetry shelves, will enable you to familiarise yourself with the market if you are thinking of submitting work to a publisher.

Local poetry groups and workshops can be a great help to a poet in improving his craft and giving him confidence in reading and talking about his work to an audience. A surprising number of them publish their own anthologies or magazines and this is as good a way as any to experience the thrill of seeing your first poem in print.

If you feel you would benefit from more concentrated guidance then you should consider attending one of the Arvon Foundation's popular and professionally-run poetry writing courses. Details are available (send SAE) from the two Arvon centres at Lumb Bank, Hebden Bridge, West Yorkshire and Totleigh Barton, Sheepwash, near Beauworthy, Devon.

Many local authorities and institutes of further education run day and evening classes in creative writing, including poetry. Your local library should have details. For those living in London the annual publication *Floodlight*, which lists all day and evening classes in the London area, is invaluable.

Your local newspaper is always on the lookout for good copy, and your poems – or at least information on your poetic activities – may be just what it's after. Of course, they may not be! But as with any other branch of writing it's up to you to 'sell' yourself.

There are two national organisations of interest to poets. The first is the Poetry Society which provides a wide range of activities and services. These include a bookshop and mail order service able to supply most contemporary poetry from stock, organising scores of readings each year at its headquarters, the National Poetry Centre, in London and helping to fund many readings elsewhere, running a critical service which provides professional advice to aspiring poets, publishing an invaluable list of practical books for poets, administering various competitions and awards and publishing the quarterly *Poetry Review* and the Poetry Society *Newsletter*. Fuller details are available from the Membership Dept., Poetry Society, 21 Earls Court Square, London, SW5 9DE.

The second is the Poetry Book Society which, as Britain's only poetry book club, is a unique way to keep up with contemporary poetry and its developing trends. All books offered by the PBS to its membership are available at discount. It also publishes the informative *PBS Bulletin* and an annual anthology of new poetry, available free to its members. Details can be obtained from the Membership Dept., Poetry Book Society, 21 Earls Court Square, London, SW5 9DE. *Note:* Although the Poetry Society and Poetry Book Society operate from the same address they are separate organisations. Correspondence, and especially *remittances*, to both organisations should not be combined.

Finally, mention should be made of the services provided by two specialist libraries: the Arts Council Poetry Library and the Scottish Poetry Library. The Arts Council Poetry Library has a first-rate collection of post-war British poetry, is well-stocked with anthologies and subscribes to all of the leading poetry magazines. It also publishes regularly updated free information lists of poetry groups and workshops in London, poetry competitions, magazines, etc. For those who cannot visit its premises in London it operates a book borrowing scheme by post. Details are available from the Librarian, Arts Council Poetry Library, 105 Piccadilly, London, W1V 0AU.

UNITED KINGDOM 121

The Scottish Poetry Library runs on similar lines, although obviously its emphasis is on contemporary Scottish poetry. Details can be obtained from the Librarian, Scottish Poetry Library, Tweedale Court, 14 High Street, Edinburgh EH1 1TE.

BRITISH MARKET FOR POETRY

MAGAZINES

Agenda
Ambit
Anglo-Welsh Review
Argo
Country Life
Countryman
Critical Quarterly
Cyphers (Ire)
Encounter
Envoi
Honest Ulsterman (Ire)
Iron
Listener
Literary Review
Litmus
London Magazine
New Statesman
Observer
Orbis
Other Poetry
Outposts
PN Review
Poetry Durham
Poetry Ireland
Poetry Nottingham
Poetry Now
Poetry Review
Poetry Wales
Rialto
Spectator
Stand
Times Literary
  Supplement
Verse
Writing Women

PUBLISHERS (only those actively prepared to look at new mss)

Allison & Busby
Anvil Press
Blackstaff Press (Ire)
Bloodaxe Books
Canongate Publishing
Jonathan Cape Ltd.
Carcanet Press
Harry Chambers/
  Peterloo Poets
Chatto & Windus
Rex Collings Ltd.
Dolmen Press (Ire)
Faber & Faber
Gallery Press (Ire)
Hippopotamus Press
New Beacon Books
Oxford University
  Press
Poetry Wales Press
Raven Arts (Ire)
Redcliffe Press Ltd.
Rivelin-Grapheme
  Press
Runa Press (Ire)
Salamander Press
Secker & Warburg
Taxus Press
Virago
Women's Press

Further reading:

Michael Baldwin. *The Way to Write Poetry.* Elm Tree Books, 1982. pbk. £4.95

Marjorie Boulton. *Anatomy of Poetry.* Routledge & Kegan Paul, 1982, 2nd ed. rev. pbk. £5.95.

Peter Finch. *How to Write Poetry.* Allison & Busby, 1985. pbk. £3.95

G.S. Fraser. *Metre, Rhyme and Free Verse.* Methuen, 1970. pbk. £2.75.

Frances Stillman. *Poet's Manual and Rhyming Dictionary.* Thames & Hudson, 1972. pbk. £4.50.

book publishers

WRITING BOOKS

Care should be taken when submitting manuscripts to book publishers. A suitable publisher should be chosen, by a study of his list of publications or an examination in the bookshops of the type of books in which he specialises. It is a waste of time and money to send the typescript of a novel to a publisher who publishes no fiction, or poetry to one who publishes no verse, though all too often this is done. A preliminary letter is appreciated by most publishers, and this should outline the nature and extent of the typescript and enquire whether the publisher would be prepared to read it (writers have been known to send out such letters of enquiry in duplicated form, an approach not calculated to stimulate a publisher's interest). It is desirable to enclose the cost of return postage when submitting the typescript and finally it must be understood that although every reasonable care is taken of material in the Publishers' possession, responsibility cannot be accepted for any loss or damage thereto.

Authors are strongly advised not to pay for the publication of their work. If a MS. is worth publishing, a reputable publisher will undertake its publication at his own expense, except possibly for works of an academic nature. In this connection attention is called to the paragraphs on **Vanity Publishing** and to the articles on **Publishers' Agreements**.

UNITED KINGDOM

*Members of the Publishers' Association

*__Abacus Press__ (1970), Abacus House, Speldhurst Road, Tunbridge Wells, Kent, TN4 0HU *T.* (0892) 29783 and 27237. *Cables:* Abacus, Tunbridgewells. *Telex:* 877440 Pburns G ref Abacus. *Director:* N. Jayasekera (Chairman). *General Manager:* Janet White; *Publishing Manager:* Mark Bicknell.
Scientific, technical with special emphasis on the applications of information technology, expert systems/artificial intelligence/knowledge engineering, cybernetics, systems science, energy and engineering science and mathematical chemistry. Some titles in science and mathematics plus small specialised trade list.

*__Abelard-Schuman, Ltd.__ A subsidiary company of **Blackie Children's Books**.

*Abson Books (1970), Abson, Wick, Bristol, BS15 5TT *T.* (0275-82) 2446. *Partners:* Anthea Bickerton, Pat McCormack.
English speaking glossaries, guides, West Region. Literary puzzle books. No fiction.

*Academic Press Inc. (London), Ltd., 24-28 Oval Road, London, NW1 7DX *T.* 01-267 4466. *Telex:* 25775 Acpres G. *Managing Director:* Joan M. Fujimoto.

*Academy Editions (1967), 7-8 Holland Street, Kensington, London, W8 4NA *T.* 01-937 6996. *Editorial:* 42 Leinster Gardens, London, W2 *T.* 01-402 2141. *Telex:* 896928 Academ G. *Director:* Dr. A. C. Papadakis.
Art, architecture, crafts, design, typography, photography, fashion, urbanism.

Actinic Press, Ltd., 311 Worcester Road, Malvern, Worcs. WR14 1AN *T.* (06845) 65045.
Chiropody and medical science.

*Addison-Wesley Publishers Ltd. (1970), Finchampstead Road, Wokingham, Berks RG11 2NZ *T.* (0734) 794000. *Telex:* 846136. *Directors:* D. Hammonds (USA), P. I. Hoenigsberg (U.K.), W. R. Stone (USA), N. W. White (U.K.).
Educational, pure and applied sciences, computing, software, business studies.

*Adlard Coles, Ltd. —see **William Collins, PLC.**

Albyn Press Ltd., 29 Forth Street, Edinburgh, EH1 3LE *T.* 031-556 9339, and 2 Caversham Street, London SW3 *T.* 01-351 4995.
Books on Scottish subjects.

*Alison Press, The, 5 Harley Gardens, London, SW10 9SW *T.* 01-373 1924 or 437 2075. *Telex:* 267613 Secker G. *T.A.* Psophidian, London, W1. *Director:* Barley Alison. An associate of **Secker & Warburg Ltd.**
Fiction, belles-lettres, biography.

Allan (Ian) Ltd., Coombelands House, Addlestone, Weybridge KT15 1HY *T.* (0932) 58511. *Telex:* 929806 Iallan G.
Transport—Railways, aircraft, shipping, road, naval and military history and reference books and magazines, travel; no fiction.

Allan (Philip) Publishers Ltd. (1973), Market Place, Deddington, Oxford, OX5 4SE *T.* Deddington (0869) 38652. *Directors:* I. P. G. Allan, J. F. Allan, S. M. E. Allan, Professor B. V. Carsberg, Professor D. E. W. Laidler, Professor M. H. Peston.
Economics, accounting and business studies.

*Allen (George) & Unwin Publishers Ltd., —see **Unwin Hyman Ltd.**

*Allen (J. A.) & Co. Ltd. (1926), 1 Lower Grosvenor Place, Buckingham Palace Road, London, SW1W 0EL. *T.* 01-834 5606 and 0090. *T.A.* Allenbooks, London. *Telex:* 28905 ref. 3810. *Managing Director:* Joseph A. Allen.
Specialist publishers of books on the horse, equestrianism including bloodstock breeding, racing, polo, dressage, horse care, veterinary and farriery.

Allen (W. H.) & Co., PLC, 44 Hill Street, London, W1X 8LB *T.* 01-493 6777. *Telex:* 28117 Whalen G. *Managing Director:* Bob Tanner, *Sales Director:* Ray Mudie.
Art, belles-lettres, biography and memoirs, current affairs, educational, fiction, films, general, history, humour, practical handbooks, reference, sociology, television, theatre and ballet, travel.

Allison & Busby, Ltd. (1968), 6A Noel Street, London, W1V 3RB *T.* 01-734 1498. *Directors:* Clive Allison, Margaret Busby, Bill Swainson, James Fraser.
Art, belles-lettres, biography and memoirs, current affairs, economics, fiction, general, history, politics, sociology, translations, poetry, children's.

Alphabooks (1978), Alpha House, South Street, Sherborne, Dorset, DT9 3LU *T.* (0935) 814944. *Telex:* 46534 Alphab G. *Directors:* Anthony Birks-Hay (Managing), Leslie Birks-Hay.
Ceramics, specialist horticulture, beekeeping, folk art, architecture, crafts.

Andersen Press Ltd. (1976), Brookmount House, 62-65 Chandos Place, Covent Garden, London WC2N 4NW *T.* 01-240 3411. *Telex:* 261212 Lit Ldn G. *T.A.* Literarius, London. *Directors:* Klaus Flugge, J. Flugge, P. Durrance.
Children's picture books and fiction. International coproductions.

***Angus and Robertson (U.K.) Ltd.**, 16 Golden Square, London, W1R 4BN *T.* 01-437 9602. *Cables:* Ausboko, London, W1. *Telex:* 897284 Arpub G. *Fax:* 01-434 2080.
Biography, children's books (fiction, non-fiction), cinema, sports, crafts, travel, humour, leisure, literature, health and beauty, Australia.

Anvil Press Poetry (1968), 69 King George Street, London SE10 8PX *T.* 01-858 2946. *Directors:* L. W. Carp, Peter Jay, Dieter Pevsner, Caroline Root, Julia Sterland.
Poetry.

Apple Press (1984), 293 Grays Inn Road, London WC1X 8QF *T.* 01-837 9604. *Telex:* 261396 Atlas G. *Directors:* Warren Bertram, Ashley Bertram, Patsy Bertram.
Leisure, domestic and craft pursuits; cookery, gardening, fitness.

***Aquarian Press Ltd, The** (1952), Denington Estate, Wellingborough, Northants, NN8 2RQ *T.* (0933) 76031. *Telex:* 311072 Thopub G. *Fax:* (0933) 72800. *Directors:* J. A. Young, D. J. Young, M. A. Cox.
Astrology, magic and occultism, the Western mystery tradition, philosophy, parapsychology and the paranormal, religion and mysticism, tarot and divination, character analysis techniques, Oriental religion and philosophies, folklore and mythology. **Crucible** imprint.

Architectural Press Ltd. (1902), 9 Queen Anne's Gate, London, SW1H 9BY *T.* 01-222 4333. *Telex:* 8953505 Archip G.
Architecture, the environment, planning, townscape, building technology; general.

Arena—see **Arrow Books Ltd.**

Argus Books Ltd., 1 Golden Square, London W1R 3AB *T.* 01-437 0626. *Telex:* 8811896 Asp G.
Model engineering, general modelling, woodworking, hobbies, maritime, railways, military, crafts, clocks, computing, electronics, video. **Amateur Winemaker** imprint. Amateur winemaking, home brewing.

Argus Specialist Publications—see **Argus Books Ltd.**

Ariel Books (1982), 35 Marylebone High Street, London W1M 4AA. *T.* 01-580 5577. *T.A.* Broadcasts London. *Telex:* 265781. Paperback imprint of **BBC Publications**.
Autobiography, cookery, antiques, self-help, science, women's interest, political science, travel.

***Armada** paperbacks—see **William Collins, PLC.**

***Arms and Armour Press** (1966), 2-6 Hampstead High Street, London, NW3 1QQ. *T.* 01-794 0922-6. *Telex:* 8951899 Armsbk G. *Cables:* Armsbooks London NW3. *Directors:* R. B. Erven (Chairman), R. Dymott, M. R. Chapman, D. Gibbons.
Military subjects (tanks, ships, aircraft, small arms, etc.).

*Arnold (E. J.) & Son Ltd. (1863), Parkside Lane, Dewsbury Road, Leeds LS11 5TD. *T.* Leeds (0532) 772112. *Telex:* 556347. *Directors:* C. Bundy (Group Managing), G. Newton (Marketing), S. E. Sharp (Publishing Director, Arnold Wheaton).
Educational (primary and secondary).

*Arnold (Edward) (Publishers), Ltd., 41-42 Bedford Square, London, WC1B 3DQ *T.* 01-637 7161. *T.A.* Scholarly, London, WC1. *Telex:* 265806 Edward G. *Founded* by Edward Arnold in 1890. *Directors:* E. A. Hamilton, B. W. Bennett, P. J. Price, M. Husk, J. G. Martyn, C. N. E. McDowall, J. E. Peck, G. N. Davies, M. W. Soper, J. W. Wallace.
Educational books in all subjects (secondary, technical, university), English language teaching, advanced works in humanities, social sciences, pure and applied science, and medicine; journals.

*Arrow Books Ltd., Brookmount House, 62-65 Chandos Place, Covent Garden, London WC2N 4NW *T.* 01-240 3411. *Telex:* 26122 Lit Ldn G. *Directors:* A. J. V. Cheetham (Chairman), C. Goulden (Managing), R. M. F. Cheetham, P. Lavery, S. A. Lenaerts, J. M. Mottram, G. Rebuck, P. C. K. Roche, R. L. Smith, R. Tucker. A division of **Century Hutchinson Ltd.**
Paperback publications, fiction and non-fiction, Hamlyn, Arena, Zenith, Century Arrow. Sparrow and Beaver (children's).

Art Trade Press Ltd., 9 Brockhampton Road, Havant, Hampshire, PO9 1NU *T.* (0705) 484943. Publishers of *Who's Who in Art*.

Ashgrove Press Ltd., (1980), 19 Circus Place, Bath, Avon, BA1 2PW *T.* (0225) 25539. *Directors:* Robin Campbell (Managing), William Allberry, Keith Nelson.
Health, healing and diet, parapsychology, countryside, local history and guidebooks, topical and controversial, general.

Aslib (The Association for Information Management) (1924), 26-27 Boswell Street, London WC1N 3JZ *T.* 01-430 2671. *Telex:* 23667. (For further details see entry under **Societies, Associations and Clubs.**)

*Associated Book Publishers (UK) Limited, 11 New Fetter Lane, London, EC4P 4EE. *T.* 01-583 9855. *Telex:* 263398. *T.A.* Elegiacs London EC4 with the following subsidiary companies:
Chapman & Hall Ltd., Current Law Publishers Ltd., E. & F. N. Spon Ltd., Eyre & Spottiswoode (Publishers) Ltd., W. Green & Son Ltd., Methuen & Company Ltd., Methuen Children's Books Ltd., Methuen Educational Ltd., Methuen London Ltd. Momentum Licensing Ltd., Police Review Publishing Co. Ltd., Routledge & Kegan Paul PLC, Stevens & Son Ltd., Sweet & Maxwell Ltd., Sweet & Maxwell, Spon (Booksellers) Ltd., Tavistock Publications Ltd. *Directors:* M. R. Turner (Chairman), C. H. Falkus (Vice-Chairman), A. R. Miles (Managing), B. M. Cardy, A. F. J. Crosthwaite Eyre, C. D. O. Evans, R. D. Green, C. C. W. Hammick, J. Jenkins, J. Naylor, A. Prideaux, D. Richards, D. G. Sampson, R. Stileman (Assistant Managing), G. Strachan, J. Potter, D. Ross, D. Silk.

Associated University Presses—see **Golden Cockerel Press.**

*Athlone Press Ltd., The (1949), 44 Bedford Row, London, WC1R 4LY *T.* 01-405 9836-7. *Telex:* 261507 ref. 1334. *Directors:* Brian Southam, Doris Southam, Clive Bingley.
Archaeology, architecture, art, economics, history, medical, music, Japan, oriental, philosophy, politics, psychology, religion, science, sociology, zoology.

Aurum Press Ltd. (1977), 33 Museum Street, London, WC1A 1LD. *T.* 01-631 4596. *Telex:* 299557 Aurum X. *Directors:* Timothy J. M. Chadwick, Michael Haggiag.
General, large format art and photographic books, travel, children's books.

Babani, Bernard (Publishing) Ltd., The Grampians, Shepherds Bush Road, London, W6 7NF *T.* 01-603 2581 and 7296. *Directors:* S. Babani, M. H. Babani, B.Sc.(ENG.).
Practical handbooks on radio, electronics and computing.

Bagster (Samuel) & Sons, Ltd. Imprint of **Marshall, Pickering Holdings Ltd.**

*****Bailey Bros. & Swinfen, Ltd.,** Warner House, Folkestone, Kent, CT19 6PH *T.* Folkestone (0303) 56501-8. *T.A.* Forenbuks, Folkestone. *Telex:* 96328.
Reference, science, general.

*****Baillière Tindall** (1826), 1 St. Anne's Road, Eastbourne, East Sussex, BN21 3UN. *T.* (0323) 638221. *T.A.* Volumists, Eastbourne. *Telex:* 877503 Volmst. *Managing Director:* Robert Kiernan, *Publishing Director:* David Inglis.
Medical, veterinary, nursing, pharmaceutical books and journals. Agents for Iowa State University Press.

Baker (Howard) Press, Ltd., 27A Arterberry Road, Wimbledon, London, SW20 8AF *T.* 01-947 5482. *Cables:* Bakerbook, London. *Directors:* W. Howard Baker, I. T. Baker, H. C. I. D. Baker, J. K. Montgomerie. *Company Secretary:* D. R. Ridgwell, A.C.I.S.
General fiction and non-fiction, political science, autobiography, biography, reference, specialist facsimile editions. Preliminary letter and synopsis with S.A.E. required before submitting unsolicited MSS.

*****Baker (John) Publishers, Ltd.,** an imprint of **A. & C. Black, plc.**

*****Bantam** paperbacks—see **Transworld Publishers Ltd.**

*****Bantam Press**—see **Transworld Publishers Ltd.**

*****Barker (Arthur), Ltd.,** 91 Clapham High Street, London, SW4 7TA *T.* 01-622 9933. *Telex:* 918066 Wpnab G. *Chairman:* Lord Weidenfeld. *Deputy Chairman:* Mark Collins. *Directors:* David Roberts (Managing), John Curtis, Richard Hussey, Rosalind Lewis, Bud Pauling, Victoria Petrie-Hay, Juliet Gardiner.
Sport, humour.

Barrie & Jenkins Ltd, Brookmount House, 62-65 Chandos Place, Covent Garden, London WC2N 4NW *T.* 01-240 3411. *Telex:* 261212 Lit Ldn G. *Directors:* A. J. V. Cheetham (Chairman), P. C. K. Roche (Managing), J. M. Mottram. An imprint of **Century Hutchinson Ltd.**
Art, antiques and collecting, shooting and rural subjects, theatre.

*****Bartholomew (John) & Son, Ltd.** (1826), 12 Duncan Street, Edinburgh, EH9 1TA *T.* 031-667 9341. *Telex:* 728134 Barts G. Cartographers, printers and publishers.
Maps, atlases and non-fiction leisure books.

*****Batsford (B. T.), Ltd.** (1843), 4 Fitzhardinge Street, London, W1H 0AH *T.* 01-486 8484. *Telex:* 943763 Crocom G ref Bat. *Directors:* A. G. Cox, Peter Kemmis Betty, Roger Huggins, Alan Finlay, Robert Beard, Timothy Auger.
Art, crafts and needlecraft, architecture, chess, costume, film and horticulture, countryside and travel, general leisure, education (secondary, technical, university).

BBC Publications, 35 Marylebone High Street, London, W1M 4AA *T.* 01-580 5577. *T.A.* Broadcasts, London. *Telex:* 265781.
Publications related to television and radio programmes.

Beaver Books—see **Arrow Books Ltd.**

*****Bedford Square Press, National Council for Voluntary Organisations,** 26 Bedford Square, London, WC1B 3HU *T.* 01-636 4066.

Social planning and policy studies, social welfare, welfare economics, community action, training, urban and rural resources. Reference books and practical guides. All publications reflect the interests and diversity of the voluntary sector.

Belitha Press Ltd. (1980), 31 Newington Green, London N16 9PU. *T.* 01-241 5566. *Telex:* 946240 Cweasy G Ref 19001760. *Directors:* Martin Pick, Treld Bicknell, Richard Hayes, Rachel Pick (non-executive), Ronald Ridout (non-executive). Children's books, mostly published in series on an international co-edition basis, books about children, and general books on Asia, preferably with potential for television tie-ins. Associated film production company Inner Eye Ltd. Sponsorship enquiries welcome.

*****Bell & Hyman Ltd.**—see **Unwin Hyman Ltd.**

*****Benn (Ernest) Ltd.**—see **A. & C. Black plc.**

Berkswell Publishing Co. Ltd., Berkswell Press, Berkswell Books (1974), 11 Rathbone Place, London W1P 1DE. *T.* 01-580 8928. *Directors:* John Stidolph (Chairman and Managing), Susan Abbott.
Royalty, heritage, sport.

Bible Society, Publishing Division, Stonehill Green, Westlea Down, Swindon, SN5 7DG *T.* (0793) 617381 *Telex:* 44283 Bibles G. *Publishing Director:* Dennis Napier.
Bibles, testaments, portions and selections in English and over 200 other languages; also books on use of Bible for personal, education, church situations.

*****Bingley (Clive), Ltd.** (1965), 7 Ridgmount Street, London WC1E 7AE. *T.* 01-636 7543.
Librarianship, information work, education, music, reference books, library catalogues.

Black (A. & C.) plc. (1807), 35 Bedford Row, London, WC1R 4JH *T.* 01-242 0946. *T.A.* Biblos, London, WC1. *Telex:* 32524 ACBLAC. *Hon. Life President:* A. A. G. Black (great-grandson of founder), *Directors:* Charles Black (Chairman and Joint Managing), David Gadsby (Joint Managing), Leonard Brown, William Still (Secretary). Proprietors of A. & C. Black (Publishers) Ltd., John Baker (Publishers) Ltd., Ernest Benn Ltd, The Dacre Press, F. Lewis (Publishers) Ltd., *q.v.* Acquired (1983) the publishing assets of E.P. Publishing Ltd.

*****Black (A. & C.) (Publishers) Ltd.** (1978), 35 Bedford Row, London, WC1R 4JH *T.* 01-242 0946. *T.A.* Biblos, London, WC1. *Telex:* 32524 ACBLAC. *Directors:* Charles Black, David Gadsby, Leonard Brown, William Still, Paul White, Paul Langridge, Jill Coleman. A subsidiary of **A. & C. Black plc.**
Children's and educational books, including music, for 3-15 years, arts and crafts, calligraphy, chess, collectors' guides, dictionaries, drama (*New Mermaid* series), drawing and painting, fishing, history, natural history, reference, sport, theatre, travel (*Blue Guides*), Autobooks. Publishers of *Who's Who* since 1897.

*****Black Swan** paperbacks—see **Transworld Publishers Ltd.**

*****Blackie & Son, Ltd.** (1809), Bishopbriggs, Glasgow, G64 2NZ. *T.* 041-772 2311. *T.A.* Blackie, Glasgow. *Telex:* 777283 Blacki G. London Office: 7 Leicester Place, London, WC2H 7BP *T.* 01-734 7521. *Directors:* J. W. G. Blackie, R. M. Miller (Chairman and Managing), Alexander D. Mitchell, Dr. A. Graeme Mackintosh, A. Rosemary Wands.
Educational (infant, primary, secondary); children's books, (fiction and non-fiction for all ages); professional, reference and text books (biological sciences, earth sciences, chemistry, food technology, engineering, physics, mathematics, business administration).

Blackie Children's Books, 7 Leicester Place, London WC2H 7BP *T.* 01-734 7521. *Telex:* 777283 Blacki G. *Directors:* R. M. Miller, A. D. Mitchell. *Children's Publisher:* Martin West.
Children's books, novelty, picture, young fiction, non-fiction.

Blackwell (Basil), Ltd. (1922), 108 Cowley Road, Oxford, OX4 1JF *T.* Oxford (0865) 722146. *Telex:* 837022. *Directors:* Nigel Blackwell (Chairman), David Martin (Managing), Sir John Brown, Julian Blackwell, Michael Holmes, Per Saugman, John Davey, Norman Drake, Ray Addicott, Terry Collins, James Nash, René Olivieri, Michael Hay.
Classical studies, economics, education, geography, history, industrial relations, linguistics, literature and criticism, modern languages, and philology, politics, psychology, social anthropology, social policy and administration, sociology, theology, business studies, law.

Blackwell Scientific Publications Ltd. (1939), Osney Mead, Oxford, OX2 0EL, 8 John Street, London WC1N 2ES, 23 Ainslie Place, Edinburgh, EH3 6AJ, 107 Barry Street, Carlton, Victoria, Australia 3053, 52 Beacon Street, Boston, Massachusetts 02108, USA., 667 Lytton Avenue, Palo Alto, California 94301, USA. *T.* Oxford (0865) 240201, Edinburgh 031-226 7232 and London 01-404 4101. *Telex:* 83355 Medbok G. *Cables:* Research, Oxford. *Directors:* Per Saugman, Keith Bowker, Nigel Palmer, Peter Pleasance, John Robson, Robert Campbell, Nigel Blackwell, Peter Saugman, Oluf Møller.
Medicine, nursing, dentistry, veterinary medicine, life sciences, earth sciences, computer science and chemistry.

Blandford Press Ltd., Link House, West Street, Poole, Dorset, BH15 1LL *T.* Poole (0202) 671171. *Telex:* 418304 Linkho G. *Fax:* (0202) 671171 ext. 250 (day); (0202) 670201 (night). *Directors:* R. B. Erven (Chairman and Managing), M. R. Chapman, G. L. Charters, C. P. Lloyd, J. Newth.
Art, educational (infants, primary, secondary, technical), crafts, gardening, history, hobbies, juvenile, militaria, music, natural history, practical handbooks, religion, transport, humour.

Blond, Anthony. An imprint of **Muller, Blond & White Ltd.**

Blond & Briggs, Ltd. An imprint of **Muller, Blond & White Ltd.**

Bloodaxe Books Ltd (1978), P.O. Box 1SN, Newcastle upon Tyne NE99 1SN *T.* 091-232 5988 *Directors:* Neil Astley, Simon Thirsk.
Poetry, fiction, drama, literary criticism.

Bodley Head, Ltd., The (1887), 32 Bedford Square, London WC1B 3EL *T.* 01-631 4434. *Telex:* 299080 Cvbcse G. *President:* Sir Hugh Greene, K.C.M.G., O.B.E. *Directors:* Max Reinhardt (Chairman), David Machin (Managing), James Michie, Quentin Hockliffe, Margaret Clark (Children's Editorial), Jill Black, Chris Holifield (Adult Publishing), Guido Waldman, Sue Curnow. Proprietors of Hollis and Carter, Putnam & Co. Ltd. Distributors for **The Nonesuch Press,** *q.v.*
Biography and memoirs, children's books (fiction, non-fiction, picture), current affairs, economics, essays, fiction, films, history, sociology, travel.

Bowker (UK), R. R., Ltd. A division of the **Butterworth Group**, Borough Green, Sevenoaks, Kent TN15 8PH *T.* (0732) 884567. *Telex:* 95678. *Fax:* (0732) 884079. *General Manager:* Phillip Woods.
Bibliographies, trade and reference directories, library and information science, electronic publishing.

Boyars, Marion, Publishers Ltd., 24 Lacy Road, London, SW15 1NL *T.* 01-788 9522. *Directors:* Marion Boyars, Arthur Boyars.

Belles-lettres and criticism, fiction, sociology, open forum series, ideas in progress series, critical appraisals series, signature series, poetry, music, travel, drama, cinema, dance, biography.

Boydell & Brewer Ltd. (1969), P.O. Box 9, Woodbridge, Suffolk, IP12 3DF.
Medieval history, literature, art history, country and sporting books. *No unsolicited MSS.*

*****BPCC Publishing Corporation Ltd.**, Maxwell House, 74 Worship Street, London, EC2A 2EN *T.* 01-377 4600. *Telex:* 885233 Macdon G. *Directors:* I. R. Maxwell (Chairman), T. Hely-Hutchinson, J. Emler, T. Hornett, H. A. Stephens. *Company Secretary:* K. P. Brown. Divisions of the Group in the U.K.: Macdonald (comprising Macdonald General, Macdonald Educational, Queen Anne Press, and Futura), Purnell Books, Caxton Publishing, BPC Publishers, Waterlows Publishers.

*****Brassey's Defence Publishers Ltd** (1886), (A member of the **Pergamon Group**), 24 Gray's Inn Road, London WC1X 8HR *T.* 01-242 2363. *Telex:* 28604. *Directors:* Maj. Gen. Anthony J. Trythall, C.B., M.A. (Managing), Jenny Shaw, B.SC(ECON), M.A. (Publishing.
Defence and national security, contemporary policy, technology, military history, reference.

British ITI Publications, 43 Welbeck Street, London, W1M 7NF *T.* 01-486 6363.
Theatre, reference, bibliography, publications for the British Centre of the International Theatre Institute and for ITI/Unesco, Paris.

*****British Museum Publications Ltd.** (1973), 46 Bloomsbury Street, London WC1B 3QQ *T.* 01-323 1234. *Telex:* 28592 Bmpubs G. *Directors:* H. J. F. Campbell, Sir Denis Hamilton, D.S.O., H.R.H. the Duke of Gloucester, H. A. Stevenson, Rt. Hon. Lord Trend, Sir David Attenborough, Professor Peter Lasko, Sir Ian Trethowan, Kevin Coombes.
Art history, archaeology, numismatics, history, oriental art and archaeology, horology, children's books.

Brockhampton Press, Ltd. An imprint of **Hodder & Stoughton Children's Books.**

Brodie (James), Ltd. (1926), 14 Queen Square, Bath, BA1 2HN *T.* 22110. *Directors:* Corinne Wimpress (Secretary), John K. Wimpress, Jeremy Wimpress.
Educational (primary and secondary) books, film strips, tape recordings, computer software.

Brown, Son & Ferguson, Ltd. (1860), 4-10 Darnley Street, Glasgow, G41 2SD *T.* 041-429 1234. *T.A.* Skipper, Glasgow.
Nautical books; Scottish books and Scottish plays. Scout, Cub Scout, Brownie and Guide story books.

Buchan & Enright, Publishers, Ltd., (1981), 53 Fleet Street, London EC4Y 1BE *T.* 01-353 4401. *Directors:* Robert Rhodes James (Chairman), J. W. H. de l'A Buchan and Dominique Enright (Joint Managing), M. P. Hills, C. W. E. R. Buchan.
General non-fiction, history, military history, biography and memoirs, field sports, natural history, fiction, humour.

*****Burke Publishing Co., Ltd.,** Pegasus House, 116-120 Golden Lane, London, EC1Y 0TL *T.* 01-253 2145. *Telex:* 27931 Burke G. *Directors:* Harold K. Starke (Chairman), Naomi Galinski (Managing).
Children's books, (fiction, non-fiction), educational (pre-school and nursery, primary, secondary).

Burke's Peerage plc, 104 New Bond Street, London W1Y 0AE *T.* 01-491 2734. *Directors:* H. B. Brooks-Baker, J. B. Gibbons.
Scholarly and popular works in the fields of genealogy, heraldry, architectural history, social history, etc.

Burns & Oates Ltd. (1847), Publishers to the Holy See, Wellwood, North Farm Road, Tunbridge Wells, Kent, TN2 3DR *T.* (0892) 44037. *Telex:* 957258 Search G. *Directors:* Charlotte de la Bedoyere, Alfred Zimmermann.
Theology, philosophy, spirituality, history, biography, literature, education and books of Catholic interest.

Burrow (Ed. J.) & Co. Ltd. (1900), Publicity House, Streatham Hill, London, SW2 4TR *T.* 01-674 1222. *Chairman:* Remo Dipré. *Managing Director:* Richard Hodges.
Guide books, street plans and maps, travel, year books, etc.

Business Books, Ltd. (1921), Brookmount House, 62-65 Chandos Place, Covent Garden, London WC2N 4NW *T.* 01-240 3411. *Telex:* 261212 Lit Ldn G. *Directors:* M. Cohen (Managing), J. M. Mottram, R. H. Trinder. A division of **Century Hutchinson Ltd.**
Business, advertising, marketing, technical and industrial, computing, reference, paperbacks.

*****Butterworths** (1818), 88 Kingsway, London, WC2B 6AB *T.* 01-405 6900 and Borough Green, Sevenoaks, Kent, TN15 8PH *T.* Borough Green (0732) 884567. *Telex:* 95678 Butwth G. *T.A.* Butterwort, London. *Directors:* W. G. Graham (Chairman and Chief Executive), D. A. Day, E. Hunter, D. J. Jackson, A. McAdam, P. J. Robinson, D. E. Saville, D. L. Summers, C. C. Whurr, P. E. Cheeseman, G. R. N. Cusworth, G. Burn, E. J. Newman. *Branches overseas:* Australia, Canada, New Zealand, Singapore, South Africa, USA.
Law, medicine, science, technology.

*****Butterworth & Co. (Publishers), Ltd.**—see **Butterworths**.

*****Calder, John (Publishers) Ltd.**, 18 Brewer Street, London, W1R 4AS *T.* 01-734 3786-7. *Director:* John Calder.
European, international and British fiction and plays, art, literary, music and social criticism, biography and autobiography, essays, humanities and social sciences, European classics. Series include: Scottish Library, New Writing and Writers, Platform Books, Opera Library, Historical Perspectives. Publishers of *Gambit*, the drama magazine, and the *Journal of Beckett Studies*.

Caliban Books (1977), 17 South Hill Park Gardens, Hampstead, London, NW3 2TD *T.* 01-435 0222. *Managing Director:* Peter Razzell.
Social history, biography, history of exploration, psychology and psychotherapy, historical ethnography, sociology.

*****Cambridge University Press** (1534), The Edinburgh Building, Shaftesbury Road, Cambridge, CB2 2RU *T.* Cambridge (0223) 312393. *T.A.* Unipress, Cambridge. *Telex:* 817256 Cupcam. U.S.A.: 32 East 57th Street, New York, N.Y., 10022. Australia: 10 Stamford Road, Oakleigh, Melbourne, Victoria 3166. *Chief Executive and Secretary of the Press Syndicate:* Geoffrey A. Cass, M.A. *Deputy Chief Executive:* Philip E. V. Allin, M.A. *Managing Director (Publishing Division):* Anthony K. Wilson, M.A. *University Publisher:* Michael H. Black, M.A. *Marketing Director:* David A. Knight, M.A. *Director of Publishing Development:* Jeremy Mynott, PH.D. *Director: American Branch:* Alan Winter, M.A. *Director: Australian Branch:* Kim W. Harris.
Archaeology, art and architecture, computer science, educational (primary, secondary, tertiary), educational software, history, language and literature,

law, mathematics, medicine, music, oriental, philosophy, science (physical and biological), social sciences, theology and religion. The Bible and Prayer book. English language teaching.

Canongate Publishing Ltd. (1973), 17 Jeffrey Street, Edinburgh, EH1 1DR *T.* 031-556 0023 and 1954. *Telex:* 72165 Canpub. *Director:* Stephanie Wolfe Murray (Managing). Associated companies: Southside (Publishers) Ltd., Q Press Ltd.
Adult general non-fiction and fiction. Children's books. **Kelpie** paperbacks.

*Cape (Jonathan), Ltd. (1921), 32 Bedford Square, London, WC1B 3EL *T.* 01-636 3344. *Telex:* 299080 Cvbcse G. *T.A.* and *Cables:* Capajon, London, WC1. *Directors:* Tom Maschler (Chairman), Graham C. Greene, C.B.E. (Managing), Liz Calder (Editorial), Anthony Colwell, Valerie Kettley, Tim Chester, Gaye Poulton, Ian Craig, Rupert Lancaster, Jill Sutcliffe.
Archaeology, biography and memoirs, children's books, current affairs, drama, economics, fiction, history, philosophy, poetry, sociology, travel.

Carcanet Press Ltd. (1969), 208 Corn Exchange Buildings, Manchester, M4 3BQ *T.* 061-834 8730. *Directors:* Michael Schmidt (Mexico), John Naylor.
Poetry, memoirs (literary), Fyfield Books, translations, biography, fiction.

*Careers Consultants Ltd. (1970), 12-14 Hill Rise, Richmond, Surrey, TW10 6UA *T.* 01-940 5668. *Directors:* A.F. Trotman, J.L. O'Reilly (Associate).
Higher education guidance, careers, lifeskills. Subsidiary of Trotman & Co. Ltd.

Cass (Frank) & Co., Ltd. (1958), Gainsborough House, 11 Gainsborough Road, London, E11 1RS *T.* 01-530 4226. *T.A.* Simfay, London E11. *Telex:* 897719 Cass G. *Directors:* Frank Cass (Managing), A. E. Cass, M. P. Zaidner.
History, African studies, Middle East studies, economic and social history, strategic studies, international affairs, development studies, academic law journals.

*Cassell Ltd. (1848), *London Office:* 1 Vincent Square, London, SW1P 2PN *T.* 01-630 7881. *T.A.* Caspeg, London, SW1. *Telex:* 28648 Caspeg. *Managing Director:* Robert Kiernan. *Imprints:* Cassell, Geoffrey Chapman, Editions Berlitz (U.K. Distribution).
Reference, religion, travel.
Head Office and Education Department: 1 St. Anne's Road, Eastbourne, East Sussex, BN21 3UN. *T.* (0323) 638221. *T.A.* Volumists, Eastbourne. *Telex:* 877503 Volmst. *Publishing Director:* Stephen White, *Schools Publisher:* Derrick Trubshaw.
Educational (primary, secondary, tertiary), ELT.

*Castle House Publications Ltd. (1978), Castle House, 27 London Road, Tunbridge Wells, Kent, TN1 1BX *T.* (0892) 39606. *Director:* D. Reinders. Distributors for D. C. Heath, Gower Medical Publishing.
Medical.

Catholic Truth Society (1868), P.O. Box 422, 38-40 Eccleston Square, London, SW1V 1PD *T.* 01-834 4392. *T.A.* Apostolic, London, SW1. *Telex:* 295542 Pavis G. *Chairman:* Rt. Rev. Bishop Alan C. Clark, D.D. *General Secretary:* David Murphy, M.A. *Editor:* Brendan Walsh.
General books of Roman Catholic and Christian interest, Bibles, prayer books and pamphlets of doctrinal, historical, devotional, or social interest. MSS. of 4,000 to 5,000 words or 2500 to 3000 words with up to six illustrations considered for publication as pamphlets; MSS. of 25,000-50,000 words will be considered for publication as paperbacks.

*Caxton & English Educational Programmes International Ltd., Maxwell House,

74 Worship Street, London, EC2A 2EN *T.* 01-377 4600. *Telex:* 885233 Macdon G.

C.B.D. Research Ltd. (1961), 154 High Street, Beckenham, Kent, BR3 1EA *T.* 01-650 7745. *Directors:* G. P. Henderson, S. P. A. Henderson, C. A. P. Henderson.
Directories, reference books, bibliographies, guides to business and statistical information.

Centaur Press, Ltd. (1954), Fontwell, Arundel, Sussex, BN18 0TA *T.* Eastergate (024-368) 3302. *Directors:* Jon Wynne-Tyson, Jennifer M. Wynne-Tyson. A preliminary letter should be sent before submitting MS.
Philosophy, environment, humane education, biography, the arts, dictionaries, reference.

*Century Arrow—see Arrow Books Ltd.

Century Communications Ltd. (1983), Brookmount House, 62-65 Chandos Place, Covent Garden, London WC2N 4NW *T.* 01-240 3411. *Telex:* 261212 Lit Ldn G. *Directors:* A. J. V. Cheetham (Chairman), D. A. R. Manderson, J. M. Mottram, R. L. Smith.
Computer books and software. A division of **Century Hutchinson Ltd.**

***Century Hutchinson Ltd.**, Brookmount House, 62-65 Chandos Place, Covent Garden, London WC2N 4NW *T.* 01-240 3411. *Telex:* 261212 Lit Ldn G. *Directors:* F. C. B. Bland (Chairman), A. J. V. Cheetham (Managing), P. G. Brearley, J. N. M. Cheetham, M. J. Cohen, J. V. Hatch, J. M. Mottram, P. C. K. Roche.
General fiction, biography and autobiography, classics, humour, illustrated editions, travel, cookery, sport, computer, children's, paperbacks, education.

***Century Hutchinson Publishing Ltd.**, Brookmount House, 62-65 Chandos Place, Covent Garden, London WC2N 4NW *T.* 01-240 3411. *Telex:* 261212 Lit Ldn G. *Directors:* A. J. V. Cheetham (Chairman), P. C. K. Roche, R. B. Bloomfield, R. M. F. Cheetham, M. J. Cohen, R. A. Cohen, D. M. Edwards, S. C. Lamb, D. A. R. Manderson, J. M. Mottram, G. R. Rebuck, R. H. Trinder.
Antiques and collecting, art, biography and memoirs, children's books (fiction and non-fiction, toy and picture books), dogs (care and breeding), current affairs, essays, fiction, general, history, humour, music, mysticism and meditation, oriental religion and philosophy, poetry, reference, classics, computers, romance, sport, thrillers, travel, films, graphics, fashion, illustrated editions, cookery.
Imprints: Barrie & Jenkins Ltd., Hutchinson & Co. (Publishers) Ltd., Hutchinson Children's Books Ltd., Rider & Co., Stanley Paul & Co., Popular Dogs Publishing Co. Ltd., Century Communications Ltd., Vermilion. A division of **Century Hutchinson Ltd.**

***Chambers (W. and R.), Ltd.** (1820), 43-45 Annandale Street, Edinburgh, EH7 4AZ. *T.* 031-557 4571. *Telex:* 727967 Words G. *T.A.* Chambers, Edinburgh. *Chairman:* A. S. Chambers. *Directors:* W. G. Henderson (Managing), R. Thomson, J. Osborne, M. S. Chambers.
Dictionaries and reference books; educational (junior, secondary), especially modern mathematics, English; general (non-fiction).

***Chapman & Hall, Ltd.** (1830), 11 New Fetter Lane, London, EC4P 4EE *T.* 01-583 9855. *Telex:* 263398. *T.A.* Elegiacs, London. *Directors:* A. R. Miles (Chairman), R. Stileman (Managing), B. West, J. Buckingham, J. Lynn-Evans, J. Potter. *Secretary:* D. G. Sampson.
Science, technology, medical.

UNITED KINGDOM

*Chapman, Geoffrey, Publishers (1957), 1 Vincent Square, London, SW1P 2PN. *T.* 01-630 7881. *T.A.* Caspeg, London SW1. *Telex:* 28648 Caspeg. *Managing Director:* Robert Kiernan. *Publisher:* Stephen Butcher.
Religious books.

*Chatto & Windus, Ltd./The Hogarth Press, Ltd. (1855/1917), 40 William IV Street, London, WC2N 4DF *T.* 01-379 6637. *Telex:* 299080 Cvbcse G. *Directors:* Carmen Callil, Christine Carswell, John Charlton, Barry Featherstone, Jeremy Lewis, Andrew Motion, Susanna Porter.
Archaeology, art, belles-lettres, biography and memoirs, cookery, crime/thrillers, current affairs, drama, essays, fiction, history, illustrated books, poetry, politics, psychoanalysis, translations, travel, hardbacks and paperbacks.

Church of Scotland Department of Communication —see **St. Andrew Press.**

*Churchill Livingstone (Medical division of **Longman Group UK Ltd.**), Robert Stevenson House, 1-3 Baxter's Place, Leith Walk, Edinburgh, EH1 3AF *T.* 031-556 2424. *T.A.* Churchliv, Edinburgh. *Telex:* 727511 Longman G. *Fax:* 031-558 1278. *Divisional Managing Director:* A. T. Stevenson.
Medical, nursing, dental, scientific, dictionaries.

Clarendon Press—see **Oxford University Press.**

Clark (Robin) Ltd. (1976), 27-29 Goodge Street, London, W1P 1FD *T.* 01-636 3992-5. *Directors:* N. I. Attallah (Chairman), R. Fraser (Managing), D. Elliott, B. Reilly. A member of the **Namara Group.**
Fiction, biography, social history, humour.

*Clark (T. & T.), Ltd. (1821), 59 George Street, Edinburgh, EH2 2LQ *T.* 031-225 4703. *T.A.* Dictionary, Edinburgh. *Directors:* T. G. R. Clark, C.A. (Managing), Geoffrey F. Green, M.A., PH.D., D. A. Ross Stewart, B.A., D. A. B. Cunningham, C.A.
Dictionaries, law, philosophy, theology and religion.

*Clarke (James) & Co., Ltd. (1859), 7 All Saints' Passage, Cambridge, CB2 3LS *T.* (0223) 350865. *Telex:* 817114 Camcom G. *Managing Director:* Adrian Brink.
Theology, religion, educational, technical, reference books.

*Collet's (Publishers) Ltd., *Registered Address and Head Office:* Denington Estate, Wellingborough, Northampton, NN8 2QT *T.* (0933) 224351. *Directors:* Dr. Eva Skelley, S. R. F. Lytton.
Politics, art, music studies, travel guides, language study materials.

*Collingridge (W. H. & L.), Ltd. An imprint of **The Hamlyn Publishing Group Ltd.**

Collings (Rex), Ltd. (1969), 6 Paddington Street, London, W1M 3LA *T.* 01-487 4201. *T.A.* Hujambo, London. *Telex:* 337340 Bookps G. *Directors:* Rex Collings, Ian Coltart.
Children's books (12 years upwards), Africana, poetry, reference books.

*Collins (William), PLC. (1819), General, Children's and Educational Book Publishing Offices, and Fontana, Armada and Grafton Paperback Publishing Offices, 8 Grafton Street, London W1X 3LA. *T.* 01-493 7070. *Telex:* 25611 Collins G. Printing and Distribution Offices and Editorial Offices for Bibles, cartographic and reference books, Westerhill Road, Bishopbriggs, Glasgow, G64 2QT *T.* 041-772 3200. *Directors:* F. I. Chapman (Chairman & Chief Executive), Sir Charles Troughton (Deputy Chairman), G. Craig, R. C. Smith, G. D. S. Blunt, M. J. Hussey, K. R. Murdoch, H. C. Paton, Sir Edward Pickering, C. G. Stanton.
General Division including Fontana and Collins Harvill; *Special Interests Division* including Collins Willow, Home and Leisure and Natural History;

Education, Reference and Professional Division; Children's Division including Fontana Lions, Dragon Books, Dinosaur Publications and Armada paperbacks; Collins Grafton including Paladin. *Associated & Subsidiary Companies:* William Collins Sons & Company Ltd; *Australia:* William Collins Pty Ltd; *Canada:* William Collins Sons & Co (Canada) Ltd; *New Zealand:* William Collins Publishers Ltd; *South Africa:* Collins Publishers (SA) (Pty) Ltd; *USA:* Collins Publishers Inc.

Archaeology, architecture, art, belles-lettres, Bibles, biography and memoirs, children's books (fiction, non-fiction, rewards, toy and picture, annuals), computer books and software, current affairs, dictionaries, directories or guide books, educational (infants, primary, secondary), essays, fiction, general history, humour, liturgical books, maps and atlases, natural history, naval and military, philosophy, practical handbooks, reference, sailing and nautical, science (history of), sports, games and hobbies, travel, theology and religion; Crime Club, Flamingo paperbacks, Fontana, Fontana Press, Fount Religious Paperbacks, Armada Children's paperbacks, Collins Harvill, Collins Willow Books, Grafton Hardbacks, Grafton Paperbacks, Grafton Trade Books, Dragon Books, Mayflower Books, Paladin Books, Panther Books, Adlard Coles Ltd, Hart Davis Educational Ltd.

*Collins Harvill,—see **William Collins, PLC.**

*Collins Willow Books,—see **William Collins PLC.**

Columbus Books Ltd (1981), 19-23 Ludgate Hill, London EC4M 7PD *T.* 01-248 6444. *Telex:* 897948 Octabs G. *Directors:* Nicholas W. Berry (Chairman), Medwyn L. Hughes (Managing), Tony B. Speakman, Eric R. Dobby, Dr. Isidore Klausner, Gill Rowley.
Cinema, travel, photography, cookery, crafts, self-help, biography, humour; general non-fiction.

Comet Books. An imprint of **W. H. Allen & Co. PLC.**

Conservative Political Centre (1945), 32 Smith Square, London, SW1P 3HH *T.* 01-222 9000. *Telex:* 8814563. *Director:* David Knapp.
Political economy, current affairs, sociology.

*Constable & Co., Ltd. (1890), 10 Orange Street, London, WC2H 7EG *T.* 01-930 0801-7. *Trade:* 062-181 6362. *T.A.* Dhagoba, London, WC2. *Telex:* 27950 ref. 830. *Directors:* Benjamin Glazebrook (Chairman and Managing), Noel Holland, R. A. A. Holt, Miles Huddleston, P. N. Marks, Richard Tomkins, Robin Baird-Smith, Jeremy Potter, John Mottram.
Fiction: general, thrillers, historical. General non-fiction: literature, biography, memoirs, history, politics, current affairs, food, travel and guide books, social sciences, psychology and psychiatry, counselling, social work, sociology, mass media.

Conway Maritime Press Ltd. (1972), 24 Bride Lane, Fleet Street, London, EC4Y 8DR *T.* 01-583 2412. *Telex:* 8814206 Popper G. *Directors:* W. R. Blackmore (Managing), D. C. Greening, R. J. Gardiner, Catherine V. Blackmore.
Maritime and naval history, ship modelling, yachting and sailing.

*Cooper (Leo), Ltd., 190 Shaftesbury Avenue, London WC2 *T.* 01-836 3141. An associate of **Martin Secker & Warburg Ltd.**

*Corgi paperbacks—see **Transworld Publishers Ltd.**

Cornwall Books—see **Golden Cockerel Press.**

*Coronet. An imprint of **Hodder & Stoughton, Ltd.**

Council for British Archaeology (1944), 112 Kennington Road, London, SE11 6RE
T. 01-582 0494. *Director:* Henry Cleere.
British archaeology—academic; no general books.

Counterpoint—see Unwin Hyman Ltd.

Country Life,—see Newnes Books.

*****Crescent Books.** An imprint of W. H. Allen & Co. PLC.

*****Croom Helm Ltd.,** 21-25 North Street, Bromley, Kent BR1 1SD. *T.* 01-466 6622.
Directors: C. Helm, D. Croom, M. Helm, B. Ackerman, R. Burns. I. McIntyre.
Humanities, social sciences, biological and medical sciences; also general books on ornithology, natural history, horticulture.

Crowood Press, The, (1982), Crowood House, Ramsbury, Marlborough, Wiltshire, SN8 2HE. *T.* Marlborough (0672) 20320. *Telex:* 449703 Telser G.
Publisher: John Dennis. *Senior Editor:* Ken Hathaway.
Sport, fishing, equestrian, climbing and mountaineering, photography, small-scale farming, natural history, chess, annuals.

Dalton (Terence), Ltd. (1966), Water Street, Lavenham, Sudbury, Suffolk, CO10 9RN *T.* (0787) 247572. *Directors:* T. R. Dalton (Managing), T. A. J. Dalton, E. H. Whitehair.
Maritime and aeronautical history, East Anglian interest and history.

Daniel (The C. W.) Company, Ltd. (1902), 1 Church Path, Saffron Walden, Essex, CB10 1JP *T.* (0799) 21909. *Directors:* Ian Miller, Jane Miller.
Natural healing, homoeopathy, diet, mysticism.

*****Darton, Longman & Todd, Ltd.** (1959), 89 Lillie Road, London, SW6 1UD *T.* 01-385 2341. *T.A.* Librabook, London, SW6. *Directors:* R. Chopping (Managing), L. L. Kay, L. J. Riddle. *Publishing Consultants:* J. M. Todd, E. A. C. Russell.
Bibles, history, ethics, theology and religion.

Darwen Finlayson, Ltd.—see Phillimore & Co., Ltd.

David & Charles Publishers plc, (1960), Brunel House, Newton Abbot, Devon, TQ12 4PU *T.* Newton Abbot (0626) 61121. *Telex:* 42904 Books Nabbot.
Directors: D. St. John Thomas (Chairman), N. Loasby, L. Springfield.
Associate Directors: S. Bryant, C. Cowan, N. Hollis, D. Porteous, C. Sage.
Adult non-fiction; practical books; specialising in craft, fishing, gardening, health, music, natural history, railways, sailing, sport, travel. Preliminary letter with outline welcomed. *Authors Guide* available on receipt of first class stamp.

Davies, Christopher, Publishers, Ltd. (1949), P.O. Box 403, Sketty, Swansea SA2 9BE *T.* (0269) 850935. *Directors:* Christopher Talfan Davies, E. C. Davies.
History, leisure books, sport, general, Welsh interest, Welsh dictionaries, *Triskele Books.*

*****Dawson, Wm., & Sons, Ltd.** (1809), Cannon House, Folkestone, Kent, CT19 5EE *T.* (0303) 57421. *T.A.* Dawbooks, Folkestone. *Telex:* 96392 Dawson G.
Directors: R. W. Hall (Chairman), D. A. Brewer (Managing), B. C. Ingleby, L. Johnson, T. R. Lowry, A. Roche, N. A. Smith.
Bibliography, reference, cartography, history.

*****Dean's International Publishing.** A division of The Hamlyn Publishing Group, Ltd.

*****Dent (J. M.) & Sons, Ltd.** (1888), Aldine House, 33 Welbeck Street, London, W1M 8LX *T.* 01-486 7233. *T.A.* Malaby, London, W1. *Telex:* 8954130 Aldine G.
Directors: V. F. Chamberlain (Chairman), Peter Shellard (Managing),

Malcolm Gerratt, Vanessa Hamilton, Patrick Johnston, John Sundell, Elizabeth Newlands, Graham Saunders, Roger Houghton, Bill Neill-Hall.
Everyman's Library, Everyman's Encyclopaedia, Everyman's Reference Library, Everyman Paperbacks, Everyman Fiction, Classic Thrillers, Mastercrime, Healthright, Master Musicians. Proprietors of the Malaby Press and the Phoenix House imprints.
Archaeology, biography, children's books (fiction, non-fiction), cookery, gardening, health and nutrition, humour, military history, music, natural history, photography, reference, science fact, literary fiction, (no poetry). Preliminary letter/synopsis and S.A.E. requested before submitting MSS.

Designer Publications Ltd., SIAD, 12 Carlton House Terrace, London SW1Y 5AH *T.* 01-930 2686-7. *Directors:* M. Sadler-Forster, A. Best, R. Fitch, Jo Parker. The publishing company of the Society of Industrial Artists and Designers.

***Deutsch, André, Ltd.** (1950), 105-106 Great Russell Street, London, WC1B 3LJ *T.* 01-580 2746-9. *T.A.* Adlib, London, WC1. *Cables:* Adlib, London, WC1. *Telex:* 261026 Adlib G. *Directors:* André Deutsch and T. G. Rosenthal (Joint Chairmen), Michael House (Deputy Managing), Diana Athill, June Bird, David Heimann, F. P. Kendall, Caroline Knox, Sheila McIlwraith, Anselm Robinson, Pamela Royds, Jeff Sains, Anthony Thwaite, Julian Tobin, Esther Whitby. *Secretary:* Michael House.
Art, belles-lettres, biography and memoirs, children's books, fiction, general, history, humour, politics, travel, photography.

Dial Industry Publications—see **Information Services Ltd.**

***Dinosaur Publications**—see **William Collins, PLC.**

Donald (John) Publishers Ltd. (1973), 138 St. Stephen Street, Edinburgh, EH3 5AA *T.* 031-225 1146. *Directors:* Gordon Angus, D. L. Morrison, J. B. Tuckwell.
Scottish history, ethnology, local history, sport, vernacular architecture.

***Dorling Kindersley Publishers Ltd.** (1984), 2 Henrietta Street, Covent Garden, London, WC2E 8PS. *T.* 01-836 5411. *Telex:* 263800 Dkpubs G. *Chairman:* Christopher Dorling. *Deputy Chairman:* Christopher Davis. *Directors:* Tim Whale (Managing), Lorraine Baird, Ian Grant, Richard Harman, Stuart Jackman, Peter Kindersley.
High quality books on non-fiction subjects, including health, cookery, gardening, crafts and reference.

Downlander Publishing (1978), 88 Oxendean Gardens, Lower Willingdon, Eastbourne, East Sussex, BN22 0RS *T.* (0323) 505814. *Patron:* Jane Gow. *President:* Nora Potter, M.B.E. *Directors:* Derek Bourne-Jones, M.A. (Oxon), F.R.S.A., Hilary Bourne-Jones.
Poetry. Preliminary letter and s.a.e. essential; no unsolicited MSS.

***Dragon Books**—see **William Collins, PLC.**

Dragon's World Ltd., Paper Tiger Books (1975), High Street, Limpsfield, Surrey, RH8 0DY. *T.* Oxted 5044. *Telex:* 95631 Dragon G. and 19 Hereford Square, London SW7 4TS. *T.* 01-373 5473. *Directors:* H. A. Schaafsma, C. M. A. Schaafsma.
Illustrated books of fantasy, mythology, science fiction, astrology, natural history, art and children's fantasy books. Series of home improvement and D.I.Y. books.

Drew, Richard, Publishing Ltd. (1981), 6 Clairmont Gardens, Glasgow, G3 7LW *T.* 041-333 9341. *Telex:* 777308. *Director:* Richard Drew.
General non-fiction, fiction, language, children's.

Dryad, P.O.Box 38, Northgates, Leicester, LE1 9BU *T.* (0533) 50405. *Telex:* 341766 Dryad G. *General Manager:* J. A. Green.
Dryad *500 series* full colour craft booklets, workcards, patterns.

Duckworth (Gerald), & Co., Ltd. (1898), The Old Piano Factory, 43 Gloucester Crescent, London, NW1 7DY *T.* 01-485 3484. *T.A.* Platypus, London, NW1. *Directors:* Ray Davies, Anna Haycraft, Colin Haycraft (Chairman and Managing), David Lines.
General, fiction, and academic.

*****East-West Publications (UK) Ltd.** (1977), Newton Works, 27-29 Macklin Street, London WC2B 5LX *T.* 01-831 6767. *Chairman:* L. W. Carp. *Editor:* B. Thompson.
General non-fiction, Eastern studies, sufism. Children's imprint: **Gallery Children's Books.**

*****Ebury Press,** Colquhoun House, 27-37 Broadwick Street, London, W1V 1FR *T.* 01-439 7144. *Telex:* 263879 Natmag G. *Publishing Director:* Roger Q. Barrett. *Editorial Director:* Maxim Jakubowski.
Cookery, health, beauty, photography, travel, transport, humour, crafts, antiques, hobbies, gardening, natural history, DIY, sport. Publishers of books from *Good Housekeeping, Cosmopolitan, Harpers and Queen,* and *She.*

Edinburgh House Press. All enquiries to: **Lutterworth Press,** *q.v.*

Edinburgh University Press, 22 George Square, Edinburgh, EH8 9LF. *T.* 031-667 1011. *T.A.* Edinpress. *Telex:* 727442 Unived.

Educational Explorers (1962), 11 Crown Street, Reading, RG1 2TQ *T.* (0734) 873103. *Directors:* C. Gattegno, D. M. Gattegno.
Educational, mathematics: *Numbers in colour with Cuisenaire Rods,* languages: *The Silent Way,* literacy, reading: *Words in Colour,* Educational films.

Element Books (1978) Longmead, Shaftesbury, Dorset, SP7 8PL *T.* (0747) 51339. *Directors:* Michael Mann, Annie Walton, Jean Allen.
Philosophy, mysticism, religion, psychology, complementary medicine and therapies, astrology and esoteric traditions. Also general, biography, history and humour under **Nadder** imprint.

Elliot Right Way Books, Kingswood Buildings, Brighton Road, Lower Kingswood, Tadworth, Surrey, KT20 6TD *T.* Mogador (0737) 832202.
Specialist in instructional and motor books, and publishers of the series *Paperfronts.* Careful consideration for all new ideas, and editorial help can be provided. Popular technical, popular educational, popular medical, pets, self-help, sport, business, general, humour, cookery, home and family, quizzes, puzzles, crosswords, paperbacks.

ELM Publications (1977), Seaton House, Kings Ripton, Cambs. PE17 2NJ *T.* (04873) 238. Sheila Ritchie.
Management and business, librarianship and information science, general non-fiction.

Elm Tree Books. An imprint of **Hamish Hamilton Ltd.**

*****Elsevier Applied Science Publishers Ltd.** (1963), Crown House, Linton Road, Barking, Essex, IG11 8JU *T.* 01-594 7272. *Telex:* 896950 Appsci G. *T.A.* Elsbark, Barking. *Publishers:* R. Lomax, N. Paskin.
Agriculture, architectural science, building and civil engineering, chemistry, food technology, materials science, petroleum technology, pollution, polymers, plastics technology.

*Encyclopaedia Britannica International Ltd. Mappin House, 4 Winsley Street, London, W1N 8EB *T.* 01-637 3371. *Telex:* 23866 Enbri G. *Managing Director:* Joe D. Adams.

English Universities Press, Ltd., The. Imprint of **Hodder & Stoughton Educational.**

Enigma Books Ltd (1981). An imprint of **Severn House Publishers Ltd.**

*EP Publishing Ltd—see **A. & C. Black plc.**

Epworth Press, Room 195, 1 Central Buildings, London, SW1H 9NR *T.* 01-222 8010. *Editorial Committee:* Rev. John Stacey, Dr. Valerie Edden, Professor Morna D. Hooker, Rev. Dr. Ivor H. Jones, Rev. Graham Slater.
Religion and Theology.

Ethnographica (1976), 19 Westbourne Road, London, N7 8AN *T.* 01-607 4074. *Directors:* Stuart Hamilton, Jane Hansom.
Ethnography, history, anthropology, social studies, arts and crafts; catalogues and books produced for museums, galleries and universities in U.K. and Overseas.

Euromonitor Publications (1972), 87-88 Turnmill Street, London EC1M 5QU *T.* 01-251 8024. *Telex:* 21120 Monref G 2281. *Directors:* T. J. Fenwick (Marketing), R. N. Senior (Managing).
Business and commercial reference, marketing information, European and International Surveys, directories.

Europa Publications Ltd., 18 Bedford Square, London, WC1B 3JN *T.* 01-580 8236. *Telex:* 21540 Europa G. *Directors:* C. H. Martin (Chairman), P. A. McGinley (Managing), J. P. Desmond, D. P. Easton, R. M. Hughes, P. G. C. Jackson, R. J. M. Joseph, A. G. Oliver, J. Quinney.
Directories, international relations, reference, year books, history, books about books.

Evangelical Press of Wales (1955), Bryntirion, Bridgend, Mid Glamorgan, CF31 4DX *T.* (0656) 55886. *Publications Secretary:* E. W. James.
Theology and religion (in English and Welsh).

*Evans Brothers Ltd. (1905), 2A Portman Mansions, Chiltern Street, London W1M 1LE. *T.* 01-935 7160. *T.A.* Byronitic, London, W1. *Telex:* 8811713 Evbook G. *Directors:* L. J. Browning (Chairman), S. T. Pawley (Managing), F. S. J. Austin, B. O. Bolodeoku (Nigerian), R. D. Hicks, B. Sandelson.
Educational books, particularly primary and secondary for Africa, the Caribbean and Hong Kong, and general books for Europe and Africa.

Exley Publications Ltd. (1976), 16 Chalk Hill, Watford, Herts, WD1 4BN *T.* Watford 50505. *Telex:* 261234 ref. H5753L. *Directors:* Richard Exley, Helen Exley.
Humour, gift books, anthologies for special occasions. No unsolicited MSS; SAE essential.

*Eyre & Spottiswoode (Publishers), Ltd., North Way, Andover, Hants, SP10 5BE *T.* (0264) 62141. *T.A.* Apt, Andover. *Telex:* 47214 Abpand. *Directors:* C. H. Falkus (Chairman), A. J. Holder (Managing Director), D. S. Ross.
Publishers of Bibles, prayer books and religious books.

*Faber & Faber Ltd. (1929), 3 Queen Square, London, WC1N 3AU *T.* 01-278 6881. *T.A.* Fabbaf, London, WC1. *Telex:* 299633 Faber G. *Directors:* Matthew Evans (Chairman and Managing), T. E. Faber, A. T. G. Pocock, O.B.E., Rosemary Goad, Giles de la Mare, Robert McCrum, Desmond Clarke, Dennis Crutcher, Will Sullein.

Archaeology, architecture, art, biography, children's books (fiction, nonfiction, picture), cookery books, current affairs, drama, fiction, films, history, literary criticism, medical and nursing, military history, music, philosophy, poetry, politics, theatre and ballet, travel. *Faber Paperbacks* cover many of the subjects shown above. *Art Books* include the following series Faber Monographs on pottery and porcelain, glass and silver.

Faber & Faber (Publishers) Ltd. (1969), 3 Queen Square, London, WC1N 3AU *T.* 01-278 6881. *T.A.* Fabbaf, London, WC1. *Directors:* T. E. Faber (Chairman), Matthew Evans, P. W. G. DuBuisson, Donald Mitchell, A. T. G. Pocock, O.B.E., Simon Jenkins, John McConnell. Holding company of **Faber & Faber Ltd.**, *q.v.*

Fabian Society (1884), 11 Dartmouth Street, London, SW1H 9BN *T.* 01-222 8877 (also controls **NCLC Publishing Society Ltd.**).
Current affairs, economics, educational, political economy, social policy.

Filmscan Ltd., Cheltonian House, Portsmouth Road, Esher KT10 9AA. *T.* (0372) 68755. *Directors:* T. S. Sherwen (Chairman), D. A. Davidson (Managing), J. Slaven, M. Hossick, J. Tuttle.
Educational video/book publishers. English language teaching (school and self-study materials), foreign language teaching, further education and training.

Financial Training Publications (1982), Avenue House, 131 Holland Park Avenue, London, W11 4UT. *T.* 01-603 4688. *Directors:* D. G. Heynes, F.C.A., A. W. MacQueen.
Law, accountancy, banking.

Fishing News Books Ltd. (1953), 1 Long Garden Walk, Farnham, Surrey, GU9 7HX *T.* (0252) 726868. *Telex:* 859500 Sharet G (F/077). *Directors:* Vivien M. Heighway, William E. Redman.
Commercial fisheries, aquaculture and allied subjects.

Flamingo paperbacks—see **William Collins, PLC**.

Focal Press, P.O. Box 63, Guildford, Surrey GU2 5BH *T.* (0483) 31261. *Telex:* 859556 Scitec G. *Publishing Director:* Tim Feest. *Editor:* Arlyn Powell.
Photography and media imprint of **Butterworths**.
Professional, technical and academic books on photography, broadcasting, film, television, radio, audio visual and communication media.

***Fontana Lions**—see **William Collins, PLC.**

Foulis, G. T. & Co. Ltd., Sparkford, Yeovil, Somerset, BA22 7JJ. *T.* North Cadbury (0963) 40635. *Telex:* 46212 Haynes G. *Directors:* J. H. Haynes (Executive Chairman), J. Scott (Managing), R. T. Grainger, A. P. Lynch, R. J. Stagg, J. R. Clew, A. C. Haynes.
Motoring/motorcycling; marque and model history; practical maintenance and renovation; related biographies; motor/motorcycle sport.

***Foulsham (W.) & Co., Ltd.** (1819), Yeovil Road, Slough, Berks, SL1 4JH *T.* (75) 26769. *Telex:* 849041 Sharet G.
General manuals, educational, school library, do-it-yourself, hobbies and games, sport, travel, art directories, electronics, computers.

***Foundational Book Company, Ltd., The**, Trade: P.O. Box 659, London, SW3 6SJ *T.* 01-584 1053.
Spiritual science.

***Fount Paperbacks**—see **William Collins, PLC**.

Fourth Estate Ltd (1984), Classic House, 113 Westbourne Grove, London W2 4UP *T.* 01-727 8993 and 243 1382 *Telex:* 299240 Donleo G. *Directors:* Victoria Barnsley, Michael Mason, John Newall.

Current affairs, literature, guide books, women's studies, popular culture, fiction.

Fowler (L. N.) & Co. Ltd. (1880), 1201-3 High Road, Chadwell Heath, Romford, Essex, RM6 4DH *T.* 01-597 2491-2.
Astrology, health and healing, mental science, yoga, psychology, religious.

Fraser (Gordon), Ltd. (1936). Editorial: Fitzroy Road, London, NW1 8TT *T.* 01-722 0077. *T.A.* Frasercard London. *Telex:* Fraser London 25848. *Distribution:* Eastcotts Road, Bedford. *Directors:* Ian G. Fraser, Margaret A. F. Moss, Alan A. F. Macpherson, Percy J. Doughty.
Fine arts, graphic art, photography, biography.

***Freeman (W. H.) & Co., Ltd.** (1959), 20 Beaumont Street, Oxford, OX1 2NQ *T.* (0865) 726975. *Telex:* 83677 Whfrmn G. *Directors:* G. Piel, L. Chaput, J. Macfarlane, G. Voaden, G. M. Borkwood.
Science, technical, medicine, politics, economics, psychology, sociology, archaeology.

***French, (Samuel), Ltd.** (1830), 52 Fitzroy Street, London, W1P 6JR *T.* 01-387 9373. *Branches:* New York, Hollywood, Toronto, Sydney *q.v. Directors:* Abbott Van Nostrand (Chairman), John Hughes (Managing), John Bedding, George Ramsey. Publishers of plays and agents for the collection of royalties.
Drama.

Futura Publications, the paperback division of **Macdonald & Company (Publishers) Ltd.,** 3rd Floor, Greater London House, Hampstead Road, London NW1 7QX *T.* 01-377 4600. *Telex:* 885233 Macdon G. *Imprints:* Futura, Troubadour, Orbit.

Gairm Publications, incorporating Alex MacLaren & Sons, (1875), 29 Waterloo Street, Glasgow, G2 6BZ *T.* 041-221 1971.
Dictionaries, language books, novels, poetry, music, quarterly magazine (Gaelic only).

Gay Men's Press—see **GMP Publishers Ltd.**

Gay Modern Classics—see **GMP Publishers Ltd.**

Gee & Son (Denbigh) Ltd. (1808), Chapel Street, Denbigh, Clwyd, LL16 3SW *T.* Denbigh (074 571) 2020. *Directors:* E. Evans, H. M. Lloyd, J. Williams. Oldest Welsh publishers. Books of interest to Wales, in Welsh and English.

***Geographia Ltd.** (1921), 105-107 Bath Road, Cheltenham, Glos. GL53 7LE *T.* (0242) 512748. *Managing Director:* B. Winkleman. A division of **John Bartholomew & Son Ltd.**
Maps, guides, and atlases.

Geographical Publications Ltd. (1933), The Keep, Berkhamsted Place, Berkhamsted, Herts, HP4 1HQ *T.* Berkhamsted (044-27) 2981. *Directors:* A. N. Clark, G. N. Clark, G. N. Blake, D. R. Denman. *Secretary:* G. N. Clark. Books on geography and land affairs, both on own account and jointly with other publishers. Publishers and general agents to World Land Use Survey and International Geographical Union.

***Gibbons (Stanley) Publications Ltd.** (1856), Unit 5, Parkside Industrial Park, Christchurch Road, Ringwood, Hants, BH24 3SH. *T.* (042 54) 2363. *Telex:* 41271 Sgp Pub G. *Directors:* S. A. Zimmerman, J. J. Curle.

Gibson, Robert & Sons Glasgow, Ltd. (1885), 17 Fitzroy Place, Glasgow, G3 7SF *T.* 041-248 5674. *Directors:* R. D. C. Gibson, R. G. C. Gibson, Dr. J. S. McEwan, M. Pinkerton, H. C. Crawford, N. J. Crawford.
Educational.

Gifford (John) Ltd. (1937), 113-119 Charing Cross Road, London, WC2H 0EB *T.* 01-437 0216. *Directors:* R. Batty, C. Batty.
Gardening, sport, natural history, travel and practical books, art, collecting antiques.

*****Ginn & Company, Ltd.** (1867), Prebendal House, Parson's Fee, Aylesbury, Bucks, HP20 2QZ *T.* Aylesbury (0296) 88411. *Telex:* 83535 Ginn G. *Directors:* N. Thompson (Chairman), W. P. Shepherd (Managing), E. F. Keartland, C. Bushnell-Wye, D. J. Miller, R. Cornford.
Educational (primary, and Caribbean primary and junior secondary).

*****Glasgow, Mary, Publications Ltd.** (1956), 140 Kensington Church Street, London, W8 4BN *T.* 01-229 9531. *Telex:* Mgpubs 311890. *Directors:* D. G. Heynes (Chairman), T. A. M. Waller (Managing), A. E. J. Bedale, S. H. I. Codrington, P. St C. Proctor, D. Raggett, L. K. Upton.
Modern languages: French, Spanish, German, and English as a foreign language; language magazines and readers, courses, films, filmstrips, tapes; geography and social studies.

GMP Publishers Ltd. (1982), P.O. Box 247, London N15 6RW *T.* 01-800 5861. *Directors:* Richard Dipple, David Fernbach, Aubrey Walter.
Publishers of books of gay and general interest: fiction, art, photography, biography, history, humour, drama, film, health, sociology, psychology and politics; **Gay Modern Classics:** a reprint list of fiction and non-fiction of the last one hundred years of particular interest to gay men; **Heretic Books:** politics, ecology, current affairs, Third World.

Godfrey Cave Associates Ltd. (1975), 42 Bloomsbury Street, London, WC1B 3QJ *T.* 01-636 9177. *Telex:* 266945 Macrol G. *Fax:* 01-636 9091. *T.A.* Godave London WC1. *Directors:* John Maxwell, John Shillingford, Peter Cox, Geoffrey Howard.
General non-fiction, reprints, remainders.

Golden Cockerel Press, 25 Sicilian Avenue, London WC1A 2QH *T.* 01-405 7979. *Directors:* Sarah Manson, Thomas Yoseloff (USA). Imprints: **Associated University Presses:** Literary criticism, art, music, history, film, theology, philosophy, Jewish studies, politics, sociology. **Cornwall Books:** Antiques, history, sport, film, general.

*****Gollancz (Victor), Ltd.** (1927), 14 Henrietta Street, London, WC2E 8QJ *T.* 01-836 2006. *T.A.* Vigollan, London, WC2. *Telex:* 265033 Vgbook G. *Directors:* Livia Gollancz, Stephen Bray, David Burnett, Jane Blackstock, Elizabeth Dobson, Malcolm Edwards, Nellie Flexner, Joanna Goldsworthy, Kate Pocock.
Biography and memoirs, children's books (fiction, non-fiction), current affairs, fiction, crime fiction, science fiction, fantasy and macabre, general, history, music, mountaineering, sociology, travel.

Gomer Press (1892), J. D. Lewis & Sons, Ltd., Gomer Press, Llandysul, Dyfed, SA44 4BQ *T.* (055 932) 2371. *T.A.* Gomerian, Llandysul. *Directors:* J. Huw Lewis, John H. Lewis.
School books in Welsh: biography, local history.

Goodchild (John) Publishers (1972), 10 Mandeville Road, Aylesbury, Bucks. HP21 8AA. *T.* (0296) 35418. *Managing Director:* John Goodchild.
Children's fiction.

*****Gower Publishing Group Ltd.** (1968), Gower House, Croft Road, Aldershot, Hampshire, GU11 3HR *T.* Aldershot (0252) 331551. *Directors:* G. R. Cyriax, N. A. E. Farrow.

Practical management and business reference, library science, engineering, industrial technology. Academic monographs on the social sciences. Reference and scholarly works in art, architecture, music, humanities.

*Grafton Books Ltd.—see **William Collins, PLC.**

*Graham & Trotman Ltd. (1972), Sterling House, 66 Wilton Road, London, SW1V 1DE *T*. 01-821 1123. *T.A.* Infobooks London. *Telex:* 298878 Gramco G. *Directors:* A. M. W. Graham, I. L. J. Pulley, N. Lott, F. W.B. Van Eysinga, D. Dissel, M. Monkhorst.
International business, international law, finance and banking, earth science, environmental science.

Granada Publishing Ltd. Now **Grafton Books Ltd.**

Gresham Books, The Gresham Press, P.O. Box 61, Henley-on-Thames, Oxfordshire, RG9 3LQ *T*. (073 522) 3789. *Chief Executive:* Mrs. M. V. Green.
Music technique, hymn books, wood engraving.

Griffin (Charles) & Co., Ltd. (1820), 16 Pembridge Road, London W11 3HL *T*. 01-229 1825.
Scientific and technical, notably statistics.

Grisewood & Dempsey Ltd. (1973), Elsley Court, 20-22 Great Titchfield Street, London, W1P 7AD *T*. 01-631 0878. *T.A.* Greatbooks, London. *Telex:* 27725. *Directors:* D. Grisewood (Managing), J. Grisewood, J. Richards, J. M. Olliver, D. Maxwell Macdonald.
Children's books, educational and general non-fiction.

*Guinness Superlatives Ltd. (1954), 33 London Road, Enfield, Middlesex, EN2 6DJ *T*. 01-367 4567. *Telex:* 23573 Gbrldn G. *Fax:* 01-367 5912. *Cables:* Mostest Enfield.
General reference books.

Gwasg Gee—see **Gee & Son (Denbigh) Ltd.**

Hale (Robert) Ltd. (1936), Clerkenwell House, 45-47 Clerkenwell Green, London, EC1R 0HT *T*. 01-251 2661. *T.A.* Barabbas, London, EC1.
Archaeology, architecture, biography and memoirs, cinema, cookery, crafts, current affairs, fiction, general history, humour, military, music, occult, practical handbooks, sports, games and hobbies, theatre and ballet, topography, travel, war.

Hambleside Publishers Ltd. (1976), 13 Southgate Street, Winchester, Hampshire, SO23 9DZ *T*. (0962) 60444. *T.A.* Hambleside, Winchester. *Telex:* 477357 Hamble G. *Directors:* A. F. Nieklrk, D. R. Yellop, R. A. Jeffery.
Sports, West African interest.

*Hamilton (Hamish), Ltd. (1931), 27 Wrights Lane, London W8 5TZ *T*. 01-938 3388. *Telex:* 917181/2 Hamish G. *Fax:* 01-937 8704. *Cables:* Hamisham, London. *Directors:* Hamish Hamilton, M.A., LL.B. (President), Christopher Sinclair-Stevenson, M.A. (Managing), Michael Brown, Peter Kilborn, Iain Harvey, Penelope Hoare, Christopher Weller, Clare Alexander, Kyle Cathie, Helen Ellis, Jane Nissen.
Belles-lettres, biography and memoirs, children's books (fiction, non-fiction), current affairs, drama, fiction, general, history, humour, music, political, theatre and ballet, travel. Also entertainment, cookery, crafts, sports, hobbies, natural history, literary reference (**Elm Tree Books**).

*Hamlyn Paperbacks—see **Arrow Books Ltd.**

*Hamlyn Publishing Group, Ltd., The (1947), Bridge House, 69 London Road, Twickenham, Middlesex TW1 3SB *T*. 01-891 6261. *Telex:* 25650 Plesbk. *Directors:* P. Hamlyn, I. Irvine, Charles Fowkes, P. Stanbury, Colin

Winchester, B. Trodd, Arthur Philo. Parent Company: **Octobus Publishing Group PLC.**

*****Hamlyn Publishing**—a division of **The Hamlyn Publishing Group Ltd.**

Hammond, Hammond & Co., Ltd. Incorporated with **Barrie & Jenkins**, *q.v.*

Hardy, Patrick, Books, (1982), 7 All Saints' Passage, Cambridge CB2 3LS *T.* (0223) 350865. *Telex:* 817114 Camcom G.
Children's fiction.

*****Harper & Row, Ltd.**, 28 Tavistock Street, London, WC2E 7PN *T.* 01-836 4635. *Telex:* 267331 Harprow G. *T.A.* Harprow, London, WC2. *Directors:* Paul Chapman (Managing), M. Dubois, B. Thomas, E. T. Razzall, Cass Canfield, Jr., N. Pomerance, N. Y. Choung, U. Bruno.
Academic, professional, medical, nursing, juveniles, religious, non-fiction, paperbacks.

Harrap Ltd. (1901), 19-23 Ludgate Hill, London, EC4M 7PD *T.* 01-248 6444. *T.A.* Harrapbook, London, EC4. *Telex:* 28673; Consol G. *Directors:* Nicholas W. Berry (Chairman), Dr. I. Isidore Klausner (Vice-Chairman), Eric R. Dobby (Managing), David L. Bangs, C. Richard Butterworth, Jean-Luc Barbanneau, Michael F. Heathcoat-Amory, Simon A. Scott, Rienk Visser, David Collins.
Bi-lingual dictionaries, reference, general, English language products.

*****Hart-Davis Educational Ltd.**—see **William Collins, PLC.**

Hart, George (1973), 73 New Bond Street, London W1Y 9DD *T.* 01-493 3321. *Telex:* 261376 Lofbnd G. *Directors:* George Hart, Grace Hart.
Personality publishers—interested in autobiographies by stage, screen, television or public-life personalities. Biographies, non-fiction, fiction. Also company histories and memoirs of business personalities.

Harvester Press Ltd., The (1969), 16 Ship Street, Brighton, Sussex, BN1 1AD *T.* (0273) 723031. *Telex:* 877101 Olship. *Directors:* John Spiers (Chairman), Mark Holland, Edward Elgar (Managing), Valerie Ewens (Secretary), Melissa Tully, Sue Roe.
History, English literature, philosophy, psychology, literary fiction. Women's studies, popular science.

*****Harvey Miller Publishers** (1968), 20 Marryat Road, London, SW19 5BD *T.* 01-946 4426. *Telex:* 265871 (Mon ref G) ref. 84 DDS 2017. *BTG:* 84:DDS 2017. *Directors:* H. I. Miller, E. Miller.
Art history, medical atlases.

Haynes, J. H. & Co. Ltd., (trading as **Haynes Publishing Group)**, Sparkford, Yeovil, Somerset, BA22 7JJ *T.* North Cadbury (0963) 40635. *Telex:* 46212 Haynes G. *Directors:* J. H. Haynes (Executive Chairman), J. Scott (Managing), P. J. Bishop, J. R. Clew, A. C. Haynes, A. P. Lynch, R. J. Stagg, P. B. Ward.
Car and motorcycle owners workshop manuals, car handbooks/servicing guides.

Haynes Publishing Group—see **J. H. Haynes & Co. Ltd.**

*****Heinemann Group of Publishers, Ltd.**, 10 Upper Grosvenor Street, London, W1X 9PA *T.* 01-493 4141. *Telex:* 8954981. *T.A.* Sunlocks, London W1, and The Windmill Press, Kingswood, Tadworth, Surrey, KT20 6TG *T.* (0737) 833511. *T.A.* Sunlocks, Tadworth. *Directors:* Paul Hamlyn (Chairman), Nicholas Thompson (Managing), B. L. Perman, P. L. Range, F.C.A.. *Secretary:* H. G. Brunger, F.C.C.A.

*****Heinemann (William), Ltd.**, 10 Upper Grosvenor Street, London, W1X 9PA *T.* 01-493 4141. *Telex:* 8954961. *T.A.* Sunlocks, London, W1 and The Windmill Press, Kingswood, Tadworth, Surrey. *T.* (0737) 833511. *T.A.* Sunlocks,

Tadworth. *Directors:* N. Thompson (Chairman), Brian Perman (Managing), Susan Boyd, Kate Gardiner, David Godwin, Clyde Hunter, T. R. Manderson, Ingrid Selberg, W. Roger Smith, Jane Turnbull. *Literary Adviser:* Roland Gant. *Secretary:* Andrew Barrett F.C.A.
Art, biography and memoirs, belles-lettres, children's books, drama, fiction, history, humour, sports, games and hobbies, technical and business, travel. Imprints: Made Simple; Kingswood Press.

*Heinemann Educational Books, Ltd., 22 Bedford Square, London, WC1B 3HH *T.* 01-637 3311. *T.A.* Hebooks, London. *Telex:* 261888. *Directors:* N. Thompson (Chairman), David Fothergill (Managing), Stephen Ashton, Mike Esplen, Richard Gale, Paul Hutchings (Secretary), Bob Osborne, Paul Lewis.
African studies, African writers, biology, chemistry, physics, mathematics, English, drama, history, geography, economics, business studies, home economics, modern languages, education, primary, English as a foreign language.

*Heinemann, William, Medical Books, Ltd., 23 Bedford Square, London, WC1B 3HH *T.* 01-637 3311 *T.A.* Hebooks, London. *Telex:* 261888.
Directors: Nicholas Thompson (Chairman), David Fothergill (Managing), Richard Barling, Paul Hutchings.
Medical, surgical, dental science, nursing, physiotherapy.

Her Majesty's Stationery Office, *Head Office,* St. Crispins, Duke Street, Norwich, NR3 1PD *T.* (0603) 622211. *Telex:* 97301. *Distribution and order point:* 51 Nine Elms Lane, London SW8 5DR *Telex:* 297138. *Government Bookshops* (retail): 49 High Holborn, WC1V 6HB *T.* 01-211 5656; London Post Orders: P.O. Box 276, London, SW8 5DT *T.* 01-622 3316; 9-21 Princess Street, Manchester, M60 8AS *T.* 061-834 7201; 13A Castle Street, Edinburgh, EH2 3AR (wholesale and retail). *T.* 031-225 6333; 258 Broad Street, Birmingham, B1 2HE *T.* 021-643 3757; Southey House, Wine Street, Bristol, BS1 2BQ *T.* (0272) 24306-7; 80 Chichester Street, Belfast, BT1 4JY *T.* (0232) 234488.
Archaeology, architecture, art, current affairs, directories or guide books, educational (infants, primary, secondary, technical, university), general, history, naval and military, practical handbooks, reference, science, sociology, year books.
As the Government Publisher, **HMSO** only publishes material sponsored by Parliament, Government Departments and other official bodies. Consequently it cannot consider unsolicited work submitted by private citizens.

Herbert Press Ltd. (1972), 46 Northchurch Road, London N1 4EJ. *T.* 01-254 4379. *Telex:* 8952022 Ctytel G. *Directors:* David Herbert, Brenda Herbert.
Art, architecture, design, crafts, nostalgia, fashion and costume, natural history, archaeology, biography, illustrated non-fiction.

Heretic Books—see GMP Publishers Ltd.

*Hilger (Adam) Ltd., Techno House, Redcliffe Way, Bristol, BS1 6NX *T.* (0272) 276693. *Telex:* 449149 Instp G.
Mathematical, physical and medical sciences, and science-based technology.

Hilmarton Manor Press (1964), Calne, Wilts SN11 8SB *T.* Hilmarton (0249 76) 208.
Fine art, photography, antiques, visual art.

Hippo Books (1980), 10 Earlham Street, London, WC2H 9RX *T.* 01-240 5753. *Telex:* 264604 Sbslon G; *Fax:* 01-240 6927. *Managing Director:* J.E. Cox. Imprint of **Scholastic Publications Ltd.**
Children's paperbacks - fiction and non-fiction.

Hippopotamus Press (1974), 26 Cedar Road, Sutton, Surrey *T.* 01-643 1970.
Editors: Roland John, Anna Martin.
Poetry, essays, criticism. Poetry submissions from new writers welcome.

HM&M Publishers Ltd. An associate company of **John Wiley & Sons Ltd.**

*****Hodder & Stoughton Ltd.**, Mill Road, Dunton Green, Sevenoaks, Kent, TN13 2YA *T.* Sevenoaks (0732) 450111. *Telex:* 95122. *T.A.* Expositor, Sevenoaks and 47 Bedford Square, London, WC1B 3DP. *T.* 01-636 9851. *Telex:* 885887. *Directors:* Philip Attenborough (Chairman), Michael Attenborough, Mark Hodder-Williams, Eric Major, Richard Morris, Alan Gordon Walker. *Secretary:* A. M. Brown.
General, fiction, religious and theology, educational, children's, medical, dictionaries, guide books, travel, sports and games.

   *****Hodder & Stoughton.** *Directors:* Eric Major (Managing), Philip Attenborough, Michael Attenborough, Tony Hammond, Ion Trewin, Clare Bristow, David Wavre, Tom Biggs-Davison, Derick Bostridge.

   *****Hodder & Stoughton Educational.** *Directors:* Brian Steven (Managing), Philip Attenborough, C. W. Davies, David Mackin, Philip Walters.

   *****Hodder & Stoughton Paperbacks.** *Directors:* A. Gordon Walker (Managing), Michael Attenborough, Philip Attenborough, Adrian Bourne, J. A. G. Wilson, David Singer.

   *****Hodder & Stoughton Children's Books.** *Directors:* David Grant (Managing), Philip Attenborough, Michael Attenborough, Graham Cook, Jane Osborn (Editorial).

*****Hogarth Press, Ltd., The**—see **Chatto & Windus Ltd./The Hogarth Press Ltd.**

Holland Press, The, 37 Connaught Street, London, W2 2AZ *T.* 01-262 6184.
Bibliography, arms and armour, music, travel, cartography, reference works of all kinds in limited editions, books of interest to collectors, specialising in reprinting in de-luxe editions, original MSS. also considered.

Hollis & Carter. An imprint of **The Bodley Head Ltd.**

*****Holmes McDougall Ltd.,** Allander House, 137-141 Leith Walk, Edinburgh, EH6 8NS. *T.* 031-554 9444. *Cables:* Educational Edinburgh. *Telex:* 727508 Holmes G.
Educational (infant, primary and secondary).

*****Holt, Rinehart & Winston,** 1 St. Anne's Road, Eastbourne, East Sussex, BN21 3UN *T.* (0323) 638221. *Telex:* 877503 Volmst. *T.A.* Volumists, Eastbourne. See **Holt-Saunders Ltd.**
Educational books (school, college, university) in all subjects.

*****Holt-Saunders Ltd.,** 1 St. Anne's Road, Eastbourne, East Sussex, BN21 3UN *T.* (0323) 638221. *Telex:* 877503 Volmst. *T.A.* Volumists, Eastbourne. *Directors:* R. Kiernan, C. J. Sehmer, D. S. B. Inglis, S. C. White, M. Bide, P. W. Mitchell.
Medical, educational, scientific, technical, school, general.

Horwood, Ellis, Ltd. (1973) Market Cross House, Cooper Street, Chichester, West Sussex, PO19 1EB *T.* (0243) 789942. *Telex:* 86402 Horwood. *Cable:* Horwood Chichester. *Directors:* Ellis Horwood, M.B.E. (Chairman), Clive Horwood, F. M. Horwood, Michael Horwood, J. Gillison, Sue Horwood.
Chemical science and engineering, computer science, artificial intelligence, cognitive science, cybernetics, engineering, environmental science, management science, mathematics, medical science, physics, astronomy, psychology, sociology, water science, medicine, food science.

*Hulton Educational Publications Ltd. Merged with **Stanley Thornes (Publishers) Ltd.,** *q.v.*

*Hutchinson & Co. (Publishers) Ltd.—see **Century Hutchinson Publications Ltd.**

*Hutchinson Educational Ltd. (1958), Brookmount House, 62-65 Chandos Place, Covent Garden, London WC2N 4NW *T.* 01-240 3411. *Telex:* 261212 Lit Ldn G. *Directors:* M. J. Cohen (Managing), C. L'Enfant, J. M. Mottram, D. Levey, P. Rowlinson, R. Trinder. An imprint of **Century Hutchinson Ltd.**
Educational (secondary, technical and vocational, university and business).

Hutchinson Children's Books Ltd., Brookmount House, 62-65 Chandos Place, Covent Garden, London WC2N 4NW *T.* 01-240 3411. *Telex:* 261212 Lit Ldn G. Children's Books Publishers. *Directors:* A. J. V. Cheetham (Chairman), P. C. K. Roche (Managing), R. M. F. Cheetham, J. M. Mottram. A division of **Century Hutchinson Ltd.**
Children's books, fiction and non-fiction, picture books.

ISL Directory Developments—see **Information Services Ltd.**

Information Services Ltd. (1983). Incorporating **Kelly's Directories, Thomas Skinner Directories, Kompass Publishers Ltd., ISL Directory Developments, Dial Industry Publications,** Windsor Court, East Grinstead House, East Grinstead, West Sussex, RH19 1XA *T.* (0342) 26972. *T.A.* Infoservices, East Grinstead. *Telex:* Infser G 95127. *Directors:* A. H. Emery, S. Brown, R. J. E. Dangerfield (Managing), T. N. Leather, D. W. Lee, G. A. Shaw.
Reference books and directories.

Institute of Physics, Techno House, Redcliffe Way, Bristol, BS1 6NX *T.* (0272) 297481. *Telex:* 449149.
Physics journals, conference proceedings, general science.

*International Textbook Co. Ltd., a member of **The Blackie Group,** Bishopbriggs, Glasgow, G64 2NZ *T.* 041-772 2311. *Telex:* 777283 Blacki G. Imprints: International Textbook Company; Leonard Hill; Surrey University Press. *Directors:* Dr. Graeme Mackintosh, Michael Miller.
Professional, reference and text books in engineering, hotel and tourism management, business administration, food technology, chemistry, physics, biological sciences.

*Inter-Varsity Press, 38 De Montfort Street, Leicester, LE1 7GP *T.* (0533) 551700.
Theology and religion.

James (Arthur) Ltd. (1935), 1 Cranbourne Road, London N10 2BT *T.* 01-883 1831 and 883 2201. *Directors:* D. M. Duncan, Jillian Tallon.
Religion, sociology, psychology.

Jane's Publishing Co. Ltd., 238 City Road, London, EC1V 2PU *T.* 01-251 9281. *Telex:* 894689. *Managing Director:* Sidney Jackson.
Military, aviation, naval, non-fiction, reference.

Jenkins (Herbert), Ltd. Incorporated with **Barrie & Jenkins,** *q.v.*

Jewish Chronicle Publications, 25 Furnival Street, London, EC4A 1JT *T.* 01-405 9252. *Telex:* 28452. *Executive Director:* M. Weinberg. Agents for Jewish Publications Society of America, Ktav, New York; Behrman House, New York; Keter, Jerusalem; Carta, Jerusalem; Sepher-Hermon, New York; Schocken, New York.
Theology and religion, reference; *Jewish Year Book, Jewish Travel Guide.*

*Johnson Publications Ltd. (1946), 130 Wigmore Street, London, W1H 0AT *T.* 01-486 6757. *Telex:* 817133. *Directors:* M. A. Murray-Pearce, Z. M. Pauncefort.

Belles-lettres, biography and memoirs, current affairs, economics, history, law, political economy, sociology, travel, medical, philosophy; perfumery. Return postage should be sent with unsolicited manuscripts.

Jordan & Sons Ltd. (1836), 15 Pembroke Road, Bristol, BS99 7DX *T*. (0272) 732861. *Telex:* 449119. *Directors:* Archie Broomsgrove, Phil Holmes, Andrew Kampe, Ralph Leake, Patrick Lockstone, Dennis Newcomb, David Ordish, James Thomas, Michael Whitwell.
Law, particularly company and family (including the *Family Law Journal*), company administration, business, finance, educational (university and professional), loose-leaf services.

*Joseph (Michael), Ltd. (1935), 27 Wrights Lane, London W8 5TZ *T*. 01-937 7255. *Telex:* 917181 and 917182. *Fax:* 01-937 8704. *Directors:* Alan Brooke (Managing), Jenny Dereham, Richard Douglas-Boyd, Keith Ireland, John Lyon, Sheila Murphy, Peter Tummons, Susan Watt, Nick Webb, Chris Weller.
Belles-lettres, biography and memoirs, current affairs, fiction, general, history, humour.

Journeyman Press Ltd., The (1974), 97 Ferme Park Road, Crouch End, London N8 9SA *T*. 01-348 9261. *T.A.* Journeyrad, London N8. *Telex:* 25247 JOU *Directors:* Peter Sinclair, Rachel Weinstein.
Fiction, poetry, art, biography, social history, politics.

Justice of the Peace Ltd. (1837), Little London, Chichester, Sussex, PO19 1PG *T*. Chichester (0234) 783637. *Directors:* Barry Rose, P. D. Madge, D. J. C. Rose.
Law, police, local government, criminology, penology.

Kelly's Directories—see **Information Services Ltd.**

Kelpie Books—see **Canongate Publishing Ltd.**

Kenyon-Deane Ltd., 311 Worcester Road, Malvern, Worcs, WR14 1AN *T*. (068 45) 65045. *Directors:* Leslie Smith, Audrey Smith.
Plays and drama textbooks. Specialists in plays for women.

*Kimber (William) & Co. Ltd. (1950), 100 Jermyn Street, London, SW1Y 6EE *T*. 01-930 0446. Trade Counter: 72-74 Paul Street, London, EC2A 4NA. *T*. 01-739 4755. *Directors:* W. T. Kimber, O. J. Colman, Audrey Kimber, F. M. de Salis, Amy Myers.
Biography and memoirs, current affairs, fiction, general, history, travel, sport, naval, military and aviation.

Kingfisher Books Ltd. (1977), Elsley Court, 20-22 Great Titchfield Street, London, W1P 7AD *T*. 01-631 0878. *T.A.* Greatbooks, London. *Telex:* 27725. *Directors:* D. Grisewood (Managing), D. Maxwell MacDonald, M. Maxwell MacDonald, J. M. Olliver, J. Richards. *Secretary:* M. Barrett.
Children's books and general non-fiction.

*Kingsway Publications Ltd., Lottbridge Drove, Eastbourne, East Sussex, BN23 6NT *T*. (0323) 27454. Geoffrey J. Booker, H. D. Fuller (Managing), Angus R. M. Hudson, Gilbert W. Kirby (Chairman), Gavin H. Reid, Geoffrey P. Ridsdale, Margaret J. Kennett.
Religious books.

*Kluwer Publishing Ltd. (1972), 1 Harlequin Avenue, Great West Road, Brentford, Middlesex, TW8 9EW *T*. 01-568 6441. *Directors:* W. E. Porter, C. B. Ancliffe (Managing), A. T. A. Drabbe, M. G. Ware, R. X. Heslop.
Law, taxation, finance, insurance, business management, medicine, farming, loose-leaf information services, books, databases, conferences.

Knight (Charles) & Co. Ltd., Tolley House, 17 Scarbrook Road, Croydon, Surrey, CR0 1SQ *T.* 01-688 4163. *Directors:* J. V. Wilson (Chairman), A. J. Fisher, E. L. Harvey, M. S. Gale, S. C. Cotter (Managing Editor). Member of the **Extel Group.**
Local government, local government law, planning and the environment.

*****Kogan Page Ltd.** (1967), 120 Pentonville Road, London, N1 9JN *T.* 01-278 0433. *Telex:* 263088 Kogan G. *Directors:* P. Kogan (Managing), B. Kogan, R. Lobatto, F.C.A., P. Newman, J. Woodall, Neil Falkner.
New technology and science, energy, business and management, personnel, training and industrial relations, transport, marketing, commodities, small business, personal finance, education and educational technology, careers and jobs, social work, general, special publications, dictionaries.

Kompass Publishers Ltd.—see **Information Services Ltd.**

*****Ladybird Books Ltd.** (1924), P.O. Box 12, Beeches Road, Loughborough, Leicestershire, LE11 2NQ *T.* Loughborough (0509) 268021. *T.A.* Ladybird, Loughborough. *Telex:* 341347 Ldbird G. *Fax:* (0509) 234672. *Directors:* T. J. Rix (Chairman), M. P. Kelley (Managing), B. D. L. Cotton, C. W. Hall, R. Smith, A. T. Warren, J. D. Williamson, M. G. P. Wymer.
Children's books, general and educational (infants, primary, junior and secondary).

Lakeland Paperbacks. Imprint of **Marshall, Pickering Holding Ltd.**

Lane, Allen—see **Viking.**

Lawrence & Wishart, Ltd., 39 Museum Street, London, WC1A 1LQ *T.* 01-405 0103. *T.A.* Interbook, London, WC1. *Directors:* R. Simon, J. Skelley (Managing Director), M. Jacques, S. Sedley, S. Hayward, E. Munro, N. Temple, W. Norris.
Current affairs, economics, history, socialism, literary criticism, philosophy, political economy, sociology.

*****Leicester University Press** (1951), Fielding Johnson Building, University of Leicester, University Road, Leicester, LE1 7RH *T.* (0533) 551860. *Telex:* 341198. *Secretary:* Peter L. Boulton, M.A.
Academic books, especially in history (including English local history and urban history), archaeology, politics and international relations, defence studies, English and foreign literature.

Letts (Charles) (Holdings) Ltd. (1796), Diary House, Borough Road, London, SE1 1DW *T.* 01-407 8891. *Telex:* 884498 Letts G. *Directors:* A. A. Letts (Chairman), J. M. Letts, T. R. Letts, R. W. Aitken, J. A. Kearns, W. J. Swords (Managing). **Charles Letts & Co. Ltd.** wholly owned publishing subsidiary.
Diary and book publishers and manufacturers.

*****Lewis (A) (Masonic Publishers), Ltd.** (1870), Terminal House, Shepperton, TW17 8AS *T.* Walton-on-Thames (0932) 228950. *Telex:* 929806 Iallan G. *Managing Director:* Ian Allan.
Masonic books.

*****Lewis (F.) Publishers, Limited.** A subsidiary of **A. & C. Black plc.**

*****Lewis (H. K.) & Co. Ltd.** (1844), 136 Gower Street, London, WC1E 6BS *T.* 01-387 4282. *T.A.* Publicavit, London, WC1. *Directors:* G. W. Edwards, R. D. Spence, J. L. Haynes.
Science, medical.

Libbey, John, & Co. Ltd. (1979), 80-84 Bondway, London SW8 1SF *T.* 01-582 5266. *Telex:* 268048 Extldn G. *Directors:* John Libbey, Eldred Smith-Gordon, G. Cahn.

Medical: nutrition, obesity, epilepsy, neurology, diabetes, biological psychiatry.

*Library Association Publishing (1981), 7 Ridgmount Street, London, WC1E 7AE *T.* 01-636 7543. *Telex:* 21897 Laldn G. *Chairman:* Sir Harry Hookway, PH.D., D. LITT, LLD., F.L.A. *Directors:* C. Ellis, M.A. (Managing), C. Bingley, M.A., F.L.A., K. Crawshaw, B.A., D.L.I.S., A.L.A., G. Cunningham, B.A., B.SC.(ECON), Mrs. E. A. L. Esteve-Coll, B.A., A.L.A., N. Higham, O.B.E., M.A., A.L.A., R. A. McKee, B.A., M.A., PH.D., A.L.A., R. G. Surridge, M.A., F.R.S.A., F.L.A., A. G. D. White, F.L.A., J. H. Wormald, B.SC., A.L.A.
Bibliographies, directories, reference works, library science.

Linden Press. Imprint of **Centaur Press, Ltd.**

*Lion Publishing P.L.C. (1972), Icknield Way, Tring, Herts, HP23 4LE *T.* (044 282) 5151. *Telex:* 825850 Lion G. *Directors:* David Alexander, Pat Alexander, Tony Wales, David Vesey (Managing), Denis Cole.
Reference, paperbacks, illustrated children's books, educational, gift books, religion and theology; all reflecting a Christian position.

*Liverpool University Press (1901), Rosalind Campbell (Secretary and Publisher), P.O. Box 147, Liverpool, L69 3BX *T.* 051-709 6022, ext. 2512, 2429. *Telex:* 627095 Unilpl G.
Academic and scholarly books in a range of disciplines. Special interests: literature, social, political, economic and ancient history, archaeology, philosophy and the natural sciences, medicine, veterinary science and urban and regional planning.

London & International Publishers Ltd (1984), 49 St. James's Street, London SW1A 1JT *T.* 01-499 5042. *Directors:* Shaie Selzer, Klaus Boehm, N. R. Reynolds, Prof. John M. Stopford, P. W. Durrance (Secretary).
Publishing under The Stock Exchange Press in finance, investment, the securities industry; sports and leisure under Sportsworld imprint.

*Longman Group Limited (1724), 5 Bentinck Street, London, W1M 5RN *T.* 01-935 0121. *T.A.* Longman, London, W1. Longman House, Burnt Mill, Harlow, Essex, CM20 2JE *T.* (0279) 26721. *Telex:* 81259 Longmn G. *T.A. and Cables:* Longman, Harlow. T. J. Rix (Chief Executive), M. G. P. Wymer (Deputy Chief Executive). *Directors:* P. Kahn, R. G. B. Duncan, M. P. Kelley, P. J. Munday, C. J. Rea, R. P. Watson, J. D. Williamson (Finance), J. Osborne, J. M. Little, P. Blackburn. Associated Companies (*q.v.*) in India, Australia, New Zealand, Uganda, Kenya, Zimbabwe, Hong Kong, Japan, Malaysia, Nigeria, The Caribbean, South Africa, U.S.A., Canada, Singapore, Botswana, Lesotho, Swaziland, Italy, Spain, Greece, France, Netherlands, West Germany, Egypt.
Atlases, audio-visual aids, children's, school, further and technical education, university, scholarly, undergraduate, post-graduate, academic, scientific, professional, dictionaries, reference, English language teaching, directories, learned journals; micro computer software, videos. Africana (including African studies and African and Caribbean literature.) Medical—see **Churchill Livingstone.** Preliminary letter recommended before submitting MSS.

*Longman Professional and Business Communications Division, including Oyez Longman Publishing Ltd and Crown Eagle Communications Ltd., 21-27 Lamb's Conduit Street, London WC1N 3NJ *T.* 01-242 2548. *Telex:* 295445 Lawtax G. *Fax:* 01-831 8119. *Directors:* L. W. Herbert, P. J. Munday, N. A. Ross, J. N. Thomas (Managing), N. D. Vandyk, J. D. Williamson, J. E. Robinson.
Books and professional journals on law, business, taxation, pensions, insurance, government contracting, finance and accountancy.

Love Stories Ltd. (1984), 1 Old Compton Street, London W1V 5PH *T.* 01-734 4752. *Directors:* Anne Dewe (Managing), Pamela Fulton, Mrinalini Srivastava.
Good novels that happen to be love stories – no formula romance. Return postage required for all unsolicited MSS.

Lowe, Peter (Eurobook Ltd), (1968), 49 Uxbridge Road, London W5 5SA *T.* 01-840 4411. *Telex:* 934610 Beurok G. *T.A.* Beurok London W5. *Directors:* P. S. Lowe, R. Lowe.
Illustrated information books, natural history, cookery, indoor gardening, health, books for young people and adults.

*****Lund Humphries Publishers Ltd.,** 124 Wigmore Street, London, W1H 9FE *T.* 01-486 5360. *Telex:* Lundhumpub 8952387. *Directors:* John Taylor, Clive Bingley, Charlotte Burri, Lionel Leventhal, Herbert Spencer.
Art, architecture, graphic art and design, Arabic language.

*****Lutterworth Press** (1799), 7 All Saints' Passage, Cambridge CB2 3LS *T.* (0223) 350865. *Telex:* 817114 Camcom G. Subsidiary of **James Clark & Co. Ltd.**
The arts, biography and memoirs, children's books (fiction, non-fiction, rewards), craft, educational, gardening, general, history, leisure, philosophy, practical, science, sociology, theology and religion, travel.

Russell Street, London, WC1B 3PE *T.* 01-636 6068. *Chairman:* D. E. Rodrigues. *Publishing Director:* J. B. Knight-Smith.
Near and Middle East & Islam, Far East, Eastern religions.

Macdonald & Evans (Publications) Ltd.—see **Pitman Publishing Ltd.**

*****Macdonald & Company (Publishers) Ltd.,** 3rd Floor, Greater London House, Hampstead Road, London NW1 7QX *T.* 01-377 4600. *Telex:* 885233 Macdon G. *Fax:* 01-389 9286. *Directors:* R. Maxwell (Chairman), K. Pickett and C. Merullo (Joint-Managing), T. Melia, A. Moon, M. Pegge, M. Tapissier, A. Samson, P. Stewart, P. Crosby, R. Bywater, J. Moulder.
An operating company within **BPCC PLC.**

*****McGraw-Hill Book Company (UK) Ltd.,** McGraw-Hill House, Shoppenhangers Road, Maidenhead, Berkshire, SL6 2QL *T.* Maidenhead (0628) 23432. *T.A.* McGraw-Hill, Maidenhead. *Telex:* 848484 Mchill G. *Directors:* Stephen Neal (Managing), Nick Stavrakakis.
Technical, scientific, professional reference, medical.

*****Macmillan Publishers, Ltd.** (book holding company), 4 Little Essex Street, London, WC2R 3LF *T.* 01-836 6633. *Telex:* 262024 Macbsk G. *T.A.* Publish, London, WC2. Brunel Road, Houndmills, Basingstoke, Hants RG21 2XS *T.* (0256) 29242. *Telex:* 858493 Macbsk G. *Foreign Cables:* Publish, London; Publish, Basingstoke. *Chairman:* Viscount Macmillan of Ovenden. *Directors:* N. G. Byam Shaw (Managing), T. J. McCormack, K. B. Stonier, A. R. Soar, M. J. Barnard, G. R. U. Todd, M. Hamilton, C. K. R. Nunneley. *Imprint:* **Macmillan Children's Books.** *Publishing Director:* M. Wace.
Children's fiction and non-fiction.

Operating Subsidiaries:

*****Macmillan Education, Ltd.,** Brunel Road, Houndmills, Basingstoke, Hants. RG21 2XS *T.* (0256) 29242. *Chairman:* A. Soar; *Directors:* J. E. Jackman (Managing), R. Balkwill, P. Bruce-Gardyne, P. Murby, D. J. Mortimer.
Primary, secondary, and college level educational books and visual aids.

*****Macmillan Press, Ltd., The.** 4 Little Essex Street, London WC2R 3LF *T.* 01-836 6633. *Chairman:* A. Soar; *Directors:* C. Paterson (Managing), T. M. Farmiloe, J. F. K. Ashby.

Academic, scientific and technical works, learned journals, economics and world affairs, publishers of Grove's Dictionary of Music and Musicians, and The Statesman's Year-Book, and other reference works.

*Macmillan London, Ltd. 4 Little Essex Street, London WC2R 3LF *T.* 01-836 6633. *Chairman:* N. G. Byam Shaw; *Directors:* P. M. Harrison (Managing), M. Wace, M. R. Alcock, J. Hale, D. Rivers, N. Chapman.
General literature, biography, fiction and children's books.
Allied and Subsidiary Companies: Macmillan Journals, Ltd., Macmillan Publishers Group Administration Ltd., Macmillan Distribution Ltd., Macmillan Production Ltd., Macmillan Accounts and Administration Ltd., Gill & Macmillan, Ltd., (*Eire*), Macmillan India, Ltd., St. Martin's Press Inc., (*U.S.A.*), Macmillan Nigeria Publishers Ltd., The Macmillan Co. of Australia Pty., Ltd., Macmillan South Africa (Publishers) (Pty.), Ltd., Macmillan Publishers (H.K.), Ltd., Macmillan Southeast Asia Pte. Ltd., Macmillan Shuppan K.K., Japan, Hospital and Social Service Publications Ltd., Globe Book Services Ltd., Macmillan Publishers (UK) Ltd., Macmillan Publishers (Overseas) Ltd., Nature Publishing Company Inc. (*U.S.A.*), Peninsula Publishers Ltd. (*Hong Kong*), Macmillan Kenya (Publishers) Ltd., The Macmillan Company of New Zealand Ltd., Macmillan Boleswa Publishers (Pty) Ltd. (*Swaziland*), Petersen-Macmillan Verlag Gmbtt (*West Germany*), Editorial Macmillan de Mexico SA de CV, The College Press (Pvt) Ltd (*Zimbabwe*), Grove's Dictionaries of Music Inc. (*USA*), Macmillan Publishers (Malaysia) SB., Macmillan China Ltd.

*MacRae, Julia, Books (1979), a division of **The House of Grolier Ltd.,** 12A Golden Square, London, W1R 4BA *T.* 01-437 0713. *Telex:* 262655 Groluk G. *Directors:* Julia MacRae (Managing), Jonathan Gillett (USA, Chairman), David Howgrave-Graham, George Taylor, Chester Fisher, Rita Ireland.
Children's books, music and general non-fiction.

Magnet—see **Methuen Children's Books Ltd.**

*Manchester University Press (1912), Oxford Road, Manchester, M13 9PL *T.* 061-273 5530, 5539. *Telex:* 668932 Mchrul G. *Publisher:* J. M. N. Spencer, M.A.
Works of academic scholarship in most branches of learning, particularly literary criticism, science and social studies, politics, philosophy and economics, history and the arts. Specific interests: international law, neuro science, nonlinear science, economic and social history, Irish studies, African studies, Latin-American studies, and the north-west region of England. Student texts at VIth form and undergraduate levels; five scholarly journals.

Mandala—see **Unwin Hyman Ltd.**

*Mansell Publishing Ltd. (1966), 6 All Saints Street, London, N1 9RL *T.* 01-837 6676. *Telex:* 28604 ref. 1647. *Director:* J. E. Duncan (Managing).
Bibliographies in all academic subject areas and monographs in urban and regional planning, Islamic studies and librarianship.

Marshall, Morgan & Scott Publications Ltd. Imprint of **Marshall, Pickering Holdings Ltd.**

Marshall, Pickering Holdings Ltd. (1928), 3 Beggarwood Lane, Basingstoke, Hants RG23 7LP *T.* (0256) 59211. *Director:* J. Hunt (Managing).
Evangelical books, theology and music.

Martin Books, Fitzwilliam House, 32 Trumpington Street, Cambridge, CB2 1QY *T.* (0223) 66733. *Telex:* 817343 Blucam G.
Cookery, gardening and other popular subjects. An imprint of **Woodhead-Faulkner (Publishers) Ltd.,** *q.v.*

Martin Brian & O'Keeffe, Ltd. (1971), 78 Coleraine Road, Blackheath, London, SE3 *T.* 01-858 5164. *Director:* Timothy O'Keeffe.
General literature including biography, fiction, history, travel, science, economics and poetry.

Martin Robertson & Co. Ltd.—now merged with **Basil Blackwell Ltd.**

***Mason (Kenneth) Publications, Ltd.** (1958), The Old Harbourmaster's, 8 North Street, Emsworth, Hampshire PO10 7DD *T.* (0243) 377977. *Directors:* Kenneth Mason, M. E. Mason, M. A. Mason, P. A. Mason.
Nautical, slimming and licensing. No poetry or fiction. Technical journals, high court law reports.

Mayflower Books Ltd.—see **William Collins, PLC.**

Meadowfield Press Ltd. (1976), I.S.A. Building, Dale Road Industrial Estate, Shildon, Co. Durham, DL4 2QZ *T.* Morpeth (0670) 55860. *Directors:* Dr. J. G. Cook, M. Cook, J. A. Verdon, A. M. Creasey.
Microbiology, zoology, archaeology, botany, biology.

Medici Society Ltd., 34-42 Pentonville Road, London, N1 9HG *T.* 01-837 7099.
Publishers of the Medici Prints, greeting cards and other colour reproductions of Old Masters and Modern Artists.
Art, nature and children's books.

Melbourne House (Publishers) Ltd., (1979), 60 High Street, Hampton Wick, Kingston-upon-Thames, Surrey KT1 4DB *T.* 01-943 3911 *Telex:* 935425 Melrso G. *Directors:* Alfred Milgrom, Naomi Besen, Geoffrey Neuth (Managing).
Computer books and software.

Melrose Press Ltd. (1969), 3 Regal Lane, Soham, Ely, Cambridgeshire, CB7 5BA *T.* Ely (0353) 721091. *T.A.* Melropres Ely. *Telex:* 81584 Mpibc G. *Directors:* Ernest Kay, Marjorie Kay, R. A. Kay, N. Lashmar, F.C.A., R. W. G. Curtis, J. Ringe, J. M. Kay, B. J. Wilson, N. S. Law.
International biographical reference works, including *International Authors & Writers Who's Who.*

Merlin Press, Ltd., 3 Manchester Road, London, E14 9BD *T.* 01-987 7959. *Directors:* M. W. Eve, Patricia Eve.
Politics, economics, history, philosophy. Publishers of *The Socialist Register.* Distributors for **Augustus M. Kelley** (USA). *No unsolicited manuscripts, please.*

Merrow Publishing Company Limited (1951), I.S.A. Building, Dale Road, Industrial Estate, Shildon, Co. Durham, DL4 2QZ *T.* Morpeth (0670) 55860. *Directors:* J. G. Cook, M. Cook, J. A. Verdon, A. M. Creasey.
Textiles, plastics, popular science, scientific.

Methodist Church, Division of Education and Youth, 2 Chester House, Pages Lane, Muswell Hill, London, N10 1PR *T.* 01-444 9845.
Theology and religion.

Methodist Publishing House (1773), Wellington Road, London, SW19 8EU *T.* 01-947 5256.
Hymn and service books. **Foundery Press:** ecumenical titles.

***Methuen & Co., Ltd.** (1889), 11 New Fetter Lane, London, EC4P 4EE *T.* 01-583 9855. *Telex:* 263398. *T.A.* Elegiacs, London. *Directors:* Alan Miles (Chairman), John Naylor (Managing), Janice Price (Assistant Managing), Carol Somerset, Jane Armstrong, Mary Ann Kernan, Julian Lynn Evans, John Potter. *Secretary:* D. G. Sampson.
Books in the humanities and social sciences for universities and colleges of education.

*Methuen Children's Books, Ltd., 11 New Fetter Lane, London, EC4P 4EE *T.* 01-583 9855. *Telex:* 263398. *Directors:* Christopher Falkus (Chairman), Joy Backhouse, Christopher Holgate, Fiona Kennedy, David Ross, C. Charles, Diane Spivey, B. Martell, Janetta Otter-Barry.
Children's books (picture, fiction, non-fiction, for young children to early teens). Children's paperbacks under **Magnet** imprint.

*Methuen Educational, Ltd. (1967), 11 New Fetter Lane, London, EC4P 4EE *T.* 01-583 9855. *Telex:* 263398. *T.A.* Elegiacs, London. *Directors:* Nick Hern, John Naylor (Chairman).
Educational (primary, secondary), education and teaching methods, educational materials.

*Methuen London Ltd., 11 New Fetter Lane, London, EC4P 4EE *T.* 01-583 9855. *Telex:* 263398. *T.A.* Elegiacs, London. *Directors:* Christopher Falkus (Chairman), Geoffrey Strachan (Managing), Clive Charles, Nicholas Hern, Chris Holgate, Elsbeth Lindner, Fiona Kennedy, Ann Mansbridge, Barry Martell, John Potter, David Ross, Diane Spivey.
General fiction, biography and memoirs, history, current affairs, topography, humour, performing arts. Please write with synopsis before submitting MSS.

*Michael Joseph Limited—see Joseph (Michael) Limited.

Miller (J. Garnet), Ltd. (1951), 311 Worcester Road, Malvern, Worcestershire WR14 1AN *T.* (068 45) 65045. *Directors:* Leslie Smith, Audrey Smith.
Antiques, children's books, drama, science, theatre.

*Mills & Boon, Ltd. (1909), 15-16 Brooks Mews, London, W1A 1DR *T.* 01-493 8131. *Telex:* 24420 Milbon G. *T.A.* Millsator, London. *Chairman:* J. T. Boon, C.B.E. *Directors:* R. J. Williams (Managing), A. W. Boon, B. C. J. Rogers, M. N. Saraceno, R. Hedley, F. Whitehead.
Romantic fiction in hardback and paperback.

Mitchell Beazley Ltd., Artists House, 14-15 Manette Street, London, W1V 5LB *T.* 01-439 7211. *Telex:* 24892 MB Book G. *Directors:* Duncan Baird (Managing), Janice Mitchell, Peter Mead (Company Secretary). Holding company controlling Mitchell Beazley International Ltd., Mitchell Beazley Encyclopaedias Ltd., Mitchell Beazley London Ltd.

Mitchell Beazley Encyclopaedias Ltd., Artists House, 14-15 Manette Street, London, W1V 5LB *T.* 01-439 7211. *Telex:* 24892 MB Book G. *Directors:* Peter Mead (Company Secretary), Duncan Baird (Managing), Michael Powell.
International reference books and encyclopaedias.

Mitchell Beazley International Ltd. (1969), Artists House, 14-15 Manette Street, London, W1V 5LB *T.* 01-439 7211. *Telex:* 24892 MB Book G. *Directors:* Duncan Baird (Managing), Peter Mead (Company Secretary), Michael Powell, Jack Tresidder, Tony Cobb, David Hight.
Astronomy, astrology, atlases, cookery, family reference books, gardening, history and culture, educational books for children, natural history, photography, pocket books, sex education, wine.

Mitchell Beazley London Ltd., Artists House, 14-15 Manette Street, London, W1V 5LB *T.* 01-439 7211. *Telex:* 24892 MB Book G. *Directors:* Duncan Baird (Managing), David Hight, Peter Mead (Company Secretary).
UK and Commonwealth publishers of all Mitchell Beazley Group titles.

Morgan-Grampian Book Publishing Co., (1977), 30 Calderwood Street, London, SE18 6QH *T.* 01-855 7777. *Telex:* 896238. *General Manager:* Ian C. Laurie.
Directories for the travel trade, automation, electronics, and engineering industries.

Mothers' Union, The (1876), 24 Tufton Street, London, SW1P 3RB *T*. 01-222 5533.
Religious, educational and social subjects connected with marriage and the family; religious books for children.

*****Mowbray (A. R.) & Co., Ltd,** Saint Thomas House, Becket Street, Oxford, OX1 1SJ *T*. (0865) 242507.
Theology and Christian religion.

*****Muller, Blond & White Ltd.,** 55-57 Great Ormond Street, London WC1N 3HZ *T*. 01-242 3355. *Telex:* 262284 ref. 3375. *Cables:* Literary Holb WC1. *Joint Managing Directors:* Antony White and Anthony Blond.
Biography and autobiography, children's books, cinema, fiction, history, natural history, humour, occult pastimes, practical, puzzles, reference and sports.

*****Muller (Frederick) Ltd.** An imprint of **Muller, Blond & White Ltd.**

*****Murray, John (Publishers), Ltd.** (1768), 50 Albemarle Street, London, W1X 4BD *T*. 01-493 4361. *T.A.* Guidebook, London, W1. *Telex:* 21312 Murray G. *Directors:* John R. Murray (Chairman), Nicholas Perren (Managing), John G. Murray, C.B.E., Hallam Murray, Keith Nettle.
General: art and architecture, biography, autobiography, fiction, letters and diaries, travel, exploration and guidebooks, Middle East, Asia, India and subcontinent, general history, health education, aviation, craft and practical, children's books.
Educational: biology, chemistry, physics, business studies, economics, management and law, English, geography and environmental studies, history and social studies, mathematics, modern languages, technical subjects. Also self teaching in all subjects in *Success Studybook* series.

National Adult School Organisation (1899), Norfolk House, Smallbrook Queensway, Birmingham, B5 4LJ *T*. 021-643 9297.
Adult education handbooks for study groups.

*****National Christian Education Council** (incorporating **Denholm House Press** and **International Bible Reading Association**), Robert Denholm House, Nutfield, Redhill, RH1 4HW *T*. Nutfield Ridge, 2411.
Books on all aspects of Christian education. Material for children's work in the Church, also R.E. and M.E. material for day schools. Activity, visual and resource material, religious drama and religious music.

Nautical Publishing Co. Ltd.—subsidiary of **Conway Maritime Press Ltd.,** *q.v.*

*****Nelson (Thomas) & Sons, Ltd.** (1798), Nelson House, Mayfield Road, Walton-on-Thames, Surrey, KT12 5PL *T*. Walton-on-Thames 246133. *Telex:* 929365 Nelson G. *T.A.* Thonelson, Walton-on-Thames. Subsidiary in Hong Kong. *Directors:* D. J. Smith (Managing), M. J. Givans, R. Tyler, G. Taylor, P. Murphy, M. McWhinnie, Alan Martin.
Educational (infant, primary, secondary), school atlases and dictionaries, English language teaching world-wide, educational books for Africa, Caribbean and S.E. Asia.

New Beacon Books (1966), 76 Stroud Green Lane, London N4 3EN *T*. 01-272 4889. *Directors:* John La Rose, Sarah White, Michael La Rose, Janice Durham.
General non-fiction, fiction, poetry, critical writings.

New Cavendish Books (1973), 23 Craven Hill, London W2 3EN *T*. 01-262 9450 and 7905. *Telex:* 8951182 Gecoms G. **White Mouse Editions Ltd.** (1979).
Specialist books for the collector.

*New English Library, Ltd. (1957), 47 Bedford Square, London, WC1B 3DP *T*. 01-323 4881. *T.A*. Expositor, London. *Telex:* 885887. *Directors:* Alan Gordon Walker (Managing), P. J. Attenborough, M. F. Attenborough, R. Morris.
Fiction and non-fiction.

*Newnes Books (incorporating **W. H. & L. Collingridge Ltd.** and **Country Life**)—a Division of **The Hamlyn Publishing Group Limited.**

*Newnes Technical Books, imprint of **Wm. Heinemann Ltd,** 10 Upper Grosvenor Street, London W1X 9PA *T*. 01-493 4141. *Publisher:* Peter Dixon.
Audio, radio, TV and video; electricity; electronics and computing, car and motor cycle mechanics. Technical trades and hobbies.

*Nicholson, Robert, Publications Ltd. (1921), 16 Golden Square, London W1R 4BN *T*. 01-437 9602.*Telex:* 897284 Arpub.*Directors:* B. Winkleman (Managing), J. Krendel. A division of **Times Books Ltd.**
Maps, guides and atlases.

*Nisbet (James) & Co., Ltd. (1810), Digswell Place, Welwyn Garden City, Herts, AL8 7SX *T*. Welwyn Garden 325491. *T.A.* Stebsin, Welwyn Garden City. *Directors:* Miss E. M. Mackenzie-Wood, Mrs. R. M. Mackenzie-Wood, A. D. M. Hill, Mrs. A. A. C. Bierrum.
Dictionaries, educational (infants, primary, secondary).

Nonesuch Press, Ltd., The. *Directors:* Dame Alix Meynell, D.B.E., Max Reinhardt, Benedict Meynell, Martin Zander. Special editions designed by the late Sir Francis Meynell. Distributors: **The Bodley Head, Ltd.,** 32 Bedford Square, London, WC1B 3EL *T*. 01-631 4434.

Normal Press, The (1889), 25 Vicarage Lane, Upper Hale, Farnham, Surrey, GU9 0PG. *Director:* L. W. Cradwick.
Educational.

Northcote House Publishers Ltd (1985), Harper & Row House, Estover Road, Plymouth, PL6 7PZ. *T*. (0752) 705251. *Telex:* 45635 Hardis G. *Directors:* R. E. Ferneyhough, B. R. W. Hulme, M. W. Beevers F.C.A.
Business and professional text and reference books, accountancy, banking, economics, computer studies, data processing, management, marketing, international business reference and specialist dictionaries, travel, police and social studies, How-To books, dance. Exclusive distributors for a number of American and European publishes.

Norton, W. W., & Company (1980), 37 Great Russell Street, London, WC1B 3NU *T*. 01-323 1579. *Telex:* 946240 ref. 19020793. *T.A.* Gavia, London WC1. *Directors:* Alan Cameron (Managing), Clarence Paget, Donald Lamm (USA), Victor Schmalzer (USA), Eric Swenson (USA).
History, biography, current affairs, sailing, English and American literature, economics, music, psychology, science.

Octopus Books Ltd. (1971), 59 Grosvenor Street, London, W1X 9DA *T*. 01-493 5841. *T.A.* Octobooks, London. *Telex:* 27278 Octobk G. *Directors:* Paul Hamlyn (Chairman), Timothy Clode (Managing), Derek Freeman, Barry Gillions, John Maynard, Bruce Powell, Paul Richardson, George Rogers, David Robertson, Geoff Cloke, David Martin.
Cookery, handicrafts, arts and antiques, children's gardening, natural history, mythology, entertainment, war histories, military, fiction.

Octopus Publishing Group PLC, (1971), 59 Grosvenor Street, London, W1X 9DA *T*. 01-493 5841 and 491 4233. *Telex:* 27278 Octobk G. *Directors:* Paul Hamlyn, (Chairman), Ian Irvine (Chief Executive), Timothy Clode (Managing), Stuart Wallis, Nicolas Thompson, Iain Burns, Robert Gavron, Sir Claus Moser, Sir Owen Green, Mike Smith.

Offord, John (Publications) Ltd. (1971), 12 The Avenue, Eastbourne, East Sussex, BN21 3YA *T.* (0323) 645871.
Specialist theatre and arts publisher. Annual theatre directories. Reference and text books for theatre and arts administration.

Oleander Press, The (1960), 17 Stansgate Avenue, Cambridge, CB2 2QZ *T.* (0223) 244688. *T.A.* Oleander. *Managing Director:* P. Ward.
Language, literature, Libya, Arabia and Middle East, Indonesia and Far East, Cambridgeshire, travel, medical history, reference. Preliminary letter required before submitting MSS.; please send s.a.e. for reply.

***Oliver & Boyd,** a Division of **Longman Group UK, Ltd.,** Robert Stevenson House, 1-3 Baxter's Place, Leith Walk, Edinburgh, EH1 3BB *T.* 031-556 2424. *T.A.* Almanac, Edinburgh. *Telex:* 727511. *Director:* R. P. Watson (Divisional Managing).
Educational material for primary and secondary schools; Scottish school books.

Open Books Publishing Ltd. (1974), Beaumont House, New Street, Wells, Somerset BA5 2LD *T.* (0749) 77276. *Directors:* P. Taylor (Managing), C. Taylor.
Academic and general non-fiction; education, child development, medicine, human behaviour, local history.

***Open University Educational Enterprises Ltd.** (1977), 12 Cofferidge Close, Stony Stratford, Milton Keynes, MK11 1BY *T.* (0908) 566744. *Telex:* 826147. *Directors:* P. Calvocoressi (Chairman), Dr. J. H. Horlock (Deputy Chairman), R. E. Cavaliero, J. D. Keir, P. S. Wright (Managing), Professor Judith Greene, C. Emsley, Dr. D. A. Elliott, J. A. Clarke, Prof. R. C. Smith.
Biological sciences, chemistry, earth and environmental sciences, economics, education, engineering and materials science, geography, history, history of art and architecture, history and philosophy of mathematics, science and technology, literature, mathematics, statistics and computing, music, philosophy and religion, physics, political science, psychology, sociology, systems. **Open University Press.** *Publisher:* John Skelton.

***Orbis Book Publishing Corporation Ltd,** the illustrated books division of **Macdonald & Company (Publishers) Ltd,** 3rd Floor, Greater London House, Hampstead Road, London NW1 7QX *T.* 01-377 4600. *Telex:* 885233 Macdon G.

***Orchard Books,** a division of **The House of Grolier Ltd** (1985), 10 Golden Square, London W1R 3AF *T.* 01-734 8738. *T.A.* Frawatts London W1. *Telex:* 262655 Groluk G. *Directors:* Judith Elliott (Managing), Jonathan Gillett (USA, Chairman), David Howgrave-Graham, Julia MacRae, George Taylor, Chester Fisher, Rita Ireland, Sandra Jordan (USA).
Children's books.

***Oriel Press, Ltd.** (1962), Stocksfield Studio, Branch End, Stocksfield, Northumberland, NE43 7NA *T.* Stocksfield (0661) 843065. *Directors:* Norman Franklin, Alan Godwin (Secretary). Bruce Allsopp (Hon. Chairman). A subsidiary company of **Routledge and Kegan Paul Ltd.**
Architecture, art, archaeology, landscape, town planning, history, librarianship, science, ecology, philosophy, religion, social concern, biography.

Orion. An imprint of **Unwin Hyman Ltd.**

***Osprey Publishing, Ltd.** (1968), 27A Floral Street, London, WC2E 9DP *T.* 01-836 7863. *Telex:* 21667.

Aviation, automotive, military, yachting, sport. See also **George Philip & Son Ltd.**

Outposts Publications (1956), 72 Burwood Road, Walton-on-Thames, Surrey, KT12 4AL *T.* Walton-on-Thames 240712. *Directors:* Howard Sergeant, Jean Sergeant.
Poetry.

*Owen, Peter, Ltd., 73 Kenway Road, London, SW5 0RE *T.* 01-373 5628 and 370 6093. *Directors:* Peter L. Owen (Managing), Beatrice Musgrave.
Art, belles-lettres, biography and memoirs, fiction, general, theatre.

Oxford Illustrated Press Ltd. (1975), Sparkford, Yeovil, Somerset, BA22 7JJ *T.* (0963) 40635. *Telex:* 46212 Haynes G. *Editorial:* Little Holcombe, Stag Lane, Newington, Oxford, OX9 8AJ *T.* Oxford 890026. *Directors:* J. H. Haynes (Executive Chairman), J. Scott (Managing), A. Lynch, Jane Marshall, R. J. Stagg, A. C. Haynes.
Well-illustrated non-fiction books, sport, leisure and travel guides, local history, car books, art books, general.

*Oxford University Press (1478). *Secretary to the Delegates:* G. B. Richardson, Oxford University Press, Walton Street, Oxford, OX2 6DP *T.* (0865) 56767. *Telex:* Clarpress, Oxford, 837330. *Oxford Publisher:* R. A. Denniston. O.U.P. Distribution Services, Saxon Way West, Corby, Northants, NN18 9ES *T.* Great Oakley (0536) 741519. *T.A.* Oxonion, Corby. *Telex:* 34313 Oxpres-G. Branches or offices *q.v.* in New York, Toronto, Melbourne, Auckland, Delhi, Bombay, Calcutta, Madras, Karachi, Cape Town, Nairobi, Dar es Salaam, Harare, Kuala Lumpur, Singapore, Hong Kong, Tokyo, Nicosia. Associated companies: **University Press Ltd.,** Ibadan, **ELTA/OUP,** Beirut.
Anthropology, archaeology, architecture, art, belles-lettres, bibles, bibliography, biography and memoirs, children's books (fiction, non-fiction, picture), commerce, current affairs, dictionaries, drama, economics, educational (infants, primary, secondary, technical, university), English language teaching, essays, general, history, hymn and service books, journals, law, maps and atlases, medical, music, oriental, philosophy, poetry, political economy, prayer books, reference, science, sociology, theology and religion. Academic books published under the imprint **Clarendon Press.**

*Oyez Longman Publishing Ltd. Division of **Longman Group Ltd.**

Pagoda Books (1982), 30 Museum Street, London WC1A 1LH. *T.* 01-637 0890. *Telex:* 23539 Vision G. *Directors:* Susan Pinkus, David Alexander.
Parenting, health, photography, natural history, fine art, children's, illustrated fiction.

*Paladin Books—see **William Collins, PLC.**

*Pan Books, Ltd. (1944), Cavaye Place, London, SW10 9PG *T.* 01-373 6070. *Directors:* S. H. Master (Managing), T. W. V. McMullan (Deputy Managing), A. R. H. Birch, N. Byam Shaw, S. Land, A. S. McConnell (Secretary), A. S. Mehta, D. L. Range, N. Thompson, G. R. Todd.
Paperback originals and reprints of notable fiction and non-fiction including novels, detective fiction, travel, adventure, war books, biography, memoirs, current affairs, humour, reference, crafts, practical handbooks, etc. Also *Piccolo*, a children's fiction and non-fiction series, *Picador*, an imprint for outstanding international fiction and non-fiction. *Educational:* Study aids for school and college students, including *Brodie's Notes* on English Literature; books for adult education, particularly in languages, business, management and professional education.

*Pandora Press (imprint of **Routledge & Kegan Paul plc**), 11 New Fetter Lane, London EC4P 4EE *T.* 01-583 9855 *Telex:* 263398. *Publisher:* Philippa Brewster.
Women's history, feminist politics, social questions, women's health, handbooks, media, reference, women's fiction, biography, travel.

*Panther Books—see **William Collins, PLC.**

Papermac—an imprint of **Macmillan London Ltd.**

Partridge Press—see **Transworld Publishers Ltd.**

*Paternoster Press, Ltd., The, Paternoster House, 3 Mount Radford Crescent, Exeter, Devon, EX2 4JW *T.* (0392) 50631.
Biblical studies, Christian theology, philosophy, ethics, history, mission.

Paul (Stanley) & Co., Ltd. (1908), Brookmount House, 62-65 Chandos Place, Covent Garden, London WC2N 4NW *T.* 01-240 3411. *Telex:* 261212 Lit Ldn G. *Directors:* R. B. Bloomfield, P. C. K. Roche, J. M. Mottram. An imprint of **Century Hutchinson Ltd.**
Sports, games, hobbies and handicrafts, sporting biographies.

Pavilion Books (1980), 196 Shaftesbury Avenue, London, WC2H 8JL *T.* 01-836 1306. *Telex:* 268639 Eperon G. *Directors:* Colin Webb, Tim Rice, Michael Parkinson.
Humour, theatre, cinema, music, sport, children's.

Pearson (C. Arthur) Books. An imprint of **The Hamlyn Publishing Group, Ltd.**

*Pelham Books, Ltd. (1959), 27 Wrights Lane, London W8 5DZ *T.* 01-937 7255. *Telex:* 917181 and 917182 Emjaybuks. *Fax:* 01-937 8704. *Directors:* Alan Brooke (Chairman), Richard Douglas-Boyd (Publisher), Muriel Gascoin, Peter Tummons.
Pears Cyclopaedia, Junior Pears Encyclopaedia, full colour encyclopaedias. Autobiographies of men and women in sport, sports handbooks, hobbies, crafts and pastimes, practical handbooks on dogs and other pets, country pursuits.

*Penguin Books Limited, Bath Road, Harmondsworth, Middlesex, UB7 0DA *T.* 01-759 1984 and 5722. *T.A.* Penguinook, West Drayton. *Telex:* 933349. *London Office:* 27 Wrights Lane, London W8 5TZ *T.* 01-938 2200. *Telex:* 917181/2. *Fax:* 01-937 8704. *Founder:* Sir Allen Lane. *Chief Executive:* P. M. Mayer. *Directors:* J. A. Broom, P. T. S. Carson, A. F. Cotton, A. S. Lacey, J. H. Rolfe, J. W. Webster, A. Wherry, P. M. M. Wright, J. R. R. Yglesias, E. M. Attenborough, C. Weller.
Penguin Books consists of reprints of novels, detective and science fiction, travel, adventure, and biography, both reprints and original works. *Pelican Books* include more serious works on general aspects of the sciences and arts, including many entirely new works. *Peregrines* are books of more academic interest. *Puffin Books* are full-length children's stories, often illustrated. *Puffin Plus* are for older children. *Penguin Classics* are new translations of the world's greatest books. *Penguin Modern Classics* consist of reprints of twentieth-century classics. *Penguin Handbooks* are a series of Practical Handbooks on many subjects of fairly widespread interest. *Penguin Specials* are books on topical subjects, in particular politics and current affairs. The *Penguin English Library* consists of some of the literary masterpieces in English produced since the fifteenth century. *Viking* and *Viking Kestrel* are the adult and children's hard-cover lists. There are also the *Buildings of England, Lives and Letters, Penguin American Library, Penguin Poets, Penguin Plays, Penguin Reference Books, Penguin Shakespeare, Penguin Travel Library, Pelican History of Art* and *King Penguins,* a larger format series of more literary fiction.

*Pergamon Press, Ltd. (1948), Headington Hill Hall, Oxford, OX3 0BW *T.* (0865) 64881. *T.A.* Pergapress, Oxford. *Telex:* 83177. *Directors:* Robert Maxwell, M.C. (Chairman), C. T. Clark (Deputy Chairman), G. F. Richards (Managing), H. A. Stephens (Deputy Managing), Jean Baddeley, D. H. Barnett, C. Bundy, I.F. Klimes, P. D. McGeough, S. C. Silkin, W. A. Snyder (USA), A. J. Steel, L. Straka (USA), R. E. W. Strange, K. Maxwell, J. R. Sharr, R. K. G. Baker, F. Cunningham. S. Wahrsager (USA), A. J. Wheaton. *Overseas:* New York, Washington, Tokyo, Toronto, Sydney, Frankfurt, Paris. *UK Subsidiary Companies:* E. J. Arnold & Sons Ltd., BPCC, plc, Bumpus, Haldane & Maxwell Ltd., Hollis Bros and ESA plc, Brassey's Defense Publishers Ltd., Information Management Techniques Ltd., Oxford Microform Publishing Services Ltd., Newport & Robinson Ltd., Pergamon Technical Services International Ltd., Aberdeen University Press Ltd., A. Wheaton & Co., Ltd., Pergamon InfoLine, Pergamon Infotech.
Economics, educational (secondary, technical, university), medical research, science, technology, engineering, sociology, energy, environment, chess, general, electronic databases.

Peterloo Poets, (1976), Treovis Farm Cottage, Upton Cross, Liskeard, Cornwall PL14 5BQ *T.* (0579) 62801. *Trustees:* Simon Curtis (Chairman), Richard H. Francis (Vice-Chairman).
Poetry.

*Phaidon Press, Ltd., Littlegate House, St. Ebbes Street, Oxford, OX1 1SQ *T.* (0865) 246681-7. *T.A.* Phaidon Oxford. *Telex:* 83308 Phaidn G. *Fax:* (0865) 251959. *Chairman:* George Riches. *Managing Director:* Derek Phillips.
Fine arts, the history of art and civilization, decorative and performing arts, archaeology, history, music, photography, art instruction, reference.

*Philip (George) & Son, Ltd. (1834), 27A Floral Street, London, WC2E 9DP *T.* 01-836 7863. *Telex:* 21667. *Directors:* R. J. Shattock (Chairman), M. A. Bovill (Managing), J. A. Bennett, R. J. Bonnett, L. M. Greeves, A. G. Poynter, D. S. Reeves, F.C.A., B. M. Willett. Imprints: **Osprey Publishing Ltd, Stanford Maritime Ltd.**
Maps, atlases, globes, travel, general trade books, educational books.

Phillimore & Co., Ltd. (incorporating **Darwen Finlayson Ltd.**), Shopwyke Hall, Chichester, Sussex, PO20 6BQ *T.* Chichester (0243) 787636. *Hon. Pres.:* Lord Darwen. *Directors:* Philip Harris, J.P. (Chairman and Managing), Noel Osborne, M.A. (Cantab). (Editorial), Ian Macfarlane, F.C.A.
Local and family history; architectural history, archaeology, genealogy and heraldry; also Darwen County History Series.

Piatkus Books (1979), 5 Windmill Street, London W1P 1HS *T.* 01-631 0710. *Telex:* 266082 Piatks G. *Directors:* Judy Piatkus (Managing), Philip Cotterell (Sales), Gill Gormode (Editorial).
Fiction, leisure, cookery, arts, women's interest, gift books, health, miscellaneous.

*Picador—see **Pan Books, Ltd.**

Piccadilly Press, (1983), 5 Golders Green Crescent, London NW11 8LA *T.* 01-209 1326. *Telex:* 295441. *Directors:* Brenda Gardner (Chairman and Managing), Philip Durrance (Secretary).
Children's hard-back books.

Pickering & Inglis, Ltd. Imprint of **Marshall, Pickering Holding Ltd.**

*Pinter, Frances (Publishers) Ltd., (1973), 25 Floral Street, London, WC2E 9DS *T.* 01-240 9233. *Telex:* 912881 Cwuktx G Attn PIN. *Directors:* Frances Pinter, Pamela Fulton, Robert Macleod, Anne Weyman.

Economics, politics, international relations, new technology, information science, computergraphics, management.

Pitkin Pictorials, Ltd. (1941), 11 Wyfold Road, London, SW6 6SG *T.* 01-385 4351. *Directors:* Norman Garrod, R. E. Willson, Dennis Potts, Eileen M. Goff.

*****Pitman Publishing Ltd.** (1845), 128 Long Acre, London, WC2E 9AN *T.* 01-379 7383. *T.A.* Ipandsons, London, WC2. *Chief Executive:* Ian Pringle.
Secretarial studies, business education, management, professional studies, information technology. M & E Handbooks; titles previously published by **Macdonald & Evans**.

Planet Books. An imprint of **W. H. Allen & Co. PLC**.

Pluto Press (1969), The Works, 105a Torriano Avenue, London, NW5 2RX *T.* 01-482 1973 *T.A.* Plutonic, London. *Directors:* Nina Kidron (Managing), Neil Middleton (Editorial).
Independent radical publishers. Current affairs, sexual politics, social science, health and medicine, political economy, trade union studies and socialist theatre, history and some fiction.

Poetry Wales Press (1981), 56 Parcau Avenue, Bridgend, Mid Glamorgan CF31 0PG. *T.* Bridgend 880649, 3480. *Director:* Cary Archard.
Poetry, literary criticism, biography – mostly with relevance to Wales.

Polygon Books (1980), 48 Pleasance, Edinburgh, EH8 9TJ *T.* 031-558 1117-8.
Scottish, fiction, social, Russian literature, general, feminist literature.

Polytech Publishing Ltd. An imprint of **Pitman Publishing Ltd**.

Poplar Press Ltd (1981), Studio 6, Kingsley House, Avonmore Place, London W14 8RY *T.* 01-602 7341. *Directors:* Linda G. Schwartz, Namir F. Al-Rahal.
How-to books on writing; science fiction; mystery/suspense fiction.

Popular Dogs Publishing Co., Ltd., Brookmount House, 62-65 Chandos Place, Covent Garden, London WC2N 4NW *T.* 01-240 3411. *Telex:* 261212 Lit Ldn G. *Directors:* R. B. Bloomfield, P. C. K. Roche, J. M. Mottram. An imprint of **Century Hutchinson Ltd**.
Practical books on breeding, care, training, and general management of dogs.

Profile Books Ltd. (Incorporating **Profile Publications Ltd.**) (1974), Unit 1, Pontiac Works, Fernbank Road, Ascot, Berks. SL5 8JH *T.* Winkfield Row (0344) 884222. *Directors:* P. E. Butler, R. E. Beckett, J. H. W. Lacy.
Aircraft, AFV's, warships, locomotives, small arms and related subjects, semi-technical part publications—these require 5,000-10,000 words, 30-50 pictures, plans for colour; case-bound books. *Writers and Their Work* series (10,000 words). Publishes *Air Pictorial* magazine.

*****P.S.I. Policy Studies Institute,** 100 Park Village East, London, NW1 3SR *T.* 01-387 2171. *Director:* Donald Derx, C.B. *Deputy Director:* W. W. Daniel. *Marketing and Publicity Manager:* Nicholas Evans. *Secretary:* Eileen M. Reid.
Economic, industrial and social policy, political institutions, social sciences.

Puffin, the children's paperback imprint of **Penguin Books,** *q.v.* 27 Wrights Lane, London W8 5TZ *T.* 01-938 2200. *Chief Editor:* Elizabeth Attenborough.

Purnell Books, 3rd Floor, Greater London House, Hampstead Road, London NW1 7QX *T.* 01-377 4600. *Telex:* 885233 Macdon G. A division of **Macdonald & Co. Publishers Ltd**.

*****Putnam & Company, Ltd.** An imprint of **The Bodley Head Ltd**.

UNITED KINGDOM

Quaritch (Bernard), Ltd. (1847), 5 Lower John Street, London, W1R 4AU *T.* 01-734 2983. *Telex:* 8955509 BQS Ldn G. *T.A.* Quaritch, London, W1. *Directors:* E. M. Dring, Lord Parmoor, P. N. Poole-Wilson, R. A. Linenthal, H. E. Radclyffe, S. D. Sainsbury, W. P. Watson.

Quartet Books, Ltd. (1972), 27-29 Goodge Street, London, W1P 1FD *T.* 01-636 3992. *Telex:* 919034 Namara G. *Directors:* N. I. Attallah (Chairman), D. Elliott, G. Grant, P. Grant, S. Pickles, C. Parker, Z. Hourani, R. Fraser. Member of the **Namara Group.**
General fiction and non-fiction, sociology, politics, topical issues, jazz, biography, crime, children's, original and reprint paperbacks.

Queen Anne Press, the sporting, sponsored and premium division of **Macdonald & Company (Publishers) Limited,** 3rd Floor, Greater London House, Hampstead Road, London NW1 7QX *T.* 01-377 4600. *Telex:* 885233 Macdon G.

Quiller Press Ltd. 50 Albemarle Street, London W1X 4BD *T.* 01-499 6529 and 1825. *Telex:* 21120.

*****Rainbird Publishing Group Ltd,** 27 Wrights Lane, London W8 5TZ *T.* 01-938 2200. *Telex:* 917181. *Fax:* 01-937 8704. *Directors:* Peter Mayer (Chairman), Valerie Reuben (Managing), Janet Liebster, John Webster, Nigel Williams. Publishers of illustrated non-fiction in the fields of general reference, travel, biography, natural history and crafts. Free-lance artists' and designers' work used.

Rapp & Whiting, Ltd. All books published by Rapp & Whiting have been taken over by **André Deutsch, Ltd.**

*****Reader's Digest Association, Ltd., The,** 25 Berkeley Square, London, W1X 6AB. *T.* 01-629 8144. *Telex:* 264631. *T.A.* Readigest, London, W1. *Directors:* R. W. Hewett (Chairman and Managing), S. N. McRae (Deputy Managing), B. C. Gray, M. R. Randolph, M. L. Stockton, M. J. Bohane.

Redcliffe Press Ltd (1976), 49 Park Street, Bristol BS1 5NT *T.* (0272) 290158. *Directors:* John Sansom, Angela Sansom.
Fine art, architecture, photography, poetry, local interest—Bristol, Bath, West Country.

Reinhardt, Max, Ltd., 32 Bedford Square, London, WC1B 3EL *T.* 01-631 4434. *Directors:* Max Reinhardt (Chairman and Managing), J. R. Hews, F.C.A., Mrs. J. Reinhardt. Proprietors of **The Bodley Head Ltd.**

*****Religious and Moral Education Press,** Hennock Road, Exeter, EX2 8RP *T.* Exeter (0392) 74121. *Telex:* 42749 Wheatn G. *Fax:* (0392) 217170. A member of the **Pergamon/BPCC** Group of Companies. *Publisher:* Simon Goodenough. Religious, moral, personal and social education.

Renwick of Otley, Printerdom, Otley, Yorkshire, LS21 1QH *T.* (0943) 465555.

Rider & Co. (1892), Brookmount House, 62-65 Chandos Place, Covent Garden, London WC2N 4NW *T.* 01-240 3411. *Telex:* 261212 Lit Ldn G. *Editorial Manager:* Oliver Caldecott. An imprint of **Century Hutchinson Ltd.**
Oriental religion and philosophy, mysticism and meditation.

*****Rivelin Grapheme Press** (1984), 199 Greyhound Road, London W14 9SD *T.* 01-381 2066. *Fax:* 01-381 6951. *Directors:* Snowdon Barnett, Winston Barnett, David Tipton.
Poetry.

Robinson Books Ltd., P.O. Box 72, London WC2H 0LU. *Directors:* R. G. Robinson, P. M. E. Robinson, H. Robinson (Managing).
Esoteric subjects, holistic medicine, philosophy, religion, new age, new sciences.

Robinson Publishing (1983), 11 Shepherd House, 5 Shepherd Street, London W1Y 7LD *T*. 01-493 1064. *Telex:* 28905 Mon. ref G ref 778. *Partners:* Nicholas Robinson, Tim Brentnall.
General fiction and non-fiction, mainly reprints.

*****Robson Books** (1973), Bolsover House, 5-6 Clipstone Street, London, W1P 7EB *T*. 01-637 5937. *T.A.* Robsobook, London, W1. *Managing Director:* Jeremy Robson.
General, biography, music, humour.

Ronald (George) (1939), 46 High Street, Kidlington, Oxford, OX5 2DN *T*. (08675) 5273. *Telex:* 837646 Talism. *T.A.* Talisman, Oxford. *Manager:* S. Lieberman.
Religion, specialising in the Baha'i Faith.

*****Rose (Barry) (Publishers), Ltd.** (1971), Little London, Chichester, Sussex, PO19 1PG *T*. Chichester (0243) 783637. *Directors:* Barry Rose, D. J. C. Rose, N. M. Marsch, P. J. Madge, R. C. Childs.
Law, local government, police, security, criminology, penology.

*****Routledge & Kegan Paul, Ltd.** (1836), 11 Fetter Lane, London EC4P 4EE *T*. 01-583 9855. *Telex:* 263398. *Directors:* Norman Franklin (Chairman), John Naylor (Managing), Robert Locke, Alan Godwin, Alan Miles, Julian Lynn-Evans, Richard Stileman.
Archaeology, art, belles-lettres, dictionaries, economics, educational (secondary, technical, university), general, geography, history, political economy, reference, science, sociology, music, occult, oriental, philosophy, psychology, literary criticism, women's studies.

Royal National Institute for the Blind, The (1868), Braille House, 338-346 Goswell Road, London EC1V 7JE. *T*. 01-837 9921. *T.A.* Pharnib, London. *Director of Publications:* Donald Bell.
Magazines and books for the blind, in Braille and Moon embossed types. Also tape-recorded books (Talking Books). For complete list of magazines see **Classified Index.**

*****Royce, Robert** (1984), 93 Bedwardine Road, London SE19 3AY *T*. 01-771 2496. *Directors:* Sir Emmanuel Kaye C.B.E., (Chairman), A. T. Hickman, R. B. Royce (Managing), J. H. K. Forster F.C.A., F.C.T. (Secretary), I. P. Williams.
Fiction, topical and historical non-fiction, fishkeeping, educational.

Saint Andrew Press, The, 121 George Street, Edinburgh, EH2 4YN. *T*. 031-225 5722. *T.A.* Free, Edinburgh, EH2 4YN. *Telex:* 727935 Chscot G. Parent company of **Church of Scotland Department of Communications.**
Theology and religion, history.

St. George's Press (1969), 37 Manchester Street, London, W1M 5PE. *T*. 01-486 5481. *Directors:* C. M. Ardito (Chairman), R. A. Duparc, The Hon. Julian Fane, J. M. Hatwell.
General (fiction and non-fiction), belles-lettres, educational (English as a foreign language).

Salamander Books Ltd. (1973), 52 Bedford Row, London WC1R 4LR. *T*. 01-242 6693. *Telex:* 261113 Salama G. *T.A.* Salamander London WC1. *Directors:* Jef Proost (Chairman), Malcolm H. Little (Managing).
Military subjects, natural history, music, gardening, hobbies.

Salamander Press (Edinburgh) Ltd. (1981), 18 Anley Road, London W14 0BY *T*. 01-602 7558 *Telex:* 826542 Teltex G. *Directors:* Tom Fenton, Mary Fenton, James Fenton, John Fuller.
Poetry, drama, general fiction, travel, memoirs.

UNITED KINGDOM

Salvationist Publishing and Supplies, Ltd., 117 Judd Street, London, WC1H 9NN. *T.* 01-387 1656.
Devotional books, theology, biography, world-wide Christian and social service, children's books, music.

Sampson Low, 3rd Floor, Greater London House, Hampstead Road, London NW1 7QX *T.* 01-377 4600. *Telex:* 885233 Macdon G. A division of **Macdonald & Co. Publishers Ltd.**

*****Saunders (W. B.) Co., Ltd.,** 1 St. Anne's Road, Eastbourne, East Sussex, BN21 3UN. *T.* (0323) 638221. *Telex:* 877503 Volmst. *T.A.* Volumists, Eastbourne. See **Holt-Saunders Ltd.**
Medical and scientific.

Saur, K. G., Ltd. (1978), Shropshire House, 2-10 Capper Street, London, WC1E 6JA. *T.* 01-637 1571. *Telex:* 946240 ref. 19006430. *Fax:* 01-580 4089.
Reference books, directories, bibliographies, books on information science, library catalogues.

*****Schofield & Sims, Ltd.** (1901), Dogley Mill, Fenay Bridge, Huddersfield, HD8 0NQ. *T.* (0484) 607080. *Telex:* 51458 Comhud G for Schosims. *T.A.* Schosims, Huddersfield. *Directors:* John S. Nesbitt (Chairman), J. Stephen Platts (Managing), J. Brierley (Sales), C. Bygott, E. J. C. Bygott, C. Nesbitt, L. M. C. Payne, E. P. C. Platts, C. N. Platts.
Educational (infants, primary, secondary, technical, music for schools).

*****Scholastic Publications Ltd.** (1964), Marlborough House, Holly Walk, Leamington Spa, Warwickshire, CV32 4LS. *T.* (092-681) 3910. *Telex:* 312138 Spls G. *London Office* **(Hippo Books)***:* 10 Earlham Street, London WC2H 9RX *T.* 01-240 5753; *Telex:* 264604 Sbslon G; *Fax:* 01-240 6927. *Directors:* J. E. Cox (Managing), M. R. Robinson Jr. (USA), R. M. Spaulding (USA), D. J. Walsh (USA).
Children's paperbacks, children's book clubs.

Scientific Publishing Co., Ltd., 40 Dalton Street, Manchester, M4 4JP. *T.* 061-205 1514.
Engineering textbooks.

*****SCM Press Ltd.,** (1929), 26-30 Tottenham Road, London N1 4BZ. *T.* 01-249 7262. *Telex:* 295068 Theolo G. *T.A.* Torchpres, London N.1. *Directors:* John Bowden (Managing Director and Editor), Mark Hammer (Production), Margaret Lydamore (Associate Editor and Company Secretary), Linda Foster (Bookroom).
Theology and religion, educational, philosophy, sociology and current affairs.

Scolar Press (1967), Gower House, Croft Road, Aldershot, Hants. GU11 3HR *T.* (0252) 331551. *Editorial:* James Price, Spelsbury House, Spelsbury, Oxford OX7 3JR *T.* (0608) 810635. An imprint of **Gower Publishing Group Ltd.**
General and academic, art and architecture, music, history, literature, bibliography and manuscript studies, medieval studies, photography and cinema, fine editions, reprints.

Scottish Academic Press Ltd. (1969), 33 Montgomery Street, Edinburgh, EH7 5JX. *T.* 031-556 2796. *Directors:* Principal J. Steven Watson, Douglas Grant, D. P. Dorward, A. A. Rodwell, R. B. R. Walker, H. Whittaker.
All types of academic books and books of Scottish interest.

Scout Association, The, Baden-Powell House, Queen's Gate, London, SW7 5JS. *T.* 01-584 7030. *T.A.* Scouting. *General Editor:* David Easton.

Technical books dealing with all subjects relevant to Scouting and monthly journal *Scouting*.

*Scripture Union Publishing (1867), Scripture Union House, 130 City Road, London, EC1V 2NJ. *T.* 01-250 1966. Christian Publishers and Booksellers. Music, bible reading aids, Sunday school materials and Christian books especially for children and young people.

Search Press, Ltd. (1962), Wellwood, North Farm Road, Tunbridge Wells, Kent, TN2 3DR. *T.* (0892) 44037. *Telex:* 957258 Search G. *Directors:* Charlotte de la Bedoyère, John M. Todd, The Hon. G. E. Noel, John Bright-Holmes (Editorial).
Philosophy, social sciences, literature, history, theology, exegesis, spirituality, educational, arts, crafts, leisure.

*Secker (Martin) & Warburg, Ltd. (Founded 1910. Reconstructed and enlarged, 1936), 54 Poland Street, London, W1V 3DF. *T.* 01-437 2075. *Telex:* 267613 Secker G. *T.A.* Psophidian, London. *Directors:* Nicolas Thompson (Chairman), Peter Grose (Managing), Barley Alison, John Blackwell, Clyde Hunter, Kate Gardiner, T. R. Manderson, Gillian Vale, Andrew Barrett (Company Secretary).
Art, belles-lettres, biography and memoirs, cinema, fiction, history, poetry, jazz, crime, politics, theatre, travel.

Severn House Publishers (1974), 4 Brook Street, London, W1Y 1AA. *T.* 01-408 2112. *Telex:* 295041. *Chairman:* Edwin Buckhalter.
Biography, music, history, natural history, fiction, romances, thrillers, detective, adventure, war, western, science fiction, film and TV tie-ins.

Shakespeare Head Press (1904), Basil Blackwell Ltd., 108 Cowley Road, Oxford, OX4 1JF.
Finely printed books; scholarly works.

Sheed & Ward Ltd. (1926), 2 Creechurch Lane, London EC3A 5AQ. *T.* 01-283 6330. *Directors:* M. T. Redfern, K. G. Darke. Publishers of books, mostly by Catholics.
History, philosophy, theology, catechetics, scripture and religion.

*Sheldon Press, Holy Trinity Church, Marylebone Road, London, NW1 4DU. *T.* 01-387 5282. *T.A.* Futurity, London, *Senior Editor:* Darley Anderson.
Popular medicine, health, self-help, psychiatry, psychology, religion, humour.

*Shepheard-Walwyn (Publishers), Ltd. (1971), Suite 34, 26 Charing Cross Road, London, WC2H 0DH. *T.* 01-240 5992. *Telex:* 261234 H5680D. *Directors:* B. K. Shaw, A. R. A. Werner.
History, political economy, philosophy, religion; books in calligraphy; Scottish interest.

Sheppard Press, Ltd.—stock acquired by **Europa Publications Ltd.,** *q.v.*

Sherratt, John & Son, Ltd., 78 Park Road, Timperley, Altrincham, Cheshire WA14 5QQ *T.* 061-973 5711.
Educational (primary, secondary, technical, university), medical, practical handbooks, collector's books.

Shire Publications Ltd. (1966), Cromwell House, Church Street, Princes Risborough, Aylesbury, Bucks, HP17 9AJ. *T.* (08444) 4301. *Directors:* J. P. Rotheroe, J. W. Rotheroe.
Discovering paperbacks, Shire Albums, Shire Archaeology, Shire Natural History, Shire Ethnography.

*Sidgwick & Jackson Ltd. (1908), 1 Tavistock Chambers, Bloomsbury Way, London, WC1A 2SG *T.* 01-242 6081. *Telex:* 8952953. *T.A.* Watergate,

London. *Directors:* Sir William Rees-Mogg (Chairman), William Armstrong (Managing), J. N. Newton (Deputy Managing), G. R. Todd, R. Smith, K. J. C. Hood, R. Yelland.
Archaeology, biography, cinema, current affairs, fiction, future history, gardening, history, military history, music (pop and classical), political economy, show business, sociology, sport, travel, wine.

Skinner (Thomas) Directories—see **Information Services Ltd.**

Smythe (Colin), Ltd. (1966), P.O.Box 6, Gerrards Cross, Bucks, SL9 8XA *T.* (0753) 886000. *Telex* (via Prestel): 295141 Txlink G; message prefix: MBX 75-3886000. *T.A.* Smythebooks, Gerrardscross. *Directors:* Colin Smythe (Managing), Peter Bander van Duren, A. Norman Jeffares, Ann Saddlemyer.
Biography, current affairs, histories, parapsychology, literary criticism, fly-fishing, folk-lore, science and fantasy fiction, Irish interest and Anglo-Irish literature.

*****Society for Promoting Christian Knowledge** (1698), Holy Trinity Church, Marylebone Road, London, NW1 4DU *T.* 01-387 5282. *T.A.* Futurity, London. *General Secretary:* P. N. G. Gilbert. *Senior Editor:* Judith Longman. *Editors:* Myrtle Powley, Philip Law.
Theology and religion. See also **Sheldon Press.**

Soncino Press, Ltd. (1929), 1st Floor, 172-176 Northcote Road, London, SW11 6RE *T.* 01-228 5928. *Directors:* P. Bloch, M. Bloch, K. Reswick.
Translations with commentaries of Hebrew classics. Theology and religion.

Southside (Publishers), Ltd. (1968). A subsidiary of **Canongate Publishing Ltd.**

*****Souvenir Press, Ltd.,** 43 Great Russell Street, London, WC1B 3PA. *T.* 01-580 9307-8 and 637 5711. *T.A.* Publisher, London. *Telex:* 24710 Souvnr G. *Directors:* Ernest Hecht, B.SC. (Econ.), B. Com (Managing), A. Hecht. *Executive Directors:* Rodney King, Jane Greenhalgh, Jeanne Manchee, Leslie Cramphorn.
Archaeology, biography and memoirs, children's books (non-fiction, rewards), educational (secondary, technical), fiction, general, humour, practical handbooks, psychiatry, psychology, sociology, sports, games and hobbies, travel, supernatural, parapsychology, illustrated books.

*****Sparrow Books**—see **Arrow Books Ltd.**

Spearman (Neville), Ltd. An imprint of **The C. W. Daniel Company Ltd.**

Spellmount Ltd., Publishers (1983), 12 Dene Way, Speldhurst, Tunbridge Wells, Kent, TN3 0NX. *T.* (089-286) 2860. *Directors:* Ian Morley-Clarke, Kathleen Morley-Clarke, John Bright-Holmes, David Burnett James.
Biography, cinema and theatre, jazz, military and naval history, music, sport.

*****Sphere Books, Ltd.,** 27 Wrights Lane, London W8 5TZ *T.* 01-937 8070. *T.A.* Spherbooks, London, W8. *Directors:* N. Webb (Managing), S. Watt, J. O'Connor, J. Tindall, B. Boote.
Paperbacks: original works and reprints.

*****Spon (E. & F. N.), Ltd.** (1834), 11 New Fetter Lane, London, EC4P 4EE *T.* 01-583 9855. *Telex:* 263398. *Directors:* P. Read, R. Stileman, B. West.
Architecture, building, surveying, engineering, applied science, energy studies.

*****Spring Books.** An imprint of **The Hamlyn Publishing Group, Ltd.**

Springwood Books Ltd., Springwood House, The Avenue, Ascot, Berks SL5 7LY *T.* (0990) 24053. *Telex:* 8813271 Gecoms G. *Directors:* Christopher Foster (Managing), T. R. Foster, LLB.
Astrology, childrens, fiction, biography, sport, history, literature, politics.

Stacey International (1974), 128 Kensington Church Street, London, W8 4BH *T.* 01-221 7166. *Telex:* 298768 Stacey G. *Directors:* Tom Stacey, C. S. Stacey.
Senior Executive: John Blackett-Ord.
Illustrated non-fiction, encyclopaedic books on regions and countries, Islamic and Arab subjects, World Affairs, art.

Stainer & Bell, Ltd. (1906), 82 High Road, London, N2 9PW *T.* 01-444 9135. *Directors:* Allen Percival, C.B.E. (Chairman), Bernard Braley, A.C.I.S. (Managing), Mrs. C. Wakefield (Secretary), Joan Braley, John Hosier, C.B.E., Rachel Percival.
Non-fiction, performing arts, religious communication.

*****Stanford Maritime Ltd.** (1973), 27A Floral Street, London WC2E 9DP *T.* 01-836 7863. *Telex:* 21667 Philip G.
Sailing, yachting, windsurfing and dinghies; cruising guides, navigation, meteorology, seamanship, historical, boatbuilding and maintenance. Textbooks for shipping professionals, deck officers and engineers. See also **George Philip & Son Ltd.**

Star Books. An imprint of **W. H. Allen & Co., PLC.**

Starke (Harold), Ltd., Pegasus House, 116-120 Golden Lane, London, EC1Y 0TL *T.* 01-253 2145. *Telex:* 27931 Burke G. *Directors:* Harold K. Starke (Chairman), Naomi Galinski (Managing), Guy W. Green.
Biography and memoirs, medical and reference.

*****Stephens (Patrick), Ltd.** (1967), Denington Estate, Wellingborough, Northants, NN8 2QD *T.* (0933) 72700. *Telex:* 311072 Thopub G. *Fax:* (0933) 72800. *Directors:* Patrick J. Stephens (Chairman), David Young (Managing), Darryl Reach, Ian Heath, Julian Rivers, Peter Winslow, F.C.A. (Secretary), David Young.
Aviation, biography, collecting, commercial vehicles, the countryside, fitness and sport, history, maritime, military and wargaming, model making, motor cycling, motoring and motor racing, photography, railways and railway modelling, pop music.

*****Stevens and Sons, Ltd.** (1889), 11 New Fetter Lane, London, EC4P 4EE *T.* 01-583 9855. *Telex:* 263398. *Directors:* C. D. O. Evans (Chairman and Managing Director), A. Prideaux, J. Jenkins, H. Jones, A. Kinahan, R. McKay, D. Tebbutt, D. Sampson (Company Secretary), Jane Belford, Mrs. B. Grandage, Mrs. C. Tullo.
Law.

Stillit Books, Ltd., 72 New Bond Street, London, W1Y 0QY *T.* 01-493 1177. *Telex:* 23475. *Director:* Gerald B. Stillit.
Stillitron audio-visual, direct method, programmed, instantaneously electronically corrected, language systems. French, German, Spanish, Italian, Arabic and English as a foreign language.

Sunflower Books, 12 Kendrick Mews, London SW7 3HG. *T.* 01-589 1862. *Telex:* 269388 Lonhan G. *Directors:* P. A. Underwood (USA), J. G. Underwood.
Travel guide books.

Sussex University Press (1971), Sussex House, Falmer, Brighton, BN1 9QZ *T.* (0273) 606755.
Publications distributed by **Scottish Academic Press Ltd.,** *q.v.*
All types of academic books.

Sutton (Alan) Publishing, Ltd. (1978), 30 Brunswick Road, Gloucester, GL1 1JJ *T.* (0452) 419575. *Telex:* 43690 Owlpen. *Directors:* Alan Sutton, Rosemary Verey, Nicholas Mander, John Milne, Robert Brown, Nicholas Mills, Peter Clifford.

History, architecture, archaeology, general, local history, travel, biography, topography, letters, diaries and journals.

Swedenborg Society, 20-21 Bloomsbury Way, London, WC1A 2TH *T.* 01-405 7986.
Theology and religion.

***Sweet & Maxwell, Ltd.** (1889), 11 New Fetter Lane, London, EC4P 4EE *T.* 01-583 9855. *Telex:* 263398. *Directors:* C. D. O. Evans (Chairman), A. Prideaux (Managing), B. M. Cardy, J. Jenkins, H. Jones, A. Kinahan, R. McKay, D. Sampson (Company Secretary), Jane Belford, D. Tebbutt, J. Potter.
Law.

Target Books. An imprint of **W. H. Allen & Co. PLC.**

***Tavistock Publications Ltd.,** 11 New Fetter Lane, London, EC4P 4EE *T.* 01-583 9855. *Telex:* 263398. *Directors:* Gill Davies, John Naylor, Carol Somerset.
Sociology, anthropology, psychology, psychiatry, social administration, social work, management studies, women's studies.

Taxus Press (1983), Forest House, 412 Hinkley Road, Leicester LE3 0WA *T.* (0533) 855404. *Publishers:* Michael Farley, Catherine Byron.
Poetry, short stories, essays.

***Taylor & Francis, Ltd.,** 4 John Street, London, WC1N 2ET *T.* 01-405 2237-9.
President: Professor Sir Nevill Mott, M.A., D.SC., F.INST.P., F.R.S. *Directors:* Professor B. R. Coles, B.SC., D.PHIL., F.INST.P. (Chairman), Professor K. W. Keohane, C.B.E., B.SC., PH.D., F.INST.P. (Vice-Chairman), A. R. Selvey, F.C.C.A., F.B.I.M. (Managing), M. I. Dawes, E. Ferguson, M.A., S. M. A. Banister, M.A., Professor H. Baum, J. H. Lavender, B.SC.
Educational (university), science: physics, and mathematics, chemistry, electronics, natural history, pharmacology and drug metabolism, medical science, astronomy, technology, history of science, ergonomics, production engineering, Falmer Press Ltd.

***Technical Press, Ltd.** An associate company of **Gower Publishing Group Ltd.**

Telegraph Publications (1920), Daily Telegraph, 135 Fleet Street, London, EC4P 4BL. *T.* 01-353 4242 ext. 3690. *T.A.* Telenews London PS4. *Publications Manager:* Christopher Milsome.
Business, personal finance, crosswords, sport, travel and guides, maps and charts, cookery and wine, painting and drawing, general.

***Temple Smith (Maurice), Ltd.** An imprint of **Gower Publishing Group Ltd.**

Teredo Books, Ltd., P.O. Box 430, Brighton, BN1 6GT *T.* Brighton (0273) 505432. *Directors:* Richard M. Cookson, Alex A. Hurst (Managing).
Maritime publications and marine art.

***Thames and Hudson Ltd.,** 30-34 Bloomsbury Street, London, WC1B 3QP *T.* 01-636 5488. *Telex:* 25992 Thbook G. *T.A.* Thameshuds, London, WC1. *Telex:* 25992. *Directors:* E. U. Neurath (Chairman), T. M. Neurath (Managing), E. Bates, J. R. Camplin, T. L. Evans, C. A. Ferguson, W. Guttmann, S. Huntley, C. M. Kaine, I. H. B. Middleton, Nikos Stangos.
Archaeology, architecture, art, photography, travel, history, biography.

Thames Publishing (1970), 14 Barlby Road, London, W10 6AR *T.* 01-969 3579. *Publishing Manager:* John Bishop.
Books about music, particularly by British composers. Preliminary letter essential.

Thomson-Leng Publications, Dundee, DD1 9QJ *T.* 23131. *T.A.* Courier, Dundee. *Telex:* 76380. London: 185 Fleet Street, London, EC4A 2HS *T.* 01-242 5086. *T.A.* Courier, London, EC4. Publishers of newspapers and periodicals.

Children's books (annuals), fiction.

*Thornes, Stanley (Publishers) Ltd. and Hulton, Old Station Drive, Leckhampton, Cheltenham, Gloucestershire, GL53 0DN *T.* (0242) 584429. *Telex:* 43593 Sthorn G. *Directors:* S. E. Thornes, R. M. Kendall, M. M. van de Weijer, P. D. Zuiderveld.
Educational (primary, secondary), mathematics, science, engineering, beauty therapy, catering, home economics, English drama, history, geography, religious studies, ELT, special needs, modern languages, botany, business studies, computing, social science.

*Thorsons Publishers Ltd. (1930), Denington Estate, Wellingborough, Northants, NN8 2RQ *T.* Wellingborough (0933) 76031. *Telex:* 311072 Thopub G. *Fax:* (0933) 72800. *Directors:* J. A. Young (Chairman), D. J. Young (Managing), D. C. J. Palmer, J. R. Hardaker, P. A. Winslow, J. G. Rivers.
Alternative medicine, health and nutrition. General books on wholefood and vegetarian cookery, vegetarian philosophy, animal rights, organic gardening, practical psychology, public speaking, hypnosis and hypnotherapy.

*Times Books Ltd. (1977), 16 Golden Square, London, W1R 4BN *T.* 01-434 3767. *Telex:* 897284 Arpub G. *Fax:* 01-434 2080. *Director:* Barry Winkleman (Managing).
Atlases, reference.

*Tiranti (Alec), Ltd. taken over by **Academy Editions**, *q.v.*

Tolley Publishing Co. Ltd., (1918), Tolley House, 17 Scarbrook Road, Croydon, Surrey, CR0 1SQ *T.* 01-686 9141. *Directors:* B. G. K. Downing (Chairman), J. V. Wilson (Managing), E. L. Harvey, A. J. Fisher, N. H. Parmee, R. E. Webb, K. R. Tingley.
Taxation, accountancy, company law and secretarial practice, employment law, social security and other law.

*Transworld Publishers Ltd., 61-63 Uxbridge Road, London, W5 5SA *T.* 01-579 2652. *Telex:* 267974 Trnspb G.
Corgi, Bantam, Bantam Press, Young Corgi, Picture Corgi, Black Swan, Partridge Press.

Triton Publishing Company Ltd. (1964), 1A Montagu Mews North, London, W1H 1AJ *T.* 01-935 8090. *T.A.* Trifem, London, W1. *Directors:* D. G. Trustcott, F.C.A., Carolyn Whitaker.
Fiction and general non-fiction.

Unicorn—see **Unwin Hyman Ltd.**

Unicorn Books, 16 Laxton Gardens, Paddock Wood, Kent TN12 6BB *T.* (0892 83) 3648. *Directors:* R. Green, M. D. Green.
Militaria, music, collecting and craft books.

United Society for Christian Literature, Robertson House, Leas Road, Guildford, Surrey, GU1 4QW *T.* Guildford (0483) 577877.
Has for over 150 years acted for the British missionary societies to assist book production in all languages by subsidy grants. *General Secretary:* Rev. Alec Gilmore, M.A., B.D.
Theology and religion.

University of Wales Press (1922), 6 Gwennyth Street, Cathays, Cardiff, CF2 4YD *T.* Cardiff (0222) 31919.
Academic and educational (Welsh and English). Publishers of *Bulletin of the Board of Celtic Studies, Welsh History Review, Studia Celtica, Llen Cymru, Y Gwyddonydd, Efrydiau Athronyddol.*

*University Tutorial Press, Ltd. — see **Unwin Hyman Ltd.**

*Unwin Hyman Ltd. (1986), Denmark House, 37-39 Queen Elizabeth Street, London SE1 2QB *T.* 01-407 0709. *T.A.* Bellhyman, London, SE1. *Telex:* 886245 Bellhy G; Ruskin House, 40 Museum Street, London WC1A 1LU *T.* 01-405 8577. *Telex:* 82626. *Directors:* Rayner Unwin (Chairman), Robin Hyman (Deputy Chairman and Managing), Nigel Britten, Mary Butler, Patric Duffy, Roger Jones, Christopher Kington, Christopher Sporborg, Mark Streatfeild, John Taylor, Patrick Gallagher (Australia).
Imprints: Trade Division: **Unwin Hyman:** Biography, travel and current affairs, crafts, design, health and childcare, sport, humour, gardening, the countryside, childrens; publishers of Pepys' Diary and J.R.R. Tolkien, **Unwin Paperbacks: Unicorn:** Fantasy fiction; **Counterpoint:** Current concerns; **Mandala:** Eastern religion. Education and International Divisions: **Bell & Hyman:** Primary and secondary educational including mathematics, science and geography; English Language Teaching; former **University Tutorial Press** titles. Academic Division **Allen & Unwin:** Tertiary: earth and life sciences, economics, humanities, social and political sciences.

*Unwin Paperbacks—see **Unwin Hyman Ltd.**

Usborne Publishing (1973), 20 Garrick Street, London, WC2E 9BJ *T.* 01-379 3535. *Telex:* 8953598 Uspub G. *Fax:* 01-836 0705. *Directors:* T. P. Usborne, Heather Amery, Jenny Tyler, David Lowe, Keith Ball.
Children's books, reference, practical, craft, natural history, computers.

Vallentine, Mitchell & Co. Ltd. (1950), Gainsborough House, 11 Gainsborough Road, London, E11 1RS *T.* 01-530 4226. *T.A.* Valmico, London. *Telex:* 897719. *Directors:* F. Cass (Managing), M. P. Zaidner.
Jewish studies.

*Van Nostrand Reinhold (UK) Co. Ltd., Molly Millars Lane, Wokingham, Berkshire, RG11 2PY *T.* (0734) 789456. *Telex:* 848268 Vnr-UK-G. *Directors:* P. A. Gardner, A. J. Davis.
Academic, aeronautics, architecture, dictionaries, economics, electrical and electronics, engineering, history, mathematics, medicine, philosophy, professional, psychology, reference, pure and applied science, sociology, technology, computers, management, marketing.

Vegetarian Society (UK), Ltd., The, Parkdale, Dunham Road, Altrincham, Cheshire, WA14 4QG *T.* 061-928 0793.
Vegetarianism, recipes, wholefood nutrition and cookery.

Verso Ltd. (1969), 6 Meard Street, London W1 *T.* 01-734 0059. *Directors:* Robin Blackburn, Neil Belton, Mike Davis, Colin Robinson, Tariq Ali.
Politics, biography, sociology, economics, history, aesthetics, philosophy.

Viking, formerly **Allen Lane,** the hardcover imprint of **Penguin Books,** *q.v.* 27 Wrights Lane, London W8 5TZ *T.* 01-938 2200. *Editorial Director:* Tony Lacey.
Fiction, general non-fiction, illustrated books; history, literature, art, archaeology, architecture and social sciences.

Viking Kestrel, the children's hardcover imprint of **Penguin Books,** *q.v.,* 27 Wrights Lane, London W8 5TZ *T.* 01-938 2200. *Chief Editor:* Sally Floyer.

*Virago Press (1974), 41 William IV Street, London WC2N 4DB *T.* 01-379 6977. *T.A.* Caterwaul London WC2. *Telex:* 299080. Chairwoman: Carmen Callil. *Directors:* Ursula Owen and Harriet Spicer (Joint Managing), Lennie Goodings, Alexandra Pringle.
Books for the general and educational market which highlight all aspects of women's lives. Fiction and non-fiction, educational and reference.

Virgin Books (1980), Portobello Dock, 328 Kensal Road, London W10 5XJ *T.*

01-968 8888. *Telex:* 892890 Virgin G. *Directors:* John Brown, Robert Devereux. A division of Virgin Publications Ltd.
Popular non fiction.

Virtue & Co., Ltd. (1819), 25 Breakfield, Coulsdon, Surrey, CR3 2UE *T.* 01-668 4632. *Telex:* 261507 ref 3393. *Directors:* Guy Virtue, Michael Virtue, R. S. Cook.
Books for the catering trade and the home.

Vision Press Ltd. (1946), c/o Trade Counter Ltd, Fulham Wharf, Townmead Road, London SW6 2SB. *T.* 01-938 2929. *Telex:* 914052 Tclond G. *Directors:* Alan Moore, B.A. (Managing), Amber G. Moore.
Art, film, history, literary criticism, music, theatre. **Artemis Press** imprint: education.

Walker Books (1979), 184-192 Drummond Street, London NW1 3HP *T.* 01-387 2000. *Directors:* Sebastian Walker, David Ford.
Children's—mainly picture books; teenage fiction.

Warburg Institute, University of London, Woburn Square, London, WC1H 0AB *T.* 01-580 9663.
Cultural history, philosophy.

Ward Lock Limited (1854), 8 Clifford Street, London, W1X 1RB *T.* 01-439 3100. *Telex:* 262364 Warlok G. *Directors:* R. Wood (Chairman), A Holmes, D. Williams, D. Holmes. Free-lance artists' and designers' work used. Member of the **Gutenberghus Group**.
Cookery, gardening, crafts, equitation, general reference, sports, children's illustrated information books, general knowledge and encyclopaedias, adult leisure, humour books.

*****Ward Lock Educational Co. Ltd.** (1964), 47 Marylebone Lane, London, W1M 6AX *T.* 01-486 3271. *Telex:* 266231 Wleco G. *Cables:* Warlock London W1. *Directors:* Au Bak Ling (Chairman Hong Kong), A. M. Alfred (Deputy Chairman), Stanley B. Malcolm (Managing), Lucy Hall, Paul M. Thompson, Au King Kwok (Hong Kong), Au Wai Kwok (Hong Kong).
Secondary and primary pupil materials, reading workshops, teachers' books, music books, educational software packages.

*****Warne (Frederick) (Publishers) Ltd.** (1865), 27 Wrights Lane, London W8 5TZ *T.* 01-938 2200. *T.A.* Warne, London, W8; and New York City. *Directors:* P. Mayer (Chairman), T. Lacey, J. Webster, A. Wherry, S. Hall. An imprint of **Penguin Books Ltd.**
Children's books, reference books including natural history and dictionaries, Observer's Pocket Series, general interest.

*****Watts, Franklin** (1969 in London, 1942 in New York), a division of **The House of Grolier Ltd.,** 12A Golden Square, London, W1R 4BA *T.* 01-437 0713. *T.A.* Frawatts, London, W1. *Telex:* 262655 Groluk G. *Directors:* David Howgrave-Graham (Managing), Jonathan Gillett (USA, Chairman), Chester Fisher, Rita Ireland, Julia MacRae, George Taylor.
Non-fiction, education (primary), juvenile, reference books.

*****Wayland (Publishers) Ltd.** (1969), 61-61A Western Road, Hove, East Sussex, BN3 1JD *T.* Brighton (0273) 722561. *Telex:* 878170 Waylan G. *Directors:* D. G. Heynes (Chairman), J. W. Lewis (Managing), F. M. Jane, P. Humphrey, K. Lilley, P. Hyem.
Educational: arts and crafts, careers, geography, history, nature, science, social studies, sport.

Webb & Bower (Publishers) Ltd. (1978), 9 Colleton Crescent, Exeter, EX2 4BY *T.* (0392) 35362. *Telex:* Webbow 42544. *T.A.* Webbower Exeter. *Fax:* (0392)

211652. *Directors:* Richard Webb, Delian Bower.
Specialises in publishing illustrated non-fiction books for the UK, USA and international co-edition markets. Arts, crafts, biography, illustrated classics, topography, travel, nostalgia, gardening, food, wine, reference, general.

*Weidenfeld, George, & Nicolson Ltd., 91 Clapham High Street, London, SW4 7TA *T.* 01-622 9933. *Telex:* 918066. *Directors:* Lord Weidenfeld (Chairman), Mark Collins (Deputy Chairman), Richard Hussey (Deputy Managing), Ted Collins, John Curtis, Michael Dover, Rosalind Lewis, Bud Maclennan, Juliet Gardiner, Victoria Petrie-Hay, David Roberts.
Anthropology, architecture, art, belles-lettres, biography and memoirs, current affairs, economics, fiction, general, history, philosophy, politics, science, sociology, sport, travel.

Wheatsheaf Books Ltd. (1979), 16 Ship Street, Brighton, East Sussex, BN1 1AD *T.* (0273) 723031 and 729585. *Telex:* 877101 Olship. *T.A.* Harvester, Brighton. *Directors:* John Spiers (Chairman), Edward Elgar (Managing), Valerie Ewens (Financial Controller), Romesh Vaitilingam (Editorial).
Economics, political science, sociology, women's studies.

Wheldon & Wesley, Ltd. Lytton Lodge, Codicote, Hitchin, Herts, SG4 8TE *T.* Stevenage (0438) 820370. *Telex:* 825562 Chacom G and 825353 Chacom G. Natural history booksellers and publishers. Agency of the British Museum (Natural History) and Hunt Botanical Library.

*Whitaker (J.) & Sons, Ltd., 12 Dyott Street, London, WC1A 1DF *T.* 01-836 8911. *Directors:* R. F. Baum, James Coates, F.L.A., A. C. E. Musk, C.V.O., David Whitaker (Chairman), Sally Whitaker (Managing).
Reference including *Whitaker's Almanack* (1869). *The Bookseller* (1858), *British Books in Print (1874), Whitaker's Cumulative Book List* (1924), and other book trade directories.

Whittet Books Ltd. (1976), 18 Anley Road, London W14 0BY *T.* 01-603 1139. *Telex:* 826542 Teltex G (Whit). *Directors:* Annabel Whittet, John Whittet, Marion Kovach.
Architecture, gardening, how-to, topography, natural history.

*Wildwood House Ltd. An associate company of **Gower Publishing Group Ltd.**

*Wiley (John) & Sons Ltd. (incorporating **Interscience Publishers**), Baffins Lane, Chichester, Sussex, PO19 1UD *T.* (0243) 784531. *T.A.* and *Cables:* Wilebook, Chichester. *Telex:* 86290 Wibook G. *Fax:* (0243) 775878. *BTG:* 83 JWP001. Subsidiary of **John Wiley & Sons Inc.**, New York. *Directors:* W. B. Wiley (Chairman) (USA), J. A. E. Higham, A. H. Neilly, Jr. (USA), M. B. Foyle (Managing), J. D. Cameron, T. L. Davies, P. W. Ferris, J. H. Wilde, The Earl of March, P. Marriage, E. van Tongeren.
Scientific, engineering, business, social science, mathematics, computing, medical.

Wiley-Heyden Ltd. An associate company of **John Wiley & Sons Ltd.**

*Wilson, Philip, Publishers Ltd. (1975), Russell Chambers, Covent Garden, London WC2E 8AA *T.* 01-379 7886. *Directors:* Philip Wilson, Peter Ling, Anne Jackson, Jane Moore.
Art.

*Witherby (H. F. & G.), Ltd., 32 Aylesbury Street, London, EC1R 0ET *T.* 01-251 5750. *Directors:* Antony Witherby, T. A. F. Witherby, D. F. Witherby.
Science (natural), sports, games and hobbies, travel.

Woburn Press, The (1968), Gainsborough House, 11 Gainsborough Road, London, E11 1RS *T.* 01-530 4226. *T.A.* Simfay, London. *Telex:* 897719 Wmp

G. *Directors:* Frank Cass (Managing), A. E. Cass, M. P. Zaidner.
Non-fiction, Woburn Educational Series.

*****Wolfe Medical Publications Ltd.,** Wolfe House, 3 Conway Street, London, W1P 6HE *T.* 01-636 4622. *T.A.* Wolfebooks London. *Telex:* 8814230. *Directors:* Peter Wolfe (Managing), P. Heilbrunn, P. Daly, Michael Manson, Colin MacPherson, John F. Dill (USA), Robert T. Grant (USA).
Colour atlases, full-colour photographic reference titles in diagnostic medicine, surgery, dentistry, veterinary medicine, pure and applied sciences.

Wolff, Oswald, Books, 8 Circus Lodge, Circus Road, London, NW8 7JL *T.* 01-286 5654. *Director:* Mrs Ilse Wolff.
German and European studies: literature and the arts, history, biography, current affairs.

Women's Press, The, (1978), 34 Great Sutton Street, London, EC1V 0DX *T.* 01-251 3007. *Telex:* 919034 Namara G. *Managing Director:* Ros de Lanerolle.
Books by women in the areas of fiction, autobiography, history, art, health, politics.

Woodhead-Faulkner (Publishers), Ltd. (1972), Fitzwilliam House, 32 Trumpington Street, Cambridge, CB2 1QY *T.* Cambridge (0223) 66733. *Telex:* 817343 Blucam G. *Directors:* A. Jessup (Chairman), M. J. Woodhead (Managing), P. J. S. Andersen, R. S. Dawes, S. G. York.
Finance and investment, management, technical, social and welfare topics.

World International Publishing Ltd., Egmont House, P.O. Box 111, Great Ducie Street, Manchester, M60 3BL *T.* 061-834 3110. *Telex:* 668609 World G. *Fax:* 061-834 0059. *T.A.* World, Manchester. *Directors:* Robin H. D. Wood (Managing), Bernie Wroe, David Sheldrake, Philip Rhodes, Don Smith, Mae Broadley, David Sheldrake.
Children's activity, gift and information books, and annuals.

*****Wright (John)** (1825), Techno House, Redcliffe Way, Bristol BS1 6NX. *T.* (0272) 290691. *Managing Director:* A. Pearce, *Editorial Director:* D. J. Kingham, *Sales Manager:* A. G. Gresford. Publishers of *The Dental Annual, The Medical Annual, The Veterinary Annual, Burns, Community Medicine, The Home Economist, Injury, International Dental Journal, Journal of Audiovisual Media in Medicine, Journal of Dentistry, Journal of Obstetrics and Gynaecology, Journal of the Royal College of Surgeons of Edinburgh, Journal of the Society of Occupational Medicine* and *International Dental Journal.*
Wholly owned by the **Institute of Physics.**

Writers & Readers Beginners Series. An imprint of **Unwin Hyman Ltd.**

*****Yale University Press London** (1961), 13 Bedford Square, London, WC1B 3JF *T.* 01-580 2693. *Telex:* 896075 Yupldn G. *T.A.* Yalepress, London.
Art, architecture, history, economics, political science, literary criticism, Asian and African studies, religion, philosophy, psychology, history of science.

*****Zed Books Ltd.** (1976), 57 Caledonian Road, London, N1 9BU. *T.* 01-837 4014. *Directors:* Paul Westlake, Anna Gourlay, Anne Rodford, Robert Molteno, Mike Pallis.
Third World issues, international politics, current affairs, ecology, women's studies, fiction.

Zenith—see **Arrow Books Ltd.**

Zomba Books (1983), Zomba House, 165-167 Willesden High Road, London NW10 2SG *T.* 01-459 8899. *Telex:* 919884 Zomba G. *Director:* Ralph Simon. *Contact:* Dede Millar.
Music, popular biographies, fashion, health, leisure.

*Zwemmer (A.), Ltd. (1951), 26 Litchfield Street, London, WC2H 9NJ *T.* 01-836 1749.
Architecture, fine and applied arts.

AUSTRALIA

*Members of Australian Book Publishers' Association

*Angus & Robertson Publishers** (1886), 4 Eden Park, 31 Waterloo Road, North Ryde, N.S.W. *T.* 887-2233. *Postal Address:* P.O. Box 290 North Ryde, NSW 2113. *Telex:* 26452. *U.K.:* 16 Golden Square, London, W1R 4BN *T.* 01-434 3767. *Chief Executive:* Richard Walsh. *Management:* Richard Walsh, Peter Ackroyd, Jennifer Rowe, Barry Smith, Stephen Cohn. General fiction and non-fiction, Australiana, poetry, pictorial, practice, veterinary, agricultural, medical, technical, children's paperbacks.

*Arnold, Edward (Australia) Pty. Ltd.** (1975), 80 Waverley Road, Caulfield East, Victoria 3145. *T.* 572-2211. *Postal Address:* P.O. Box 234 Caulfield East, Victoria 3145. *Telex:* AA35974. *Cables:* Edarnold. *Chairman:* E.A. Hamilton (UK). *Directors:* B. W. Bennett (UK), T. M. Coyle, (Managing), B. E. Fordham. Educational, primary and secondary, academic, general non-fiction, professional, technical.

Artlook Books (1979), The Old Maltings Theatre, 39 Stuart Street, Perth 6000. *Postal Address:* P.O. Box 132 Aberdeen Street, Perth. *T.* 328 9188. *Directors:* John Harper-Nelson (Chairman), Helen Weller (Managing), Guy Weller. Australiana, fiction, poetry, children's, history, general.

*Australasian Publishing Co., Pty., Ltd.,** Corner Bridge Road and Jersey Street, Hornsby, N.S.W. 2077. *T.* 476-2000. *Telex:* AA23274. *Directors:* G. A. Rutherford, G. C. Greene, K. A. Harrap, J. D. Cody, J. E. Bullivant. General, fiction, juvenile, education, art and technical.

*Australian Council for Educational Research, Ltd., The,** P.O. Box 210, Hawthorn, Victoria, 3122. *T.* 03-819 1400. Educational books.

*Blackwell Scientific Publications (Australia) Pty. Ltd.,** 107 Barry Street, Carlton, Victoria, 3053. *T.* 347 0300. *T.A.* Blackwell, Melbourne.

*Brooks Waterloo Publishers,** 36 Albert Road, South Melbourne, Victoria, 3205. *T.* 03-699 5000. *Telex:* AA 151018. Education, primary and secondary; management, general.

*Butterworths Pty. Limited,** 271-273 Lane Cove Road, North Ryde, N.S.W. 2113 *T.* 02-887-3444. *Telex:* AA22033. *Fax:* 02-887 4251.

*Cambridge University Press Australian Branch,** 10 Stamford Road, Oakleigh, Melbourne 3166. *T.* 568 0322 and 93 Albion Street, Surry Hills, Sydney 2010. *T.* 212 6014. *Director:* Kim W. Harris.

CBS Publishing (Australia) Pty Ltd., 9 Waltham Street, Artarmon, N.S.W. 2064 *T.* 02-439 3633.

*Collins, William, Pty Ltd.,** 55 Clarence Street, Sydney, N.S.W. 2000. *T.* 290-2066. *Directors:* J. C. Clement, A. A. Leuteneggar, N. Topham, T. T. Hughes, G. R. Beachley. General literature, fiction, children's books, Bibles. Head Office: 8 Grafton Street, London, W1X 3LA.

Currawong Press Pty. Ltd., The, 6 Calypso Avenue, Mosman, NSW 2088. Books of general appeal by Australian authors, mainly non-fiction.

French, Samuel (Australia) Pty. Ltd., represented by Dominie Pty. Ltd., Drama Department, 8 Cross Street, Brookvale, N.S.W. 2100. *T.* 930201. Publishers of plays and agents for the collection of royalties for Samuel French Ltd., incorporating Evans Plays and Samuel French Inc., The Society of Authors, A.C.T.A.C., and Bakers Plays of Boston.

*Golden Press Pty. Ltd.,** 5-01 Henry Lawson Business Centre, Birkenhead Point, Drummoyne, N.S.W. 2047. *T.* 819-9111. General children's books, and educational.

*Heinemann Publishers Australia Pty. Ltd.,** 85 Abinger Street, Richmond, Victoria, 3121. *T.* 429-3622. *Cables:* Hebooks, Melbourne. *Telex:* 35347. *Managing Director:* Sandy Grant. Educational and general non-fiction.

*Hill of Content Publishing Co. Pty., Ltd.** (1965), 86 Bourke Street, Melbourne, 3000 *T.* 654 3144. *T.A.* Colbook, Melbourne. *Telex:* AA37396. *Directors:* M. Slamen, M. G. Zifcak, P. Shaw, Michelle Anderson. Australiana, health, history, educational, general.

*Hodder and Stoughton (Australia) Pty. Ltd.,** 2 Apollo Place, Lane Cove, N.S.W. 2066. *T.* 428 1022. *Telex:* 24858. *Directors:* Philip Attenborough, Edward Coffey (Managing), John Carroll, Margaret Hamilton, Richard Morris, Barrie Coffey, John Vermeer. Fiction, general, educational, children's, religious, hardback and paperback.

Horwitz Grahame Books Pty. Ltd., including **Horwitz Publications, Martin Educational** and **Carroll's,** 506 Miller Street, Cammeray, 2062. *T.* 929-6144. *Cables:* Horbooks, Sydney. *Telex:* AA27833. *Facsimile:* (02) 957 1814. *Directors:* S. D. L. Horwitz (Chairman), L. J. Moore (Managing), M. C. Phillips (Deputy Managing), R. B. Fuller, B. B. Nash. Fiction (paperback and hardbound), educational (primary, secondary and tertiary), reference books, non-fiction, technical, cookery.

*Jacaranda Wiley Ltd.,** 65 Park Road, Milton, Queensland 4064. *T.* (07) 369 9755. *Telex:* AA 41845; 90 Ormond Road, Elwood, Victoria 3184. *T.* 03-531 8677; 140A Victoria Road, Gladesville, N.S.W., 2111. *T.* 02-816-2758; 159 Halifax Street, Adelaide, S.A., 5000. *T.* 08-232-0240. Also New Zealand, Hong Kong, *q.v. Managing Director:* K. J. Collins; *General Managers:* Q. Smith, G. Browne, P. Donoughue, B. Brennan. Educational, technical, atlases, software.

*Kangaroo Press Pty Ltd** (1980), 3 Whitehall Road, Kenthurst, New South Wales 2156. *T.* 02-654 1502. *Telex:* AA 176432 Duroff. *T.A.* Kangaroops Sydney. *Fax:* 02-651 2118. *Directors:* David Rosenberg, Priscilla Rosenberg. Gardening, craft, Australian history and natural history, collecting, fitness.

Lansdowne Editions (unit of **RPLA Pty Ltd.**), 176 South Creek Road, Dee Why West, N.S.W. 2099. *T.* (02) 981-0444. *Telex:* AA121546. *Chief Executive:* Graham Fill. *Publishing Manager:* Anne Wilson. Limited editions—art, nature, literature and Australiana.

Lansdowne Press (unit of **RPLA Pty Ltd.**) and incorporating the imprints of **Lansdowne Press, Robinsons & Broadbents Maps and Guides.** 176 South Creek Road, Dee Why West, N.S.W. 2099. *T.* (02) 981-0444. *Telex:* AA121546. *Chief Executive:* Kevin Weldon. *Publishing Manager:* Anne Wilson. Practical books on Australian lifestyle, craft, children's art, Australiana, maps, guides.

Law Book Company Ltd., The, 44-50 Waterloo Road, North Ryde, N.S.W. 2113 *T.* 887 0177.

*Longman Cheshire Pty. Ltd.,** Longman Cheshire House, Kings Gardens, 91-97 Coventry Street, South Melbourne, Victoria, 3205. *T.* 03-697 0666. *Telex:* AA33501. *Fax:* 03-699 2041. *Managing Director:* N. J. Ryan. Educational publishers.

*Lothian Publishing Co. Pty. Ltd.,** 11 Munro Street, Port Melbourne, Victoria 3207

T. 03-645 1544. *Telex:* AA39476. *Directors:* Louis A. Lothian (Chairman), P. H. Lothian (Managing), K. A. Lothian. Juveniles, health, gardening, general literature.

*Macmillan Company of Australia Pty. Ltd., The,** 107 Moray Street, South Melbourne, 3205. *T.* 699 8922. *T.A.* Scriniaire, Melbourne. *Telex:* AA34454. 6-8 Clarke Street, Crows Nest, 2065, N.S.W. *T.* 438-2988. *Managing Director:* K. B. Stonier. All types of books.

Melbourne House (Australia) Pty. Ltd., (1979), 96-100 Tope Street, South Melbourne, Victoria, 3205. *T.* 03-699 6155. *Telex:* AA34785 Melpub. *Directors:* Alfred Milgrom, Naomi Besen. Computer books and software.

*Melbourne University Press,** 268 Drummond Street, Carlton, Victoria, 3053. *T.* 347 3455. *Postal Address:* P.O. Box 278, Carlton South, Victoria, 3053. Prepared to consider works of academic, scholastic or cultural interest, educational textbooks and books of reference. Terms of publication are royalty, commission or profit-sharing agreements, according to the nature of the work. Representatives: Britain and Europe, H.B. Sales, Enterprise House, Ashford Road, Ashford, Middlesex TW15 1XB, England; North America, International Scholarly Book Services Inc.; Tokyo, Hong Kong and Singapore, United Publishers Services Ltd. *Chairman:* Professor J. R. Poynter. *Director:* P. A. Ryan, M.M., B.A.

*Nelson (Thomas) Australia,** 480 La Trobe Street, Melbourne, Victoria, 3000. *T.* 329 5199. *Telex:* AA33088.

*O'Neil, Lloyd, Pty Ltd** (1973), 56 Claremont Street, South Yarra, Victoria 3141. *T.* 03-241-9901. *Telex:* AA36472. *Directors:* Lloyd J. O'Neil (Chairman), Peter J. Hyde, Robert P. Sessions. Australian history, natural history, art, pictorial and general works relating to Australia.

*Oxford University Press, Australia,** *Managing Director:* Sandra McComb. 7 Bowen Crescent, Melbourne, Victoria 3004. *Postal address:* G.P.O. Box 2784Y, Melbourne, Victoria 3001. *Cables:* Oxonian, Melbourne. *T.* 267-7466. *Telex:* AA 35330 ref. Oxonian. Australian history, biography, literary criticism, general, including children's books, but excluding fiction. School books in all subjects.

Pacific Publications (Aust.) Pty. Ltd., 76 Clarence Street, Sydney, N.S.W., 2000. *T.* 02-20231. *Postal address:* G.P.O. Box 3408, Sydney, N.S.W., 2001. General and reference for Pacific Islands market and agricultural/technical.

*Penguin Books Australia Ltd.,** (1946), (P.O. Box 257), 487 Maroondah Highway, Ringwood, Victoria, 3134. *T.* 871 2400. *T.A.* Penguinook, Melbourne. *Directors:* G. Beattie, P. J. Field, R. E. Ford, T. D. Glover (Managing), B. F. Johns (Publishing), P. M. Mayer, T. J. Rix, N. J. Ryan, J. C. Strike, J. W. Webster. Fiction, general non-fiction, current affairs, sociology, economics, environmental, anthropology, politics, children's.

*Pitman Publishing Pty. Ltd.,** Kings Gardens, 95 Coventry Street, South Melbourne, Victoria, 3205. *Telex:* AA30107. *Chairman:* Neil Ryan; *Managing Director:* Tudor Day; *Marketing Director:* Paul Reekie; *Company Secretary:* Stewart Opie. Technical, educational, general, commercial, legal and art and crafts. Exclusive agent throughout Australia for Longman (trade books); Pitman Publishing Ltd, London; ABC Publications; Watson Guptill; Howard Sams; Copp Clark Pitman, Canada; Que Corporation.

Reed Books Pty. Ltd., 2 Aquatic Drive, Frenchs Forest, N.S.W. 2086. *T.* (02)451-8122. *Directors:* D. A. MacLellan, C. J. B. Scott. General.

Rigby Publishers, Division of **RPLA Pty Ltd.,** 176 South Creek Road (P.O. Box

60), Dee Why, N.S.W. 2099. *T.* 02-981 0444. *Telex:* AA121546. *Fax:* 02-982 6001. *Publisher:* Anne Wilson. General (with emphasis on Australian), reference, technical, fiction, paperbacks and children's fiction.

Shakespeare Head Press, 5-01 Henry Lawson Business Centre, Birkenhead Point, Drummoyne, N.S.W. 2047 *T.* 819-9111. Educational. A Division of **Golden Press Pty. Ltd.**

Sun Books Pty. Ltd. (1965), 107 Moray Street, South Melbourne, Victoria 3205. *T.* 699 8922. *T.A.* Sunbooks. *Directors:* K. B. Stonier, J. Rolfe, N. G. Byam Shaw. Paperbacks—fiction, non-fiction, educational, especially Australian titles. Subsidiary of **The Macmillan Company of Australia Pty. Ltd.**

***Sydney University Press** (1964), Press Building, University of Sydney, N.S.W., 2006. *T.* 660 4997. *T.A.* Sydpress. *Director:* David New. Social sciences and the humanities.

***University of Queensland Press** (1948), P.O. Box 42, St. Lucia, Queensland, 4067 *T.* 377 2127. *General Manager:* L. C. Muller. Scholarly works, tertiary texts, Australian fiction, poetry, history, and some general interest books.

***Wild & Woolley** (1974), P.O. Box 41, Glebe, New South Wales 2037. *T.* 692-0166. *Director:* Pat Woolley. Fiction, literary criticism, political cartoons, drug information, politics. Australian authors only.

CANADA

The paragraph prefixing 'US Publishers' applies to this section also
*Members of the Canadian Book Publishers' Council
†Members of the Association of Canadian Publishers

†**Anansi Press Ltd., House of** (1967), 35 Britain Street, Toronto, M5A 1R7 *T.* 416-363-5444. *Directors:* Ann Wall (President), Harald Bohne, James Polk, Norma Goodger. Distributed by **Kershaw Publishing Co. Ltd.,** 7 Bury Place, London WC1A 2LA *T.* 01-430 2460. Poetry, fiction, non-fiction. Only Canadian writers.

Book Society of Canada, Limited, The —see **Irwin Publishing Inc.**

***Butterworths,** 2265 Midland Avenue, Scarborough, Ontario, M1P 4S1 *T.* 416-292 1421.

Canada Publishing Corporation (1844), 164 Commander Boulevard, Agincourt, Ontario, M1S 3C7 *T.* 416-293-8141. *T.A.* Gagepub, Toronto. Publishers of elementary, secondary, post-secondary, university textbooks, medical and general reading publications, business education and vocational materials for high school and college. Professional and reference material.
Agents for: Financial Post, Fraser Institute, George G. Harrap, Macmillan London Ltd., Andrews & McMeel, Forkner Publishing Corp., Wm. Morrow, Scott Foresman Inc., South-Western, Urban & Schwarzenberg, Wilshire Book, Bordas (Paris), Special Learning Corp, Fairmont Press, C.B.I., Hearst Books, Ivory Tower, Quill, Mondia Editeurs.

Canadian Stage and Arts Publications, George Hencz, 52 Avenue Road, Toronto, Ontario, M5R 2G2 *T.* 416-921-2601, 921-5188. Primarily interested in children's books of an educational nature, art books and fiction.

***Collier Macmillan Canada, Inc.,** (1958), 50 Gervais Drive, Don Mills, Ontario, M3C 3K4 *T.* 449-6030. *Director:* Ray Lee (President). Academic, technical, medical, educational, children's and adult, trade, computer books and software.

*Collins (Wm.) Sons & Co. (Canada), Ltd.,** 100 Lesmill Road, Don Mills, Ontario, M3B 2T5. *T.* 416-445-8221. *Telex:* 06-966673. Publishers of general literature, fiction, children's books, Bibles and paperbacks. Publishers in Canada for Wm. Collins, Sons & Co., Ltd., Totem Books, Pan Books Ltd., André Deutsch, Ltd., Harvill Press, Ltd., Ladybird Books, Arrow Publications Ltd., Granada Publishing, Adlard Coles Ltd., Colour Library International, Fontana, Farrar, Strauss & Giroux, Inc., Severn House, Piatkus Books, Mysterious Press.

*Copp Clark Pitman,** 495 Wellington Street West, Toronto, M5V 1E9 *T.* 416-593-9911. *Telex:* 06-217849. *President:* Stephen J. Mills, *Vice President Marketing:* Brian O'Donnell, *Publication Director:* Linda Scott. Educational textbooks for elementary, secondary and college, technical and business education. Preliminary letter required before submitting manuscript.

Dodd, Mead & Company (Canada), Ltd., 481 University Avenue, Toronto, M5G 2E9 *T.* 416-598-1114. General publishers.

*Dominie Press Limited,** 1361 Huntingwood Drive, Agincourt, Ontario, M1S 3J1 *T.* 416-291-5857.

*Doubleday Canada Ltd.** (1937), 105 Bond Street, Toronto, Ontario, M5B 1Y3 *T.* 416-977-7891. *President:* Peter Maik; *Vice-Presidents:* H. Ford, G. Cholack, J. Neale. *Secretary and Treasurer:* D. Z. McBride. General trade fiction and non-fiction, school textbooks, Dell mass market.

†Douglas & McIntyre Ltd. (1964), 1615 Venables Street, Vancouver, B.C., V5L 2H1 *T.* 604-254-7191. *Directors:* J. J. Douglas, Scott McIntyre. General non-fiction specialising in Canadian biography, art, outdoors and recreation, Northwest Coast anthropology; fiction. Children's books and high quality graphic books. Agents for Thames & Hudson, British Museum Publications.

†Fitzhenry & Whiteside Limited (1966), 195 Allstate Parkway, Markham, Ontario L3R 4T8 *T.* 416-477-0030. *Directors:* R. I. Fitzhenry, Cecil L. Whiteside, Anthony Eckstein, Hilda Fitzhenry, Robert W. Read, Thomas Richardson, Sharon Fitzhenry. Trade, educational, college books.

*Gage Publishing Ltd—see Canada Publishing Corporation.**

*General Publishing Co., Limited,** 30 Lesmill Road, Don Mills, Ontario, M3B 2T6 *T.* 416-445-3333. Fiction, non-fiction, elementary, secondary, college and technical; mass market paperbacks.

*Harlequin Enterprises Ltd.** (1949), 225 Duncan Mill Road, Don Mills, Ontario, M3B 3K9 *T.* 416-445-5860. *Telex:* 06-966697. *Directors:* David A. Galloway (Chairman), Brian Hickey (President). Romance, heroic adventure.

Hodder & Stoughton, Ltd., 1361 Huntingwood Drive, Agincourt, Ontario, M1S 3J1 *T.* 416-291 5857.

*Holt, Rinehart & Winston of Canada, Ltd.,** 55 Horner Avenue, Toronto, Ontario, M8Z 4X6 *T.* 416-255-4491.

†Hurtig Publishers (1967), 10560 105 Street, Edmonton, Alberta, T5H 2W7 *T.* 403-426-2359. *President:* M. G. Hurtig. Reference, humour, biography, political science, Canadiana, energy, environment.

*†Irwin Publishing Inc.,** 180 West Beaver Creek Road, Richmond Hill, Ontario L4B 1B4 *T.* 416-731-3838. *Telex:* 06-964577. *President:* J. W. Irwin, *Controller:* W. A. Boake. *General Manager:* Russell A. Culver. Educational books at the elementary, high school and college levels. General trade books, including fiction, non-fiction and young adult.
Represent in Canada: Allison & Busby Ltd., B. T. Batsford, Bell & Hyman, Heinemann Educational, Heinemann Medical, Hulton Educational, William

Kimber, John Murray, Phaidon Press, Continental Press, McDonald Publishing, Hudson Hills Press, McDougal Littell & Co., Open Court Publishing (educational programs only), Stein & Day, Marcel Broquet.

*†**McClelland & Stewart, Limited** (1906), 481 University Avenue, Toronto, M5G 2E9 *T.* 416-598-1114. *Chairman and President:* Avie Bennett. General and educational.

†**McGill-Queen's University Press,** 849 Sherbrooke Street West, Montreal, Quebec H3A 2T5 *T.* 514-392-4421 and Queen's University, Kingston, Ontario K7L 3N6 *T.* 613-547-6614. Academic.

***McGraw-Hill Ryerson Ltd.,** 330 Progress Avenue, Scarborough, Ontario, M1P 2Z5 *T.* 416-293-1911. Educational and trade books.

***Macmillan of Canada** (1905), a Division of **Canada Publishing Corporation,** 29 Birch Avenue, Toronto, Ontario M4V 1E2 *T.* 416-923-7329. Trade book publishers.

***Methuen Publications** (1965), a Division of the Carswell Co., Ltd., 2330 Midland Avenue, Agincourt, Ontario, M1S 1P7 *T.* 416-425-9200. *Vice President and General Manager:* F. D. Wardle. General trade, school and college textbooks.

***Nelson Canada** (1914), 1120 Birchmount Road, Scarborough, Ontario, M1K 5G4 *T.* 416-752-9100. *Telex:* 06-963813. *Directors:* Alan G. Cobham (President), Barry G. Jones, Helmut C. Batke, Ross M. Inkpen, Douglas R. Fletcher, Thomas R. Tyrrell, Martin Keast, Peter McBride. Elementary, high school, college textbooks; measurement and guidance, children's library.

†**Oberon Press,** 401A Delta Ottawa, Ottawa, Ontario, K1R 7S8 *T.* 613-238-3275. General.

***Oxford University Press (Canada),** 70 Wynford Drive, Don Mills, Ontario, M3C 1J9 *T.* 416-441-2941. *Cables:* Frowde, Toronto. *Telex:* OUP-Tor-06-966518. *Fax:* 416-441-0427. *Manager:* M. Morrow. General, educational, medicine, religious, juvenile and Canadiana.

*****PaperJacks Ltd.,** *Editorial:* 330 Steelcase Road East, Markham, Ontario L3R 2M1 *T.* 416-475-1261.

*****Prentice-Hall Canada, Inc.,** (1960), 1870 Birchmount Road, Scarborough, Ontario, M1P 2J7 *T.* 293-3621. *Telex:* 065-25184. *Directors:* W. A. Matheson, E. E. Campbell, R. E. Snyder. Educational (elementary, secondary, post-secondary), general history, natural history, politics, sports.

*****Stoddart Publishing Co. Ltd,** 30 Lesmill Road, Don Mills, Ontario M3B 2T6 *T.* 416-445-3333. Fiction and non-fiction.

†**University of Toronto Press,** University of Toronto, Toronto, M5S 1A6 *T.* 416-978-2231 (Editorial); 416-978-2239 (Administration).

INDIA

*Members of the Federation of Indian Publishers

*****Ajanta Books International** (1975), 1-UB Jawahar Nagar, Bungalow Road, Delhi 110 007 *T.* 2917375, 2926182. *Proprietor:* S. Balwant. Social sciences and humanities, specialising in: politics, sociology, management, history, literature (Indian, Sanskrit and Western), education, linguistics, philosophy, archaeology, library science, fiction.

Allied Publishers Private Limited, 15 J. N. Heredia Marg, Ballard Estate, Bombay 400 038 *T.* 261959; 17 Chittaranjan Avenue, Calcutta 700 072, *T.* 277023; 13/14 Asaf Ali Road, New Delhi 110 002, *T.* 275001; 751 Mount Road, Madras

600 002, *T.* 89430; 5th Main Road, Gandhinagar, Bangalore 560 009, *T.* 72081, 3-5-1129 Kachiguda Cross Road, Hyderabad 500 027, *T.* 43132. Publishers of school and college textbooks; economics, education, psychology, sociology, and general books on current affairs and Oriental art. Exclusive agents in India for: A. & C. Black (Publishers) Ltd., Arlington Books, Applied Science Publishers Ltd., Basil Blackwell Ltd., Duckworth (Gerald) & Co. Ltd., John Murray (Publishers) Ltd., and William Heinemann Ltd.

Asia Publishing House, imprint of **Jaisingh & Mehta Publishers Pvt. Ltd.,** Bhogilal Hargobindas Building, 18/20 K. Dubash Marg, Bombay, 400 023 *T.* 225353, 225425. *Telex:* 1171665 Quip In; Indra Palace, Connaught Circus, New Delhi, 110 001. *New York Representative:* Apt Books Inc., 141 East 44th Street, New York, N.Y. 10017. Literature, general, including art, biography, economics, politics, world affairs, education, history, library, science, philosophy and psychology, science and technology, publish Air India's inflight magazine.

Atma Ram & Sons (1909), Post Box 1429, Kashmere Gate, Delhi, 110 006 *T.* 2518159, 2523082. *Cables:* Books Delhi. *Managing Proprietor:* Ish Kumar Puri; *Senior Director:* Sushil Puri; *General Manager:* Ashutosh Pury. *Branch:* 17 Ashok Marg, Lucknow. Art, literature, reference, biography, fiction, economics, politics, education, history, philosophy, psychology, science, technology. Books published in English and Hindi languages. Translations and reprints of foreign books undertaken. Booksellers and importers of foreign books on a large scale.

B.I. Publications Pvt. Ltd., 54 Janpath, New Delhi, 110001. *T.* 325313. *Telex:* 031 63352 BI IN. *Chairman:* R. D. Bhagat. Scientific, technical, medical, business and industrial management, educational, children's, reference and general.

Blackie & Son, Publishers Pvt. Ltd., Blackie House, 103-5 Walchand Hirachand Marg, Post Box 381, Bombay 400 001. *T.* 261410, 269408. *Branch:* Bharat Buildings, P.B. 3724, 93 Anna Salai, Madras, 600 002. *T.* 811225, and 11 G.F., Virat Bhavan, Plot No. 1.D., Dr. Mukharjee Nagar, Community Centre, New Delhi.

***Chand, S., & Co. Ltd.** (1917), Ram Nagar, New Delhi 110055. *T.* 772080. *Telex:* 031-2185. *T.A.* Eschand, New Delhi. *Directors:* S. L. Gupta, Rajendra Kumar Gupta, Ravindra Kumar Gupta. Science, technology, medicine, educational books, children's books.

***Children's Book Trust** (1957), Nehru House, 4 Bahadur Shah Zafar Marg, New Delhi 110002. *T.* 3316970. *T.A.* Childtrust, New Delhi. *Executive Trustee:* K. Shankar Pillai. Children's books.

English Book Depot (1923), 15 Rajpur Road, Dehra Dun (U.P.), 248 001. *T.* 23792, 23187. *Directors:* Dev Dutt and Sandeep Dutt. Military science, agriculture, forestry, geology and petroleum.

***Heritage Publishers** (1973), 4348 Madan Mohan Street, 4c Ansari Road, Daryaganj, New Delhi 110002. *Proprietor:* B. R. Chawla. Social science, Indology, humanities.

***Hind Pocket Books Pvt. Ltd.,** G. T. Road, Shahdara, Delhi, 110032. *T.* 353814, 202046. *T.A.* Pocketbook Delhi. Paperbacks in Indian languages and English. *Managing Director:* D. N. Malhotra.

Indian Press (Publications) Private, Limited, 36 Pannalal Road, Allahabad (U.P.) *T.* 53190. *T.A.* Publikason. Branches and agencies in all principal towns of India. Publishers of *Saraswati Hindi Monthly Magazine*, and school, college, university and general books in Hindi, Bengali, English; Gurumukhi, Urdu, Marathi, Nepali languages. *Managing Director:* D. P. Ghosh.

Kothari Publications, Jute House, 12 India Exchange Place, Calcutta, 700001. *T.* 22-9563, 22-6572, 45-0009. *Cable:* Zeitgeist. *Proprietor:* Ing. H. Kothari of Sujangarh, Rajasthan. Technical, general and reference books. *Who's Who* series in India. Agents for many foreign publishers.

Little Flower Co., The (1929), Bhurangam Buildings, P.B. 1028, 43 Ranganathan Street, Thyagarayanagar, Madras, 600017. *T.* 441538. *T.A.* Lifco, Madras. Lifco books. General, fiction, technical, dictionaries, astrology, medicine, legal, commercial, educational and religious.

Macmillan India Ltd., 2/10 Ansari Road, Darya Ganj, New Delhi 110 002. *Branches:* Bombay: Mercantile House, Magazine Street, Raey Road (East), Bombay, 400010; Bangalore: 12-A Mahatma Gandhi Road, Bangalore 560001; Madras: 40 Peters Road, Royapettah, Madras 600 014. Associate Company of Macmillan Publishers Ltd., London. Publishers of educational, scientific, humanities, literature, technical, medical, and general books. Agents in India, Burma, Ceylon, Nepal and Bangladesh for: Gill & Macmillan Ltd., Dublin, The Hamlyn Publishing Group Ltd., W. & R. Chambers.

National Book Trust, India (1957), A-5 Green Park, New Delhi 110 016 *T.* 664667, 664020.

Natraj Publishers, 17 Rajpur Road, Dehra Dun, U.P., 248001. *T.* 23382. *Partners:* Sohan Lall and Upendra Arora. Specialist books on military science, forestry, agriculture and geology.

*Orient Longman Ltd., Regd. Office: 5-9-41/1, Bashir Bagh, Hyderabad 500 029, and regional offices at 17 Chittaranjan Avenue, Calcutta, 700 072; Kamani Marg, Ballard Estate, Bombay, 400 038; 160 Anna Salai, Madras, 600 002; 1/24 Asaf Ali Road, New Delhi, 110 002. Educational, scientific, technical, medical, general and children's. Associated with the Longman Group Ltd. Agents and distributors in India for Longman Group Ltd.; U.N.E.S.C.O., Paris; Penguin Books, Ltd.

*Oxford University Press (Indian Branch). *General Manager:* R. Dayal. *Head Office:* Post Box 43, YMCA Library Building, Jai Singh Road, New Delhi 110001; *Branch Office:* Post Box 7035, 2/11 Ansari Road, Daryaganj, New Delhi, 110002; Post Box 31, Oxford House, Apollo Bunder, Bombay, 400039; G.P.O. Box 530, Faraday House, P17 Mission Row Extension, Calcutta, 700013; Post Box 1079, Oxford House, Anna Salai, Madras, 600006. *Cables:* Oxorient, Delhi, Oxonian, Delhi, Oxonian, Bombay, Oxonian, Calcutta, Oxonian, Madras. *T. Head Office:* New Delhi 321190, 321322, 322769; *Branch Office:* New Delhi 27-3841-2, 27-7812, Bombay 202-1029, 202-1198, 202-1396; Calcutta 26-3533, 26-3534, 23-4832; Madras 47-2267, 47-2268, 47-2299. Publishers in all subjects. Agents in India, Burma, Sri Lanka and Nepal for Faber & Faber Ltd., and Ginn & Co. Ltd. (selected titles). It distributes books for the following university presses: Harvard, Princeton and Stanford.

Pustak-Bhandar, Govind Mitra Road, Patna, PIN 800 004 *T.* 50341. *Founder:* Acharya Ramlochan Saran. *Partners:* M. S. Singh, Dr. S. S. Singh, S. R. Saran, J. B. Saran. Literary, scientific, and educational books in English, Hindi, Nepali, Bengali, Urdu, Maithili, Sanskrit, Oriya. Comic books for children; publishes children's monthly magazine in Hindi *Balak* and Hindi family monthly magazine *Anand Digest.*

*Rajpal & Sons, Kashmere Gate, Delhi, 110006. *T.* 2523904 and 2519104. *T.A.* Rajpalsons, Delhi. Literary criticism, social and general, humanities, textbooks, juvenile literature, Hindi and English. *Managing Partner:* Vishwanath.

Ranjan Gupta (1969), 22/3-C Galiff Street, Calcutta 700004. *T.* 55-4387.

Specialising in rare books of Indology, Indian philosophy, religion, art, literature, history, linguistics, periodicals.

Rupa & Co., P.O. Box 12333, 15 Bankim Chatterjee Street, Calcutta, 700073. *T.* 34-4821. *T.A.* Rupanco, Calcutta-73.

Shiksha Bharati (1955), Madarsa Road, Kashmere Gate, Delhi 110006. *T.* 2519104. Textbooks, popular science and children's books in Hindi and English; also juvenile literature. *Managing Partner:* Veena Malhotra.

***Sterling Publishers Pvt. Ltd.,** (1964) L-10 Green Park Extension, New Delhi, 110016. *T.* 669560. *Directors:* O. P. Ghai (Chairman), S. K. Ghai (Managing), Mrs. Vimla Ghai. Agriculture, biography, computer science, cookery, economics and commerce, education, history and Indology, language and literature, law, library science, management, medicine, military, philosophy and religion, politics, psychology and sociology.

***Tata McGraw-Hill Publishing Co. Ltd.** (1970), 12/4 Asaf Ali Road, New Delhi 110 002. *T.* 273105, 271303, 263087. *Telex:* 31-2257 Tmhd In. *T.A.* Corinthian, New Delhi. *Directors:* J. J. Bhabha (Chairman), S. A. Sabavala, Dr. Francis A. Menezes, Dr. Malcolm S. Adiseshiah, J. C. Dastur, N. R. Subramanian, Joseph L. Dionne, Donald L. Fruehling, Frederick G. Perkins. Engineering, sciences, management, humanities, social sciences, computer science, electronics.

***Taraporevala (D. B.) Sons & Co., Private, Ltd.** (Original firm established 1864), 210 Dr. Dadabhai Naoroji Road, Bombay, 400 001. *T.* 261433. *Directors:* Mrs. Manekbai J. Taraporevala and Miss Sooni J. Taraporevala. *Chief Executive:* Prof. Russi J. Tapaporevala. Books on India and on Indian interest, fine arts, handicrafts, pictorial albums, business, economics, education, electronics, psychology, cookery, domestic economy, pets, hobbies, reference, languages, religion, philosophy, mysticism, occult sciences, law, history, culture, mythology, sociology, health, medical, sex, science, technology, self-improvement, self-instruction, sports, Indian classics.

Thacker & Co., Ltd., P.O. Box 190, 18-20 Kaikushru Dubash Marg (Rampart Row), Bombay 400 023. *T.* 242667, 242683, 242745. *T.A.* Booknotes, Bombay. *Chairman:* K. M. Diwanji. *Chief Executive:* Dhanraj K. Bhagat. *Managing Director:* J. M. Chudasama. Banking, gardening, cooking. Distributors for Ladybird Books, Penguin, RotoVision, Walter Foster, Pan, Fontana, Hamlyn.

Theosophical Publishing House, The, Adyar, Madras, 600020. *T.* 412904. *T.A.* Theotheca, Madras 600020. Theosophical, mystical and occult literature. Publishers of *The Theosophist*, official organ of the President, Theosophical Society. *Editor:* Mrs. Radha Burnier, International President of The Theosophical Society. *Manager:* R. Gopalaratnam.

***Vikas Publishing House Pvt Ltd.,** (1969), 5 Ansari Road, New Delhi 110 002 *T.* 273601, 279743, 866536. *Telex:* 592-252 Viph/In. *T.A.* Vikasbooks, New Delhi. *Managing Director:* Narendra Kumar. Science and technology, humanities and social sciences.

***Vision Books Pvt. Ltd.,** (1975). Head Office: Madarsa Road, Kashmere Gate, Delhi 110 006 *T.* 2517001, 2514274, 2512267; Editorial Office: 36-c Connaught Place, New Delhi 110 001. *T.* 352081, 312978. *T.A.* Visionbook New Delhi. *Directors:* Sudhir Malhotra (Managing), Kapil Malhotra, Vishwanath. Fiction (including Indo-Anglian and translation from Indian languages and other languages), Indian culture, politics, biography, travel, poetry, drama management, military, religion, anthropology, mountaineering, education, international relations. *Imprints:* Vision Books, Orient Paperbacks, Anand Paperbacks, Naya Sahitya.

*Wiley Eastern Ltd. (1966), 4835/24 Ansari Road, Daryaganj, New Delhi, 110 002 *T.* 276802, 261487. *T.A.* Wileyeast. *Branches:* Bangalore, Bombay, Calcutta, Hyderabad, Madras. *Chief Executive:* A. Machwe. *Directors:* W. Bradford Wiley, A. H. Neilly, Jr., E. B. Desai, A. R. Kundaji, F. N. Mulla, K. K. Lalkaka, B. D. Bharucha. Biology, physics, chemistry, mathematics, engineering sciences, humanities and social sciences.

THE REPUBLIC OF IRELAND AND NORTHERN IRELAND

*Members of the Irish Publishers' Association

Academy Press Ltd. (1976), 17 Brighton Square, Rathgar, Dublin 6 *T.* 01-962946. *Director:* Sean Browne.
Irish history, Anglo-Irish literature, literary criticism, art and art history.

*Appletree Press Ltd. (1974), 7 James Street South, Belfast, BT2 8DL *T.* (0232) 243074 and 246756. *Telex:* 265871 Monref G ref. ATP001 and Suite 521, Irish Life Centre, Talbot Street, Dublin *T.* 746611. *Director:* John Murphy.
Academic, biography, cookery, educational, guide books, history, literary criticism, music, photographic, social studies, sport, travel.

*Arlen House Ltd., The Women's Press (1975), Kinnear Court, 16-20 South Cumberland Street, Dublin 2. *T.* 01-717383. *Directors:* Louise Barry, Mary Cullen, Margaret MacCurtain, Catherine Rose, Ann Blackwell, Jennifer Kelly.
Women's studies, biography, literature, poetry, fiction.

*Blackstaff Press Ltd. (1971), 3 Galway Park, Dundonald BT16 0AN *T.* (02318) 7161. *Directors:* Michael Burns, Anne Tannahill.
Fiction, poetry, biography, history, art, academic, natural history, sport, politics, philosophy, music, education, fine limited editions.

Blackwater Press, The, an imprint of **Folens & Co. Ltd.,** *q.v.*
General non-fiction, Irish interest.

*Boethius Press Ltd. (1973), Clarabricken, Clifden, Co. Kilkenny. *T.* Kilkenny (056) 29746. *Directors:* L. J. Hewitt, J. M. Hewitt, Mrs. J. M. Hewitt.
Irish and London topography, gardens, botany, Irish studies.

*Brandon Book Publishers Ltd (1982), Cooleen, Dingle, Co. Kerry. *T.* 066-51463. *Directors:* Steve MacDonogh, Bernard Goggin.
Fiction, literature, politics, history, folklore, sport.

*Brophy Educational Books Ltd (1977), 108 Sundrive Road, Dublin 12. *T.* 01-973061 and 971617. *Directors:* Kevin T. Brophy (Managing), Mary Brophy.
School texts; sport, entertainment, general non-fiction, drama. *Imprints:* **Brophy Books, Canavaun Books.**

Canavaun Books, an imprint of **Brophy Educational Books.**

Catholic Communications Institute of Ireland, Inc.—see **Veritas Publications.**

*Dolmen Press, Ltd., The Lodge, Mountrath, Portlaoise. *T.* (0502) 32213. *Directors:* Liam Miller, Josephine P. Miller, Thomas Kinsella, William C. Browne, Alec Reid.
Irish literature and books of Irish interest. Childrens books (under **Brogeen Books** imprint).

*Eason & Son Ltd. (1886), 66 Middle Abbey Street, Dublin 1. *T.* 733811. *Publishing Director:* W. H. Clarke.
Irish non-fiction, including Irish Heritage Series.

Educational Company of Ireland, The, P.O.Box 43a, Ballymount Road, Walkinstown, Dublin 12. *T.* Dublin 500611. *Executive Directors:* F. J. Maguire

(Chief Executive), J. M. Davin, F.C.A. (Secretary), S. O'Neill, Ursula Ní Dhálaigh, P. McGann, R. McLoughlin. A trading unit of Smurfit Ireland Ltd. Educational MSS. on all subjects in English or Gaelic.

Fallon (C. J.) Ltd. (1927), Lucan Road, Palmerstown, Dublin 20. *T.* 265777. *Directors:* H. J. McNicholas (Managing), P. Tolan (Secretary), N. White (Editorial).
Educational text books.

Folens & Co., Ltd., Airton Road, Tallaght, Co. Dublin. *T.* 515311.
Educational (primary, secondary, comprehensive, technical, in English and Irish), educational children's magazines.

*****Four Courts Press** (1969), Kill Lane, Blackrock, Co. Dublin. *T.* 01-850922. *Directors:* Michael Adams, Gerard O'Flaherty.
Theology.

Gallery Press (1970), 19 Oakdown Road, Dublin 14. *T.* 01-985161. *Director:* Peter Fallon. *Allied Company:* Deerfield Publications Inc., Massachusetts.
Poetry, drama, occasionally fiction. Also, hand-printed limited editions poetry.

*****Gill & Macmillan, Ltd.** (1968), Goldenbridge, Inchicore, Dublin 8. *T.* 531005.
Biography or memoirs, educational (primary, secondary, university), history, philosophy, sociology, theology and religion, literature.

Goldsmith Press, The (1972), Newbridge, Co. Kildare. *Directors:* D. Egan, V. Abbott, P. Mulreid, R. Garvey.
Literature, art, Irish interest, poetry. *ERA* Review (annually), *Goldsmith Poetry Calendar* (annually).

*****Institute of Public Administration** (1957), 59 Lansdowne Road, Dublin 4. *T.* 686233; Publications: 697011. *T.A.* Admin, Dublin. *Deputy Assistant Director and Head of Publishing:* James D. O'Donnell. *Assistant Manager:* Iain McAulay.
Government, economic, law, social policy and administrative history.

*****Irish Academic Press** (1974), Kill Lane, Blackrock, Co. Dublin. *T.* 01-850922. Publishes under the imprints **Irish University Press, Irish Academic Press** and **Ecclesia Press**. *Directors:* Michael Adams, Frank Cass, John Mladinich, Gilbert Raff, Michael Philip Zaidner.
Scholarly books especially in history and law.

Longman, Browne & Nolan, now incorporated in **Educational Company of Ireland,** *q.v.*

*****Mercier Press, The** (1945), P.O. Box 5, 4 Bridge Street, Cork. *T.* Cork 504022. *Telex:* 75463. *Directors:* Capt. J. M. Feehan, J. C. O'Connor, P. W. McGrath, D. J. Keily, C. U. O. Marcaigh, M. Feehan, L. McNamara, J. F. Spillane, A. C. Devitt.
Irish literature, folklore, history, politics, humour, ballads, education, theology.

O'Brien Educational (1976), 20 Victoria Road, Rathgar, Dublin 6. *T.* 979598 and 740354. *Directors:* Michael O'Brien, Seamus Cashman, Bride Rosney.
Humanities, science, environmental studies, history, geography, English, Irish, art, commerce, music, careers, media studies.

O'Brien Press Ltd., The (1974), 20 Victoria Road, Rathgar, Dublin 6. *T.* 979598. *Directors:* Michael O'Brien, Valerie O'Brien.
Folklore, nature, fiction, architecture, topography, history, general, illustrated books, music, sport, anthropology, children.

*****Poolbeg Press Ltd.** (1976), Knocksedan House, Forrest Great, Swords, Co. Dublin. *T.* 401133. *Telex:* 24639. *Director:* Philip MacDermott. *Editor:*

Sean McMahon.
Irish fiction, including short stories; general non-fiction.

Raven Arts Press (1979), P.O. Box 1430, Finglas, Dublin 11. *Publisher:* Dermot Bolger.
Modern Irish poetry and literature.

Runa Press, The (1942), 2 Belgrave Terrace, Monkstown, Dublin. *T.* 801869 and 805000.
Belles-lettres, educational (university), essays, poetry, science, philosophy.

School and College Publishing Ltd. (1968), Taney Road, Dundrum, Dublin 14. *T.* 988554, 988398, 988075. *Directors:* Patrick M. O'Brien, Geraldine O'Brien.
Educational books for primary and secondary schools.

*****Stationery Office** (1922), St. Martins House, Waterloo Road, Dublin 4. *T.* 689066. *T.A.* Enactments Dublin.
Parliamentary publications.

Turoe Press Ltd. (1977), 69 Jones Road, Dublin 3. *T.* 01-786913. *Directors:* Michael Fenton, Margaret MacCurtain, Terry Prone, Michael Roberts, Catherine Rose.
Sociology, social issues, social history, reference, practical.

*****Veritas Publications,** a division of the **Catholic Communications Institute of Ireland, Inc.,** Veritas House, Lower Abbey Street, Dublin 1 *T.* 788177.
Religion, including social and educational works, and material relating to the media of communication.

*****Ward River Press Ltd.** (1980), Knocksedan House, Forrest Great, Swords, Co. Dublin. *T.* 401133. *Telex:* 24639. *Directors:* Bernadette MacDermott, Philip MacDermott, Margaret Daly, Breda Purdue, Kieran Devlin, Ivan Kerr.
Irish non-fiction, art books, art prints, mass-market fiction.

*****Wolfhound Press** (1974), 68 Mountjoy Square, Dublin 1 *T.* 740354. *Publisher:* Seamus Cashman.
Literary studies and criticism, fiction, art, biography, history, children's, law.

NEW ZEALAND

*Membership of the New Zealand Book Publishers' Association

*****Auckland University Press** (1966), University of Auckland, Private Bag, Auckland. *T.* (09) 737 654. *Chairman of University Press Committee:* K. J. Hollyman. *Managing Editor:* R. D. McEldowney. Represented by Oxford University Press. New Zealand studies—especially history and literature. Works of scholarship in general.

*****Bush Press Communications Ltd.** (1979), P.O. Box 33-029, Takapuna, Auckland 9 *T.* 09-495-649. *Governing Director and Publisher:* Gordon Ell. Outdoor and wildlife books, guides, New Zealand non-fiction.

*****Butterworths of New Zealand, Ltd.,** 33-35 Cumberland Place, Wellington. *T.* 851-479.

*****Caxton Press, The,** 113 Victoria Street, Christchurch, P.O. Box 25-088. *T.A.* Imprint, Christchurch. *Directors:* B. C. Bascand, E. B. Bascand. Fine printers and publishers since 1935 of New Zealand books of many kinds, including verse, fiction, biography, history, natural history, travel, children's books. Publish literary quarterly *Landfall (q.v.).*

Century Hutchinson New Zealand Ltd., (1977), P.O. Box 40-086, 32-34 View Road, Glenfield, Auckland 10. *T.* 444-7197 and 7524. *Telex:* 60824. *Directors:* J. Mottram (Chairman), L. Earney (Managing), S. McCloud, M. L. Burnett,

D. Ling. Fiction, junior books, educational and university, sports and pastimes, religion, non-fiction.

*Collins (William) Publishers Ltd., P.O. Box 1, Auckland. *T.* 09-444-3740. *Cables:* Folio Auckland. *Telex:* NZ21685. *Fax:* 09-444 1086. (Parent Company **William Collins, Sons & Co., Ltd.,** 8 Grafton Street, London W1X 3LA. *Directors:* Terry T. Hughes (Managing), Ruth Hamilton (Publishing), Ross Marwick (Marketing). Publishers of general literature, fiction, bibles, children's books, reference books, educational, technical, paperbacks.

*Heinemann Publishers (N.Z.), Ltd., P.O. Box 36064, Northcote, Auckland, 9. *T.* 419 0119. *Telex:* Hebooks NZ 61902. William Heinemann, Ltd.; Wm. Heinemann Medical Books, Ltd.; Secker & Warburg, Ltd.; Heinemann Educational Books; representing also BBC Publications, John Murray (Publishers), Ltd., Daily Express, Lutterworth Press, Book Society of Canada, Shepheard-Walwyn Ltd. *Chairman:* Nicolas Thompson. *Managing Director:* D. J. Heap. *Directors:* G. W. McEwan (Educational), P. J. Redgrove, C. Hunter, G. R. Stevens (Secretary). Secondary and tertiary textbooks, specialist and technical titles, New Zealand literature.

*Hodder & Stoughton Ltd., P.O. Box 3858, Auckland 1. *Showroom:* 46 View Road, Glenfield, Auckland 10. *T.* 444-3640. *T.A.* Expositor, Auckland. *Telex:* NZ21422.

*Jacaranda Wiley Ltd., 4 Kirk Street, Grey Lynn, Auckland 2. *T.* 764620. *Postal Address:* C.P.O. 2259, Auckland 1. *Head Office:* Milton, Queensland, 4064, Australia, *q.v.*

*Longman Paul Limited, Private Bag, Takapuna, Auckland 9. *T.* 444-4968. *Telex:* NZ 21041. Publishers of New Zealand educational books.

*McIndoe, John, Ltd. (1968), 51 Crawford Street, P.O. Box 694, Dunedin. *T.* 770-355. *Directors:* M. M. McIndoe, F. B. McKenzie, R. S. Simpson. All categories.

*Mallinson Rendel Publishers Ltd., (1980), 5A Grass Street, P.O. Box 9409, Wellington. *T.* 857-340. *Directors:* Ann Mallinson, David Rendel. Childrens, general New Zealand books, aviation.

*New Zealand Council for Educational Research (1933), Box 3237, Education House, 178-182 Wills Street, Wellington 1. *T.* 847 939. *T.A.* Edsearch. Education, including educational administration and planning, vocational education and adult learning, special education, families, women and parents, rural education, early childhood education, higher education, Maori schooling, educational achievement tests, etc.

*Oxford University Press, 5 Ramsgate Street, Ellerslie, Auckland 5. *Postal address:* P.O. Box 11-149 Ellerslie, Auckland 5. *T.* 590-460 and 596-914. *Telex:* NZ 60777. *Cables:* Oxonian, Auckland. *N.Z. Manager:* Jeff Olson. *Managing Editor:* Anne French.

*Pitman Publishing New Zealand Ltd., P.O.Box 38 688, 28 Fitzherbert Street, Petone, Wellington. *T.* 683-623. *Chairman:* Neil Ryan; *Managing Director:* Gil McGahey. Technical, educational, general, commercial, medical, legal, art and crafts, music, languages.

*Price Milburn & Co., Ltd., Corner Waione and Kirkaldie Streets, Petone. *T.* 687179. *Telex:* NZ 30656. *Postal Address:* Private Bag, Petone. *Directors:* H. Anderson, A. Dunnett, F. Dodd, D. K. Kerr, N. B. Lambert, P. J. McGurk, P. Singh. Children's fiction, primary school texts, especially school readers and social studies. Publishers for N.Z. Educational Institute.

*Reed Methuen, 39 Rawene Road, Birkenhead, Auckland 10. *Postal Address:* Private Bag, Birkenhead, Auckland 10. *T.* 486 039. *Telex:* NZ21944 Abpub. General.

*Richards Publisher, Ray (1977), 3-49 Aberdeen Road, Castor Bay, Auckland. *Postal Address:* P.O. Box 31240 Milford, Auckland. *T.* 410 4681. *Directors:* Ray Richards, Barbara Richards, Nicki Richards. Publishers for organisations; especially history, biography, military, equestrian, agriculture.

Sweet & Maxwell (N.Z.) Ltd., 39 Rawene Road, Birkenhead, Auckland 10. *T.* 486-039. *Telex:* NZ21944 Abpub. *Postal Address:* Private Bag, Birkenhead, Auckland 10. Law, accounting.

Taylor (Alister), Publishing Ltd. (1971), P.O. Box 83, Russell, Bay of Islands. *T.* Russell 37-633. *T.A.* Taylor, Russell, NZ. *Telex:* NZ2583 Alister Taylor. *Managing Directors:* Alister Taylor, Deborah Coddington. Publishers of New Zealand books; general, limited edition art books, contemporary N.Z. art, horses, poetry, fiction, N.Z. social and political history.

*Victoria University Press (1974), Victoria University of Wellington, Private Bag, Wellington. *T.* 721-000. *Chairman of the Publications Committee:* Professor G. R. Hawke. *Editor:* Fergus Barrowman. Academic, scholarly books on New Zealand history, sociology, political history, architecture, economics, law, zoology, biology; also fiction, plays.

*Viking Sevenseas Ltd., 23b Ihakara Street, Paraparaumu. *T.* 058-71990. *T.A.* Vikseven. *Managing Director:* M. B. Riley. Factual books on New Zealand only.

*Whitcoulls Publishers. *Head Office and Editorial:* Whitcoulls Publishers, Private Bag, Christchurch 1. *T.* 794580. *T.A.* Whitcoulls, Christchurch. *Telex:* NZ4205. Publishers of New Zealand books of all descriptions, general and educational.

OTHER COMMONWEALTH PUBLISHERS

GHANA

Emmanuel Publishing Services, P.O. Box 5282, Accra *T.* 25238. *Cables:* Emmapus Accra. *Director:* E. K. Nsiah. Representing Oxford University Press, Faber & Faber Ltd., G. Philip & Son Ltd., University Press Ltd., Ibadan, Nigeria.

Moxon Paperbacks (1967), P.O. Box M 160, Accra. *T.* 665397. *T.A.* Moxon, Accra. *Partners:* James Moxon, Oliver Carruthers, Mark Gilbey. Crime, current affairs, biography, travel, fiction.

Sedco Publishing Ltd., Sedco House, Tabon Street, North Ridge, Accra. *T.* 221332. *Postal Address:* P.O. Box 2051, Accra.

HONG KONG

Jacaranda Wiley Ltd., 19D 257 Gloucester Road, Causeway Bay, Hong Kong. *T.* 5-762346. *Head Office:* Milton, Queensland 4064, Australia, *q.v.*

Longman Group (Far East) Ltd., G.P.O. Box 223, Hong Kong. *T.* 5-618171-5.

Macmillan Publishers (China) Limited, 19/F Warwick House, Taikoo Trading Estate, Quarry Bay, Hong Kong. *T.* 5-636206, 5-620101, 5-643115, 5-643125, 5-643135. *Cables:* Macpublish, Hong Kong. *Telex:* 85969. *Fax:* 5-8110743. *Directors:* N. Byam Shaw (Chairman), Ken Derrick, Robert Gaff, Michael Hamilton, Rupert Li, Brian Stonier. Educational (all subjects) and general.

Oxford University Press, 18/F Warwick House, Taikoo Trading Estate, 28 Tong Chong Street, Quarry Bay, Hong Kong. *T.* 5-610221-4, 5-651351-8. *Cables:*

Oxonian, Hong Kong. *Telex:* HX65522.

KENYA

Longman Kenya Ltd., P.O. Box 18033, Nairobi. *T.* 541345-7. *Telex:* 22724.

Nelson, Thomas, & Sons Ltd., P.O. Box 18123, Nairobi. *T.* 555766.

Oxford University Press (East & Central Africa), J. Clarke (Regional Manager), P.O.B. 72532, 1st Floor, Science House, Monrovia Street, Nairobi, Kenya. *Cables:* Oxonian Nairobi. *T.* Nairobi 336377.

MALAYSIA

Heinemann Educational Books (Asia), Ltd. (1963), 2 Jalan 241, Section 51A, 46100 Petaling Jaya, Selangor. *T.* 7750033, 7750250, 7750141. *Telex:* Hebkl MA 37504.

Longman Malaysia Sdn. Berhad, 2nd Floor, 3 Jalan Kilang A, off Jalan Penchala, Petaling Jaya, Selangor. *T.* 03-520466. *Telex:* LMSB MA37600. *T.A.* Freegrove, Kuala Lumpur.

Oxford University Press (East Asia), R. E. Brammah (Regional Manager), Regional Office, 7 Jalan Semangat, P.O. Box 523, Jalan Sultan, 46760 Petaling Jaya, Selangor, Malaysia. *T.* 7551744, 7551841, 7551958. *Telex:* MA37283; Enshu Building, 3-3-3- Otsuka, Bunkyo-ku, Tokyo, Japan. *T.* (942)-0101-3. *Telex:* 2723520.

NIGERIA

African Universities Press, Pilgrim Books Ltd., PMB 5617 Ibadan. *Head Office:* Plot 1, Block P., New Oluyole Industrial Estate, Phase 2, Ibadan-Lagos Expressway, Ibadan. *Cables:* Pilgrim Ibadan. *Telex:* 20311-Box 078. *Directors:* Emmanuel A. Jaja, J. E. Leigh. Educational, Africana.

Evans Brothers (Nigeria Publishers), Ltd., Jericho Road, P.M.B. 5164, Ibadan. *T.* 417570, 417601, 417626. *Telex:* 31104 Edbook NG.

Longman Nigeria, Ltd., Private Mail Bag, 21036, Ikeja. *T.* Lagos 963007, 963176, 964370. *Telex:* 26639.

Macmillan Nigeria Publishers, Ltd., Oluyole Industrial Estate, Scheme 2, Lagos-Ibadan Expressway, Near Methodist High School, P.O. Box 1463, Ibadan, Oyo State. *T.* 316894, 316896-7. *Warehouse and Accounts:* Ilupeju Industrial Estate, Mushin, P.O. Box 264, Yaba, Lagos. *T.* 961188. *Directors:* Olu Anulopo, I. Ademokun, J. O. Dada, N. G. Byam Shaw, Geoff Denner, Prof. Babs Fafunwa, C. R. Harrison, Dr. Tai Solarin, A. Hikima, J. O. Ojelere.

University Press Limited, (in association with Oxford University Press), *Managing Director:* M. O. Akinleye, Three Crowns Building, Jericho, Ibadan. *Postal Address:* Private Mail Bag 5095, Ibadan. *T.* Ibadan 0-22 411356, 412386, 412313 and 413117. *T.A.* and *Cable:* Oxonian Ibadan. *Trade Department:* UPL Jericho, Ibadan. *Postal Address:* P.M.B. 5142, Ibadan. *T.A.* and *Cable:* Frowde, Ibadan. *Telex:* 31121.

SINGAPORE

Butterworth & Co. (Asia) Pte. Ltd., P.O. Box 770, Crawford Post Office, Singapore 9119.

Federal Publications (S) Pte Ltd. (1957), Times Jurong, 2 Jurong Port Road, Singapore 2261. *T.* 2658855. *T.A.* Fedpubs, Singapore. *Telex:* Timesj RS35846. *General Manager:* Y. H. Mew. Educational, children's books and general reference books.

Heinemann Publishers Asia (Pte) Ltd. (1963), 41 Jalan Pemimpin, Apartment

03-05, Singapore, 2057. *T.* 2583255. *Telex:* Hebooks RS24299.

Oxford University Press Pte. Ltd., Unit 221 Ubi Avenue 4, Singapore 1440. *T.* 7431066. *Telex:* RS37960 Oxpres. *Cables:* Oxonian, Singapore.

TANZANIA
Longman Tanzania Ltd., P.O. Box 3164, Dar es Salaam. *T.* Dar es Salaam 29748. *T.A.* and *Cables:* Longman, Dar es Salaam.

Oxford University Press (East & Central Africa), P.O.B. 5299, Maktaba Road, Dar es Salaam. *T.* Dar es Salaam 29209. *Cables:* Oxonian, Dar es Salaam.

UGANDA
Longman Uganda Ltd., P.O. Box 3409, Kampala. *T.* Kampala 42940.

ZAMBIA
Temco Publishing Ltd., P.O. Box 30886, Lusaka. *T.* 211883. *Telex:* ZA45250.

ZIMBABWE
Collins, William, International Ltd., P.O. Box 2800, Harare. *T.* 721413. *Cables:* Fontana.

Longman Zimbabwe (Pvt.) Ltd., P.O. Box ST 125, Southerton, Harare. *T.* Harare 62711-4. *T.A.* Longman, Harare.

Oxford University Press, P.O.B. 3892, 317-320 Roslin House, Baker Avenue, Harare. *T.* 727848. *Cables:* Oxonian, Harare.

SOUTH AFRICA
*Members of South African Publishers' Association.

Balkema (A. A.) Pty Ltd. (1931), P.O. Box 3117, 93 Keerom Street, Cape Town, 8000. *T.* 236721. *Director:* A. A. Balkema. Africana series, fine art, architecture, nature. Balkema academic and technical publications. South African historical and biographical studies. Learned journals and annuals. Distribution outside South Africa: A. A. Balkema, P.O. Box 1675, Rotterdam, Netherlands; and for USA and Canada: I.P.S., P.O. Box 230, Accord, MA02018.

Books of Africa (Pty) Ltd., 39 Atlantic Road, Muizenberg 7951, P.O. Box 1516, Cape Town, 8000. *T.* 888-316. *Directors:* T. V. Bulpin, M. Bulpin. Books on any subject about Africa.

*****Butterworth Publishers (Pty) Ltd.,** 8 Walter Place, Waterval Park, Mayville, Durban 4091 *T.* 294247. *T.A.* and *Cables:* Butterlaw, Durban. *Telex:* 620730SA. *Postal Address:* P.O. Box 792, Durban 4000.

*****Collins Publishers (SA) (Pty) Ltd.,** 10-14 Watkins Street, Denver Ext. 4, Johannesburg. (P.O. Box 61342, Marshalltown, 2107). *T.* 616-1822. *Cables:* Fontana, Johannesburg. *Telex:* 4-23702SA. General publications, fiction, reference books, bibles, juveniles, school textbooks and paperbacks.

Delta Books (Pty) Ltd. (1980), P.O. Box 41021, Craighall, 2024. 111 Central Street, Houghton, Johannesburg 2196. *T.* 728-7121. *Directors:* Adriaan Donker, Karin Donker. Natural history, gardening, cookery, sport, health, practical and pictorial books.

*****Donker (Ad.) (Pty) Ltd.** (1973), P.O. Box 41021, Craighall, 2024. 111 Central Street, Houghton, Johannesburg 2196. *T.* 728-7121. *Directors:* Adriaan Donker, Karin Donker, Michael Chapman. Africana, literature, history, academic, biography.

Hodder & Stoughton Southern Africa, P.O. Box 548, Bergvlei, Sandton 2012. *T.* 786-0001. *Telex:* 4-24235 SA.

*Juta & Company Ltd. (1853), P.O. Box 1010, Johannesburg, 2000. *T.* 23-5521 and P.O. Box 30, Cape Town, 8000. *T.* 71-1181. Educational and legal publishers. General and educational booksellers and importers.

Longman Penguin Southern Africa (Pty) Ltd.,—see Maskew Miller Longman (Pty) Ltd.

*Lovedale Press, Private Bag X 1346, Alice Ciskei. *T.* Alice 278, 167. Educational, religious and general book publications for African market.

Macdonald Purnell (Pty) Ltd., Head Office: 10 Burke Street, Randburg. *Postal Address:* P.O. Box 51401 Randburg 2125. *Telex:* 4-24985 SA *T.A.* Purprint. *Chairman:* R. Maxwell, M.C. *Managing Director:* Malcolm Edwards. Publishers of books of South African interest and stockists of general and juvenile books for the BPCC Group, Apple Press, Arnold Wheaton, Aidan Ellis, Grosset & Dunlap, Lion Publishing, Macdonald & Co., Mitchell Beazley, Purnell & Co., Time Life, Virtue.

*Macmillan South Africa (Publishers) (Pty) Ltd., Braamfontein Centre, Jorissen Street, Braamfontein, Johannesburg (P.O. Box 31487, Braamfontein, 2017). *T.* 339-4841. Publishers of academic, educational and general books as well as those of South African interest.

*Maskew Miller Longman (Pty) Ltd., Howard Drive, Pinelands 7405 *T.* 53-7750. *Postal Address:* P.O. Box 396, Cape Town, 8000. Educational and general publishers and booksellers; school stationery requirements.

*Oxford University Press (Southern African Branch), Neville Gracie, *General Manager.* 5th Floor, Harrington House, 37 Barrack Street, Cape Town, 8001. *Postal Address:* Box 1141, Cape Town, 8000. 306 Hyde Park Corner, Jan Smuts Avenue, Craighall 2196. *Postal Address:* P.O. Box 41390, Craighall 2024. 4th Floor Dales House, 36 Gardiner Street, Durban 4001. *Postal Address:* P.O. Box 37166, Overport 4067. *Cables:* Oxonian Cape Town; Oxonian Johannesburg; Oxonian Durban. *T.* Cape Town 021-45 7266; Johannesburg 011-7883617; Durban 031-304-7202. *Telex:* Capetown 9550022.

Philip (David) Publisher (Pty) Ltd. (1971), P.O. Box 408, Claremont, 7735, Cape Province. *T.* 21-64-4136. *T.A.* Philipub, Cape Town. *Telex:* 527566 Philipub. *Directors:* David Philip, Marie Philip, Academic, history, social sciences, biography, belles-lettres, Africana, reference books, fiction, children's books.

Pitman Publishing Co. S.A. (Pty) Ltd. (1974), P.O. Box 396, Cape town, 8000. *T.* 53-7750. Division of **Maskew Miller Longman (Pty) Ltd.**

*Ravan Press (Pty) Ltd. (1972), 23 O'Reilly Road, Berea, Johannesburg 2001. *Postal Address:* P.O.Box 31134 Braamfontein, 2017. *T.* 643 5552. *Directors:* R. M. Kirkwood, P. Randall. African studies: history, politics, theology. Fiction, new black writing; children's, educational.

Science Press (Pty) Ltd., The (1981), P.O. Box 41021, Craighall 2024. 111 Central Street, Houghton, Johannesburg 2196. *T.* 728 7121. *Directors:* Adriaan Donker, Karin Donker. Medical and scientific books and journals.

*Shuter and Shooter (Pty), Ltd. (1925), Church Street, Pietermaritzburg, Natal. *T.* 58151. *Telex:* 6-43771SA. *T.A.* Shushoo. *Directors:* M. N. Prozesky (Managing), C. L. S. Nyembezi, C. A. Roy, W. N. Vorster, R. J. Watkinson, L. van Heerden, E. O. Oellermann, J. S. Craib, G. Walker, J. A. Wilken, D. F. Ryder.

*Struik Publishers and Distributors (Pty) Ltd. (1957), 2nd Floor, Struik House, cnr. Jack Craig and Oswald Pirow Streets, Foreshore, P.O. Box 1144, Cape Town, 8000. *T.* 21-6740. *T.A.* Dekena, Cape Town. *Telex:* 526713SA. *Fax:* 216744. *Directors:* G. Struik (Managing), P. Struik, W. Reinders, P. Borchert,

D. Wilkins, N. Pryke, P. Isaac.

*Van Schaik (J. L.) (1914), P.O. Box 724, Pretoria, 0001. *T.* 012-21-2441. *Telex:* 3-22340 SA. Publishers of books in English, Afrikaans and African languages. Specialists in Afrikaans books.

Winchester Press (Pty) Ltd. (1967), P.O. Box 52605, Saxonwold 2132. *T.* 442-8789. *Managing Director:* G. A. Winchester-Gould. Travel, natural history, Africana.

Witwatersrand University Press, 1 Jan Smuts Avenue, Johannesburg, 2001. *T.* 716 2029.

UNITED STATES

The following is a selected list; it includes a few of the very many smaller firms, and few of the specialist publishers. The introductory note 'Writing Books' applies also to US publishers.

*Members of the Association of American Publishers Inc.

Abingdon Press, Editorial and Business Offices: 201 Eighth Avenue S., P.O. Box 801, Nashville, Tennessee, 37202. *T.* 615-749 6403. *Vice-President* and *Editorial Director:* Ronald P. Patterson. Lay, professional, academic, reference and family books—primarily directed to the religious market.

Academy Chicago Publishers (1975), 425 North Michigan Avenue, Chicago, Illinois, 60611. *T.* 312-644-1723. *Cables:* Racksole Chicago. *Directors:* Anita Miller, Jordan Miller. Fiction, mystery, biography, travel, books of interest to women; quality reprints.

And/Or Press Inc. (1974), P.O. Box 522, Berkeley, California 94701. *T.* 415-548-2124. Health and nutrition, travel, life styles, computers.

Andrews, McMeel and Parker Inc. (1933), 4400 Johnson Drive, Fairway, Kansas, 66205. *T.* 913-362 1523. *Vice-President* and *Editorial Director:* Donna Martin. General trade publishing, with emphasis on how-to-do-it and cartoon books.

*Arbor House Publishing Co. (1969), 235 East 45th Street, New York, N.Y., 10017. *T.* 212-599 3131. *Publisher:* Eden Collinsworth. General fiction and non-fiction.

*Ashley Books Inc. (1971), P.O. Box 768, Port Washington, New York, N.Y. 11050. *T.* 516-883-2221. *Directors:* Simeon Paget (Managing), Billie Young (President). Consumer, fiction, cookery, medical and health.

*Atheneum Publishers (1960), 115 Fifth Avenue, New York, 10003. *T.* 212-614-1300. General, fiction, poetry, drama, juveniles.

*Atlantic Monthly Press, 8 Arlington Street, Boston, Massachusetts, 02116. *T.* 617-536 9500. *Editor-in-chief:* Harold Evans. *Editor-in-chief, Children's Books:* Melanie Kroupa. (Books distributed by Little Brown & Co.) MSS. of permanent interest, fiction, biography, autobiography, history, current affairs, social science, poetry, belles-lettres, natural history, children's books. The opportunity of serialising our books in whole or in part in *The Atlantic* is frequently of assistance in advancing the interests of the author.

*Avon Books (1941), The Hearst Corporation, 1790 Broadway, New York, N.Y., 10019. *T.* 212-399 4500. *T.A.* Avon Books. *President and Publisher:* Rena Wolner. All subjects, fiction and non-fiction.

Baker (Walter H.) Company (1845), 100 Chauncy Street, Boston, Mass., 02111. *President:* M. Abbott Van Nostrand. *Editor:* John B. Welch. Plays and books on the theatre. Also agents for plays. *London agents:* Samuel French, Ltd., 52 Fitzroy Street, London, W1P 6JR.

UNITED STATES

*Bantam Books Inc. (1945), 666 Fifth Avenue, New York, N.Y., 10103. *T.* 212-765-6500. *Cables:* Bantambook New York. *Chairman of the Executive Committee:* Olaf Paeschke, *Chairman and Co. Chief Executive Officer:* Louis Wolfe, *President and Co-Chief Executive Officer:* Alberto Vitale, *Treasurer:* John Choi. Fiction, classics, biography, health, business, general non-fiction, social sciences, religion, sports, science, audio tapes, computer books.

Barnes (A. S.) & Co., 9601 Aero Drive, San Diego, California 92123. *T.* 619-560-5163. General publishers.

Beacon Press, 25 Beacon Street, Boston, Mass., 02108. *T.* 617-742 2110. General non-fiction in fields of religion, ethics, philosophy, current affairs, history, literary criticism, psychology, sociology and women's studies.

Beech Tree Books, a division of **William Morrow & Co., Inc.,** 105 Madison Avenue, New York, N.Y. 10016. *T.* 212-889-3050. *Publisher:* James D. Landis. General literature fiction and non fiction.

*Better Homes and Gardens Books (Publishing Group, Meredith Corporation), 1716 Locust Street, Des Moines, Iowa, 50336. *T.* 515-284-2685. *Managing Editor:* Dove Kirchnor. Publishes non-fiction in all family and home service categories including decorating, gardening, do-it-yourself and how to do it books. Publisher suggests outline be submitted first.

Bluejay Books Inc., (1983), 1123 Broadway, Suite 306, New York, N.Y. 10010. *T.* (212) 206-1538. *Directors:* Joan D. Vinge (President), James Frenkel (Vice-President), Joann J. Hill (Treasurer), Frank Balazs (Secretary). Science fiction, fantasy and related non fiction.

*Bobbs-Merrill Company, Inc., The, acquired by **Macmillan Publishing Company,** *q.v.*

*Bowker (R. R.) Co., 205 East 42nd Street, New York, N.Y. 10017. *T.* 212-916-1600. Outside North America: **Bowker Publishing Co.,** Borough Green, Sevenoaks, Kent TN15 8PH, England. Bibliographies and reference tools for the book trade and literary and library worlds. Reference and 'how-to' books for graphic arts, music, art, corporate communications, computer industry, cable industry, and information industry.

Braziller, George, Inc. (1954), 1 Park Avenue, New York, N.Y., 10016. *T.* 212-889-0909. *Telex:* 422144. *President:* George Braziller. *Editors:* Beatrice Rehl, Deirdre Mullane. Philosophy, science, art, architecture, history, biography, fiction, environment, ecology, poetry.

*Cambridge University Press (American branch), 32 East 57th Street, New York, N.Y., 10022. *T.* 212-688-8885.

*CBS Educational & Professional Publishing (1866), 383 Madison Avenue, New York, N.Y., 10017. *T.* 872-2000. A subsidiary of **CBS** General publishers. Fiction, history, biography, etc.; college and school textbooks of all kinds; children's; technical; reference; religious; dictionaries. Imprints: **Holt Rinehart and Winston, Dryden Press, Saunders College.**

*Collier Macmillan International, 866 Third Avenue, New York, N.Y., 10022-6299. *T.* 212-702 2000. *Cable Address:* Pachamac, N.Y. *London:* Macmillan Distribution Ltd., Houndmills, Basingstoke, Hants. RG21 2XS *T.* (0256) 29242; *Australia:* Collier Macmillan Australia, Methuen L.B.C. Ltd., 31 Market Street, Sydney, N.S.W. 2000; *New Zealand:* Associated Book Publishers (N.Z.) Ltd., 61 Beach Road, Auckland; *Canada:* Collier Macmillan Canada Inc., 50 Gervais Drive, Don Mills, Ontario; *South Africa:* Macmillan South Africa (Publishers) (Pty) Ltd:, Braamfontein Centre, Jorissen Street, Braamfontein, Johannesburg 2001. Publishers of encyclopaedias, text and reference books, paperbacks, general trade and juvenile books.

*Columbia University Press, 562 West 113th Street, New York, N.Y., 10025. *T.* 212-316 7100. *England:* 15A Epsom Road, Guildford, Surrey, GU1 3JT. Scholarly work in all fields and serious non-fiction of more general interest.

Concordia Publishing House (1869), 3558 S. Jefferson Avenue, St. Louis, Mo., 63118. *T.* 314-664-7000. Religious books, prayer books, children's religious books.

Contemporary Books Inc. 180 North Michigan Avenue, Chicago, Illinois, 60601. *T.* 312-782-9181. *President:* Harvey Plotnick. Non-fiction.

*Continuum Publishing Corp., The (1980), 370 Lexington Avenue, New York, N.Y., 10017. *T.* 532-3650. *President* and *Publisher:* Werner Mark Linz. General non-fiction, education, literature, psychology, politics, sociology, literary criticism.

*Cornell University Press (including Comstock Publishing Associates) (1869), 124 Roberts Place, Ithaca, New York, 14851 *T.* 607-257-7000. Scholarly books. *Agents Overseas:* Trevor Brown Associates, Suite 7B, 26 Charing Cross Road, London WC2H 0LN.

*Coward-McCann Inc., 200 Madison Avenue, New York, N.Y., 10016. *T.* 212-576-8900. *Cables:* Comagan, N.Y. *Publisher:* Phyllis Grann. *Editor-in-Chief Coward Juvenile Books:* Refra Wilkin. General publishers. Fiction, juveniles, religion, biography, mystery, history.

*Crane, Russak & Company, Inc., 3 East 44 Street, New York, N.Y., 10017. *T.* 212-867-1490. *Cables:* Cranium, New York. A member of the Taylor & Francis Group. Information science and computers, strategy and foreign affairs, earth sciences, scientific journals.

*Crown Publishers, Inc., 225 Park Avenue South, New York, N.Y., 10003. *T.* 254-1600. *President:* Alan Mirken. *Editor-in-Chief:* Betty A. Prashke. General fiction, non-fiction, illustrated books and children's books.

Devin-Adair Publishers, Inc., (1911), 6 North Water Street, Greenwich, Connecticut, 06870. *T.* 203-531-7755. Conservative politics, health and ecology, Irish topics, homeopathy, and holistic health books.

*Dodd, Mead & Co., Inc., 79 Madison Avenue, New York, N.Y., 10016. *T.* 685-6464. Fiction, children's books, biography, belles-lettres, mysteries, social issues, how-to books, business, holistic health, company sponsored books.

*Doubleday & Company, Inc., 245 Park Avenue, New York, 10167. *T.* 212-984 7561. *T.A.* Doubday, New York. *London:* 100 Wigmore Street, W1H 9DR. *T.* 01-935 1269. Trade, general fiction and non-fiction, adventure and crime. Anchor Press—books for young readers. Religious.

*Dryden Press —see CBS Educational & Professional Publishing.

*Dutton (E.P.), Division of New American Library, 2 Park Avenue, New York, N.Y., 10016. *T.* 212-725-1818. General publishers. General non-fiction, including biographies, adventure, history, travel; fiction, mysteries, juveniles, quality paperbacks.

*Facts on File Inc. (1940), 460 Park Avenue South, New York N.Y. 10016. *T.* 212-683-2244. *Telex:* 238552. *Cables:* Factsfile New York. *U.K. Office:* Collins Street, Oxford OX4 1XJ. *President:* Howard Epstein, *Executive Vice President and Publisher:* Edward W. Knappman. *UK and European Manager:* Alan Goodworth. Information books and services for colleges, libraries, schools and general public.

Farrar, Straus & Giroux, Inc. (incorporating Hill and Wang), 19 Union Square

West, New York City, N.Y., 10003. *T.* 212-741-6900. *T.A.* Farrarcomp, New York. *Telex:* 667428. General publishers.

French (Samuel), Inc., 45 West 25th Street, New York, N.Y., 10010. *T.* 212-206-8990. Play publishers and author's representatives (dramatic).

Godine, David R., Publisher Inc. (1970), Horticultural Hall, 300 Massachusetts Avenue, Boston, Massachusetts, 02115. *T.* 617-536-0761. *President:* David R. Godine. Fiction, photography, history, natural history, art, biography, children's, poetry.

*****Greene (Stephen) Press** (1957), 15 Muzzey Street, Lexington, Mass. 02173 *T.* 617-861-0170. *Editorial Director:* Thomas Begner. Americana, conservation and nature, country living, cook books, sports: skiing, snowshoeing, kayaking, riding, orienteering, crafts, general adult non-fiction, etc.

Greenwillow Books, a division of **William Morrow & Co., Inc.,** 105 Madison Avenue, New York, N.Y., 10016. *T.* 212-889-3050. *Senior Vice-President/Editor-in-Chief:* Susan Hirschman. Children's books only.

*****Grosset & Dunlap, Inc.,** 51 Madison Avenue, New York, N.Y., 10010. *T.* 212-689-9200. Adult non-fiction, juveniles, popular reference books, children's picture books, series books, activity books, and religious books.

Harcourt Brace Jovanovich, Inc. (1919), 111 Fifth Avenue, New York, N.Y., 10003. *T.* 212-614-3000. *Chairman and President:* William Jovanovich. *U.K. office:* 24-28 Oval Road, London, NW1 7DX. *T.* 01-485 7074. General, textbook and educational tests publishers. Fiction, biography, travel, juveniles, poetry, current events, history.

*****Harper & Row, Publishers** (1817), 10 East 53rd Street, New York, N.Y., 10022. *T.* 212-207-7000. *Cable Address:* Harpsam, N.Y. *Telex:* 12-5741(dom.), 62-501(intl). *London:* 28 Tavistock Street, London, WC2E 7PN. Fiction, history, biography, poetry, science, travel, juvenile, educational, business, technical, medical and religious.

*****Harvard University Press,** 79 Garden Street, Cambridge, Mass., 02138. *T.* 617-495-2600. *London:* 126 Buckingham Palace Road, London, SW1. *T.* 01-730-9208.

Hastings House Publisher. A Division of **The Gallen Fund, Inc.,** 260 Fifth Avenue, New York, N.Y. 10001 *T.* (212) 889-9624. *President:* Richard Gallen, *Vice-President:* Peter Skutches, *Editorial Director-Juvenile Book Editor:* Judy Donnelly, *Editorial Director-Communication Arts Editor:* Joanne Dolinar, *Editorial Manager:* Raphaela Seroy. General, travel, graphic arts, sports, cookery and wines, children's books, communication arts (television, film, radio).

*****Heath (D. C.) and Co.,** a division of **Raytheon Co.,** 125 Spring Street, Lexington, Mass., 02173. *T.* 617-862-6650. Elementary, secondary, college textbooks.

*****Holiday House** (1935), 18 East 53rd Street, New York, N.Y., 10022. *T.* 212-688-0085. *Directors:* John Briggs (President), Margery Cuyler, Kate Briggs, David R. Rogers. General children's books.

*****Holt, Rinehart and Winston** —see **CBS Educational & Professional Publishing.**

*****Houghton Mifflin Company** (1832), 2 Park Street, Boston, Mass., 02108. *T.* 617-725-5000. Fiction, biography, history, works of general interest of all kinds, both adult and juvenile, also school and college textbooks in all departments, and standardised tests. Best length: 75,000-180,000 words; juveniles, any reasonable length.

Keats Publishing Inc. (1971), 27 Pine Street, P.O. Box 876, New Canaan,

Connecticut, 06840. *T.* (203) 966-8721. *Directors:* Nathan Keats (President), An Keats (Editor-in-Chief), Gilbert Raff. Natural health, medical, regional and religious books.

***Knopf (Alfred A.), Inc.** (1915), a division of **Random House, Inc.,** 201 East 50th Street, New York, N.Y., 10022. *T.* 212-751 2600. *T.A.* Knopf, New York. General literature, fiction, belles-lettres, sociology, politics, history, nature, science, etc.

Lake, David S., Publishers, 19 Davis Drive, Belmont, California 94002. *T.* 415-592-7810. Elementary/High school special education materials. Textbooks, reading materials, teacher-aids, high school education materials, management and training materials.

***Lippincott (J. B.) Co.** (1792), East Washington Square, Philadelphia, Pa., 19105. *T.* 215-238-4200. *Cables:* Lippcot, Phila. Medical and nursing books and journals. A division of **Harper & Row Publishers Inc.**

***Little, Brown and Company,** 34 Beacon Street, Boston, Mass., 02106. *T.* 617-227-0730. *Cables:* Brownlit, Boston. General literature, especially fiction, non-fiction, biography, history, trade paperbacks, books for boys and girls, college, law, medical books. Art and photography books under the **New York Graphic Society Books** imprint.

Lothrop, Lee & Shepard Books (1859), a division of **William Morrow & Co., Inc.,** 105 Madison Avenue, New York, N.Y., 10016. *T.* 212-889-3050. *Vice-President/Editor-in-Chief:* Dorothy Briley. Children's books only.

Lyle Stuart, Inc. (1956), 120 Enterprise Avenue, Secaucus, New Jersey 07094 *T.* 212-736-1141. Trade books, hard back and paperbacks covering a wide range of subjects of adult interest.

***McGraw-Hill Book Co.,** 1221 Avenue of the Americas, New York, N.Y., 10020. *T.* 212-512-2000. Professional and reference: engineering, scientific, business, architecture, encyclopaedias. College textbooks. High school and vocational textbooks: business, secretarial, career. Trade books. Microcomputer software; training courses for industry. See also McGraw-Hill Book Company (UK) Ltd., McGraw-Hill House, Maidenhead, England, and McGraw-Hill Ryerson Ltd. of Canada.

McKay David, Co., Inc., 2 Park Avenue, New York, N.Y., 10016. *T.* 340-9800. *T.A.* Davmacay. *President:* James Louttit. Non-fiction. Distributed by Fodor's Travel Guides.

***Macmillan Publishing Company** (A division of **Macmillan Inc**), (1896), 866 Third Avenue, New York, N.Y., 10022. *T.* 212-702-2000. *T.A.* Pachamac, N.Y. *Chairman of the Board and President:* Jeremiah Kaplan. *President, General Books Division:* Bruno Quinson. *Senior Vice-President/Publisher:* Hillel Black. General books.

***Messner, Julian** (a division of **Simon & Schuster**), 1230 Avenue of the Americas, New York, N.Y., 10020. *T.* 212-245-6400. General non-fiction for ages through high school.

Methuen Inc. (1977), 29 West 35th Street, New York, N.Y. 10001. *T.* (212) 244-3336. *T.A.* Algernon New York. *Telex:* 6801368 Methuen UW. *Directors:* John von Knorring, Ed Sands. *Scientific publisher:* Ashak Rawji. *Editorial Director for the Humanities:* William Germano. Literary criticism, drama, history, psychology, women's studies, academic, scientific, technical.

Morehouse-Barlow Co., Inc., 78 Danbury Road, Wilton, Conn. 06897. *T.* 203-762-0721. *Chairman of the Board:* Stanley Kleiman. *President:* Ronald C. Barlow. *Editorial Director:* Stephen S. Wilburn. Religious books, secondary level texts, seminary texts.

Morrow Jr. Books, a division of **William Morrow & Co., Inc.,** 105 Madison Avenue, New York, N.Y., 10016. *T.* 212-889-3050. *Vice-President/Editor-in-Chief:* David Reuther. Children's books only.

*****Morrow (William) & Co., Inc.,** 105 Madison Avenue, New York, N.Y., 10016. *T.* 212-889-3050. Allen Marchioni (Chairman and C.E.O.), Sherry Arden (President and Publisher, Adult Trade), James D. Landis (Senior V.P., Publisher, Beech Tree Books), Susan Hirschman (Senior V.P. Editor-in-Chief Greenwillow Books), Dorothy Briley (V.P. Editor-in-Chief Lothrop, Lee & Shepard), David Reuther (V.P., Editor-in-Chief Morrow Jr. Books). General literature, fiction and juveniles. Interested in works dealing with American and non-fiction foreign life and history. Royalty.

Nelson (Thomas), Inc. (1978), Nelson Place at Elm Hill Pike, P.O. Box 141000, Nashville, Tennessee 37214-1000 *T.* 615-889-9000. Publishers of bibles, religious, non-fiction and fiction general trade.

Norton, W. W., & Company, Inc., 500 Fifth Avenue, New York, 10110. *T.* 212-354-5500. General fiction and non-fiction, music, boating, psychiatry, family therapy, social work, reprints, college texts, science.

Ottenheimer Publishers Inc. (1890), 300 Reisterstown Road, Baltimore, Maryland, 21208. *T.* 301-484-2100. *Telex:* 198110. *Directors:* Allan T. Hirsh, Jr., Allan T. Hirsh, III. Juvenile and adult non-fiction, reference.

*****Overlook Press, The,** 12 West 21st Street, New York, NY 10010. *T.* 212-675 0585. *Telex:* 233776. *T.A.* Vikpress. Fiction, non-fiction, poetry, how-to manuals.

*****Oxford University Press, Inc.,** 200 Madison Avenue, New York, N.Y., 10016. *T.* 212-679-7300. *Cables:* Frowde, New York. Scholarly, professional, reference, all non-fiction, bibles, college textbooks, religion, medicals, music.

*****Pantheon Books,** a division of **Random House, Inc.,** 201 East 50th Street, New York, N.Y., 10022. *T.* 572 2404. Fiction, mysteries, belles-lettres, translations, philosophy, history and art, sociology, psychology, juvenile.

Pergamon-Brassey's International Defence Publishers (1984), (member of the **Pergamon Group**), 1340 Old Chain Bridge Road, McLean, Virginia 22101. *T.* 703-442 0900. *Telex:* 90-1811. *Senior Executive:* Franklin D. Margiotta, PH.D. All aspects of contemporary defence policy and national security.

Pinnacle Books Inc., 1430 Broadway, New York, N.Y., 10018. *T.* 212-719 5900. *President and Publisher:* Sondra T. Ordover. Fiction, men's adventure, historical and contemporary romance, mystery, suspense, family sagas, non-fiction, women's health.

*****Praeger Publishers** (a division of **CBS Educational & Professional Publishing**), 521 Fifth Avenue, New York, N.Y., 10175. *T.* (212) 599 8400. *T.A.* Prabooks, New York. Non-fiction on international relations, social sciences, economics, reference, contemporary issues, urban affairs, psychology, education, biology, medicine.

*****Prentice-Hall, Inc.** (1913), Englewood Cliffs, New Jersey, 07632. *Overseas representative:* Prentice-Hall International, Inc., 66 Wood Lane End, Hemel Hempstead, Hertfordshire, HP2 4RG *T.* (0442) 58531. *Cables:* Prenhall, Hemel, England. *Telex:* 82445. Text, technical and general non-fiction, business selling and management books, juveniles; biographies and autobiographies. Free-lance artists' and designers' work used.

*****Putnam's (G. P.) Sons,** 200 Madison Avenue, New York, N.Y., 10016. *T.* 212-576-8900. *President* and *Publisher:* Phyllis Grann. *Executive V.P:* Robert Copp. *Marketing Director:* Neil Sigman. Publications of books in all divisions of literature. History, economics, political science, natural science, and standard literature. Also an important group of fiction. Children's books.

Quill Paperbacks, a division of **William Morrow & Co., Inc.,** 105 Madison Avenue, New York, N.Y., 10016. *T.* 212-889-3050. *Managing Editor:* Allison Cerier. General literature fiction and non-fiction.

*****Rand McNally & Company,** P.O. Box 7600, Chicago, Illinois, 60680. *T.* 312-673-9100. Trade, publications including juvenile and adult non-fiction, maps, guides, atlases, globes; banking publications. *Chairman:* Andrew McNally III. *President:* Andrew McNally IV.

*****Random House, Inc.,** 201 East 50th Street, New York, N.Y., 10022. *T.* 212-751-2600. General publishers.

*****Rawson Associates,** A Division of the **Scribner Book Companies,** 115 Fifth Avenue, New York, N.Y., 10003. *T.* 212-614-1403. *President:* Kennett L. Rawson. *Executive Vice-President:* Eleanor S. Rawson. Adult non-fiction and fiction.

Revell (Fleming H.) Co., Old Tappan, New Jersey, 07675. *T.* 201-768-8060. Religious books.

Ronin Publishing Inc., Box 1035, Berkeley, California 94701. *T.* 415-540 6278. Management, humour. Preliminary letter essential; no unsolicited manuscripts or art work.

*****St Martin's Press, Inc.,** 175 Fifth Avenue, New York, N.Y., 10010. *T.* 212-674-5151. *T.A.* Saintmart, New York. Trade, reference, college.

Saunders College—see CBS Educational & Professional Publishing.

*****Schocken Books Inc.,** (1945), 62 Cooper Square, New York, N.Y., 10003. *T.* 212-475-4900. *T.A.* Schockenus, New York. Education, Judaica and holocaust studies, women studies, social sciences, literature, literary criticism.

*****Scribner's (Charles) Sons (1846),** 115 Fifth Avenue, New York, N.Y., 10003. *T.* 212-614 1300. General publishers of standard books in education, biography, history, science, fiction, belles-lettres, juveniles.

*****Simon & Schuster,** 1230 Avenue of the Americas, New York, N.Y., 10020. *T.* 212-245-6400. *President:* Richard Snyder. *Publisher:* Dan Green. *Editor-in-Chief:* Michael V. Korda. General non-fiction, fiction, biography, detective, humour, occasional novelty books. Manuscripts not addressed to an editor by name will be returned unread.

*****Stanford University Press,** Stanford, California, 94305. *T.* 415-723-9434. Scholarly non-fiction.

Strawberry Hill Press (1973), 2594 15th Avenue, San Francisco, California, 94127. *T.* 415-664-8112. *President:* Jean-Louis Brindamour, PH.D, *Executive Vice-President and Art Director:* Ku Fu-Sheng, *Treasurer:* Edward E. Serres. Health, self-help, cookbooks, philosophy, religion, history, drama, science and technology, biography, mystery, Third World. No unsolicited MSS, preliminary letter and return postage essential.

*****Taplinger Publishing Co., Inc.** (1955), 132 West 22nd Street, New York, N.Y., 10011. *T.* 212-741-0801. *T.A.* Taplinpub. Calligraphy, literature (including translated works into English), music, art and art criticism, non-fiction, popular fiction.

Theatre Art Books, 153 Waverly Place, New York, N.Y., 10014. *T.* 212-675-1815. *Director:* George Zournas. *Consultant:* Rosamond Gilder. Successor to the book publishing department of Theatre Arts (1921-1948). Theatre, dance and allied books—costume, materials, tailoring, etc., a few plays.

Tuttle (Charles E.), Co., Inc. (1949), 28 South Main Street, Rutland, Vermont, 05701-0410. *T.* 802-773-8930 and Suido I-chome, 2-6 Bunkyo-ku, Tokyo 112, Japan. *T.* 811-7106-9. *T.A.* Tuttbooks, Tokyo. *President:* Charles E. Tuttle. Oriental art, culture, history, manners and customs, Americana.

***University of California Press**, 2120 Berkeley Way, Berkeley, California, 94720. Publishes scholarly books, books of general interest, series of scholarly monographs, and scholarly journals. *London:* University of California Press Ltd., 126 Buckingham Palace Road, London SW1W 9SD. *T.* 01-730 9208.

***University of Chicago Press**, 5801 South Ellis Avenue, Chicago, Ill., 60637. *T.* 312-962-7700. *London:* 126 Buckingham Palace Road, SW1W 9SD. *T.* 01-730-9208. The Press publishes scholarly books and monographs, religious, medical and scientific books, general trade books, Chicago visual library micropublications, and 45 scholarly journals.

University of Illinois Press (1918), 54 East Gregory Drive, Champaign, Illinois, 61820. *T.* 217-333-0950. *Director:* Richard L. Wentworth. American studies (history, music, literature), poetry, working-class and ethnic studies, anthropology, communications, special education and childhood development, urban and regional planning.

***Van Nostrand Reinhold Co. Inc.** (1848), 115 Fifth Avenue, New York, N.Y. 10003 *T.* 212-254-3232. *President:* James Connolly. Reference, encyclopedias, handbooks: architecture, business, design, energy, medicine, science and technology.

***Vanguard Press, Inc.**, 424 Madison Avenue, New York, N.Y., 10017. *T.* 753-3906. *Cables:* Vangpress, N.Y. *Director:* Miss Evelyn Shrifte, *Editor-in-Chief:* Bernice Woll. General trade publishers, fiction, non-fiction and juveniles.

***Viking Penguin Inc.** (1925), 40 West 23 Street, New York, N.Y., 10010. *T.* 807 7300. *President:* Alan Kellock. *Editor-in-Chief, Adult Books:* Kathryn Court. *Consulting Editor:* Malcolm Cowley. *Editors:* Amanda Vaill, William Strachan, Charles Verrill, Daniel Frank, Nan Graham, Gerald Howard, Patricia Mulcahy. *Editorial Director, Viking Kestrel:* Regina Hayes. *Publisher, Elisabeth Sifton Books:* Elisabeth Sifton. General books, fiction, non-fiction, juveniles, biography, sociology, poetry, art, travel. Viking Kestrel junior books.

Walker & Co. (1960), 720 Fifth Avenue, New York, N.Y., 10019. *T.* 265-3632. Samuel S. Walker Jr. (President). General publishers, biography, history, religion, philosophy, natural history, and adventure, world affairs, criticism, detective fiction, romances, westerns, juveniles, early childhood education, parenting.

Warne (Frederick) & Co., Inc., 40 West 23rd Street, New York, N.Y. 10010 *London:* 27 Wrights Lane, London W8 5TZ. Juvenile and young adult books. Subsidiary of **Viking Penguin Inc.**

***Warner Books Inc.** (1973), 666 Fifth Avenue, New York, N.Y. 10103. *T.* 212-484-2900. *T.A.* Warcom. *President:* Laurence J. Kirshbaum. Fiction and non-fiction, hardcovers, trade paperbacks, mass market paperbacks.

***Watts (Franklin), Inc.**, a subsidiary of **Grolier Inc.**, 387 Park Avenue South, New York, N.Y., 10016. *T.* 212-686 7070. K-12 and College text. Adult trade.

***Westminster Press**, 925 Chestnut Street, Philadelphia, Pennsylvania. 19107. *T.* 215-928-2700. Fiction, non-fiction, juveniles, and religious.

Winchester Press Inc., 220 Old New Brunswick Road, Piscataway, N.J. 08854 *T.* 201-981-0820. *Vice-President:* Frank Gil. Outdoor, sport, nature, conservation, natural history, games, collecting.

Writer's Digest Books, 9933 Alliance Road, Cincinnati, Ohio 45242 *T.* 513-984-0717. *Telex:* 5106000623 FW Pub Cin. Market Directories, books for writers, photographers, songwriters, plus selected how-to trade titles. **North Light** imprint: Art instruction and graphic arts books.

***Yale University Press,** 302 Temple Street, New Haven, Connecticut, 06520. *T.* 203-436-7584. *Postal Address:* 92A Yale Station, New Haven, Connecticut, 06520. *Director:* John G. Ryden. Scholarly books.

BOOK PACKAGERS
*Members of the Book Packagers Association.

Most of the firms listed below are 'packagers' who devise books and sell them to publishers. They frequently offer opportunities for freelance authors, illustrators and designers.

Adkinson Parrish Ltd. Associate company of **Macdonald & Co. Publishers Ltd.**, *q.v.*

Adkinson, Robert, Ltd (1982), 7-8 Greenland Place, London NW1 0AP *T.* 01-485 4445. *Telex:* 295029 Robadk G. *Directors:* Robert Adkinson, Clare Howell. Production of international co-editions of illustrated books on wine and food, leisure, travel, photography and the decorative arts.

Aladdin Books Ltd. (1980), 70 Old Compton Street, London, W1V 5PA *T.* 01-734 5186. *Telex:* 21115 Aladin. *Directors:* Charles Nicholas, Charles Matheson, Lynn Lockett. Full design and book packaging facility.

Albion Press Ltd. (1984), 9 Stewart Street, Oxford, OX1 4RH. *T.* (0865) 723401. *Telex:* 83138 Telkay G. *Directors:* Emma Bradford, Neil Philip. Quality integrated illustrated titles specialising in literature, social history, fine and graphic arts, children's books. Supply finished books. Publishers' commissions undertaken. Freelance artists' and designers' work used.

*****Alphabet and Image Ltd** (1972), Alpha House, South Street, Sherborne, Dorset, DT9 3LU *T.* (0935) 814944. *Telex:* 46534 Alphab G. *Directors:* Anthony Birks-Hay, Leslie Birks-Hay. Complete editorial, picture research photographic, design and production service for illustrated books on ceramics, beekeeping, folk art, horticulture, architecture, crafts, history.

Antler Books Ltd. (1980), 11 Rathbone Place, London W1P 1DE. *T.* 01-580 9276 and 8928. *Directors:* John Stidolph, Dr. Susan Abbott. Packaging—production and printing of books and magazines. Picture research, editorial, design services. Supplies film to publishers. Part of **Berkswell Publishing Co. Ltd.**

Beanstalk Books Ltd. (1983), 89 Park Hill, London SW4 9NX. *T.* 01-720 9109 and 673 8508. *Telex:* 8950459 Aspac G. *Directors:* Shona McKellar, Penny Kitchenham. Specialists in highly illustrated books for adults and children and novelties; editorial, design and production service.

*****Belitha Press Ltd.** (1980), 31 Newington Green, London N16 9PU *T.* 01-241 5566. *Telex:* 946240 Cweasy G Ref 19001760. *Directors:* Martin Pick, Treld Bicknell, Richard Hayes, Rachel Pick (non-executive), Ronald Ridout (non-executive). Conception, editing, design and production, offering authors and illustrators close involvement at each stage. Specialises in high quality international co-editions for children and general books for adults on Asia, preferably with potential for television tie-ins. Associated film production Company, Inner Eye Ltd. Sponsorship enquiries welcome.

Bison Books Ltd. (1974), 176 Old Brompton Road, London SW5 0BA *T.* 01-370 3097. *Telex:* 888014 Bison G. *Director:* S. L. Mayer. Non-fiction illustrated titles principally history, military history, weaponry, natural history, transport.

Booth, David, (Publishing) Ltd. (1980), 8 Cranedown, Lewes, East Sussex BN7 3NA *T.* (0273) 472309. *Telex:* 878236 DPB G. *Directors:* D. Booth, S. A. Birch.

International co-edition children's books packagers, specialising in pop-up and novelty books, both fiction and non-fiction.

*Breslich & Foss** (1978), Golden House, 28-31 Great Pulteney Street, London W1R 3DD *T.* 01-734 0706. *Telex:* 27950 ref. 2257. *Directors:* Paula G. Breslich, K. B. Dunning. Books produced from MS to bound copy stage from in-house ideas. Specialising in the arts, sport, health, crafts, gardening.

*Calmann, John, and King Ltd.** (1976), 71 Great Russell Street, London WC1B 3BN *T.* 01-831 6351. *Directors:* Marianne J. Calmann, Elisabeth Ingles, Laurence King. Illustrated books on art, history, nature, architecture for international co-editions.

Cameron Books (1976), 2A Roman Way, London, N7 8XG *T.* 01-609 4019. *T.A.* Cameron London N7. *Directors:* Ian A. Cameron, Jill Hollis. Illustrated non-fiction including fine arts, the decorative arts and crafts, antiques, collecting, natural history, social history, films, food, and children's non-fiction. **Edition** (1975). Design, editing, typesetting, production work for other publishers.

Dorling Kindersley Ltd. (1974), 9 Henrietta Street, Covent Garden, London, WC2E 8PS *T.* 01-836 5411. *Telex:* 8954527. *Editorial Director:* C. J. Davis. Illustrated reference books. Specialists in international co-editions.

*Eddison/Sadd Editions Ltd.** (1982), 2 Kendall Place, London W1H 3AH *T.* 01-486 3621. *Telex:* 265871 Monref G ref. WXX019. *Directors:* Nicholas J. Eddison, Graham D. Sadd, Ian N. Jackson. Illustrated non-fiction books for the international co-edition market.

Elvendon Press (1978), The Old Surgery, High Street, Goring-on-Thames, Reading, Berks. RG8 9AW *T.* (0491) 873003. *Directors:* R. N. Hurst, B. R. Hurst. Complete packaging service. Specialise in cookery, nutrition.

*Equinox (Oxford) Ltd.** (1981), Littlegate House, St. Ebbes Street, Oxford OX1 1SQ *T.* Oxford 251499. *Directors:* G. J. Riches (Chairman), B. T. Lenthall (Managing), M. G. Desebrock, M. Ritchie, D. M. Phillips, A. Peebles. Illustrated reference titles for the international market.

Grisewood & Dempsey Ltd. (1973), Elsley Court, 20-22 Great Titchfield Street, London W1P 7AD *T.* 01-631 0878. *Telex:* 27725 Gridem G. *T.A.* Greatbooks, London. *Directors:* D. Grisewood, J. Grisewood, D. Maxwell MacDonald, J. M. Olliver, J. C. Richards. Packaging. General non-fiction; children's information books.

Hamilton House Publishing (1975), 17 Staveley Way, Brixworth Industrial Park, Northampton, NN6 9EL *T.* (0604) 881889. *Directors:* Tony Attwood, Philippa Attwood. Mostly tv and radio tie-ins, but all concepts considered.

*Holland & Clark Ltd** (1981), 53 Calton Avenue, Dulwich Village, London SE21 7DF *T.* 01-693 3204. *Telex:* 897012 Trabus G. *Directors:* Philip Clark, Julian Holland. Illustrated non-fiction for the international market, including natural history, windsurfing and other sports, children's reference books and sponsored titles.

*Lennard Books Ltd.** (1979), Mackerye End, Harpenden, Herts. AL5 5DR. *T.* (05827) 69636. *Directors:* A. K. L. Stephenson, K. A. A. Stephenson, R. H. Stephenson, D. Pocknell. Book production company originating and developing illustrated books: sport, leisure activities, entertainment. Design, editorial and general production services.

Lexus Ltd. (1980), 181 Pitt Street, Glasgow, G2 4DR *T.* 041-221 5266. *Director:* P. M. Terrell. Reference book publishing (especially bilingual dictionaries) as contractor, packager, consultant. Translation, word processing.

Lincoln, Frances, Ltd. (1981) Apollo Works, 5 Charlton Kings Road, London NW5 2SB. *T.* 01-482-3302. *Telex:* 21376. *Directors:* Frances Lincoln (Managing), J. S. Nicoll. Illustrated books suitable for international coeditions, art, archaeology, architecture, design, gardening, natural history, childcare, cookery, health, DIY, decorating, photography, computers, children's books.

***Market House Books Ltd.** (1981), 2 Market House, Market Square, Aylesbury, Bucks HP20 1TN. *T.* (0296) 84911. *Directors:* Dr. Alan Isaacs, Dr. John Daintith, P. C. Sapsed. Compilation of dictionaries and reference books.

***Marshall Editions Ltd.** (1977), 170 Piccadilly, London, W1V 9DD *T.* 01-629 0079 *T.A.* Marsheds, London W1. *Telex:* 22847 Marsh G. *Directors:* Bruce Marshall, John Bigg, Barbara Anderson, Candy Lee. Editorial, art and production services.

New Leaf Books Ltd. (1973), BCM, New Leaf, London WC1N 3XX *T.* 01-435 3056. *Telex:* 261507 ref. 3228. *Directors:* Michael Wright, Susan Wright. Complete creation of illustrated book projects (mainly how-to) from concept to finished product with or without production services.

***Oregon Press Ltd, The,** (1981), Faraday House, 8 Charing Cross Road, London WC2H 0HG. *T.* 01-240 2504 and 3239. *Directors:* Michael Rainbird, Mary Anne Sanders. High quality illustrated non-fiction.

***Phillips, Phoebe, Editions** (1977), 6 Berners Mews, London W1P 3DG *T.* 01-637 7933 and 1673. *Directors:* Phoebe Phillips, (US), Tessa Clark. Packagers of international co-editions in all general subjects.

Price, Mathew, Ltd (1983), 242A Canbury Park Road, Kingston-upon-Thames, Surrey KT2 6LG *T.* 01-541 0784. *Telex:* 24667 Impemp G. *Chairman:* Mathew Price. Illustrated fiction and non-fiction children's books for all ages for the international market.

***Quarto Publishing Ltd.** (1976), **QED Publishing Ltd.** (1977), **Quill Publishing Ltd.** (1979), **Quintet Publishing Ltd.** (1984), **QDOS Ltd.** (1985), The Old Brewery, 6 Blundell Street, London N7 9BH *T.* 01-609 2222. *Telex:* 298844 Quarto G. *T.A.* Quartopub. *Directors:* L. F. Orbach, R. J. Morley, A. N. Campbell. International co-editions.

Roxby & Lindsey Holdings Ltd. (1974), 98 Clapham Common Northside, London, SW4 9SG *T.* 01-720 8872. *Telex:* 261234 ref. H5654D. *Directors:* Hugh Elwes, L. G. Allgood, Charles Fitzherbert, Henry Scrope, Lady Francis Seymour (Editorial), P. J. Garrigan (Secretary), Anne Hunt (Foreign Rights). International book packagers through subsidiary companies.

***Sadie Fields Productions Ltd.** (1983), 16 Pembridge Crescent, London W11 3DX. *T.* 01-221 3355. *Telex:* 262284 ref. 1255. *Fax:* 01-229 9651. *Directors:* Sheri Safran, David Fielder. Creates and produces international co-productions of pop-up, novelty and picture and board books for children.

Sceptre Books (1982), Time and Life Building, New Bond Street, London W1Y 0AA *T.* 01-499 4080. *Telex:* 22557. *Managing Director:* David Owen. Conceive, design, edit and produce finished books; work with publishers on joint ventures.

***Shuckburgh Reynolds Ltd.** (1978), 289 Westbourne Grove, London W11 2QA *T.* 01-727 9636. *Directors:* Montagu Curzon-Herrick, David Reynolds, Julian Shuckburgh. Design, editorial services, market research, picture research, manufacturing consultancy, literary agency, production of finished books.

***Thames Head Ltd.,** (1981), Avening, Tetbury, Gloucestershire, GL8 8NB. *T.* (045 383) 2136. *Telex:* 946240 Cweasy G ref 19018495. *Editorial:* Blakes, Much Hadham, Herts. SG10 6BT. *T.* (027 984) 2167. *Directors:* David Playne, Martin

Marix Evans. Illustrated international co-editions, general non-fiction, militaria, history, guides and practical crafts.

Ventura Publishing Ltd. 11-13 Young Street, London W8 5EH *T.* 01-221 6395. *Telex:* 8953658 Venpub G. *Directors:* R. D. Ellis (Managing), D. Hall. Specialise in production and design of high quality children's novelty books including the *Where's Spot?* lift-the-flap books by Eric Hill. Illustrated adult leisure and general interest non-fiction for the international co-edition market.

BOOK CLUBS

A book club supplies its subscribing members, usually monthly, with its chosen book at less than the price of the publisher's original edition, and offers to them at the same time an alternative title to the first choice. Members undertake to purchase a minimum number of books in a club's programme of publication over the period covered by their subscription. The bargain appeal of the clubs is made possible by the guaranteed circulation of their choices, which in the case of a successful club can be very large indeed.

Some Book Clubs publish simultaneously with the trade edition, whereas others produce their choices after a delay of some months. The price paid by subscribers for their choices will reflect the time delay, if any, between trade and Book Club publication.

The author's remuneration is normally in one payment on a royalty basis in respect of the number of copies sold of the club edition, and in some cases the author can obtain before publication a guarantee of a minimum figure.

Academy Book Club, Namara Group, 51 Beak Street, London W1R 3LF *T.* 01-437 2131.

Artists' Book Club (Monthly), Musterlin Ltd., P.O. Box 178, Oxford, OX1 1SX *T.* (0865) 243557. *Managing Director:* Jean-Claude Peissel.

Artists' Choice, (Quarterly) Artists' Choice Ltd., P.O. Box 3, Huntingdon, Cambridgeshire PE18 0QX *T.* Bythorn (080-14) 201.

Book Club Associates, Smith/Doubleday House, 87 Newman Street, London, W1P 4EN *T.* 01-637 0341.

> *Monthly Book Clubs*
>   Ancient & Medieval History Book Club
>   Book of the Month Club
>   History Guild
>   The Literary Guild
>   Master Storytellers
>   Military Book Society
>   Mystery & Thriller Guild
>   World Books
> *Quarterly Book Clubs*
>   About Britain
>   Arts Guild
>   Aviation Book Club
>   Cricket Book Club
>   Encounters
>   Executive Book Club
>   Home Computer Club (6 p.a.)
>   Military Guild
>   On the Road
>   Railway Book Club
>   Readers Choice
>   World of Nature
> *Series*
>   Good Housekeeping Step-by-Step Cookery Series
>   Great English Classics
>   Kings and Queens
>   20th Century Classics

Bookmarx Club, (Quarterly), IS Books Ltd., 265 Seven Sisters Road, London, N4 2DE *T.* 01-802 6145.

Books for Children, (Monthly), Park House, Dollar Street, Cirencester, Gloucestershire, GL7 2AN *T.* (0285) 67081.

Bookworm Club, The, Children's Club in Schools (6 p.a.), Heffers Booksellers, 20 Trinity Street, Cambridge CB2 3NG.

The Folio Society, 202 Great Suffolk Street, London, SE1 1PR *T.* 01-407 7411. *Showroom:* The Folio Gallery, 5 Royal Arcade, 28 Old Bond Street, London W1X 3HD.

Gay Bookclub, The, (Quarterly), GMP Publishers Ltd., P.O. Box 247, London N15 6RW *T.* 01-800 5861.

The Leisure Circle, (Quarterly), York House, Empire Way, Wembley, Middlesex, HA9 0PF *T.* 01-902 8888.

Letterbox Library, (Quarterly), Childrens Books Co-operative, 5 Bradbury Street, London N16 8JN *T.* 01-254 1640.

New Left Review, (Bi-Monthly), 15 Greek Street, London, W1V 5LF. *T.* 01-734 8839.

Odhams Leisure Group Ltd., (Subsidiary of K.L.P. Group Plc), Sanders Lodge Estate, Rushden, Northants. NN10 9RZ *T.* (0933) 58621. Women's interest series: cookery, needlecraft, children's products.

Poetry Book Society, (Quarterly), 21 Earls Court Square, London SW5 9DE *T.* 01-244 9742.

Pooh Corner Book Club, For all things Pooh, High Street, Hartfield, East Sussex, TN7 4AE *T.* (089 277) 453.

Puffin Bookclub, (Quarterly), Penguin Books, Bath Road, Harmondsworth, Middlesex, UB7 0DA *T.* 01-759 1984. Two clubs: Junior for 4 – 8 year olds; Older for 8 – 13 year olds.

Readers Union Ltd., P.O. Box 6, Brunel House, Newton Abbot, Devon, TQ12 2DW *T.* (0626) 69881.

- Anglers Book Society
- Arena Book Society
- Belief: The Religious Book Society
- Birds and Natural History Book Society
- Country Book Society
- Craft Book Society
- Craftsman Book Society
- Equestrian Book Society
- Field Sports Book Society
- Gardeners Book Society
- Joy of Photography Book Society
- Maritime Book Society
- Music Book Society
- Nationwide Book Service
- Needlecraft Book Society
- Phoenix Book Society
- Photographic Book Society
- Ramblers and Climbers Book Society

Red House Children's Book Club, (8 p.a.), The Industrial Estate, Station Lane, Witney, Oxfordshire, OX8 6YQ *T.* (0993) 71144.

Scholastic Publications Ltd, Marlborough House, Holly Walk, Leamington Spa, Warwickshire CV32 4LS *T.* (092 681) 3910. *Telex:* 312138 Spls G.

Scottish Book Club Ltd, (Quarterly), The Thistle Mill, Station Road, Biggar, Scotland ML12 6BW *T.* (0899) 21001.

Women's Press Book Club, The, (Quarterly), The Women's Press Ltd., 34 Great Sutton Street, London, EC1V 0DX *T.* 01-253 0009.

INTERNATIONAL STANDARD BOOK NUMBERING (ISBN)

The Standard Book Numbering (SBN) system was introduced in this country in 1967. It became the International Standard Book Numbering (ISBN) system three years later.

The overall administration of the international system is done from Berlin, by the International ISBN-Agentur, Staatsbibliothek Preussicher Kulturbesitz, D-1000 Berlin 30, Potsdamerstr. 33, West Germany.

In this country the system is administered by the Standard Book Numbering Agency Ltd., 12 Dyott Street, London, WC1A 1DF. The Agency was set up before the scheme became international which is why that word does not appear in its title.

Over the years a number of misconceptions have grown up about ISBNs, and this article endeavours to put right some of these.

The Standard Book Numbering Agency gets a large number of telephone calls, many of which follow a common pattern. For instance:

Are they legal? Do we have to have them?

There is no legal requirement for a book to carry an ISBN. But it is useful to educational authorities, certain library suppliers, public libraries and some computer using distributors, and is now essential to booksellers using the teleordering system. The introduction of Public Lending Right has also made ISBNs of importance to authors.

I am about to publish a book. Must I deposit a copy with the ISBN Agency to obtain copyright?

No. Copyright is obtained by the simple act of publication. However, by law, a copy of every new book must be deposited at the Copyright Receipt Office of the British Library, 2 Sheraton Street, London, W1V 4BH. The copyright office issues a receipt, and this has, in the past, proved useful when a dispute has arisen over the date of publication.

Titles deposited are catalogued by the British National Bibliography, which records ISBNs where available. Perhaps a confusion about copyright and ISBNs arises from this, but the ISBN, of itself, has nothing to do with copyright.

What are the fees for ISBNs?

No charge is made for the allocation of an ISBN. Various publishers who allocate their own, usually ask the agency to supply a computer print out of all the ISBNs available to the publisher, with check digits calculated. A small charge is made for this print out.

If the publisher does not allocate his own ISBNs, not only is there no charge, he may not even know about them. For a few years after the system was introduced, books catalogued by the BNB or Whitakers may have been assigned ISBNs by the Agency for listing purposes, without reference to the publisher. However with the widespread use of numbers it is now customary to consult all publishers before any are assigned.

Are you a Government Department?

No. Our parent company pays taxes; we get no subsidy from anyone. In most other countries the costs *are* borne by the state, through the national library system which frequently administers the scheme overseas.

Do I need an ISBN for a Church Magazine?

No. But you may need an ISSN (International Standard Serial Number). These are obtainable from the U.K. National Serials Data Centre, the British Library, 2 Sheraton Street, London, W1V 4BH.

Incidentally, a yearbook can have both an ISBN and an ISSN.

We would prefer to have our own identifier as we do not consider ourselves within the English speaking group.

This comes from publishers with devolution in mind. Usually Welsh, less often Irish. The group system within the ISBN scheme is not quite so categoric as to be dictated by language considerations only. A group is defined as a "language, geographic or other convenient area". There is no strict logic applied, just pragmatism as to what is most *convenient* for trading purposes.

I would prefer not to be involved with ISBNs, but there is this Public Lending Right, and the author says . . .

Well, yes. ISBNs have now taken on a new significance; they help authors towards a little more money. The recording system for P.L.R. dues is machine based, and uses ISBNs where available. It is more convenient for the libraries who provide the sample loan statistics if ISBNs are printed in books, but this is not a legal requirement and the system *can* work without ISBNs. However, it works better, and with lower overheads (and so more money available to be allocated to authors) if ISBNs *are* in books.

I want my book to reach as wide a market as possible, so I must have an ISBN.

The ISBN will not automatically sell a book. If the book, like that famous mousetrap, is a better one, the world will beat a path to its door. However, the ISBN will oil the wheels of distribution and it is therefore advisable to have one.

Will you supply an ISBN for a carton of assorted painting books?

No. In the words of the ISBN manual (available from the SBN agency at £3.00, cash with order), 'an ISBN identifies one title, or edition of a title, from one specific publisher, and is unique to that title or edition'. It is not designed for a carton of assorted painting books.

How does a publisher who knows nothing about the system and does not want regularly to allocate his own numbers, get an ISBN?

The agency is willing to supply ISBNs for future books, to all the small publishers who have neither the continuity of staff, nor the facilities for assigning their own. This offer extends not only to new books, but also to new editions and reprints. The only details requested at the time of allocation are title, edition and binding and, if he has not had ISBNs before, the name of the publisher, as quoted in the book, his address, and an approximate idea of how many titles a year he is likely to publish. A standard application form, for new publishers, is available from the Agency.

If, at any stage, a publisher who has not previously assigned his own ISBNs wishes to take over the allocation of his own numbers from the agency, no objection will be made. But it is essential that due warning is given. Otherwise the publisher will assign one number to a given title, and the agency may well assign a completely different number.

Reproduced by kind permission of the Standard Book Numbering Agency Ltd.

VANITY PUBLISHING

A reputable publisher very rarely asks an author to pay for the production of his work, or to contribute to its cost, or to undertake to purchase copies. The only exception is in the case of a book of an extremely specialised nature, with a very limited market or perhaps the first book of poems by a new writer of some talent. In such instances, especially if the book is a good one making a contribution to its subject, an established and reliable publisher will be prepared to accept a subvention from the author to make publication possible, and such financial grants often come from scientific or other academic foundations or funds. This is a very different procedure from that of the *vanity publisher* who claims to perform, for a fee to be paid by the author, all the many functions involved in publishing a book.

In his efforts to secure business the vanity publisher will usually give exaggerated praise to an author's work and arouse equally unrealistic hopes of its commercial success. The distressing reports we have received from embittered victims of vanity publishers underline the importance of reading extremely carefully the contracts offered by such publishers. Often these will provide for the printing of, say, two thousand copies of the book, usually at a quite exorbitant cost to the author, but will leave the 'publisher' under no obligation to bind more than a very limited number. Frequently, too, the author will be expected to pay the cost of any effective advertising, while the 'publisher' makes little or no effort to promote the distribution and sale of his book. Again, the names and imprints of vanity publishers are well-known to literary editors, and their productions therefore are rarely, if ever, reviewed or even noticed in any important periodical. Similarly, such books are hardly ever stocked by the booksellers.

We repeat, therefore, except in rare instances never pay for publication, whether for a book, an article, a lyric, or a piece of music. If a work is worth publishing, sooner or later a publisher will be prepared to publish it at his own expense. But if a writer cannot resist the temptation of seeing his work in print, in book form, or in an anthology, even though he has to pay a substantial sum, he should first discover just how much or how little the publisher will provide and will do in return for the payment he demands.

theatre, tv radio, agents

MARKETING A PLAY

JULIA JONES
Society of Authors

As soon as a play is written, it is protected under the Copyright laws of this country. No formalities are necessary here to secure copyright protection but it is a good plan to deposit a copy with the bank and take a dated receipt for it, so as to be able to prove the date of its completion, if this should be necessary at some time either, for example, to enforce a claim for infringement of copyright or to rebut such a claim. The copyright belongs to the author unless and until he parts with it and this he should never do, since the copyright is in effect the sum total of all his rights in his work. He should, so far as possible deal separately with the component rights which go to make up the copyright and grant limited licences for the principal rights with, where customary or necessary, limited interests in the ancillary rights. A West End production agreement (see below) illustrates this principle.

The author can try to market the play himself, but once a play is accepted, it is wise to have professional assistance. There is no standard author's contract in this country; all points are, therefore, open for negotiation and the contractual complications are best handled by a reputable literary agent.

Although most ambitious young playwrights visualise a West End opening for their plays, the first step, except for the established dramatist, is usually to try to place the play with a repertory company known to be interested in presenting new plays. It is wise to write to the company first, giving salient details, such as type of play, size of cast, number of sets, etc., and ask if the management would be willing to read it. This saves the frustration and expense of copies of the play being kept for long periods by managements who have no interest in it. (Do not send your only copy of the play away—this seems obvious, but many authors have suffered the torment of having to rewrite from memory when the only copy has been lost.) It is also possible to get a first production by entering the play for the various competitions which appear from time to time, but in this case great care should be taken to study the rules and ensure that the organisers of the competition do not acquire unreasonably wide rights and interests in the entries.

Many repertory companies will give a new play a try-out production in the hope that it will be seen by London managements and transfer to the West End. For the run at the repertory company's own theatre the company will receive a licence for a given period from a fixed date and pay the author a royalty of between 6 per cent and 10 per cent calculated on the gross box office receipts. In return for the risk involved in presenting a new play, the repertory company will expect a share in the author's earnings from subsequent professional stage productions of the play during a limited period (usually two years). Sometimes on transfer the West End management will agree to take over responsibility for part or all of this payment.

The contract, for repertory or West End production, or for the use of any other rights in the play, should specify precisely the rights to which it refers, the territory covered, the period of time covered, the payments involved and make it clear that all other rights remain the property of the author.

For a first-class production in the West End of London, usually preceded by a short provincial tour, the author's contract will include clauses dealing with the following main heads of agreement. The substance, as well as the phrasing of these clauses will vary considerably, but those given below probably represent the average, as do the figures in brackets, which must not be assumed to be standard:

1. *U.K. Option.* In consideration of a specified minimum sum (between £500 and £1000) as a non-returnable advance against royalties, the Manager shall have the exclusive option for a specified period (usually six months) to produce the play in a first-class theatre in the West End of London (preceded possibly by a tour of specified number of weeks) with an extension for a further period upon payment of a further similar sum.

2. *U.K. Licence.* When the Manager exercises his option he shall have the U.K. licence for a specified period (three or five years) from the date of the first performance under the licence such licence to terminate before the expiry of the specified period if

(a) the play is not produced before a specified date;
(b) (i) less than a specified number (between 50 and 75) of consecutive professional performances are given and paid for in any year; or
(ii) the Manager has not paid at the beginning of any year a non-returnable advance against royalties. This variant on clause (b) (i) prevents the rights being tied up for a year while waiting to check if the qualifying performances have been given and is thus desirable from the author's point of view.

3. *U.S. Option.* If the Manager gives a specified number (usually 24) of consecutive performances in the West End he shall have an option exercisable within a specified period of the first West End performance (six weeks) to produce the play on Broadway on payment of a specified non-returnable advance on royalties (between £500 and £1000).

4. *U.S. Licence.* When the Manager exercises his option the Broadway licence shall be for a specified period (3 years) on terms not less favourable than those specified in the Minimum Basic Agreement of the Dramatists' Guild of America.

5. *Other Rights.* Provided the play has run for the qualifying period (usually 24 performances) the Manager acquires interests in some of the other rights as follows:

(i) *Repertory.* The author should reserve these rights paying the Manager a share (one-third) of his royalties for a specified period (two years after the end of the West End run or the expiry of the West End licence whichever is the shorter.) The author agrees not to release these rights until after the end of the West End run without the Manager's consent, this consent not to be unreasonably withheld. It is recommended that a play should be released to theatres on the A list immediately after the end of the West End run, and to theatres on the B list within three months from the end of the West End run, if an option for a tour has not been taken up by then, otherwise at the end of the tour. The Theatres on these lists are those recommended by the Theatres' National Committee for immediate and early release of plays to repertory.

(ii) *Amateur.* The author should reserve these rights and pay the Manager no share in his royalties, but should undertake not to release these rights for an agreed period, to allow the repertory theatres to have maximum clear run.

(iii) *Radio, Television, and Video.* The author should reserve these rights but it may well be in his interest not to release them until some time after the end of the West End run. During the run of the play in the West End, however, the Manager may arrange for an extract from the play to be broadcast or televised for publicity purposes, the author's fee for such broadcast or television performances being paid to him in full without any part of it going to the Manager.

(iv) *Film.* If the Manager has produced the play for the qualifying period it is expected that the author will pay him a percentage (often 20 per cent) of the author's net receipts from the disposal of the film rights, if these rights are disposed of within a specified period (one year) from the last West End performance. If the Manager has also produced the play on Broadway for the qualifying period the author is expected to allow him a further percentage (20 per cent) of the author's net receipts from the disposal of the film rights if the rights are disposed of within a specified time (one year) of the last Broadway performance. This is a field where the established dramatist can, not unnaturally, strike a much better bargain than the beginner. In no case, however, should the total percentage payable to the Manager exceed 40 per cent.

(v) *Foreign Language.* These rights should be reserved to the author, the Manager receiving no share of the proceeds.

(vi) *Cassette.* These rights should be specifically reserved to the author.

Other clauses which should appear include:

(a) A royalty clause setting out the royalties which the author shall receive from West End and touring performances of the play—usually a scale rising from 5 per cent through 7½ per cent to 10 per cent. If the author is registered for VAT, provision for VAT should be included here.

(b) Cast approval, etc. The author should be consulted about the casting and the director of the play, and in some cases may be able to insist on approval of the casting of a particular part.

(c) Rehearsals, scripts, etc. The author should be entitled to attend all rehearsals of the play and no alteration in the title or script should be made without the author's consent. All approved alterations in or suggestions for the script should become the author's property. In this clause also should appear details about supply of tickets for the author for opening performances and any arrangements for tickets throughout the West End run.

(d) Credits. Details of billing of the author's name on posters, programmes and advertising matter should be included.

(e) Lord Chamberlain's Licence. The Theatres Act 1968 abolishes the power of the Lord Chamberlain to censor stage plays and play licences are no longer required. However, it is obligatory for managers to deposit a copy of the script on which the public performance of any new play is based with the Keeper of Manuscripts, British Library, London, WC1, within one month of the performance.

(f) The author will normally warrant that the play contains nothing that is obscene or defamatory or that infringes copyright.

There must also be:

(g) An accounting clause giving details of payment and requiring a certified statement of box office receipts.

(h) A clause giving the conditions under which the agreement may be assigned or sub-leased.

(i) A termination clause, stating the conditions under which the agreement shall terminate.

ARRANGEMENTS FOR OTHER RIGHTS AFTER THE FIRST-CLASS RUN OF THE PLAY

Repertory. The author or his representative will license repertory performances for a fixed royalty on the gross box office receipts—usually 10 per cent for a new play immediately after its West End run, dropping perhaps to 7½ per cent in later years.

Amateur. The author or his representative will license amateur performances of the play for a flat fee (normally between £15 – £25).

Publication. A firm specialising in acting editions of plays may offer to publish the play in which case it will expect to license amateur performances and collect the fees on a commission basis (20 per cent to 50 per cent). The publication contract will also usually provide for the author to receive a royalty of 10 per cent of the published price of every copy sold.

Radio and Television. Careful negotiation is required and care should be taken that repeat fees for repeat performances are included in the contract in addition to the initial fee for the first broadcast.

Film Rights. Professional advice is absolutely necessary when dealing with a film contract as there are many complications. The rights may be sold outright or licensed for a number of years—usually not less than 7 or 10 or more than 15. The film company normally acquires the right of distribution throughout the world in all languages and expects a completely free hand in making the adaptation of the play into a film.

Foreign Rights. It is usual to grant exclusive foreign language rights for the professional stage to an agent or translator who will arrange for a translation to be prepared and produced—it is wise to ask for evidence of the quality of the translator's work unless the translator is very well known. The financial arrangement is usually an advance against royalties for a given period to enable a translation to be prepared and then a licence to exploit the translation for a further period after production (usually five years).

MARKETS FOR PLAYS

It is not easy for a new or comparatively unknown writer to find a management willing to present his play. The Royal Court Theatre and some other similarly enterprising organisations present a number of plays by new authors. The new and inexperienced writer may find it easier to persuade amateur drama groups or provincial repertory theatres to present his work. A further possible market may be found in the smaller fringe theatre companies.

The Stage reports productions of most new plays first produced by repertory theatres and a study of this journal may reveal other potential new markets for plays.

The Arts Council of Great Britain publishes a brochure *Theatre Writing Schemes*, which gives details of various forms of assistance available to playwrights and to theatres wishing to commission new plays. The help given by the Arts Council includes Bursaries (including the John Whiting Award), help to writers who are being commissioned or encouraged by a theatre company, and Supplements to authors' royalties. There is a number of Resident Dramatists' Attachment Awards available and some support is available towards the costs of writers' workshops. Copies of the brochure and further information may be obtained from The Drama Director, The Arts Council of Great Britain, 105 Piccadilly, London, W1V 0AV.

It is probable that competitions for full-length and one-act plays and other special opportunities for new plays will be announced after the *Yearbook* has gone to press, and writers with plays on the stocks would do well to watch carefully for announcements in the Press. *The Observer, The Author, Drama, Amateur Stage,* and *The Stage,* are the journals in which announcements are most likely to appear.

Sketches for revues, concert parties, and broadcasting, and plays for youth organisations are in demand. Sketches are usually bought outright, but in any case authors should make quite certain of what rights they will be disposing before accepting any offer.

In every case it is advisable to send a preliminary letter before submitting a manuscript. Suggestions for the preparation of manuscripts will be found in the article **Making a Book** .

Writers of plays are also referred to **Marketing a Play** and to the section on **Television**, a medium which provides a very big market for the writers of plays.

In the following lists of theatres an asterisk * denotes that Theatre Club membership is required.

LONDON

***Bush Theatre,** Shepherd's Bush Green, London, W12 8QD *T.* 01-602 3703 (Administration); 01-743 3388 (Box Office).

Codron, Michael, Ltd., Aldwych Theatre Offices, Aldwych, London WC2B 4DF *T.* 01-240 8291.

Cooney Presentations, Ray, Ltd., 1-3 Spring Gardens, Trafalgar Square, London, SW1A 2BD *T.* 01-839 5098-9.

English Stage Company Ltd., Royal Court Theatre, Sloane Square, London, SW1W 8AS *T.* 01-730 5174.

Freedman Panter Ltd., 95 Wardour Street, London W1V 3TE *T*. 01-434 4301.

Gale, John, Strand Theatre, Aldwych, London, WC2B 5LD *T*. 01-240 1656.

Greenwich Theatre Ltd., Greenwich Theatre, Crooms Hill, London, SE10 8ES *T*. 01-858 4447.

Hampstead Theatre, Swiss Cottage Centre, London, NW3 3EX *T*. 01-722 9224.

Hyman, Bruce, Associates Ltd, 46 Carnaby Street, London W1V 1PE *T*. 01-734 8875.

Kenwright, Bill, Ltd. 59 Shaftesbury Avenue, London, W1V 7AA *T*. 01-439 4466.

*****King's Head Theatre,** 115 Upper Street, London, N1 1QN *T*. 01-226 1916.

Knightsbridge Theatrical Productions Ltd., 2 Goodwin's Court, St. Martin's Lane, London, WC2N 4LL *T*. 01-836 7517.

Libby Productions Ltd., Toby Rowland, Prince of Wales Theatre, Coventry Street, London W1V 8AS *T*. 01-930 4031.

Lyric Theatre Hammersmith, King Street, London W6 0QL. *T*. 01-741 0824.

National Theatre, South Bank, London, SE1 9PX *T*. 01-928 2033.

New Half Moon Theatre, 213 Mile End Road, London, E1 4AA *T*. 01-791 1141.

*****Orange Tree Theatre,** 45 Kew Road, Richmond, Surrey TW9 2NQ. *T*. 01-940 0141.

*****Pentameters,** Three Horseshoes, Heath Street, London, NW3. *T*. 01-435 6757.

Polka Children's Theatre, 240 The Broadway, London, SW19 1SB *T*. 01-542 4258.

Portman Theatrical Productions, 30 St. James's Square, London, SW1Y 4JH *T*. 01-930 9241.

Questors Theatre, Mattock Lane, Ealing, London, W5 5BQ *T*. 01-567 0011.

Royal Shakespeare Company, Barbican Theatre, Barbican, London, EC2Y 8DS *T*. 01-628 3351.

Saunders, Peter, Ltd., Vaudeville Theatre Offices, 10 Maiden Lane, London, WC2E 7NA *T*. 01-240 3177.

*****Soho Poly Theatre,** 16 Riding House Street, London, W1P 7PD *T*. 01-636 9050 and 580 6982.

Tennent, H. M., Ltd., Globe Theatre, Shaftesbury Avenue, London, W1 *T*. 01-437 3647.

Theatre Royal, Stratford East, Gerry Raffles Square, Stratford, London, E15 1BN *T*. 01-534 7374.

Tricycle Theatre Company, The, Tricycle Theatre, 269 Kilburn High Road, London, NW6 7JR *T*. 01-624 5330 and 8168.

Triumph Apollo Productions Ltd., Suite 4, Waldorf Chambers, 11 Aldwych, London, WC2B 4DA *T*. 01-836 0186.

Unicorn Theatre for Children, Arts Theatre, 6-7 Gt. Newport Street, London, WC2H 7JB *T*. 01-379 3280. (Plays for children up to age of 12 only.)

*****Warehouse Theatre,** 62 Dingwall Road, Croydon CR0 2NE. *T*. 01-681 1257.

White, Michael, 13 Duke Street, St. James's, London, SW1Y 6DB *T*. 01-839 3971.

Young Vic, 66 The Cut, Waterloo Road, London, SE1 8LZ *T*. 01-633 0133.

PROVINCIAL

Abbey Theatre, Lower Abbey Street, Dublin, 1 *T.* 748741. The Abbey Theatre mainly produces plays in Irish or English written by Irish authors or on Irish subjects. Foreign plays are however regularly produced.

Belgrade Theatre, Belgrade Square, Coventry, CV1 1GS *T.* (0203) 56431.

Birmingham Repertory Theatre, Ltd., Broad Street, Birmingham, B1 2EP *T.* 021-236 6771.

Bristol Old Vic Company, Theatre Royal, King Street, Bristol, BS1 4ED *T.* 277466.

Chester Gateway Theatre Trust, Ltd., Gateway Theatre, Hamilton Place, Chester, CH1 2BH *T.* (0244) 44238.

Chichester Festival Theatre Productions Company Ltd., Chichester Festival Theatre, Oaklands Park, Chichester, Sussex, PO19 4AP *T.* (0243) 784437.

Churchill Theatre Trust Ltd., High Street, Bromley, Kent BR1 1HA. *T.* 01-464 7131.

Colchester Mercury Theatre Ltd., Balkerne Gate, Colchester, Essex, CO1 1PT *T.* (0206) 577006.

Coliseum Theatre, The, Fairbottom Street, Oldham, OL1 3SW *T.* 061-624 1731.

Contact Theatre Company, University Theatre, Devas Street, Manchester, M15 6JA *T.* 061-273 7531.

Crucible Theatre Trust Ltd., The Crucible Theatre, Norfolk Street, Sheffield, S1 1DA *T.* (0742) 760621.

Derby Playhouse, Ltd., Theatre Walk, Eagle Centre, Derby, DE1 2NF *T.* (0332) 363271.

Druid Theatre Company, Druid Lane Theatre, Chapel Lane, Galway, Eire *T.* (091) 68617 and 68660.

Duke's Playhouse, The, Moor Lane, Lancaster, LA1 1QE *T.* (0524) 67461.

Dundee Repertory Theatre, Tay Square, Dundee, DD1 1PB *T.* 27684.

Everyman Theatre, Regent Street, Cheltenham, GL50 1HQ *T.* (0242) 512515.

Farnham Repertory Company, Ltd., The Redgrave Theatre, Brightwells, Farnham, Surrey, GU9 7SB *T.* Farnham (0252) 727000.

Field Day Theatre Company, Northern Counties Building, 22 Waterloo Place, Derry, Northern Ireland, BT48 6BU. *T.* 260196.

Glasgow Citizens' Theatre, Ltd., Gorbals, Glasgow, G5 9DS *T.* 041-429 5561.

Grand Theatre, Singleton Street, Swansea, SA1 3QJ *T.* (0792) 475242.

Harrogate Theatre, Oxford Street, Harrogate, Yorkshire HG1 1QF *T.* (0423) 502710.

Hornchurch Theatre Trust, Ltd., The, The Queen's Theatre, Billet Lane, Hornchurch, Essex, RM11 1QT *T.* Hornchurch 56118.

Horseshoe Theatre Co., The Shrubbery, Cliddesden Road, Basingstoke, Hants, RG21 3ER *T.* (0256) 55844.

Key Theatre, Embankment Road, Peterborough, PE1 1EF *T.* (0733) 52437.

Leeds Playhouse, Calverley Street, Leeds, LS2 3AJ *T.* (0532) 442141. (Particularly work with a northern bias.)

Leicester Haymarket Theatre, Belgrave Gate, Leicester, LE1 3YQ *T.* (0533) 530021. *Telex:* 341019 Lehay G.

Liverpool Repertory Theatre, Ltd., The Playhouse, Williamson Square, Liverpool, L1 1EL *T.* 051-709 8478.

Lyceum Studio—see **Royal Lyceum Theatre Company Ltd.**

Lyceum Theatre, Heath Street, Crewe, Cheshire, CW1 2DA *T.* (0270) 215523.

Merseyside Everyman Theatre Company Ltd., 5 – 9 Hope Street, Liverpool, L1 9BH *T.* 051-708 0338.

New Victoria Theatre, Etruria Road, Newcastle under Lyme ST5 0LU. New purpose built theatre in the round, presenting new plays, adaptations, documentaries.

Northampton Repertory Players, Ltd., Royal Theatre and Opera House, Guildhall Road, Northampton, NN1 1EA *T.* (0604) 38343.

Northcott Theatre, Stocker Road, Exeter, Devon EX4 4QB *T.* (0392) 56182.

Nottingham Playhouse, Nottingham Theatre Trust Ltd., Wellington Circus, Nottingham, NG1 5AF *T.* (0602) 474361.

Nuffield Theatre, University Road, Southampton. *T.* (0703) 585633.

Octagon Theatre, Howell Croft South, Bolton, BL1 1SB *T.* 29407.

Oxford Playhouse Company, (Anvil Productions Ltd.), Beaumont Street, Oxford, OX1 2LW *T.* (0865) 723238.

Palace Theatre, Clarendon Road, Watford, WD1 1JZ *T.* 35455.

Palace Theatre Trust Ltd., London Road, Westcliff-on-Sea, Essex SS0 9LA *T.* (0702) 347816.

Peacock Theatre, The Abbey Theatre, Lower Abbey Street, Dublin 1. *T.* 748741. The experimental theatre associated with the Abbey Theatre and presents mostly new writing as well as exploring the entire canon of world drama.

Perth Repertory Theatre, Ltd., 185 High Street, Perth, PH1 5UW *T.* (0738) 38123.

Phoenix Arts Centre, Newarke Street, Leicester, LE1 5TA *T.* 555627. Community Arts Centre with resident theatre company.

Plymouth Theatre Royal, Theatre Royal, Royal Parade, Plymouth, Devon, PL1 2TR *T.* (0752) 668282.

Royal Exchange Theatre Company Ltd., The Royal Exchange, St. Ann's Square, Manchester, M2 7DH *T.* 061-833 9333.

Royal Lyceum Theatre Company Ltd., Royal Lyceum Theatre, Grindlay Street, Edinburgh, EH3 9AX *T.* 031-229 7404; and Lyceum Studio.

St. Andrews Byre Theatre, Abbey Street, St. Andrews, KY16 9LA *T.* (0334) 76288.

Salisbury Playhouse, Malthouse Lane, Salisbury, Wiltshire SP2 7RA *T.* (0722) 20117.

Scarborough Theatre Trust Ltd., The Stephen Joseph Theatre-in-the-Round, Valley Bridge Parade, Scarborough, Yorkshire YO11 2PL *T.* (0723) 370540/1/2.

Swan Theatre, The Moors, Worcester, WR1 3EF *T.* (0905) 27463.

Thorndike Theatre, Church Street, Leatherhead, Surrey, KT22 8DF *T.* (0372) 376211.

Tynewear Theatre Company, Barras Bridge, Newcastle upon Tyne NE1 7RH *T.* (091) 232 3366.

Vance, Charles, Ltd., Leas Pavilion Theatre, Folkestone, CT20 2DP *T.* 59097.

Watermill Theatre Ltd., Bagnor, Newbury, Berkshire, RG16 8AE *T.* (0635) 45834.

Windsor Theatre Company (Capoco Ltd.), Theatre Royal, Windsor, SL4 1PS *T.* (0753) 863444.

Wolsey Theatre, The, Civic Drive, Ipswich, Suffolk IP1 2AS *T.* (0473) 218911.

Worthing and District Connaught Theatre Trust, Ltd., Connaught Theatre, Union Place, Worthing, West Sussex, BN11 1LG *T.* (0903) 35334.

York Citizens' Theatre Trust, Ltd., Theatre Royal, St. Leonard's Place, York, YO1 2HD *T.* (0904) 58162.

Yvonne Arnaud Theatre Management Ltd., Yvonne Arnaud Theatre, Millbrook, Guildford, Surrey, GU1 3UX *T.* (0483) 64571.

TOURING COMPANIES

Avon Touring Theatre Co., The Albany Centre, Shaftesbury Avenue, Montpelier, Bristol, BS6 5LL *T.* (0272) 555436.

Black Theatre Co-Operative, Unit 1, 2nd Floor, 61-71 Collier Street, London N1 9BE *T.* 01-833 3785 and 2046.

Common Stock Youth Theatre, 182 Hammersmith Road, London, W6 7DJ *T.* 01-741 3086 and 748 6980.

Foco Novo, 1-2 Alfred Place, London WC1E 7EB *T.* 01-580 4722.

Gay Sweatshop Theatre Co., 90 Cranfield Gardens, London, NW6 3EE.

Hull Truck Theatre Co. Ltd., Spring Street Theatre, Spring Street, Hull HU2 8RW *T.* (0482) 224800.

Joint Stock Theatre Group, 123 Tottenham Court Road, London, W1P 9HN *T.* 01-388 9719. Plays created from workshops.

Live Theatre, 8 Trinity Chare, Quayside, Newcastle upon Tyne NE1 3DF. *T.* (091) 261 2694.

London Bubble, The (Bubble Theatre Company), 5 Elephant Lane, London SE16 4JD *T.* 01-237 4434.

M6 Theatre Company, Theatre Workshop, Heybrook School, Park Road, Rochdale, Lancashire, OL12 9BJ *T.* (0706) 355898.

Major Road Theatre Company, 29 Queens Road, Bradford, West Yorkshire BD8 7BS *T.* (0274) 480251.

Monstrous Regiment, 4 Elder Street, E1 6BT *T.* 01-247 2398.

Northumberland Theatre Company, The Playhouse, Bondgate Without, Alnwick, Northumberland NE66 1PQ. *T.* (0665) 602586.

Orchard Theatre Company, 108 Newport Road, Barnstaple, N. Devon, EX32 9BA *T.* (0271) 71475.

Paines Plough, The Writers Company, 123 Tottenham Court Road, London, W1P 9HN *T.* 01-380 1188.

Pentabus Theatre Company, The Old Primary School, Abberley Avenue, Areley Kings, Stourport-on-Severn, Worcs., DY13 0LH. *T.* Stourport (02993) 6288.

Perspectives Theatre Co-operative Ltd., c/o Mansfield Community Arts Centre, Leeming Street, Mansfield, Notts. NG18 1NG. *T.* (0623) 35225. Has a policy of employing writers for new work.

Quicksilver Theatre of Thelema, 4 Enfield Road, London N1 5AZ. *T.* 01-241 2942.

MARKETS FOR PLAYS 217

Red Ladder Theatre Co., New Blackpool Centre, Cobden Avenue, Lower Wortley, Leeds, LS12 5PB. *T.* (0532) 792228.

Solent People's Theatre, The Heathfield Centre, Valentine Avenue, Sholing, Southampton SO2 9EQ *T.* (0703) 443943.

Theatre Centre, Hanover School, Noel Road, Islington, London N1 8BD. *T.* 01-354 0110.

Touring Theatre London, Sue Charman, Lympstone, Grange Road, St Mary's Platt, Sevenoaks, Kent TN15 8ND *T.* (0732) 882678; (0703) 443943 (c/o **Solent Peoples Theatre**).

Women's Theatre Group, 5 Leonard Street, London, EC2A 4AQ *T.* 01-251 0202. Women writers only.

PUBLISHERS SPECIALISING IN THE PUBLICATION OF PLAYS

(For other particulars regarding Publishers, see under **'UK Publishers,'** and **'US Publishers'**.)

Atheneum Publishers, 597 Fifth Avenue, New York, N.Y. 10017.

Baker (Walter H.) Company, 100 Chauncy Street, Boston, Mass., 02111.

ETG (English Theatre Guild), Ltd., part of Chappell Music Ltd., 129 Park Street, London W1Y 3FA *T.* 01-629 7600.

Faber & Faber Ltd., 3 Queen Square, London, WC1N 3AU.

French (Samuel), Ltd., 52 Fitzroy Street, London W1P 6JR.

French (Samuel) Inc., 45 West 25th Street, New York, N.Y. 10010.

Kenyon-Deane Ltd., 311 Worcester Road, Malvern, Worcestershire, WR14 1AN.

Macmillan Education Ltd., Houndmills, Basingstoke, Hants, RG21 2XS.

Methuen London Ltd., 11 New Fetter Lane, London, EC4P 4EE.

Miller (J. Garnet), Ltd., 311 Worcester Road, Malvern, Worcestershire WR14 1AN.

New Playwrights' Network, 35 Sandringham Road, Macclesfield, Cheshire, SK10 1QB *T.* (0625) 25312.

(For a list of periodicals dealing with the Theatre see the **Classified Index**.)

MARKETS FOR SCREENPLAYS

JEAN McCONNELL

There have been setbacks for the British Film Industry recently. Nevertheless, a market still exists – particularly in regard to material being made for television, with which many film companies are now very actively engaged.

The recommended approach is through a recognised literary agent, but most film companies have a story department to whom material can be sent for consideration. But it is a good idea to check with the company first to make sure it is worth your while.

It is a fact that many of the feature films these days are based on already best-selling books, but there are some companies, particularly those with a television outlet, which will sometimes accept unsolicited material if it seems to be exceptionally original. It is obviously sensible to try to sell your work to a company which is currently in active production, such as those listed below. *But again remember the best way to achieve success is through the knowledge and efforts of a literary agent.*

When a writer submits material direct to a company, some of the larger ones, usually those American based, may request that a Release Form be signed before they are prepared to read it. This document is ostensibly designed to absolve the company from any charge of plagiarism if they should be working on a similar idea; also to limit their liability in the event of any legal action. The writer must make up his own mind whether he wishes to sign this but, in principle, it is not highly recommended.

Burrill Productions, 51 Lansdowne Road, London W11 2LG *T.* 01-727 1442. *Telex:* 896691 TLXIR G (Message prefix: Nikelodeon).

Children's Film and Television Foundation Ltd., Thorn EMI Elstree Studios, Borehamwood, Herts, WD6 1JG *T.* 01-953 1600, ext. 371.

Walt Disney Productions, Ltd., 31-32 Soho Square, London, W1V 6AP *T.* 01-734 8111. *Telex:* 21532 (will only consider material submitted through an agent).

Forstater, Mark, Productions Ltd., 42a Devonshire Close, Portland Place, London W1N 1LL *T.* 01-631 0611.

Goldcrest Film and Television Ltd., (1981), 180 Wardour Street, London W1V 3AA *T.* 01-437 8696. Submissions to Scripts and Projects Department.

Hammer Film Productions, Ltd., EMI Elstree Studios, Borehamwood, Herts, WD6 1JG *T.* 01-953 1600.

ITC Entertainment Ltd., 45 Seymour Street, London, W1A 1AG *T.* 01-262 8040. *Telex:* 261807.

Klinger, Michael, 19 Watford Road, Radlett, Herts. *T.* Radlett 3255-6-7. *Telex:* 8951182 Gecoms G. *Cables:* Klingfilm Radlett.

London Cannon Films Creative Affairs, 138 Wardour Street, London, W1V 3TA *T.* 01-437 9844. Material only accepted through agents.

London Film Productions Ltd., 44a Floral Street, London WC2E 9DA *T.* 01-379 3366. *Telex:* 896805.

Opix Films, 5 Carlisle Street, London W1V 5RG *T.* 01-437 6788 and 1451.

Paramount Pictures (UK), Ltd., 162 Wardour Street, London, W1V 4AB *T.* 01-437 7700. Material only accepted through agents.

MARKETS FOR SCREENPLAYS

Twentieth Century-Fox Productions Ltd., Twentieth Century House, 31 Soho Square, London, W1V 6AP *T.* 01-437 7766.

Tyburn Productions Ltd., Pinewood Studios, Iver Heath, Bucks, SL0 0NH *T.* (0753) 651700. *Telex:* 847505. Submissions to Gillian Garrow, Director of Research and Development.

United Artists Corporation, Ltd., c/o Pinewood Studios, Pinewood Road, Iver Heath, Bucks, SL0 0NH *T.* (0753) 654522.

Universal Pictures Ltd. (MCA), 139 Piccadilly, London, W1V 9FH *T.* 01-629 7211 (will pass on material for consideration by the U.S. office, and prefer submissions through an agent).

Warner Bros. Productions Ltd., 135 Wardour Street, London, W1V 4AP *T.* 01-437 5600 (will only consider material submitted through an agent).

Welbeck Film Distributors Ltd., 52 Queen Anne Street, London, W1M 9LA *T.* 01-935 1186.

Zenith Productions Ltd., 8 Great Titchfield Street, London W1P 7AA *T.* 01-637 7941. *Head of Development:* Scott Meek.

SCREENPLAYS FOR FILMS

JEAN McCONNELL

Despite the old saying that the plot of the best movie can be written on a postcard, film companies do not actually welcome a plot on a postcard. Nor is it enough simply to send a story in narrative form. You should be prepared to write your idea into a full screenplay. In consequence, it is advisable to check as far as possible in case a company is already working on a similar idea and your efforts likely to be wasted.

LAY-OUT

1. Use A4 size typing paper.
2. It is not necessary to put in elaborate camera directions. A shooting script will be made later. Your job is to write the master scenes, clearly broken down into each incident and location.
3. Your screenplay will tell your story in terms of visual action and dialogue spoken by your characters. If you intend it to be a full-length feature film, running about 1½ hours, your script will be about 100-130 pages long.
4. The general lay-out of a page of screenplay can be seen from the specimen page. The following points should be noted.

(a) Each scene should be numbered on the left, and given a title which indicates whether the scene is an interior or an exterior, where it takes place, and a rough indication of the lighting conditions, i.e. Day or Night. The situation of each scene should be standardised; don't call your 'sitting room' a 'lounge' the next time you come to it, or people will think you mean a different place.

(b) Note that the dialogue is spaced out, with the qualifying directions such as '(frowning)' on a separate line, slightly inset from the dialogue. Double space each speech from the previous one.

(c) Always put the names of the characters in CAPITALS, except when they occur in the actual dialogue. Double space the stage directions from the dialogue, but single space the lines of the stage directions themselves.

(d) Leave at least a 1½ inch margin on the left hand and a reasonably wide right-hand margin. It is false economy to cram the page. You will, of course, type on one side of the page only.

(e) If you have to make a correction, cross it out neatly and type the whole section out again. But don't irritate your reader with too many corrections. Better to re-type the page.

(f) Only give the camera directions when you feel it to be essential. For instance, if you want to show something from a particular character's point of view, or if you think you need it to make a point, i.e. 'HARRY approaches the cliff edge and looks down. LONG SHOT—HARRY'S POINT OF VIEW. ALICE fully-clad is walking into the sea. CUT TO: CLOSE UP OF HARRY'S HORRIFIED FACE.' Note the camera directions are put in capital letters on a separate line, as in the specimen page.

PREPARATION OF MANUSCRIPT

1. Make at least two copies, and never send your very last copy out to anyone. It will invariably be lost.
2. The length of your manuscript will depend on whether you are submitting a feature film, a short film for children, say, or a documentary. But it is better to present a version which is too short rather than too long.

13 (continued)

    She moves across the barn to the door, where she turns.

                       ELIZABETH
          I still think the police ought to know.

    She goes out. ALAN stands immobile until her footsteps retreat, and then he sighs with relief. He darts quickly to the large wine vat, climbs up and begins heaving at the lid.

                                                  CUT TO:

14 EXT. FARMYARD DAY

    DONALD intercepts ELIZABETH as she crosses yard.

                        DONALD
          What does he say?

                       ELIZABETH
  Nothing.

                        DONALD
          (frowning)
          Right! Now it's my turn.
    He starts for the barn. ELIZABETH watches him anxiously.

                                                    CUT TO:

15 INT. BARN DAY

    Donald's shadow falls across the threshold. He hesitates while his eyes get used to the gloom.

                        DONALD
          Alan?

    ALAN lets the lid of the vat fall and jumps down. He stands quite still as DONALD crosses the barn and stands staring at him. The two men are silent a moment.

                        DONALD
          (then, with realisation)
          You knew it was there, didn't you?

CLOSE SHOT — DONALD'S POINT OF VIEW
ALAN'S face is haggard.

                        ALAN
          I hoped to God it wouldn't be.

3. Prepare the title page in the same way as for a story or article to an editor, except that it is not necessary to state the number of words.
4. If you give a list of characters, do not suggest the actor or actress you would like to play it. This is a decision to be made elsewhere and relies on many factors about which you cannot know. Don't attach character sketches, as these should appear in the body of the screenplay.
5. Bind your screenplay, giving it a front and back cover, and securing the pages firmly.

SUBMISSION

Attach a stamped, addressed envelope to your manuscript whether sending it through an agent or direct. But do remember that if film companies state that they will only consider material sent through an agent, they definitely mean it.

Most companies have Story Departments to which you should address your material. As Story Editors are very busy people, you can make their life easier by complying with the following rules.
1. If you have based your screenplay on someone else's published work you should make the fact clear in a covering letter, stating *(a)* that the material is no longer in copyright, or *(b)* that you yourself own the copyright, or at least an option on it, or *(c)* that you have not obtained the copyright, but have reason to believe that there would be no difficulty in doing so.
2. Apart from a note of any relevant credits you may already possess, do not regale the Editor with your personal details, unless they bear a direct relation to the material submitted. For instance, if your story concerns a brain surgeon, then it would be relevant for the Editor to know that you actually are one. Otherwise, trust your work to stand on its own merit.
3. There is no need to mention if your work has been turned down by other companies, however regretfully. The comments of others will not influence a Story Editor one way or the other.
4. Don't pester the company if you don't get a reply, or even an acknowledgement, for some weeks. Most companies will formally acknowledge receipt and then leave you in limbo for at least six weeks. However, after a passage of three months or more, a brief letter asking politely what has happened is in order. A telephone call is unlikely to be helpful. It is possible the company may have liked your work enough to have sent it to America, or to be getting further readers' opinions on it. This all takes time. If they don't like it, you will certainly get it back in due course.
5. Accept that this is really a tough market; for which there are at least three reasons. One, films cost so much to make these days that the decision to go ahead is only taken after a great many important factors have been satisfied and an even greater number of important people are happy about it. Two, the number of films made is small in relation to, say, books published or TV plays produced. Three, writing a screenplay calls for knowledge and appreciation of the technicalities of film-making, as well as the ability to combine dialogue, action and pictures, visualising the story throughout in the language of the cinema.
6. Try to get an agent. A good agent will give you a fair opinion of your work. If he thinks it worthwhile, then he is the one who will know the particular film company to whom he can sell it.

(List of Agents who handle film material will be found at the end of **Literary Agents** Section.)

WRITING FOR TELEVISION

BILL CRAIG
Past-President of The Writers' Guild of Great Britain

"Television Drama" is a generic term which covers several varied and specialist areas of writing for the domestic screen. Since each differs from the others in terms of requirements and rewards and since each is definable in Copyright terms, let's start by identifying them.

The television play is a one-off creation of a single mind and talent and absolutely the property of its author. As a form it is the vehicle for the talents of newest and least-experienced writers in the medium and also for those who are held in the highest regard. It is (for practical reasons) the traditional point of entry for the tyro. There has been some reduction in the number of plays produced annually but the BBC and certain ITV companies are still in the market for 30, 60 and 90 minute slot-length works. If the bad news is that they get several thousand unsolicited manuscripts every year, then the good news is that they are all read. No script-unit will risk missing out on an undiscovered genius.

The same observations (with some modification) would apply to the original series or serial: that is, a multi-part work of sole-authorship and of finite length. They tend to be written by established television writers who have a proven ability to go the necessary distance but a new writer with an attractive idea can come in through this door.

What's the procedure? Invest some time and talent and write the play. A commission on a synopsis is unlikely without some evidence that you can write interesting action, dialogue and characters. With the finite series/serial—write the first episode and synopsise the rest.

The situation-comedy is the most highly-paid area of television writing – and understandably so. It calls for a quirky and idiosyncratic mind and its overriding imperative—to make the viewer laugh—subordinates all of the other dramatic tools to this end. If it's difficult to play Beethoven's *Ninth* on a one-stringed fiddle, then it's Hell to do it for a run of six episodes. The sit-com is unique in screen drama insofar as most of them are played before live studio audiences. Once upon a time, they were constructed round individual comedians. Some still are, but for several years now the practice has been to cast according to the script with actors who can play comedy. And that's not a bad thing, is it?

Again, this form is an original in Copyright terms, though dual-authorships are not uncommon. A synopsis is pretty useless (ever tried to explain a joke?) so write the pilot-script and briefly indicate where you can go with other episodes.

We now come to a significant point of departure and go into those areas where the Copyright is split with another party.

First, the drama-series: *Bergerac, The Gentle Touch, Upstairs Downstairs,* et al. These are definable as a series of original and self-contained scripts using the same characters and backgrounds throughout. The format—that is, the characters and general ambience—will be owned or leased by the production organisation. They represent a substantial part of television drama but it is rare for a writer without previous screen experience to be commissioned to write for them. It is quite pointless to submit a speculative script or synopsis: the series you are seeing now was recorded months ago.

The daily or bi-weekly serial *(Coronation Street, Crossroad, Triangle, Take the High Road, Emmerdale Farm)* will occasionally try out new writers but the production pressures on reliability and deadline delivery dates don't allow for too many risks to be taken outside what is usually an established and pretty permanent writing team.

The dramatisation and the adaptation. Terms which are interchanged in an ignorantly casual manner; they are not the same thing. A dramatisation is the conversion of a prose-work to a screenplay. An adaptation is a similar conversion of a dramatic work. The difference is considerable and the screen credit should reflect this fact.

There has been a great increase in the number of dramatisations made from novels. Again, these are usually written by writers with a track-record in television but occasionally the author of the book to be dramatised will be approached to write the screenplay. If you don't come under either of those headings, then you probably wouldn't get very far by simply suggesting that you'd like to dramatise this or that novel. Adaptations are usually "in-house" works.

All of which leaves uncovered an odd and often lucrative area—the format. It is possible to sell an idea for a series without ever having written a script. But make sure that your submission is as detailed as it possibly can be in terms of background, main characters and development. Doing it the simple way in this instance can mean finding out that fifty other people have had the same simple idea. And selling an idea carries no guarantee that you'll be asked to write the scripts.

Script lay-out and presentation. Use A4. Type it or have it typed. Blank margin about four inches on the left hand side. Directions and character names in capitals, dialogue in capitals and lower case, double spaced. Don't go mad with directions, keep them functional and indicative. Don't be intimidated by camera directions: use them only when they make a dramatic point you want to get across.

Number and head the scenes thus: 1. INT. JOE'S ROOM. DAY
Avoid nonsense action directions such as "Her inner resilience manifests itself in a way reminiscent of the wind howling across her native moors". If you mean she's from Yorkshire, just say it.

There are several books on the subject of layout and technique. Two which come to mind are *Writing for Television* by Malcolm Hulke and *The Way to Write for Television* by Eric Paice.

Given success to your efforts, you will be contracted under the terms of the relevant agreement between the British Broadcasting Corporation or the Independent Television Companies Association and the Writers' Guild of Great Britain, 430 Edgware Road, London W2 1EH. The Guild has sole bargaining rights in the television drama rates, its agreements are complex and comprehensive and several of the rights and benefits contained in them are available to Guild members only.

Payments are made in stages. BBC—half on commission, half on acceptance. ITCA—half on commission, a quarter on delivery, a quarter on acceptance.

The foregoing comments apply mainly to programmes produced by the British Broadcasting Corporation or the ITV companies. The increasingly-important independent production sector should not, however, be ignored since many of their productions are primarily intended for television screening.

These programmes are made by either entirely independent production organisations (e.g. *The Irish R.M.*, Little Bird Productions Ltd.) or subsidiaries of the ITV companies (e.g. *Minder*, Euston Films/Thames Television.)

Generally speaking, the scripts are laid out in film format (see **Screenplays for Films**) although some, since they produce on tape, might prefer the television format. The procedures described above for submitting unsolicited work should be observed.

Contracts should conform to the terms laid down by the agreement between The Writers' Guild of Great Britain and the British Film and Television Producers Association/Independent Programme Producers Association. Again, the Agreement is comprehensive and covers all forms and aspects of screen drama. Payment is made in four stages: Treatment, First Draft, Second Draft and Principal Photography. Further exploitation is also covered.

Further useful information and addresses may be found in a booklet called *Contacts*. The 1986-87 edition is available, price £3.00 including postage, from *The Spotlight*, 42-43 Cranbourn Street, London WC2H 7AP.

BROADCASTING: RADIO AND TV
BRITISH BROADCASTING CORPORATION

For fuller information see the BBC publication *Writing for the BBC*—a guide for writers on possible markets for their work within the BBC. The latest, 7th edition, is out of print but may be obtained in public libraries. The 8th edition is in preparation and at the time of going to press was expected to be published during 1987.

TELEVISION

Drama.—Original plays dealing with contemporary problems are most wanted. Plays needing only a few sets and characters start at an advantage. Specially-shot film sequences should only be written into a script if essential for the story. No standardised layout is expected in unsolicited scripts. Dialogue should be set out in a way that makes it clearly distinguishable from 'stage directions' and sound/visual effects. Further details about length and type of plays currently required are available from Script Unit.

All scripts should be clearly typed and sent to Head of Script Unit, BBC Television Centre, London, W12 7RJ, from whom a leaflet, *BBC Television Script Requirements* is available.

RADIO

Short Stories.—Short stories specially written for broadcasting will be considered. A short story written for a fifteen-minute broadcasting space should be between 2300 and 2500 words in length.

Drama Department.—The Department broadcasts several hundred new plays and adaptations every year, in addition to series and serials, dramatic features and readings. There is therefore a very large market regularly available to the freelance writer. A free leaflet, *Notes on Radio Drama,* giving basic guidance on the technique of radio writing and also on the market is available from the Script Editor, (Radio Drama), BBC, Broadcasting House, Portland Place, London W1A 1AA to whom all submissions should be addressed.

Music.—The music policy of the BBC, dedicated to the encouragement of the best music old and new, continues to enlarge its range. Audition sessions for professional soloists and ensembles are held every week, except in July and August, with an outside professional assessor on the listening panel.

A Music Panel of distinguished musicians meets regularly to advise on the suitability for performance of the large number of MSS. constantly submitted. The BBC also commissions from British composers works of various kinds. These have included opera and works for special occasions. Incidental music is also commissioned for features and drama. In the case of music commissioned by the BBC the original score is now returned to the composer at his request and not as in the past automatically retained by the BBC.

Light Entertainment.—Careful consideration is given to new ideas for Light Entertainment programmes by the Script Editor and senior members of the Light Entertainment Department. The chief requirement is originality; the vast majority of scripts sent in are merely variations of existing programmes. A particular need exists for topical sketches and 'one-liners' for programmes such as *Week Ending*. In general it is inadvisable to write scripts for a particular star artist unless the writer has a really intimate knowledge of the artist's work; and even then the material for 'solo' performances (as distinct from scripts for comedy series) is almost invariably provided by the artists themselves. No real decision can be reached on a new proposition until the completed script is seen: but the Script Editor is prepared to look at detailed synopses and specimen dialogue and offer opinions if requested. Fees are a matter for negotiation with the Corporation's Copyright Department. Typewritten scripts should be addressed to the Script Editor (Light Entertainment), BBC Broadcasting House, London, W1A 1AA.

BROADCASTING RIGHTS AND TERMS

Contributors are advised to check latest details of fees with the B.B.C.

Specially written material for television: For the period to 31st December 1986 the rates for one performance of a 60-minute original television play were a minimum of £2675 for a play written by a beginner and a 'going rate' of £4212 for an established writer, or *pro rata* for shorter or longer timings. Half the fee is paid on a work being commissioned and half on its acceptance as being suitable for television. If the work is submitted it is paid for on acceptance. Fees for a 50-minute episode in a series during the same period were a minimum of £2200 for a beginner and a 'going rate' of £3186 for an established writer. Fees for a 50-minute dramatisation were a minimum of £1545 for a beginner and a £2268 'going rate' for an established writer. All fees are subject to negotiation above the minima.

Specially written material for radio: Fees are assessed on the basis of the type of material, its length, the author's status and experience in writing for radio. For the period to 31st December 1986 fees for one performance of specially written radio dramas in English (other than educational programmes) were £14.40 a minute for beginners and a 'going rate' of £21.75 a minute for established writers. Fees for submitted material are paid on acceptance, and for commissioned material half on commissioning and half on acceptance as being suitable for broadcasting.

Short stories specially written for radio: Fees range from £77.50 for 15 minutes.

Stage plays for television: Fees for stage plays are negotiable.

Published material for radio (for the period to 31st December 1986:

Domestic service: Dramatic works: £7.45 per minute; Prose works: £7.45 per minute; Prose works required for adaptation into dramatic form: £5.80 per minute; Poems: £7.45 per half minute.

External Services: English language services: Dramatic works: £3.51 per minute for up to five broadcasts; Prose works: £3.51 per minute for up to five broadcasts; Prose works required for adaptation into dramatic form: £2.66 per minute for up to five broadcasts; Poems: £3.51 per *half* minute for up to five broadcasts. For Foreign language services one fifth of the rate for English language services.

Published prose and poems for television: prose works, £11.60 per minute; poems £13.50 per half minute.

Repeats in BBC programmes: Further proportionate fees are payable for repeats.

Use abroad of recordings of BBC programmes: If the BBC sends abroad recordings of its programmes for use by overseas broadcasting organisations on their own networks or stations, further payments accrue to the author, usually in the form of additional percentages of the basic fee paid for the initial performance. This can apply to both sound and television programmes.

Value Added Tax: A self-billing system for V.A.T. was introduced in January 1978 for programmes made in London. This now covers radio, external services and television.

TALKS FOR TELEVISION

Contributors to talks will be offered the standard Television talks contract which provides the BBC certain rights to broadcast the material in a complete, abridged and/or translated manner, and which provides for the payment of further fees for additional usage of the material whether by television, domestic radio and external broadcasting. The contract also covers the assignment of material and limited publication rights. Alternatively a contract taking all standard rights may be negotiated. Fees are arranged by the contract authorities in London and the Regions.

TALKS FOR RADIO

Contributors to talks for domestic Radio and External Broadcasting may be offered either the standard talks contract which takes rights and provides for residual payments as does the Television standard contract above or be offered an ARR (All Rights) Contract which takes all broadcasting and non-paying audience rights where the contribution is of a short, ephemeral nature, not exceeding an air-time of five minutes and which has set fees or disturbance money payable, or an ARC contract where no payment is made which provides an acknowledgement that a contribution may be used by the BBC.

ADDRESSES

Letters addressed to speakers c/o the BBC will be forwarded, but may be opened before being forwarded. Letters marked "Personal" are forwarded unopened.

LONDON

Head Office: Broadcasting House, London, W1A 1AA *T.* 01-580 4468. *Telex:* 265781. *T.A. & Cables:* Broadcasts, London.

Television: Television Centre, Wood Lane, London, W12 7RJ *T.* 01-743 8000. *Telex:* 265781. *T.A.* Telecasts, London.

Publications: 35 Marylebone High Street, London W1M 4AA *T.* 01-580 5577. *T.A.* Broadcasts, London.

External Broadcasting: P.O. Box 76, Bush House, Strand, London WC2B 4PH *T.* 01-240 3456. *Telex:* 265781. *T.A. & Cables:* Broadbrit, London.

BBC NATIONAL REGIONS

Northern Ireland: Broadcasting House, 25-27 Ormeau Avenue, Belfast, BT2 8HQ *T.* (0232) 244400.

Scotland: Broadcasting House, Queen Margaret Drive, Glasgow, G12 8DG *T.* 041-339 8844.
Edinburgh Office: Broadcasting House, Queen Street, Edinburgh, EH2 1JF *T.* 031-225 3131.
Aberdeen Representative: Broadcasting House, Beechgrove Terrace, Aberdeen, AB9 2ZT *T.* (0224) 25233.

Wales: Llantrisant Road, Llandaff, Cardiff, CF5 2YO *T.* (0222) 564888.
Bangor Office: Broadcasting House, Meiron Road, Bangor, Gwynedd, LL57 2BY *T.* (0248) 362214.
Swansea Office: 32 Alexandra Road, Swansea SA1 5DZ *T.* (0792) 54986.

BBC ENGLISH REGIONAL BROADCASTING

North-West Region: New Broadcasting House, P.O. Box 27, Oxford Road, Manchester, M60 1SJ. *T.* 061-236 8444.

North-East Region: Broadcasting House, 54 New Bridge Street, Newcastle-upon-Tyne, NE1 8AA. *T.* (0632) 20961.
Broadcasting Centre, Woodhouse Lane, Leeds, LS2 9PX. *T.* 021-472 5353.

Midland Region: Broadcasting Centre, Pebble Mill Road, Birmingham, B5 7SA. *T.* (0532) 441188.

East and South-East Region: Elstree Centre, Clarendon Road, Borehamwood, Herts, WD6 1JF. *T.* 01-953 6100.

South and West Region: Broadcasting House, 21 – 33B Whiteladies Road, Clifton, Bristol, BS8 2LR. *T.* (0272) 32211.

OTHER REGIONAL ADDRESSES

Norwich: St. Catherine's Close, All Saints Green, Norwich, NR1 3ND. *T.* (0603) 28841.

Southampton: South Western House, Canute Road, Southampton, SO9 1PF. *T.* (0703) 26201.

Plymouth: Broadcasting House, Seymour Road, Mannamead, Plymouth, PL3 5BD. *T.* (0752) 29201.

OVERSEAS OFFICES

U.S.A.: 630 Fifth Avenue, New York, N.Y., 10111, U.S.A. *T.* 212-581-7100. *Cables:* Broadcasts, New York City. *Telex:* 620150.

Canada: Suite 1220, Manulife Centre, 55 Bloor Street West, Toronto, Ontario *T.* 925-3891. *Cables:* Loncalling, Toronto. *Telex:* 06-23577.

Cairo Bureau, Flat 42, 23 Kasr El Ni1 Street, P.O. Box 2040, Cairo, Egypt. *T.* Cairo 745898 and 748040. *Telex:* 94169 Mytim Un.

South East Asia Bureau: P.O. Box 434, Maxwell Road Post Office, Singapore 9008 *Telex:* RS 35414.

South American Office: Casilla de Correo, 1566 Buenos Aires, Argentina. *T.* 3926439. *Telex:* Florida 734.

Australia and New Zealand: Westfield Towers, 100 William Street, Sydney, N.S.W.2011, Australia. *T.* Sydney 3586411. *Cables:* Loncalling, Sydney. *Telex:* 20705.

India: 1 Nizamuddin East, New Delhi 110013. *T.* 616108. *Telex:* 31 2927 Bbc in. *Cables:* Loncalling, Newdelhi.

France: 155 rue du Faubourg Saint-Honoré, BP 487 08, 75366 Paris, Cedex 08 *T.* 561-9700. *Cables:* Broadbrit, Paris. *Telex:* 650341.

Germany: BBC Buero, 1 Berlin 12, Savignyplatz 6, W. Germany. *T.* West Berlin 316773, 316263. *Telex:* Berlin 184469.

Belgium: P.O. Box 50, International Press Centre, 1041 Brussels. *T.* Brussels 736-8015. *Telex:* 25912.

BBC LOCAL RADIO STATIONS

Local Radio also affords opportunities for writers to submit short stories and plays. A number of stations hold play-writing or short story competitions where the winners have their work broadcast. Others consider original work from local writers. Material should be submitted to the Programme Organiser.

Bedfordshire, BBC Radio Bedfordshire, P.O. Box 476, Luton LU1 5BA. *T.* (0582) 459111.

Birmingham, BBC Radio WM (West Midlands), Pebble Mill Road, Birmingham, B5 7SD *T.* 021-472 5141. *Telex:* 339210.

Bristol, BBC Radio Bristol, 3 Tyndalls Park Road, Bristol, BS8 1PP *T.* (0272) 741111. *Telex:* 449170.

Cambridgeshire, BBC Radio Cambridgeshire, Broadcasting House, 104 Hills Road, Cambridge, CB2 1LD *T.* (0223) 315970. *Telex:* 817776.

Cleveland, BBC Radio Cleveland, P.O. Box 1548, Broadcasting House, Newport Road, Middlesbrough, Cleveland, TS1 5JA *T.* (0642) 225211. *Telex:* 58203.

Cornwall, BBC Radio Cornwall, Phoenix Wharf, Truro, Cornwall TR1 1UA. *T.* (0872) 75421. *Telex:* 45728.

Cumbria, BBC Radio Cumbria Hilltop Heights, London Road, Carlisle, CA1 2NA *T.* (0228) 31661. *Telex:* 64165.

Derby, BBC Radio Derby, 56 St. Helen's Street, Derby, DE1 3HY *T.* (0332) 361111. *Telex:* 37257.

Devon, BBC Radio Devon, P.O. Box 100, St. David's Hill, Exeter, Devon EX14 4DB. *T.* (0392) 215651. *Telex:* 42440.

Essex, BBC Essex, 198 New London Road, Chelmsford, Essex CM2 9AB *T.* (0245) 262393.

Furness, BBC Radio Furness, Broadcasting House, Hartington Street, Barrow-in-Furness, Cumbria *T.* (0229) 36767.

Guernsey, BBC Radio Guernsey, Commerce House, Les Banques, St. Peter Port, Guernsey *T.* (0481) 28977. *Telex:* 4191456.

Humberside, BBC Radio Humberside, 63 Jameson Street, Hull, HU1 3NU *T.* (0482) 23232. *Telex:* 527031.

Jersey, BBC Radio Jersey, Broadcasting House, Rouge Bouillon, St. Helier, Jersey *T.* (0534) 70000. *Telex:* 4192381.

Kent, BBC Radio Kent, 30 High Street, Chatham, Kent, ME4 4EZ *T.* (0634) 462843. *Telex:* 965011.

Lancashire, BBC Radio Lancashire, King Street, Blackburn, Lancashire, BB2 2EA *T.* (0254) 62411. *Telex:* 63491.

Leeds, BBC Radio Leeds, Broadcasting House, Woodhouse Lane, Leeds, LS2 9PN *T.* (0532) 442131. *Telex:* 557230.

Leicester, BBC Radio Leicester, Epic House, Charles Street, Leicester, LE1 3SH *T.* (0533) 27113. *Telex:* 34401.

Lincolnshire, BBC Radio Lincolnshire, Radio Buildings, P.O. Box 219, Newport, Lincoln, LN1 3DF *T.* (0522) 40011. *Telex:* 56186.

London, BBC Radio London, 35A Marylebone High Street, London, W1A 4LG *T.* 01-486 7611. *Telex:* 267223.

Manchester, BBC Radio Manchester, P.O. Box 90, New Broadcasting House, Oxford Road, Manchester, M60 1SJ *T.* 061-228 3434. *Telex:* 668708.

Merseyside, BBC Radio Merseyside, 55 Paradise Street, Liverpool, L1 3BP *T.* 051-708 5500. *Telex:* 629364.

Newcastle, BBC Radio Newcastle, Crestina House, Archibold Terrace, Newcastle-upon-Tyne, NE2 1DZ *T.* (0632) 814243. *Telex:* 537007.

Norfolk, BBC Radio Norfolk, Norfolk Tower, Surrey Street, Norwich, Norfolk, NR1 3PA *T.* (0603) 617411. *Telex:* 975515.

Northampton, BBC Radio Northampton, P.O.Box 1107, Abingdon Street, Northampton NN1 2BE *T.* (0604) 20621. *Telex:* 311812.

Nottingham, BBC Radio Nottingham, York House, Mansfield Road, Nottingham, NG1 3JB *T.* (0602) 415161. *Telex:* 37464.

Oxford, BBC Radio Oxford, 242-254 Banbury Road, Oxford, OX2 7DW *T.* (0865) 53411. *Telex:* 83571.

Sheffield, BBC Radio Sheffield, Ashdell Grove, 60 Westbourne Road, Sheffield, S10 2QU *T.* (0742) 686185. *Telex:* 54400.

Shropshire, BBC Radio Shropshire, 2-4 Boscobel Drive, Shrewsbury, Shropshire SY1 3TT *T.* (0743) 248484.

Solent, BBC Radio Solent, South Western House, Canute Road, Southampton, SO9 4PJ *T.* (0703) 31311. *Telex:* 47420.

Stoke-on-Trent, BBC Radio Stoke-on-Trent, Conway House, Cheapside, Hanley, Stoke-on-Trent, Staffordshire, ST1 1JJ *T.* (0782) 24827. *Telex:* 36104.

Sussex, BBC Radio Sussex, Marlborough Place, Brighton, BN1 1TU *T.* (0273) 680231. *Telex:* 87313.

York, BBC Radio York, 20 Bootham Row, York, YO3 7BR. *T.* (0904) 641351. *Telex:* 57444.

INDEPENDENT BROADCASTING

Independent Broadcasting Authority, 70 Brompton Road, London, SW3 1EY *T.* 01-584 7011. The Authority does not produce programmes, and material intended for broadcasting on the Authority's service should be addressed to the programme contractors, who are responsible for supplying programmes for transmission.

Channel Four Television Company Ltd., 60 Charlotte Street, London, W1P 2AX *T.* 01-631 4444. Commissions programmes (does not make them) for broadcast during the whole week throughout the United Kingdom.

TELEVISION

Material required by the Programme Contractors as listed below depends upon the contract held by the Company, i.e. London mid-week programmes will obviously differ from those for the Midlands. In all cases scripts are preferred to synopses. Programmes should be planned with natural breaks for the insertion of advertisements. These companies also provide some programmes for Channel 4.

Anglia Television Ltd., Anglia House, Norwich, NR1 3JG *T.* (0603) 615151. Brook House, 113 Park Lane, London, W1Y 4DX *T.* 01-408 2288. Provides programmes for the East of England during the whole week and drama and natural history programmes. Original dramas are welcomed. Writers should contact the Head of Anglia Drama Dept.

Border Television, PLC, The Television Centre, Carlisle, CA1 3NT *T.* (0228) 25101. 33 Margaret Street, London, W1N 7LA *T.* 01-637 4363. Provides programmes for The Borders and the Isle of Man, during the whole week. Occasionally scripts are commissioned from outside sources. Suggestions should be sent to the Controller of Programmes in Carlisle.

Central Independent Television PLC, Central House, Broad Street, Birmingham, B1 2JP *T.* 021-643 9898. East Midlands Television Centre, Nottingham, NG7 2NA *T.* (0602) 863322. Provides programmes for the East and West Midlands area during the whole week.—Central's requirements are constantly changing, and interested professional writers are asked to contact the Script Unit in Nottingham for information. Writers are advised to send photo-copies rather than original unsolicited manuscripts.

Channel Television, The Television Centre, St. Helier, Jersey, C.I. *T.* (0534) 73999. Provides programmes for the Channel Islands during the whole week—relating mainly to Channel Islands news and current affairs.

Grampian Television PLC, Queens Cross, Aberdeen, AB9 2XJ *T.* (0224) 646464. *Telex:* 73151. Albany House, 68 Albany Road, West Ferry, Dundee, DD5 1NW *T.* (0382) 739363. 23-25 Huntly Street, Inverness IV3 5PR *T.* (0463) 242624. 29 Glasshouse Street, London W1R 5RG *T.* 01-439 3141. Provides programmes for North Scotland during the whole week.

Granada Television Limited, Granada Television Centre, Manchester, M60 9EA *T.* 061-832 7211 and 36 Golden Square, London, W1R 4AH *T.* 01-734 8080. Provides programmes for North-West England throughout the week. Granada has for some time largely pursued a policy of initiating its own dramatic material, e.g. *Strangers*, *Bulman*, *Time for Murder* or adaptations of established works like *The Jewel in the Crown, Brideshead Revisited, Lost Empires, The Death of The Heart, The Adventures of Sherlock Holmes*. It is, therefore, advisable for writers to make their approach through agents who would have some knowledge of Granada's current requirements.

HTV Ltd., HTV Wales, The Television Centre, Culverhouse Cross, Cardiff, CF5 6XJ *T.* (0222) 590590. HTV West, The Television Centre, Bristol, BS4 3HG *T.* (0272) 778366. 99 Baker Street, London, W1M 2AJ *T.* 01-486 4311. The Television Centre, Pontcanna, Cardiff CF1 9XL *T.* (0222) 590590. The Civic Centre, Mold, Clwyd CG7 1YA *T.* (0352) 55331. Provides programmes for Wales and West of England during the whole week. Produces programmes for home and international sales.

LWT, South Bank TV Centre, London, SE1 9LT *T.* 01-261 3434. Provides programmes for London area from Friday 5.15 p.m. to Sunday Close Down.

Scottish Television, PLC, Cowcaddens, Glasgow, G2 3PR *T.* 041-332 9999. The Gateway, Edinburgh, EH7 4AH *T.* 031-557 4554. Provides programmes for Central Scotland during the whole week, *Material:* Scripts for contemporary plays and ideas and formats for programmes with a Scottish or international flavour. Approach in the first instance to the Head of Drama, Robert Love.

Television South PLC (TVS), Television Centre, Southampton, SO9 5HZ *T.* (0703) 34211; Television Centre, Vinters Park, Maidstone ME14 5NZ *T.* (0622) 54945 and 60-61 Buckingham Gate, London, SW1 *T.* 01-828 9898. Provides programmes for the South and South East of England during the whole week.

Thames Television, PLC, Thames Television House, 306 Euston Road, London, NW1 3BB *T.* 01-387 9494 (Features). Teddington Lock, Teddington, Middlesex, TW11 9NT *T.* 01-977 3252 (Drama/Light Entertainment). Provides programmes for the London area from Monday to Friday 5.15 p.m.
Material required: Drama Department: Most of the material produced by the Drama Department is specially commissioned, and it is advisable that a preliminary letter should be sent before submitting any unsolicited scripts. Correspondence should be addressed to Charlotte Hargreaves, Script Executive.
Light Entertainment Department: Material is generally specially commissioned but the Light Entertainment Department invites scripts for 30-minute situation comedies, also material for sketch shows. Submissions to Light Entertainment, Thames Television PLC.

TSW-Television South West Ltd., Derry's Cross, Plymouth PL1 2SP *T.* (0752) 663322. Provides programmes for South-West England during the whole week.

Tyne Tees Television, Ltd., The Television Centre, City Road, Newcastle upon Tyne, NE1 2AL *T.* (091) 261 0181. London: 15 Bloomsbury Square, London WC1A 2LJ *T.* 01-405 8474. Provides programmes for North-East England during the whole week.

Ulster Television, plc, Havelock House, Ormeau Road, Belfast, BT7 1EB *T.* (0232) 228122. 6 York Street, London, W1H 1FA *T.* 01-486 5211. Provides programmes for Northern Ireland during the whole week. Company staff provide majority of scripts, but occasionally they are commissioned from other sources.

Yorkshire Television, Ltd., The Television Centre, Leeds, LS3 1JS *T.* (0532) 438283. *Telex:* 557232. Television House, 32 Bedford Row, London, WC1R 4HE *T.* 01-242 1666. *Telex:* 295386. Yorkshire Television is a Network Company which produces many programmes for the ITV Network and the Yorkshire area throughout the week.

Independent Television News, Ltd., ITN House, 48 Wells Street, London, W1P 4DE *T.* 01-637 2424. Provides the national and international news programmes for all ITV areas.

TV-am Limited, Breakfast Television Centre, Hawley Crescent, London, NW1 8EF *T.* 01-267 4300. A national service of Independent breakfast television seven days a week.

INDEPENDENT LOCAL RADIO

There is no central commissioning of scripted material on behalf of the many Independent Local Radio companies. Several of the major companies commission and produce dramatic works and some also undertake scripted readings. Further details can be obtained from the **Association of Independent Radio Contractors,** Regina House, 259-269 Old Marylebone Road, London NW1 5RA *T.* 01-262 6681.

ILR Aberdeen: NorthSound Radio, 45 Kings Gate, Aberdeen, AB2 6BL *T.* (0224) 632234.

ILR Ayr: West Sound, Radio House, 54 Holmston Road, Ayr, KA7 3BD *T.* (0292) 283662.

ILR Belfast: Downtown Radio, P.O. Box 96, Kiltonga Industrial Estate, Newtownards, Northern Ireland, BT23 4ES *T.* (0247) 815555.

ILR Birmingham: BRMB Radio, P.O. Box 555, Radio House, Aston Road North, Aston, Birmingham, B6 4BX *T.* 021-359 4481-9.

ILR Bournemouth: Two Counties Radio, 5-7 Southcote Road, Bournemouth, BH1 3LR *T.* (0202) 294881.

ILR Bradford: Pennine Radio, P.O. Box 235, Pennine House, Forster Square, Bradford, BD1 5NP *T.* (0274) 731521.

ILR Brighton: Southern Sound, Radio House, Franklin Road, Portslade, Sussex BN4 2SS *T.* (0273) 422288.

ILR Bristol: GWR, P.O. Box 963 Watershed, Canons Road, Bristol, BS99 7SN *T.* (0272) 279900.

ILR Bury St. Edmunds: Saxon Radio, Long Brackland, Bury St. Edmunds, Suffolk IP33 1JY *T.* (0284) 701511.

ILR Cardiff: Red Dragon Radio, Radio House, West Canal Wharf, Cardiff, CF1 5JX *T.* (0222) 384041.

ILR Coventry: Mercia Sound, Hertford Place, Coventry, CV1 3TT *T.* (0203) 28451.

ILR Doncaster: Radio Hallam, P.O. Box 194, Hartshead, Sheffield, S1 1GP *T.* (0742) 71188.

ILR Dundee/Perth: Radio Tay, P.O. Box 123, Dundee, DD1 9UF *T.* (0382) 29551.

ILR East Kent: Invicta Radio, 15 Station Road East, Canterbury CT1 2RB *T.* (0227) 67661.

ILR Edinburgh: Radio Forth, Forth House, Forth Street, Edinburgh, EH1 3LF *T.* 031-556 9255.

ILR Exeter/Torbay: DevonAir Radio, The Studio Centre, 35-37 St. David's Hill, Exeter, EX4 4DA *T.* (0392) 30703.

ILR Glasgow: Radio Clyde, Clydebank Business Park, Clydebank, Glasgow G81 2RX *T.* 041-941 1111.

ILR Gloucester & Cheltenham: Severn Sound, P.O. Box 388, Old Talbot House, 67 Southgate Street, Gloucester, GL1 1TX *T.* (0452) 423791.

ILR Great Yarmouth & Norwich: Radio Broadland, St. George's Plain, Colegate, Norwich NR3 1DD *T.* (0603) 630621.

ILR Guildford: County Sound, The Friary, Guildford, Surrey, GU1 4YX *T.* (0483) 505566.

ILR Hereford/Worcester: Radio Wyvern, 5-6 Barbourne Terrace, Worcester WR1 3JM *T.* (0905) 612212.

ILR Humberside: Viking Radio, Commercial Road, Hull HU1 2SA *T.* (0482) 25141.

ILR Inverness, Moray Firth Radio, P.O. Box 271, Inverness, IV3 6SF *T.* (0463) 224433.

ILR Ipswich: Radio Orwell, Electric House, Lloyds Avenue, Ipswich, IP1 3HZ *T.* (0473) 216971.

ILR Leeds: Radio Aire, P.O. Box 362, Leeds, LS3 1LR *T.* (0532) 452299.

ILR Leicester: Leicester Sound, Granville House, Granville Road, Leicester LE1 7RW *T.* (0533) 551616.

ILR Liverpool: Radio City, P.O. Box 194, 8-10 Stanley Street, Liverpool, L69 1LD *T.* 051-227 5100.

ILR London (General and Entertainment Service): Capital Radio, Euston Tower, London, NW1 3DR *T.* 01-388 1288.

ILR London (News & Information Service): London Broadcasting Company (LBC), Gough Square, London, EC4P 4LP *T.* 01-353 1010.

ILR Luton/Bedford: Chiltern Radio, Chiltern Road, Dunstable, Bedfordshire, LU6 1HQ *T.* (0582) 666001.

ILR Maidstone & Medway: Invicta Radio, 37 Earl Street, Maidstone, ME14 1PS *T.* (0622) 679061.

ILR Manchester: Piccadilly Radio, 127-131 The Piazza, Piccadilly Plaza, Manchester, M1 4AW *T.* 061-236 9913.

ILR Northampton: Hereward Road, P.O. Box 1557, 73 Abington Street, Northampton NN1 2HW.

ILR Nottingham: Radio Trent, 29-31 Castle Gate, Nottingham, NG1 7AP *T.* (0602) 581731.

ILR Peterborough: Hereward Radio, P.O. Box 225, 114 Bridge Street, Peterborough, Cambs., PE1 1JX *T.* (0733) 46225.

ILR Plymouth: Plymouth Sound, Earl's Acre, Alma Road, Plymouth, PL3 4HX *T.* (0752) 27272.

ILR Portsmouth: Radio Victory, P.O. Box 257, 247 Fratton Road, Portsmouth, PO1 5RT *T.* (0705) 827799.

ILR Preston & Blackpool: Red Rose Radio, P.O.Box 301, St. Paul's Square, Preston, Lancashire, PR1 1YE *T.* (0772) 556301.

ILR Reading: Radio 210 Thames Valley, P.O. Box 210, Reading, RG3 5RZ *T.* (0734) 413131.

ILR Reigate & Crawley: Radio Mercury, Broadfield House, Brighton Road, Crawley RH11 9TT *T.* (0293) 519161.

ILR Sheffield & Rotherham: Radio Hallam, P.O. Box 194, Hartshead, Sheffield, S1 1GP *T.* (0742) 71188.

ILR Southend/Chelmsford: Essex Radio, Radio House, Clifftown Road, Southend-on-Sea, Essex, SS1 1SX *T.* (0702) 333711.

ILR Stoke-on-Trent: Signal Radio, Studio 257, 67-73 Stoke Road, Stoke-on-Trent, Staffordshire ST4 2SR *T.* (0782) 417111.

ILR Swansea: Swansea Sound, Victoria Road, Gowerton, Swansea, SA4 3AB *T.* (0792) 893751.

ILR Swindon/West Wiltshire: GWR, Old Lime Kiln, High Street, Wootton Bassett, Swindon, Wiltshire, SN4 7EX *T.* (0793) 853222.

ILR Teesside: Radio Tees, 74 Dovecot Street, Stockton-on-Tees, Cleveland, TS18 1HB *T.* (0642) 615111.

ILR Tyne & Wear: Metro Radio, Long Rigg, Swalwell, Newcastle upon Tyne, NE99 1BB *T.* (0632) 883131.

ILR Wolverhampton & Black Country: Beacon Radio, P.O. Box 303, 267 Tettenhall Road, Wolverhampton, WV6 0DQ *T.* (0902) 757211.

ILR Wrexham & Deeside: Marcher Sound/Sain-Y-Gororau, The Studios, Mold Road, Gwersyllt, Wrexham, Clwyd LL11 4AF *T.* (0978) 752202.

Independent Radio News (IRN). A subsidiary of LBC which acts as a news agency for all other ILR Companies by providing spoken and other live material and a teleprinter service. Address as LBC above.

OVERSEAS RADIO AND TELEVISION COMPANIES

AUSTRALIA

Australian Broadcasting Corporation, Box 9994, GPO, Sydney, NSW 2001. Manager for Europe: Australian Broadcasting Corporation, 54 Portland Place, London, W1N 4DY. The Australian Broadcasting Corporation is a statutory authority established by Act of Parliament and responsible to Parliament. It provides television and radio programmes in the national broadcasting service and operates Radio Australia. It operates six symphony orchestras and stages concerts throughout Australia.

ABC television restricts its production resources to work closely related to the Australian environment. For this reason scripts submitted from outside Australia in the field of television drama and short stories have little chance of success. ABC radio also looks principally to Australian writers for the basis of its drama output. However, ABC radio is interested in reading or auditioning new creative material of a high quality from overseas sources and this may be submitted in script or taped form. No journalistic material is required. Talks on international affairs are commissioned.

Federation of Australian Commercial Television Stations, 13th Floor, 447 Kent Street, Sydney, 2000. *T.* 264 5577. *T.A.* Facts, Sydney. There are at present 50 commercial television stations in Australia; all are members of FACTS. Our enquiries thus far show that the following six stations accept freelance material:

ATN Channel 7, Amalgamated Television Services Pty. Ltd., Television Centre, Epping, NSW 2121. *T.* 858-7777. *T.A.* Telecentre, Sydney. *Telex:* AA 20250. Willing to consider original television material of all types, especially 60 minute drama series, 30 minute situation-comedy series and 30 minute children's drama series if they have received a 'C' classification. Material should have an *Australian* background and deal with *Australian* characters. For series submit sample script with some future story-lines.

BTQ Channel 7, Brisbane TV Limited, Sir Samuel Griffith Drive, Mt. Coot-Tha, GPO Box 604, Brisbane 4001. *T.* (07)369 7777. *T.A.* Beeteeque. Writers should be Australian-based. Children's Educational-type series, children's entertainment programmes and local drama (Queensland writers only).

HSV Channel 7, Herald-Sun Television Pty. Ltd., GPO Box 215D, Melbourne, Victoria 3001. *T.* 03-699-7777. For requirements see entry for ATN Channel 7.

National Nine Network (TCN 9 Sydney; GTV 9 Melbourne; QTQ, 9 Brisbane; NWS 9 Adelaide; STW 9 Perth), 3rd Floor, 54 Park Street, Sydney, NSW 2000. *T.* 268-0666. *Telex:* A20514. *Executive Vice-President:* Lynton Taylor. Also **P.B.L. Productions.** *Chairman:* Lynton Taylor. *Executive Producer:* Jane Deknatel. Interested in receiving material from freelance writers strictly on the basis of payment for material or ideas used. No necessity for writers to be Australian-based, but membership of the Australian Writers' Guild is helpful.

NSW Channel 9, Southern Television Corporation Pty. Ltd., 202 Tynte Street, PO Box 9, North Adelaide, South Australia 5006. *T.* 267 0111. *T.A.* Newsnine, Adelaide. *Telex:* 82238. *Fax:* (08) 267-3996.

STW Channel 9, Swan Television & Radio Broadcasters Limited, PO Box 99, Tuart Hill, Western Australia 6060. *T.* 349 9999. *T.A.* Swantel, Perth. *Telex:* AA92142. *Fax:* (09) 349-2110. Writers should be Australian-based.

CANADA

Canadian Broadcasting Corporation, PO Box 500, Station 'A', Toronto, M5W 1E6 Ontario. *T.* 416-925-3311.

Canadian Radio-television and Telecommunications Commission, Ottawa, Ontario, K1A 0N2 *General information: T.* (819) 997-0313—the federal authority which regulates telecommunications and the broadcasting system in Canada.

INDIA

All India Radio, Broadcasting House, Parliament Street, New Delhi, 110 001, is a part of the Ministry of Information and Broadcasting of the Government of India which operates the broadcasting network in the country. There are 90 centres covering almost the entire area of the country and catering for the various social, cultural and linguistic needs of the people. Programmes consist of music, talks, plays, discussions, documentary features and special audience programmes for women, children, industrial workers and rural audience.
External Services Division of All India Radio broadcasts programmes in 25 languages. Programmes consist of news, daily commentary and press review, talks, interviews, discussions and music, mainly Indian (classical, light, film and folk). These are broadcast in two major services: General Overseas Service in English, and the Urdu Service. The West Asian service broadcasts programmes in Arabic, Dari, Persian, Pushtu and Baluchi. East African countries are served by the Swahili service. The French service is directed to South East Asia and North West Africa. Other area-oriented services are in Russian, Burmese, Chinese, Indonesian, Sinhala, Thai, Nepali and Tibetan languages. For Indians abroad, there are services in Bengali, Gujarati, Hindi, Konkani, Punjabi, Sindhi, Tamil and Urdu. The object of these programmes is to entertain Indians abroad and keep them in touch with the events and developments in India. Also a special weekly programme for ethnic Indians in U.S.A., Canada and U.K.
Programmes for the youth or 'Yuva Vani' are broadcast from many stations of All India Radio. This service is mainly for the youth by the youth.
The Commercial Service was introduced from AIR Bombay-Pune-Nagpur on November 1, 1967 and it is now being broadcast on 31 AIR stations. Sponsored programmes were first introduced in the Bombay-Pune-Nagpur beam in May, 1970. Later on the programmes were extended to all the 31 Commercial Centres. Commercial advertisements were introduced on the Primary Channel in 1982.

Television: There are 24 television centres.

IRELAND

Radio Telefís Eireann, Donnybrook, Dublin 4. *T.* 693111. *Telex:* 25268. The Irish national broadcasting service operating radio and television.
Television: script requirements: original television plays, minimum length 52 minutes, preferably set in Ireland or of strong Irish interest. Plays should be sent to the Head of Drama. Before submitting material to Current Affairs, Features, or Young People's programmes, authors are advised to write to the department in question.
Radio: talks and short stories (length 14 minutes) in Irish or English suitable for broadcasting: features, dramatic or narrative and plays are welcomed and paid for according to merit. Plays should run 30, 45, 60, 75 or 90 minutes. MSS. should be addressed as follows: R.T.E., Radio 1, Radio Centre, Donnybrook, Dublin 4.

OVERSEAS RADIO AND TELEVISION COMPANIES 239

At present there is no independent local radio or commercial television in the Republic of Ireland.

NEW ZEALAND

Broadcasting Corporation of New Zealand, PO Box 98, Wellington. *T.* (04) 721-777. *Telex:* NZ31031. *Chairman:* Hugh Rennie. *Chief Executive:* Nigel Dick. The BCNZ operates a radio service **Radio New Zealand (RNZ)** and a television service **Television New Zealand (TVNZ).** The BCNZ publishes a weekly magazine, the *Listener,* and administers the New Zealand Symphony Orchestra.

Radio New Zealand, The Director-General, Beverley Wakem, PO Box 2092, Wellington, C1. *T.* 721-777. *Telex:* NZ31031. A 24 hour service of the Broadcasting Corporation of New Zealand controlling three public radio networks (one commercial), and also a limited shortwave service directed primarily to the Southwest Pacific Islands and Southeastern Australia.

Television New Zealand. The Director-General, Julian Mounter, PO Box 3819, Auckland. *T.* 770630. Runs two networks, Television One and Television Two, which provide two equally attractive complementary programmes. The audience split between the two networks is 50/50. Both networks transmit morning, afternoon and evening, seven days a week, and more than one-third of programme content is produced in New Zealand.

SOUTH AFRICA

South African Broadcasting Corporation, PO Box 8606, Johannesburg 2000. *T.* 714-9111. The South African Broadcasting Corporation, established in terms of the Broadcasting Act No. 22 of 1936 as amended, operates five national networks: Radio South Africa, Radio Suid-Afrika, Radio 5, Radio Orion, and Radio Allegro, and seven regional services, Radio Highveld, Radio Port Natal, Radio Good Hope, Radio Lotus, Radio Jacaranda, Radio Algoa, Radio Oranje. The nine radio services in Nguni and Sotho languages broadcast in Zulu, Xhosa, Southern Sotho, Northern Sotho, Tswana, Venda, Tsonga, Swazi and Ndebele. The SABC introduced an External Service on May 1st 1966 known as Radio RSA, *The Voice of South Africa* which transmits programmes to all corners of the world. This service echoes around the world in eleven languages to carry a positive and objective message about South Africa, its peoples and their achievements, their culture, tradition and ideals. The languages used are English, Afrikaans, Portuguese, French, German, Dutch, ChiChewa, Swahili, Lozi, Tsonga and Spanish.

Plays.—Most types are produced—classical and modern dramas, comedies and thrillers, original radio plays and adaptations of stories, etc. Contributions are welcomed in all sections. The most convenient lengths are 30, 60 and 90 minutes. The Afrikaans network also accepts high quality material for translation. Programmes are typical of modern commercial radio, and serials of 15-minute episodes are widely used. Series of self-contained episodes of 15, 30 or 60 minutes are also acceptable. Variety programmes of 30 minutes' duration are always in demand.

Feature Programmes.—Material of topical, scientific and historical interest of 30 to 60 minutes' duration is welcomed.

Talks.—Most are commissioned locally, but outstanding material of particular interest may be submitted. Most suitable length is 5, 10 and 15 minutes.

Short Stories.—There are occasional openings for short stories of 1500-1800 words.

Light Entertainment.—Variety material, light entertainment scripts, and light plays with music may be submitted. The SABC particularly needs first-class variety material.

Youth and Children's Programmes.—Plays, talks, stories, and serials may be submitted. Lengths: plays, up to 15 minutes, and 30 minutes for youth; stories, from 5 to 10 minutes.

It should be stressed that all outside contributors should take into consideration the fact that Radio South Africa caters for a South African public, a public, that is to say, with its own needs, ideas, and tastes.

Television: There are four television services in seven languages: TV1 transmits in English and Afrikaans; TV2 transmits in Zulu and Xhosa; TV3 transmits in South Sotho, North Sotho and Tswana and TV4 is an entertainment and sports channel transmitting in English and Afrikaans.

UNITED STATES

American Broadcasting Company, ABC News, 8 Carburton Street, London, W1P 7DT *T.* 01-637 9222.

CBS News, European Broadcast Centre, 68 Knightsbridge, London, SW1X 7LL *T.* 01-581 4801. *Telex:* 916319.

NBC News Worldwide, Inc., 8 Bedford Avenue, London, WC1B 3NQ *T.* 01-637 8655. *Telex:* 27765.

LITERARY AGENTS

The Association of Authors' Agents (see **Societies**) is the trade association of British agents. Members meet regularly and commit themselves to observe a code of practice in the conduct of their business. They are designated with an asterisk in the following list. All agents listed below were circulated with a questionnaire with a view to providing pertinent information and are asked to keep this information up to date.

It should be noted that most agents do not charge a fee for marketing or placing manuscripts. Some firms charge a reading fee which is refunded on acceptance of the material. Most agents in this list will suggest revision of worth-while manuscripts where necessary, suggesting in the first instance that revision should be done by the author. In certain cases, an agency is prepared to recommend a qualified person not connected with their agency to undertake revision. In a few cases where agencies themselves are prepared to undertake revision, this fact is clearly stated. In their own interests writers are strongly recommended to think twice before agreeing to pay for revision. Some agents are prepared to give an author a report and advice on a MS. and they make an appropriate charge for this. The reference to 'Short MSS.' in many of the following entries is almost invariably to short stories and not to journalistic articles.

Literary agents exist to sell saleable material. It must be remembered that, while they are looking for new writers and are often prepared to take immense pains with a writer whose work, in their opinion, shows potential quality or distinctive promise, agents do not exist to teach people how to write. Short manuscripts, unless they are of an exceptional nature, are unlikely to be profitable or even to pay an agent for the work involved. Writers must not expect agents, publishers or editors to comment at length on unsuitable work submitted to them, although often they are asked to do so. Every writer must expect disappointments, especially at the outset of his career, but if he has something to say and knows how to say it, then eventually (if he is patient) he will learn how to satisfy an editor's requirements, or alternatively he will learn that he should give up attempting to write and turn to some other form of activity. He must not expect other people to tell him his mistakes, although not infrequently a new writer is helped in this way by an agent, editor or publisher who has detected a spark of promise in a manuscript submitted to him.

If a writer of some proven ability is contemplating using an agent, he is advised in his own interests *to write a preliminary letter* to ascertain whether the agent will consider him as a potential client. He should also enquire the agent's terms if they are not given in the entry in the following pages. Reputable agents do not accept work unless they consider it to be of a marketable standard and an author submitting work to an agent for the first time *should therefore enclose return postage*. It is also advisable for a writer not to send work to more than one agent at the same time. This is not only a waste of time, but could cause complications.

This list of literary agents does not purport to be exhaustive. If any who are not included would like to receive a copy of the questionnaire and to be considered for inclusion, application should be made to the publishers.

*Membership of The Association of Authors' Agents.

A & B Personal Management Ltd., (1982). *Directors:* R. W. Ellis, P. R. Ellis. 5th Floor, Plaza Suite, 114 Jermyn Street, London, SW1Y 6HJ. *T.* 01-839 4433. *Telex:* 21901 Jwppl G. *T.A.* Abpersman London SW1.
  Full-length and short MSS. (home 12½%, overseas 15%). Theatre, films, television, radio (12½%). No reading fee, but return postage required.

*Alexander, Jacintha, Associates (1981), 47 Emperor's Gate, London, SW7 4HJ. *T.* 01-373 9258. *Proprietor:* Jacintha Alexander; *Associate:* Julian Alexander. Full length MSS (home 15%, US 20%, translations 20%). Theatre, films, television, radio (10%). Will suggest revision. Works in conjunction with agents in New York and Europe. No reading fee, but preliminary letter with S.A.E. essential.

Aske, Stephen, Ltd. (1929). *Director:* Rowena McKelvie, Wildacre, The Warren, Ashtead, Surrey, KT21 2SL. *T.* Ashtead 74475.
Full-length MSS. (home 10%, overseas 20%). Theatre, films, television, sound broadcasting (10%). Represented in the USA and works in conjunction with agents in most European countries. No reading fee.

Authors' Alliance (1911). Mrs. Deborah Greenep, 23 Mill Hill, Alresford, Hants, S024 9DD.
Full-length MSS. (home and overseas 10%). Theatre (10%), films (10%), television and sound broadcasting (10%). Does not accept articles or short stories. No reading fee. Preliminary enquiry. S.A.E. please.

*Blake Friedmann Literary, TV & Film Agency (1977). *Directors:* Carole Blake, Julian Friedmann. 37-41 Gower Street, London WC1E 6HH *T.* 01-631 4331. *Telex:* 27950 ref. 3820.
Full-length MSS. fiction and non-fiction, no poetry or plays, (home 15%, overseas 20%). Specialise in film, television and video rights; place journalism and short stories. Represented in Europe, Canada, South America, Japan; and in USA by Roslyn Targ Literary Agency Inc. Preliminary letter and synopsis preferred. No reading fee.

Bolt, David, Associates, 12 Heath Drive, Send, Surrey, GU23 7EP. *T.* Woking (04862) 21118.
Full-length MSS. (home 10%, overseas 19%; all other rights including film, video and television 10%). No unsolicited short stories or play scripts. Will sometimes suggest revision. Works in association with overseas agencies worldwide. Preliminary letter preferred.

Burston, Diane (1984), 46 Cromwell Avenue, Highgate, London N6 5HL *T.* 01-340 6130.
Full-length and short MSS (home 10%, overseas 20%, USA 15%). Television, radio (10%). No reading fee.

Byrne, Myles (Starfinder Agency). *Director:* Myles Byrne, Suite 5, Linosa Court, 81 Pevensey Road, Eastbourne, East Sussex BN22 8AD *T.* (0323) 643231.
Full length MSS. Theatre, film, radio, television, fiction, non-fiction, biography, autobiography. Not poetry or children's books. Preliminary synopsis preferred. S.A.E. essential with all scripts in case of return. Represented in European countries, U.S.A. and world coverage.

*Campbell Thomson & McLaughlin, Ltd. *Directors:* John McLaughlin, John Parker, Timothy Webb, Charlotte Bruton, Hal Cheetham. 31 Newington Green, London, N16 9PU *T.* 01-249 2971. *T.A.* Peterlaine, London, N16.
Full-length book MSS. (home 10%, overseas up to 20% including commission to foreign agent). No poetry, plays or television scripts or short stories. U.S.A. agents represented: Raines & Raines, 71 Park Avenue, New York, N.Y., 10016; The Fox Chase Agency, Inc., 401 East 34th Street, New York, N.Y., 10016. Representatives in most European countries. No reading fee, but return postage required. Subsidiary company: **Peter Janson-Smith Ltd.**

*Carnell Literary Agency (1951). Pamela Buckmaster, Danes Croft, Goose Lane, Little Hallingbury, Herts. CM22 7RG *T.* (0279) 723626.

All mss. except poetry. Specialises in science/fantasy fiction. Works in conjunction with many foreign agents. Home 10%, overseas 10% or 19% through sub-agent. No reading fee, but s.a.e. essential. Preliminary letter preferred.

Christy and Moore—see Sheil, Anthony, Associates, Ltd.

*Clarke, Serafina (1980), 98 Tunis Road, London W12 7EY *T.* 01-749 6979.
Full-length MSS. (home 10%, overseas 15-20%). Theatre, films, television, radio (10%). Works in conjunction with agents overseas. No reading fee, but preliminary letter and return postage essential.

*Clowes, Jonathan, Ltd. (1960). *Directors:* Jonathan Clowes, Ann Evans, Donald Carroll, Enyd Williams. 22 Prince Albert Road, London, NW1 7ST. *T.* 01-722 7674. *Telex:* 23973 Clowes G. *T.A.* Agenclow, London, NW1.
Full-length MSS. (home and overseas 10%). Theatre, films, television and sound broadcasting (10%). Works in association with agents in most foreign countries. No reading fee but preliminary letter essential.

Cochrane, Elspeth, Agency (1967). *Director:* Miss Elspeth Cochrane, 11-13 Orlando Road, London, SW4 0LE. *T.* 01-622 0314.
Full-length MSS. (home and overseas 10%). Theatre, films, television, sound broadcasting (10%). No reading fee.

Coles, Dianne, Literary Agency (1980). *Directors:* Dianne Coles, J. C. Reynolds (Managing). The Old Malthouse, St. John's Road, Banbury, Oxfordshire, OX16 8HX. *T.* Banbury (0295) 50731.
Full-length MSS., fiction and non-fiction (home and overseas 10%). No plays, children's books, articles or short stories. No reading fee, but return postage must be enclosed with MS. Preliminary letter advisable.

Colin, Rosica, Limited (1949). *Directors:* Sylvie Marston, Joanna Marston. 1 Clareville Grove Mews, London, SW7 5AH. *T.* 01-370 1080. *T.A.* Colrep, London, SW7.
All full-length MSS. (home 10%, overseas 20%). Theatre, films, television and sound broadcasting (10%). Works in U.S.A., European countries and overseas. No reading fee.

Conway-Gordon, Jane, (1982), 213 Westbourne Grove, London W11 2SE. *T.* 01-229 4451.
Full length mss, theatre, films, television, radio (home 10%, overseas 20%). Represented in all foreign countries. No reading fee but preliminary letter and return postage essential.

Creative Agency, The, (1984). *Partners:* Tristan Ashman, Toni Ashman, 30 Rathmore Road, London SE7 7QW. *T.* 01-305 0654.
Full-length MSS (home 10%, overseas 20%). Television (20%). Works in conjunction with agents throughout the world. No reading fee.

*Crew, Rupert, Limited (1927). *Directors:* F. R. Crew, K. A. Crew, D. Montgomery, S. Russell. King's Mews, London, WC1N 2JA. *T.* 01-242 8586. *T.A.* Authorship, Holb., London.
International business management for authors and feature writers desiring world representation by a highly geared, personal service, available only to a limited clientele. Preliminary letter. Commission 10%-20% by arrangement. No reading fees. Also acts independently as publishers' consultants.

Cruickshank, Harriet (1983), 97 Old South Lambeth Road, London SW8 1XU *T.* 01-735 2933.
Full-length and short MSS (home 10%, overseas varies). Theatre, films, television, radio (10%). Works with agents abroad.

Curtis Brown. *Directors:* Peter Murphy and Michael Shaw (Joint Managing), Diana Baring, Andrew Best, Felicity Bryan, Tim Curnow (Australia), Sue Freathy, George Greenfield, Robert Loder, Anne McDermid, Anthea Morton-Saner, Elizabeth Stevens. 162-168 Regent Street, London W1R 5TB *T.* 01-437 9700. *Telex:* 261536. *Cables:* Browncurt, London W1. Part owner with Curtis Brown Ltd, New York, of Curtis Brown Associaties Ltd., 10 Astor Place, New York, N.Y. 10003. *T.* 212-473 5400, and of Curtis Brown Ltd., 303 Davenport Road, Toronto, Ontario, Canada M5R 1K5 *T.* (416) 922-9006. Sole owner of Curtis Brown (Australia) Pty. Ltd., 27 Union Street or P.O. Box 19, Paddington, Sydney, N.S.W. 2021, Australia. *T.* (612) 331 5301.
Agents for the negotiation in all markets of novels, general non-fiction, children's books, academic, professional and specialist works and associated rights. (Home 10%, USA 15%, Canada and Foreign 20%). Preliminary letter essential; no reading fee. MSS. for films, theatre, television and radio. Also agents for directors and designers.

Davis-Poynter, Reg, 118 St. Pancras, Chichester, West Sussex PO19 4LH *T.* (0243) 779047 and 11 Bolt Court, Fleet Street, London EC4A 3DQ *T.* 01-353 9365.
Full-length MSS (home 15%, overseas 20%). Theatre, films, television, radio (10%). Works with agents in Germany, Scandinavia, Japan, Italy, France, USA. No reading fee but preliminary letter and return postage essential. Also acts as publishing consultant.

De Wolfe, Felix (1946). *Principal:* Felix de Wolfe. 1 Robert Street, Adelphi, London, WC2N 6BH. *T.* 01-930 7514. *T.A.* Hayhill, London, WC2.
Theatre, films, television, sound broadcasting, fiction. Works in conjunction with many foreign agencies.

Dorman, John (1983), The Old Parsonage, Lower Brailes, Banbury, Oxon, OX15 5HT *T.* Brailes (0608 85) 584.
Non-fiction only, specializing in sport, leisure, health and fitness. Full-length and short MSS (home 10%, overseas 15%). Theatre, films, television, radio (15%). No reading fee, but preliminary letter essential.

Eady, Toby, Associates Ltd (1967). *Directors:* Toby Eady, M. A. Siepmann. *Associates:* Celestria Noel, Philip Pollock, Alex de Jonge. 5 Gledhow Gardens, London SW5 0BL *T.* 01-370 6292.
Full length and short MSS (home 10%, overseas 15-20%). Theatre, films, television, radio (10%). *USA office:* P.O. Box 1556, Fdr Station, New York NY 10150. No reading fee.

E.T.G. (English Theatre Guild, Ltd.), (1938) part of **Chappell Music Ltd.,** 129 Park Street, London W1Y 3FA *T.* 01-629 7600.
Specialise in stage plays. Occasional radio, film and television. Works in conjunction with overseas agents. Preliminary letter essential.

Fact & Fiction Agency Ltd. *Directors:* Roy Lomax, Vera Lomax. 16 Greenway Close, London, NW9 5AZ. *T.* 01-205 5716.
Television, radio (home 10%, overseas 15%). By introduction only.

*Farquharson, John, Ltd. (1919). *Directors:* George Greenfield, Vivienne Schuster, Vanessa Holt, Michael Shaw, Jane Gelfman (USA). 162-168 Regent Street, London W1R 5TB *T.* 01-437 9700.
Full-length MSS. (home 10%, overseas 20% including commission to foreign agents). U.S.A. Branch: John Farquharson Ltd., 250 West 57th Street, New York, N.Y. 10107. Works in conjunction with agents throughout the world. No reading fee.

Film Link Literary Agency (1979). *Director:* Yvonne Heather, 31 Oakdene Drive, Tolworth, Surrey, KT5 9NH. *T.* 01-330 3182.
Full-length MSS. (home 10%, overseas 15-20%). No short stories or poetry. Will suggest revision where appropriate. Works in conjunction with overseas agents. Preliminary letter, synopsis and S.A.E. essential.

Film Rights Ltd (1932). *Directors:* D. M. Sims, Maurice Lambert, Laurence Fitch. 4 New Burlington Place, Regent Street, London W1X 2AS. *T.* 01-437 7151.
Theatre, films, television and sound broadcasting (10%). Represented in U.S.A. and abroad.

Fitch, Laurence, Ltd. (1952) (incorporating The London Play Company) (1922). *Directors:* F. H. L. Fitch, L. Ruscombe-King, Joan Potts, W. Corlett. 4 New Burlington Place, Regent Street, London, W1X 2AS. *T.* 01-437 7151.
Theatre, films, television and sound broadcasting. Also works with several agencies in New York and in Europe.

Foster, Jill, Ltd. (1976). *Director:* Jill Foster, 35 Brompton Road, London, SW3 1DE. *T.* 01-581 0084/5.
Full-length and short MSS. (10%). No novels or short stories. Theatre, films, television, sound broadcasting (10%). No reading fee. Preliminary letter preferred.

*****Fraser & Dunlop Scripts, Ltd.** (1959)—in association with Robin Dalton Associates, and with Fraser & Dunlop, Ltd. (1949). Kenneth Ewing, Richard Wakeley, Tim Corrie, Mark Lucas. 91 Regent Street, London, W1R 8RU. *T.* 01-734 7311. *Telex:* 28965 Script G. *T.A.* Frasanlop London.
Full-length MSS. (home 10%, overseas 10-20%, including any overseas agent's commission). Theatre, films, television and sound broadcasting (10%). Negotiates with several U.S. agencies. No reading fee.

French (John) Artists Agency, Ltd. *Director:* John French. 26-28 Binney Street, London, W1Y 1YN *T.* 01-629 4159.
All MSS, home and overseas (10%). Theatre, films, television, radio (10%). Reading service available, details on application. S.A.E. must be enclosed with all MSS.

Gillon Aitken Ltd., *Director:* Gillon Aitken. 29 Fernshaw Road, London, SW10. *T.* 01-351 7561.
Full-length MSS. (home 10%, U.S.A. 15%, translations 20%). Theatre, films, television, radio (10%). Unheralded submissions not welcome.

Glass, Eric, Ltd. (1932). *Directors:* Eric Glass, Janet Crowley. 28 Berkeley Square, London W1X 6HD. *T.* 01-629 7162. *T.A.* Blancheric, London, W1. *Telex:* 296759 Kallin G; ref. 101.
Full-length MSS only. Theatre, films, television, and sound broadcasting. Will occasionally recommend someone for revision of promising material if the author is unable to undertake it. No reading fee. Sole represetatives of the French Society of Authors (Societé des Auteurs et Compositeurs Dramatiques).

Goodwin Associates (1977), 12 Rabbit Row, Kensington Church Street, London W8 4DX *T.* 01-299 8805.
Dramatic works only—theatre, films radio, TV.

Green, Christine, Author's Agent (1984), 8 Albany Mews, Albany Road, London SE5 0DQ *T.* 01-703 9285.
Full-length and short MSS. (home 10%, overseas 20%). Theatre, films, television, radio (10%). Works in conjunction with agencies in Europe and Scandinavia. No reading fee.

*Greene, Elaine, Ltd. (1962). *Directors:* Elaine Greene (U.S.A.), Ilsa Yardley, Timothy Webb. 31 Newington Green, Islington, London, N16 9PU. *T.* 01-249 2971. *T.A.* Peterlaine, London, N16.
Full-length MSS. (home 10%, U.S.A. 15%, translation rights 20%); film, television, sound broadcasting (10%). Works in conjunction with agencies in most countries. No reading fees. No unsolicited manuscripts accepted without an introductory letter from the author describing the work and unless return postage is included.

Gregory, Jane (1982), 4 Westwick Gardens, London W14 0BU *T.* 01-603 9998. *Telex:* 268141 Metmak G.
Full-length and short MSS (home 10%, overseas 20%). Films, television, radio (10%). No reading fee.

Grossman, David, Literary Agency Ltd. (1976). *Director:* David Grossman. 110-114 Clerkenwell Road, London EC1M 5SA *T.* 01-251 5046-7. *Telex:* 263404 Bk Biz G.
Full-length and short MSS. (home 10%, overseas 15-20% including foreign agent's commission). Theatre, films, television, radio (10%). Works in conjunction with agents in New York, Europe, Japan. No reading fee, but preliminary letter required.

Hall, June, Literary Agency (1979). *Proprietor:* Mrs. June Hall; *Associates:* Roger Schlesinger, Sara Fisher, Caroline Sheldon, 19 College Cross, London, N1 1PT. *T.* 01-609 5991.
Full-length MSS. only and no plays or poetry. Terms on application with s.a.e. Represented in all major foreign markets, and works in conjunction with agencies and publishers in U.S.A. No reading fee, return postage and preliminary letter essential.

Harrison, Alec, and Associates (1954). *Senior Partner:* Alec Harrison. International Press Centre, Shoe Lane, London, EC4A 3JB. *T.* Upminster (04022) 24523. *T.A.* Litalic, London, EC4.
Full-length MSS. (home 10%, overseas 19% where another agent is concerned). Short MSS. (home 15%, overseas 15%-25%). Films (10%), television and sound broadcasting (10% for series, 15% for single items). 'In the main, all the people we handle are professional writers who come to us on recommendation. The great bulk of the material we handle is non-fiction, such as educational books and autobiographies, which often have to be ghosted. Most of our work is commissioned. For syndication we work with literary agents in almost every country in the world.' No reading fee.

Hatton & Baker Ltd. (1980). *Directors:* Richard Hatton, Terence Baker, 18 Jermyn Street, London, SW1Y 6HN. *T.* 01-439 2971. *Telex:* 263026 Hatbak. Films, television, radio (10%). No reading fee.

Headline Enterprises Ltd. (1971). *Directors:* Malcolm Hamer, Jill Foster, 35 Brompton Road, London, SW3 1DE. *T.* 01-584 8568.
Full-length non-fiction MSS. (home up to 15%, overseas up to 20%). No reading fee.

*Heath, A. M. & Co., Ltd. (1919). *Directors:* Mark Hamilton, Michael Thomas, William Hamilton. 40-42 William IV Street, London, WC2N 4DD. *T.* 01-836 4271. *T.A.* Script, London, WC2. *Cables:* Script, London.
Full-length MSS. (home 10%, U.S.A. 15%, translation 20%). Theatre, films, television and sound broadcasting (15%). Agents in U.S.A. and all European countries and Japan. No reading fee.

Higham, David, Associates Ltd. (1935). *Directors:* Bruce Hunter, Jacqueline Korn, Anthony Crouch, John Rush, Elizabeth Cree, Anthony Goff. 5-8 Lower John Street, Golden Square, London, W1R 4HA. *T.* 01-437 7888. *Cables:* Highlit London, W1. *Telex:* 28910.
Agents for the negotiation of all rights in fiction, general non-fiction, children's books, plays, film and television scripts and academic works (home 10%, USA 15%, translation 19%). U.S.A. Associate Agency: Harold Ober Associates Inc. Represented in all foreign markets. Preliminary letter and return postage essential. No reading fee.

Hoskins, Valerie (1983). *Proprietor:* Valerie Hoskins. 10 Connaught Square, London W2 2HG *T.* 01-723 8066. *Telex:* 27475 Sepbof G.
Theatre, films, television and radio *only*. (10% home and maximum 20% overseas.) No reading fee, but SAE appreciated. Works in conjunction with overseas agents. Preliminary letter essential.

Howard, Theresa, Associates, (1984). *Proprietor:* Theresa Howard, B.A., 78 Killyon Road, Clapham, London, SW8 2XT. *T.* 01-627 3084.
Theatre, films, television, radio (home 10%, overseas 12½%). No fiction or general MSS. Dramatic Associate for Lawrence Pollinger Ltd and Carcanet Press. No reading fee but send S.A.E.

*****Hughes Massie Ltd.** (1912). *Directors:* Brian Stone, Gillon Aitken, Anne-Louise Fisher. 29 Fernshaw Road, London SW10 0TG *T.* 01-351 7561. *Telex:* 298391. Full-length MSS. (home 10%, U.S.A. 15%, translations 20%, including 10% to local agents). Theatre, films, television, sound broadcasting (10%). U.S.A. Associates: Harold Ober Associates Inc., 40 East 49th Street, New York 10017. Works in conjunction with agents in most European countries, Israel and Japan. No reading fee, but return postage and preliminary letter essential.

Imison, Michael, Playwrights Ltd (formerly Dr Jan Van Loewen Ltd). *Directors:* Michael Imison, M.A., Alan Brodie, B.A., LL.B., Candace Imison, B.A., 28 Almeida Street, London N1 1TD. *T.* 01-354 3174.
Specialise in stage plays, also cover radio, TV, film (home 10%, overseas 12½%), preliminary letter essential, no fiction or general MSS. New York Office: Michael Imison Playwrights Ltd., 105 West 70th Street, No. 1R, New York, N.Y. 10023. *T.* 212-874-2671. Australian Office: Michael Imison Playwrights Ltd., 98-106 Kippax Street, Surry Hills, Sydney, N.S.W. 2010. *T.* 212-2766. Represented in all major countries. No reading fee, but send S.A.E.

Intercontinental Literary Agency (1965). *Director:* Anthony Guest Gornall. 6-7 Buckingham Street, London, WC2N 6BJ. *T.* 01-839 1612. *T.A.* Interlitag. Concerned only with translation rights exclusively for all authors of A. D. Peters & Co., London, Harold Matson Co. Inc., New York, The Sterling Lord Agency, New York.

International Copyright Bureau Ltd. (1905). *Directors:* Joy Westendarp, J. C. H. Hadfield (Secretary), Suite 8, 26 Charing Cross Road, London WC2H 0DG *T.* 01-836 5912 *T.A.* Volscius London WC2.
Theatre, films, television, radio (home 10%, overseas 19%). Works in conjunction with agents in New York and most foreign countries. Preliminary letter essential.

International Literary Management (1969). *Directors:* Nicholas Thompson, Tessa Heron. Forest House, Horningsham, Warminster, Wiltshire BA12 7LW. *T.* Maiden Bradley (09853) 312.
Comprehensive management for writers. Commission by arrangement. No reading fees but professional readers' reports arranged on request. Please write or telephone before submitting material.

International Scripts (1979). *Directors:* H. P. Tanner, J. Lawson. *Agent:* Sheelagh Thomas. 1 Norland Square, Holland Park, London W11 4UE *T.* 01-229 0736.
Full-length and short MSS. (10% home, 20% overseas). First works 15%. Theatre, films, television, radio (20%). No poetry. Works with overseas agents world-wide.

Irvine, Mary (1974), 11 Upland Park Road, Oxford OX2 7RU *T.* (0865) 513570.
Full-length and short MSS (home 10%, USA 15%, translations 20%). Works with agents in USA, Europe, Japan. No reading fee. Preliminary letter and return postage required.

*****Johnson, John, (Authors Agent) Ltd.** (1956). Clerkenwell House, 45-47 Clerkenwell Green, London, EC1R 0HT. *T.* 01-251 0125. *T.A.* Litjohn London.
Full-length and short MSS. (home 10%, overseas 10%, if foreign agent is concerned maximum of 20%), theatre, television, sound broadcasting (10%). Works in conjunction with agents in US and many European countries. No reading fee, but send S.A.E. please.

Juvenilia (1973). *Proprietor:* Mrs. Rosemary Bromley, Avington, Winchester, Hants, SO21 1DB. *T.* (096278) 656.
Full-length MSS. for the children's market, fiction and non-fiction (home 10%, overseas from 15%). No verse. Short stories only if specifically for picture books, radio or TV. Theatre, films, television, radio (10%). No unsolicited MSS.; preliminary letter with S.A.E. and full details essential. No reading fee. Postage for acknowledgement and return of material imperative. Full production and design in association with Elizabeth Weaver Ltd.

*****Kelly, Frances, Agency** (1978). *Director:* Frances Kelly. 111 Clifton Road, Kingston-upon-Thames, Surrey KT2 6PL *T.* 01-549 7830.
Full-length and short MSS. (home 10%, overseas 20%). Television, radio (10%). Non-fiction: general and academic, reference and professional books; all subjects. *U.S. Associate:* The Balkin Agency, 850 West 176 Street, New York, N.Y. 10033. No reading fee, but no unsolicited MSS; return postage and preliminary letter requested.

Lemon & Durbridge Ltd., 24 Pottery Lane, Holland Park, London W11 4LZ *T.* 01-229 9216-7 and 727 1346. *Telex:* 27618 Author G.
Theatre, film, television, radio only (10%). No novels. Works in conjunction with agents in U.S.A. and all foreign countries. No reading fee, but return postage and preliminary letter essential.

Little, Christopher, Literary Agent (1976), 49 Queen Victoria Street, London, EC4N 4SA. *T.* 01-236 5881. *Telex:* 883968 Heads G.
Full-length MSS. (home 20%, overseas 20%). Films, television (20%). No reading fee.

Lloyd-George & Coward (1959). *Directors:* W. Lloyd-George, B. G. Coward, Nicolette Milnes Walker, M.B.E., 11-12 Fairfax Place, Dartmouth, Devon, TQ6 9AE. *T.* Dartmouth (080 43) 2448.
Full-length MSS. (home 10%, overseas 20%). No reading fee but return postage requested; preliminary letter advisable.

London Independent Books, Ltd. (1971). *Directors:* Carolyn Whitaker, Patrick Whitaker. 1A Montagu Mews North, London, W1H 1AJ. *T.* 01-935 8090. *T.A.* Trifem, London, W1.
Full-length MSS. (home 15%, overseas 20%). Films, television and sound broadcasting (15%). Will suggest revision of promising MSS. No reading fee.

*****London Management,** (1959). Heather Jeeves, Tony Peake. 235 Regent Street, London, W1A 2JT. *T.* 01-493 1610. *Telex:* 27498.

Full-length MSS fiction and non-fiction (home 10% U.S.A. and translation 20% including 10% to local agents). Theatre, films, television, sound broadcasting (10%). Preliminary letter and synopsis required. No reading fee.

MacLean Dubois (Writers & Agents) (1978). *Associates:* Charles MacLean, R. A. A. McCall-Smith, S. A. Scott, P. A. Maguire, R. F. C. Miers. 10 Rutland Square, Edinburgh EH1 2AS. *T.* 031-229-6185.
Full length and short MSS (home 10%, overseas 15%). Editing, copywriting and book packaging services also available.

***Marlu Literary Agency Ltd.** (1980). *Director:* Mary Hall Mayer, 26 Stratford Road, London, W8 6QD. *T.* 01-937 5161 and 6191. *Telex:* 268141 Metmak G.
Full-length MSS. (home 10%, overseas 20%). Will suggest revision. Represented in all major countries and works in conjunction with agents and publishers in USA. No reading fee but preliminary letter and return postage essential.

Marsh & Sheil Ltd., (1985), 43 Doughty Street, London WC1N 2LF. *T.* 01-405 7473. *Telex:* 946240 Cweasy G ref. 19008160(Easylink). Anthony Sheil, Paul Marsh, Gill Coleridge.
Translation rights only.

Marvin, Blanche, 21A St. John's Wood High Street, London, NW8 7NG. *T.* 01-722 2313.
Full-length MSS. (home and overseas 10%). Theatre, films, television, sound broadcasting (10%). No reading fee but postage extra. Return postage essential.

***MBA Literary Agents Ltd.** (1971). *Directors:* Diana Tyler, John Richard Parker, 45 Fitzroy Street, London, W1P 5HR. *T.* 01-387 2076.
Full-length MSS. (home 10%, overseas 20%). Theatre, television, radio (10%), films—negotiable. No reading fee. Works in conjunction with agents in most countries.

Milne, Richard, Limited (1956). *Directors:* R. M. Sharples, K. N. Sharples. 28 Makepeace Avenue, Highgate, London, N6 6EJ. *T.* 01-340 7007.
Specialising in scripts for films, television, sound broadcasting (10%). Unable to represent any additional authors at present.

Morris, William, Agency (U.K.) Ltd (1965). *Managing Director:* Steve Kenis. *Literary Department:* Lavinia Trevor. 31-32 Soho Square, London W1V 6AP *T.* 01-434 2191. *Telex:* 27928 Wmlnd G. *T.A.* Willmorris London.
Full-length MSS, fiction and non-fiction (home 10%, overseas 20%). Also theatre, film, television, radio (10%). *U.S. Office:* William Morris Inc., New York. No reading fee. Preliminary letter requested.

Mulvany, Jolie, Literary Agency (1979). *Director:* Jolie Mulvany (U.S.A.). 85c Linden Gardens, London, W2 4EU *T.* 01-229 8042. *T.A.* Literarybooks London W2.
Full-length adult book MSS. only. No poetry, short stories, articles or plays (home 10%, overseas 20%). Films, television, radio (10%; where co-agent is involved 15%). Will suggest revision. Agent for Ray Peekner Literary Agency, USA. Represented in Europe. No reading fee but return postage requested. Preliminary letter essential.

***Noach, Maggie, Literary Agency** (1982), 21 Redan Street, London W14 0AB *T.* 01-602 2451.
Full-length and short MSS (home 10%, overseas 20%). Films (10%-15%), television (15%), radio (10%). Works with agents in USA and most foreign countries. No reading fee, but preliminary letter essential.

***Nurnberg, Andrew, Associates Ltd.,** Clerkenwell House, 45-47 Clerkenwell Green, London, EC1R 0HT. *T.* 01-251 0321. *Cables:* Nurnbooks, London. *Telex:* 23353.

Specialising in the sale of translation rights of English and American authors into European languages.

*Owen, Deborah, Ltd. (1971). Deborah Owen, Judith Dooling, 78 Narrow Street, Limehouse, London, E14 8BP. *T.* 01-987 5119.
Full-length MSS. (home 10%, overseas 15%). All types of literary material except plays, scripts, children's books or poetry. No unsolicited MSS. without preliminary letter and S.A.E.

*Paterson, Mark & Associates (1955). *Proprietor:* Mark Paterson. 10 Brook Street, Wivenhoe, Colchester, Essex CO7 9DS *T.* (0206 22) 5433-4. *T.A.* Paterson, Colchester. *Telex:* 988805 Patem G.
Full-length MSS including clinical psychology and psychiatry (20% including subagent's commission). No short stories or articles. No reading fee.

Pawsey, John. Hollybrae, Hill Brow Road, Liss, Hants. GU33 7PS *T.* (0730) 893065.
Full-length popular fiction and non-fiction MSS., television and radio (home 10%, overseas 19%). No unsolicited material, poetry, short stories or original film and stage scripts. Preliminary letter and return postage with all correspondence essential. Works in association with agencies in the U.S.A. and Europe. Will suggest revision if MS. sufficiently promising. No reading fee.

Penman Literary Agency (1950). *Director:* Leonard G. Stubbs, F.R.S.A., 175 Pall Mall, Leigh-on-Sea, Essex, SS9 1RE. *T.* Southend (0702) 74438.
Full-length novel MSS. (home 10%, overseas 15%). Also theatre, films, television, sound broadcasting (10%). Revision undertaken by agency at author's request; fees depending upon amount of revision required. No reading fee.

Peterborough Literary Agency (1973). Jane Holloway. *Manager:* Ewan MacNaughton. 135 Fleet Street, London, EC4P 4BL. *T.* 01-353 4242, ext. 3681/3683. *T.A.* Telesyndic, London. *Telex:* London 22874 Telesyndic.
Rates (home 10%, overseas 20%). New and established authors. Non-fiction only. No reading fee but preliminary letter with S.A.E. essential.

*Peters, A. D., & Company, Ltd. (1924). *Directors:* Michael Sissons (Managing), Anthony Jones, Pat Kavanagh, Norman North, Kenneth Howard, Caroline Dawnay. 10 Buckingham Street, London, WC2N 6BU. *T.* 01-839 2556.
Associated agencies: Literistic Ltd., 264 Fifth Avenue, New York, N.Y., 10001. Sterling Lord, 660 Madison Avenue, New York, N.Y., 10021. Intercontinental Literary Agency (foreign language rights), 6 Buckingham Street, London, WC2N 6BJ. Specialists in the negotiation of all rights in general fiction and non-fiction, film and television scripts, plays, and certain specialist and academic works. No unsolicited manuscripts accepted without an introductory letter from the author describing the work and unless return postage included. *Rates of commission:* 10% on all work negotiated except 20% in U.S.A. and on foreign language rights. No reading fee.

Pollinger, Laurence, Limited. *Directors:* Gerald J. Pollinger, Margaret Pepper. *Secretary:* Denzil De Silva. 18 Maddox Street, London, W1R 0EU. *T.* 01-629 9761. *T.A.* Laupoll, London, W1.
Authors' agents for all material with the exception of original film stories, poetry and free-lance journalistic articles. Dramatic associate, Theresa Howard, *q.v.* Terms are a commission of 15% of the amounts obtained, except on translation sales, where the total commission of 20% may include the commission to the associate in the territory concerned. No reading fee. An editorial contribution may be requested.

*Pollinger, Murray (1969), 4 Garrick Street, London, WC2E 9BH. *T.* 01-836 6781. *T.A.* and *Cables:* Chopper, London, WC2.

Agents for the negotiation in all markets of novels for both adults and children and general non-fiction, including film, television and broadcasting rights in book material. (Home 10%, U.S.A. 15%, translations 20%). Preliminary letter and synopsis required; also names of agents and publishers previously contacted. No reading fee.

*Power, Shelley, Literary Agency Ltd/INPRA (1976). *Director:* Shelley Power. P.O. Box 149a, Surbiton, Surrey KT6 5JH. *T.* 01-398 7723. *T.A.* Barpress, Surbiton, Surrey.
Full-length MSS (home 10%, overseas 19%). No children's books, poetry or plays. Works in conjunction with agents in Europe and U.S.A. No reading fee, but preliminary letter essential.

PVA Management Ltd. *Directors:* Paul Vaughan (Managing), Peter Plant, Maureen Clark. Alpha Tower, Paradise Circus, Birmingham, B1 1TT *T.* 021-643 4011.
Full-length and short MSS. (home and overseas 15%). Theatre, films, television, radio (15%).

Radala & Associates (1970). *Directors:* Richard Gollner, István Siklós. 17 Avenue Mansions, Finchley Road, London, NW3 7AX. *T.* 01-794 4495.
Full-length MSS. (10% U.K., 15% overseas). Fiction and non-fiction. Books, films, television, sound broadcasting. Comprehensive service for computer book publishers and software producers in the U.S.A., Australia and the U.K. placing European rights with specialist as well as general publishers.

Rae, Douglas (Management) Ltd. (1975). *Directors:* Douglas Rae (Managing), Jenne Casarotto. 28 Charing Cross Road, London, WC2H 0DB. *T.* 01-836 3903-4.
Full-length MSS. (home 10%, overseas 15%). Theatre, films, television (10%).

Ramsay, Margaret, Ltd. (1953). *Directors:* M. Ramsay, Tom Erhardt. 14A Goodwin's Court, St. Martin's Lane, London, WC2N 4LL. *T.* 01-836 7403, 01-240 0691 and 01-836 6807.
MSS. Theatre, films, television, sound broadcasting only (commission 10%). Works in conjunction with agents in U.S.A. and in all foreign countries. Preliminary letter essential. No reading fee.

*Rogers, Deborah, Ltd. (1967). *Directors:* Deborah Rogers, Patricia White (U.S.A.). *Consultant:* Ann Warnford-Davis. 49 Blenheim Crescent, London, W11 2EF. *T.* 01-221 3717. *Telex:* 25930 Debrog G. *T.A.* Debrogers, London, W11.
Full-length book MSS. including children's books (home 10%, U.S.A. 15%, translations 20%). *U.S.A. Associate:* International Creative Management, 40 West 57th Street, New York, N.Y. 10019. No unsolicited MSS considered without a preliminary letter describing work and giving publishing history. No reading fee but return postage with MSS essential.

Ryder, Herta (1984), c/o Toby Eady Associates Ltd., 7 Gledhow Gardens, London SW5 0BL *T.* 01-370 6292 and 948 1010.
Full-length and short MSS. (home 10%, USA 15%, overseas 20%). Represented by agents in all major foreign countries. No reading fee.

*Sayle, Tessa, Agency. *Publishing:* Tessa Sayle. *Film, TV and Theatre:* Penny Tackaberry. 11 Jubilee Place, London, SW3 3TE. *T.* 01-352 4311, 01-352 2182. *T.A.* Bookishly, London SW3.
Full-length MSS. (home 10%, overseas 20%). Plays, films, television, sound broadcasting (10%). U.S.A. Associates: Liz Darhansoff Literary Agency, 1220 Park Avenue, New York, N.Y. 10028. Represented in all foreign countries. No reading fee.

Sharkey, James, Associates Ltd (1983). *Literary Executive:* Sebastian Born. 3rd Floor Suite, 15 Golden Square, London W1R 3AG *T.* 01-434 3801-6. *Telex:* 295251 Jsalon G.

Full-length MSS (home 10%, overseas 20%). Theatre, films, television, radio (10%). Works with various agencies in USA. No reading fee.

*Sheil, Anthony, Associates, Ltd. (1962), incorporating Christy & Moore, Ltd. (1912). 43 Doughty Street, London, WC1N 2LF. *T.* 01-405 9351. *T.A.* Novelist, London. *Telex:* 946240 Cweasy G ref. 19008175 (Easylink). Anthony Sheil, Giles Gordon, Gill Coleridge, Paul Marsh, Janet Fillingham, Mic Cheetham, Lois Wallace (U.S.A.).
Full-length MSS. (home 10%, U.S.A. 20%, translations 20%). Theatre, films, television, sound broadcasting (10%). *U.S.A. associates:* Wallace & Sheil Agency, Inc., 177 East 70th Street, New York, N.Y. 10021. *T.* (212) 570 9090. Translations: see **Marsh & Sheil Ltd.** Preliminary letter and return postage essential.

Sheri Safran Literary Agency Ltd. (1979). *Director:* Sheri Safran, 16 Pembridge Crescent, London, W11 3DX. *T.* 01-221 3355. *Telex:* 262284 ref. 1255. *Fax:* 01-229 9651.
Non-fiction titles for, by and about women; and children's books. Preliminary letter with outline or partial MSS together with return postage and self addressed envelope (home 15% overseas 20%). See also: **Sadie Fields Productions Ltd. (Book Packagers).** No reading fee.

Sheldon, Caroline, Literary Agency (1985), 23 Cumberland Street, London SW1V 4LS *T.* 01-821 8051.
Full-length MSS (home 10%, overseas 15-20%). General adult fiction, women's fiction, non-fiction and children's books. No reading fee, but synopsis and first three chapters with return postage required.

Simmons, Jeffrey, 10 Lowndes Square, London, SW1X 9HA. *T.* 01-235 8852.
Full-length MSS. (home from 10%, overseas from 15%). Will suggest revision. No reading fee, but preliminary letter essential.

*Simon, Richard Scott, Ltd. (1971). *Directors:* Richard Simon, Vivien Green, 32 College Cross, London N1 1PR *T.* 01-607 8533. *T.A.* Simonpure London.
Full-length and short MSS (home 10%, U.S. 15%, overseas 20%). *U.S. Associate:* Georges Borchardt Inc. No reading fee, but no unsolicited manuscripts without preliminary letter and return postage. *U.K. representatives* of Andrew Wylie Agency.

Smith, Carol. (1976). Carol Smith. 25 Hornton Court, Kensington High Street, London, W8 7RT. *T.* 01-937 4874.
Full-length and short MSS. (home 10%, U.S.A. 15%, translation 20%). Will suggest revision of promising MSS. Works in conjunction with many foreign agencies. No reading fee, but preliminary letter essential. Please enclose return postage.

Solo Literary Agency Ltd. (1978). *Directors:* Don Short (Managing), Wendy Short (Secretary), 8 Bouverie Street, London, EC4Y 8BB. *T.* 01-583 9372. *Telex:* 858623. Specialising in celebrity and autobiographical books. Fiction from established authors only (home 15%, overseas 20%).

Spokesmen—see **Curtis Brown.**

*Stein, Abner. *Director:* Abner Stein. 10 Roland Gardens, London, SW7 3PH. *T.* 01-373 0456 and 370 7859.
Full-length and short MSS. (home 10%, U.S.A. 19%, foreign 19%). No reading fee.

Tauber, Peter, Press Agency (1950). *Directors:* Peter Tauber, Martha Tauber, Robert Tauber. 94 East End Road, London, N3 2SX. *T.* 01-346 4165. *T.A.* Tauberpres, London N3.

Full length MSS only (20% worldwide). No scripts, poetry or children's. No unsolicited MSS, preliminary letter, synopsis and S.A.E. essential.

Thurley, Jon, M.A. (1976), 213 Linen Hall, 156-170 Regent Street, London W1R 5TA. *T.* 01-437 9545-6.
Literary and Dramatic work for all media. Commission: home 10%, overseas 20%. American and European representation arranged geared to specific projects. No reading fee.

*****Unna, Harvey, & Stephen Durbridge, Ltd.** (1975). *Directors:* Stephen Durbridge, Girsha Reid, Wendy Gressor. *Consultant:* Harvey Unna. 24-32 Pottery Lane, Holland Park, London, W11 4LZ. *T.* 01-727 1346. *Cables:* Undur, London, W11. Specialise in dramatic works for all media; handle also book MSS. Widely represented in most European and overseas countries. Commission charged by agency 10% in all instances: where sub-agents are employed overseas, additional commission by arrangement, but not exceeding 9%. No reading fee.

Van Loewen, Dr. Jan, Ltd.—see **Michael Imison Playwrights Ltd.**

Vestey, Lorna (1971). *Principal:* Mrs. Lorna Vestey. 33 Dryburgh Road, London, SW15.
Full-length MSS. (home 10%, U.S.A. 15%, other overseas 20%). Films, television, sound broadcasting (10%). Will occasionally suggest revision. No reading fee, but return postage essential. No unsolicited MSS.

*****Victor, Ed Ltd.** (1976). *Directors:* Ed Victor, Carol Ryan, Dasha Shenkman, Caroline Daubeny, Leon Morgan. 162 Wardour Street, London, W1V 4AT. *T.* 01-734 4795. *T.A.* Victorious, London W1. *Telex:* 263361.
Full-length MSS but no short stories, film/TV scripts, poetry or plays. (home 15%, U.S.A. 15%, translation 20%). Theatre, film, television, sound broadcasting rights (15%). Represented in all foreign markets. U.K. representatives of Knox Burger Associates, Ltd., Peter Lampack Agency Inc. No unsolicited manuscripts without preliminary letter.

Vosper, Margery, Ltd. (1932). Suite 8, 26 Charing Cross Road, London, WC2H 0DG. *T.* 01-836 5912. *T.A.* Volscius, London, WC2.
Theatre, films, television and sound broadcasting (home 10%, overseas 19%). Works in conjunction with agents in New York, and most foreign countries. Preliminary letter essential.

Walker, S., Literary Agency (1939). *Directors:* S. Walker, E. K. Walker, A. Oldfield, C-L. Oldfield. 199 Hampermill Lane, Oxhey, Watford, WD1 4PJ. *T.* Watford 28498.
Full-length novels only (home 10%, overseas 20% including 10% to overseas agent). Do not handle short topical articles, poetry or stories for juveniles. Works in conjunction with agencies in most European countries, and also negotiates directly with foreign publishers. No reading fee but preliminary letter and return postage essential.

*****Watson, Little Ltd.** *Directors:* Sheila Watson, Amanda Little. Suite 8, 26 Charing Cross Road, London WC2H 0DG *T.* 01-836 5880.
Full-length MSS (home 10%, overseas 19%; all other rights including film, software, video and television 10%). No short stories or play scripts. Will sometimes suggest revision. Works in association with US agency and many foreign agencies. Preliminary letter please.

*****Watt, A. P. Ltd.** (1875). *Directors:* Hilary Rubinstein, Caradoc King, Linda Shaughnessy, Rod Hall. 26/28 Bedford Row, London, WC1R 4HL. *T.* 01-405 6774. *T.A.* Longevity, London. *Telex:* 297903 Apwatt G.

Full-length MSS; dramatic works for all media (home 10%, U.S. and foreign 20% including commission to U.S. or foreign agent). No poetry. Works in conjunction with agents in U.S.A. and most European countries and Japan. No reading fee. Preliminary letter please.

UNITED STATES LITERARY AGENTS

*Membership of the Society of Authors' Representatives

It has long been customary among literary agencies that the agent retains a 10% commission on domestic sales and up to 20% on foreign sales, subject to various exceptions and special policies established by each agent individually. Some agencies charge a reading fee for unsolicited MSS. and for the work of beginners and new writers, such fees sometimes being refunded on the acceptance of the material. Members of the Society of Authors' Representatives do not charge a reading fee. In all cases, and in their own interests, writers are advised to send a preliminary letter and to ascertain terms before submitting MSS.

American Play Company Inc., 19 West 44th Street, Suite 1206, New York, N.Y., 10036. *T.* 212-921-0545. *President:* Sheldon Abend.

*****Bach, Julian, Literary Agency Inc.,** 747 Third Avenue, New York, N.Y., 10017. *T.* 753-2605. *Telex:* 668359. *Cables:* Turtles, New York.

Balkin Agency, The, *Director:* Richard Balkin. 850 West 176th Street, New York, N.Y., 10033. *T.* 212-781-4198.
Full-length MSS. only (home 15%, overseas 20%). Adult non-fiction only. Query first. May suggest revision. Agents in all major countries. *British representative:* Marlu Literary Agency. No reading fee.

Berger, Bill, Associates Inc. *President:* William P. Berger; *Vice-President* and *Treasurer:* Henriette E. Neatrour. 444 East 58th Street, New York, N.Y., 10022. *T.* 212-486-9588.
Full-length and short MSS. (home 10%, Great Britain 15%, translations 20%). Films, television, radio (10%). No reading fee.

*****Berman, Lois,** The Little Theatre Building, 240 West 44th Street, New York, N.Y., 10036. *T.* 212-575-5114.
Dramatic writing only (and only by recommendation).

Blassingame, McCauley & Wood (1978). *Directors:* Eleanor Wood, Ralph M. Vicinanza. 432 Park Avenue South, Suite 1205, New York, N.Y., 10016. *T.* 212-532-7377.
No unsolicited MSS; preliminary letter with return postage essential. *Commission:* 10% domestic, 20% foreign.

*****Borchardt, Georges, Inc.** (1967). *Directors:* Georges Borchardt, Anne Borchardt. 136 East 57th Street, New York, N.Y., 10022. *T.* 212-753-5785. *T.A.* Literary New York. *Telex:* 423421 Literary.
Full-length and short MSS. (home 10%, British 15%, translations 20%). Theatre, films, television, radio (10%). Agents in most foreign countries. No unsolicited MSS. No reading fee.

*****Brandt & Brandt Literary Agents Inc.,** 1501 Broadway, New York, N.Y., 10036. *T.* 212-840-5760. *T.A.* Bromasite New York.
Full-length and short MSS. (home 10%, overseas 15-20%). Theatre, films, television and radio (10%). *British representative:* A. M. Heath & Co. Ltd. No reading fee.

*Brann, Helen, Agency Inc., The,** 157 West 57th Street, New York, N.Y., 10019. *T.* 212-247-3511.

*Brown, James, Associates Inc.**—see **Curtis Brown Associates Ltd.**

*Curtis Brown Associates Ltd., *President:* Peter L. Ginsberg. 10 Astor Place, New York, N.Y., 10003. *T.* 212-473 5400.

*Cushman, John, Associates Inc.**—see **Curtis Brown Associates Ltd.**

Darhansoff, Liz, Literary Agency, 1220 Park Avenue, New York, N.Y. 10128 *T.* 212-534 2479.
Full-length and short MSS (home 10%, overseas 20%). Theatre, films, television, radio (10%). Works with agents throughout Europe; Tessa Sayle Agency in U.K. No reading fee.

*Daves, Joan** (1952), 59 East 54th Street, New York, N.Y., 10022. *T.* 212-759-6250. *Cables:* Jodabooks, New York.
Full-length MSS. (home 10%, overseas 20%). Theatre, films, television, radio (10%). No reading fee. No unpublished writers.

*Diamant, Anita,** 310 Madison Avenue, New York, N.Y., 10017. *T.* 212-687-1122.

*Donadio, Candida, & Associates, Inc.,** 231 West 22nd Street, New York, N.Y., 10011. *T.* 212-691-8077.
Literary and dramatic.

Dorese Agency, Alyss Barlow Dorese, 41 West 82nd Street, New York, N.Y., 10024. *T.* 580-2855.

*Elmo, Ann, Agency. *Directors:* Ann Elmo, Lettie Lee. 60 East 42nd Street, New York, N.Y., 10165. *T.* 661-2880.
Full-length fiction and non-fiction MSS. (home 15%, overseas 20%). Theatre, films, television (15%). Will suggest revision when MSS. is promising. Works with foreign agencies. No reading fee.

Fishbein, Frieda, Ltd., 353 West 57th Street, New York, N.Y., 10019. *T.* 212-247-4398.

Fles, Barthold, 501 Fifth Avenue, New York, N.Y., 10017. *T.* 687-7248.
Books only, fiction and non-fiction, adult and juvenile; no picture books.

*Fox Chase Agency Inc., The,** 401 East 34th Street, New York, N.Y., 10016. *T.* 212-752-8211.

*Freedman Dramatic Agency, Inc., Robert A.** (formerly **Harold Freedman Brandt & Brandt Dramatic Dept., Inc.)**, 1501 Broadway, Suite 2310, New York, N.Y., 10036. *T.* 212-840-5760.

*French, Samuel, Inc.,** 45 West 25th Street, New York, N.Y., 10010. *T.* 212-206-8990.

Jay Garon-Brooke Associates Inc., 415 Central Park West, New York, N.Y., 10025. *T.* 212-866-3654. Writer must be referred by an editor or a client. Will not read unsolicited MSS. *London:* Abner Stein, *T.* 01-373 0456.

Goodman Associates, Literary Agents (1976), *Partners:* Arnold P. Goodman, Elise Simon Goodman, 500 West End Avenue, New York, N.Y. 10024 *T.* 212-873-4806. *Telex:* 238198 Tlxa UR.
Adult book length fiction and non-fiction (home 15%, overseas 20%). No reading fee.

Greenburger, Sanford, J., Associates, Inc., 55 Fifth Avenue, New York, N.Y., 10003. *T.* 212-206-5600.

*Gregory, Blanche C., Inc.,** Two Tudor City Place, New York, N.Y., 10017. *T.* 212-697 0828.

*Hawkins, John & Associates, Inc. (formerly **Paul R. Reynolds, Inc.**) (1893), 71 West 23rd Street, Suite 1600, New York, N.Y., 10010. *T.* 212-807-7040. *Cable Address:* Carbonato, New York.

Hill, Frederick, Associates, (1979). 2237 Union Street, San Francisco, California 94123. *T.* 415-921-2910.
Full-length and short MSS. (home 15%, overseas 20%). Will suggest revision. Works in conjunction with agents in Scandinavia, France, Germany, Holland, Japan, Spain, Mexico, Brazil. *UK representative:* Marlu Literary Agency. No reading fee.

*International Creative Management, Inc., 40 West 57th Street, New York, N.Y., 10019. *T.* 212-556-5600.

*JCA Literary Agency Inc., Suite 4-A, 242 West 27th Street, New York, N.Y., 10001. *T.* 212-807-0888.

King, Daniel P. (1974), 5125 North Cumberland Boulevard, Whitefish Bay, Wisconsin 53217. *T.* 414-964-2903. *Telex:* 724389.
Specialist in mystery and crime fiction and non-fiction.

*Kroll, Lucy, Agency, 390 West End Avenue, New York, N.Y., 10024. *T.* 212-877-0627. *T.A.* Lucykroll, New York.

*Lantz Office Inc., The, 888 Seventh Avenue, New York, N.Y., 10106. *T.* 212-586-0200 and 9255 Sunset Boulevard, Los Angeles, California 90069. *T.* 213-858-1144.

Larsen, Michael-Elizabeth Pomada Literary Agents (1972). *Partners:* Michael Larsen and Elizabeth Pomada, 1029 Jones Street, San Francisco, California 94109 *T.* 415-673 0939.
Full-length MSS. (home 15%, overseas 20%). Films, television, (10%). Works in conjunction with agents in Europe, Israel, Japan, South America. Preliminary letter, with S.A.E., essential.

*Lescher & Lescher, Ltd. (1966). *Directors:* Robert Lescher, Susan Lescher. 155 East 71st Street, New York, N.Y., 10021. *T.* 212-249-7600. *T.A.* Micawber.
Full-length and short MSS. (home 10-15%, overseas 20%). No reading fee.

*Levine Literary Agency, Ellen, Inc. (1980). *President:* Ellen Levine. Suite 1205, 432 Park Avenue South, New York, N.Y., 10016. *T.* 212-899-0620.
Full-length MSS. (home 10%, overseas 20%). In conjunction with co-agents, theatre, films, television, (10%). Will suggest revision. Works in conjunction with agents in Europe, Japan, Israel, Argentina. *UK representative:* A. P. Watt. No reading fee; preliminary letter essential.

*Literistic, Ltd., (1979). *Directors:* Peter Matson, Michael Sissons, Anthony Jones. 264 Fifth Avenue, New York, N.Y. 10001. *T.* 212-696-4770. *Cables:* Literistic New York.
Full-length and short MSS. (home 10%, overseas 19%). Theatre, films, television, radio (10%). Will suggest revision. Represented in Europe. *UK representative:* A. D. Peters & Co. No reading fee.

*McCauley, Gerald, Agency, Inc. 141 East 44th Street, New York, N.Y., 10017. *T.* 914-232 5700. *Postal address:* P.O. Box AE, Katonah, New York 10536.

McCauley, Kirby, Ltd., 432 Park Avenue South, Suite 1509, New York, N.Y., 10016. *T.* 212-683-7561. *Directors:* Kirby McCauley, Kay McCauley. *Foreign Rights:* Ralph Vicinanza. 432 Park Avenue South, Suite 1205, New York, N.Y. 10116.

McIntosh, McKee & Dodds Inc., 276 Fifth Avenue, New York, N.Y., 10001. *T.* 212-679-4490. *Cables:* Halmatson.

*McIntosh & Otis Inc. (1928), 475 5th Avenue, New York, N.Y., 10017.

*Marton, Elisabeth. Elisabeth Marton, Tonda Marton. 96 Fifth Avenue, New York, N.Y., 10011. *T.* 212-225-1908.

*Matson, Harold, Company Inc. (1937), 276 Fifth Avenue, New York, N.Y., 10001. *T.* 212-679-4490. *Cables:* Halmatson.
Full-length MSS. (home 10%, U.K. 19%, translation 19%). No unsolicited MSS. No reading fee.

*Merrill, Helen, Ltd. 361 West 17th Drive, New York, N.Y., 10011. *T.* 212-691-5326.

Miller, Peter, Agency Inc. (1976). *President:* Peter Miller. P.O. Box 764, Midtown Station, New York, N.Y. 10018. *T.* 212-221-8329.
Full-length and short MSS (home 15%, overseas 25%). Films, television (10-20%). Works in conjunction with agents in Germany, Japan, Spain. Preliminary enquiry with synopsis and resumé essential.

Mills, Robert P., Ltd. c/o Richard Curtis Associates, 164 East 64th Street, New York, N.Y., 10021. *T.* 212-371-9481.

*Morris, William, Agency Inc., 1350 Avenue of the Americas, New York, N.Y., 10019. *T.* 212-586-5100.

New Wave, Authors' Representatives (1984). *Director:* Gene Lovitz, 2544 North Monticello Avenue, Chicago, Illinois, 60647. *T.* 1-312-342-3338.
Full-length and short MSS (home 10% overseas 15%). Films, television (15%). Particularly interested in historical romance novels, horror, mysteries, experimental. Reading fee charged to unpublished authors.

*Ober, Harold, Associates Inc. *Directors:* Dorothy Olding, Claire M. Smith, Phyllis Westberg. 40 East 49th Street, New York, N.Y., 10017. *T.* 759-8600. *T.A.* Litober. *Telex:* 236112.
Full-length MSS. (home 10%, British 15%, overseas 20%). Theatre, films, television, radio (10%). Will suggest revision. *London representative:* David Higham Associates. No reading fee.

*Oscard Associates, Fifi, Inc. *President:* Fifi Oscard, *Vice-President:* Charles W. Hunt. 19 West 44th Street, New York, N.Y. 10036. *T.* 212-764-1100.
Full-length MSS (home 15%, overseas 20%). Theatre, films, television, radio (10%). Will suggest revision. Works in conjunction with many foreign agencies. No reading fee, but no unsolicited submissions.

Porter, Dierks & Lovitz, Literary Brokers, 2544 North Monticello Avenue, Chicago, Illinois, 60647. *T.* 1-312-342-3338. *Directors:* Roy E. Porter, Jack C. Dierks, Gene Lovitz.
Non-fiction, fiction, juveniles, poetry (home 10%, overseas 10% unless another agent used). Will suggest revision. Reading fee charged for unpublished authors.

*Raines & Raines (1961). *Directors:* Theron Raines, Keith Korman. 71 Park Avenue, New York, N.Y., 10016. *T.* 212-684-5160. *T.A.* Rainesbuck New York.
Full-length MSS. (home 15%, overseas 20%). Works in conjunction with overseas agents. No unsolicited MSS.

*Roberts, Flora, Inc., 157 West 57th Street, New York, N.Y., 10019. *T.* 355-4165.

*Rodell, Marie-Frances Collin Literary Agency (1948). *Director:* Frances Collin. 110 West 40th Street, New York, N.Y., 10018. *T.* 212-840-8664. *Cables:* Rodellitag, New York.
Full-length and short MSS. (home 15%, overseas 25%). Theatre, films, television, radio (10%). Works in conjunction with agents throughout the world. No reading fee.

*Rosenstone/Wender, 3 East 48th Street, 4th Floor, New York, N.Y., 10017. *T.* 212-832-8330.

*Russell & Volkening Inc., 50 West 29th Street, New York, N.Y., 10001. *T.* 212-684-6050.

*Schaffner, John, Associates Inc. (1948). *Directors:* Timothy Schaffner, Patrick Delahunt. 114 East 28th Street, New York, N.Y. 10016. *T.* 212-689-6888(89). *T.A.* Shafflit.
Full-length MSS. (home 10% and overseas 7½%). *British representative:* A. M. Heath & Co. Ltd. No reading fee.

*Schulman, Susan F., Literary & Dramatic Agents Inc., 454 West 44th Street, New York, N.Y., 10036. *T.* 212-877-2216.
Agents for negotiation in all markets (with coagents) of fiction, general non-fiction, children's books, academic and professional works, and associated subsidiary rights including plays, film and television. (home 10%, United Kingdom 7½%, overseas 20%). Return postage required.

Scott Meredith Literary Agency Inc. (1941). *President:* Scott Meredith, *Vice-Presidents:* Jack Scovil, Theodore Chichak, *Subsidiary Rights:* Jonathan Silverman, William T. Haas. 845 Third Avenue, New York, N.Y., 10022. *T.* 212-245-5500. *Cables:* Scottmere. *T.A.* Esemela 224705.
Full-length and short MSS. (home 10%, overseas 20%). Theatre, films, television, radio (10%). Will read unsolicited MSS., queries, outlines. Single fee charged for readings, criticism and assistance in revision. London: Mark Hamilton, A. M. Heath & Co. Ltd.

*Sheedy, Charlotte, Literary Agency, 145 West 86th Street, New York, N.Y., 10024. *T.* 873-4768.

Shukat Company Ltd. The, *President:* Scott Shukat; *Partner:* Lawrence J. Weiss. 340 West 55th Street, Suite 1-A, New York, N.Y. 10019. *T.* 1-212-582-7614.
Theatre, films, novels, television, radio (15%). No reading fee. No unsolicited material accepted.

Singer Communications Inc. *Directors:* Natalie Carlton (Acting President), Kurt Singer (Chairman). 3164 West Tyler Avenue, Anaheim, California, 92801. *T.* 714-527-5650. *T.A.* Singerbook.
Full-length MSS. including romance, westerns, biography (home 15%, overseas 20%); short MSS. (home 10%, overseas 15%). Films, television, radio (15%, overseas 20%). Represented in most countries abroad.

Spectrum Literary Agency, The, 432 Park Avenue, South, Suite 1205, New York, N.Y., 10016. *T.* 212-532-7377.
No unsolicited MSS. Send query with S.A.E.

*Spitzer, Philip G., Literary Agency, 1465 3rd Avenue, New York, N.Y., 10028. *T.* 212-628-0352.

*Sterling Lord Agency Inc., 660 Madison Avenue, New York, N.Y., 10021. *T.* 212-PL 1-2533. *T.A.* Lordage. *Representatives: London:* A. D. Peters, *q.v. Europe:* Intercontinental Literary Agency, *q.v. Japan:* The Tuttle-Mori Agency Inc.

Swanson, H. N., Inc. (1934), 8523 Sunset Boulevard, Los Angeles, California, 90069. *T.* 213-652-5385. *T.A.* Swanie. *Directors:* H. N. Swanson, Ben Kamsler.
Full-length MSS. (home 10%, overseas 20%). Theatre, films, television, radio. No reading fee.

*Targ, Roslyn, Literary Agency, Inc. *President:* Roslyn Targ. 105 West 13th Street, New York, N.Y., 10011. *Cable:* Rosbooks, New York. *Telex:* 62193.
Full-length MSS (home 10%, overseas 20%). Films, television, radio (10%). Will suggest revision. Affiliates in most foreign countries. No reading fee.

Wahl, Austin, Agency, Ltd. (1935). *President:* Thomas Wahl. Suite 342, Monadnock Building, 53 West Jackson Boulevard, Chicago, Illinois, 60604. *T.* 312-922-3331.

Full-length and short MSS. (home 15%, overseas 20%). Theatre, films, television (10%). No reading fee.

*Wallace & Sheil Agency, Inc. (1974). *Directors:* Lois Wallace, Anthony Sheil. 177 East 70th Street, New York, N.Y., 10021. *T.* 212-570-9090. *Cables:* Aswaslit, New York.
Full-length and short MSS. (home 10%, U.K. 20%, overseas 20%). Theatre, films, television, radio (10%). Will suggest revision. *British representatives:* Anthony Sheil Associates in England. Translation, Marsh & Sheil Ltd. No unsolicited manuscripts.

Watkins/Loomis Agency, Inc., 150 East 35th Street, New York, N.Y., 10016. *T.* 212-LE2-0080. *Cables:* Anwat, Newyork. *London:* A. P. Watt & Son.

Williams Wesley Winant (1976). *Directors:* William A. Winant III, William W. Winant II. 180 East 79th Street, New York, N.Y., 10021. *T.* 212-RE-4-0988.
Full-length and short MSS. (home 10%, overseas 15%). Theatre, films, television, radio (10%). Will suggest revision. No reading fee.

Writers House Inc. (1974), *President:* Albert Zuckerman. 21 West 26th Street, New York, N.Y. 10010. *T.* 212-685 2400. *Telex:* 620103 Writers.
Full-length MSS (home 10%, overseas 20%). No reading fee.

*Yost, Mary, Associates, Inc. (1958). *President:* Mary B. Yost. 59 East 54th Street, New York, N.Y., 10022. *T.* 212-980-4988. *T.A.* Mybooks.
Full-length and short MSS. (home and overseas 10%). Works with individual agents in all foreign countries. Will suggest revision. No reading fee.

OTHER LITERARY AGENTS

Most of the agents whose names and addresses are given below work in association with an agent in London.

In all cases, and in their own interests, writers are advised to send a preliminary letter and to ascertain terms before submitting MSS. or books.

ARGENTINA

International Editors Co., Avenida Cabildo 1156, 1426 Buenos Aires. *T.* 784-4613. *Telex:* 24518 Blibro AR.

Lawrence Smith B.A. (1938), Avenida de los Incas 3110, Buenos Aires, 1426. *T.* 552-5012. *Cables:* Litagent, Baires.

AUSTRALIA

Curtis Brown (Australia) Pty., Ltd., 27 Union Street, Paddington, N.S.W., 2021. *T.* 331-5301 and 33 6161. *Cables:* Browncurt.

Yaffa Syndicate Pty, Ltd., 432-6 Elizabeth Street, Surry Hills, Sydney, N.S.W. 2010. *Postal Address:* Box 606, G.P.O. Sydney, N.S.W. 2001. *T.* 699 7861. *Telex:* AA 121887 Yaffa.
Largest and oldest established Australian syndicate and literary agency.

BRAZIL

Dr. J. E. Bloch Literary Agency, Mrs. Karin Schindler, Caixa Postal 19051, 04599 São Paulo, S.P. *T.* 241-9177 and 9077. *Cables:* Copyright Sãopaulo.

Ms Ana Maria Santeiro, Agencia Literaria Carmen Bacells, Rua João Lira 97-202, Leblon, 22430 Rio de Janeiro, RJ. *T.* 294-3248. *Cables:* Copyright Rio. *Telex:* (021) 33961 Alcp.

CANADA

Curtis Brown Canada Ltd., 303 Davenport Road, Toronto, Ontario M5R 1K5 *T.* 416-922 9006. *Telex:* 06-218392 Colbert Tor.

CZECHOSLOVAKIA

Dilia Theatrical and Literary Agency Vyšehradská 28, 128 24 Prague 2. *T.* 296651-5. *Telex:* 121367 dili c.

Lita Slovak Literary Agency, ul. Cs. armády 37, 815-30 Bratislava. *T.* 550-25, 591-79, 328-223, 328-549. *T.A.* Lita Bratislava.

DENMARK

A/S Bookman, Fiolstraede 12, DK-1171, Copenhagen K. *T.* 01-14-57-20.

Inter-Media, Kantorparken 4, 8240 Risskov. *T.* 06-211796 and 06-215615.

Leonhardt Literary Agency aps, Studiestraede 35, DK-1455 Copenhagen K. *T.* 01-132523. *Cables:* Leolitag.

Licht & Licht, Maglemosevej 46, DK-2920, Charlottenlund. *T.* (01) 61 09 08. *Cables:* Literagent.

FINLAND

A/S Bookman, 12 Fiolstraede, DK-1171, Copenhagen K. *T.* 01-14-57-20.

Licht & Licht, Maglemosevej 46, DK-2920, Charlottenlund. *T.* (01) 61 09 08. *Cables:* Literagent.

FRANCE

Mrs. W. A. Bradley, 18 Quai de Bethune, 75004 Paris. *T.* 354-75-14.

Bureau Litteraire International Marguerite Scialtiel, Geneviève Ulmann, 14 rue Chanoinesse, 75004 Paris. *T.* (1) 43 5471 16.

D.M. Agence Littéraire (formerly **McKee & Mouche**), 12 rue du Regard, 75006 Paris. *T.* 45-48-45-03 and 42-22-42-33. *Telex:* 214889 F.

Agence Hoffman, 77 Boulevard Saint-Michel, 75005 Paris. *T.* 3265694. *Cables:* Aghoff. *Telex:* 203605.

La Nouvelle Agence, Mary Kling, 7 rue Corneille, 75006 Paris. *T.* 43-25-85-60.

Mme Michelle Lapautre, 6 rue Jean Carriès, 75007 Paris. *T.* 4734-82-41. *Telex:* 205 247 (France).

Mme. Greta Strassova, 4 rue Git-Le-Coeur, 75006 Paris. *T.* 4633-34-57.

GERMANY

Paul & Peter Fritz AG Literary Agency (formerly **Linder AG**), Jupiterstrasse 1, 8032 Zürich, Switzerland. *Postal Address:* Postfach, 8032 Zürich. *T.* (01) 53 41 40. *Telex:* 55123 ch.

Geisenheyner & Crone, Gymnasiumstrasse 31B, 7000 Stuttgart-1. *T.* 0711-293738.

Agence Hoffmann, Seestrasse 6, 8000 Munich 40. *T.* (089) 396402. *Telex:* 521 5661.

Liepman AG., Ruth Liepman, Eva Koralnik, Ruth Weibel, Maienburgweg 23, 8044 Zürich, Switzerland. *T.* (01) 47 76 60. *Cables:* Litagent. *Telex:* Litag 56739.

Literarische Agentur Brigitte Axster, Hüttenstrasse 38, D 4000 Düsseldorf 1. *T.* 0211-376625.

Mohrbooks Literary Agency, Rainer Heumann, Klosbachstrasse 110, Postfach, CH-8030 Zürich, Switzerland. *T.* (01) 251-16-10. *Telex:* 56830.

Niedieck Linder AG, Holzgasse 6, CH-8039 Zürich-Postfach. *T.* 01 202 14 50. *Telex:* 56096 nck ch.

Thomas Schlück, Literary Agency, Hinter der Worth 12, 3008 Garbsen 9. *T.* 05131-93053. *Telex:* 923419 Litag d.

HUNGARY

Artisjus. Agency for Literature, Theatre and Music of the Hungarian Bureau for Copyright Protection, Vörösmarty tér 1, Budapest V. *Post address:* H-1364 Budapest PB 67. *T.* 184-704. *Cables:* Artisjus. *Telex:* 226527 Arjus H.

ICELAND

Sveinbjorn Jonsson Literary and Dramatic Agent (1960), P.O. Box 438, Gardastraeti 21, 121 Reykjavik. *T.* 1-28110 and 1-613206.

ITALY

Agenzia Letteraria Internazionale SRL, 41 via Manzoni, 20121 Milan. *T.* 6572465, 6572594, 6572596. *Telex:* 323574 Linali I.

Dais Literary Agency, Via Santa Maria in Monticelli 67, 00186 Rome. *T.* 655356.

ILA—International Literary Agency—U.S.A. (1969). I-18010 Terzorio-IM. *T.* 0039 184-48-40-48. *T.A.* Friedmann 1-18010 Terzorio-IM, also c/o Wreschner, 10 West 73rd Street, New York 10023 *T.* 212-877-2605. Publishers' Agent, interested in bestsellers and mass market books.

News Blitz International (1949), Via Cimabue 5, 00196 Rome. *T.* 36 01 489, 36 00 620, 36 19 014. *T.A.* Blitz, Rome.

JAPAN

Orion Press, 58, 1-Chome, Kanda-Jimbocho, Chiyoda-ku, Tokyo, 101. *T.A.* Orionserv, Tokyo. *Telex:* J24408 Orionagy.

NETHERLANDS

International Drama Agency, Francis Lonnee, P.O. Box 30030, 1003 BA Amsterdam. *T.* 020-36 77 54.

Internationaal Literatuur Bureau B.V., Menno Kohn, Postbus 10014, 1201 DA, Hilversum. *T.* 035-13500. *Telex:* 73201 ILB.

Hans Keuls, International Bureau Voor Auteursrecht BV., Verdiweg 171, 3816 KD Amersfoort. *T.* 033-752-778.

Prins & Prins Literary Agents (Henk Prins), de Lairessestraat 6, P.O. Box 5400, 1007 AK Amsterdam. *T.* 76 10 01.

Rombach & Partners, Bentveldsweg 100, P.O. Box 121, 2110 AC Aerdenhout.

United Dutch Dramatists, Hemmo B. Drexhage, de Perponcherstraat 116, 2518 TA The Hague. *T.* 070-46 97 38.

NEW ZEALAND

Lockhart, Joseph, Associates Ltd. (1980), *Chairman:* Ellen Butland, 1-519 Richardson Road, Mt. Roskill, Auckland 4. *Postal Address:* 1-519 Richardson Road, Mt. Roskill, Auckland 4. *T.* 694-378.

Richards Literary Agency (1976). *Partners:* Ray Richards, Barbara Richards, Nicki Richards. 3-49 Aberdeen Road, Castor Bay, Auckland 9. *Postal Address:* P.O. Box 31240, Milford, Auckland 9. *T.* 469-681.
Full-length MSS, films, television, radio (home 10%, overseas 10-20%) Preliminary letter, synopsis with SAE required. No reading fee.

NORWAY

A/S Bookman, 12 Fiolstraede, DK-1171, Copenhagen K. *T.* 01-14-57-20.

Licht & Licht, Maglemosevej 46, DK-2920 Charlottenlund. *T.* (01) 61 09 08. *Cables:* Literagent.

Suzanne Palme Literary Agency, Oscarsgt. 60, Oslo 2. *Postal Address:* P.O. Box 7112, Homansbyen, 0307 Oslo 3. *T.* 44 81 74. *Cables:* Palmebook.

PORTUGAL

Ilidio da Fonseca Matos, Rua de S. Bernardo, 68-3, 1200 Lisbon. *T.* 66 97 80, 70 94 45. *Cables:* Ilphoto.

SOUTH AFRICA

Frances Bond, Literary Agency (1985), 32b Stanley Teale Road, Westville North 3630, Natal. *T.* 031-824532.

International Press Agency (Pty) Ltd., P.O. Box 67, Howard Place 7450. *T.* 53-1926. *London Office:* Mrs. S. Power, P.O. Box 149A, Surbiton, Surrey, KT6 5JH. *T.* 01-398 7723.

SPAIN

Miss Carmen Balcells, Agencia Literaria Carmen Balcells, Diagonal 580, Barcelona 21. *T.* 200-89-33, 200-85-65. *Cables:* Copyright, Barcelona. *Telex:* 50 459 Copy E.

International Editors Co., S.A., Rambla Cataluña 63, 3º-1ª, 08007 Barcelona. *T.* 215-88-12. *Telex:* 98478 Rght E.

Julio F. Yañez, Agencia Literaria, Via Augusta 139, 6º-2ª, 08021 Barcelona. *T.* 200 7107. *Telex:* 97348 GNLT-E.

SWEDEN

A/S Bookman, 12 Fiolstraede, DK-1171, Copenhagen K. *T.* 01-14-57-20.

Gösta Dahl & Son, AB, Aladdinsvägan 14, S-161 38 Bromma. *T.* 08-25 62 35.

Licht & Licht, Maglemosevej 46, DK-2920 Charlottenlund. *T.* (01) 61 09 08. *Cables:* Literagent.

Arlecchino Teaterförlag, Gränsvägen 14, S-131 41 Nacka. *T.* 08-718 17 18.

AGENTS SPECIALISING IN PLAYS, FILMS, TELEVISION AND RADIO

Full particulars about Agents and Notes to which special attention is called will be found on the preceding pages.

*U.S.A. Literary Agents

A & B Personal Management Ltd
Authors' Alliance
*Berger, Bill, Associates Inc.
*Borchardt, Georges, Inc.
*Brandt & Brandt Literary Agents Inc.
*Brown, James, Associate Inc.
Burston, Diane
Byrne, Myles
Clarke, Serafina
Clowes, Jonathan
Cochrane, Elspeth, Agency
Colin, Rosica, Ltd.
Conway-Gordon, Jane
Cruickshank, Harriet
Curtis Brown
*Darhansoff, Liz, Literary Agency
Davis-Poynter, Reg
De Wolfe, Felix
Dorman, John
Eady, Toby, Associates Ltd
*Elmo, Ann, Agency
E.T.G. (English Theatre Guild, Ltd)
Fact & Fiction Agency Ltd.
Film Rights, Ltd.
Fitch, Laurence, Ltd.
Foster, Jill, Ltd.
Fraser & Dunlop Scripts, Ltd.
French, John, Artists Agency Ltd
Gillon Aitken Ltd
Glass, Eric
Goodwin Associates
Green, Christine
Gregory, Jane
Grossman, David, Literary Agency
Harrison, Alec, and Associates
Hatton & Baker Ltd
Higham, David, Associates, Ltd.
Hoskins, Valerie
Howard, Theresa, Associates
Hughes Massie, Ltd.
Imison, Michael, Playwrights Ltd
International Scripts
Johnson, John, (Authors Agent) Ltd.
Juvenila
Kelly, Frances, Agency
*Larsen, Michael-Elizabeth Pomada
*Levine Literary Agency, Ellen, Inc.
*Literistic, Ltd.
Little, Christopher Literary Agent.
London Independent Books, Ltd.
Marvin, Blanche
*Miller, Peter, Agency Inc.
Milne, Richard
Morris, William, Agency (UK) Ltd.
Mulvany, Jolie
Noach, Maggie, Literary Agency
*Ober, Harold, Associates Inc.
*Oscard Associates, Fifi, Inc.
Paterson, Mark & Associates
Penman Literary Agency
Peters, A. D., & Company, Ltd.
Pollinger, Laurence, Ltd.
PVA Management Ltd.
Radala & Associates
Rae, Douglas
Ramsay, Margaret, Ltd.
*Rodell, Marie-Frances Collin Literary Agency
Rogers, Deborah, Ltd.
Sayle, Tessa, Agency
*Schulman, Susan
*Scott Meredith Literary Agency Inc.
Sharkey, James, Associates Ltd.
Sheil, Anthony, Associates, Ltd.
*Shukat Co. Ltd.
*Singer Communications Inc.
*Targ, Roslyn
Thurley, Jon
Unna, Harvey and Stephen Durbridge, Ltd.
Vestey, Lorna
Vosper, Margery, Ltd.
*Wahl, Austin, Agency Inc.
*Wallace & Sheil Agency Inc.
Watt, A. P. Ltd.
*Williams Wesley Winant

CHARACTER MERCHANDISING

A number of agents specialise in the handling of rights connected with the promotion of characters from books, television programmes etc., or with the books and programmes themselves. This is a selective listing, both of agents and of properties handled.

BBC Merchandising, BBC Enterprises Ltd., Room C201, Woodlands, 80 Wood Lane, London W12 0TT *T.* 01-576 0555.
Properties include *The Archers, Mrs Beeton, Bertha, The Collectors, Doctor Who, Dogtanian and the Three Muskehounds, EastEnders, Grange Hill, Howard's Way, Ivor the Engine, Jimbo and the Jet Set, Magic Roundabout, Mop and Smiff, Mysterious Cities of Gold, Play School, Pole Position, Postman Pat, The Tripods, Ulysses 31.*

Copyright Promotions Ltd., 90-91 Tottenham Court Road, London, W1P 9HE. *T.* 01-580 7431.
Properties include *The Mr. Men, Little Miss, Danger Mouse, Victoria Plum, Pink Panther, Tom and Jerry, Wind in the Willows, Willo-the-Wisp, Towser, Bananaman, My Little Pony, Rainbow Brite, Alias the Jester, Creepy Crawlies, Roland Rat, Mask, Telebugs, The Pondles, James the Cat, Bertie Bassett.*

Copyrights Company Ltd, The, 22 Crawford Place, London, W1H 1JE *T.* 01-723 6034. *Telex:* 298830 Bearup.
Properties include *Beatrix Potter, Paddington Bear, Brambly Hedge,* and other book-related properties for merchandise licensing.

Fern Hollow Productions Ltd., Macdonald & Co. (Publishers) Ltd., 3rd Floor, Greater London House, Hampstead Road, London NW1 7QX *T.* 01-377 4600. *Telex:* 885233 Macdon G. *Fax:* 01-387 9286. *Contact:* Clarissa Cridland. Property: *Fern Hollow.*

Marvel Licensing, 23 Redan Place, London W2 4SA *T.* 01-221 1232.
Properties include *The Marvel Super Heroes, Acorn Green, Heathcliff, Inspector Gadget, Dungeons & Dragons.*

Noddy Subsidiary Rights Company Ltd., Macdonald & Co. (Publishers) Ltd., 3rd Floor, Greater London House, Hampstead Road, London NW1 7QX *T.* 01-377 4600. *Telex:* 885233 Macdon G. *Fax:* 01-387 9286. *Contact:* Clarissa Cridland. Property: *Noddy.*

Withers (John) Enterprises Ltd., 11 Owen Mansions, Queens Club Gardens, London W14 9RS *T.* 01-385 5072.

art, music prizes, clubs

OPPORTUNITIES FOR FREELANCE ARTISTS
CAMILLA BRYDEN-BROWN

FINE ART

Opportunities for freelance artists are more numerous than is generally supposed. For fine art such as painting, it is best to contact galleries, of which there are many in this country, particularly in London. It is worth remembering, though, that they have the choice of a large market and specialise in a fairly limited field. If you want to exhibit at these galleries, perhaps to have a one-man show, it is advisable to find out about the type of exhibitions they hold. This you can do by visiting each gallery yourself and assessing the current work. It is best to visit likely galleries frequently in order to get to know their work and how they function. (*The Arts Review Yearbook* (£9.95, plus £2.50 postage and packing), published by Arts Review, 16 St. James's Gardens, London W11 4RE *T*. 01-603 7530 and 8533, contains a guide to London Galleries—including a description of the type of work in which they specialise—together with a list of Regional Galleries.) If you decide to approach a gallery, it is usual to write to the director with a short description, and photographs of some of your work, with a stamped addressed envelope for their return. The photographs should be clear, but not necessarily up to reproduction quality. It is possible to take the photographs yourself, but most towns have commercial photographers who work freelance for industry. Ask for an estimate first. Some of the greetings-card manufacturers already listed in this book are interested in paintings for reproduction. It would be wiser to write to them, if possible enclosing good colour transparencies of your work, before becoming involved in the expense of packing and sending paintings by post or carrier. Other useful reference books for the artist are the *London Art and Artists Guide*, 4th edition (£5.95) and *The Artists Directory*, 2nd edition (£6.95) published by Art Guide Publications, 28 Colville Road, London, W11 2BS *T*. 01-229 4669.

One of the best methods of displaying and selling paintings is at the annual Summer Exhibition at the Royal Academy in London. Anyone can submit work, which is put to the Selection Committee and the Hanging Committee. Sending in days are in March and these dates must be strictly adhered to. A handling fee allows artists to enter up to three pieces of work at £7.50 per entry. Should any subsequently be hung and sold the Royal Academy charges commission at 25% plus VAT. Full details will be found in the leaflet of regulations entitled *Notice to Artists* which is obtainable from mid-February each year from The Registry, The Royal Academy of Arts, Piccadilly, London, W1V 0DS. This leaflet refers to the exhibition of the coming summer of that year. If requests for it are sent at other times of the year the Royal Academy can only send the leaflet from the previous February. Other exhibitions are listed in *Arts Review* (£1.40 fortnightly).

ILLUSTRATION AND DESIGN

For a career in the field of illustration and design it is advisable to have a training in illustration, and also in typography if possible. Although the latter is not absolutely essential, it is helpful to the artist and to the publisher. Artists who launch into freelance work often do so gradually from the security of full-time employment, probably in the same field. It is useful to have the experience of working with a publisher or in an advertising agency or a studio first, as this gives the artist valuable background knowledge of suppliers and sources of work. Training in illustration can be obtained through a recognised course at art school, or through employment in a studio. Either method is an advantage, for even the most brilliantly gifted illustrator should know how to think in terms of printed work and to realise how work will reduce and reproduce.

Once an artist feels competent to accept commissions it is important to be available and reliable. Both these attributes are essential, and busy clients will not be bothered with artists who say vaguely that they had to go away or that the children were ill. Freelance work is a business, and will stand or fall by the competence or otherwise of the staff—you.

THE FOLIO

Artists who have already been in full-time employment in an advertising agency or publishing house will know of clients who are prepared to give them commissions, or they probably would not have started on the freelance venture, and if one commission is a success it will very often lead to another. For all artists, but particularly those with no connections, it is essential to make up a professional folio of work, spending some time and money on it, and showing as versatile a range of work as possible. For instance, it should include work in line, pencil, ink, line and tone, two or more colour line and full colour, and be on a variety of subjects. There are excellent folders, plastic envelopes or elaborate specimen books or cases containing plastic folders, for sale at most shops which stock equipment for designers. An overall colour scheme for your presentation helps to make your work look well-organised and professional. Designs or samples should be neatly trimmed and mounted on coloured cover paper (try black if in doubt) of a size to fit the folder or envelope. Paste the specimens of work on the cover paper, but do not use petroleum-based rubber solution if the sample of work is to be enclosed in a plastic envelope.

Gradually you will collect together printed specimens as the commissions increase, and your folio of work should be brought up to date all the time. Always get as many samples as you can beg, although if it is a book you will probably only get one copy. In this case, see if you can get some extra dust-jackets so that if the first one becomes worn you can replace it, and if necessary buy more copies of the book if that should also become worn. The publisher may well give you a discount on books on which you have worked. Any book specimens should be kept separately in plastic bags, but it would be expedient to ask for spare block pulls of your illustrations early on in the proceedings, and they should be mounted up in your specimen book. Try to keep your specimens immaculate.

PUBLISHERS

When the specimen folder is complete it is time to type letters to the production manager of as many publishing houses as practicable, asking for an interview in order to show your work, whether for illustrations or for book-jackets, or both. It would be wise to design an attractive personal stationery range which can be an excellent advertisement of your work. There are print shops that will produce your design very well and advise you if you are not skilled in typography or finished artwork. Usually they print by lithography quickly and at a reasonable price. A letterheading, preferably A4 because this is the most popular size and therefore is easily filed, can also be used as a compliment slip, invoice and estimate if necessary. A business card can be very useful. Space these letters out, or you may find yourself with too many appointments in one week. The production managers will usually grant you interviews (be on time), since they are interested in seeing new work, and they will probably be helpful about prices too, if you have no experience in this field. Book-publishing houses as a rule are not able to pay as highly as advertising agencies or popular magazines but they are usually fair. Do not overlook educational departments of publishing houses for there is considerable scope for illustrating modern school books. You may have to accept low fees to begin with until you know your market and your worth, but you will be gaining valuable knowledge and experience.

At each interview it would be a good idea to ask if there is anyone else in the firm who would be interested in seeing your work, such as the advertising manager or in some firms the editors, who occasionally commission artists. Do not expect to be seen by other people in the firm at the same time as your first interview, but be prepared to come back another time. It would be better not to leave your samples to be seen by other people, particularly if you have only one folio. You will be needing your folio for other interviews, and there is a very real danger that it will go astray, or that specimens will be damaged beyond use, with no redress. If your work is liked and your first commission is satisfactory, you will often find that your work has been recommended to other people in similar fields.

ARTISTS' AGENTS

Advertising agencies frequently use the services of artists' agents, who can be good or bad, but if you are accepted on the books of a good one life will be much easier for you. Agents generally work very hard on behalf of both clients and artists: they take the brief, negotiate the price and commission you to do the work, usually taking 25 to 30 per cent of the fee. Although this percentage may seem high, you should remember that they do a lot of work on your behalf and invariably manage to get a more professional fee for you than you can obtain for yourself, even after the percentage has been deducted.

FEES

There is no definite rule in assessing fees. A simple method of calculation is to decide upon a weekly salary and the number of hours of work for a normal week. This salary is then divided by the number of hours, which gives a basic hourly rate. Rent, rates, heating, telephone and other general studio costs should be considered, materials bought especially for a commission have to be added to the invoice concerned. As a rough guide one third of a fee will be payable to the Inland Revenue. Time spent at meetings with clients and the travelling time and cost involved should be added to the time sheet.

This solution may appear to be simple but it will be seen that the hourly rate is high. Many clients offer low fees and it is sometimes necessary to choose between accepting work at little or no return when the result is a good specimen of work, or to do without work. One of the greatest problems to the freelance artist are the artists in full-time employment who are prepared to accept commissions out of hours for a lower fee. With no studio overheads and a regular salary they spoil the market for the serious professional.

ADVERTISING AGENCIES

Advertising agencies employ art buyers who are very skilled and capable people and should be approached by a letter similar to that previously described, giving details of the type of work at which you are best. Here again, once you have obtained the interview and shown your work, you might ask if there is anyone else who would be interested, not necessarily at that moment.

STUDIOS

Studios exist in most cities, and the type of their work varies; some specialise in purely commercial work in finished lettering and finished artwork, and they employ highly skilled and extremely able artists. Often their work involves the use of airbrushes and photographic skills, but they do sometimes employ freelance artists for specific commissions, and may well like to have photocopies of your work on file in case they need drawings or diagrams for catalogues or similar uses. Technical drawing is called technical drawing with good reason and requires specific training. If you feel your work would be of interest to a studio, write to the studio manager and ask for an interview. Should they ask for photographs of your work, a commercial photographic studio will prepare these for you. If you wish to have photographs made, the photographic studio will help you with the details and give you prices before they take on the work.

GRAPHIC DESIGNERS

A graphic designer, who may be running a one-man studio of his own and doing freelance design and typography (designing for printing), may also use illustrators from time to time. Graphic designers are difficult to track down, but once you have found one you are likely to be on the trail of many others. They will not be able to use your work all the time, even if they like it, as not all their commissions require drawings. The more versatile you are the more opportunities are available to you, and artists skilled only in very specialised fields, such as lettering and illumination, usually know where to offer their work.

IMPORTANCE OF RELIABILITY

Remember also that once you have started to get commissions, you must be accurate and reliable, as well as available. If you are given a date for the work, it must be presented on time, even if this means sitting up half the night before. Do not, for example, fall back on the excuse of mild illness or you will lose sympathy and understanding should you have the misfortune to be more seriously ill. Once you have received the commission you are part of a team, even though you may not know the other members of it. There are often unforeseen events which hold up production anyway, and it is as well to see that you do not come to be considered one. It is wise to take trouble over the presentation, and you have only yourself to blame if you have not protected your finished work adequately. It is distressing to have one's precious work destroyed or damaged, the more so if it means doing it all again.

You will discover that once you have started freelance work your commissions will build up gradually, although most artists have some periods when there is little work available. Use these 'rests' advantageously to prepare more specimen drawings and to experiment with new techniques and equipment, and to make sure your folio is ready to show again. At such times you should be looking for new outlets, visiting more agencies and publishers, or checking with the ones you have visited in the past.

Above all decide whether or not you really want to do this work: are you sure it is not just a pleasant day-dream with the appeal of being called an artist? It is hard work, but if you have ability and are consistent, reliable, enthusiastic and optimistic, even at those times when there is a lull, then you will be happy and successful.

ARTISTS AND DESIGNERS

CODE OF PROFESSIONAL CONDUCT

This is an abbreviated version of the Code of Professional Conduct issued by the *Society of Industrial Artists and Designers*. A complete copy is available from 12 Carlton House Terrace, London SW1Y 5AH *T.* 01-930 1911 (35p. to members; 65p to non-members). See also entry in **Societies.**

Introduction

1. This Code issued by the Society of Industrial Artists and Designers establishes a workable pattern of professional conduct for the benefit of its members and of those who employ their services.
2. All members of the Society undertake as a condition of membership that they will abide by this Code.
3. The Council of the Society has empowered its Conduct Committee to question any member thought to be behaving in a manner contrary to this Code and may as a result of the Committee's report reprimand, suspend or expel that member.
4. When members are working or seeking work abroad they will observe the rules of professional conduct currently in use in that country.

The designer's professional responsibilities

5. Designers work primarily for the benefit of their clients or their employers. Like everyone engaged in professional activities, designers have responsibilities not only to their clients or employers but also to their fellow practitioners and to society at large. It follows therefore that designers who are members of the Society accept certain obligations specifically in regard to these responsibilities.

The designer's responsibility to his client or employer

6. Good professional relations between a designer and an employer or client depend on the designer's acceptance of the need to be professionally and technically competent and on his/her ability to provide honourable and efficient advice and performance.
7. They will also depend on the reliance which the employer or client can place on a designer's integrity in all confidential matters relating to his/her business.
8. No member may work simultaneously for more than one employer or client known to be in competition, without their knowledge and approval. Similarly no member, or his/her associates or staff, may divulge information confidential to their client or employer without their consent, subject to any requirement under law.
9. The Society believes that it is in the interest of the design profession and of industry that the employment of qualified designers should be increased. Members may therefore promote their own services and those of their profession in a manner appropriate to the various fields of practice in which they work. It is essential however, that any claims made by them, or by those acting for them, are factually correct, honourable and clear as to their origin, and that the effect shall not be at variance with this Code nor cause harm to their fellow members.
10. It is normal for designers to be paid for their professional services, whether executive or advisory. The Society recommends methods of charging which it considers appropriate for various types of work, but members will use their own judgement in agreeing fees with their clients.

11. The Society recommends conditions of engagement to enable proper working relationships to be established between members and their clients.

12. Whereas members will make for their clients the best possible trading arrangements with contractors, manufacturers and suppliers, their responsibilities to contractors or suppliers are as professionally important as is their responsibilities to their clients. They must therefore be prepared to act as impartial arbitrators, if need be, to ensure fair dealing on both sides.

13. Whilst acting for a client, members may not divert to their own advantage any discounts, reductions or other financial benefits offered as inducement by contractors, manufacturers or suppliers. Similarly members must disclose any financial involvement which they may have with contractors or suppliers they may recommend.

14. On the other hand, if a member is also a manufacturer, retailer or agent in his/her own right, a member may accept those financial terms which are normally honourably offered within the trade, provided they accrue to his company or his organisation and not to himself privately.

15. Although the relationship between a staff designer and employer may well differ from that between consultant and client, the employed designer, who is a member of the Society, shall accept a responsibility to the employer on the same terms of professional integrity and confidentiality.

The designer's responsibility to his fellow practitioners

16. From time to time members may find themselves called upon to comment on other designers' work and in a consultative capacity may reasonably be expected to do so. Personal opinion must play a significant part in any criticism, but members should be aware of the fine dividing line between objective and destructive criticism. Personal denigration amongst members is regarded as intolerable and the Society will support any member who is shown to have been so affronted.

17. Similarly the Society regards copying or plagiarism with intent as wholly unprofessional.

18. No member shall knowingly seek to supplant another designer currently working on a project whether satisfactorily or not. There are occasions when more than one designer may be engaged on the same project. Where, however, a member suspects that his/her engagement may supplant rather than augment the service of another, he/she shall seek an assurance from the client that any previous association with another designer has been terminated.

19. Neither shall a member charge nor receive a fee, neither make nor receive a gift or other benefit, from a fellow member, in recognition of a recommendation to a post or an assignment.

20. Members should assure themselves that competitions they may be invited to assess or may wish to enter are in accordance with the Society's regulations for holding of design competitions.

MARKETS FOR ARTISTS
ART AGENTS AND COMMERCIAL ART STUDIOS

In their own interests Artists are advised to make preliminary enquiries before submitting work, and to ascertain terms of work. Commission varies but averages 25 per cent. **The Association of Illustrators** (full details under **Societies**), provides a valuable service for illustrators, agents and clients.

A.L.I. Press Agency, Ltd., Boulevard Anspach 111-115, B9—1000 Brussels, Belgium. *T.* 02 512.73.94. *Director:* G. Lans. Cartoons, comics, strips, puzzles, entertainment features, illustrations for covers, posters on order or in syndication. All feature material for newspapers and magazines. The biggest choice in picture stories for children and adults. Art studio. Market for transparencies.

Allied Artists Ltd 15 Heddon Street, Regent Street, London, W1R 7LF *T.* 01-437 5788-9. *Director:* G. R. Mills. Specialising in realistic figure illustration particularly for magazines, bookjackets, video and advertising, and also other illustration styles for promotions and publishing. Extensive stocks of second rights illustrations for syndication.

Associated Freelance Artists Limited, 19 Russell Street, London, WC2B 5HP *T.* 01-836 2507-8. *Directors:* Eva Morris, Doug FitzMaurice. Freelance illustrators mainly in children's and educational fields; strip illustration; book design; character merchandising.

Beint & Beint (1976), Lupus House, 11-13 Macklin Street, London WC2B 5NH *T.* 01-240 0805. *Proprietor:* Michele Beint. Illustrations in a variety of styles for advertising, design groups and some publishing.

Craddock, John (1981), Ground Floor, 66 Carter Lane, London EC4V 5EA *T.* 01-698 6814. *Partners:* John Craddock, Vi Craddock. All types of illustration: figure, food, story, humour, caricature for advertising, magazine and book publishing, newspapers, public relations. *Commission:* 25%.

David Lewis Management (1974), Worlds End Studios, 134 Lots Road, London, SW10 0RJ *T.* 01-351 4333. *Director:* David Lewis. High quality illustration applicable to book publishing and magazines. Return postage with samples essential. *Average rate of commission:* 25%.

Fleming, Ian, Associates Ltd (1970), 1 Wedgwood Mews, 12-13 Greek Street, London, W1V 5LW *T.* 01-734 8701. *Managing Director:* Ian Fleming. Illustration and lettering for advertising and publishing. *Rate of commission* 33⅓%.

Garden Studio, The (1929), 11-13 Broad Court, Covent Garden, London, WC2B 5QJ *T.* 01-836 3653. *Managing Agent:* John Havergal. All illustration markets covered. *Commission* 25%.

Gossop (R.P.) Ltd. (1923), 4 Denmark Street, London, WC2H 8LP. *T.* 01-836 1058. *Directors:* Bronson Gossop, Kathleen Wheston. Illustration, book decoration, educational drawings and diagrams, maps, graphic design for publicity, and jackets. *Rate of commission:* 20 to 25 per cent.

Hodgson, John, Agency (1965), 3 Bromley Place, London W1P 5HB *T.* 01-580 3773. Illustrations for advertising, publishing, editorial. *Rate of commission:* 25%.

Jones, Libba (1983), Dale Cottage, Dale End, Brassington, Derbyshire DE4 4HA *T.* (062 985) 353. Professional artwork and illustrations for ceramics, greetings cards, jigsaw puzzles, calendars, stationery, and prints/posters. Submission of samples required for consideration.

Juvenilia. *Proprietor:* Mrs. Rosemary Bromley, Avington, Winchester, Hants, SO21 1DB *T.* (096278) 656. Professional artwork for the children's market considered. Picture books—particularly author illustrated. No games or play books. Preliminary letter with S.A.E. Terms 20%. Return postage for artwork and acknowledgement imperative. Production and design in association with Elizabeth Weaver Ltd.

Linden Artists Ltd (1962) 86 Petty France, London SW1H 9EA *T.* 01-222 3050 and 4065. Illustrations for advertising, publishing, packaging. *Rate of commission:* from 25%.

London Art Services Ltd., 175 Bermondsey Street, London SE1 3VW *T.* 01-403 4181. Artists, designers, illustrators and photographers. Art studio offering service in illustration, lettering, general art work, photography.

Martin, John & Artists, Ltd., 5 Wardour Street, London, W1V 3HE *T.* 01-734 9000. *Directors:* W. Bowen-Davies, C. M. Bowen-Davies, L. L. Kemp. *Production Manager:* W. Bowen-Davies. Illustrations for children (educational and fictional), dust jackets, paperbacks, magazines, encyclopaedias, advertising.

Meiklejohn Illustration (1971), 28 Shelton Street, Covent Garden, London, WC2H 9JN. *T.* 01-240 2077. All types of illustration.

Middleton (N.E.), Ltd., 44 Great Russell Street, London, WC1B 3PA *T.* 01-580 1999. General.

Miss Carter Publications (1972), 25 Silverwell Street, Bolton BL1 1PP *T.* (0204) 386608. *Partners:* Keith and Patricia Lee. Fine art print publishers and artists agents.

Mundy, Maggie (1983), 216 King Street, London W6 0RA *T.* 01-741 5862. Realistic figurative work for all aspects of publishing and advertising, including technical, medical and natural history. *Rate of commission:* 25%.

Oxford Illustrators Ltd (1968), Aristotle Lane, Oxford OX2 6TR *T.* (0865) 512331. Studio of full-time illustrators working exclusively for publishers—science, technical, medical, biological, botanical, engineering, computer, electrical, educational. Recent installation producing computer generated diagrams, graphs, etc.

Rogers & Co., Artists' Agents (1906), 11 Bishop's Court, Chancery Lane, London WC2A 1EB *T.* 01-405 1821. *Proprietor:* K. M. Woolley.

Specs Art Agency (1982), Billbrook House, Winchcombe Street, Cheltenham, Glos., GL52 2NW, *T.* (0242) 515951. *Director:* Roland Berry. High quality illustration work for advertisers, publishers and all other forms of visual communication.

Temple Art Agency (1939), 11 Bishop's Court, Chancery Lane, London, WC2A 1EB *T.* 01-405 8295. Children's book illustration; picture strips; magazine illustrations; historical reconstruction.

Woodward, Michael, Associates (1980), Barkston Towers, Barkston Ash, Tadcaster, North Yorkshire LS24 9PS *T.* (093 781) 7598. *Telex:* 55293 Chacom G. *Fax:* (093 781) 7727. *Proprietor:* Michael R. Woodward. Art library and international art agency, specialising in posters, prints, greetings cards, stationery products, etc. Terms on application. Freelance artists considered on submission of samples.

Young Artists (1970), 2 Greenland Place, London, NW1 0AP *T.* 01-267 9661. Book covers, editorial, advertising. *Average rate of commission:* 30%.

DRAWINGS, DESIGNS AND VERSES FOR CARDS, ETC.

*Member of the Greeting Card and Calendar Association.

In their own interest artists are advised to write giving details of the work which they have to offer, and asking for requirements before submitting the work.

*__Arnold Barton Cards Ltd.__, Church Bridge Works, Henry Street, Church, Lancashire BB5 4EL. *T.* Accrington (0254) 382121. Designs suitable for reproduction as greeting cards from experienced artists only.

Arnold (Joseph) & Co. Ltd., Church Bridge Works, Accrington, Lancashire, BB5 4EL *T.* Accrington (0254) 382121. Publishers for **Webb Ivory, Studio Cards.** Designs suitable for reproduction as greeting cards from experienced artists only.

*__Athena International,__ P.O. Box 13, Bishops Stortford, Herts. CM23 5PQ. *T.* (0279) 58351. *Art Director:* Stewart F. E. Stott. Designs for greetings cards, gift tags, gift wrap, and general stationery. Paintings and illustrations of a professional standard for reproduction as prints and posters. S.A.E. essential for return of work.

C.C.A. Stationery Ltd., Eastway, Fulwood, Preston, PR2 4WS. *T.* (0772) 794508. Publishers of personalised wedding stationery and Christmas cards. Pleased to consider any original artwork but verses not required.

Carfax Cards (1927), 42 Glentham Road, London SW13 9JL *T.* 01-748 1122. Artwork for greeting cards, postcards, prints. Christmas, occasions, humour. No verses.

Castle Cards Co. Ltd., Great George Street, Preston, PR1 1TJ *T.* (0772) 59267. *Joint Managing Directors:* P. Packer, G. King. *Design Manager:* Jean Ashton. Greeting cards, mini-notes, Christmas cards. Designs and verses on all subjects.

De Montfort Cards Ltd (1984), 37-41 Bedford Row, London WC1R 4JH *T.* 01-430 2388. *Directors:* Charles Mathew, Veronica Mathew, Peter Crick. Artwork and drawings for all occasions and Christmas greeting cards.

Dryad, P.O. Box 38, Northgates, Leicester LE1 9BU *T.* (0533) 50405 *Telex:* 341766 Dryad G. Dryad *500 Series,* full colour craft booklets, workcards and patterns.

*__Elvin, Simon, Ltd__ (1978), Wooburn Industrial Park, Wooburn Green, Bucks., HP10 0PE *T.* (06285) 26711. *Directors:* S.P. Elvin, J.E. Elvin. Drawings.

Felix Rosenstiel's Widow & Son, Ltd., Fine Art Publishers, 33-35 Markham Street, London, SW3 3NR *T.* 01-352 3551. Invite offers of Originals of a professional standard for reproduction as Picture Prints for the Picture Framing trade. Oil paintings and strong Water-colours. Any type of subject considered. Also subjects for decorative stationery trade.

*__Fine Art Graphics Ltd.__ (Incorporating **Raphael Tuck & Sons Ltd.**), Dawson Lane, Dudley Hill, Bradford BD4 6HW *T.* (0274) 689514. *Directors:* D. T. Barnes (Chairman), G. B. Barnes, R. F. Kerry, J. P. Parker. Fine art, greeting card and calendar publishers.

*__Jarrold & Sons Ltd__ (1770), Colour Publications, Barrack Street, Norwich, NR3 1TR *T.* (0603) 660211 *Telex:* 97497. *T.A.* Jarrold, Norwich. *Directors:* P.J. Jarrold, R.E. Jarrold, A.C. Jarrold, T. Watt, D. Clark, R. Bussey, G. Bloxsom, P. Merttens. Drawings, transparencies (35mm or larger). Postcards, calendars, pictorial books on natural history, topography, hobbies, architecture.

Kardonia Ltd., Farrier Street, Worcester, WR1 3BH *T.* (0905) 611294.

Medici Society, Ltd., The, 34-42 Pentonville Road, London, N1 9HG *T.* 01-837 7099. Requirements: paintings suitable for reproduction as large prints or greeting cards. Preliminary letter and return postage essential.

Miss Carter Publications (1972), 25 Silverwell Street, Bolton BL1 1PP *T.* (0204) 386608. Oil and watercolour paintings to professional standards.

*****Royle Publications, Ltd.,** Royle House, Wenlock Road, London, N1 7ST *T.* 01-253 7654. Greeting cards, calendars, prints and gift wrap. Only accept work in colour.

*****Rust Craft Greeting Cards (U.K.) Ltd.,** Mill Street East, Dewsbury, West Yorkshire, WF12 9AW *T.* Dewsbury 465200.

*****Sharpe (W.N.) Ltd.** Bingley Road, Bradford BD9 6SD *T.* (0274) 42244. Greetings cards, gift wrap. Artwork in colour, verses considered.

Solomon & Whitehead (Guild Prints) Ltd., Lynn Lane, Shenstone, Staffs, WS14 0DX. *T.* 480696. Fine Art prints framed and unframed.

Tatt, Noel, Ltd., (1954) Nash House, Nash Hill, Lyminge, Folkestone, CT18 8ED *T.* (0304) 211644. *Directors:* Noel Tatt, Vencke Tatt, Derek Bates, Anthony Sharpe. Greetings cards, prints, postcards.

Thomas Leach Limited, 54 Ock Street, Abingdon-on-Thames, Oxfordshire, OX14 5DE *T.* Abingdon (0235) 20444. (Address to Edward Jones.) Sketches of religious subjects suitable for reproduction as Christmas or Easter Cards.

*****Universal Greetings Ltd.,** Church Bridge Works, Church, Nr. Accrington, Lancashire BB5 4EL. *Director:* D. Espley (Managing). Enquiries to Alison Spenceley (Publisher).

*****Valentines of Dundee, Ltd.,** P.O. Box 74, Kinnoull Road, Dundee, DD1 9NQ *T.* (0382) 814711. Everyday greeting cards, Christmas cards, gift wraps, social stationery, St. Valentine's Day, Easter, Mother's Day, Father's Day, calendars. Address to *The Director of Product Management*.

*****Wilson Bros. Greeting Cards Ltd.,** Church Bridge Works, Church, Lancashire BB5 4EL *T.* (0254) 390813.

MARKETS FOR PHOTOGRAPHERS

Photographers are advised to study carefully the detailed requirements of journals at the beginning of the *Yearbook*. Book publishers, especially those issuing technical books and school books, will be glad to know the range of subjects covered by a photographer.

GREETINGS, VIEWCARD, CALENDAR AND COLOUR SLIDES

A preliminary letter to ascertain requirements is advisable.
So far as colour is concerned, and most of the firms mentioned below are concerned with colour, usually colour transparencies are required. Very few firms will consider 35mm. frames; 5 in. x 4 in. is preferred, and 3¼ x 2¼ is acceptable. 2¼ in. square is the minimum size acceptable to film libraries and agencies. Only top quality transparencies should be submitted; inferior work is never accepted.
Postage for return of photographs should be enclosed.

*Member of the Greeting Card and Calendar Association

***Arnold Barton Cards Ltd.** Church Bridge Works, Henry Street, Church, Lancashire BB5 4EL *T*. Accrington (0254) 382121. Photographs for reproduction as greeting cards.

***Athena International,** P.O. Box 13, Bishops Stortford, Herts. CM23 5PQ. *T*. (0279) 58351. *Art Director:* Stewart F. E. Stott. Professional quality transparencies for posters, prints and postcards, preferably not 35 mm. S.A.E. essential for return of work.

C.C.A. Stationery Ltd., Eastway, Fulwood, Preston PR2 4WS *T*. (0772) 794508. Personalised wedding stationery, Christmas cards.

Castle Cards Co. Ltd., Great George Street, Preston, PR1 1TJ *T*. (0772) 59267. *Joint Managing Directors:* P. Packer, G. King. *Design Manager:* Jean Ashton. Everyday and Christmas greeting cards. Transparencies, preferably not 35mm.

De Montfort Cards Ltd (1984), 37-41 Bedford Row, London WC1R 4JH *T*. 01-430 2388. *Directors:* Charles Mathew, Veronica Mathew, Peter Crick. Transparencies, preferrably 5" x 4" for all occasion and Christmas greetings cards.

Dennis (E.T.W.) & Sons, Ltd., Printing House Square, Melrose Street, Scarborough, Yorkshire, YO12 7SJ *T*. Scarborough (0723) 361317. Interested in first class transparencies for reproduction as local view postcards and calendars. 3¼ x 2¼ in. or 35 mm. transparencies ideal for postcard reproduction.

***Dixon (J. Arthur), DRG (UK) Ltd.,** Forest Side, Newport, Isle of Wight, PO30 5QW *T*. Isle of Wight (0983) 523381. Greeting cards, postcards, gift wrap and booklets.

Kardonia, Ltd., Farrier Street, Worcester, WR1 3BH *T*. (0905) 611294.

Lowe Aston Calendars, Ltd., Saltash, Cornwall, PL12 4HL *T*. Saltash (075 55) 2233. Calendar printers.

Medici Society, Ltd., The, 34-42 Pentonville Road, London, N1 9HG *T*. 01-837 7099. Photographs suitable for reproduction as greeting cards.

Mowbray (A.R.), & Co. Ltd, Saint Thomas House, Becket Street, Oxford, OX1 1SJ. 2¼ in. square colour transparencies for parish magazine covers. Seasonal scenes, human interest subjects. Also unusual black and white photographs for editorial articles.

*Royle Publications, Ltd., Royle House, Wenlock Road, London, N1 7ST *T.* 01-253 7654. Colour transparencies required for two calendars, *Moods of Nature* and *Gardens of Britain*. Natural landscape photography taken in Britain and abroad or pictures of ornate flower gardens in Britain.

*Salmon (J.), Ltd., 100 London Road, Sevenoaks, Kent, TN13 1BB *T.* Sevenoaks 452381. Picture postcards, calendars and greeting cards.

Tatt, Noel Ltd., (1954) Nash House, Nash Hill, Lyminge, Folkestone, CT18 8ED *T.* (0304) 211644. *Directors:* Noel Tatt, Vencke Tatt, Derek Bates, Anthony Sharpe. Transparencies for greeting cards, prints and postcards.

Vision International (1979), 30 Museum Street, London WC1A 1LH *T.* 01-636 9516. *Telex:* 23539.

*Wilson Bros. Greeting Cards, Ltd., Church Bridge Works, Church, Lancashire BB5 4EL *T.* (0254) 390813.

PHOTOGRAPHIC AGENCIES AND PICTURE LIBRARIES

THE FREELANCE PHOTOGRAPHER AND THE AGENT
Bruce Coleman

Photographic agencies and libraries have a dual role in the service they provide. They meet the needs and demands of Picture Editors, Picture Researchers and Art Buyers and, at the same time, provide a service to the freelance photographer. The enterprising photographer, wishing to penetrate the publishing market, would do well to consider employing the services of an agent whose knowledge of current trends and client contact will gear the photographer's output to the requirements of the markets. The complexities of reproduction rights are best left to an agent—that's if the photographer wishes to protect the copyright of his work!

Selecting the right agent very much depends on the type of work the photographer is producing and he should, therefore, take a look at several agencies before choosing the one he thinks will be of advantage to him. Some agents, for example, work in the syndication area, selling news and topical pictures to the world's press; others are in the stock business maintaining a library of photographers' work orientated to the editorial market. Agents normally do not sell pictures outright but lease them for a specific use and fee from which they deduct a commission. A good photograph in the hands of a good agent can be published several times over and bring in royalties for many years.

Before submitting your work to an agent, a preliminary letter is recommended enquiring if (1) he is accepting new photographers and (2) details of his specific needs.

The agent will wish to see an initial presentation of at least two hundred photographs and the photographer should indicate the number of photographs he plans to submit in the course of a year. Agents are keen to encourage the active photographer who can supply a regular stream of good quality work. Serious attention should be given to the caption of every picture as this can often mean the difference between a sale or a rejection. A caption should be brief and legible and an example of a good nature caption would be:

>   Spotted Hyena (C. crocuta)
>   Serengeti
>   Aggressive behaviour

or, a geographical caption:

>   Canada: Northwest Territories
>   Eskimo fur trappers and dogsled

Some time spent on the presentation of your work, editing for composition, content, sharpness and in the case of transparencies, colour saturation, will create a favourable impression. When submitting original colour transparencies, to ensure they are protected from damage and also to facilitate easy examination place them in clear plastic sleeves, never between glass. Do not submit transparencies which you may require for personal use as it is quite impossible for an agent to recall pictures at short notice from his client.

One final point, never supply similar photographs to more than one agent as the problems created by almost identical pictures appearing, say, on a calendar or a greeting card can be embarrassing and costly to rectify. Indeed, for this reason, many agents insist on an exclusive arrangement between themselves and their photographers.

*Member of The British Association of Picture Libraries and Agencies

A-Z Botanical Collection, Ltd., Holmwood House, Mid Holmwood, Dorking, Surrey, RH5 4HE *T.* Dorking (0306) 888130. Colour transparencies, minimum size 2¼ in. square, of all subjects of a botanical nature.

***Ace Photo Agency** (1980), 22 Maddox Street, London W1R 9PG *T.* 01-629 0303. General library: people, industry, travel, commerce, skies, sport, music and natural history. World wide syndication. *Terms:* 50%. S.A.E. for enquiries.

Aerofilms Limited (1919), Gate Studios, Station Road, Boreham Wood, Herts, WD6 1EJ *T.* 01-207 0666. *Fax:* 01-207 5433. Comprehensive library of vertical and oblique aerial photographs of U.K., large areas with complete cover.

Alexander, Bryan and Cherry, Photography (1973), 33 Mount Pleasant, Arundel, West Sussex. BN18 9BD *T.* (0903) 882897. Arctic regions with emphasis on Eskimos and Lapps.

***All-Sport Photographic Ltd.** (1972), All-Sport House, Greenlea Park, Prince George's Road, Colliers Wood, London SW19 2JD *T.* 01-685 1010. International sport and leisure.

Allen, J. Catling, Rev., Hope House, 29 Lovaine Place, North Shields, Tyne & Wear, NE29 0BU *T.* (091) 2583701. Library of colour transparencies (35 mm.) and black and white photographs of Bible Lands, including archaeological sites and the religions of Islam and Judaism. Medieval abbeys and priories, cathedrals and churches in Britain. Also historic, rural and scenic Britain. (Not an agent or buyer).

American History Picture Library, 3 Barton Buildings, Bath BA1 2JR *T.* (0225) 334213. Photographs, engravings, colour transparencies covering the exploration, social, political and military history of North America from 15th to 20th century. Conquistadores, Civil War, Gangsters, Moon landings, etc. Prints and photos purchased.

***Ancient Art & Architecture Photo Library,** 6 Kenton Road, Harrow-on-the-Hill, Middlesex, HA1 2BL *T.* 01-422 1214. *Telex:* 268048. Specialising in the civilisations of the Middle East, Mediterranean countries, Europe, Asia, Americas, from ancient times to recent past, their arts, architecture, landscapes, beliefs, peoples past and present.

***Angel, Heather,** Highways, 6 Vicarage Hill, Farnham, Surrey, GU9 8HJ *T.* Farnham (0252) 716700. Colour transparencies (35 mm. and 2¼ in. square) and monochrome prints with world-wide coverage of natural history and biological subjects including gardens, close-ups, photomicrographs and underwater images. Detailed catalogues on request.

***Animal Photography Ltd.** (1955), 4 Marylebone Mews, New Cavendish Street, London, W1M 7LF *T.* 01-935 0503. Horses, dogs, cats, East Africa, Galapagos.

***Aquila Photographics,** P.O. Box 1, Studley, Warwickshire, B80 7JG *T.* Studley (052 785) 2357. Specialists in ornithological subjects, but covering all aspects of natural history in both colour and black and white.

Arctic Camera, Derek Fordham (1978), 66 Ashburnham Grove, Greenwich, London, SE10 8UJ *T.* 01-692 7651. Mainly colour transparencies of all aspects of Arctic life and environment.

***Ardea London Ltd.,** 35 Brodrick Road, London, SW17 7DX *T.* 01-672 2067 and 8787. *T.A.* Ardeaphotos. *Telex:* 896691 Tlxir G. Su Gooders. Specialist worldwide natural history photographic library of animals, birds, plants, fish, insects, reptiles.

Asian Affairs, Royal Society for, 2 Belgrave Square, London, SW1X 8PJ *T.* 01-235 5122. Archive library of original 19th and 20th century black-and-white photographs, glass slides, etc., of Asia. Publishes *Asian Affairs* 3 times p.a.

***Aspect Picture Library Ltd** (1971) 40 Rostrevor Road, London SW6 5AD *T.* 01-736 1998 and 731 7362. *Telex:* 297606 Polyis G. General library including wildlife, tribes, cities, industry, science, space.

Associated Press (The), Ltd., (News Photo Department), The Associated Press House, 12 Norwich Street, London EC4A 1BP *T.* 01-353 1515. *T.A.* Appho, Telex, London. News and feature pictures. Negatives preferred.

Aviation Photographs International (1970), 23 Bankside, Swindon, SN1 4JZ *T.* (0793) 47179. All types of aviation. Assignments undertaken.

Aviation Picture Library (Austin J. Brown) (1970), 3 Berkeley Crescent, Clifton, Bristol, BS8 1HA *T.* (0272) 213109 and 49894. Worldwide aviation photographic library, all aspects of industry. Aerial photos of South West England and Caribbean. Travel photos of U.K., U.S.A., West Indies. Material taken since 1960. Commissions undertaken.

B. & B. Photographs (1974), Dodds, Clifford Chambers, Stratford upon Avon, Warwickshire, CV37 8HX *T.* (0789) 204636. 35 mm. colour library of horticulture (especially pests and diseases) and biogeography (worldwide), natural history (especially Britain) and biological education.

Band, Alan, Associates, 25 Longdown Road, Farnham, Surrey, GU10 3JL *T.* (0252) 713022. *Telex:* 858623 Telbur G. International news and feature picture service for British and overseas publishers.

***Barnaby's Picture Library,** 19 Rathbone Street, London, W1P 1AF *T.* 01-636 6128-9. Requires photographs for advertising and editorial publication. Photographs not purchased, sender retains copyright.

Bassano & Vandyk Studios, incorporating **Elliott & Fry,** 35 Moreton Street, London, SW1V 2NY *T.* 01-821 9182. Specialists in historical portraits, royals, composers, politicians, academics, actors, writers, etc.

***BBC Hulton Picture Library,** 35 Marylebone High Street, London, W1M 4AA *T.* 01-927 4735. Historical picture library founded by *Picture Post*, containing over ten million pictures on all topics, up to 1980. Now includes the *Standard/Express* library. Agents in the UK for Bettmann/UPI, New York.

Beaumont, Alan, Dr., 52 Squires Walk, Lowestoft, Suffolk, NR32 4LA *T.* (0502) 60126. World-wide collection of monochrome prints and colour transparencies (35 mm. and 6 x 7 cm.) of natural history, countryside, windmills and aircraft. No other photographers required.

Benson, Stephen, Slide Bureau, 45 Sugden Road, London, SW11 5EB *T.* 01-223 8635. World: agriculture, archaeology, architecture, commerce, everyday life, culture, environment, geography, science, tourism. Speciality: South America, the Caribbean, Australasia and Nepal. Assignments undertaken.

BIPS-Bernsen's International Press Service, Ltd., 9 Paradise Close, Eastbourne, East Sussex BN20 8BT *T.* (0323) 28760. (For full details see under **Syndicates, News and Press Agencies.**)

Blake, John, Picture Library (1975), 26 Malvern Drive, Thornbury, Bristol, Avon BS12 2HY *T.* (0454) 418321 and 413240. England, Scotland and Wales: landscapes, architecture, churches, gardens, countryside. General topography of Iceland, Switzerland, Tenerife, Mid-West and West U.S.A., France, Spain. Horse Trials including Badminton and Gatcombe Park. *Terms:* 50%.

Bodleian Library, Oxford, OX1 3BG *T.* (0865) 244675. Photographic library of 30,000 35 mm. (5" x 4" to order) colour transparencies, of subjects mostly from medieval manuscripts with iconographical index to illuminations.

Bord, Janet and Colin, Melysfan, Llangwm, Corwen, Clwyd LL21 0RD *T.* (049 082) 472. Library of black and white photographs and colour transparencies, specialising in the prehistoric and Roman sites of Britain, but also covering rural and scenic Britain in general, e.g. landscapes, wild flowers, villages, churches. Also strange phenomena. Do not act as agents for other photographers.

Boxing Picture Library, 3 Barton Buildings, Bath BA1 2JR *T.* (0225) 334213. Prints, engravings and photos of famous boxers, boxing personalities and famous fights from 18th century to recent years.

*****Bridgeman Art Library,** 19 Chepstow Road, London, W2 5BP *T.* 01-727 4065, 229 7420. *Telex:* 265208 Art Pix. Documentary and fine art collection; specialists in top quality colour transparencies relating to the arts: European and Oriental paintings and prints, Christmas material, antiques, arms and armour, history, natural history, maps, manuscripts, sculpture, topography, transport.

*****Britain on View Photographic Library,** official photographic library for British Tourist Authority and English Tourist Board. Thames Tower, Black's Road, London W6 9EL *T.* 01-846 9000. General UK travel including many special subjects. Colour, black and white. Mon. to Fri. 11 am – 1 pm, 2 – 4 pm.

Brown, Hamish, 21 Carlin Craig, Kinghorn, Fife, KY3 9RX *T.* Kinghorn (0592) 890422. Photographs and 35 mm. transparencies of Scottish topographical, Morocco, mountain ranges of Europe, Africa, India and South America.

Bryan, Malcolm, 6 Old London Road, Knockholt, Nr. Sevenoaks, Kent, TN14 7JN. *T.* (0959) 32601. *Telex:* 8951182 Gecoms G. Motor sport, motoring, profiles, general sport.

Camerapix, News and feature picture agency (1960), P.O. Box 45048, Nairobi, Kenya. *T.* 23511 or 334398. *Telex:* 22576. Covers the whole of Africa (except South Africa) and the Middle East. Contemporary African—social, general, political and nature. African wildlife.

*****Cash, J. Allan, Photolibrary, (J. Allan Cash Ltd.),** 74 South Ealing Road, London, W5 4QB *T.* 01-840 4141. Worldwide photographic library; travel, landscape, natural history, wild life. Details available for photographers interested in contributing.

*****Central Press Photos, Ltd., The,**—see **Photo Source Ltd.**.

*****Cephas Picture Library** (1982), 20 Trafalgar Drive, Walton on Thames, Surrey KT12 1NZ *T.* (0932) 241903. People, places, agriculture, industry, religion, architecture, travel, food and wine, crafts; especially France—wine industry modern architecture.

Christmas Archives (1978), Wassail House, 64 Severn Road, Cardiff CF1 9EA *T.* (0222) 41120. (For full details see under **Editorial, Literary and Production Services.**)

*****City Syndication Ltd.** (1980), 47 Fleet Street, London EC4Y 1BJ *T.* 01-583 0080. *Managing Director:* David Fowler. Specialists in portrait photographs of leading national and international personalities; also politics, trade unions, entertainment, sport and royalty. Some outside contributions considered, but write for details. *Terms:* 50%.

Coleman, Bruce, Inc., 381 Fifth Avenue, New York, N.Y., 10016 *T.* 212-683-5227. *Telex:* 429093. *President:* Norman Owen Tomalin. Specialising exclusively in colour transparencies. All formats from 35 mm. acceptable. All subjects required.

*****Coleman, Bruce, Ltd.,** 17 Windsor Street, Uxbridge, Middlesex, UB8 1AB *T.* (0895) 57094. *Telex:* 932439. Colour transparencies on natural history, ecology, environment, geographical, archaeological, anthropology, agriculture, science subjects and social documentary.

Colorific Photo Library, Garden Offices, Gilray House, Gloucester Terrace, London, W2 3DF *T.* 01-723 5031. Handling photographs of top international photographers, most subjects currently on file, upwards of 150,000 images. Also represents *Life, Sports Illustrated* and *Discover* magazines. New York agencies: Black Star, Contact Press Images Inc., J. B. Pictures, Wheeler Pictures,. Visages, Los Angeles; Cosmos, Paris; Focus, Germany; Camara Tres, Brazil.

*****Colour Library International**—see **Photo Source Ltd**.

*****C.P.L. (Camerapix Picture Library),** 8 Ruston Mews, London W11 1RB *T.* 01-221-0077. *Telex:* 263996. Africa, Middle East, Asia; portraits, agriculture, industry, tribal cultures, landscapes. Wildlife including rare species. Islamic portfolio; Mecca, Medina, Muslim pilgrimage. Further material available from collection held in Nairobi.

Craven Photographics, (1980), 1 Hothfield Terrace, Skipton, North Yorkshire BD23 2AX *T.* (0756) 61149. North country subjects, especially featuring Yorkshire. Also Bird of Paradise collection on Papua New Guinea. *Terms:* 50%.

Cross Sections, James Cross, 52 Crockford Park Road, Addlestone, Weybridge, Surrey, KT15 2LX *T.* (0932) 847554. Transparencies and monochromes, specialising in natural history. Also travel. Other photographers' work not accepted.

Cutten, John H., Associates, 76 Northways, London, NW3 5DL *T.* 01-586 6696. Psychical Research. Library includes many portraits of notable personalities from the 19th century to present day. Transparencies of philosophers, psychologists, scientists. Also historical and unusual.

*****Daily Telegraph Colour Library,** 135 Fleet Street, London, EC4P 4BL *T.* 01-353 4242 ext. 3686-7-8. Over 300,000 transparencies covering a wide range of subjects: technology, industry, health, countries, people, transport, sport and landscapes; comprehensive space exploration collection. See also **Daily Telegraph Syndication.**

Dance Library, The (1983), 175 Blythe Road, London W14 0HL *T.* 01-603 1164. Contemporary and historical dance: classical ballet, jazz, tap, disco, popping, ice dancing, musicals, variety, folk, tribal rites and rituals.

Das Photo (1975), Cherry Trees, Queen's Road, Bisley, Woking, Surrey, GU24 9AP *T.* Brookwood (04867) 3395 and Chalet le Pin, Domaine de Bellevue 181, 5482 Septon, Belgium. *T.* (086) 32 24 26. Arab countries, Americas, Europe, Amazon, folklore, world festivals, archaeology, people, Biblical, markets, sailing, motor bikes.

Davies, Barry (1983), 25 Elder Grove, Llangunnor, Carmarthen, Dyfed SA31 2LQ *T.* 233625. Natural history, landscape, travel (especially Egypt), children, outdoor activities, sports.

*****Davis, James, Travel Photography,** 30 Hengistbury Road, New Milton, Hants. BH25 7LU. *T.* (0425) 610328. *Proprietor:* James Davis. Stock transparency library specialising in world-wide travel photographs. Supply tour operators, publishers, advertising agents, etc. Terms 50% to photographers.

Dickson, Gordon, (1975) Flagstones, 72 Catisfield Lane, Fareham, Hants. P015 5NS *T.* (0329) 42131. Colour transparencies of fungi, in natural habitat; also butterflies, moths, beetles.

*Dixon, C.M., The Orchard, Marley Lane, Kingston, Canterbury, Kent CT4 6JH *T.* (0227) 830075. Europe and Ethiopia, Iceland, Sri Lanka, Tunisia, Turkey, USSR. Main subjects include agriculture, archaeology, architecture, clouds, geography, geology, horses, industry, meteorology, mosaics, mountains, occupations, people.

English, T. Malcolm, B.A., L.R.P.S., M.R.AE.S., 3 The Bakery, Silver Street, Stevington, Beds. MK43 7QN. *T.* (02302) 4150. Aviation photographic library specialising in military, historic and air weapons.

*Evans, Greg, Photo Library (1979), 19 Charlotte Street, London W1P 1LB *T.* 01-636 8238-9. World-wide travel, UK travel, people, industrial, commercial, social, animals, food and sports. Commissions undertaken. *Terms:* 50%.

*Evans, Mary, Picture Library, 1 Tranquil Vale, Blackheath, London, SE3 0BU *T.* 01-318 0034. Over two million historical illustrations from antiquity to the recent past. Also runs of British and foreign illustrated periodicals. Special collections: Sigmund Freud Copyrights, Society for Psychical Research, and London University Harry Price Collection.

*Eyeline Photos (1979), Berwyn House, Mead Close, Cheltenham GL53 7DX *T.* (0242) 513567. *Telex:* 43432 DSA G ref Eyeline. Sports particularly sailing and powerboating. *Terms:* 50%.

*Feature-Pix Colour Library (Travel Photographic Services Ltd.), 21 Great Chapel Street, London, W1V 3AQ *T.* 01-437 2121. *Directors:* Gerry Brenes, Joan Brenes. Colour transparencies (2¼ in. sq. or larger), on travel and allied subjects. Undertake photography on assignment for tour operators, National Tourist Offices. *Terms:* 50% to photographer.

Focus Picture Library, 75A Selby Road, Garforth, Leeds, LS25 1LR *T.* (0532) 863016. Transparencies, 35 mm. & 6 x 9 cm. Landscapes, rivers, buildings, British Isles, especially Yorkshire and Northern Counties. Also popular European regions, especially Greece. Assignments undertaken. No new photographers.

Foord, Ron and Christine, 155B City Way, Rochester, Kent, ME1 2BE *T.* (0634) 47348. Colour picture library of wild flowers, British and European, insects and other natural history subjects. Gardens, horticulture, scenery and countryside generally.

Fortean Picture Library, Melysfan, Llangwm, Corwen, Clwyd, LL21 0RD *T.* (049 082) 472. Library of colour and black and white pictures covering all strange phenomena: UFOs, Loch Ness Monster, ghosts, Bigfoot, witchcraft, etc.

Fotolink Picture Library, Twyman House, 31-39 Camden Road, London, NW1 9LR *T.* 01-482 0478. A world travel and documentary picture library with specialist section on industrial subjects. Require colour transparencies (6 x 6 or 6 x 7 cm.) of tourist locations of the world, and industrial subjects. Preliminary enquiry for details. *Rates:* 50%.

Fotomas Index, 74 Newman Street, London W1P 3LA *T.* 01-636 4148. Specialises in supplying pre-20th century (mostly pre-Victorian) illustrative material to publishing and academic worlds, and for television and advertising. Complete production back-up for interior decor and exhibitions.

Fotosports International (1969), The Barn, Swanbourne, Bucks. MK17 0SL *T.*

(029672) 773; and 227 27th Manhattan Beach, California 90266, USA. *T.* 213-545 9368. Sports events and players, domestic, European, international. American football, athletics, cricket, golf, motor sport, tennis, soccer.

***Fox Photos**—see **Photo Source Ltd.**

***Frank Lane Picture Agency Ltd.,** 19 Dors Close, Kingbury, London NW9 7NT *T.* 01-205 9486. Natural history and meteorology.

Free, John B. Dr., 17 Oakfield Road, Harpenden, Hertfordshire, AL5 2NJ *T.* (05827) 5856. Natural history, agriculture, archaeology. Colour transparencies on: bees and bee keeping, insects and small invertebrates, tropical crops and flowers, people, occupations and religious life in Arabia, Bangladesh, India, Iran, Japan, Mexico, Nepal, Thailand, Mediterranean countries. No other photographers required.

Frost Historical Newspaper Collection, 8 Monks Avenue, New Barnet, Herts, EN5 1DB. *T.* 01-440 3159. (For full details see under **Editorial, Literary, and Production Services.**)

Gadsby, Brian (Visual Life), Middle Barmston Farm, District 15, Washington, Tyne & Wear, NE38 8LE *T.* (091) 416 5454 and 2859179. Colour (2¼ sq., 645 cm. and 35 mm.) and black and white prints. Wide range of subjects but emphasis on travel, children, natural history.

Garratt, Colin (1969), The Square, Newton Harcourt, Leicestershire LE8 0FQ. *T.* (053759) 2068. Steam locomotives of the world.

***Geoscience Features,** 6 Orchard Drive, Wye, Nr. Ashford, Kent, TN25 5AU *T.* Wye (0233) 812707. *Director:* Dr. Basil Booth. Colour library (35 mm to 5 in-4 in). Natural history, ecology, geology, geography, macro/micro, natural phenomena. Americas, Africa, Australasia, Europe, Indian Sub-Continent, S.E. Asia. Incorporates K.S.F. colour library.

Geoslides, 4 Christian Fields, London, SW16 3JZ *T.* 01-764 6292. *Director:* John Douglas. Geographical and general interest of subjects from Africa, Asia, Antarctic, Arctic and sub-Arctic areas. Photographs from space. Australian cover through Associate Picture Library: Blackwoods S.A. Interested only in large recent collections of relevant colour transparencies, regionally based. *Terms:* 50% on UK sales. Photographs for all types of publications, television, advertising.

Globe Photos Inc., 275 7th Avenue, New York, N.Y., 10001. *T.* 212-689 1340. *Telex:* Stkphto 426758. *Cables:* Globephoto New York. Picture stories for magazines or stock photos. Colour transparencies only. Send International Reply Coupons for return of material.

Glover John (1979), 2 Struan Cottages, Church Fields, Witley, Godalming, Surrey GU8 5PP *T.* (042 879) 3322. Gardening, U.K. landscapes, native flora. Commissions undertaken.

***Godwin's, Fay, Photo Files** (1979), 36 Camden Square, London, NW1 9XA *T.* 01-267 1034. Colour and black and white photographs covering portraits of writers, landscapes of the British Isles, North Sea oil, Yorkshire mills, welfare services, education.

Gower Scientific Photos, Middlesex House, 34-42 Cleveland Street, London W1P 5FB *T.* 01-580 9327. *Telex:* 21736. Natural history: high quality photomicrography and photomacrography. Medicine: Up to date imaging techniques of normal structure and functions. Contact: Rosemary Allen.

Graham, Tim (1970), 31 Ferncroft Avenue, London, NW3 7PG *T.* 01-435 7693. British Royal Family in this country and on tours; background pictures on royal homes, hobbies, sports, cars etc. English and foreign country scenes.

Greater London Photograph Library, 40 Northampton Road, London, EC1R 0HB *T.* 01-633 6759. Over 350,000 photographs of London and the London area from *c.* 1860 to present day. Especially strong on local authority projects—schools, housing, open spaces, etc.

Greek Island Photos (1985), Willowbridge Enterprises, Willowbridge, Stoke Road, Bletchley, Milton Keynes, Bucks MK2 3JZ *T.* (0908) 643242. Country and urban facets of most Greek islands. Commissions undertaken.

*****Griggs, Susan, Agency** (1968), 17 Victoria Grove, London W8 5RW *T.* 01-584 6738. *T.A.* Susanpix, London, W8. *Telex:* 8956130. 35 mm. colour transparencies. World-wide travel and people, industry, girls, decorating, mood shots. Library list sent on request.

Haas, Robert, Photo Library (1978), 11 Cormont Road, Camberwell, London, SE5 9RA *T.* 01-326 1510. Holland, Greek Islands, Morocco, Scottish oil industry, Nottinghill Carnival, skies. *Specialities:* people; New York City.

*****Harding, Robert, Picture Library,** 17A Newman Street, London, W1P 3HD *T.* 01-637 8969. *Cables:* Rohard W1. Photographic library. Require photographs for editorial publications which must be of outstanding quality. Telephone or write for details.

Harper Horticultural Slide Library, 219 Robanna Shores, Seaford, Virginia, 23696, U.S.A. *T.* 804-898 6453. 80,000 35 mm. slides of plants and gardens.

Historical Picture Service, 3 Barton Buildings, Bath BA1 2JR *T.* (0225) 334213. Engravings, prints and photographs on all aspects of history from ancient times to 1920. Special collection Old London: buildings, inns, theatres, many of which no longer exist.

Hodgson, Pat, Library, Jasmine Cottage, Spring Grove Road, Richmond, Surrey, TW10 6EH *T.* 01-940 5986. Small social history collection of 19th century engravings. Special picture research in 19th century periodicals, prints, etc. also undertaken. Modern black-and-white photographs: topographical and archaeological.

Horticultural Photo Supply Service, The Good Gardeners' Association, Arkley Manor Farm, Rowley Lane, Arkley, Barnet, Herts, EN5 3HS *T.* 01-449 7944 (evenings).

Hosking, Eric, O.B.E., Hon.F.R.P.S., F.I.I.P., and **David Hosking,** A.R.P.S., 20 Crouch Hall Road, London, N8 8HX *T.* 01-340 7703. Natural history subjects, especially birds covering whole world. Also Dr. D.P. Wilson's unique collection of marine photographs.

*****Hutchison Library, The** (1976), 118b Holland Park Avenue, London W11 4UA *T.* 01-229 2743. General colour library; worldwide subjects: agriculture, environments, festivals, human relationships, industry, landscape, peoples, religion, towns, travel.

Images Photo Agency (1982), 4th Floor, Min Yip Building, 67 Jervois Street, Hong Kong. *T.* 5-442255. *Directors:* Chris Smith, Neil Farrin. General photographic library; also pictures of old Hong Kong. *Terms:* 50%.

Irish International News Service, Barry J. Hardy, P.C., 12 Greenlea Park, Terenure, Dublin 6 *T.* 906183.

JS Library International (1979) 101A, Brondesbury Park, London, NW2 5JL *T.* 01-451-2668 and 459-0223. *Telex:* 912881 JSH. The Royal Family; world wide travel pictures. Also stage and screen celebrities.

Jones, E. Lloyd, 8 Windsor Court, Deganwy, Gwynedd, LL31 9TN *T.* (0492) 84456. Welsh lakes and waterfalls, also Scottish and Irish scenes. Rarer wild flowers, ancient Welsh monuments. Assignments undertaken.

Kemp, Roger Clive, Bellair Cottage, Bellair Terrace, St. Ives, Cornwall TR26 1JR *T.* (0736) 795568. Devon, Cornwall and the Isles of Scilly; candid studies of Pop Stars since 1960, and portraits of Westcountry writers and artists; bodybuilders, glamour, craftspeople. Represents a number of Westcountry photographers, specialising in regional and general subjects. *Terms:* 50%. Photographs not purchased.

*****Keystone Press Agency, Ltd.**—see **Photo Source Ltd.**

Lakeland Life Picture Library (1979), Langsett, Lyndene Drive, Grange-over-Sands, Cumbria LA11 6QP *T.* (044 84) 3565. English Lake District: industries, crafts, sports, shows, customs, architecture, people. Not an agency.

Lancashire Picture Agency Ltd. (1984), 12 Bark Street, Bolton, Lancs BL1 2BQ *T.* (0204) 31719 and (070 682) 6910. Covers assignments for news contacts and publishers and operates a picture library specialising on news, sport (mainly snooker), landscapes, mountaineering, northern subjects and general interest. Assignments undertaken for public relations and commercial photography, including audio visual presentations.

Lensmen Ltd., Press P.R. Photo Agency, Lensmen House, Essex Street, East, Dublin 2. *T.* Dublin 773447.

Les & Joyce, 133 Barton Hill Road, Torquay, Devon, TQ2 8HY *T.* (0803) 37254. Photo illustrators; landscape, architecture, pets, children, craft. Black and white and up to 4 x 5 colour. Not an agency.

MacQuitty International Collection, The, 7 Elm Lodge, River Gardens, Stevenage Road, London, SW6 6NZ *T.* 01-385 6031. 300,000 photographs covering aspects of life in 60 countries: archaeology, art, buildings, flora and fauna, gardens, museums, people and occupations, scenery, religions, methods of transport, surgery, acupuncture, funeral customs, fishing, farming, dancing and music, pot making, sports, food, wine, jewellery and oriental subjects. Period: 1920 to present day.

Mander (Raymond) and Joe Mitchenson Theatre Collection (a Registered Charity), 5 Venner Road, Sydenham, London, SE26 5EQ *T.* 01-778 6730 and 658 7725. Prints, drawings, photographs, programmes, etc., theatre, opera, ballet, music hall, and other allied subjects including composers, playwrights, etc. All periods. Available for books, magazines, T.V.

Mansell Collection, Ltd., 42 Linden Gardens, London, W2 4ER *T.* 01-229 5475.

Massey Stewart, John, 20 Hillway, Highgate, London, N6 6QA *T.* 01-341 3544. Many countries, particularly Europe (including Britain), Asia, U.S.A. and Canada; large collection of Russia past and present; also Alaska, Mongolia, South Korea, etc.

*****Mathews, S. & O.,** Stitches Farm House, Eridge, East Sussex TN3 9JB *T.* Rotherfield (089285) 2848. British life and landscape, architecture, topography and flora.

May, Robin, Collection, 5 Ridgway Place, London, SW19 4EW *T.* 01-946 9007. Library specialises in Western Americana and the theatrical arts.

Merrill, John N., Yew Cottage, West Bank, Winster, Matlock, Derbyshire, DE4 2DQ *T.* Winster (062 988) 454. English and Welsh National Parks, Derbyshire and the Peak District, N.W. Scotland, Hebridean islands, St. Kilda, Fair Isle, Orkneys, Shetland, west coast of Ireland and islands, long distance footpaths,

Tour of Mont Blanc, Alps, Pyrenees, Appalachian Trail and Pacific Crest Trail, U.S.A., Himalayas, and English cathedrals, also the whole of the British coastline.

Midland Colour Library (1978), P.O. Box 24, Bilston, West Midlands WV14 8JW *T.* 021-520-4933. Aircraft, abstracts, landscapes, people, Midland scenes.

Model Picture Library and K.A.P.P.A. (1975), 29 Nearton End, Swanbourne, Milton Keynes, Bucks. MK17 0SL *T.* (029 672) 427. *Telex:* 826715 Aero G. Transparencies: human interest, science, travel, girls.

*****Monitor International,** 17-27 Old Street, London, EC1V 9HL *T.* 01-253 7071. *Telex:* 24718. *Picture Editor:* Bernard Usher. International picture agency. Features and personality portraits, from sport, politics, entertainment, business, general subjects.

Mountain Visions, (1984), Graham and Roslyn Elson, 15 Whiteledges, St. Stephens Road, London W13 8JB. *T.* 01-998-6309. Colour transparencies of mountaineering, skiing, and associated travel, in Europe, N. Africa, Himalayas, Arctic, Far East and Australia.

*****Muscroft, David, Snooker Photography** and **David Muscroft Picture Library** (1977) 16 Broadfield Road, Heeley, Sheffield, S8 0XJ *T.* (0742) 589299. Snooker; most other sports, Northern England news, personalities, features, events. Falkland Islands from 1880.

Mustograph Agency, The, 19 Rathbone Street, London, W1P 1AF *T.* 01-636 6128-9. Britain only. General subjects of countryside life, work, history and scenery.

National Motor Museum, Beaulieu, Photographic Library, Beaulieu, Hants SO4 7ZN *T.* Beaulieu (0590) 612345. All aspects of motoring, cars, commercial vehicles, motor cycles, traction engines, etc. Illustrations of period scenes and motor sport. Also large library of 5 in. x 4 in. and smaller colour transparencies of veteran, vintage and modern cars, commercial vehicles and motor cycles.

Natural History Photographic Agency—see **NHPA**.

News Blitz International, 5 Via Cimabue, 00196 Rome, Italy. *T.* 36 00 620, 361-90-14, 36 01 489. (see **Syndicates, News and Press Agencies.**)

*****NHPA** Little Tye, 57 High Street, Ardingly, West Sussex RH17 6TB. *T.* (0444) 892514. Represents 50 of the world's leading natural history photographers specialising in a wide range of fauna and flora.

Northpix (1976), 75A Bold Street, Liverpool, L1 4EZ *T.* 051-708 6044. News, sport, features; wire facilities.

Orion Press, 55 1-Chome, Kanda Jimbocho, Chiyoda-ku, Tokyo, 101. *T.* (03) 295-1400. *Cable:* Orionserv, Tokyo. *Telex:* J2 4447 Orionprs.

*****OSF Picture Library,** Oxford Scientific Films Ltd., Long Hanborough, Oxford, OX7 2LD *T.* (0993) 881881. Comprehensive colour transparencies of plant and animal life worldwide. Illustrated articles on natural history topics. Agents for *Animals Animals* and *Earth Scenes*, New York. Representatives in New York, Tokyo, Milan, Barcelona, Frankfurt, Copenhagen, Paris.

Osborne, Christine, Pictures including **Middle East Pictures & Publicity** (1975), 53a Crimsworth Road, London SW8 4RJ *T.* 01-720 6951. Muslim countries socio-economic, Middle East, Asia, Pacific countries. Travel and food, over 60 countries.

Pardoe, Rosemary, 38 Marina Village, Preston Brook, Runcorn, Cheshire, WA7 3BQ. Heraldic subjects, especially royal arms in churches, hatchments; also inn signs (heraldic and general). Not an agency.

Peerless, Ann & Bury, 22 King's Avenue, Minnis Bay, Birchington-on-Sea, Kent, CT7 9QL *T.* Thanet (0843) 41428. Art, architecture, geography, history, social and cultural aspects in India, Pakistan, Bangladesh, Sri Lanka, Thailand, Malaysia and parts of the Middle East, Egypt and Africa. Specialist material on world religions: Hinduism, Buddhism, Jainism, Sikhism.

*Photo Library International,** P.O. Box 75, Leeds, LS7 3NZ *T.* (0532) 789321. Colour transparencies 35 mm. to 10 x 8. Most subjects. New material always welcome.

*Photo Source Ltd, The,** Unit C1, Enterprise Business Estate, 2 Mill Harbour, Mastmaker Road, London E14 9TE *T.* 01-987 1212. *Telex:* 888258. All aspects of daily life, events, places, personalities from 1900 to present day; major colour stock library. Incorporating libraries of Central Press Photos Ltd., Colour Library International, Fox Photos, Keystone Press Agency Ltd.

*Photographers' Library, The** (1978), 81A Endell Street, Covent Garden, London, WC2H 9AG *T.* 01-836 5591. Requires material on worldwide travel, industry, agriculture, commerce, sport, people, leisure, girls, scenic. Colour only. Terms: 50%.

Photographic Society, The Royal (1853), The R.P.S. National Centre of Photography, The Octagon, Milsom Street, Bath, BA1 1DN *T.* (0225) 62841. Exhibitions; library of books, photographs and photographic equipment.

*Photoresources,** The Orchard, Marley Lane, Kingston, Canterbury, Kent CT4 6JH *T.* (0227) 830075. Ancient civilisations, art, archaeology, world religions, myth, and museum objects covering the period from 30,000 B.C. to A.D. 1900.

Pictor International, Ltd., Twyman House, 31-39 Camden Road, London, NW1 9LR *T.* 01-482 0478. *Telex:* 21497. International photographic library—all subjects, especially industry technology, people. Transparencies 6 x 6 minimum. *Rates:* 50%.

Pictor International, Piazza Bertarelli 1, 20122 Milan. *T.* 02-8050710. General photo libraries: Milan, London, Paris.

Pictor International (formerly **Leo Aarons**), 14 rue Rougemont, 75009 Paris, *T.* 246-1205 and 770-3088. General photo libraries: Paris, London, Milan. Genuine international sales network.

Pictorial Press, Ltd. 30 Aylesbury Street, London, EC1R 0BL *T.* 01-253 4023. *Telex:* 24744 Caslon G. *Directors:* A. F. Gale, K. V. Gale, S. M. Gale. Handles features, personalities especially royalty and pop music, nudes, historical cars and transport, teenage life, military, especially Second World War; also landscapes, families, people at work. SAE essential.

Picturepoint, Ltd., Hurst House, 157-169 Walton Road, East Molesey, Surrey KT8 0DX *T.* 01-941 4520. Have ready world-wide markets for high quality colour transparencies. Any subject other than *news*. Minimum of 250 pictures in first submission. Send by Registered Mail enclosing stamps or I.R.C. for returns. *Terms:* 5 year contract, 50% commission.

Pitcher, Sylvia (1968), 75 Bristol Road, Forest Gate, London, E7 8HG *T.* 01-552 8308 and 4th Floor, 59 Charlotte Street, London, W1P 1LA *T.* 01-636 6015. Specialist in rural south east USA, including musicians, blues, jazz, country.

Pixfeatures (Mr. P.G. Wickman), 5 Latimer Road, Barnet, Herts. *T.* 01-449 9946. Picture-features, preferably topical. Especially for sale to German, South African, Spanish and American magazines. 35% of all sales, unless otherwise arranged.

*Planet Earth Pictures: Seaphot Ltd (1969) 4 Harcourt Street, London W1H 1DS *T.* 01-262 4427. Marine, surface and underwater; natural history and environments on land and underwater; people, places; space.

*Popperfoto (Paul Popper, Ltd.), 24 Bride Lane, London, EC4Y 8DR *T.* 01-353 9665-6. *Telex:* 8814206. Offer and require documentary photos (black and white and colour) from all countries of the world. Collection includes Exclusive News Agency, Odhams Periodicals Photo Library, Conway Picture Library, United Press International (UPI) Library and Planet.

Power Pix International Picture Library (1968), 35 North Street, Tillingham, Essex CM0 7TR *T.* (0621 87) 614. World wide travel, people and views, girl and "mood pix"; sub-aqua including tropical fish, yachting, civil and military aircraft, natural history. *Terms:* 50%.

Pratt, Derek, (1976) 11 Ashchurch Park Villas, London, W12 9SP. *T.* 01-743 1824. British inland waterways; canals, and rivers; bridges, aqueducts, locks; waterway holidays, boats, fishing; town and countryside scenes.

*Premaphotos Wildlife, 2 Willoughby Close, King's Coughton, Alcester, Warwicks, B49 5QJ *T.* Alcester (0789) 762938. Library of 35 mm. transparencies of own work only by K.G. Preston-Mafham and Dr. R.A. Preston-Mafham. Wide range of natural history subjects from around the world. All work done in the field.

Press Association Photos (the news picture service of The Press Association), 85 Fleet Street, London, EC4P 4BE *T.* 01-353 7440.

Radio Times Hulton Picture Library—now **BBC Hulton Picture Library,** *q.v.*

Rich Research (1978), 13 Knoll House, Carlton Hill, St. John's Wood, London, NW8 9XD *T.* 01-624 7755. *Director:* Diane Rich. Professional picture research and fee negotiation. Illustrations found for books, films, television, advertising agencies and exhibitions. Fast access to world-wide sources.

*Ronan, Ann, Picture Library, Wheel Cottage, Bishops Hull, Taunton, Somerset, TA1 5EP *T.* Taunton (0823) 52737. Woodcuts, engravings, etc., of history of science and technology from c.1500 – c.1900.

S & G Press Agency, Ltd., 68 Exmouth Market, London, EC1R 4RA *T.* 01-278 1223. Send photographs, but negatives preferred. Press photographs and vast photo library.

Saxon Wildlife Films Ltd., (incorporating the library of **Michael Leach** A.R.P.S.), Byways, Shebdon, Stafford ST20 0PU. *T.* (078 579) 333. General wildlife subjects, particularly mammals and special emphasis on urban wildlife.

*Science Photo Library (1979), 2 Blenheim Crescent, London, W11 1NN *T.* 01-727 4712. Scientific photography of all kinds—space, medicine, technology, microscopic life. Undertakes scientific photo research.

*Sefton Photo Library, 30-30A Mason Street, Manchester, M4 5EY *T.* 061-834 9423 and 832 7670. *Director:* Sefton Samuels, F.R.P.S., N.U.J. Speciality Library on all aspects of the North of England. Other areas around Britain, and the world; general subjects. Submissions considered from other photographers. Assignments undertaken.

Sharp, Mick, (1981), Eithinog, Waun, Penisarwaun, Caernarfon, Gwynedd, LL55 3PW *T.* Llanberis 872425. Archaeology, ancient monuments, historic buildings, churches and general landscape of the British Isles and Brittany. Archaeological sites and courtyard houses in Iraq.

Skye Agencies, Calum Mackenzie Neish, Portnalong, Isle of Skye. *T.* Portnalong (047-872) 272. *Telex:* 75317. News, features and picture agency for the Inner Hebrides and adjacent mainland (Skye and Lochalsh District).

Slide File, The, (1978) 79 Merrion Square South, Dublin, 2. *T.* 686086. Specialise in Northern Ireland and Eire: landscapes, wild life, Irish agriculture and industry, Irish people and their traditions, Celtic archaeological heritage, Gaelic and other sports.

Society for Cultural Relations with the USSR (SCR)—see **The Elsie Timbey Collection.**

Smith, Patrick, Associates Ltd. (1964), Woodcote, Ffordd y Fulfran, Upper Borth, Dyfed, SY24 5NN *T.* (097081) 296. South London 1950-77, rural mid-Wales. Single pictures and features.

Source Photographic Archives (1974), Woodhouse, Captain's Hill, Leixlip, County Kildare. *T.* 244411. *Director:* Thomas Kennedy. Mostly recent photographs by living photographers on many different subjects.

Southern Media Services, P.O. Box 140, Springwood, New South Wales 2777, Australia. *T.* (047) 514967. *Proprietors:* Nic van Oudtshoorn, Daphne van Oudtshoorn. Stock colour library, also illustrated features.

*Spectrum Colour Library, 146 Oxford Street, London, W1N 9DL *T.* 01-637 3682. Require high quality colour transparencies for all markets. Need all subjects except topical or "hot news" pictures—list of requirements available on receipt of stamped, addressed envelope.

*Sporting Pictures (UK) Ltd., 7A Lambs Conduit Passage, Holborn, London, WC1 4RG *T.* 01-405 4500. *Director:* Crispin J. Thruston. *Librarian:* Steve Brown. Specialising in sports, sporting events, sportsmen.

Stiles, Peter, Picture Library, 12 Farncombe Road, Worthing, Sussex BN11 2BB. *T.* (0903) 31276. Most subjects covered, but specialises in views, natural history and horticulture. Picture sequences and illustrated features. Own pictures only. Commissions undertaken.

*Stone, Tony, Worldwide, 28 Finchley Road, St. John's Wood, London, NW8 6ES *T.* 01-586 3322. International colour transparency library. Subjects required: travel, children, natural history, commerce, industry, historic transport, etc. *Terms* 50-50.

Sutcliffe Gallery, 1 Flowergate, Whitby, Yorkshire, YO21 3BA *T.* Whitby (0947) 602239. Collection of 19th-century photography all by Frank M. Sutcliffe, HON. F.R.P.S. (1853-1941). Especially inshore fishing boats and fishing community, also farming interests. Period covered 1872 to 1910.

*Syndication International (1986) Ltd., Orbit House, 9 New Fetter Lane, London, EC4A 1AR *T.* 01-822 2019. Colour and black-and-white news and feature photography.

Theatre Museum, Victoria & Albert Museum, South Kensington, London, SW7 2RL. *T.* 01-589 6371, ex. 428. The Theatre Museum is not a picture library, but has extensive collections of prints, drawings, playbills, programmes, press cuttings, photographs, theatre documents including the Enthoven Collection, the Guy Little Photographic Collection, the London Archives of the Dance, the Dame Marie Rambert-Ashley Dukes Ballet Collection, the M.W. Stone Toy Theatre Collection, the Gerald Morice Puppetry Collection, the British Puppet Theatre Guild's Collection of Puppets, the Harry R. Beard Theatre Collection, the Antony Hippisley Coxe Circus Collection, the British Council's and the Arts Council of Great Britain's collections of theatre designs and the collections of the British Theatre Museum Association and the Friends of the Museum of Performing Arts. From April 1987: The Old Flower Market, Covent Garden, London WC2.

Timbey, Elsie, Collection (1943), Society for Cultural Relations with the USSR, 320 Brixton Road, London SW9 6AB *T.* 01-274 2282. Russian and Soviet life and history. Comprehensive coverage of cultural subjects: art, theatre, folk art, costume, music. Also posters and theatre props, artistic reference and advice.

*****Topham Picture Library,** (1928), P.O. Box 33, Edenbridge, Kent, TN8 5PB *T.* Cowden (034-286) 313. *Telex:* 95351. Historic Library: personalities, warfare, royalty, topography, France, natural history. World news file from original sources: UPI, INP, Press Association, Central News, Planet News, Alfieri, Pictorial Press, Private Eye cartoons.

Transworld Feature Syndicate (UK) Ltd., Tubs Hill House, Sevenoaks, Kent TN13 1BL *T.* (0732) 458204-7.

Travel Photo International, 8 Delph Common Road, Aughton, Ormskirk, Lancashire, L39 5DW *T.* (0695) 423720. Touristic interest including scenery, towns, monuments, historic buildings, archaeological sites, local people. Specialising in travel brochures and books. *Terms:* 50%.

Travel Trade Photography, Colour Library, 18 Princedale Road, London, W11 4NJ *T.* 01-727 5471. *Principal:* Teddy Schwarz. Landscapes, townscapes, ancient monuments and buildings of historical interest in England and foreign countries, peoples, and their customs. Return postage essential. *Terms:* 50%.

*****Tropix Photographic Library** (1973), 156 Meols Parade, Meols, Wirral, Merseyside, L47 6AN. *T.* 051-632 1698. All human and environmental aspects of tropics and sub-tropics, also non-tropical developing countries. Interested in new collections, particularly West Africa and Caribbean. Also North-West England. Preliminary enquiry essential. *Terms:* 50%.

Ulster Photographic Agency (1985), 22 Casaeldona Park, Belfast BT6 9RB *T.* (0232) 795738. All aspects of life in Ulster and Ireland; also motoring and motorsport. *Terms:* 50%.

*****Universal Pictorial Press & Agency, Ltd.** (1929), New Bridge Street House, 30-34 New Bridge Street, London, EC4V 6BN *T.* 01-248 6730. *Telex:* 8952718 Unipix G. Suppliers of a daily press and library service to the national and provincial press, periodicals and television companies throughout the British Isles and overseas. Notable political, company, academic, legal, diplomatic, church, military, pop, arts, entertaining and sports personalities and well-known views and buildings.

Van Hallan, Bill Bates, 16 Blenheim Road, Basing, Basingstoke, Hampshire RG24 0HP *T.* (0256) 465217.

Vickers, John, Theatre Collection, 27 Shorrolds Road, London, SW6 7TR *T.* 01-385 5774. Archives of British theatre and portraits of actors, writers and musicians by John Vickers from 1938-1974.

Vidocq Photo Library (1983), 9 Vicarage Street, Frome, Somerset BA11 1TX *T.* (0373) 64548. Worldwide travel pictures, natural history, architecture, outdoor activities, sports, landscapes, aircraft, animals, children. *Terms:* 60% to photographer.

*****Vision International** (1979) 30 Museum Street, London WC1A 1LH *T.* 01-636 9516. *Telex:* 23539. *T.A.* Visint London. Travel, fine art, gardens and plants, wildlife, natural history, architecture, landscapes, medicine, pregnancy, birth, child development, abstracts.

Warner, Simon, Whitestone Farm, Stanbury, Keighley, West Yorkshire, BD22 0JW *T.* Haworth (0535) 44644. Landscape/countryside pictures, featuring especially Yorkshire. Commissions accepted. No other photographers.

Weimar Archive (1983), 8-9 The Incline, Coalport, Telford, Shropshire TF8 7HR *T.* (0952) 580500. Modern Germany, specialising in Weimar Republic, rise of Hitler and Nazi anti-Semitism.

*****Werner Forman Archive** (1975), 36 Camden Square, London, NW1 9XA *T.* 01-267 1034. Art, architecture, archaeology, history and peoples of ancient, oriental and primitive cultures.

Western Americana Picture Library, 3 Barton Buildings, Bath BA1 2JR *T.* (0225) 334213. Prints, engravings, photographs and colour transparencies on the American West, cowboys, gunfighters, Indians, including pictures by Frederic Remington and Charles Russell, etc. Interested in buying pictures on American West.

Westlake, Roy J., A.R.P.S. Photo Library, 20 The Knoll, Woodford, Plympton, Plymouth, PL7 4SH *T.* (0752) 336444. Britain, especially the West Country. Landscape subjects suitable for book illustrations, calendars, greeting cards, travel brochures, etc. Also camping, caravanning and inland waterways subjects in Britain, including rivers and canals. Other photographers work not accepted.

Whitelaw Library (1980), 29 Granby Avenue, Harpenden, Herts., AL5 5QP. *T.* (05827) 4751. Landscapes and buildings in England; specializing in windmills, follies, dovecotes, market crosses, curiosities, Hertfordshire. Other photographers work not required.

Widdicombe, Derek G., Country Wide Photographic Library, Oldfield, High Street, Clayton West, Huddersfield, HD8 9NS *T.* (0484) 862638. Landscapes, seascapes, architecture, human interest of Britain and abroad, moods and seasons, buildings and natural features. Holds copyright of Noel Habgood, F.R.P.S. Collection.

Wilderness Images (1977), 70 Foster Road, Kempston, Bedford MK42 8BU *T.* (0234) 854848. The Canadian Rockies, British Columbia, Alberta.

Wilderness Photographic Library, *Director:* John Noble, F.R.G.S. 2 Kent View, Kendal, Cumbria LA9 4HE *T.* (0539) 28334. Mountain and wilderness regions, travel and adventure, and associated aspects; also Antarctic exploration and wildlife.

Wildlife Matters Photographic Library (1980), Dr. John Feltwell, F.R.E.S., F.L.S., M.I.BIOL., Marlham, Henley Down, Battle, East Sussex, TN33 9BN. *T.* Crowhurst (042 483) 566. Entomology, specially butterflies, ecology, practical and urban conservation, nature reserves, wild and garden flowers of Europe, Mediterranean flora and fauna, aerial habitats.

*****Woodmansterne Publications Ltd.,** Watford Business Park, Watford, WD1 8RD *T.* (0923) 28236 and 45788. Britain, Europe, Holy Land; architecture, cathedral and stately home interiors; general art subjects; museum collections; natural history, butterflies, geography, volcanoes, transport, space; opera and ballet; major state occasions; British heritage.

Woodward, Zenka, Picture Library, 19 Gallows Hill, King's Langley, Hertfordshire, WD4 8PG *T.* King's Langley 63242. International pictorial documentation of the ancient and recent past—engravings, woodcuts, paintings, photographs, etc.

Wren, Murray, Picture Library, 3 Hallgate, London, SE3 9SG *T.* 01-852 7556. Outdoor nudes; nudist holiday resorts and activities in Europe and elsewhere.

PICTURE RESEARCH
JUDITH HARRIES

Picture research is the term given to the selection, procurement and collection of illustrations suitable for reproduction. In recent years this trade has developed and diversified enormously, so that it is no longer largely confined to supplying the requirements of book and magazine publishers. Picture researchers are widely used by packaging companies, advertising agencies and film, television and video companies. However an account of the methods applying to publishing research will provide the fullest general guide to the craft. Publishers either employ a researcher full-time, or submit their requests to freelance researchers, and some commercial picture libraries offer their own research facilities.

A picture researcher is responsible, to a large extent, for the publisher's end product. The publisher's needs may be highly specialised, but there is nearly always a choice of pictures. The researcher makes this initial choice, whether it be between different views of a subject or between pictures of a different quality. For example, when asked for a picture of the Eiffel Tower the researcher would be quite correct in either presenting a worm's eye view, an aerial view, or both. In this case quality would really mean different techniques, i.e., a picture illustrating the architectural structure of the tower or a picture indicating the splendid view it gives of Paris. The only indication an editor may give in his request may be whether he requires a portrait or a landscape shaped picture. The researcher is also responsible for copyright permission, correct acknowledgement and providing the editor with all the information about the photograph as a basis for caption copy. A picture researcher fully employed by a group of publishers, or one publisher, is expected to attend to everything. This includes the payment of all reproduction fees (new editions to be remembered) and the safe return of any material from the printer to the source. If not directly involved in these final stages the freelance researcher can at least check their completion. Costs must be kept down at all times (in the case of a freelance researcher this will ensure that she never lacks work).

Publishers who employ a permanent researcher will always be appreciative of any material which does not have to be returned, being formed into a picture library of their own, or a reference "bank".

Picture research can cover a tremendous variety of topics but there is a fundamental core to the actual research. For me, the process from beginning to end, forms the following pattern.

BOOKING IN OF PROJECTS

Each separate request is booked-in, just as a production department books in a manuscript. The title, author, date of publication, number of copies going into print, the sales market, and the budget allocation for pictures are noted. General information is wanted by anyone who may supply a picture, certain facts may influence their decision. For example, publication date may be far ahead, and the picture wanted elsewhere (you then offer to have a copy made at your expense), or sometimes in the case of a syndication department, or a foreign source, the number of copies going into print affects the permission fee. Remember to set some of your budget aside for extras, which will probably include any photocopying you want done, and print fees. (Some agencies keep their stock in negative form only.)

Colour transparencies are very valuable and require special attention. They are usually signed for and the indemnity for loss or damage varies enormously. It may be £50 or £500 for each transparency. The loan period is usually one month and if a transparency is not returned on the requested date the borrower is asked to pay a holding fee. This fee, for each transparency for every week it is held, varies with each library or agency.

The *British Association of Picture Libraries (BAPLA)* was founded in 1975. A great majority of commercial picture libraries and several institutional libraries are members of the Association. Their aim is to promote fair and honest trading within the profession and between members and their clients. *Address:* P.O. Box 284, London W11 4RP.

TYPE OF RESEARCH

The line of research depends entirely on the type of picture one is looking for. It is not logical to go to a photograph library dealing in news pictures for an engraving, nor is it ideal to go to the same library for a photograph of a bar of chocolate when you can approach the maker of that particular bar and be given a picture with no reproduction fee. So, content and design dictate the direction on one's research. Many professional authors (scientists, doctors, engineers, architects, etc.) submit illustrations with their manuscripts, or their needs are highly specialised, and the research clear-cut. The author may have an idea of the illustrations he wants, but not every picture asked for will be available, and the researcher involved should have access to the manuscript so that substitutes can be found. *Most important*, at this stage, is the checking of any information necessary to obtain the picture required. "Wants" may be expressed loosely, e.g. "Royalty visiting the Empire and Colonies in 1907." In this case one would need to know which of the royal family was referred to and which country, before approaching a source. It is much more efficient to do the fact finding before contacting any would-be source, as it just slows up the process having your list queried by an agency, or a picture library.

Reference libraries are of great service to a picture researcher for information. When there is no obvious source for a particular picture one can work backwards from printed material. This applies when a "want" is expressed in general terms, e.g. "a twentieth-century woodcut". One can go straight to books on the subject, select a number of artists and examples of their work from which a choice can be made. The source is then traceable from the library book. Useful libraries in London are:

    British Library Reading Room   Victoria and Albert Museum
    London Library   Library
    United States Reference Library,   Westminster Central
      US Embassy   Reference Library

CONTACTING SOURCES

It is a good idea to visit, at some time, picture agencies and libraries with whom you will be constantly dealing. It is necessary to be familiar with their stock, and *their* system. It is particularly helpful if you can single out one member of their staff, and deal with that person whenever possible. Personal relations may be vital when you need a certain picture in a hurry, but cannot leave your office. Many projects can be dealt with, as time goes on and you accumulate more information, over the telephone or by sending out want lists. A want list should be specific to each source, as it is a waste of time and effort to have a number of agencies and libraries duplicating the request. An agency's time is just as valuable as the researcher's, and where a wide choice is involved a visit can eliminate a research fee, but please telephone first. Many agencies operate an appointment system and they do so because they can deal more efficiently with the client's request.

Most important, at this stage, is to see that every picture is clearly marked with the agency's name. It is also a good idea to count the number of pictures, and write the figures down, even if the agency sends its own list. This will eliminate any disagreement about the number of pictures supplied. This is to be followed up by noting down the number of pictures you return (and the date) either as unsuitable for selection, or when a definite choice has been made.

COVER PICTURE AND CAPTIONS COPY

A researcher is not responsible for deciding on cover material but is often asked to provide suitable material for selection by the editor and the art department. If a picture reproduced inside a book is repeated on the cover the researcher may quite reasonably ask for a reduction on the cover rate remembering that a cover rate is usually double that of an "inside" reproduction fee. At this point you make certain that all pictures have their correct captions, and that all relevant information has been passed on to the Publisher or Editor. It is a good idea to discuss any print fees or reproduction rates at the beginning of the assignment with each individual source. These rates can vary enormously.

LAST STAGES

A researcher employed by a publisher would now write to each source, confirming what pictures were being used. An acknowledgement list to be included in the book would also be prepared at this point.

A freelance researcher should retain a copy of the list of pictures supplied to the publisher. (This list will be of sources, and costing.) Reproduction fees are usually paid on publication day, although it is a good policy to pay freelance photographers on completion of their work. (Their work can be irregular, and this arrangement is advantageous to both.) After publication, the final task is to ensure the safe return of any material from the printer (and this includes the cover picture) back to you. A permanently employed researcher is usually responsible for the safe return of any material back to its source. If a picture is damaged, or lost, you must see that it is paid for. In the case of photographs worked on by the art department you are responsible for paying for a replacement print. A freelance researcher does not usually have these responsibilities.

FURTHER HINTS

Professional picture researchers jot down every useful source, and a card index system is a time-saving one. Useful addresses, ranging from collections and agencies to freelance photographers, and private individuals are filed in categories, e.g. Scientific, Geographical, Political, Transport, etc. Against each source one can note useful details such as: research fee (if required), willingness to send material through the post, how prompt their service is, and if one must make an appointment in advance of a visit. The card index provides quick reference, but a comprehensive file is necessary. This can be made by dividing a looseleaf file into three sections:

In the *first* section file any literature from public collections, museums, government offices, and other official bodies, such as permission conditions, reproduction details, and application forms;

in the *second* section, keep a complete record of the detailed fees of all sources;

the *last* section will be a comprehensive version of your quick-reference card index file, i.e. a complete subject list from each source (where available). It will include any up-to-date information on new subjects they cover. These lengthy subject lists cannot be accommodated on a simple card index.

SOURCES

These are endless and international. The obvious ones being: public collections, publishers, photographers, agencies, and commercial picture libraries. One is guided to these and others through books such as those listed below (and of course the pages immediately preceding this article!) The first two books listed below are invaluable to all users of photographs and vital to every picture researcher's reference shelf.

The Picture Researcher's Handbook: An International Guide to Picture Sources—and How to Use Them (Hilary and Mary Evans), 3rd edition, Saturday Ventures. Obtained direct from Saturday Ventures, 11 Granville Park, London, SE13 7DY. Full price £21.95, including postage and packing. Professional discount available on request.

Directory of British Photographic Collections, published by William Heinemann on behalf of The Royal Photographic Society. The Directory, as its title implies (and for the first time), comprehensively lists all the photographic collections in the British Isles. It gives a detailed description of each collection, including subject matter and all other relevant details specific to each collection; location; number of photographs; type and size; owner/custodian; historical data; photographer; further sources of information; accessibility; details of inspection, loan, sale and reproduction.

World of Learning, Europa Publications, London (annually). Lists museums, learned societies, universities, galleries, etc.

International Directory of Arts, Verlag Muller KG, of Frankfurt. A comprehensive 2-volume directory of museums, galleries, universities, academies, collections, associations, dealers, publishers, collectors, etc., throughout the world. Technical data appears in English, French, German, Italian and Spanish.

The State Association of the Press Photographic Agencies and Archives in Western Germany. Bundesverband der Pressebild—Agenturen Bilderdierste und Bildarchive e.V. 8000 München 22-Maximilianstr. 17.

Official Museum Directory of America and Canada (Latest edition 1970) Ed. U.S. association of museums. Crowell-Collier Education Corporation.

Guide to the Special Collections of Prints and Photographs in the Library of Congress, Paul Vanderbilt. Government Printing Office, Washington.

Picture Sources 4, Ed. Ernest H. Robl. Special Libraries Association, 235 Park Avenue South, New York, N.Y. 10003, $35.00 pbk. Should be available for consultation at most major libraries.

The Libraries, Museums and Art Galleries Year Book (new edition in preparation). James Clarke, Cambridge, England.

Picture Source Book for Social History, Allen & Unwin, London 1961. A 6-volume work with a wealth of pictures, indicating their sources.

Sources of Illustration 1500-1900, Adams & Dart, London 1971.

EXHIBITIONS

These are now becoming an excellent opportunity of seeing a wide variety of photography, both foreign and British, and include the work of many young photographers. Exhibitions are held in a number of places and, more and more, the daily newspapers are drawing attention to them, as well as reviewing the exhibitions. The weekly *British Journal of Photography* also lists current exhibitions. The Photographers' Gallery, besides giving us an opportunity to see some marvellous photography, has a very good bookstand where one may look at (and buy!) books on early and contemporary photography. There is also a study centre. A number of exhibitions of photography are sponsored by the Arts Council of Great Britain. Both the Photographers' Gallery and the Arts Council have advance mailing lists, and some specialist galleries in London are listed below.

Camera Work, 121 Roman Road, London, E2.
Half Moon Gallery, 27 Alie Street, London, E1.
Kodak Photographic Gallery, The, 246 High Holborn, London, WC1.
Photographers' Gallery, 5 & 8 Great Newport Street, London, WC2.
Serpentine Gallery, Kensington Gardens, London, W2.
Victoria and Albert Museum, South Kensington, London, SW7.
Whitechapel Art Gallery, High Street, London, E1.

The galleries listed below are located outside London and exclusively show photography, both Victorian and Contemporary. The Gallery of Photography in Southampton, is particularly good about forwarding details of their exhibitions and lectures. It is always a good idea to be on as many mailing lists as possible.

Gallery of Photography, The University, Southampton.
John Hayward Gallery, Southampton.
Impressions Gallery of Photography, 17 Colliergate, York, YO1 2BN.
National Museum of Photography and Film, Bradford.
Open Eye Gallery, Whitechapel, Liverpool.
The Photogallery, The Forresters Arms, Shepherd Street, St. Leonards-on-Sea, East Sussex.
The Photographers' Corridor, University College, Cardiff.
The Photographic Gallery, 41 Charles Street, Cardiff.
Royal Photographic Society, National Centre of Photography, The Octagon, Milson Street, Bath, BA1 1DN.
Side Photographic Gallery, 9 Side, Newcastle-upon-Tyne.
Sutcliffe Gallery, 1 Flowergate, Whitby.

PICTURE RESEARCH COURSE

The Unwin Foundation Book House Training Centre offers training in picture research. It is part of a course designed for those working in book publishing, and there may be more programmes for other applicants and some evening classes. The objective of the course is to give a professional approach to the search for and use of suitable sources; to make picture researchers aware of all the implications of their task: suitability for reproduction, legal and financial aspects, efficient administration.

Details of the course, with the outline of the programme, may be obtained from the Training Assistant, Book House Training Centre, 45 East Hill, Wandsworth, London, SW18 2QZ *T*. 01-874 2718/4608.

The London School of Publishing now offers a course in picture research twice a year—Spring and Autumn. Each course lasts ten weeks and there is one lecture a week. Further details may be obtained from Mark Featherstone, 47 Red Lion Street, London, WC1R 4PF. *T*. 01-405 9801.

The Art of Picture Research by Hilary Evans (David & Charles) is a useful introduction to picture research as a profession. It covers everything from qualifications needed to do picture research to everyday aspects of the job and also covers career opportunities. Available from Saturday Ventures, 11 Granville Park, London SE13 7DY £13.50, including postage and packing.

S.P.R.Ed. (SOCIETY OF PICTURE RESEARCHERS AND EDITORS)

S.P.R.Ed. was formed in 1977 as a professional body with a Code of Practice for picture researchers and editors. It is a meeting-place for people to discuss ideas, share problems and exchange information. It aims to provide a number of services and has established a Freelance Register for those members available for freelance work and provides a Freelance Engagement Form for freelance researchers wishing to use a standard contract.

S.P.R.Ed. holds regular monthly meetings and publishes a bi-monthly newsletter which can be purchased on a yearly subscription by non-members. Advertising space can also be bought in this newsletter.

Those interested in further details should write to The Secretary, BM Box 259, London, WC1N 3XX. *T.* 01-404 5011.

MUSIC PUBLISHERS

UNITED KINGDOM MUSIC PUBLISHERS

Copyright in musical compositions comprises (*a*) the right of publication in print and sale of printed copies; (*b*) the right of public performance, and (*c*) the right to use the work for the purpose of making gramophone records, sound films or other similar contrivances. The musical composer should bear that in mind when entering into an agreement for the publication of his work.

Mr. Rutland Boughton's warning to amateurs given many years ago, still stands. He said that amateurs, "like the more hardened professional composers, find pleasure in seeing their musical thoughts in print. Because of that human weakness they become the prey of tenth-rate publishers, who offer to issue their music for them (however poor and ineffective it may be) *if they will pay for the privilege. If a piece of music is worth publishing a publisher will be willing to pay for it in cash or royalty.*" Music publishers requiring work for issue on cash or royalty terms no more advertise in the public press for music and lyrics than a first-class publisher of books advertises for MSS. on that basis.

The Publishers in the following list are all members of the Performing Right Society except those marked †. The list does not include all publisher-members of the Performing Right Society.

Lyrics without a musical setting are not accepted unless stated by individual firms

Arcadia Music Publishing Co., Ltd., P.O. Box 1, Rickmansworth, Herts, WD3 3AZ *T.* 01-584 6671. Light orchestral.

Banks Music Publications (Ramsay Silver), The Old Forge, Sand Hutton, York, YO4 1LB *T.* (0904) 86472. Publishers of choral and instrumental music.

Belwin-Mills Music Ltd., 250 Purley Way, Croydon, CR9 4QD *T.* 01-681 0855. *Telex:* 8953180. Orchestral, instrumental, choral and vocal works by classical and contemporary composers, educational music, instrumental tutors, textbooks, band music, guitar, keyboard, popular music.

Black (A & C) (Publishers) Ltd. (1978), 35 Bedford Row, London, WC1R 4JH *T.* 01-242 0946. *T.A.* Biblos, London, WC1. *Telex:* 32524 ACBLAC. Song books and instrumental books for children.

Boosey & Hawkes Music Publishers, Ltd., 295 Regent Street, London, W1R 8JH *T.* 01-580 2060. General and educational.

Bosworth & Co., Ltd. (1889), 14-18 Heddon Street, London, W1R 8DP *T.* 01-734 4961, 0475. Orchestral, chamber, instrumental, operetta, church, educational, piano, violin and part-songs.

Bourne Music Ltd., 34-36 Maddox Street, London, W1R 9PD *T.* 01-493 6412, 6583. Popular and educational music.

Cambridge University Press (1534). The Edinburgh Building, Shaftesbury Road, Cambridge, CB2 2RU *T.* Cambridge (0223) 312393. *T.A.* Unipress, Cambridge. *Telex:* 817256 Cupcam. *Chief Executive and Secretary of the Press Syndicate:* Geoffrey A. Cass, M.A. *Deputy Chief Executive:* Philip E.V. Allin, M.A. *Managing Director* (Publishing Division): Anthony K. Wilson, M.A. *University Publisher:* Michael H. Black, M.A. *Marketing Director:* David A. Knight, M.A. Books on music and history of music; music books for schools.

Campbell Connelly Group of Companies, 78 Newman Street, London, W1P 3LA *T.* 01-636 7777. General and popular.

MUSIC PUBLISHERS

Chappell Music Ltd., 129 Park Street, London, W1Y 3FA *T.* 01-629 7600. Brussels, Hamburg, Johannesburg, Los Angeles, Madrid, Milan, Bussum, Nashville, New York, Paris, Stockholm, Sydney, Tokyo, Toronto, Zurich.

Chester Music—J. & W. Chester/Edition Wilhelm Hansen London Ltd. (1860), 7-9 Eagle Court, London, EC1M 5QD *T.* 01-253 6947. *Telex:* 919934. *T.A.* Guarnerius, London, EC1. Concert and educational works.

Cramer Music (1824), 99 St. Martin's Lane, London, WC2N 4AZ *T.* 01-240 1612. General and educational.

De Wolfe, Ltd., 80-88 Wardour Street, London, W1V 3LF *T.* 01-439 8481-6. Symphonic recorded orchestral (English and foreign). Comprehensive library of recorded music on disc and tape. Extensive effects library. Original film scores. Recording studio.

Dix, Ltd. (1922)—see **EMI Music Publishing Ltd.**

†**East-West Publications (UK) Ltd.** (1977), Newton Works, 27-29 Macklin Street, London WC2B 5LX *T.* 01-831 6767. *Chairman:* L. W. Carp. *Editor:* B. Thompson. Piano, guitar, recorder and vocal music.

EMI Music Publishing Ltd., 138-140 Charing Cross Road, London, WC2H 0LD *T.* 01-836 6699. *Telex:* 269189. *Fax:* 01-240 9814. *T.A.* and *Cables:* Emimus London WC2. Comprising B. Feldman & Co. Ltd., Robbins Music Corp. Ltd., KPM Music Group, Francis, Day & Hunter Ltd., Keith Prowse Music Publishing Co. Ltd., and Screen Gems-EMI Music Ltd.

Faber Music, Ltd. (1966), 3 Queen Square, London, WC1N 3AU (Subsidiary of Faber & Faber, Ltd. (1929). *T.* 01-278 6881. *Telex:* 299633 Faber G. *T.A.* Fabbaf, London, WC1. *Directors:* Donald Mitchell (Chairman), Martin Kingsbury (Vice Chairman), Patrick Carnegy, Giles de la Mare, Peter du Sautoy, Piers Hembry, A. T. G. Pocock, O.B.E., Sally Cavender, James Fleming. A general list of the highest quality, comprising both old and new music, and music books.

Fairfield Music Co., Ltd., Borough Green, Sevenoaks, Kent, TN15 8DT *T.* Borough Green (0732) 883261. London Showroom: 8 Lower James Street, London, W1. *T.* 01-734 8080. Contemporary orchestral, instrumental, chamber and film music.

Feldman (B.) & Co., Ltd.—see **EMI Music Publishing Ltd.**

Fentone Music Ltd., Fleming Road, Earlstrees, Corby, Northants. NN17 2SN *T.* (0536) 60981. *T.A.* Fentone, Corby. Agents for Fenette Music, Earlham Press, both of Corby, VEB Breitkopf & Härtel, Friedrich Hofmeister, Deutscher Verlag für Musik, Pro Musica Verlag, F.E.C. Leuckart Musikverlag, all of Germany. Columbia Music Co., Washington, D.C., Neil A. Kjos Music Co., all of USA. Edizioni Bèrben, Ancona, Italy, F & R. Walsh Publications, London, Hänssler Verlag, Stuttgart.

Forsyth Bros., Ltd. (1857), 126 Deansgate, Manchester, M3 2GR *T.* 061-834 3281. Educational piano and instrumental music. Modern Teaching material. U.K.Distributors of *Music Minus One.*

Francis, Day & Hunter, Ltd.—see **EMI Music Publishing Ltd.**

Glocken Verlag, Ltd. (1946), 12-14 Mortimer Street, London, W1N 7RD *T.* 01-580 2827. *Cables:* Operetta, London, W1. *Telex:* 888735 Jowein G. *Directors:* R. M. Toeman, S. Buchman. Musical works by Franz Lehar.

†**Gresham Books,** The Gresham Press, P.O. Box 61, Henley-on-Thames, Oxfordshire RG9 3LQ *T.* (073 522) 3789. *Chief Executive:* Mrs. M. V. Green. Hymn books for churches and schools.

Gwynn, Cwmni Cyhoeddi (Cyf.), Stâd Ddiwydiannol, Penygroes, Gwynedd, Cymru LL54 6DB. *T.* Penygroes (0286) 881797. Publishers of Welsh Educational and International Choral Music. Official music publishers to the Welsh Folk Song Society, The Welsh Folk Dance Society, The Court of the National Eisteddfod.

Hughes & Son, Publishers, Ltd. (1820), Clôs Sophia, Cardiff CF1 9XY *T.* (0222) 43421. *Telex:* 497146. Welsh music, Welsh language, television related material, educational publications.

Kalmus, Alfred, A., Ltd., 2-3 Fareham Street, Dean Street, London, W1V 4DU *T.* 01-437 5203-4. *Trade:* 38 Eldon Way, Paddock Wood, Tonbridge, Kent, TN12 6BE *T.* 089-283 3422. Sole representatives of Universal Edition A.G., Vienna, Universal Edition (London) Ltd, Universal Edition, A.G. Zurich, Universal Edition S.P.A., Milan; Theodore Presser Co, Lea Pocket Scores, Hargail Music Inc., International Music Co, Boelke-Bomart Inc., Peer-Southern, Serious Music Division, European American Music Distributors Corp, Bourne Music, Belmont Music, Kelton Publications, Summy Birchard, Trio Associates, all U.S.A.; Doblinger Edition, Vienna, Polish Editions, Cracow (complete (Chopin-Paderewski), Supraphon, Prague, Harmonia, Uitgrave, Hilversum, Artia, Prague, Panton, Prague, Berandol, Canada, Billaudot, France, Boccaccini and Spada, Italy, Aldo Bruzzichelli, Italy, Breitkopt & Härtel, Wiesbaden, Moeck Verlag, West Germany, Musikwissenschaftlicher Verlag, Austria, Musica Rara, France, Fraser-Enoch, Kent, Musical New Services, Dorset; Arcadia Music, Olivan Press, London; Price Milburn, New Zealand, Israel Music Institute, Tel Aviv, Broekmans & Van Poppel, Amsterdam. Serious music of all types.

Keith Prowse Music Publishing Co., Ltd.—see **EMI Music Publishing Ltd.**

Lengnick (Alfred) & Co., Ltd. (1892), Purley Oaks Studios, 421A Brighton Road, South Croydon, CR2 6YR *T.* 01-660 7646. Music publishers and importers. Publishers of Brahms' and Dvorak's works. Specialise in educational music, leading publishers of English contemporary music. Always ready to consider MSS. of any type. Agents for CeBeDeM (Brussels); Iceland Music Information Centre (Iceland).

Leonard, Gould & Bolttler, 60-62 Clerkenwell Road, London, EC1M 5PY *T.* 01-253 6346. General and educational.

MCA Music, Ltd., 139 Piccadilly, London, W1V 9FH *T.* 01-629 7211.

Maurice (Peter) Music Co., Ltd., The,—see **EMI Publishing Ltd.**

Novello & Co., Ltd. (1811), Borough Green, Sevenoaks, Kent, TN15 8DT *T.* Borough Green (0732) 883261. London Showroom: 8 Lower James Street, London, W1. *T.* 01-734 8080. Classical and modern orchestral, instrumental, vocal and choral music, church music, school and educational music books.

†**Novello Hire Library,** incorporating **Goodwin & Tabb,** Borough Green, Sevenoaks, Kent, TN15 8DT. *T.* Borough Green (0732) 883261. Vocal, choral and orchestral hire libraries.

Octava Music Co., Ltd. (1938), 12-14 Mortimer Street, London, W1N 7RD *T.* 01-580 2827. *Cables:* Operetta, London, W1. *Telex:* 888735 Jowein G.

Oxford University Press (Oxford University Press established 1478. Music Dept. constituted 1923). Music Department. Walton Street, Oxford OX2 6DP *T.* (0865) 56767. Orchestral, instrumental, operatic, choral, vocal works, church and organ music by early and modern composers, educational music, courses, and books on music.

MUSIC PUBLISHERS

Paterson's Publications Ltd., 10-12 Baches Street, London, N1 6DN *T.* 01-253 1638. Pianoforte, vocal, choral, orchestral, instrumental, educational and bagpipe music; also musical greetings cards.

Peters Edition, Ltd. (1938), 10-12 Baches Street, London, N1 6DN *T.* 01-253 1638. Copyright/Hire: *T.* 01-251 5094; Promotion/Editorial: *T.* 01-251 6732. *T.A.* Musipeters, London. Peters Edition, Hinrichsen Edition, Collection Litolff. Classical and modern (piano, organ, other instrumental, vocal, choir and brass band) music.

Polyphone Music Co., Ltd., The P.O. Box 1, Rickmansworth, Herts, WD3 3AZ *T.* 01-584 6671. Light orchestral.

†**Reynolds Music**—see **EMI Publishing Ltd.**

Ricordi (G.) & Co. (London), Ltd. (1808), The Bury, Church Street, Chesham, Bucks, HP5 1JG *T.* (0494) 783311 and 784427. *T.A.* Ricordi, Chesham. Publishers of Italian opera, music for piano, classical and contemporary, operatic arias, songs, choral large scale works and part songs for all voices, orchestral works, classical and contemporary, instrumental, string, woodwind, brass tutors, exercises, etc., guitar music of all types.

Roberton Publications, The Windmill, Wendover, Aylesbury, Bucks, HP22 6JJ *T.* Wendover (0296) 623107. *Partners:* Kenneth Roberton, Margaret Roberton. Choral and educational; also piano, chamber, orchestral, and music for all instruments. Represent Lawson-Gould Music Publishers Inc., New York; Leslie Music Supply, Oakville, Ontario; Paraclete Press, Orleans, Massachusetts; Paul Price Publications, New Jersey.

Schott & Co., Ltd. (1835), 48 Great Marlborough Street, London, W1V 2BN *T.* 01-437 1246. Music of a serious and educational nature is considered including music for recorders, guitar and orchestra.

Sea Dream Music (1976), 236 Sebert Road, Forest Gate, London, E7 0NP *T.* 01-534 8500. *Senior Partner:* S.A. Law. Christian based rock, blues and folk.

Sheet Music Publishing (1978) 41 Dynham Road, London NW6 2NT *T.* 01-328 6752. *Director:* Peter J. Scally. Library music, pop, jazz, country, classical, disco, Latin American, children's series, tutors for schools.

Smith, R. & Co., Ltd. (1857), P.O. Box 210, Watford, Herts. *Delivery:* Unit 2, Paramount Industrial Estate, Sandown Road, Watford, Herts, WD2 4YG *T.* Watford 34146.

Sphemusations, Gramercy House, 12 Northfield Road, Onehouse, Stowmarket, Suffolk, IP14 3HF *T.* Stowmarket (0449-61) 3388. Serious music, brass band, choral, instrumental and educational. Records of modern works. Tapes.

Stainer & Bell, Ltd., P.O. Box 110, 82 High Road, East Finchley, London, N2 9PW *T.* 01-444 9135. Book and music publishers including the imprints of **Augener, Belton Books, Galliard, Stainer & Bell, A. Weekes, Joseph Williams.**

Swan & Co. (Music Publishers), Ltd., P.O. Box 1, Rickmansworth, Herts, WD3 3AZ *T.* 01-584 6671. Light orchestral.

Sylvester Music Co., Ltd., 80-82 Wardour Street, London, W1V 3LF *T.* 01-437 4933-4. Popular and orchestral music. Comprehensive library of recorder music on disc and tape. Extensive effects library. Specially composed scores. Transfers to tape and film.

Thames Publishing (1970), 14 Barlby Road, London, W10 6AR *T.* 01-969 3579. Serious music of all types, particularly vocal, choral and instrumental. Manuscripts welcome *but should always be preceded by a letter.*

United Music Publishers, Ltd. (1932), 42 Rivington Street, London EC2A 3BN T. 01-729 4700. Agents for the principal French music publishing houses and specialise in the sale of French, Spanish and other foreign music. Also contemporary English works.

Universal Edition (London), Ltd., 2-3 Fareham Street, Dean Street, London, W1V 4DU T. 01-437 5203-4. Serious music of all types.

Warren & Phillips, (1906), 126 Deansgate, Manchester, M3 2GR T. 061-834 3281. Educational piano and instrumental music. Modern teaching material.

Weinberger (Josef), Ltd. (1885), 12-14 Mortimer Street, London, W1N 7RD T. 01-580 2827 (4 lines). *Cables:* Operetta, London, W1. *Telex:* 888735 Jowein G. *Directors:* S. Buchman, R. M. Toeman. *Executive Directors:* G. Barker, K. Dixon, G. Kingsley, J. Schofield. Theatrical and music publishers.

Workers' Music Association (1936), 17 Prideaux House, Prideaux Place, London, WC1X 9PR. T. 01-278 8374. General music organisation with emphasis on the social aspects of music. Publications, music courses.

OVERSEAS MUSIC PUBLISHERS

IRELAND

Boethius Press Ltd (1973), Clarabricken, Clifden, Co. Kilkenny. T. Kilkenny (056) 29746. *Directors:* L. J. Hewitt, J. M. Hewitt, Mrs. J. M. Hewitt. Early music in facsimile and edition, opera, history of musical education.

NEW ZEALAND

Price Milburn Music Ltd., P.O. Box 995, Wellington T. 721542; and CPO Box 2496 Auckland T. 33372. *Directors:* Peter Zwartz, Marianne Dunkley. Music and books by New Zealand composers, and music and books about music for use in schools. Distributors of music and books about music from overseas publishers.

UNITED STATES

Associated Music Publishers, Inc., 866 Third Avenue, New York, N.Y. 10022. T. (212) 702 5500.

Belwin-Mills Publishing Corporation, 1776 Broadway, New York, N.Y. 10019. T. 212-245-1100.

Birch Tree Group Ltd. (1876), Box 2072, Princeton, New Jersey 08540. T. 609-683-0090. *President:* W. Stuart Pope. *Divisions:* **Summy-Birchard Music.** Educational music teaching methods, music publishing for choral, band, piano. **Suzuki Method International.** Promotion and distribution for the world outside Japan of the Suzuki Teaching Method.

Boosey & Hawkes, Inc., 24 West 57th Street, New York, N.Y. 10019. T. (212) 757-3332. Symphonic, opera, ballet, concert, and educational music.

Bourne Co., 5 West 37th Street, New York, N.Y. 10018. T. (212) 679 3700. Publishers of popular, standard, choral, educational wind band, instrumental, production and film music.

Chappell/Intersong Music Group—USA, 810 Seventh Avenue, New York, N.Y. 10019. T. 212-399-6910.

Church (John) Company, c/o Theodore Presser Co., Bryn Mawr, Pennsylvania, 19010. T. 215-525-3636. Established 1854. Considers suitable MSS. from composers. Does not use or buy songs or lyrics unless with a musical setting. Publication at the firm's expense only.

Dean, Roger, Publishing, 501 East Third Street, Dayton, Ohio 45401. *T.* 513-228-6118. Manuscripts for schools and colleges. Division of **The Lorenz Corporation.**

Ditson (Oliver) Company, c/o Theodore Presser Co., Bryn Mawr, Pennsylvania, 19010. *T.* 215-525-3636. Established 1793. Considers suitable MSS. from composers. Does not use or buy songs or lyrics unless with a musical setting. Publication at the firm's expense only.

Elkan-Vogel, Inc., c/o Theodore Presser Co., Bryn Mawr, Pennsylvania, 19010. *T.* 215-525-3636. Considers suitable MSS. from composers. Does not use or buy songs or lyrics unless with a musical setting. Publication at the firm's expense only.

Gray Publications, H.W. division of **Belwin-Mills Publishing Corp.,** 1776 Broadway, New York, N.Y., 10019.*T.* 212-245-1100. Choral music of all types and arrangements. Organ music, sacred songs.

Heritage Music Press, The, 501 East Third Street, Dayton, Ohio, 45401. *T.* 513-228-6118. Division of **The Lorenz Corporation.** Manuscripts for elementary, junior-high and high schools (secondary schools).

Hinrichsen Edition, C.F. Peters Corporation, 373 Park Avenue South, New York, N.Y. 10016. *T.* 212-686-4147. Classical and contemporary music.

International Music Company, 5 West 37th Street, New York, N.Y. 10018. *T.* 212-683-7900. Publishers of music for instrumental solo, duet, trio, quartet, quintet, large ensembles, voice; study scores, opera scores; concerto and aria orchestral parts on hire.

Laurel Press, 40 Music Square East, Nashville, Tennessee 37203 *T.* 615-244 5588. Division of **Lorenz Creative Services**. Gospel music.

Lorenz Publishing Co., 501 East Third Street, Dayton, Ohio, 45401. *T.* 513-228-6118. Considers for purchase anthems and church organ voluntaries. Division of **The Lorenz Corporation.**

Mercury Music Corporation, c/o Theodore Presser Co., Bryn Mawr, Pennsylvania, 19010. *T.* 215-525-3636. Considers suitable MSS. from composers. Does not use or buy songs or lyrics unless with a musical setting. Publication at the firm's expense only.

Merion Music, Inc., c/o Theodore Presser Co., Bryn Mawr, Pennsylvania, 19010. *T.* 215-525-3636. Established 1953. Considers suitable MSS. from composers. Does not use or buy songs or lyrics unless with a musical setting. Publication at the firm's expense only.

Mills Music Inc., 1776 Broadway, New York, N.Y. 10019. *T.* 212-245-1100.

Peters, C.F., Corporation, 373 Park Avenue South, New York, N.Y. 10016. *T.* 212-686-4147. (Edition Peters, Hinrichsen Edition, and other European music publications, in U.S.A.).

Presser (Theodore) Co., Bryn Mawr, Pennsylvania, 19010. *T.* 215-525-3636. Established 1883. Considers suitable MSS. from composers. Does not use or buy songs or lyrics unless with a musical setting. Publication at the firm's expense only.

Sacred Music Press, The, 501 East Third Street, Dayton, Ohio, 45401. *T.* 707-785-2408. *Editor:* Dale Wood. Division of **The Lorenz Corporation.**

Schirmer, G., Inc., 866 Third Avenue, New York, N.Y. 10022. *T.* (212) 702-5500.

Sonshine Productions, 40 Music Square East, Nashville, Tennessee 37203 *T.* 615-244 5588. Division of **Lorenz Creative Services.** Contemporary sacred music.

Triune Music Inc, 40 Music Square East, Nashville, Tennessee 37203 *T.* 615-244 5588. Division of **Lorenz Creative Services.** Sacred music.

Warner Bros. Music, 9000 Sunset Boulevard, Penthouse, Los Angeles, California, 90069. *T.* 213-273-3323. *Cables:* Wang, Los Angeles. Includes, among others, the following companies: WB Music Corp., Warner-Tamerlane Publishing Corp., Harms Inc., M. Witmark, Remick, Advanced, New World Music Corp., Pepamar Music Corp., Schubert Music Publishing Corp., Weill-Brecht-Harms Company Inc., Viva Music Inc., Zapata Music Inc., Curtom Publishing Co. Inc., Rodart Music Corp., Jalynne Corp, Twentieth Century Fox Music Corp., House of Gold Music, Foster Frees Music Inc., Pendulum Music.

MECHANICAL-COPYRIGHT PROTECTION SOCIETY LTD.

The Society was formed in 1910 by a group of music publishers in anticipation of the introduction of new legislation which for the first time would provide for the protection of copyright material by mechanical reproduction.

This became effective on the introduction of the Copyright Act 1911 when only the music box, piano roll, cylinder and disc recordings were known.

Since those days the Society has grown with the technical advances into sound film, radio and television recordings, magnetic tape, videocassettes, and now grants licences in all matters affecting recording rights, both in the U.K. and throughout the world by virtue of its affiliation with other similar organisations and agencies.

Membership of the Society is open to all music copyright owners, composers, lyric writers and publishers. There is no entrance fee or subscription.

Enquiries for membership should be addressed to the Membership Department, Elgar House, 41 Streatham High Road, London, SW16 1ER *T.* 01-769 4400.

THE PERFORMING RIGHT SOCIETY, LTD.

The Performing Right Society is an Association of Composers, Authors and Publishers of copyright musical works, established in 1914 to collect royalties for the public performance, broadcasting and diffusion by cable of such works and their use by diffusion services; also to restrain unauthorised use thereof.

Licences are granted which convey the necessary permission for the public performance of any of the works of its members and those of the affiliated national societies of more than 30 other countries. The combined membership thus represented by the Society is about 500,000. Over 200,000 places of entertainment are covered by the Society's licence in the British Isles alone.

The Society does not control the performance of non-musical works (plays, sketches, etc.), but its licence is required for the use of its international repertoire in variety, as overture, entr'acte or exit music, or for any other form of live or mechanical performances (excluding operas, operettas, musical plays, specially written music for plays, revues or pantomimes, (apart from interpolations therein of independent items) and ballets).

The constitution of the Society is that of a Company limited by guarantee having no share capital. The General Council consists of twelve composers and authors and twelve music publishers elected by the members from among their own number. The Society is not a profit-making organisation, the whole of the royalties it collects being distributed amongst its members and the affiliated societies after deduction of administration expenses and contributions to the P.R.S. Members' Fund, established for the benefit of necessitous members and their dependants.

There are two distributions of general performing fees each year, and two distributions of broadcasting fees. The Annual General Meeting is usually held in July.

Applicants for membership are required to pay an initial admission fee, but no further subscriptions or fees are charged. All composers of musical works and authors of lyrics or poems which have been set to music, are eligible for membership, provided that they satisfy the current membership criteria.

The Society has available for free loan a documentary film *What Price Music?* For details of this and for further information contact the Public Relations Department at PRS, 29-33 Berners Street, London, W1P 4AA *T.* 01-580 5544.

LITERARY PRIZES AND AWARDS

In the past year many special awards and prizes have been offered for novels, short stories and works of non-fiction. Details of these awards, as they are offered, will be found in such journals as *The Author*. Book Trust (*q.v.*) publish a useful *Guide to Literary Prizes, Grants and Awards*, (£2.75 including postage). The number of permanent literary prizes in Great Britain is small compared with America, where there are scores of literary awards.

The Age Australian Book of the Year Award
Founded in 1974, this annual award of two prizes of $3000 each is given, one to a work of imaginative writing, the other to a non-fiction work. Authors must be Australian by birth or naturalisation. Publishers only must submit books (maximum two works of imaginative writing and/or three works of non-fiction). Details from the Literary Editor, *The Age*, 250 Spencer Street, Melbourne, Victoria, Australia 3000.

The Alexander Prize
Candidates for the Alexander Prize may choose their own subject for an Essay, but they must submit their choice for approval to the Literary Director, Royal Historical Society, University College London, Gower Street, London, WC1E 6BT *T*. 01-387 7532.

The American Book Awards
Books written by U.S. citizens and published by U.S. publishers are eligible for this annual prize of $10,000 in each of two categories: fiction and non-fiction. Runners-up in each category will receive $1,000. A Louise Nevelson Sculpture is given to the winners. Books are entered by publishers by July 31st each year. Details from The American Book Awards Inc., 155 Bank Street, Studio 1002d, New York, N.Y. 10014.

The Hans Christian Andersen Medals
The Hans Christian Andersen Medals are awarded every two years to an author and an illustrator who by the outstanding value of their work are judged to have made a lasting contribution to literature for children and young people. Details from International Board on Books for Young People, British Section, Book Trust, Book House, 45 East Hill, London, SW18 2QZ *T*. 01-870 9055.

Angel Literary Award
Prizes of £1000 and £500 are awarded annually to writers living and working in East Anglia. One prize is given for a work of fiction and one for non-fiction. Further details from Caroline Gough, Angel Hotel, Angel Hill, Bury St. Edmunds, Suffolk, IP33 1LT.

Arts Council of Great Britain
Writers' Bursaries
The Arts Council will award three bursaries of £5,000 to writers whose work is of outstanding literary quality.
Details are available from the Literature Department, Arts Council of Great Britain, 105 Piccadilly, London W1V 0AU. *T*. 01-629 9495.

The Arts Council/An Chomhairle Ealaíon, Ireland
Bursaries for Creative Writers
In 1986 awards totalling £30,000 were offered to creative writers of poetry, fiction and drama to enable them to concentrate on or complete writing projects. At least the same amount will be distributed in 1987.

Denis Devlin Memorial Award for Poetry
This award, value approximately £1000, is made triennially for the best book of poetry in the English language by an Irish citizen published in the preceding three years. The next award will be made in 1989.

Macaulay Fellowship
Fellowships, value £3,000, are awarded once every three years to writers under 30 years of age (or in exceptional circumstances under 35 years) in order to help them to further their liberal education and careers. The cycle of awards is: Literature (1987), Visual Arts (1988), Music (1989).

The Marten Toonder Award
This award is given to an artist of recognised and established achievement on a rotating cycle as follows: Visual Arts (1987), Music (1988), Literature (1989). Candidates must be Irish-born (Northern Ireland is included). Value £3,000.

Prize for Poetry in Irish
This is Ireland's major award to Irish-language poetry; it is given triennially for the best book of Irish-language poetry published in the preceding three years. The next award will be made in 1989. Value £1,000.

Travel Grants
Creative artists (including writers) may apply at any time of the year for assistance with travel grants to attend seminars, conferences, workshops, etc. Applications are assessed four times each year.

Further details may be obtained from The Arts Council (An Chomhairle Ealaíon), 70 Merrion Square, Dublin, 2 *T.* (01) 764685.

Arvon Foundation International Poetry Competition
This competition, founded in 1980, is awarded biennially for previously unpublished poems written in English. First prize £5,000 plus other cash prizes. Full details from Arvon Foundation Poetry Competition, Kilnhurst, Kilnhurst Road, Todmorden, Lancashire, 0L14 6AX.

The Astra Prize for Medical Writing
Thanks to the generosity of Astra Pharmaceuticals Ltd, who have taken over the funding of this prize from Abbott Laboratories Ltd, the Medical Writers Group of the Society of Authors is again offering a prize of £1,000 for a medical textbook. The closing date for entries, which must be submitted by publishers, is 30 June. Details from the Secretary, MWG, 84 Drayton Gardens, London SW10 9SB.

Authors' Club First Novel Award
The award was instituted in 1954 and is made to the author of the most promising first novel published in the United Kingdom during each year. The award takes the form of a silver mounted and inscribed quill plus £200 and is presented to the winner at a dinner held in the Club. Entries for the award are accepted from publishers and must be full length novels—short stories are not eligible—written and published in the United Kingdom during the year.

The Authors' Foundation
The Foundation, which was founded in 1984 to mark the centenary of the Society of Authors, provides grants to authors for specific projects which have been commissioned by a British publisher. The aim is to provide funding (in addition to a proper advance) for research, travel or other necessary expenditure. Novels and poetry are not excluded, but preference is given to works of non-fiction.

Application should be in the form of a letter sent to the Authors' Foundation at the Society of Authors, giving reasons for the application (including information about the basic terms of the publishing contract). The closing date for applications is 30 June.

The Phoenix Trust has been merged with the Foundation, which hopes to provide grants totalling at least £10,000 in 1987.

The Alice Hunt Bartlett Prize
The Poetry Society prize of £500 is awarded annually to the author of a volume of poetry comprising not less than 20 poems or 400 lines published in English and presented in duplicate to the Society's library in the year of publication. The closing date in each year is 31st January. Special consideration is given to newly emerging poets so far as merit warrants. In the event of the poems being translations into English the prize is divided equally between the author and the translator.

H. E. Bates Short Story Competition
This annual prize is awarded for a short story—maximum length 2000 words-to anyone resident in Great Britain. The first prize is for £50, other prizes to a total value of £50. Further details from Tourist Information Centre, 21 St. Giles Street, Northampton *T.* (0604) 22677.

The David Berry Prize
Candidates for the David Berry Prize of £100 may select any subject dealing with Scottish History within the reigns of James I to James VI inclusive, provided such subject has been previously submitted to and approved by the Council of the Royal Historical Society, University College London, Gower Street, London, WC1E 6BT *T.* 01-387 7532.

Best Book of the Sea Award
This award of £500 founded in 1970 and sponsored by King George's Fund for Sailors is given each year for a work of non-fiction which contributes most to the knowledge and/or enjoyment of those who love the sea. A second award of £250 may be given at the discretion of the judges for a book of outstanding merit. Books must be published in the UK and sent to 1 Chesham Street, London SW1X 8NF *T.* 01-235 2884.

The James Tait Black Memorial Prizes
The James Tait Black Memorial Prizes, founded in memory of a partner in the publishing house of A. and C. Black Ltd., were instituted in 1918 and since 1979 have been supplemented by the Scottish Arts Council. Two prizes, of £1000 each are awarded annually: one for the best biography or work of that nature, the other for the best novel, published during the calendar year. The prize winners are announced normally in the February following the year of the awards. The adjudicator is the Professor of English Literature in the University of Edinburgh.

Publishers are invited to submit a copy of any biography, or work of fiction that in their judgement may merit consideration for the award. Copies should be sent to the Department of English Literature, David Hume Tower, George Square, Edinburgh, EH8 9JX, marked "James Tait Black Prize". They should be submitted as early as possible, with a note of the exact date of publication. Co-operation on this point is essential to the work of the adjudicator.

By the terms of the bequest, and by tradition, eligible novels and biographies are those written in English, originating with a British publisher, and first published in Britain in the year of the award; but technical publication elsewhere, simultaneously or even a little earlier, does not disqualify. Both prizes may go to the same author; but neither to the same author a second time.

The Boardman Tasker Prize
This annual prize of £1,000, founded in 1983, is given for a work of fiction, non-fiction or poetry, the central theme of which is concerned with the mountain environment. Authors of any nationality are eligible but the work must be published or distributed in the United Kingdom. Further details from

Mrs. Dorothy Boardman, 56 St. Michael's Avenue, Bramhall, Stockport, Cheshire, SK7 2PL.

The Booker Prize

This annual prize for fiction of £15,000 is sponsored by Booker plc, and administered by the National Book League. The prize is awarded to the best novel in the opinion of the judges, published each year. The Prize is open to novels written in English by citizens of the British Commonwealth, Republic of Ireland, Pakistan, Bangladesh and South Africa and published for the first time in the U.K. by a British publisher. Entries are to be submitted only by U.K. publishers who may each submit not more than four novels with scheduled publication dates between the last presentation date and 30 September of the current year, but the judges may also ask for other eligible novels to be submitted to them. Entry forms and further information are available from the Publicity Officer, Book Trust, Book House, 45 East Hill, London, SW18 2QZ *T*. 01-870 9055.

Katharine Briggs Folklore Award

An award of £50 and an engraved goblet is given annually for a book in English, having its first original and initial publication in the U.K., which has made the most distinguished contribution to folklore studies. The term folklore studies is interpreted broadly to include all aspects of traditional and popular culture, narrative, belief, customs and folk arts. Details from the Publicity Officer, The Folklore Society, University College London, Gower Street, London, WC1E 6BT *T*. 01-387 5894.

The British Academy Research Awards

These are made annually (in the case of Learned Societies or group research applications) and quarterly (in the case of individual applications) to scholars conducting advanced academic research for the humanities and normally resident in the U.K. The main headings under which an application would be eligible are: (*a*) Travel and maintenance expenses in connection with an approved programme of research; (*b*) Fieldwork; (*c*) Provision of mechanical or photographic aids for research; (*d*) Costs of preparation of research for publication; (*e*) In special cases, aid to the publication of research. Successful applicants are normally expected to publish the results within two years. Details and application forms from The British Academy, 20-21 Cornwall Terrace, London NW1 4QP.

British Airways Commonwealth Poetry Prize

An annual prize totalling £11,000 sponsored by British Airways and comprising £5000 for the best published poet; £2000 for the best first-time published poet; £1000 each for individual world Commonwealth area awards. Extra £2500 fund for sponsored readings by winners. Open to all published Commonwealth poets, including U.K. Entries in non-English officially-recognised languages accepted with translation. Closing date is 30 June. Details are available from the Poetry Prize Administrator, Commonwealth Institute, Kensington High Street, London W8 6NQ. *T*. 01-603 4535.

The British Film Institute Book Award

Founded in 1984, this annual prize of £1000 is given for any book, biography, reference work, collected essays, etc., on film or television which advances the public's understanding of those media. Details from Wayne Drew, Press Officer, British Film Institute, 127 Charing Cross Road, London WC2H 0EA.

Burnley Express and National & Provincial Building Society Award of Children's Book of the Year

An annual prize of £250, plus a crystal decanter, founded in 1985, is given to the writer of the most outstanding work of fiction written for children between the ages of 5 and 14. The closing date is 30th April; details from A. McColm, Chairman, Children's Book of The Year, *Burnley Express*, Bull Street, Burnley BB11 1DP.

Canadian Authors Association Awards
The awards consist of a silver medal and $5000 and apply in (i) fiction, (ii) non-fiction, (iii) poetry, (iv) drama (for any medium). These annual awards are to honour writing that achieves literary excellence without sacrificing popular appeal and are given to works by Canadian authors. Further details from the Canadian Authors Association, 121 Avenue Road, Suite 104, Toronto, Ontario, M5R 2G3 *T.* 416-364 4203.

Children's Book Award
Founded in 1980 by The Federation of Children's Book Groups this award is given to authors of works of fiction for children under 14 years of age, published in the United Kingdom. Children participate in the judging of the award. Details from Martin G. Kromer, 22 Beacon Brow, Bradford, West Yorkshire BD6 3DE *T.* (0274) 575301.

The Children's Book Circle Eleanor Farjeon Award
In 1965 the Children's Book Circle instituted an annual award to be given for distinguished services to children's books and to be known as the Children's Book Circle Eleanor Farjeon Award in memory of the much-loved children's writer. A prize of (minimum) £500, may be given to a librarian, teacher, author, artist, publisher, reviewer, television producer or any other person working with, or for children through books. The award is sponsored by Books for Children.

Children's Book of the Year Awards
The Children's Book Council of Australia makes annual awards in three sections. (1) Book of the Year (for literary merit, quality of production and appeal to children.) Book Council Medal, plus Literature Board cash award. (2) Picture Book of the Year (for younger children.) Medal and Visual Arts Board cash award. (3) Junior Book of the Year (for middle readers.) Medal given.
The Literature Board of the Australia Council gives $4,500 to be distributed at the discretion of the Council to the winners in the Book of the Year section. The Visual Arts Board of Australia Council gives $3,000 to be distributed to the winners in the Picture Book of the Year section. Candidates must be Australian citizens, or authors normally resident in Australia. Information from Children's Book Council of Australia, P.O. Box 420, Dickson, A.C.T. 2602, Australia.

Cholmondeley Awards
In 1965, the Dowager Marchioness of Cholmondeley established these non-competitive awards, for which submissions are not required, for the benefit and encouragement of poets of any age, sex or nationality. In 1986 the total value of the awards was £3,200. The Scheme is administered by the Society of Authors.

Collins Biennial Religious Book Award
This £2000 prize was founded in 1969 to commemorate the 150th Anniversary of the founding of Wm. Collins Sons & Co. Ltd. It is given biennially to a living citizen of the United Kingdom, the Commonwealth, the Republic of Ireland, and South Africa for a book which in the judges' opinion has made the most distinguished contribution to the relevance of Christianity in the modern world. Details from Wm. Collins PLC, 8 Grafton Street, London, W1X 3LA *T.* 01-493 7070.

The Constable Trophy

An annual competition supported by the five Northern based Regional Arts Associations for fiction writers living in the North of England (Cumbria, the North East, North and South Humberside, Lincolnshire, Yorkshire, Lancashire, Merseyside and Cheshire) for a previously unpublished novel. The winning entry will receive a prize of £1,000 and a silver cup and will be considered for publication by Constable & Co. Ltd., as may up to two runners-up. The winning novel will also receive an advance of £1,000 against royalties on publication. Full details from The Literature Department, Northern Arts, 10 Osborne Terrace, Newcastle upon Tyne NE2 1NZ.

Thomas Cook Travel Book Awards

Awards are given annually in two categories to encourage the art of travel writing. (*a*) Travel Books award value £2000, (*b*) Guide Books, £1000. Books written in English and published between 1st November and 31st October are eligible. Details from the Book Trust, Book House, 45 East Hill, London, SW18 2QZ, *T*. 01-870 9055.

Catherine Cookson Cup Short Story Competition

This annual prize of £150 for a short story was founded in 1978 and is open to anyone resident in Great Britain. It is organised by the Hastings Writers' Group, 7 Harlequin Gardens, St Leonards-on-Sea, East Sussex TN37 7PF.

The Duff Cooper Memorial Prize

Friends and admirers of Duff Cooper, first Viscount Norwich (1890-1954), contributed a sum of money which has been invested in a Trust Fund. The interest is devoted to an annual prize for a literary work in the field of biography, history, politics or poetry published in English or French during the previous twenty-four months. There are two permanent judges (the present Lord Norwich, and the Warden of New College, Oxford) and three others who change every five years.

The Rose Mary Crawshay Prizes

One or more Rose Mary Crawshay prizes are awarded each year. The Prizes, which were originally founded by Rose Mary Crawshay in 1888, are awarded to women of any nationality who, in the judgement of the Council of the British Academy, have written or published within three calendar years next preceding the date of the award an historical or critical work of sufficient value on any subject connected with English literature, preference being given to a work regarding Byron, Shelley, or Keats.

John Creasey Memorial Award

The award was founded in 1973 following the death of John Creasey, to commemorate his foundation of the Crime Writers Association. It is given annually, for a first published crime fiction novel, by the Crime Writers Association, P.O. Box 172, Tring, Herts. HP23 5LP.

Current Crime Silver Cup

This is an annual award given for the best British crime novel. The choice is made by readers of *Current Crime*. Further details from Forensic Publishing Co., 87 London Street, Chertsey, Surrey KT16 8AN.

The Isaac Deutscher Memorial Prize

This prize of £100 was founded in 1968 and is awarded each year to the author of an essay or full-scale work, published or in manuscript, in recognition of an outstanding research and writing in the Marxist tradition of Isaac Deutscher. Material should be submitted before 1st May of the current year to The Isaac Deutscher Memorial Prize, c/o Lloyds Bank, 68 Warwick Square, London, SW1V 2AS.

The European Poetry Translation Prize

Founded in 1983 a prize of £500 is given every two years for a published volume of poetry which has been translated into English from a European language. It is administered by the Poetry Society, 21 Earls Court Road, London SW5 9DE.

Christopher Ewart-Biggs Memorial Prize

This Prize of £2000 is awarded annually to the writer, of any nationality, whose work contributes most to peace and understanding in Ireland; to closer ties between the peoples of Britain and Ireland; or to co-operation between the partners of the European Community. Eligible works must be published during the current year and can be written in either English or French. Entry forms are available from 30 Sherwood Court, Bryanston Place, London W1H 5FL *T.* 01-262 4778.

The Geoffrey Faber Memorial Prize

As a memorial to the founder and first Chairman of the firm, Messrs. Faber & Faber Limited established in 1963 the Geoffrey Faber Memorial Prize. With the financial assistance of the Arts Council of Great Britain the Prize of £500 is awarded annually: and it is given, in alternate years, for a volume of verse and for a volume of prose fiction. It is given to that volume of verse or prose fiction first published originally in this country during the two years preceding the year in which the award is given which is, in the opinion of the judges, of the greatest literary merit.

To be eligible for the prize the volume of verse or prose fiction must be by a writer who is: (*a*) not more than 40 years old at the date of publication of the book; (*b*) a citizen of the United Kingdom and Colonies, of any other Commonwealth state, of the Republic of Ireland or of the Republic of South Africa.

There are three judges who are reviewers of poetry or of fiction as the case may be; and they are nominated each year by the editors or literary editors of newspapers and magazines which regularly publish such reviews.

Messrs. Faber & Faber invite nominations from such editors and literary editors. No submissions for the prize are to be made.

Prudence Farmer Poetry Prize

This poetry prize was founded in 1974 and is awarded annually for the best poem *printed during the previous year* in the *New Statesman* (14-16 Farringdon Lane, London, EC1R 3AU).

The Kathleen Fidler Award

An annual award of £500 is given to an author of any age or nationality for a novel for the 8-12 age range, which must be the author's first attempt for this age range. Details from Book Trust, Scotland, 15a Lynedoch Street, Glasgow G3 6EF. *T.* 041-332 0391.

Sir Banister Fletcher Prize Trust

The late Sir Banister Fletcher, who was President of the Authors' Club for many years, left the Authors' Club a sum of money to be held upon trust: "to apply the income thereof in or towards the provision of an annual prize for the book on architecture or the arts which, in the opinion of the Committee...shall be most deserving of it, such prize to be known as the Sir Banister Fletcher Prize".

The Committee of the Club decided that the prize be awarded annually for the best book on architecture or the fine arts. The award, which is £200, is presented to the winner at a dinner held in the Club.

The John Florio Prize
This prize was established in 1963 for the best translation into English of a twentieth century Italian work of literary merit and general interest, published by a British publisher during the preceding two years under the auspices of the Italian Institute and the British-Italian Society, and named after John Florio. Details from the Secretary, The Translators' Association, 84 Drayton Gardens, London, SW10 9SB.

E. M. Forster Award
The distinguished English author, E. M. Forster, bequeathed the American publication rights and royalties of his posthumous novel *Maurice* to Christopher Isherwood, who transferred them to the American Academy and Institute of Arts and Letters (633 West 155th Street, New York, N.Y. 10032), for the establishment of an E. M. Forster Award, to be given from time to time to an English writer for a stay in the United States. Applications for this award are not accepted.

Gold Dagger Award and Silver Dagger Award
Founded in 1955 and awarded annually for a novel of any crime fiction published in the United Kingdom to a novelist from any country. The panel of 9 judges are reviewers or writers of crime fiction. Given by the Crime Writers Association, P.O. Box 172, Tring, Herts HP23 5LP.

Gold Dagger Award for Non-Fiction
Founded in 1977 and awarded annually for a non-fiction crime book to an author published in the United Kingdom. Chosen by the Trustee of Prizes and four judges of different professions. Given by the Crime Writers Association.

E. C. Gregory Trust Fund
A number of substantial awards are made annually from this Fund for the encouragement of young poets who can show that they are likely to benefit from an opportunity to give more time to writing. A candidate for an Award must: (*a*) be a British subject by birth but *not* a national of Eire or any of the British dominions or colonies and be ordinarily resident in the United Kingdom or Northern Ireland; (*b*) be under the age of thirty at 31st March in the year of the Award (i.e. the year following submission); (*c*) submit for the consideration of the Judges a published or unpublished work of belles-lettres, poetry or drama poems (not more than 30 poems). Entries for the Award should be sent not later than 31st October to the Society of Authors, 84 Drayton Gardens, London, SW10 9SB.

Guardian Fiction Prize
The *Guardian*'s annual prize of £1000 for a work of fiction published by a British or Commonwealth writer. The winning book will be chosen by the Literary Editor in conjunction with the *Guardian*'s regular reviewers of new fiction.

Guardian Award for Children's Fiction
The *Guardian*'s annual prize of £250 for an outstanding work of fiction for children by a British or Commonwealth writer, instituted in 1967. Further details from Stephanie Nettell, 24 Weymouth Street, London W1N 3FA *T*. 01-580 3479.

The Hawthornden Prize
The Hawthornden Prize, for which books do not have to be specially submitted, may be awarded annually to the author of what, in the opinion of the Committee, is the best work of imaginative literature published during the preceding calendar year by a British author under forty-one years of age. It was founded by the late Miss Alice Warrender in 1919 and is administered by The Society of Authors.

The Felicia Hemans Prize for Lyrical Poetry
The Felicia Hemans Prize of books or money is awarded annually for a lyrical poem, the subject of which may be chosen by the competitor. Open to past and present members and students of the University of Liverpool only. The prize shall not be awarded more than once to the same competitor. Poems, endorsed "Hemans Prize", must be sent in to the Registrar, The University of Liverpool, P.O. Box 147, Liverpool L69 3BX *T.* 051-709 6022, on or before May 1st. Competitors may submit either published or unpublished verse, but no competitor may submit more than one poem.

David Higham Prize for Fiction
This prize of £1000 which was founded in 1975 is awarded annually to a citizen of the British Commonwealth, Republic of Ireland, South Africa or Pakistan for a first novel or book of short stories written in English and published during the current year. Entry forms are available from Book Trust, Book House, 45 East Hill, London, SW18 2QZ *T.* 01-870 9055. Publishers only may submit books.

Historical Novel Prize
The prize, value £2,000 was founded in 1977 in memory of Georgette Heyer and is awarded annually for an outstanding full-length previously unpublished historical novel. Details from: The Bodley Head, 32 Bedford Square, London, WC1B 3EL or Transworld Publishers, Century House, 61-63 Uxbridge Road, London, W5 5SA.

Winifred Holtby Memorial Prize
The prize will be for the best regional novel of the year written in the English language. The writer must be of British or Irish nationality, or a citizen of the Commonwealth. Translations, unless made by the author himself of his own work, are not eligible for consideration. If in any year it is considered that no regional novel is of sufficient merit the prize may be awarded to an author, qualified as aforesaid, of a literary work of non-fiction or poetry, concerning a regional subject.
Publishers may submit novels published during the current year to The Royal Society of Literature, 1 Hyde Park Gardens, London, W2 2LT.

International Poetry Competition
Prizes totalling £1000 are awarded biennially for the best three poems. Open to anyone over sixteen writing in English. Details from the Greenwich Festival, 25 Woolwich New Road, London, SE18. *T.* 01-317 8687.

The Martin Luther King Memorial Prize
A prize of £100 is awarded for a literary work reflecting the ideals to which Dr. Martin Luther King dedicated his life: viz. a novel or non-fiction book, poetry collection, essay, play, TV, radio or motion picture script, first published or performed in the United Kingdom during the calendar year preceding the date of the award. Details from John Brunner, c/o NatWest Bank, 7 Fore Street, Chard, Somerset TA20 1PJ. No enquiries answered without s.a.e.

The Allen Lane Award
The Allen Lane Award established in 1985 carries a prize of £2,000, plus guaranteed publication in Penguin paperback, and is given annually to one book selected from those published by the three Penguin hardcover companies, Viking, Hamish Hamilton or Michael Joseph. The winning title, by a British or Commonwealth author under 40 years of age, will be a work of non fiction in the area of literature or history which in the opinion of the judges best exemplifies the spirit of Allen Lane.

The Library Association Besterman Medal

The Library Association Besterman Medal is awarded annually for an outstanding bibliography or guide to the literature first published in the United Kingdom during the preceding year. Recommendations for the award are invited from members of the Library Association, who are asked to submit a preliminary list of not more than three titles. The following are among the criteria which will be taken into consideration in making the award: (i) the authority of the work and the quality and kind of the articles or entries; (ii) the accessibility and arrangement of the information; (iii) the scope and coverage; (iv) the quality of the indexing; (v) the adequacy of the references; (vi) the up-to-dateness of the information; (vii) the physical presentation; (viii) the originality of the work.

The Library Association Carnegie Medal

The Library Association Carnegie Medal is awarded annually for an outstanding book for children written in English and receiving its first publication in the United Kingdom during the preceding year. It was instituted by the Library Association, whose work owes so much to the benefactors of the Carnegie Trust, to commemorate the centenary of Andrew Carnegie's birth in 1835.

Recommendations for the award are made by members of the Library Association and the decision rests with a Panel of the Youth Libraries Group. Consideration is given not only to the literary quality and suitability of the work, but also to the type, paper, illustrations and binding. It should be added that the award is not necessarily restricted to books of an imaginative nature.

The Library Association Kate Greenaway Medal

The Kate Greenaway Medal is intended to recognise the importance of illustrations in children's books. It is awarded to the artist, who, in the opinion of the Library Association, has produced the most distinguished work in the illustration of children's books first published in the United Kingdom during the preceding year. Books intended for younger as well as older children are included and reproduction will be taken into account. Recommendations are invited from members of the Library Association who are asked to submit a preliminary list of not more than three titles.

The Library Association McColvin Medal

The Library Association McColvin Medal is awarded annually for an outstanding reference book first published in the United Kingdom during the preceding year. The following types of book are eligible for consideration: (i) encyclopedias, general and special; (ii) dictionaries, general and special; (iii) biographical dictionaries; (iv) annuals, yearbooks and directories; (v) handbooks and compendia of data; (vi) atlases. Recommendations for the award are invited from members of the Library Association, who are asked to submit a preliminary list of not more than three titles. The following are among criteria which will be taken into consideration in making an award; (i) the authority of the work and the quality and kind of the articles or entries; (ii) the accessibility and arrangement of the information; (iii) the scope and coverage; (iv) the style; (v) the relevance and quality of the illustrations; (vi) the quality of the indexing; (vii) the adequacy of the bibliographies and references; (viii) the up-to-dateness of the information; (ix) the physical presentation; (x) the originality of the work.

The Library Association Wheatley Medal

The Library Association Wheatley Medal is awarded annually for an outstanding index published during the preceding three years. Printed indexes to any type of publication may be submitted for consideration. Recommendations for the award are invited from members of the L.A. and the Society of Indexers, publishers and others. The final selection is made by a committee consisting of representatives of the L.A. Cataloguing and Indexing Group and the Society of Indexers, with power to co-opt. The award is made to the compiler of the winning index to a work which must have been published in the United Kingdom.

The Sir William Lyons Award
The Lyons Award of £500 is to encourage young people in automotive journalism, including broadcasting, and to foster interest in motoring and the motor industry through these media. It is awarded to any person of British nationality resident in the United Kingdom under the age of 22 and consists of writing two essays and an interview with the Award Committee. Further details from the Chief Executive, Jean Peters, 2 Pembroke Villas, The Green, Richmond, Surrey TW9 1QF.

Roger Machell Prize
An annual award of £2,000 (sponsored by Hamish Hamilton) for a book on the performing arts, including music, ballet, the theatre, film or television. Work submitted must be in the English language and the work of one author, of over 50,000 words, to have been first published in the UK. Closing date for entries 30 November. Full details from the Society of Authors, 84 Drayton Gardens, London SW10 9SB.

The Enid McLeod Literary Prize
This annual prize of £100 is given for a full-length work of literature which contributes most to Franco-British understanding. It must be written in English by a citizen of the U.K., British Commonwealth, the Republic of Ireland, Pakistan, Bangladesh, or South Africa, and first published in the U.K. Further details from the Secretary, Franco-British Society, Room 636, Linen Hall, 162-168 Regent Street, London W1R 5TB *T.* 01-734 0815.

Katherine Mansfield Menton Short Story Prize
This prize of 10,000 French francs is given every three years for a volume of English short stories. The books must have been printed in English and appeared in the U.K., Eire or The Commonwealth, and should be submitted by agents or publishers to the English Centre of the International P.E.N., 7 Dilke Street, London, SW3 4JE *T.* 01-352 6303. An award will be made in 1987.

Arthur Markham Memorial Prize
A prize for a short story, essay or poems on a given subject is offered annually as a memorial to the late Sir Arthur Markham. Candidates must be manual workers in or about a coal mine, or have been injured when so employed. Full details can be obtained from The Registrar and Secretary, The University, Sheffield, S10 2TN.

Kurt Maschler Award
An annual prize of £1000 was founded in 1982 and is given to a British author/artist or one resident in Britain for more than ten years. It is given for a children's book in which text and illustrations are of excellence and enhance and balance each other. Details from Book Trust, Book House, 45 East Hill, London, SW18 2QZ *T.* 01-870 9055.

The Somerset Maugham Trust Fund
The purpose of these annual awards, totalling about £4,000, is to encourage young writers to travel, to acquaint themselves with the manners and customs of foreign countries, and, by widening their own experience, to extend both the basis and the influence of contemporary English literature. Mr. Maugham urged that in the selection of prize-winners, originality and promise should be the touchstones: he did not wish the judges to "play for safety" in their choice.

A candidate for the award must be a British subject by birth and ordinarily resident in the United Kingdom or Northern Ireland. He or she must, at the time of the award, be under thirty-five years of age, and must submit a published literary work in volume form in the English language, of which he or she is the sole author. The term "literary work" includes poetry, fiction, criticism, history and biography, belles-lettres, or philosophy, but does not include a dramatic work. A candidate who wins an award must undertake to spend not less than three months outside Great Britain and Ireland, and to devote the prize to the expenses of this sojourn.

Any questions relating to the terms of the award should be addressed to The Society of Authors, 84 Drayton Gardens, SW10 9SB, to which candidates should send the literary work they wish to submit for an award. Three copies of one published work (which are non-returnable) should be submitted by a candidate, and it must be accompanied by a statement of his or her age, place of birth, and other published works.

The closing date for the submission of books to be considered is December 31st.

The Vicky Metcalf Awards for Short-Fiction and a Body of Work.

These awards are given annually to stimulate writing for children. $2,000 prize for Body of Work and $1,000 prize for Short-Fiction are given to Canadian authors. Details from Canadian Authors' Association, 121 Avenue Road, Suite 104, Toronto, Ontario, M5R 2G3.

MIND Book of the Year—the Allen Lane Award

This £1,000 award, inaugurated in memory of Sir Allen Lane in 1981, is given to the author of any book published in the current year which outstandingly furthers, in the opinion of the judges, public understanding of the prevention, causes, treatment or experience of mental illness or mental handicap. The award is administered by MIND, the National Association for Mental Health. Further details from Christine Shaw, MIND, 22 Harley Street, London, W1N 2ED *T*. 01-637 0741.

The Mofolo-Plomer Prize

This prize, founded in 1975, is awarded annually for a literary work, written in English, by a South African writer, whether resident in South Africa or abroad. The value of the prize is R1000. Full details from The Mofolo-Plomer Prize Committee, c/o Ravan Press (Pty) Ltd., P.O. Box 31134, Braamfontein 2017, South Africa. *T*. Johannesburg 642-5235.

The Mother Goose Award

The award, sponsored by Books for Children, is open to all artists having published a first major book for children during the previous year. Only books first published in Britain will be considered and this includes co-productions where the illustration originated in Britain. The award is presented annually at Easter and is in the form of a bronze egg together with a cheque for £500. Recommendations for the award are invited from publishers and should be sent to each panel member. Full details and names and addresses of the panel members from Sally Grindley, Books for Children, Park House, Dollar Street, Cirencester, Glos. GL7 2AN.

National Book Council of Australia Awards

These awards, sponsored by the National Book Council and supported by the Literature Board of the Australia Council, are one of the two major features of Australian Book Week, held annually. The awards are for books of the highest literary merit and are the only awards of which the prizes are shared by author and publisher. The first prize of $6000 is divided, the author receives $5000 and the publisher $1000. The second prize of $4000 will also be divided; the author receiving $3500 and the publisher $500. The second prize must be for a book of a different category from that winning the first prize. Details from the Awards Secretary, Level 5, 1 City Road, South Melbourne, Victoria 3205, Australia. *T.* 614 5111.

National Poetry Competition
Now established as the major annual poetry competition in Britain. Prizes of £2000, £1000, £500, 5 of £100, 10 of £50. Entry fees of £2.00 per poem, maximum entry of 10 poems, length of each poem not to exceed 40 lines. Run in association with BBC Radio 3. Results announced on a special BBC Radio 3 programme broadcast in December. Details and entry forms from National Poetry Competition, National Poetry Centre, 21 Earls Court Square, London SW5 9DE.

John Newbery Medal
This annual prize which was founded in 1922 is given for children's literature to a citizen or resident of the U.S.A. The judges are 15 members of the Association for Library Service to Children (ALSC), a division of the American Library Association (committee members change annually) and the prize is given to the author of the most distinguished contribution to American literature for children published in the U.S. during the preceding year. Further details from ALSC, The American Library Association, 50 East Huron Street, Chicago, Illinois 60611.

The Nobel Prize
The Nobel Prize in Literature is one of the awards stipulated in the will of the late Alfred Nobel, the Swedish scientist who invented dynamite. The awarding authority is the Swedish Academy Källargränd 4, S-111 29 Stockholm, Sweden. No direct application for a prize will, however, be taken into consideration. For authors writing in English it was bestowed upon Rudyard Kipling in 1907, upon W. B. Yeats in 1923, upon George Bernard Shaw in 1925, upon Sinclair Lewis in 1930, upon John Galsworthy in 1932, upon Eugene O'Neill in 1936, upon Pearl Buck in 1938, upon T.S. Eliot in 1948, upon William Faulkner in 1949, upon Bertrand Russell in 1950, upon Sir Winston Churchill in 1953, upon Ernest Hemingway in 1954, upon John Steinbeck in 1962, upon Samuel Beckett in 1969, upon Patrick White in 1973, upon Saul Bellow in 1976 and upon William Golding in 1983. The Nobel Prizes are understood to be worth about £128,000 each. They number five (*a*) Physics, (*b*) Chemistry, (*c*) Physiology or Medicine, (*d*) Literature, and (*e*) Promotion of Peace.

The Noma Award for Publishing in Africa
Established in 1979, this annual book prize of $3,000 is available to African writers and scholars whose work is published in Africa. The principal aim of the Award is to encourage publication of works by African writers and scholars in Africa. The prize is given to the author of an outstanding new book published (during the preceding twelve months) by a publisher domiciled on the African continent or its offshore islands, in any of these three categories: (i) scholarly or academic, (ii) books for children, (iii) literature and creative writing, including fiction, drama, and poetry. Any original work in any of the indigenous or official languages of Africa is eligible for consideration. Full details from The African Book Publishing Record, P.O. Box 56, 52 St Giles, Oxford OX1 3EL.

Odd Fellows (Manchester Unity) Social Concern Annual Book Awards
A prize worth £1000 is awarded for the book, or pamphlet of not less than 10,000 words, in an area of social concern (to be specified each year). Entries must be published in the current year; must be written by citizens of Britain, the Commonwealth, Republic of Ireland, Pakistan or South Africa; and must

first have appeared in English. Entry forms are available from Book Trust, Book House, 45 East Hill, London, SW18 2QZ *T.* 01-870 9055.

Oppenheim-John Downes Memorial Trust
Awards, varying from £50 to £1500 depending on need, from this Trust Fund are given each December to deserving artists of any kind including writers, musicians, artists who are unable through poverty to effectively pursue their vocation. Applicants must be over 30 years of age and of British birth. Full details and Application for an Award form from the Trust, c/o 5 Breams Building, Chancery Lane, London, EC4A 1HL, enclosing s.a.e.

The Other Award
A commendation is given annually to a number of children's books published in Britain in a 12 month period. The Award was founded in 1975 and further details are available from The Other Award, 4 Aldebert Terrace, London, SW8 1BL. (Please enclose S.A.E.)

Catherine Pakenham Memorial Award
Young women journalists (over 18 and under 30 years of age), resident in Britain, are eligible for this annual award which was founded in 1970 in memory of Lady Catherine Pakenham. The award of £500 is given for an article or TV or radio script (not a short story). Applications for entry forms should be sent to Roy Wright, *The Standard*, 118, Fleet Street, London EC4P 4JT (an enclosed S.A.E. essential), after July 20th for that year's competition.

Parents Magazine Best Book for Babies Award
An annual award of £1000 for the best book for the under-fours—babies and toddlers. Eligible books must be published in the year ending 31 May, in the United Kingdom. A shortlist of ten books is chosen in February and the winner presentation is in May. Details and entry form from Book Trust, Book House, 45 East Hill, London SW18 2QZ.

Radio Times Drama Awards
Founded in 1973 and now given biennially, these awards, totalling at present £15,000, are given for an original play for radio and also for television. Full details of the award will be given in *Radio Times* in January 1988.

Radio Times Radio Comedy Awards
Founded in 1985 and now given biennially, these Awards, totalling at present £4,000, are given for an original radio comedy script with the potential to become a series. Full details in *Radio Times* in January 1987, or on request after that date by sending an S.A.E. to Radio Times Radio Comedy Awards, 35 Marylebone High Street, London, W1M 4AA. Closing date 30 June 1987.

FAW Barbara Ramsden Award
The award was founded by public subscription in 1971 to honour Barbara Ramsden, M.B.E., an editor of distinction. This major Australian literary award for quality writing is made each year to both author and then in symbolic recognition of the importance of the publishing process to the publisher's editor. The winners are each presented with a plaque specially designed by Andor Meszaros. There is no restriction of category and more than one work may be submitted. The award is administered by the Victorian fellowship of Victorian Writers, of which Barbara Ramsden was a foundation member. Details of this award and other national awards, organised by this body from The Secretary, Victorian Fellowship of Australian Writers, 1/317 Barkers Road, Kew, Victoria 3101. *T.* 03-817 5243.

Trevor Reese Memorial Prize
Founded in 1979, a prize of £500 is given every two years for an historical monograph on Imperial or Commonwealth history published in the last two

years. Details from The Director, Institute of Commonwealth Studies, 27-28 Russell Square, London WC1B 5DS.

The Margaret Rhondda Award

This award, first made in July 1968 on the tenth anniversary of Lady Rhondda's death, and afterwards every three years, is given to a woman writer as a grant-in-aid towards the expenses of a research project in journalism. It is given to women journalists in recognition of the service which they give to the public through journalism. Closing date for next award December 31st, 1989. Further details from The Society of Authors, 84 Drayton Gardens, London, SW10 9SB.

The John Llewellyn Rhys Memorial Prize

The prize of £500, inaugurated by the late Mrs. Rhys in memory of her husband who was killed in 1940, and administered jointly by the trustees and the National Book League, is offered annually to the author of the most promising literary work of any kind published for the first time during the current year. The author must be a citizen of this country or the Commonwealth, and not have passed his or her 35th birthday by the date of the publication of the work submitted. Entry forms and further information are available from the John Llewellyn Rhys Memorial Prize, c/o Book Trust, Book House, 45 East Hill, London, SW18 2QZ *T.* 01-870 9055. Publishers only may submit books.

The Rogers Prize

This prize of the value of £100, will be offered by the Senate, for an essay or dissertation on the subject of Advance in Surgery. The Prize is open to all persons whose names appear on the Medical Register of the United Kingdom. The essay or dissertation must be submitted to the Secretary to the Scholarships Committee, University of London, Senate House, London, WC1E 7HU (from whom further particulars may be obtained) not later than 30th June.

Romantic Novelists' Association Award

The Annual Award for the best Romantic Novel of the Year is open to non-members as well as members of the Romantic Novelists' Association. Novels must be published between January 1st and December 31st of year of entry. Two copies of the novel required. The Netta Muskett Award is for unpublished writers in the romantic novel field who must join the Association as Probationary members. MSS. entered for this award must be specially written for it. No Award will be made unless a MSS. is accepted for publication through the Association. Details from the Hon. Secretary, Mrs Dorothy Entwistle, 20 First Avenue, Amersham, Bucks HP7 9BJ.

The Royal Society of Literature Award under the W. H. Heinemann Bequest

The purpose of this foundation is to encourage the production of literary works of real worth. The prize shall be deemed a reward for actual achievement. Works in any branch of literature may be submitted by their publishers to the verdict of the Royal Society of Literature which shall be final and without appeal. Prose fiction shall not be excluded from competition, but the Testator's intention is primarily to reward less remunerative classes of literature: poetry, criticism, biography, history, etc. Any work originally written in the English language, shall be eligible. The recipient of a Prize shall not again be eligible for five years.

Runciman Award

Established in 1985 by the Anglo-Hellenic League for a literary work wholly, or mainly, about Greece. The £1000 prize is sponsored by the Onassis Foundation and to be eligible must be published in its first English edition in the U.K. Details from the Book Trust, Book House, 45 East Hill, London SW18 2QZ. *T.* 01-870 9055.

Ryman New Writers' Award

Founded in 1986 this annual award is for a novel, short story, children's story, poetry, song lyric by a previously un-published writer. £500 is given in each category, plus guaranteed publication. Details from P.O. Box 38, London SW3 3NL.

The Schlegel-Tieck Prize

This prize was established in 1964 under the auspices of the Society of Authors and its Translators Association to be awarded annually for the best translation published by a British publisher during the previous year. Only translations of German twentieth-century works of literary merit and general interest will be considered. The work should be entered by the publisher and not the individual translator. Details may be obtained from the Secretary, The Translators Association, 84 Drayton Gardens, SW10 9SB.

Scottish Arts Council Awards

A limited number of Book Awards, value £750 each, are made each year by the Scottish Arts Council to published books of literary merit written by Scots or writers resident in Scotland. These awards are for new writing as well as for work by established authors, and there is also a Scottish Arts Council Publication Award of £250 to be made to a Scottish-based publishing house only in recognition of high standards of publishing and which will normally be restricted to books already submitted to the Book Awards panel. Books are submitted by the author's publisher yearly, in the spring and autumn. Details from the Literature Department, The Scottish Arts Council, 19 Charlotte Square, Edinburgh, EH2 4DF T. 031-226 6051. Also writers' bursaries are awarded twice a year to Scottish writers or writers resident in Scotland displaying professional standing and with a record of publication. Applications from writers should be supported by an appropriate referee.

The Scott Moncrieff Prize

This prize was established in 1964 under the auspices of the Society of Authors and its Translators Association to be awarded annually for the best translation published by a British publisher during the previous year. Only translations of French twentieth century works of literary merit and general interest will be considered. The work should be entered by the publisher and not the individual translator. Details from the Secretary, The Translators Association, 84 Drayton Gardens, London, SW10 9SB.

The Signal Poetry for Children Award

A prize of £100 is given annually for an outstanding book of poetry published for children in Britain and the Commonwealth during the previous year, whether single poet or anthology and regardless of country of original publication. Articles about the winning book are published in *Signal* each May. Not open to unpublished work. Further details from The Thimble Press, Lockwood, Station Road, South Woodchester, Stroud, Glos., GL5 5EQ.

Silver Dagger Award—for details see under Gold Dagger Award.

Sinclair Prize for Fiction

First awarded in 1982 this £5,000 prize is sponsored by Sinclair Research Ltd. and is awarded to the author of the best unpublished full-length novel which, in the opinion of the judges, is not only of great literary merit, but also of major social and political significance. The panel of judges will be chosen by the National Book League in conjunction with Sinclair Research Ltd. Novels must be not less that 50,000 words, written originally in English and must be submitted by the author. Closing date is 31 July. Full details and entry form from Book Trust, Book House, 45 East Hill, London, SW18 2QZ T. 01-870 9055.

Ally Sloper Award

Founded in 1976, this is an annual award which is presented at the annual convention of British strip/comic artists, and is given to veteran strip cartoonists only, for work in newspapers and comics. The award is given by Denis Gifford on behalf of the Association of Comic Enthusiasts. Full details are available from 80 Silverdale, Sydenham, London, SE26.

Smarties Prize

Established in 1985 to encourage high standards and stimulate interest in books for children of primary school age. £1000 for book for under 7's; £1000 for over 7's; £1000 for innovation: book outstanding in its format, presentation or packaging. Grand Prix of £7000 for overall winner chosen from the above 3 category winners. Eligible books must be published between 1 January and 31 October of the year of presentation and be written in English by a citizen of the U.K., or an author resident in the U.K., and published in the U.K. Prize is sponsored by Rowntree Mackintosh. Details from Book Trust, Book House, 45 East Hill, London SW18 2QZ *T.* 01-870 9055.

The W. H. Smith Annual Literary Award

A prize of £4,000 is awarded annually to a Commonwealth author (including a citizen of the United Kingdom) whose book, written in English and published in the United Kingdom, within 12 months ending on December 31st preceding the date of the Award, in the opinion of the judges makes the most outstanding contribution to literature. Further details are available from W. H. Smith & Son Ltd., Strand House, 7 Holbein Place, London SW1W 8NR *T.* 01-730 1200 ext. 5458.

Southern Arts Literature Prize

The £1000 prize is awarded annually for a published novel, poetry, or literary non-fiction to writers living within the Southern Arts region. Details from The Literature Officer, Southern Arts Association, 19 Southgate Street, Winchester, Hants, SO23 9DQ *T.* (0962) 55099.

Winifred Mary Stanford Prize

The prize was founded in 1977 by Mr. Leonard Cutts in memory of his wife who died in 1976. The prize of £1000 is awarded biennially and is open to any book published in the U.K. in the English language which has been inspired in some way by the Christian faith, written by a man or woman 50 years of age or under at the date of publication. The subject of the book may be from a wide range, including poetry, fiction, biography, autobiography, biblical exposition, religious experience and witness. Books must have been published in the two years prior to the award which is made at Easter. Literary merit will be a prime factor in selection. Submission by publishers only to the Secretary to the Judges, Winifred Mary Stanford Prize, c/o Hodder & Stoughton, 47 Bedford Square, London WC1B 3DP *T.* 01-636 9851.

E. Reginald Taylor Essay Competition

A prize of £100, in memory of the late E. Reginald Taylor, F.S.A., is awarded annually for the best unpublished essay submitted during the year. The essay, not exceeding 7500 words, should show original research on a subject of archaeological, art-historical or antiquarian interest within the period from the Roman era to A.D. 1830. The successful competitor may be invited to read the essay before the Association and the essay may be published in the *Journal* of the Association if approved by the Editorial Committee.

Competitors are advised to notify the Hon. Editor in advance of the intended subject of their work. The essay should be submitted not later than 31st

December to the Hon. Editor, Dr. Martin Henig, British Archaeological Association, Institute of Archaeology, 36 Beaumont Street, Oxford OX1 2PG.

The Dylan Thomas Award
This annual award of £1000 was established in 1983 to honour the contribution made to English letters by Dylan Thomas and to encourage writers working in two literary genres in which Dylan Thomas's work is justly celebrated—poetry and short-story writing. The award is made in alternate years for poetry and short stories and is open to writers throughout the U.K. Full details of the rules obtainable from The Dylan Thomas Award, The Poetry Society, 21 Earls Court Square, London SW5 9DE *T.* 01-373 7861/2.

Times Educational Supplement Information Book Awards
There are two annual awards of £500 to the authors of the best information books—one for children up to the age of 9, the other for children aged 10-16. The books must be published in Britain or the Commonwealth. Details from the Times Educational Supplement, Priory House, St. John's Lane, London EC1M 4BX *T.* 01-253 3000.

The Tom-Gallon Trust
This Trust was founded by the late Miss Nellie Tom-Gallon and is administered by the Society of Authors. An award is made biennially from this Fund to fiction writers of limited means who have had at least one short story accepted for publication. The latest award of £500 will be made in 1987. Authors wishing to enter should send to the Secretary, Society of Authors, 84 Drayton Gardens, SW10 9SB: (i) a list of their already published fiction, giving the name of the publisher or periodical in each case and the approximate date of publication; (ii) one published short story; (iii) a brief statement of their financial position; (iv) an undertaking that they intend to devote a substantial amount of time to the writing of fiction as soon as they are financially able to do so; (v) a stamped addressed envelope for the return of the work submitted. Closing date for next award 20th September 1988.

The Betty Trask Awards
The Betty Trask Awards are for the benefit of young authors under 35 and are given on the strength of a first novel (published or unpublished) of a romantic or traditional, rather than experimental nature. They stem from a generous bequest by the late Miss Betty Trask (who died in 1983) and are administered by the Society of Authors. It is expected that prizes totalling at least £17,500 will be presented each year. The winners are required to use the money for a period or periods of foreign travel. Full details of the conditions of entry can be obtained from the Society of Authors, 84 Drayton Gardens, London SW10 9SB.

The Travelling Scholarship
This is a non-competitive award, for which submissions are not required (see article: **The Society of Authors**).

The Dorothy Tutin Award
This award of a carriage clock, donated by Johnathon Clifford, was founded in 1980, and is presented to the person whom it is felt has done the most to encourage the writing and love of poetry in the U.K. Details from Johnathon Clifford, 153 Coles Lane, Sutton Coldfield, West Midlands, B72 1NP.

UEA Writing Fellowship
Funded by the University and by the Eastern Arts Association, this Fellowship is offered annually, to be held in the School of English and American Studies at the University of East Anglia for the Summer Term.

The duties of the Fellowship will be discussed at interview. It will be assumed that one activity will be the pursuit of the Fellow's own writing. In addition, the Fellow will be expected to take part in some of the following activities: (a) contributing to the teaching of a formal course in creative writing; (b) running a regular writers' workshop on an informal extra-curricular basis; (c) being available for a specified period each week to advise individual students engaged in writing; (d) giving an introductory lecture or reading at the beginning of the Fellowship; (e) organizing one or two literary events involving other writers invited from outside the University; (f) making some contribution to the cultural and artistic life of the region (by, for instance, a public lecture or reading). The salary for the Fellowship will be £2,000 plus free flat. Applications for the Fellowship should be lodged with the Establishment Officer, University of East Anglia, Norwich, NR4 7TJ by 1st October of each year.

The Universe Literary Prize
In 1981 *The Universe* inaugurated an annual Literary Prize worth £500 which will be awarded to the book which in the opinion of the judges best supports and defends Christian values. The theme changes each year. Books written in English and published in Britain and Ireland during the current year are eligible. Details from *The Universe*, 33-39 Bowling Green Lane, London EC1R 0AB *T*. 01-278 7321.

Wandsworth All London Literary Competition
The competition is open to writers of 16 years and over who live, work or study in the Greater London Area. Awards are made periodically in two classes, Poetry and Short Story, the prizes totalling £500 in each class. Entries must be previously unpublished work. The award is sponsored by the Greater London Arts Association, and the judging is under the chairmanship of Martyn Goff, Director of the National Book League. Further details from Assistant Director of Leisure and Amenity Services (Libraries and Arts), Wandsworth Town Hall, High Street, London, SW18 2PU.

Wattie Book of the Year Award
This annual award, sponsored by the Wattie Group since 1967, is run by the Book Publishers Association of New Zealand, and is given for the best book taking into account writing and illustration, design and production, and impact on the community. Authors must be New Zealanders or resident in New Zealand. It is New Zealand's major literary award; 1st prize $9,000, 2nd $4,000, 3rd $2,000, and open only to books published by B.P.A.N.Z. members. Details from Wattie Award, Box 44146, Auckland 2.

The Welsh Arts Council's Awards to Writers
Prizes of £1000 each are awarded to the authors of books published during the previous calendar year which, in the Literature Committee's opinion, are of exceptional literary merit. The Tir na nOg Prize is awarded for children's books. The Council also organizes competitions from time to time. For further details of the Welsh Arts Council's policies, write to the Literature Department, Welsh Arts Council, Museum Place, Cardiff, CF1 3NX *T*. (0222) 394711.

Whitbread Literary Awards
Awards to be judged in two stages and offering a total of £22,500 prize money open to five categories: Novel, First Novel, Children's Novel, Biography/Autobiography, Poetry. The winner in each category will receive a Whitbread Nomination Award of £1,000. The five nominations will go forward to be judged for the Whitbread Book of the Year. The overall winner receives £18,500 (£17,500 plus £1,000 Nomination Award). Writers must have lived in Great Britain and Ireland for five or more years. Submissions only from publishers. Further details may be obtained from The Booksellers Association, 154 Buckingham Palace Road, London SW1W 9TZ *T*. 01-730 8214.

John Whiting Award
Founded in 1965, this prize of £3,500 is given annually. Eligible to apply are any writers who have received during the previous two calendar years an award through the Arts Council new theatre writing schemes, or who have had a premier production by a theatre company in receipt of an annual subsidy. Details from the Drama Director, Arts Council of Great Britain, 105 Piccadilly, London, W1V 0AU *T.* 01-629 9495.

Francis Williams Illustration Awards
These awards are given every five years to practising illustrators, for any book, published or distributed in Great Britain in which illustration is a major element, including newly illustrated editions of the classics. Illustrations of a purely technical nature and photographs are excluded. The most recent competition was in 1982. Further details from The Victoria and Albert Museum Library, South Kensington, London SW7 2RL, or Book Trust, Book House, 45 East Hill, London, SW18 2QZ.

H. H. Wingate Prize
Awarded to the book which best stimulates an interest in and awareness of Jewish concern among a wider reading public. Books must be published in English and authors normally resident in the UK, Israel, the British Commonwealth, South Africa, Pakistan or Republic of Ireland are eligible. The Prize is worth £3,000 and is awarded annually in December. Details from Book Trust, Book House, 45 East Hill, London SW18 2QZ *T.* 01-870 9055.

Wolfson Literary Awards for History
The Awards were established in 1972 to pay tribute to a lifetime's contributions to the study of history and also to encourage the writing of scholarly history for the general public. No application is necessary, but further details from M. Paisner, Messrs. Paisner & Co., Bouverie House, 154 Fleet Street, London, EC4.

Yorkshire Arts Association Writers Awards
Yorkshire Arts awards a number of bursaries of £250 each to assist in a writer's development and to encourage recognition of the writer's work. The Panel supports writing where the creative use of imagination is the major element in the finished work, although it will consider local history, biography and social documentary. Applicants must be living, working or studying in the Yorkshire Arts Association region. Details from the Literature Officer, Yorkshire Arts Association, Glyde House, Glydegate, Bradford BD5 0BQ.

Yorkshire Post Literary Awards
A prize of £1,000 is awarded for the Book of the Year and a prize of £800 for the Best First Work each year. Also annual awards of £500 each are made for works which in the opinion of the Panel of Judges have made the greatest contribution to the understanding and appreciation of Music and Art. Nominations are only accepted from publishers and should arrive (together with one copy of the book) by 15th December in the case of main prizes, by 16th January in the case of the Art and Music Awards. Correspondence to Caroline Colmer, Secretary of the Book Awards, Yorkshire Post Newspapers Ltd., P.O. Box 168, Wellington Street, Leeds, LS1 1RF *T.* (0532) 432701 ext. 512.

Young Observer Teenage Fiction Prize
This annual prize of £600 was founded in 1981 and is given to an author for the best full-length novel written for teenagers published between 1st July and 30th June each year. Details from *Young Observer, Observer Magazine*, 8 St. Andrew's Hill, London, EC4V 5JA *T.* 01-236 0202.

SOCIETIES, ASSOCIATIONS AND CLUBS

Academi Gymreig Yr. *President:* Dr. John Gwilym Jones; *Chairman:* R. Gerallt Jones; *Treasurer:* Gwenlyn Parry; *Administrator:* Marion Arthur, 3rd Floor, Mount Stuart House, Mount Stuart Square, The Docks, Cardiff CF1 6DQ *T.* (0222) 492064. The Society was founded in 1959 to promote creative writing in the Welsh language. Existing members elect new members on the basis of their contribution to Welsh literature or criticism. The society publishes a literary magazine, *Taliesin*, books on Welsh literature, and translations of modern European classics into Welsh. It is currently engaged in the production of a new English/Welsh Dictionary. The society's activities are open to all.

Academi Gymreig, Yr: English Language Section. *President:* A. G. Prys-Jones; *Chairman:* Tony Curtis; *Administrator:* Mrs. Ceri George, 3rd Floor, Mount Stuart House, Mount Stuart Square, The Docks, Cardiff CF1 6DQ *T.* (0222) 492025. This section was founded in 1968 to provide a meeting-point for writers in the English language who are of Welsh origin and/or take Wales as a main theme of their work. Membership at present is by invitation and members pay an annual subscription. Associate Membership is open to all interested individuals or organisations. Although it is an autonomous body, members of the English Language Section co-operate with members of the parent body for joint conferences and similar activities.

Agricultural Journalists, Guild of, c/o *Farmers Weekly*, Carew House, Wallington, Surrey SM6 0DX *T.* 01-661 4703. *President:* Peter Bell; *Chairman:* Peter Grimshaw; *Hon. General Secretary:* Don Gomery. Established to promote a high standard among journalists who specialise in agricultural matters and to assist them to increase their sources of information and technical knowledge. Membership is open to those earning their livelihood wholly or mainly from agricultural journalism.

American Correspondents in London, Association of, *President:* Helen Westwood, c/o ABC News, 8 Carburton Street, London W1P 7DT *T.* 01-637 7211.

American Publishers, Association of, Inc. (1970), *President:* Nicholas A. Veliotes. *Executive Vice President:* Thomas D. McKee, 220 East 23rd Street, New York, N.Y. 10010. *T.* 212-689-8920. *Senior Vice-President:* Richard P. Kleeman, 2005 Massachusetts Avenue N.W., Washington, D.C. 20036. A confederation of more than 300 member houses which is the major voice of the publishing industry in the United States. Members drawn from all regions of the country, publish the great majority of printed materials sold to American schools, colleges and libraries, bookstores, and by direct mail to homes. Their basic products comprise books in the categories of school and college textbooks, general trade, reference, religious, technical, professional, scientific, and medical—both hard cover and paperback. They also publish scholarly journals, and produce a range of educational materials including computer software, classroom periodicals, maps, globes, films and filmstrips, audio and video tapes, records, cassettes, slides, transparencies, and test materials.

Art and Design, National Society for Education in (1888), 7A High Street, Corsham, Wiltshire, SN13 0ES *T.* (0249) 714825. *General Secretary:* John Steers, N.D.D., A.T.C., D.A.E. A professional association of principals and lecturers in colleges and schools of art and of specialist art, craft and design teachers in other schools and colleges. Has representatives on National and Regional Committees which are the concern of those engaged in Art and Design Education. Publishes *Journal of Art and Design Education* (3 p.a.).

SOCIETIES

Artists, Federation of British, 17 Carlton House Terrace, London, SW1Y 5BD *T.* 01-930 6844. *Secretary-General:* Oliver Warman, R.B.A. Administers 12 major National Art Societies at The Mall Galleries, The Mall, London, SW1.

Artists' League of Great Britain, The (Incorporated 1909). Bankside Gallery, 48 Hopton Street, London, SE1 9JH *T.* 01-928 7521. Run by Artists for Artists and renders advice and assistance with problems met with in their professional capacity. *Annual Subscription:* £10.00.

Artists Union (1972), 9 Poland Street, London, W1V 3DG *T.* 01-437 1984. Represents and protects the interests of visual artists in this country and assists and advises its members on problems connected with their work. *Annual Subscription:* £10.00.

Arts (1863), 40 Dover Street, London, W1X 3RB *T.* 01-499 8581. *Secretary:* Christopher Miers. *Subs:* £280. For men and women connected with or interested in the arts.

Arts Council of Great Britain, 105 Piccadilly, London, W1V 0AU *T.* 01-629 9495. *Chairman:* Sir William Rees-Mogg; *Secretary-General:* Luke Rittner. To develop and improve the knowledge, understanding and practice of the arts, and to increase their accessibility to the public throughout Great Britain. The arts with which the Council is mainly concerned are dance and mime, drama, literature, music and opera, and the visual arts, including photography and arts films. **Scottish Arts Council:** 19 Charlotte Square, Edinburgh, EH2 4DF *T.* 031-226 6051. **Welsh Arts Council:** Holst House, Museum Place, Cardiff, CF1 3NX *T.* (0222) 394711.

Asian Affairs, Royal Society for, (1901), 2 Belgrave Square, London, SW1X 8PJ *T.* 01-235 5122. *President:* The Lord Denman, C.B.E., M.C., T.D.; *Chairman of Council:* Sir Michael Wilford, G.C.M.G.; *Secretary:* Miss M. FitzSimons. For the study of all Asia past and present. Fortnightly lectures etc. Library. *Publication: Asian Affairs,* three times a year, free to members. *Subscription:* £25.00 London members, £20 members more than 60 miles from London and overseas; £2.00 Junior (under 25); £50 Affiliated.

Aslib, The Association for Information Management, (1924), Information House, 26-27 Boswell Street, London, WC1N 3JZ *T.* 01-430 2671. An association which promotes the effective management and use of information in industry, central and local government, education and the professions. For particulars of membership apply: The Director.

Assistant Librarians, Association of (1895), c/o The Library Association, 7 Ridgmount Street, London, WC1E 7AE (Group of the Library Association, *q.v.*). *President:* Mrs R. Aldrich, A.L.A. *Hon. Secretary:* Miss C. M. Campbell, B.A., A.L.A. Publish library text books and bibliographical aids.

Australia, Children's Book Council of, *National Executive:* P.O. Box 420, Dickson, A.C.T., 2602.

Australia Council, Northside Gardens, 168 Walker Street, North Sydney, New South Wales 2060, Australia. *T.* (02) 923 3333. *Chairperson:* Professor Donald Horne, A.O.
The Australia Council is a statutory authority which provides a broad range of support for the arts in Australia. Established in 1968 as The Australian Council for the Arts (supporting mainly the performing arts), it was restructured in 1973 to embrace music, theatre, film/radio/television, literature, visual arts, crafts, Aboriginal arts and community arts. (In June 1976 the activities of the film/radio/television board were transferred to the Australian Film Commission and in 1984 the design arts were included.) In March 1975, by Act of Parliament, the Australia Council was established as an independent authority.

The Council is involved in the administration of grants, public information services, policy development, research, international activities, and advisory services to many other organisations including government bodies. A wide range of projects and activities, both individual and group, receive Australia Council funds. Support includes grants made to enable artists to study, and living allowances to permit others (notably writers) to 'buy time' to follow their creative pursuits. Some of the major initiatives of the Council in past years, include: negotiation with international bodies for the touring of exhibitions, a Public Lending Right scheme for Australian authors (which is now administered by the Department of Arts, Heritage & Environment); copyright protection; moral rights for artists; art and working life; women in the arts; Arts Law Centre; a Provident Fund for performers; Artist-in-Residence schemes at tertiary institutions, and increased employment for Australian artists in all fields. Australia Council publications include information booklets, directories, research reports, newsletters, program reviews and an Annual Report.

Literature Board, The, Australia Council, P.O. Box 302, North Sydney, New South Wales 2060. Because of its size and isolation and the competition its literature meets from other English speaking countries, Australia has always needed to subsidise writing of creative and cultural significance. The Literature Board, one of the eight Boards of the Australia Council, was created in 1973, taking over the duties of the earlier Commonwealth Literary Fund, established in 1908.

The Board's chief objective is the support of the writing of all forms of creative literature—novels, short stories, poetry, plays, biographies, history and works on the humanities. The Board also assists with the publication of literary magazines and periodicals. It has a publishing subsidies scheme and it initiates and supports projects of many kinds designed to promote Australian literature both within Australia and abroad.

About two-thirds of the Board's expenditure in recent years has gone to writers in the form of direct grants including Fellowships and New Writers' Assistance Grants (living allowances), Special Purpose Grants and Emeritus Fellowships. Category A Fellowships (valued at $25,000 per year) are living allowances to assist published writers of substantial achievement to complete a major project or projects. Category B Fellowships (valued at $17,000 per year) are living allowances for developing writers of potential who may or may not have had a work published or performed. New Writers' Assistance Grants (maximum value $8,000) are to assist writers to meet living expenses while writing a particular literary work. Special Purpose Grants (maximum value $4,000) are to assist writers with research, travel and other expenses involved in writing a literary work of cultural significance. Emeritus Fellowships are paid at varying rates to senior writers of distinction.

Australia, The Library Association of, 376 Jones Street, Ultimo, Sydney, N.S.W. 2007. *T.* 692 9233. *Executive Director:* Jenny Adams. The Association is an Australia-wide organisation incorporated by Royal Charter in 1963 with c. 7,500 members, of whom c. 5,500 are profesional members. The objects of the Association are (*a*) to promote, establish and improve libraries and library services; and (*b*) to improve the standard of librarianship and the status of the library profession. It publishes the *Australian Library Journal* four times a year, and the newsletter *Incite* twenty-one times a year, as well as a range of specialist publications to cater for the interests of members in different types of libraries. The governing body of the Association is the General Council.

Australian Book Publishers' Association, 161 Clarence Street, Sydney, N.S.W., 2000. *T.* (02) 29 5422. *Telex:* AA121822 SY 508.

The Association aims to foster original and licensed publishing in Australia, to help improve the Australian book industry as a whole. There are over 150 member firms.

Australian Library Promotion Council, State Library of Victoria, 328 Swanston Street, Melbourne, Victoria 3000. A national body campaigning to raise the level of public awareness of the value, role and importance of libraries in Australia, and providing information and advice. Consists of representatives appointed by organisations affiliated to the Council in the fields of writing, publishing, bookselling and library and information service. Publishers of the annual *Bookmark Diary and Directory*, which consists of a diary coupled with a comprehensive directory containing information of interest to all interested in and involved with books.

Australian Society of Authors, The, 22 Alfred Street, Milsons Point, N.S.W., 2061 *T.* 92-7235. *President:* Elizabeth Jolley, *Executive Officer:* Denise Yates.

Australian Writers, The Society of, Australia House, Strand, London, WC2B 4LA. Formed in 1952 to further the cause of Australian writers and Australian writing wherever possible.

Australian Writers' Guild Ltd (1962), 171 New South Head Road, Edgecliff, NSW 2027 *T.* 326 1900. *Executive Officer:* Angela Wales. A trade union and professional association dedicated to promoting and protecting the professional interests of writers for stage, screen, television and radio. *Subscription:* Full members: $70.00 Entrance, $108.00 p.a. Associates: $50.00 Entrance, $54.00 p.a.

Authors (1891) (at the Arts Club). 40 Dover Street, London, W1X 3RB *T.* 01-499 8581. *Secretary:* Huldine Ridgway. *Subscription:* £300.

Authors' Agents, The Association of (1974), 49 Blenheim Crescent, London, W11 *T.* 01-221 3717. *President:* Deborah Rogers; *Vice President:* Andrew Nurnberg; *Secretary;* Michael Thomas; *Treasurer:* Andrew Hewson. Maintains a code of professional practice to which all members of the Association commit themselves; holds regular meetings to discuss matters of common professional interest; and provides a vehicle for representing the view of authors' agents in discussion of matters of common interest with other professional bodies.

Authors' Guild of Ireland, Ltd., 282 Swords Road, Dublin, 9. *T.* 375974. *Directors:* John K. Lyons, John McDonnell, Mrs. Iseult McGuinness. A society for the protection of copyright owned and managed, on a non-profit basis, by Full Members who must be owners of copyright in literary or dramatic works by reason of authorship, or who are the personal successors of such authors. Agents for the control of performing rights and collection of royalties in Ireland. *Secretary:* Tom Mooney.

Authors' Lending and Copyright Society Limited (ALCS), 7 Ridgmount Street, London, WC1E 7AE *T.* 01-580 2181. *President:* Lord Willis. Independent, non-profit-making collecting society for the collective administration of literary rights in the spheres of reprography, lending right, audio and video recording and cable television. Membership, £5 annually, open to authors, successor membership to authors' heirs. See **Article**.

Authors' Representatives, Inc., Society of (1928), 39½ Washington Square South, New York, N.Y., 10012 *T.* 212-228-9740.

Authors, The Society of, 84 Drayton Gardens, London, SW10 9SB *T.* 01-373 6642. *President:* Sir Victor Pritchett, C.B.E.; *General Secretary:* Mark Le Fanu. The Society was founded in 1884 by Sir Walter Besant with the object of representing, assisting, and protecting authors. It is a limited company and an independent trade union. The Society's scope has been continuously extended;

specialist associations have been created for translators, broadcasters, educational, medical, technical and children's writers (details will be found elsewhere in this issue). Members are entitled to legal as well as general advice in connection with the marketing of their work, their contracts, their choice of a publisher, etc., and also to have litigation in which their work may involve them conducted by the Society and at the Society's expense provided the Committee of Management is satisfied that the member's case is sound in law and that the proceedings are justified. Annual Subscription: £50 (£45 by direct debit). Full particulars of membership from the Society's offices. (See article: **The Society of Authors.**)

Aviation Artists, The Guild of (incorporating **The Society of Aviation Artists**), affiliated to the Federation of British Artists, 11 Great Spilmans, London, SE22 8SZ *T.* 01-693 3033. *President:* Frank Wootton, P.G.AV.A.; *Secretary:* Mrs. Y. C. Bonham. A Guild of painters formed in 1971 to promote all forms of avaiation art through the organisation of Exhibitions and Meetings. Annual Exhibition June/July. Entrance Fee £10. Annual Subscription (exhibiting) Associate £20.00, Full Members £25, Overseas £14, Friends Non-Exhibiting £15.

BAPLA (British Association of Picture Libraries and Agencies) (1975), P.O. Box 4, Andoversford, Cheltenham, Glos. GL54 4JS. *Secretary:* Liz Moore. *Administrator:* Corinna Rock, *T.* 024-289 373. BAPLA is a trade association formed to promote fair and honest trading within the profession, and between members and their clients. To this end it published a Code of Professional Standards and Fair Practice and a set of Recommended Terms and Conditions for the Submission and Reproduction of Photographs. BAPLA makes a constant effort to promote the fact that photographs, prints, drawings, have a copyright and that this copyright has a commercial value, that if any picture has the impact to promote a product, sell a book, it also has a market value for being so used.

Bibliographical Society (1892), British Library, Humanities and Social Sciences, Great Russell Street, London WC1B 3DG. *President:* T. J. Brown; *Hon. Secretary:* Mrs. M. M. Foot. Acquisition and dissemination of information upon subjects connected with historical bibliography.

Blackpool Art Society, The (1884). *President:* Audrey Tebay. *Hon. Secretary:* Jack Tebay, 17 Leeds Road, Blackpool FY1 4HQ *T.* (0253) 33986. *Studio:* Wilkinson Avenue, off Woodland Grove, Blackpool. Summer and Autumn exhibition (members' work only). Studio meetings, practical, lectures, etc., out-of-door sketching.

Blind Authors' Association (1983), Brierdene, Croit-e-Quill Road, Lonan, Isle of Man. *T.* (0624) 781 349. To enable blind authors and beginners to have access through the medium of tape-recordings, all essential information concerning markets for their work and, for the beginner, instruction and advice. *Subscription:* £3.00 p.a.

Book House Ireland (1983), 65 Middle Abbey Street, Dublin, 1. *T.* 730108. *Administrator:* Clara Clark. Represents Clè, The Irish Book Publishers' Association and The Booksellers' Association of Great Britain and Ireland (Irish Branch); provides a joint secretariat for both associations; book trade information and resource centre, produces regular newsletters, runs courses, has function rooms, a library and co-ordinates trade and social events for the Irish book industry. *Subscription:* £50.00 per annum.

Book Packagers Association (1985), 147-149 Gloucester Terrace, London W2 6DX *T.* 01-723 7328. *Secretary:* Rosemary Pettit. To represent the interests of book packagers; to exchange information; to provide services such as standard contracts and meeting facilities at book fairs.

Book Trust, (formerly **National Book League**). Book House, 45 East Hill, Wandsworth, London, SW18 2QZ *T.* 01-870 9055. Founded in 1925 as the National Book Council, and incorporated as an educational charity. The name and the constitution of the National Book League was changed in September 1986 and is now known as **Book Trust.** *President:* Sir Charles Troughton, C.B.E., M.C., T.D.; *Director:* Martyn Goff, O.B.E., F.R.S.A. The Book Trust's principal aim is to foster the growth of a wider and more discriminating interest in books. The membership now exceeds 4,000. Among the Trust's services to its members are a lending library of books about books, and the use of the Book Information Service and The Centre for Children's Books which holds a reference collection of the last 24 months of children's publications and provides an information service for queries about children's books. Book lists on many subjects are published. The Trust organises touring exhibitions which are shown in many parts of the country. It also takes part in research projects and administers many literary prizes, including the £15,000 Booker Prize; also The School Bookshop Association. The headquarters is a meeting-place for members. The Trust produces a quarterly newsletter, *Booknews,* circulated to members. Membership is open to all. Annual subscription £9.00. Special facilities and subscriptions for libraries, schools and other corporate bodies. Full details from the Publicity Officer.

Books Across the Sea, The English-Speaking Union of the Commonwealth, Dartmouth House, 37 Charles Street, London, W1X 8AB *T.* 01-408 0013. The English Speaking Union of the United States, 16 East 69th Street, New York, N.Y., 10021. World voluntary organisation devoted to the promotion of international understanding and friendship. Exchanges books with its corresponding BAS Committees in New York, Australia, Canada and New Zealand. The books exchanged are selected to reflect the life and culture of each country and the best of its recent publishing and writing. The books are circulated among members and accredited borrowers, bulk loans are made to affiliated schools and public libraries. New selections are announced by bulletin, *The Ambassador Booklist*.

Booksellers Association of Great Britain and Ireland (1895), 154 Buckingham Palace Road, London, SW1W 9TZ *T.* 01-730 8214-6. *Director:* T. E. Godfray. To protect and promote the interests of booksellers engaged in selling new books.

British Academy, 20-21 Cornwall Terrace, London NW1 4QP *T.* 01-487 5966. *President:* Professor Sir Randolph Quirk, C.B.E.; *Foreign Secretary:* Professor E. W. Handley, C.B.E.; *Treasurer:* Professor Peter Mathias, C.B.E.; *Secretary:* P. W. H. Brown.

British Amateur Press Association (1890), 78 Tennyson Road, Stratford, London E15 4DR. To promote the Fellowship of writers, artists, editors, printers and publishers and other craftsmen, and to encourage them to contribute to, edit and print and publish, as a hobby, magazines and literary works produced by letterpress and other processes.

British American Arts Association (UK), 49 Wellington Street, London, WC2E 7BN *T.* 01-379 7755. *Director:* Jennifer Williams. Acts as an information service and clearing house for exchange between Britian and the United States in all the arts fields—literature, poetry, theatre, dance, music, visual arts. Counsels artists, administrators, organizations and sponsors on opportunities to promote, perform, show and tour their work; does not run programmes or give funds.

British Artists, Royal Society of, 17 Carlton House Terrace, London, SW1Y 5BD *T.* 01-930 6844. *President:* Peter Garrard, R.P., N.E.A.C.; *Keeper:* Oliver Warman. Incorporated by Royal Charter for the purpose of encouraging the study and practice of the arts of painting, sculpture and architectural designs. Annual Open Exhibition at the Mall Galleries, The Mall, London SW1.

British Association of Industrial Editors, The (1949). 3 Locks Yard, High Street, Sevenoaks, Kent, TN13 1LT *T.* (0732) 459331. The objects include development of the qualifications of those engaged in producing house journals and other forms of employee communications and to work for improved standards in all types of employee communications; and to provide a consultancy service on all matters relating to house journals. Membership is open to men and women engaged in, or who have a valid interest in industrial, commercial or organisational communication.

British Copyright Council, The, Copyright House, 29-33 Berners Street, London, W1P 4AA *T.* 01-580 5544. *Chairman:* Denis de Freitas, O.B.E.; *Vice Chairmen:* Maureen Duffy, Michael Freegard, Tom Phillips; *Secretary:* Geoffrey Adams; *Treasurer:* Kenneth Brookes. Its purposes are to defend and foster the true principles of creators' copyright and their acceptance throughout the world, to bring together bodies representing all who are interested in the protection of such copyright, and to keep watch on any legal or other changes which may require an amendment of the law.

British Council, The, 10 Spring Gardens, London, SW1A 2BN *T.* 01-930 8466. *Chairman:* Sir David Orr, M.C., LL.D.; *Director General:* Sir John Burgh, K.C.M.G., C.B. The British Council's aim is to promote a wide knowledge and appreciation of Britain and the English language abroad and to develop closer cultural relations with other countries. It was established in 1934 and received a Royal Charter in 1940. It is now a worldwide organisation with offices in about 80 countries and its programmes of cultural, educational, scientific and technical co-operation provide ready access to British ideas, expertise and experience. In everything it does the British Council aims to establish relationships between people and between institutions.

The Council has around 111 lending and reference libraries throughout the world which cater for the serious reader and act as show-cases for the latest British publications. They vary in size from small reference collections and information centres to comprehensive libraries equipped with up-to-date reference works, on-line facilities and a selection of British periodicals. Bibliographies of British books on special subjects are prepared on request. Working in close collaboration with the Book Development Council (International Division of the Publishers Association), the British Council organises over 200 separate book exhibitions each year for showing overseas. These exhibitions, some of which are shown many times in different places, range from small specialist displays of 100 or so books to the big fair exhibit of nearly 5,000 books representing 250 British publishers which is mounted annually at Frankfurt.

The Council publications include *British Book News,* a monthly guide to books published in Britain and other Commonwealth countries; *Writers and Their Work,* a series of brochures on classic and contemporary authors; and *Nexus,* a series designed for the teacher, student and general reader of Commonwealth literature in English. The Council has also produced several series of recordings including *Commonwealth Writers,* interviews of leading writers speaking about their work; *Critics on Criticism,* critics discussing major current approaches to the study of English literature; and *Recorded Interviews,* leading British novelists and dramatists describing their major works and careers as writers. A catalogue of publications, covering the arts, books, libraries and publishing, education and training, English language teaching and Information for and about overseas students, is available on request.

The Council acts as the agent of the Oveseas Development Administration for two schemes of book aid for developing countries: the Books Presentation Programme under which books and periodicals are presented to institutional libraries; and the Low-Priced Books Scheme which subsidises the production of tertiary-level textbooks for sale in specified countries at greatly reduced prices under the imprint of the English Language Book Society.

Each year the Council organises about 300 tours in dance, drama, music and opera and around 80 fine art, photographic and documentary exhibitions. It also organises about 17 British film weeks and participates in over 30 international film festivals.

The Council is an authority on teaching English as a second or foreign language and gives advice and information on curriculum, methodology, materials and testing through its English Language and Literature Division.

Further information about the work of the British Council is available from: Press and Information Department at the headquarters in London or from British Council offices and libraries overseas.

British Directory Publishers, Association of, Imperial House, 17 Kingsway, London, WC2B 6UN. *Correspondence* to 154 High Street, Beckenham, Kent BR3 1EA. *Chairman:* K. S. Aukstolis. To provide for the exchange of information between members on the technical, commercial and management problems arising in Directory Publishing. Maintains code of Professional Practice.

British Film Institute, 127 Charing Cross Road, London, WC2H 0EA *T.* 01-437 4355. *Telex:* 27624. *Director:* Anthony Smith.

The general object of the British Film Institute is "to encourage the development of the art of the film, to promote its use as a record of contemporary life and manners, to foster study and appreciation of it from these points of view, to foster study and appreciation of film for television and television programmes generally, to encourage the best use of television." Its divisions include the National Film Archive and the National Film Theatre on the South Bank. The Institute has also helped to set up 33 Film Theatres outside London. Through its information service, its *Monthly Film Bulletin* (which gives credit and reviews of every feature film released in Britain), its quarterly *Sight and Sound*, and its Education Department it provides materials and services for film and television education. The annual subscription for Members £14.30 including *Sight and Sound*, and NFT programme (post free), or £24.00 including *Sight and Sound, Monthly Film Bulletin* and programme (post free). Associateship (National Film Theatre) (London) £9.25 (including programme post free), £6.90 to full-time students at recognised education establishments.

British Institute of Professional Photography, Amwell End, Ware, Herts, SG12 9HN *T.* Ware 4011-2. (Founded 1901, Incorporated 1921.) *Principal Objects:* Professional Qualifying Association; to represent all who practise photography as a profession in any field; to improve the quality of photography; establish recognised examination qualifications and a high standard of conduct; to safeguard the interests of the public and the profession. *Membership:* approx. 3500. Admission can be obtained either via the Institute's examinations, or by submission of work and other information to the appropriate examining board. Fellows, Associates and Licentiates are entitled to the designation Incorporated Photographer or Incorporated Photographic Technician. *Meetings:* The Institute organises numerous meetings and conferences in various parts of the country throughout the year. *Publications:* A monthly journal, *The Photographer* and an annual Register of Members and *guide to buyers of photography*, plus various pamphlets and leaflets on professional photography.

British Kinematograph, Sound and Television Society (founded 1931. Incorporated 1946), 110-112 Victoria House, Vernon Place, London, WC1B 4DJ *T.* 01-242 8400. *Secretary:* W. Pay. Aims to encourage technical and scientific progress in the industries of its title. Publishes technical information, arranges international conferences and exhibitions, lectures and demonstrations, and encourages the exchange of ideas.

British Science Fiction Association, Ltd., The (1958). *President:* Arthur C. Clarke; *Membership Secretary:* Sandy Brown, 18 Gordon Terrace, Blantyre, Scotland, G72 9NA. For authors, publishers, booksellers and readers of science fiction, fantasy and allied genres. Publishes informal magazine, *Matrix*, of news and information, *Focus*, an amateur writers' magazine, and critical magazine, *Vector*; editor David V. Barrett, 23 Oakfield Road, Croydon, Surrey CR0 2UD.

British Science Writers, Association of, c/o British Association for the Advancement of Science, Fortress House, 23 Savile Row, London W1X 1AB. *Chairman:* Dr. Robert Walgate; *Secretary:* Ursula Laver. An association of science writers, editors, and radio, film, and television producers concerned with the presentation and communication of science, technology and medicine. Its aims are to improve the standard of science writing and to assist its members in their work. Activities include visits to research establishments, luncheon meetings for those concerned with scientific policy, and receptions for scientific attachés and Parliamentarians.

British Sculptors, Royal Society of, 108 Old Brompton Road, London, SW7 3RA *T.* 01-373 5554. *President:* John W. Mills; *Hon. Treasurer:* John Ravera; *Secretary:* Maureen O'Connor. Aims to promote and advance the Art of Sculpture. Informs and advises its members on professional matters; provides an advisory service to the general public.

British Theatre Association (1919), (The British Theatre Play Library) The Darwin Infill Building, Regents College, Inner Circle, Regents Park, London NW1 4NS *T.* 01-387 2666. *Director:* Jane Hackworth-Young. The British Play Library holds the most comprehensive collection of plays in the world and any member of the public may come and read on the premises without charge. The Reference, Lending and Play Sets Sections comprise the largest Theatre Library in the country and the Information Service can answer any question on British Theatre. Training courses for amateurs, professionals and University drama departments. Record and Tape Department. Publishes: *Drama* (quarterly).

Broadcasting Group, The Society of Authors (1979), 84 Drayton Gardens, London, SW10 9SB *T.* 01-373 6642. A specialist unit within the framework of the Society of Authors exclusively concerned with the interests and special problems of radio and television writers.

Brontë Society, The, Brontë Parsonage, Haworth, nr. Keighley, BD22 8DR *T.* Haworth (0535) 42323. *President:* Mrs Jocelyn E. Kellett, B. COMM. *Chairman of the Council:* R. A. Scatchard, M.B.E., *Hon. Secretary:* Mrs. C. M. Geldard. Examination, preservation, illustration of the memoirs and literary remains of the Brontë family; exhibitions of MSS. and other subjects. Publishes: *The Transactions of the Brontë Society* (Annual), *Bibliography of the Manuscripts of Charlotte Brontë,* and *Haworth Parsonage, the home of the Brontës.*

Bulwer-Lytton Circle, The (1973), High Orchard, 125 Markyate Road, Dagenham, Essex, RM8 2LB. *Secretary:* Eric Ford. Promotion of scholarship and research in the life, work and times of Bulwer-Lytton and his family. *Subscription* £2.00 p.a.

Byron Society (International) (1971), Byron House, 6 Gertrude Street, London, SW10 0JN. *T.* 01-352 5112. *Hon. Treasurer:* Mrs. Elma Dangerfield, O.B.E. To promote research into the life and works of Lord Byron by seminars, discussions, lectures and readings. Publishes *The Byron Journal* (annual). *Subscription:* £9.00 p.a.

Caldecott, Randolph, Society (1983). *Secretary:* Kenn Oultram, Clatterwick Hall, Little Leigh, Northwich, Cheshire, CW8 4RJ *T.* (0606) 891303 (office hours). To encourage an interest in the life and works of Randolph Caldecott, the Victorian artist, illustrator and sculptor. Meetings: London, Chester. *Subscription:* £5.00-£8.00 p.a.

Canadian Authors' Association, 121 Avenue Road, Suite 104, Toronto, Ontario, M5R 2G3. *T.* 416-364-4203. *President:* W. D. Valgardson; *Executive Director:* Ginny Sumodi.

Canadian Book Publishers' Council. Consists of 50 educational and trade publishers; maintains offices at 45 Charles Street East, 7th Floor, Toronto, Ontario M4Y 1S2 *T.* 416-964-7231. Interested in advancing the cause of the publishing business by co-operative effort and encouragement of high standards of workmanship and service. Co-operates with other organisations interested in the promotion and distribution of books. Canadian Book Publishers' Council has three divisions, the School Group concerned with primary and secondary school instructional materials, the College Group concerned with post-secondary materials, and the Trade Group concerned with general interest adult and children's books. *Executive Director:* Jacqueline Hushion.

Canadian Periodical Publishers' Association (1973), 2 Stewart Street, Toronto, Ontario M5V 1H6 *T.* 416-362-2546. *Executive Director:* Dinah Hoyle. A trade association representing members' interests to provincial and federal governments, and providing services to Canadian magazines, including retail distribution. Resource centre for information about Canadian magazines.

Canadian Poets, League of (1966), 24 Ryerson Avenue, Toronto, Ontario, M5T 2P3 Canada. *T.* 416-363 5047. *Executive Director:* Anglea Rebeiro. To promote the interests of poets and to advance Canadian poetry in Canada and abroad.

Canadian Publishers, Association of (1976—formerly Independent Publishers Association 1971), 70 The Esplanade, 3rd Floor, Toronto, Ontario M5E 1R2 *T.* 416-361-1408. *Executive Director:* Marcia George. Represents the interests of Canadian publishers in Canada and abroad; facilitates the exchange of information and professional expertise among its members.

Lewis Carroll Society (1970), *Secretary:* Kenn Oultram, Clatterwick Hall, Little Leigh, Northwich, Cheshire CW8 4RJ *T.* (0606) 891303 (office hours). To encourage an interest in the life and works of Lewis Carroll. Meetings at birthplace: Daresbury, Cheshire. *Subscription:* £3.00 p.a.

Cartoonists Club of Great Britain. *Secretary:* Mike Turner, 11 Simons Lane, Colchester, Essex *T.* (0206) 67283. Aims to encourage social contact between members and endeavour to promote the professional standing and prestige of cartoonists. *Annual sub.:* New members £15; Full members £15, Associate £15.

Catholic Writers Guild, *Hon. Secretary:* 1 Leopold Road, London W5 3PB *T.* 01-992 3954. For Catholic writers, journalists and those working in public relations and broadcasting. Monthly meetings. *Subscription:* £5.00 p.a.

Chesterton Society, The (1974), 20 Valleyside, Hemel Hempstead, Herts HP1 2LN

T. (0442) 61828. *Secretary:* P. M. S. Pinto. To promote interest in the life and work of Chesterton and those associated with him or influenced by his writings. *Subscription:* £10 p.a., includes journal *The Chesterton Review* (Q.) and newsletters.

Children's Book Council of Australia, P.O. Box 420, Dickson, A.C.T. 2602, Australia. The Council, a non-profit organization, exists to encourage reading among children of all ages, to promote better writing, illustration and book production, and to encourage the sharing of literature. *Reading Time*, the official journal of the Council, is published 4 times a year. *Subscription:* $12.00.

Children's Writers Group, 84 Drayton Gardens, London, SW10 9SB *T.* 01-373 6642. *Secretary:* Diana Shine. A subsidiary organisation for writers of children's books, who are members of the Society of Authors.

Civil Service Authors, Society of, *Secretary:* Miss Betty Richards, 16 Palmerston Road, Twickenham, Middlesex, TW2 7QX. Aims to encourage authorship both by present and past members of the Civil Service and to provide opportunities for social and cultural relationships between civil servants who are authors or aspirant authors. Literary competitions are held annually for members only. *Annual Subscriptions:* £6.50. S.A.E. for enquiries.

John Clare Society, The (1981), Tudor Court, 86 Glinton Road, Helpston, Peterborough PE6 7DQ *T.* (0733) 252485. Promotes a wider appreciation of the life and works of the poet John Clare. *Subscription:* £5.00 p.a.

Classical Association. *Secretary (Branches):* Miss H. M. Jones, 18 Valley Close, Pinner, Middlesex HA5 3UR. *Secretary (Council):* Professor J. Percival, Department of Classics, University College, P.O. Box 78, Cardiff, CF1 1XL.

William Cobbett Society, The (1976), *Hon. Secretary:* J. R. Grey, 17 Arle Close, Alresford, Hants. SO24 9BG. *T.* (096 273) 2350. To make the life and work of William Cobbett better known. *Subscription:* £3.00 p.a.

Comann Leabhraichean, An, (Gaelic Books Council), (1968), Department of Celtic, University of Glasgow, Glasgow, G12 8QQ *T.* 041-339 8855, ext. 5190. *Chairman:* Professor Derick S. Thomson. Stimulates Scottish Gaelic publishing by awarding publication grants for new books, commissioning authors, setting literary competitions and providing editorial services and general assistance to writers and readers. Also publishes a catalogue of all Scottish Gaelic books in print and a magazine of book news. Runs a mobile bookselling service in the Highlands and Islands of Scotland and supports, and sometimes organises, literary evenings. Enquiries to the Editorial Officer.

Comics Enthusiasts, The Association of, (1978). *Founder:* Denis Gifford, 80 Silverdale, Sydenham, London SE26. A society for those interested in comics and strip cartoons from both the collecting and professional angles. *Comic Cuts*, the society's journal (9 p.a.). Annual membership £5; specimen issue 50p.

Commonwealth Press Union (1909), Studio House, 184 Fleet Street, London, EC4A 2DU *T.* 01-242 1056. Organisation of newspapers, periodicals, news agencies throughout the Commonwealth. *Director:* Lieut-Colonel Terence Pierce-Goulding, M.B.E., C.D.

Composers' Guild of Great Britain, The, 10 Stratford Place, London, W1N 9AE *T.* 01-499 4795. The Composers' Guild was created in June 1945 under the aegis of The Incorporated Society of Authors, Playwrights, and Composers. In 1948 it was formed into an independent body under the title of The Composers' Guild of Great Britain. Its function is to represent and protect the interests of composers of music in this country and to advise and assist its members on problems connected with their work. *Annual subscription:* £20.00, Associate membership £15.00. Further particulars obtained from the General Secretary of the Guild.

Confédération Internationale des Sociétés d'Auteurs et Compositeurs-Congrès Mondial des Auteurs et Compositeurs, 11 Rue Keppler, 75116 Paris, France. *T.* 720-5937. *T.A.* Interauteurs, Paris.

Joseph Conrad Society (U.K.), The (1973). *Chairman:* Mrs. Juliet McLauchlan; *President:* Dr. Wit Tarnawski; *Vice-President:* Philip Conrad; *Secretaries:* S. Tyley and R. G. Hampson, The English Dept., Royal Holloway and Bedford New College, Egham Hill, Egham, Surrey TW20 0EX. Maintains close and friendly links with the Conrad family. Activities include an Annual Gathering, with lectures and discussions; publication of the *Conradian* and a series of pamphlets; and maintenance of a study centre in London.

Contemporary Arts, Institute of, The Mall, London, SW1Y 5AH *T.* 01-930 0493. A centre which aims at encouraging collaboration between the various arts, the promotion of experimental work and the mutual interchange of ideas. Exhibitions, theatre, music, dance, poetry, lectures, cinema and discussions, all play a part in the programme.

Copyright Council of New Zealand Inc., P.O. Box 11168, Wellington. *T.* 724430. *Chairman:* Bernard Darby. *Secretary:* Fred Smith.

Crime Writers' Association (1953), P.O. Box 172, Tring, Herts. HP23 5LP. For professional writers of crime novels, short stories, plays for stage, television and sound radio, or of serious works on crime. Full membership £15.00 annually; overseas $25.00 and country £20.00. Associate membership open to publishers, journalists, booksellers specialising in crime literature. Publishes *Red Herrings* monthly.

Critics' Circle, The (1913). *President:* John Percival; *Vice-President:* David Nathan; *Hon. General Secretary:* Peter Hepple, 47 Bermondsey Street, London SE1 3XT. *T.* 01-403 1818. *Objects:* To promote the art of criticism, to uphold its integrity in practice, to foster and safeguard the professional interests of its members, to provide opportunities for social intercourse among them, and to support the advancement of the arts. Membership is by invitation of the Council. Such invitations are issued only to persons engaged professionally, regularly and substantially in the writing or broadcasting of criticism of drama, music, films, or ballet.

Cromwell Association, The (1935), *Press Liaison Officer:* B. Denton, 10 Melrose Avenue, off Bants Lane, Northampton NN5 5PB *T.* (0604) 582516. Encourages the study of Oliver Cromwell and his times, holds academic lectures and meetings, publishes annual journal *Cromwelliana*, erects memorials at Cromwellian sites. *Subscription:* £10.00 p.a.

Cyngor Llyfrau Cymraeg—see **Welsh Books Council**.

Designers, Society of Industrial Artists and, *Director:* Michael Sadler-Forster, 12 Carlton House Terrace, London, SW1Y 5AH *T.* 01-930 1911. The S.I.A.D. is the chartered body representing professional designers in some 40 different categories of design. It unites in a single organisation those who are concerned with design in engineering, consumer products, textiles, graphic design, visual communications, interiors and exhibitions. The Society is concerned with standards of competence, professional conduct and integrity; it makes a significant contribution to the establishment of high standards in design education, and represents the views and interests of professional designers in government and other official bodies. Designer Registers maintained by the Society and containing a visible record of members' work assist industry and government bodies in the selection of designers for freelance commissions and staff appointments. *Designer* is the independent magazine published by the

Society 11 times per annum. The Society's Code of Conduct is included in **Art, Music, Prizes, Clubs**. Conditions of Engagement, competition regulations and other documentation is available from the Society's office.

Dickens Fellowship (1902), *Headquarters:* The Dickens House, 48 Doughty Street, London, WC1N 2LF *T.* 01-405 2127. *Hon. Secretary:* Alan Watts. House occupied by Dickens 1837-9. Membership rates and particulars on application. Publication: *The Dickensian*.

Dorman (Sean) Manuscript Society (1957), 4 Union Place, Fowey, Cornwall, PL23 1BY. For mutual help among part-time writers in England, Scotland and Wales only. Circulating manuscript parcels affording constructive criticism, with Remarks Book. Special circulator for advanced writers. Technical discussion circulators. *Writing* (2 p.a.) buys verse and articles on journalism. (Editor: Barbara Horsfall, 87 Brookhouse Road, Farnborough, Hants GU14 0BU.) *Subscription:* £3.50 p.a. (after initial six months' trial period at £1.50).

Early English Text Society (1864), St. Peter's College, Oxford OX1 2DL. *Hon. Director:* Professor John Burrow; *Executive Secretary:* T. F. Hoad. To bring unprinted early English literature within the reach of students in sound texts. *Annual subscription:* £15.00.

Edinburgh Bibliographical Society (1890), c/o National Library of Scotland, Edinburgh, EH1 1EW *T.* 031-226 4531 ext. 256. *Secretary:* I.C. Cunningham; *Treasurer:* E. D. Yeo.

Educational Writers Group, 84 Drayton Gardens, London, SW10 9SB *T.* 01-373 6642. A specialist unit within the membership of The Society of Authors.

Edwardian Studies Association (1975), High Orchard, 125 Markyate Road, Dagenham, Essex, RM8 2LB. Promotion of integrated approach to studies of Edwardians—Shaw, Wells, Conrad, etc. Publishes: *Edwardian Studies*.

Eighteen Nineties Society, The, 17 Merton Hall Road, Wimbledon, London SW19 3PP. *President:* Brian Reade. *Chairman:* C. C. Gould. *Secretary:* Dr. G. Krishnamurti. Founded in 1963 as The Francis Thompson Society, it widened its scope in 1972 to embrace the entire artistic and literary scene of the eighteen-ninety decade. Its activities include exhibitions, lectures, poetry readings. Publishes biographies of neglected authors and artists of the period; also check lists, bibliographies, etc. Its Journal appears periodically, and includes biographical, bibliographical and critical articles and book reviews. The Journal is free to members, and is not for public sale. All correspondence to the *Hon. Secretary,* 97-D Brixton Road, London SW9 6EE.

George Eliot Fellowship, The (1930). *President:* Jonathan G. Ouvry. *Secretary:* Mrs. K. M. Adams, 71 Stepping Stones Road, Coventry, CV5 8JT *T.* (0203) 592231. Promotes an interest in the life and work of George Eliot and helps to extend her influence. Monthly meetings are arranged and an annual magazine is produced. *Annual subscription:* £4.00.

English Association, 1 Priory Gardens, Bedford Park, London, W4 1TT *T.* 01-995 4236. *President:* Professor F. T. Prince; *Secretary:* Dr. Ruth Fairbanks-Joseph.

English Speaking Board (International), Ltd., 32 Roe Lane, Southport, Merseyside, PR9 9EA *T.* (0704) 34587. *President:* Christabel Burniston, M.B.E.; *Director:* Kenneth Hastings; *Chairman:* Klaus Neuberg. *Aim:* to foster all activities concerned with English speech. The Board conducts examinations and training courses for teachers and students where stress is on individual oral expression. The examination auditions include talks, prepared and unprepared. Examinations are also held for those engaged in technical or industrial concerns, and for those using English as an acquired language. Three times a year, in January, May and September, members receive the English Speaking

Board Journal, *Spoken English*. Articles are invited by the editor on any special aspect of spoken English. Members can also purchase other publications at reduced rates. Individual membership £8 per annum. Residential summer conference held annually, July-August. A.G.M. in London in the spring.

Fabian Society, 11 Dartmouth Street, London, SW1H 9BN *T.* 01-222 8877.

Fantasy Society, The British (1971), 15 Stanley Road, Morden, Surrey SM4 5DE. *President:* Ramsay Campbell. *Secretary:* Di Wathen. The Society was formed for devotees of fantasy, horror, and related fields, in literature, art and the cinema. Publications include *British Fantasy Newsletter* (Bi-M.) featuring news and reviews and *Dark Horizons* (the bi-annual magazine) which features fiction and articles. There is a small-press library and an annual convention and fantasy awards sponsored by the Society. Membership fees are £8 per annum.

Fine Art Trade Guild, The (1910) incorporating The Printsellers Association (1847), 192 Ebury Street, London, SW1W 8UP *T.* 01-730 3220. *Clerk of the Guild:* John D. Mountford. For the promotion and improvement of all aspects of the Fine Art Trade.

Folklore Society, The (1878), c/o University College, Gower Street, London, WC1E 6BT *T.* 01-387 5894. *Hon. Secretary:* A. Roy Vickery. Collection, recording and study of folklore.

Foreign Press Association in London (1888). *President:* R. Hill, *Hon. Secretary:* A. Takahata. *Registered Office:* 11 Carlton House Terrace, London, SW1Y 5AJ *T.* 01-930 0445 and 8883. *Objects:* The promotion of the professional interests of its members. Membership open to overseas professional journalists, men or women, residing in the United Kingdom. Entrance fee, £85.00; annual subscription, £62.50.

FPS (Free Painters & Sculptors), 15 Buckingham Gate, London, SW1E 6LB. *Secretary:* Marjorie Wadsworth. Open Bi-annual London Exhibition. Provincial Exhibitions for Members. Exhibits the work of progressive-minded artists, irrespective of their differing points of view; to provide opportunities for members to meet and discuss their work by means of lectures, discussions or other ways appropriate. Loggia Gallery and Sculpture Garden available for members to exhibit. *T.* 01-828 5963. (Weekdays 6-8 p.m., Sat. and Sun. 2-6 p.m.)

Freelance Photographers, Bureau of (1965), Focus House, 497 Green Lanes, London, N13 4BP *T.* 01-882 3315. *Head of Administration:* John Tracy. To help the freelance photographer by providing information on markets, and free advisory service. Membership fee £25.00 per annum.

Gaelic Books Council—see **Comann Leabhraichean, An**

Gay Authors Workshop (1978), 36 Earlham Grove, Forest Gate, London E7 9AW. *Secretary:* Martin Foreman. To encourage writers who are gay and to present readings of their work. Anthology in preparation. London members meet twice monthly. Members throughout Britain. Membership £4.00.

Graphic Artists, Society of (1919), 9 Newburgh Street, London, W1V 1LH. *President:* Mrs Lorna B. Kell. Membership open to both men and women. Annual open exhibition. Drawings and prints in any medium, including collages and constructions.

Greeting Card and Calendar Association, The, 6 Wimpole Street, London, W1M 8AS *T.* 01-637 7692. Publishes *Greetings* bi-monthly.

Hakluyt Society (1846), c/o The Map Library, The British Library: Reference Division, Great Russell Street, London, WC1B 3DG. *T.* 025-125 4207. *President:* Professor David Beers Quinn; *Hon. Secretaries:* Mrs. Sarah Tyacke and T. E. Armstrong, M.A., PH.D Publication of original narratives of voyages, travels, naval expeditions, and other geographical records.

Thomas Hardy Society Ltd., The (1967). *Secretary:* Mrs Kate N. Fowler, Park Farm, Tolpuddle, Dorchester, Dorset DT2 7HG *T.* Puddletown (030 584) 651. *Subscription:* £6.00 (US $12.00) p.a.

Harleian Society (1896), College of Arms, Queen Victoria Street, London, EC4V 4BT. *Chairman:* J. Brooke-Little, M.V.O., M.A., F.S.A., Norroy and Ulster King of Arms. *Secretary:* P. Ll. Gwynn-Jones, Lancaster Herald of Arms. Instituted for transcribing, printing and publishing the heraldic visitations of Counties, Parish Registers and any manuscripts relating to genealogy, family history and heraldry.

Illustrators, The Association of (1973), 1 Colville Place, London W1P 1HN *T.* 01-636 4100. To further and promote better relationships between illustrators, agents and clients which will result in the raising of standards and through which individual illustrators can support the common good of illustrators as a whole. Gallery space available for hire.

Illustrators, Society of Architectural and Industrial (1975), P.O. Box 22, Stroud, Gloucestershire, GL5 3DH. *T.* Brimscombe (0453) 882563. *Administrator:* Eric Monk. A professional body to represent all who practise architectural, industrial and technical illustration, including the related fields of model making and photography.

Independent Literary Agents Association, Inc., 55 Fifth Avenue, New York, N.Y. 10003. *T.* 212-206 5600.

Independent Producers, The Association of (1976), 17 Great Pulteney Street, London, W1R 3DG *T.* 01-437 9191 and 734 1581. *Fax:* 01-437 0086. *Chairman:* Simon Perry. *Directors:* Sally Davies. To encourage production of films and to broaden the base of finance and exhibition beyond that which is currently available for film-makers in the U.K. Membership is open to anyone active in the film and television industries. Information service, seminars, production workshops, monthly magazine, annual handbook.

Independent Publishers Guild (1962), 147-149 Gloucester Terrace, London, W2 6DX *T.* 01-723 7328. Membership is open to publishing companies and packagers, associate membership to companies or individuals who have not yet published three books and supplier membership to companies or individuals (but not printers or binders) who are specialists in fields allied to publishing. Offers a forum for the exchange of ideas and information and represents the interests of its members. £25 or £30 p.a.

Indexers, The Society of. Objects: (1) to improve the standard of indexing; (2) to maintain a Register of Indexers (for details see article: **Indexing;** (3) to act as an advisory body on the qualifications and remuneration of indexers; (4) to publish or communicate books, papers and notes on the subject of indexing; (5) to raise the status of indexers and to safeguard their interests. Membership is open to those who are interested in indexing and all aspects of information retrieval. There is no entrance fee. *Annual Subscription:* £15.00. Copies of the Society's journal, *The Indexer*, are sent free to members. *Secretary:* Mrs H. C. Troughton, 16 Green Road, Birchington, Kent CT7 9JZ *T.* (0843) 41115.

Indian Publishers', The Federation of, Federation House, 18/1-C Institutional Area, J.N.U Road, New Delhi 110067. *T.* 654847.

International Amateur Theatre Association, The Darwin Infill Building, Regents College, Inner Circle, Regents Park, London NW1 5NS. *Secretariat:* 19 Abbey Park Road, Grimsby, DN32 0HJ *T.* (0472) 43424. To encourage, foster and promote exchanges of theatre; student, educational, puppet theatre activities

SOCIETIES 341

at international level. To organise international seminars, workshops, courses and conferences, and to collect and collate information of all types for international dissemination, and within the United Kingdom.

Irish Book Publishers Association, Book House Ireland, 65 Middle Abbey Street, Dublin 1. *T.* 730108. *President:* Michael Adams. *Administrator:* Clara Clark.

Richard Jefferies Society, The (1950), 6 Chickerell Road, Swindon, Wilts., SN3 2RQ *T.* (0793) 21512. *President:* Prof. W. J. Keith (Toronto). *Hon. Secretary:* Cyril Wright. Promotes interest in the life, works and associations of Richard Jefferies; helps to preserve buildings and memorials, and co-operates in the development of a Museum in his birthplace. Provides a service to students, lecturers, readers and writers. The Society arranges regular meetings in Swindon, and occasionally elsewhere. Outings and displays are organised. The membership is worldwide. *Annual subscription:* £1.50.

Johnson Society, The, Johnson Birthplace Museum, Breadmarket Street, Lichfield, Staffordshire, WS13 6LG *T.* (0543) 264972. *Secretary:* Mary A. Salloway. To encourage the study of the life and works of Dr. Samuel Johnson; to preserve the memorials, associations, books, manuscripts, letters of Dr. Johnson and his contemporaries; preservation of his birthplace.

Johnson Society of London (1928). *President:* The Revd Dr. E. F. Carpenter, K.C.V.O.; *Secretary:* Miss Stella Pigrome, Round Chimney, Playden, Rye, East Sussex, TN31 7UR *T.* Iden (079 78) 252. To study the life and works of Doctor Johnson, and to perpetuate his memory in the city of his adoption.

Journalists, The Institute of, R. F. Farmer, O.B.E. (*General Secretary*), Bedford Chambers, Covent Garden, London, WC2E 8HA *T.* 01-836 6541. The senior organisation of the profession, founded in 1884 and incorporated by Royal Charter 1890. Men and women are equally eligible for Fellowship (F.J.I.) and Membership (M.J.I.). Maintains a successful Employment Register and has considerable accumulated funds for the assistance of members; offers a service of free legal advice to members in matters relating to their professional activities and employment. A Free-lance Division maintains close co-operation between editors and publishers and free-lances. A directory and panel of free-lance writers on special subjects are available for the use of editorial publishers. There are also Special Sections for Public Relations Officers and broadcasters. Occasional contributors to the press may be eligible for election as Affiliates. Certificated as an independent trade union. *Subscriptions:* related to earnings, maximum £100.00; Affiliate £45.

Keats-Shelley Memorial Association (1903). *Chairman:* The Countess of Birkenhead; *Patron:* H.M. Queen Elizabeth the Queen Mother. *Hon. Secretary:* Mrs. C. M. Gee, Keats House, Wentworth Place, Keats Grove, London, NW3 2RR *T.* 01-435 2062. Occasional meetings; annual *Review* and progress reports. Supports house in Rome where John Keats died, and celebrates the poets Keats, Shelley, Byron, and Leigh Hunt. Subscription to "Friends of the Keats-Shelley Memorial," minimum £5.00 per annum.

Kent and Sussex Poetry Society, centre Tunbridge Wells, formed in 1946 to create a greater interest in Poetry. *President:* Laurence Lerner; *Chairman:* Mary Colloff; *Hon. Secretary:* Bill Headdon, 41 Harries Road, Tunbridge Wells, TN2 3TW *T.* (0892) 40381. *Annual Subscription:* adults, £4.00; country members £2.00; students, £1.00. Well-known poets address the society, a Folio of members' work is produced and a full programme of recitals, discussions and readings is provided.

Kipling Society, The, *President:* Sir Angus Wilson; *Hon. Secretary:* Norman Entract, 18 Northumberland Avenue, London, WC2N 5BJ *T.* 01-930 6733.

Aims: To honour and extend the influence of Kipling, to assist in the study of Kipling's writings, to hold discussion-meetings, to publish a quarterly journal and to maintain a Kipling Reference Library. Membership details on application.

Lancashire Authors' Association, The (1909), "for writers or lovers of Lancashire literature and history." *President:* L.M. Angus-Butterworth, M.A., F.S.A.SCOT.; *General Secretary:* J. D. Cameron, M.B.E., Kings Fold, Pope Lane, Penwortham, Preston PR1 9JN *T.* (0772) 742236. *Subscription:* £5.00 p.a. Publishes *The Record* (Q.).

Lancashire Dialect Society, The (1951). *President:* Professor G. L. Brook; *Secretary:* Paul Salveson, 6 Alfred Street, Farnworth, Bolton. *T.* (0204) 73985. Fosters the study of Northern dialects and their preservation in speech and writing. *Annual subscription:* £2.00. Journal and Newsletter published annually.

Learned and Professional Society Publishers, The Association of (1972). Aims to promote and develop the publishing activities of learned and professional organisations which produce journals and other publications. Membership is open to professional and learned societies and to individuals with publishing interests: details are available from the Secretary, A. I. P. Henton, Sentosa, Hill Road, Fairlight, Nr Hastings, East Sussex TN35 4AE *T.* Hastings (0424) 812354.

Library Association, 7 Ridgmount Street, London, WC1E 7AE. *T.* 01-636 7543. *Telex:* 21897 Laldn G. *President:* Sir Harry Hookway, *Chief Executive:* G. Cunningham, B.A., B.SC(ECON). Founded in 1877 to promote bibliographical study and research and the better administration of libraries, and to unite all persons interested in library work. Conferences and meetings are held, publications issued and a library and information department maintained. The monthly journal, *The Library Association Record*, is distributed free to all members. Subscription varies according to income.

Linguists, Institute of, 24A Highbury Grove, London, N5 2EA *T.* 01-359 7445 or 6386. *General Secretary:* A. Bell. To provide language qualifications. To encourage Government and industry to develop the use of modern languages and encourage recognition of the status of professional linguists in all occupations. To promote the exchange and dissemination of information on matters of concern to linguists.

Literary Societies, Alliance of. *Secretary:* Mrs. Kathleen Adams, 71 Stepping Stones Road, Coventry, CV5 8JT *T.* (0203) 592231. An informal alliance of a number of Literary Societies formed to give mutual help in preserving particularly properties with literary associations.

Literature, Royal Society of (1823), 1 Hyde Park Gardens, London, W2 2LT. *T.* 01-723 5104. Fellows and Members. Men and women. *Chairman of Council:* Brian Fothergill, F.S.A., F.R.S.L.; *Secretary:* Mrs. P.M. Schute. For the advancement of literature by the holding of lectures, discussions, readings, and by publications. Administrators of the Dr. Richards' Fund and the Royal Society of Literature Award, under the W.H. Heinemann Bequest and the Winifred Holtby Memorial Prize.

Little Presses, Association of (1966), 89A Petherton Road, London, N5 2QT *T.* 01-226 2657. *Co-ordinator:* Bob Cobbing. A loosely knit association of individuals running little presses who have grouped together for mutual self-help, while retaining their right to operate autonomously. Membership fee: £6.00 p.a. Publications include: *Poetry and Little Press Information, Catalogue of Little Press Books in Print.*

Little Theatre Guild of Great Britain. *Secretary:* Marjorie Havard, 19 Abbey Park Road, Grimsby, DN32 0HJ. *T.* (0472) 43424. To promote close co-operation between Little Theatres, to maintain and further the highest standards in the art of theatre. Membership is confined to independent play producing organisations which control their own established theatres.

London Writer Circle. For mutual help among writers of all grades. Lectures, study groups, MS. clubs, discussions, competitions. *Subs.:* £7.00 (town); £3.50 (country). Entrance fee: 25p. *Hon. Secretary:* Miss M.E. Harris. *Enrolment Secretary:* Mrs. A. Miller, 28 Knowsley Road, London SW11 5BL.

Marine Artists, Royal Society of, 17 Carlton House Terrace, London, SW1Y 5BD *T.* 01-930 6844. *President:* John Worsley. To promote and encourage marine painting. Open Annual Exhibition.

Master Photographers Association, TMT House, 1 West Ruislip Station, Ickenham Road, Ruislip, Middlesex, HA4 7DN *T.* Ruislip 30876. *Telex:* 884 389 (TMTCo). To promote and protect professional photographers. *Subscription:* £38.00 a year. Members can qualify for awards of Associateship and Fellowship.

Mechanical-Copyright Protection Society Ltd., Elgar House, 41 Streatham High Road, London, SW16 1ER *T.* 01-769 4400. *Telex:* 946792 Mcps G. *Managing Director:* R. W. Montgomery. See **Article.**

Medical Journalists Association (1966), 14 Hovendens, Sissinghurst, Kent TN17 2LA *T.* (0580) 713920. Formed by doctor-writers and journalist/broadcasters specialising in medicine and the health services. Aims to improve the quality and practice of medical journalism. Administers major awards for medical journalism and broadcasting. £15.00 p.a. *Chairman:* J. Cowhig. *Hon. Secretary:* Tony Thistlethwaite.

Medical Writers Group, 84 Drayton Gardens, London, SW10 9SB *T.* 01-373 6642. *Secretary:* Philippa MacLiesh. A specialist unit within the membership of the Society of Authors.

Miniature Painters, Sculptors and Gravers, Royal Society of (1895), 17 Carlton House Terrace, London, SW1Y 5BD *T.* 01-930 6844. *President:* Suzanne Lucas. *Secretary:* Oliver Warman. Open Annual Exhibition: November/December.

Miniaturists, The Hilliard Society of, (1982), 15 Union Street, Wells, Somerset BA5 2PU *T.* (0749) 74472 and 72918. *Secretary:* Mrs. S. M. Burton. To promote the art of miniature painting; annual exhibition; exchanges views through quarterly newsletter; puts patrons in touch with artists.

Miniaturists, Society of (1895), *Director:* Leslie Simpson. Castle Gallery, Castle Hill, Ilkley, West Yorkshire LS29 9DT. *T.* (0943) 609075.

William Morris Society (1955), Kelmscott House, 26 Upper Mall, London W6 9TA *T.* 01-741 3735. *Secretary:* Dr. R. S. Smith. To spread knowledge of the life, work and ideas of William Morris. Publishes a *Newsletter* (Q.), and a *Journal* (2 p.a.).

Motoring Writers, The Guild of, 2 Pembroke Villas, The Green, Richmond, Surrey TW9 1QF *T.* 01-940 6974. *Chief Executive:* Jean Peters. To raise the standard of motoring journalism. For writers, broadcasters, photographers on matters of motoring, but who are not connected with the motor industry.

Music Publishers Association Ltd. (1881), 7th Floor, Kingsway House, 103 Kingsway, London, WC2B 6QX *T.* 01-831 7591. *Secretary:* P.J. Dadswell. The only trade organisation representing the U.K. music publishing industry;

protects and promotes its members' interests in copyright, trade and related matters. A number of sub-committees and groups deal with particular interests. Details of subscriptions available.

Musical Association, The Royal, c/o Rosemary Dooley, 5 Church Street, Harston, Cambridge CB2 5NP *T.* (0223) 871028.

Musicians, Incorporated Society of, 10 Stratford Place, London, W1N 9AE *T.* 01-629 4413. *President:* 1986: Louis Carus. *General Secretary:* David Padgett-Chandler. Representative body of professional musicians; its objects are the promotion of the art of music and maintenance of the honour and interests of the musical profession. *Subscription:* £45.00 p.a.

Name Studies in Great Britain and Ireland, Council for, *Chairman:* R. L. Thomson; *Hon. Secretary & Treasurer:* I. A. Fraser, School of Scottish Studies, University of Edinburgh, 27 George Square, Edinburgh, EH8 9LD. The advancement, promotion and support of research into the place-names and personal names of Great Britain and Ireland and related regions in respect of, i) the collection, documentation, and interpretation of such names, ii) the publication of the material and the results of such research, iii) the exchange of information between the various regions. Acts as a consultative body on Name Studies. Membership consists of representatives from relevant British and Irish organisations and a number of individual scholars elected by Council and usually domiciled in one of the relevant countries. Membership is by invitation, and members pay a small annual subscription. Publishes an annual newsletter, *Nomina*, which includes news of research in progress, publications, courses in name studies, reviews, short articles, notes and queries; edited by Dr. Alexander Rumble, Dept. of Palaeography, University of Manchester, Oxford Road, Manchester M13 9PL.

National Book League now **Book Trust**, *q.v.*

National Graphical Association—see **NGA 82**

National Society of Painters, Sculptors & Printmakers (1930), Ladye Place Cottage, Ferry Lane, Shepperton, Middlesex TW17 9LQ. *President:* Ernest Fedarb, P.R.O.I. An annual open exhibition representing all aspects of art for artists of every creed and outlook.

National Union of Journalists. Head Office: Acorn House, 314 Gray's Inn Road, London, WC1X 8DP *T.* 01-278 7916. A trade union for working journalists with 32,689 members and 183 branches throughout the U.K. and the Republic of Ireland, and in Paris, Brussels and Geneva. Its wages and conditions agreements cover the whole of the newspaper press, news agencies and broadcasting, the major part of periodical and book publishing, and a number of public relations departments and consultancies, information services and Prestel-Viewdata services. Administers disputes, unemployment, benevolent, and provident benefits. Official publications: *The Journalist, Freelance Directory* and policy pamphlets.

New English Art Club, 17 Carlton House Terrace, London, SW1Y 5BD *T.* 01-930 6844. *Chairman:* William Bowyer, R.A., R.W.S., R.P. For persons interested in the art of painting, and the promotion of fine arts. Open Annual Exhibition.

New Zealand Book Marketing Council, Box 11377, Wellington 1 *T.* 726 333. *Administrative Director:* Liz Melhuish, *Marketing Director:* Ian Grant. *Chairman:* R. Goddard.

New Zealand, Book Publishers Association of, Inc., Box 44146, Point Chevalier, Auckland 2. *T.* 892-533. *Director:* Gerard Reid; *President:* Graham Beattie.

Newspaper Press Fund, Dickens House, 35 Wathen Road, Dorking, Surrey,

RH4 1JY *T.* Dorking (0306) 887511. *Secretary:* P.W. Evans. For the relief of hardship amongst member journalists, their widows, and dependants. Limited help is available for non-member journalists and their dependants.

Newspaper Publishers Association, Ltd., The, 6 Bouverie Street, London, EC4Y 8AY *T.* 01-583 8132.

Newspaper Society, Whitefriars House, Carmelite Street, London, EC4Y 0BL *T.* 01-583 3311. *Director:* Dugal Nisbet-Smith; *Secretary:* C. Gordon Page, A.C.I.S.

NGA 1982, National Graphical Association, Graphic House, 63-67 Bromham Road, Bedford, MK40 2AG *T.* (0234) 51521.

Oil Painters, Royal Institute of (1883), 17 Carlton House Terrace, London, SW1Y 5BD *T.* 01-930 6844. *President:* Krome Barratt, P.R.O.I., R.B.A., F.M.S. Membership (R.O.I.) open to all. Annual Exhibition is open to all artists.

Painter-Etchers and Engravers, Royal Society of (1880), Bankside Gallery, 48 Hopton Street, London, SE1 9JH *T.* 01-928 7521. *President:* H.N. Eccleston, O.B.E., R.W.S. *Secretary:* Michael Spender. Spring Exhibition open to non-members; Autumn Exhibition for members only. Particulars from the Secretary.

Painters in Water Colours, Royal Institute of (1831), 17 Carlton House Terrace, London, SW1Y 5BD *T.* 01-930 6844. *President:* Charles Bone. Membership (R.I.) open to all. Annual Exhibition open to all artists.

Painters in Water-Colours, Royal Society of (founded 1804), Bankside Gallery, 48 Hopton Street, London, SE1 9JH *T.* 01-928 7521. Maurice Sheppard, M.A. (R.C.A.) (*President*), Michael Spender (Secretary). Membership (R.W.S.) open to British and overseas artists. An election of Associates is held usually in March of each year, and applications for the necessary forms and particulars should be addressed to the Secretary by February. Open Exhibition held in July. Exhibitions: April/October.

Pastel Society, The (1899), 17 Carlton House Terrace, London, SW1Y 5BD *T.* 01-930 6844. *President:* Leigh Parry. Membership open to all. Pastel and drawings in pencil or chalk. Annual Exhibition open to all artists working in dry media.

Mervyn Peake Society, The (1975). *Hon. President:* Sebastian Peake; *Chairman:* John Watney, Flat 36, 5 Elm Park Gardens, London, SW10 9QQ. Devoted to recording the life and works of Mervyn Peake. Publishes a journal and news letter. *Annual subscription:* £8 (U.K. and Europe): £5 for students; £10 all other countries.

P.E.N., International. A world association of writers. *International President:* Francis King, C.B.E. *International Secretary:* Alexandre Blokh, 38 King Street, London, WC2E 8JT *T.* 01-379 7939. *Cables:* Lonpenclub, London, WC2. *President of English Centre:* Michael Holroyd. *General Secretary of English Centre:* Josephine Pullein-Thompson, M.B.E., 7 Dilke Street, London, SW3 4JE *T.* 01-352 6303.

P.E.N. was founded in 1921 by C.A. Dawson Scott under the presidency of John Galsworthy, to promote friendship and understanding between writers and defend freedom of expression within and between all nations. The initials P.E.N. stand for Poets, Playwrights, Editors, Essayists, Novelists—but membership is open to all writers of standing (including translators), whether men or women, without distinction of creed or race, who subscribe to these fundamental principles. P.E.N. takes no part in state or party politics; it has given care to, and raised funds for, refugee writers, and also administers the P.E.N. Writers In Prison Committee which works on behalf of writers imprisoned for exercising their right to freedom of expression, a right implicit in the P.E.N. Charter to which all members subscribe. Through the P.E.N.—UNESCO Translations' Scheme the two bodies co-operate to promote the translations of works by writers in the lesser-known languages. International Congresses are held most years. The 48th Congress was held in New York in January 1986, and the 49th in Hamburg in June 1986.

Membership of the English Centre is £16.00 per annum for country members, £20.00 for London members. Associate membership is available for writers not yet eligible for full membership and persons connected with literature. Membership of any one Centre implies membership of all Centres, at present 85 autonomous Centres exist throughout the world. The English Centre has a programme of literary lectures, discussion, dinners and parties. A yearly *Writers' Day* is open to the public.

Publications: The P.E.N.; P.E.N. International (bi-lingual, Fr.-Eng., reviews of books in languages of limited currency; sponsored by UNESCO); *The Survival and Encouragement of Literature in Present Day Society* (Archive Press) 1979; New Bulletins published by various Centres; English Centre edited a series of annual anthologies of contemporary poetry; *New Poems*— 1952-62; from 1965 the volume appeared biennially and from 1972 to 1977 annually. From 1978 to 1983 PEN and the Arts Council and Hutchinson combined to published *New Poetry* and *New Stories* annually. From 1984, in partnership with Quartet Books, the English Centre publish prose and poetry anthologies, *P.E.N. New Fiction* and *P.E.N. New Poetry,* in alternate years.

Penman Club, The, 175 Pall Mall, Leigh-on-Sea, Essex, SS9 1RE *T.* Southend 74438. *President:* Trevor J. Douglas. *General Secretary:* Leonard G. Stubbs, F.R.S.A. Literary Society for writers throughout the world, published and unpublished. Members in almost every country. Benefits of membership include criticism of all MSS. without additional charge. Marketing and general literary advice, also use of large writers' library. *Subscription:* £5.25 p.a. S.A.E. for Prospectus from the General Secretary.

Performing Right Society, Ltd. (1914), 29-33 Berners Street, London, W1P 4AA *T.* 01-580 5544. See **Article.**

Periodical Publishers Association, Imperial House, Kingsway, London WC2B 6UN *T.* 01-379 6268. *Executive Director:* Michael Finley.

Periodical Writers Association of Canada (1976), 24 Ryerson Avenue, Toronto, Ontario M5T 2P3 *T.* 416-868 6913. To protect and promote the interests of periodical writers in Canada.

Personal Managers' Association, Ltd., The, *Liaison Secretary:* Alison Shelley, Redfern House, Woodside Hill, Chalfont St. Peter, Bucks SL9 9TF. *President:* Peter Dunlop. An association of Personal Managers in the theatre, film and entertainment world generally.

Photographers Association, International, (1983) Central House, New North Road, Exeter, Devon, EX4 4HF *President:* R. L. Sarendon. To facilitate the exchange of information, expertise, and cultural relationships between those interested in photography in the United Kingdom and overseas. Fosters contacts between enthusiasts and professionals, establishes links with similar organisations in U.K. and overseas to promote international understanding of the importance of photography in conservation, education, exploration, science and the performing arts. Fellowship and Associateship is open to both men and women. Membership details on application.

Photographic Society, The Royal (1853), The RPS National Centre of Photography, The Octagon, Milsom Street, Bath, BA1 1DN *T.* (0225) 62841. Aims to promote the general advancement of photography and its applications.

Publish *The Photographic Journal* monthly, £40.00 p.a., overseas £45.00 p.a. and *The Journal of Photographic Science,* bi-monthly £65.00 p.a., overseas £75.00.

Player-Playwrights (1948), 1 Hawthorndene Road, Hayes, Bromley, Kent BR2 7DZ. Weekly meetings in Central London. A society for the benefit of experienced playwrights and newcomers to play and T.V. writing. Members' plays tried out followed by discussion and friendly criticism. *Annual subscription:* £5.00. Meetings: 70p each.

Playwrights Workshop (1949). A meeting place where those people in the Manchester area interested in drama can meet to discuss playwriting in general and their own plays in particular. Details of places and times of meetings from *Hon. Secretary:* Robert Coupland, 22 Brown Street, Altrincham, Cheshire WA14 2EU *T.* 061-928 3095.

Poetry Society, The (1909) Incorporated, 21 Earls Court Square, London, SW5 9DE *T.* 01-373 7861 and 2551. *Chairman:* Alan Brownjohn; *Director* and *General Secretary:* Brian Mitchell; *Treasurer:* John Cotton. The Society is a national body entirely devoted to the encouragement of the art. It publishes *Poetry Review* quarterly, runs poetry readings, children's events, verse-speaking examinations and administers various prizes and competitions. It incorporates the National Poetry Secretariat which sponsors poetry readings. It houses a poetry bookshop.

Portrait Painters, Royal Society of (1891), 17 Carlton House Terrace, London, SW1Y 5BD *T.* 01-930 6844. *President:* David Poole. Annual Exhibition when work may be submitted by non-members with a view to exhibition.

Beatrix Potter Society (1980), High Banks, 26 Stoneborough Lane, Budleigh Salterton, Devon EX9 6HL. *Chairman:* Christopher Hanson-Smith; *Secretary:* Brian Riddle, 24 Warren Road, Wanstead, London E11 2NA. To promote the study and appreciation of the life and works of Beatrix Potter as author, artist, diarist, farmer and conservationist. *Subscription:* U.K. £5.00, overseas £12.00.

Press Council, The (1953), Independent. *Chairman:* Rt. Hon. Sir Zelman Cowen. *Director:* Kenneth Morgan, O.B.E., 1 Salisbury Square, London, EC4Y 8AE *T.* 01-353 1248.

Private Libraries Association (1956), Ravelston, South View Road, Pinner, Middlesex, HA5 3YD. *President:* John Russell Taylor. *Hon. Editor;* David Chambers. *Subscriptions:* £16.00 per annum. International society of book collectors and private libraries. Publications include the quarterly *Private Library*, annual *Private Press Books*, and other books on book collecting.

Publishers Association, 19 Bedford Square, London, WC1B 3HJ. Established 1896. *T.* 01-580 6321-5. *Telex:* 267160 Pubass G. *Fax:* 01-636 5375. *Chief Executive:* Clive Bradley; *Deputy Secretary:* Peter Phelan; *Director Book Marketing Council (UK):* Maggie van Reenen; *Director Book Development Council (International):* Anthony Read. *Director Educational Publishers Council (Schools) and University, College and Professional Publishers Council:* John Davies; *Director Management Services:* Philip Flamank. The national association of British publishers whose over-all membership represents some 258 members (embracing 585 companies, starred in the list of British Publishers given earlier in this book).

Radclyffe International Philosophical Association, The (1955), BM-RIPhA, Old Gloucester Street, London WC1N 3XX. *President:* William Mann, F.R.I.PH.A., *Secretary General:* John Khasseyan, F.R.I.PH.A. *Objects:* To dignify those achievements which might otherwise escape formal recognition; to promote the interests and talent of its members; to encourage their good fellowship and to form a medium of exchange of ideas between members. *Entrance fee:* £10.00. *Subscription:* £15.00 (Fellows, Members and Associates). Published authors and artists usually enter at Fellowship level.

Railway Artists, Guild of, (1979). *Hon. Administrator:* F. P. Hodges, 45 Dickins Road, Warwick, CV34 5NS. *T.* (0926) 499246. To forge a link between artists depicting railway subjects and to give members a corporate identity; also stages railway art exhibitions.

Regional Arts Associations. The Arts Council of Great Britain, as well as local authorities, local education authorities, industry, charitable trusts and private patrons, provides funds for Regional Arts Associations which promote and develop the arts in their regions.

With their grasp of regional needs and demands they are well equipped to provide a service of information, help and guidance to all kinds of arts organisations in their area, and in many cases can provide financial assistance. They can take the initiative in promoting activities themselves and in planning and co-ordinating regional tours. Most of them issue periodically a magazine or broadsheet containing a calendar of forthcoming events. Some R.A.A.s offer transport subsidies to parties travelling to various kinds of performances, etc.

Representatives of all the associations meet as the Council of Regional Arts Associations (CORAA), Litton Lodge, 13A Clifton Road, Winchester, Hampshire, SO22 5BP *T.* (0962) 51063.

The subsidy responsibility for many activities in England and Wales has been transferred from the Arts Council of Great Britain to the Regional Arts Associations, but the Arts Council retains as direct beneficiaries a number of the larger organisations, including certain regional theatre companies and major festivals.

Annual Subscriptions for Full Membership (Organisations) and Associate Membership (Individuals) vary between the Associations and details may be obtained from the addresses listed below. Membership entitles one to the periodicals and broadsheets and to other benefits. There are at present no regional arts associations in Scotland and all enquiries should be addressed to The Scottish Arts Council, 19 Charlotte Square, Edinburgh, EH2 4DF *T.* 031-226 0651.

East Midlands Arts (1969), Mountfields House, Forest Road, Loughborough, Leicestershire, LE11 3HU *T.* (0509) 218292. *Director:* John Buston. Derbyshire (excluding High Peak District), Leicestershire, Northamptonshire, Nottinghamshire. Also funds the Buckinghamshire Arts Association.

Eastern Arts Association (1971), 8-9 Bridge Street, Cambridge, CB2 1UA *T.* (0223) 357 596. *Director:* Jeremy Newton. Specialist officers for each art form. Bedfordshire, Cambridgeshire, Essex, Hertfordshire, Norfolk and Suffolk.

Greater London Arts (1966), Angel House, 9 White Lion Street, London N1 9PD *T.* 01-837 8808. *Director:* Pat Abraham. The area of the 32 London Boroughs and the City of London.

Lincolnshire and Humberside Arts (1964), St. Hugh's, Newport, Lincoln, LN1 3DN *T.* (0522) 33555. *Director:* Clive Fox. Lincolnshire and Humberside.

Merseyside Arts (1968), Bluecoat Chambers, School Lane, Liverpool, L1 3BX *T.* 051-709 0671. *Director:* Peter Booth. Liverpool City Council, the district councils of Ellesmere Port & Neston, Halton, Knowsley, Sefton, St. Helens, West Lancashire and Wirral and the Cheshire, Lancashire.

North Wales Arts Association (1967), 10 Wellfield House, Bangor, Gwynedd, LL57 1ER *T.* (0248) 353248. *Director:* D. Llion Williams, Clwyd, Gwynedd and District of Montgomery in the County of Powys.

North West Arts (1966), 12 Harter Street, Manchester, M1 6HY *T.* 061-228 3062. *Director:* Raphael Gonley. Greater Manchester, High Peak District of Derbyshire, Lancashire (except District of West Lancashire), Cheshire (except Ellesmere Port and Halton Districts). Publish monthly *The Artful Reporter*.

Northern Arts (1961), 10 Osborne Terrace, Newcastle-upon-Tyne, NE2 1NZ *T.* 091-281 6334. *Director:* Peter Stark. Cumbria, Cleveland, Metropolitan County of Tyne and Wear, Northumberland and Durham.

South East Arts Association (1973), 10 Mount Ephraim, Tunbridge Wells, Kent, TN4 8AS *T.* (0892) 41666. *Director:* Christopher Cooper. Kent, East Sussex and Surrey. Publish 11 times per year *Arts Diary* for Kent, East Sussex and Surrey as well as annual poetry or short story anthologies, information for new and aspiring writers, directories of artists, craftsmen and authors etc.

South-east Wales Arts Association (1973), Victoria Street, Cwmbran, Gwent, NP44 3YT *T.* (063-33) 67530. *Director:* H.C.H. Perks. South Glamorgan, Mid-Glamorgan, Gwent, Districts of Radnor and Brecknock in the County of Powys, and the City of Cardiff.

South West Arts (1956), Bradninch Place, Gandy Street, Exeter, Devon, EX4 3LS *T* (0392) 218188. *Director:* Martin Rewcastle. Avon, Cornwall, Devon, Dorset (except Districts of Bournemouth, Christchurch and Poole), Gloucestershire, Somerset.

Southern Arts Association (1968), 19 Southgate Street, Winchester, Hants, SO23 9DQ *T.* (0962) 55099. *Director:* Bill Dufton; *Literature Officer:* Keiren Phelan. Berkshire, Hampshire, Isle of Wight, Oxfordshire, West Sussex, Wiltshire, Bournemouth, Christchurch and Poole, Districts of Dorset.

West Midlands Arts (1971), Brunswick Terrace Stafford, ST16 1BZ *T.* (0785) 59231. *Director:* Geoff Sims. County of Hereford and Worcester, Metropolitan County of West Midlands, Shropshire, Staffordshire, Warwickshire.

West Wales (Association for the) Arts (1971), Dark Gate, Carmarthen, Dyfed, SA31 1QL *T.* (0267) 234248. *Director:* Carwyn Rogers. Dyfed and West Glamorgan.

Yorkshire Arts Association (1969), Glyde House, Glydegate, Bradford, West Yorkshire, BD5 0BQ *T.* (0274) 723051. North, South and West Yorkshire. Offers a range of awards and schemes to help writers and those who promote literary activity in the region. Provides grants to festivals, literary societies, poetry-reading groups, etc. Bursaries to authors. Appoints short-term 'placements' for creative writers.

Ridley Art Society (1889), 35 Fitzjames Avenue, London, W14 0RR. *President:* Professor Carel Weight, R.A.; *Chairman:* J. F. Richardson; *Hon. Secretary:* Mrs. Brenda Sykes. To encourage a high standard of painting, draughtsmanship and sculpture. An exhibition is held annually and candidates for membership can submit four works.

Romantic Novelists' Association The. *Chairman:* Sheila Walsh, 35 Coudray Road, Southport, Merseyside PR9 9NL. *Hon. Secretary:* Mrs. Dorothy Entwistle, 20 First Avenue, Amersham, Bucks HP7 9BJ. To raise the prestige of Romantic Authorship. Open to romantic and historical novelists. See also under **Literary Awards.**

Royal Academy of Arts, Piccadilly, London, W1V 0DS *T.* 01-734 9052. Academicians (R.A.) and Associates (A.R.A.) are elected from the most distinguished artists in the United Kingdom. Major loan exhibitions throughout the year with the Annual Summer Exhibition, May to August. Also runs art schools for 80 students, mainly post-graduate, in painting and sculpture.

Royal Birmingham Society of Artists, 69A New Street, Birmingham, B2 4DU *T.* 021-643 3768. *President:* W. Alex Jackson; *Hon. Secretary:* Tom Barker, R.B.S.A. The Society has its own galleries and rooms prominently placed in the city centre. Members (R.B.S.A.) and Associates (A.R.B.S.A.) are elected annually. There are two annual Spring Exhibitions open to all artists and an Autumn Exhibition of Members' and Associates' works. *Annual Subscription* (Friends of the R.B.S.A.): £5.00 entitles subscribers to season ticket for painting days, criticisms and lectures organised by the Society and to submit work for the Annual Friend's Exhibition in July. Further details from the Hon. Secretary.

Royal Literary Fund, The (1790), 144 Temple Chambers, Temple Avenue, London EC4Y 0DT *T.* 01-353 7150. Grants made to necessitous authors of some published work of approved literary merit or their dependants. *President:* Arthur Crook; *Secretary:* Antony MacKenzie Smith.

Royal Society, The (1660), 6 Carlton House Terrace, London, SW1Y 5AG *T.* 01-839 5561. *President:* Sir Andrew Huxley; *Treasurer:* Sir John Mason, *Secretaries:* Sir David Smith, Professor R. J. Elliott; *Foreign Secretary:* Sir Arnold Burgen. Promotion of the natural sciences (pure and applied) through meetings, publications, grants and awards.

Royal Society of Arts, John Adam Street, Adelphi, London, WC2N 6EZ *T.* 01-930 5115. Founded in 1754. Sir Peter Baldwin (*Chairman of the Council*), Christopher Lucas (*Secretary*). Fellowship is open to both men and women. The aims of the Society, as indicated by its full title, are, "The encouragement of Arts, Manufactures and Commerce."

Royal West of England Academy (1844), Queens Road, Clifton, Bristol, BS8 1PX *T.* (0272) 735129. *President:* Mary Fedden, R.W.A. *Organising Secretary:* Jean McKinney. Aims to further the interests of practising painters and sculptors. Holds art exhibitions and is a meeting place for artists and their work.

Ruskin Society of London, The (1985) *Hon. Secretary:* Miss O. E. Madden, 351 Woodstock Road, Oxford OX2 7NX *T.* (0865) 515962. To promote literary and biographical interest in John Ruskin and his contemporaries. *Annual subscription:* £5.00.

Dorothy L. Sayers Historical and Literary Society, The (1976), *Chairman:* Dr Barbara Reynolds. *Secretary:* Christopher J. Dean, Rose Cottage, Malthouse Lane, Hurstpierpoint, W. Sussex BN6 9JY *T.* (0273) 833444. To promote and encourage the study of the works of Dorothy L. Sayers; to collect relics and reminiscences about her and make them available to students and biographers, to hold an annual seminar, to publish proceedings and pamphlets and a bi-monthly bulletin. *Annual subs.:* £4.00.

Scientific and Technical Communicators, The Institute of (1972), 17 Bluebridge Avenue, Brookmans Park, Hatfield, Herts, AL9 7RY *T.* (0707) 55392. *President:* Ray Burgess, F.I.S.T.C.; *Secretary:* Mrs. Eileen Parkinson. A professional body for those engaged in the communication of scientific and technical information. *Objects:* to establish and maintain professional standards, to encourage and co-operate in professional training and to provide a source of information on, and to encourage research and development in, all aspects of scientific and technical communication. *The Communicator* is the official quarterly journal of the Institute, and *The Communicator—News Supplement*, a newsletter (6 times p.a.).

Scottish Academy, Royal (1826), Princes Street, Edinburgh, EH2 2EL *T.* 031-225 6671. *President:* H. Anthony Wheeler, P.R.S.A.; *Secretary:* R. R. Steedman,

R.S.A.; *Treasurer:* W.J.L. Baillie, R.S.A.; *Administrative Secretary:* W. T. Meikle. Academicians (R.S.A.) and Associates (A.R.S.A.) and non-members may exhibit in the Annual Exhibition of Painting, Sculpture and Architecture. Annual Exhibition dates approximately mid April to early August, Festival Exhibition August/September. Royal Scottish Academy Diploma Collection, normally between October and January. Royal Scottish Academy Student Competition held in March.

Scottish Arts, 24 Rutland Square, Edinburgh, EH1 2BW *T.* 031-229 1076. *Honorary Secretary:* W. B. Logan. *T.* 031-229 8157. *Subs.:* Full £154.00, but various reductions. Art, literature, music.

Scottish Arts Council, The—see **Arts Council of Great Britain.**

Scottish History Society (1886), Department of Modern History, The University, Dundee DD1 4HN. *Hon. Secretary:* Annette M. Smith, PH.D. The Society exists to publish documents illustrating the history of Scotland.

Scottish Newspaper Proprietors' Association, Edinburgh House, 3-11 North St. Andrew Street, Edinburgh, EH2 1JU *T.* 031-557 3600. *President and Chairman:* Derek J. R. Smail. *Director:* J. B. Raeburn, A.C.I.S. To promote and safeguard newspaper interests.

Scottish Publishers' Association, The, (1974) 25a South West Thistle Street Lane, Edinburgh EH2 1EW *T.* 031-225 5795. *Director:* Judy Moir. *Publicist:* Alison Harley. To assist Scottish publishers primarily in the publicity, promotion and marketing of their books and to provide information and advice on all aspects of publishing.

Screenwriters Workshop, London (1983), 20 Jeffreys Street, London NW1 9PR *T.* 01-482 0527. Formed by a group of film and television writers to serve as a forum for contact, discussion and practical criticism. Membership open to anyone interested in writing for film and television, and to anyone working in these and related media. *Annual subscription:* £12. Send SAE for further details.

Shakespearean Authorship Trust. *Hon. Secretary:* Dr. D. W. Thomson Vessey, 26 Ouse Walk, Huntingdon, Cambridgeshire PE18 6QL. *Hon. Treasurer:* John Silberrad, Dryads' Hall, Woodbury Hill, Loughton, Essex IG10 1JB. *Aims:* The advancement of learning with particular reference to the social, political and literary history of England in the sixteenth century and the authorship of the plays and poems commonly attributed to William Shakespeare. *Annual Subscription:* £10.00. Subscribers receive *The Bard*, published twice yearly by the Trust, and are entitled to use the Trust's library.

Shaw Society, The, 6 Stanstead Grove, Catford, London, SE6 4UD. *T.* 01-690 2325. *Secretary:* Barbara Smoker. Improvement and diffusion of knowledge of the life and works of Bernard Shaw and his circle. Meetings in London, annual festival at Ayot St. Lawrence; publication: *The Shavian.*

Sherlock Holmes Society of London, The (1951). *President:* Frank A. Allen, F.P.S.; *Chairman:* Bernard Davies; *Hon. Secretary:* Capt. W. R. Michell, R.N., J.P., The Old Crown Inn, Lopen, near South Petherton, Somerset TA13 5JX *T.* South Petherton (0460) 40717. *Objects:* to bring together those who have a common interest as readers and students of the literature of Sherlock Holmes; to encourage the pursuit of knowledge of the public and private lives of Sherlock Holmes and Dr. Watson; to organize meetings and lectures for the discussion of these topics; to co-operate with other bodies at home and abroad that are in sympathy with the aims and activities of the Society. *Subscription*, including two issues of *The Sherlock Holmes Journal:* £9.00 p.a. within 50 miles of Baker Street, £7.50 p.a. outside this radius, overseas £9.00 or $20.00.

Singapore Book Publishers Association, P.O. Box 846, Colombo Court Post Office, Singapore, 0617. *President:* Mr. Koh Hock Seng; *Hon. Secretary:* Peh Chin Hua.

SLADE—Society of Lithographic Artists, Designers, Engravers & Process Workers—see NGA 1982.

Society of Authors—see Authors, The Society of.

Songwriters, Composers and Authors, British Academy of, (1947), 148 Charing Cross Road, London WC2H 0LB *T.* 01-240 2823. *General Secretary:* Marilyn Worsley. To give advice and guidance to its songwriter members.

South African Publishers Association, P.O. Box 326, Howard Place 7450, South Africa. *T.* (021) 53-8907.

SPREd—Society of Picture Researchers and Editors, BM Box 259, London, WC1N 3XX *T.* 01-404 5011. A professional organisation whose purpose is to bring picture researchers and editors together to meet, compare views, pool experience, resolve problems and in general improve the professional status of picture people. Will recommend suitable researchers for a project. See article: **Picture Research.**

Strip Illustration, Society of, 7 Dilke Street, Chelsea, London SW3 4JE. Founded in 1977 by a group of professionals, the Society is open to artists, writers, editors, and anyone professionally concerned with comics, newspaper strips, and strip illustration. Monthly Newsletter, monthly meetings, and an annual convention.

Sussex Playwrights' Club. Founded in 1935. Members' plays are read by local actors before an audience of Club members. The Club from time to time sponsors productions of members' plays by local drama companies. Details: Hon. Secretary, Sussex Playwrights' Club, 2 Princes Avenue, Hove, East Sussex BN3 4GD.

Syndicat des Conseils Litteraires Français, 117 boulevard Saint-Germain, 75006 Paris.

Syndicat National de l'Edition (the French publishers' association), 35 Rue Gregoire de Tours, 75279 Paris 06. *T.* 329 21-01.

Technical Writers Group, 84 Drayton Gardens, London, SW10 9SB *T.* 01-373 6642. *Secretary:* Julian Chancellor. A specialist unit within the membership of the Society of Authors.

Theatre Research, The Society for. *Hon. Secretaries:* Kathleen Barker and Derek Forbes, 77 Kinnerton Street, London, SW1X 8ED. Publishes annual volumes and journal, *Theatre Notebook*, and holds lectures.

Theatre Writers' Union (1976), Actors Centre, 4 Chenies Street, London WC1E 7EP *T.* 01-631 3619. The Union's principles include the furthering of the interests of all writers working in the theatre, particularly the subsidised theatre; the negotiation of minimum terms contracts with representative organisations across the entire theatrical spectrum, the improvement of theatre writers' status and the protection of their rights; the encouragement of new writing in the theatre; the pressing for adequate expenditure on theatre writing by various funding bodies; the development of regional script centres, providing cheap photocopying facilities. Membership fee from £20.00 p.a.

Edward Thomas Fellowship, The (1980), 20a Waldegrave Gardens, Strawberry Hill, Twickenham, Middlesex TW1 4PG *T.* 01-892 7895. *Hon. Secretary:* Alan A. Martin. To perpetuate the memory of Edward Thomas, foster an interest in his life and work, to assist in the preservation of places associated with him and to arrange events which extend fellowship amongst his admirers. *Annual* subscription: £4.00.

Francis Thompson Society, The, now incorporated in **The Eighteen Nineties Society,** *q.v.*

Translators Association, The (1958), 84 Drayton Gardens, London, SW10 9SB *T.* 01-373 6642. *Secretary:* Julian Chancellor. A specialist unit within the membership of the Society of Authors, exclusively concerned with the interests and special problems of writers who translate foreign literary or dramatic work into English for publication or performance in Great Britain or English-speaking countries overseas. Members are entitled to general and legal advice on all questions connected with the marketing of their work, such as rates of remuneration, contractual arrangements with publishers, editors, broadcasting organisations, etc. The annual subscription is £45 by direct debit, £50 by cheque and includes membership of the Society of Authors. Full particulars may be obtained from the offices of the Association.

Translators' Guild Ltd, c/o 26-27 Boswell Street, London WC1N 3JZ. All correspondence to be addressed to the *Secretary*. The Translators' Guild is a professional association which restricts its qualified entry to those who have passed the translators' examinations in technical, scientific, commercial or social science fields. Affiliate membership (non-qualified) and student membership are also possible. Members of the Guild are listed in an Index which shows the languages and subjects they are qualified to handle.

Travel Writers, The British Guild of, *Hon. Chairman:* Peter McGregor Eadie, 31 Riverside Court, Caversham, Reading, Berks. RG4 8AL *T.* (0734) 481384. To assist members by arranging meetings and discussions to extend the range of their knowledge and experience and by writing seriously and conscientiously about travel to contribute to the growth of public interest in the knowledge of the subject.

Turner Society, The (1975), B.C.M. Box Turner, London, WC1N 3XX. *President:* Henry Moore, O.M., C.H.; *Chairman:* Stanley Warburton; *Secretary:* Dr. Selby Whittingham (*T.* 01-373 5560). To foster a wider appreciation of all facets of Turner's work; to encourage exhibitions of his paintings, drawings and engravings. Publishes: *The Turner Society News. Subscriptions:* £5.00; Overseas: £6; Corporate: £10.

Typographic Designers, Society of, *President:* David Playne, F.S.T.D., F.S.I.A.D.; *Chair:* Angela Reeves, F.S.T.D., F.S.I.A.D. *Hon. Secretary:* Peter Hatch, F.S.T.D., F.S.I.A.D., Wellington House, Church Road, Ashford, Kent TN24 1PE *T.* (0233) 24618. Founded in 1928, the Society has been recognised as the authoratative organisation for the typographic profession in the U.K. It advises and acts on matters of professional practice, provides a better understanding of the craft and the rapidly changing technology in the graphic industries by lectures, discussions and through the journal *Typo/graphic* and the Newsletter. Typo/graphic students are encouraged to first gain Licentiateship of the Society as the accepted yard stick by employers by an annual assessment of submitted work to a sponsored professional brief. The STD is a full member of The International Council of Graphic Design Associations, ICOGRADA, which brings professionals together for a General Assembly, Congress and exhibition of work, every three years.

United Society for Christian Literature (1799), Robertson House, Leas Road, Guildford, Surrey, GU1 4QW *T.* Guildford 577877. *President:* Lord Luke. *Chairman:* David G. Temple. *General Secretary:* Rev. Alec Gilmore, M.A., B.D. To aid and undertake Christian publishing at home and overseas.

United Society of Artists, 17 Carlton House Terrace, London, SW1Y 5BD

T. 01-930 6844. *President:* Robert Hill, R.O.I., N.E.A.C. Membership by election on application. Annual Exhibition open to all non-members.

Jules Verne Circle, The (1978) 6 High Orchard, 125 Markyate Road, Dagenham, Essex, RM8 2LB. *Secretary:* Eric Ford. Promotion of scholarship and research in the life, work and times of Jules Verne. *Subs:* £2.00 p.a.

Edgar Wallace Society (1969), 7 Devonshire Close, Amersham, Bucks HP6 5JG *T.* (024 03) 5398. *Organiser:* John A. Hogan. To promote an interest in the life and work of Edgar Wallace through the *Crimson Circle* magazine (Q.). *Subscription:* £6.00 p.a.

Watercolour Society, British, *Director:* Leslie Simpson, Castle Gallery, Castle Hill, Ilkley, West Yorkshire LS29 9DT *T.* (0943) 609075.

Mary Webb Society (1972), *Secretaries:* Mrs. H. M. Dormer, 6 Ragleth Road, Church Stretton, Shropshire SY6 7BN *T.* (0694) 722755 and Mrs. A. Parry, 4 Lythwood Road, Bayston Hill, Shrewsbury. *T.* Bayston Hill 2766. To further an interest in the life and works of Mary Webb by meetings, lectures and excursions.

H. G. Wells Society, The (1960), Department of Language and Literature, Polytechnic of North London, Prince of Wales Road, Kentish Town, London, NW5 3LB. *Secretary:* Christopher Rolfe. Promotion of an active interest in and encouragement of an appreciation of the life, work and thought of H. G. Wells. Publishes *The Wellsian* (annually) and *The Newsletter* (quarterly). *Subscription:* £4.00 per annum.

Welsh Arts Council, The—see Arts Council of Great Britain.

Welsh Books Council/Cyngor Llyfrau Cymraeg, Castell Brychan, Aberystwyth, Dyfed, SY23 2JB *T.* (0970) 4151-3. *Director:* Alun Creunant Davies. Founded in 1961 to encourage and increase the interest of the public in Welsh literature and to support authors of popular books in the Welsh language. With the establishment of Publicity, Editorial, Design and Marketing Departments, the Council promotes all aspects of book production in Wales and provides a service for Welsh-language books and English-language books of Welsh interest. Also distributes the government grant for Welsh-language publications.

West Country Writers' Association, The. *President:* Christopher Fry, F.R.S.L.; *Chairman:* Rosemary Jeffrey; *Hon. Secretary:* Dorothy Stiffe, 9 Firs Glen Road, West Moors, Dorset BH22 0EB. *T.* Ferndown 873728. Founded in 1951 by Waveney Girvan for the purpose of fostering the love of literature in the West Country. An Annual Week-end Congress is held in a West Country city. There are Regional Meetings of Members, a Newsletter-cum-magazine, and correspondence between members. Membership is by invitation of the Committee. *Annual Subscription:* £5.

Wildlife Artists, Society of, 17 Carlton House Terrace, London, SW1Y 5BD *T.* 01-930 6844. *President:* Robert Gillmor. To promote and encourage the art of Wildlife painting and sculpture. Open Annual Exhibition.

Charles Williams Society (1975), 26 Village Road, Finchley, London N3 1TL. *Secretary:* Mrs. Gillian Lunn. To promote interest in Charles Williams' life and work and to make his writings more easily available.

Women Artists, Society of (1855), 17 Carlton House Terrace, London, SW1Y 5BD. *T.* 01-930 6844. *President:* Barbara Tate. Annual Exhibition, pictures, sculpture and crafts. Annual Exhibition. Open to all women.

Women Writers and Journalists, Society of, (1894) *Acting Secretary:* Jean Marian Stevens, 3 Nettlecroft, Hemel Hempstead, Herts HP1 1PQ. For women writers and artists. Lectures, monthly lunch-time meetings. Free literary advice for members. *The Woman Journalist.* (3 p.a.) *Subscription:* Town £12.00; Country £9.00; Overseas £5.00.

Worshipful Company of Musicians (1500), 4 St. Paul's Churchyard, London, EC4M 8BA *T.* 01-236 2333. *Clerk:* W. R. I. Crewdson.

Worshipful Company of Stationers and Newspaper Makers (1403), Stationers' Hall, London, EC4M 7DD *T.* 01-248 2934. *Master:* Allen F. Thompson, M.C. *Clerk:* Captain P. Hames, R.N. One of the Livery Companies of the City of London. Connected with the printing, publishing, bookselling and allied trades.

Writers' Guild of Great Britain, The, 430 Edgware Road, London, W2 1EH *T.* 01-723 8074-5-6. See also **Article**.

Writers' Union of Canada, The, The Writers' Centre, 24 Ryerson Avenue, Toronto, Ontario, M5T 2P3 *T.* (416) 868-6914. *National Chairman:* Rudy Wiebe.

Yachting Journalists' Association, (1973). *Secretary:* Timothy Jeffery, *Yachting World*, Quadrant House, The Quadrant, Sutton, Surrey, SM2 5AS. *T.* 01-661 3857. To further the interests of yachting journalists and boating. *Subscription:* £5.00 p.a.

Yorkshire Dialect Society, The (1897). The aims of the Society are to encourage interest in: (1) Dialect speech; (2) the writing of dialect verse, prose and drama; (3) the publication and circulation of dialect literature and the performance of dialect plays; (4) the study of the origins and the history of dialect and kindred subjects—all dialects, not only of Yorkshire origin. *Annual subscription:* £2.50; life membership, £52.50. *Meetings:* the Society organises a number of meetings during the year—details from the Hon. Secretary. *Annual Publications: Transactions* and *The Summer Bulletin* free to members, list of other publications on request. *Hon. Secretary:* Gerald Williams, Fieldhead House, West Street, Hoyland, Barnsley, S74 9AG *T.* Barnsley 742203.

Francis Brett Young Society (1979), *Secretary:* Mrs. M. Bowater, 5 Norbury Drive, Withymoor Village, Brierley Hill, West Midlands DY5 3DP *T.* Brierley Hill (0384) 72735. To provide opportunities for members to meet, correspond, and to share the enjoyment of the author's works. *Annual subscription:* £3.00.

GET CLUED UP WITH A & C BLACK

WRITING A THRILLER
André Jute

WRITING CRIME FICTION
H R F Keating

Take some expert advice on writing from two leading authorities in their field. H. R. F. Keating well known author of the Inspector Ghote novels, and André Jute an internationally successful thriller writer offer practical information and guidance on all aspects. The two books cover how to choose a theme, character creation, plot, research, writing, cutting and rewriting to finally submitting the finished manuscript for publication.

WRITING
A THRILLER
André Jute

WRITING
CRIME FICTION
H. R. F. Keating

£4.95 each

copyright
tax, services

BRITISH COPYRIGHT

E. P. SKONE JAMES, M.A.

GENERALLY

It is not possible, in a short article such as this must be, to examine the law of British copyright in detail. The general principles are explained, and attention is drawn to many points of special interest. Expert legal advice should be sought in difficult cases.

The Copyright Act, 1956 ("the Act"), which substantially replaces the Copyright Act, 1911, ("the Act of 1911"), received the Royal Assent on November 5, 1956, and came into operation on the 1st June 1957. The Act has been amended by the Design Copyright Act 1968, which came into operation on the 25th October 1968, and which deals with the relationship between copyright under the Act and copyright under the Registered Designs Act 1949. Also by the Copyright (Amendment) Act 1971, which came into operation on the 17th February 1971 and which permits applications to the Performing Right Tribunal to review its orders under Section 27. Again by the Copyright Act 1956 (Amendment) Act 1982, which came into force on the 13th July 1982, and the Copyright (Amendment) Act 1983 which came into force on 13th July 1983 and which amended Section 21 of the Act concerned with criminal offences. Again by the Cable and Broadcasting Act 1984, which came into force as to the provisions relevant to this article on the 1st January 1985, and which established a new form of copyright in cable programmes and made consequential amendments to the Act. Most recently by the Copyright (Computer Software) Amendment Act 1985 (the 1985 Act) which came into force on the 16th September 1985 and which provided for the protection of computer programs as literary works.

The Act, though more complicated, will not, it is thought, be found to have made substantial changes affecting the rights of writers and artists. The Act provides (Section 45(5)) that no copyright shall subsist otherwise than by virtue thereof, and the Seventh Schedule to the Act contains lengthy transitional provisions which assume that the provisions of the Act have always been in force, but then proceed to modify its provisions in respect of works which were in existence before its commencement. Thus, devolutions of title to copyright works valid under the Act of 1911 are to be treated as remaining valid, and, in general, copyright which subsisted in works under the Act of 1911, will continue to subsist under the Act. Again, the proviso to Section 3, and Section 4 of the Act of 1911, which dealt respectively with the right, 25 years after the death of the author of a published work, to reproduce the work without infringement of the copyright therein if the necessary notice had been given, and, the right to apply to the Judicial Committee of the Privy Council for a compulsory licence in certain circumstances, and the proviso to Section 5(2) of the Act of 1911 are repealed by the Act: but, if the necessary notice has been given under such proviso before Section 3 is repealed, then, as respects reproductions of that work by the person who gave the notice, after the repeal of Section 3, such proviso is to have effect as if re-enacted in the Act (Paragraph 9, 7th Schedule of the Act), and in the case of an assignment or licence before 1957 under the Act of 1911 there will still be a reverter to the personal representatives of the author at the end of twenty-five years from his death. This proviso has been the subject of substantial litigation in the courts (see, for instance, *Chappell & Co. Ltd.* v. *Redwood Music Ltd.* 1980 2 A.E.R. 817 (H.L.)). The Act also made the necessary changes in the law to enable this country to ratify the Brussels Convention and the Universal Copyright Convention.

In March 1977 the Report of the Whitford Committee to consider the law of copyright and designs was presented to Parliament; Cmnd. 6732. It contains a large number of recommendations for revising the law of copyright and recommends the abolition of registered design protection under the Registered Designs Act 1949. Two of the major recommendations were, first that there should be a system of blanket licensing to cater for all user requirements for facsimile copies; secondly that a levy system should be introduced to apply to the sale of all equipment of a type suitable for private recording, with an additional annual licence fee in the case of educational recording payable under a blanket licensing scheme. These recommendations arise because of the problems created by the increased availability and use of reprographic machines, such as photo copiers and of audio and visual precording equipment, such as tape recorders. The Government published a Green Paper (Cmnd. 8302 July 1981) following some of the Whitford Committee recommendations, on others putting forward divergent views and inviting debate. In December 1983 a further Green Paper was published (Cmnd. 9117) entitled Intellectual Property Rights and Innovation. Another Green Paper was published in February 1985 (Cmnd. 9445) entitled the Recording and Rental of Audio and Video Copyright material. In April 1986 the Government published a White Paper (Cmnd. 9712) entitled Intellectual Property and Innovation containing the Government's proposals *inter alia* for the reform of the law of copyright and related rights taking into account, for this purpose, the Whitford Committee's Report and the 1981 and 1985 Green Papers. The White Paper stated the Government's intention to legislate on the lines set out in the White Paper as soon as the parliamentary timetable permits.

In 1979 the Public Lending Right Act was passed establishing public lending right. It came into force on 1st March 1980 (1980 S.I. No.83 (C.5)). Such right is not part of an author's copyright and is virtually not a 'right' at all. The object of the Act is to provide payments to authors out of a Central Fund, such payments being dependent on the number of times a book is lent from certain libraries and most of the important matters are left to be dealt with by a scheme. The present scheme is set out in the Appendix to 1982 S.I. No. 719 (as amended). The only right an author has arises when his book has been registered and the Registrar of Public Lending Right has determined the sum (if any) due by way of public lending right. Once this has happened the author can recover such sums from the Registrar as a debt due. The amount any particular author will receive is likely to be small.

NATURE OF COPYRIGHT

Copyright protection is not given to ideas or systems, plots or themes, however original; it is aimed solely to prevent the copying of literary, musical, dramatic or artistic works, sound recordings, films, television and sound broadcasts and published editions of works. The idea, theme or plot must therefore be reduced into material form before protection can be claimed, and then the protection given is to the form and not to the idea. If the idea is reproduced in a quite different form, this is not an infringement of copyright. However ideas, for instance an idea for a television series, may be protected under the law of confidence; *Fraser* v. *Thames Television Ltd.* 1984 Q.B. 44.

Another basic principle of copyright law is that it does not give a monopoly even to the form selected, since it is directed to preventing copying, and not to giving an absolute title to any particular form of words, or of artistic production. Copyright protection is given to dictionaries and directories and to photographs, but this does not mean that another may not lawfully produce independently an almost identical work; he is only guilty of infringement if he copies the earlier work.

A further important matter in regard to copyright protection is that, in the United Kingdom and most European countries at least (see *post* "Works protected abroad"), no formalities are required. Copyright protection is afforded as soon as the page of manuscript is written, the sketch is drawn or the melody is composed provided certain conditions are complied with. The work does not need to be printed or published, no form of registration is needed, no "copyright reserved" or other copyright notice is required. To claim ownership of copyright by virtue of a copyright notice has no effect under United Kingdom law in relation to such ownership. To do so wrongly might give rise to claims under section 43 of the Act (see *post* "Other Remedies") or for "passing off". Publishers are required to deliver certain copies of published books to certain prescribed libraries (Section 15 of the Act of 1911 as amended, which is not repealed by the Act), but failure to do this does not affect the copyright, though it may give rise to liability for penalties (sub-section (6)). Copies of scripts of certain new plays are required to be delivered to the British Museum under the Theatres Act 1968.

KIND OF WORKS PROTECTED

Literary, dramatic and artistic works are defined in the Act (Sections 48(1) and 3(1); see also definitions of "sculpture", "engraving", "photograph", "building", "construction", "drawing", "manuscript", "writing"). Computer programs (undefined) are protected as literary works by the 1985 Act. Musical works are not defined by the Act, but it is thought sufficient if the work is recorded in some permanent form whether sheet music or a tape, for instance. Furthermore, copyright may subsist in arrangements of music, even if made unlawfully; *Redwood Music Ltd.,* v *Chappell & Co. Ltd.* 1982 R.P.C. 109.

It has been decided that the expression "literary" does not involve any qualification of style, but covers any work expressed in print or writing, so long as it is substantial enough to involve some literary skill and labour of composition (see *Exxon* post). And a similarly slight degree of skill and labour is imposed in regard to other classes of works.

Thus selections of poems, abridgements, notes to school textbooks, arrangements of music, football championship fixtures list and other compilations are protected, provided that it is established that the production has involved a certain amount of intellectual endeavour, and is not merely mechanical. Thus, in *Independent Television Productions Ltd.* v. *Time Out Ltd.* and *The B.B.C.* v. *Time Out Ltd.* 1984 F.S.R. 64, held copyright in programme schedules of television programmes. Again in *British Northrop Ltd.* v. *Texteam Blackburn*

Ltd. 1973 F.S.R. 241 drawings of such items as screws and bolts were held not too simple to lack originality. But it has been decided that copyright does not subsist in prototypes of chairs and settees as works of artistic craftsmanship: *George Hensher Ltd.* v. *Restawhile Upholstery (Lancs) Ltd.* 1974 2 W.L.R. 700 (H.L.). Again copyright could subsist in a translation of an existing work entirely separate from copyright in the work.

Under the Act of 1911 (Section 22), artistic works intended for use as industrial designs were not protected under such Act, but could be protected under the Patents and Designs Acts, 1907-31. If the author of such a work failed to register the work as a design he lost both his artistic and designs copyright. Under the Act (Section 10) the author was not required to register his design until it was actually about to be licensed for industrial use, and, even if so licensed without registration, its artistic copyright was preserved, except in regard to industrial use (see *Dorling* v. *Honnor Marine Ltd.* 1964, 2 W.L.R. 195). On the other hand, the protection against industrial use would endure only for the period of fifteen years provided by its registration. This position has been changed by the Design Copyright Act 1968 in respect of works created after its coming into force. The 1968 Act amends section 10 of the Act in such a way that industrial use will not affect copyright under the Act except to limit the period of protection against industrial use in relevant cases. The position as to pre-1968 works is not made clear by the 1968 Act.

Protection under the Registered Designs Act, 1949, requires certain formalities of registration, and a Patent Agent should be consulted.

Sound recordings, films, television, sound broadcasts and cable programmes are defined in the Act as amended (Sections 12 (9), 13 (10), 14 (10) and 14A; and see *post* "Sound recordings", "Films", "Broadcasting and Television and Cable Programmes", "Published Editions").

PUBLISHED EDITIONS

The Act provides for the first time that a separate copyright is to subsist in every published edition of any literary, dramatic or musical work first published in the United Kingdom, or of which the publisher was a qualified person at the date of first publication. The publisher is entitled to such copyright (Section 15 of the Act).

Copyright in published editions subsists until the end of the period of twenty-five years from the end of the calendar year in which the edition was first published, and such copyright is infringed by making, by any photographic or similar process, a reproduction of the typographical arrangement of the edition.

TITLES AND PSEUDONYMS

The title of a book or story is normally not protected under the Act since it is too short to be treated as a literary work. Nor are single invented words such as "Exxon"; *Exxon Corporation* v. *Exxon Insurance etc. Ltd.* 1982 R.P.C. 69. If, however, a title is taken, and used in such a way as to cause confusion, a "passing off" action can often be brought successfully.

A similar cause of action arises if an author's pseudonym is used by another in such a way as to cause the public to believe that the second work is by the first author.

Apart from agreement, if an author has been writing for a periodical under a particular pen name, and ceases to contribute, he is entitled to use the pen name elsewhere, and the periodical is not entitled to continue to use it (and see *post* "Anonymous and Pseudonymous works").

TO WHOM COPYRIGHT PROTECTION IS GIVEN

In general the person to be protected is the author. This means for instance the person who has actually written the book, made the translation, drawn the picture, and so on; in the case of a photograph it means the person who, when the photograph is taken, is the owner of the material on which it is taken. A person who has merely suggested a theme, or supplied information, is not an author. This follows from the general principle stated above that protection is given to form and not ideas; it is the author of a form with whom copyright law is concerned. This may lead to difficulties in deciding who is the author of a computer program.

However, where a literary, dramatic or artistic work is made by an author in the course of his employment by the proprietor of a newspaper, magazine or similar periodical under a contract of service or apprenticeship, and is so made for the purpose of publication in a newspaper, etc., such proprietor is entitled to the copyright in the work, but only in so far as the copyright relates to such publication: the remainder of the copyright remains in the author (Section 4 (2) of the Act). Subject to this, in the case of photographs and portraits, engravings and sound recordings (Section 4 (3) and 12 (4) of the Act), if the original is ordered, and paid for, the copyright vests in the client, and not in the artist, photographer or maker.

But, if in a case not falling within either Section 4 (2) or Section 4 (3), a work is made in the course of the author's employment by another person under a contract of service or apprenticeship, that other person, and not the author, is entitled to the copyright in the work (Section 4 (4) of the Act). As to the difficulties in deciding whether a contract is a contract of service or a contract for services see *Beloff* v. *Pressdram Ltd.* 1973 F.S.R. 33. In the case of a full-time employee, work done for the employer out of hours will remain the copyright of the servant.

OWNERSHIP OF COPYRIGHT WORKS

The ownership of a work in which copyright subsists is an entirely separate matter from the ownership of the copyright in the work and each can be separately dealt with. (See, for instance, *ante* "To whom copyright protection is given" and *post* "Assignment of copyright" "Films" "Sound Recordings"). Problems frequently arise where A employs B to produce a copyright work, for instance architects, advertising agents and illustrators, not only in relation to ownership of the entitled to the copyright, or only to a licence to use and if so, what is the extent of the licence?), but also in relation to ownership of the work itself. To a large extent the latter is a question of fact in each case the most important fact being the terms of the contract between A and B. Care should therefore be taken to ensure that such a contract contains clear terms dealing with this matter. If nothing is said in the contract, it may well be that A will be entitled to the work produced by B if A has paid B all moneys due under the contract (see *Gibbon* v. *Pease* (1905)1 K.B. 810), though probably not B's working papers and the like (see *Chantrey Martin* v. *Martin* (1953)2 Q.B. 286).

ANONYMOUS AND PSEUDONYMOUS WORKS

Copyright in published literary, dramatic or musical works, and artistic works other than photographs, which are anonymous or pseudonymous, subsists until the end of the period of fifty years from the end of the calendar year in which the work was first published, unless, at any time before the end of that period, it is possible for a person, without previous knowledge of the facts, to ascertain the identity of the author (or one or more of the authors in the case of joint works), by reasonable enquiry (Second Schedule to the Act). However, publication of a work under two or more names is not pseudonymous unless all the names are pseudonyms.

The normal period of copyright is fifty years from the end of the calendar year in which the author died. In certain circumstances, therefore, a shorter period of protection only is obtained (see also "Duration of copyright protection" *post*).

JOINT AUTHORS

Joint authorship involves that two or more persons must have collaborated to produce a single work. Each must have taken some part in producing jointly the work protected; as has been seen, a man who merely suggests the idea or theme is not an author at all. Again, if the parts produced by each are easily separable, it is not a case of joint authorship, but each owns a separate copyright in each part (Section 11 (3) of the Act). The Act provides that, with certain exceptions, references therein to the author of a work are to be construed in relation to a work of joint authorship as a reference to all the authors of the work (Third Schedule to the Act). The more important exceptions are that, for the purposes of establishing copyright in literary, dramatic, musical and artistic works, it is sufficient if only one of the joint authors satisfies the necessary conditions. Further, if one or more of the joint authors does not satisfy the necessary conditions to establish copyright in the joint work, then the remaining author or authors are to be considered the person or persons entitled to the copyright in each work. In the case of a work of joint authorship, neither can deal with the copyright without the consent of the other or others, but, on the other hand, each can bring actions against the other or third parties for any infringement. Other matters of importance to joint authors are referred to under "Duration of copyright protection" *post*.

ASSIGNMENT OF COPYRIGHT

An assignment of copyright must be in writing and signed by or on behalf of the assignor (Section 36 (3) of the Act), but no other formality is required. If signed on behalf of the assignor, the person signing must have the authority of the assignor to sign; see *Beloff* v. *Pressdram Ltd.* 1973 F.S.R. 33. Copyright may be assigned for certain areas, or for a certain period, or the right may be assigned to do certain of the acts which the copyright owner has the exclusive right to do (e.g. the right to make adaptations, the right to perform, and publishing rights). The right to do acts not separately mentioned in the Act may now be assigned separately.

Future copyright (that is, copyright which will, or may, come into existence in respect of any future work, or on the coming into operation of any of the provisions of the Act, or in any other future event), will vest, on the coming into existence of the copyright, in the assignee under a purported assignment of such copyright, without any further document: such assignment must, however, be in writing, and signed by or on behalf of the prospective owner of such copyright (Section 37 (1) of the Act). In drafting publishing agreements and other transactions, authors will therefore have carefully to consider these provisions.

LICENCES

A mere licence to publish or perform or to do other acts which the copyright owner has the exclusive right to do, does not require to be in writing (unless exclusive, and then only to enable the licensee to sue), but may be implied from conduct (see *Solar Thomson Engineering Co. Ltd.* v. *Barton* 1977 R.P.C. 537 licence implied from wording of patent). Licences in writing may be granted by a prospective owner of copyright in relation to his prospective interest therein

(Section 37 (3) of the Act). The principal distinction between the position of an assignee and a licensee is that the former can, but the latter cannot, except in the case of an exclusive licence in writing, sue third parties for the infringement of the right. Other distinctions are referred to under "Publishing Agreements" *post*. However, if a licence (in the Act called an "exclusive licence") is made in writing, and signed by or on behalf of the owner or prospective owner of copyright, authorising the licensee exclusively to do any of the acts which the copyright owner has the exclusive right to do, then the licensee has (except against the owner of the copyright) the same remedies for damages, etc., as if the licence had been an assignment, subject to the owner of the copyright, either being joined as Plaintiff or added as Defendant in certain circumstances (Section 19 of the Act). A licensee, like an assignee, may make alterations in the work unless the terms of the licence expressly or impliedly forbid alterations being made and the courts will readily imply such a term (*Frisby* v. *BBC* 1967 2 W.L.R. 1204). The extent of an implied licence to use an architect's plans has been considered in *Blair* v. *Osborne & Tomkins* 1971 2 W.L.R. 503 and *Stovin-Bradford* v. *Volpoint Properties Ltd.*, 1971 3 W.L.R. 256.

No copyright licence is required in respect of out of copyright works, though it is not always easy to ascertain whether or not a work is still in copyright. Art galleries, for instance, often charge a fee for the right to enter the gallery and to take a photograph of a work of art there, but this is normally a condition of entry into the gallery and has nothing to do with copyright. In many cases the work of art will be out of copyright or, if in copyright, the gallery will probably not be the owner of such copyright and should not permit the photograph to be taken. In either of which cases the gallery would not be entitled to charge a fee in respect of copyright.

It has recently been held by the House of Lords, in *British Leyland etc Ltd.* v. *Armstrong etc Ltd.* 1986 2 W.L.R. 400 that the owners of the copyrights in drawings for car spare parts were not allowed to derogate from grant to prevent the manufacture of parts solely for repair. The basis of this decision is novel and would appear to go further than implied licence.

WHAT CONSTITUTES INFRINGEMENT

Copyright is infringed by the doing or the authorising of the doing of certain restricted acts, without the licence of the copyright owner. Authorise means to grant or purport to grant a third person the right to do the act complained of, whether the intention is that the grantee shall do the act on his own account or only on account of the grantor: *Amstrad etc PLC* v. *The British Phongraphic Industry Ltd.* 1986 F.S.R. 159. Thus copyright is infringed by the reproduction of any substantial part of a copyright work without permission. Such infringements are proved by a detailed comparison of similarities, and proof is often difficult in the case of compilations which, of necessity, resemble one another; in such cases, copying may be proved from the coincidence of trifling errors. In considering whether the part taken is substantial, more regard is had to the importance than to the quantity of what is taken; *Ladbroke (Football) Ltd.* v. *William Hill (Football) Ltd.* 1964 1 W.L.R. 273. Thus, to take a few bars of the essential melody of a tune may constitute an infringement. An infringement is committed whether the copying has been directly from the original, or through an intervening copy, and may be committed where the copying is from memory; *Francis Day & Hunter, Ltd.* v. *Bron* 1963 2 W.L.R. 868. See *Solar* supra as to the risks of infringing, even where an independent designer is used, because of the instructions which he has to be given to produce the work by a person with knowledge of the copyright work or of an object made therefrom.

Other modes of infringement are: to publish an unpublished work, (if already published in the relevant territory the only infringement of a similar kind may be sale with knowledge; see below and *Infabrics Ltd.* v. *Jaytex Ltd.* (H.L.) 1982 A.C.1.), to make an adaptation of a work, which latter includes making a version of the work in which the story or action is conveyed wholly, or mainly, by means of pictures in a form suitable for reproduction in a book, or in a newspaper, magazine or similar periodical, making a translation, dramatising a book and making a novel of a play. (See the 1985 Act as to reproduction in relation to computers and as to adaptations of computer programs.) (See also "Performance", "Films", "Records", "Broadcasting and Television and Cable Programmes" *post*, and "Published Editions", *ante*.) It has been held that to parody a work, such as a picture or a play, may not be an infringement if the parody amounts to an original work and does not reproduce a substantial part of the Plaintiff's work (*Joy Music, Ltd.* v. *Sunday Pictorial Newspapers* (1920), *Ltd.* 1960 2 W.L.R. 645, *Schweppes Ltd.* v. *Wellingtons Ltd.* 1984 F.S.R. 210). Further, to copy an idea or concept as against the form in which it is expressed, is not an infringement; *L.B. (Plastics) Ltd.* v. *Swish Products Ltd.* 1979 F.S.R. 145 (H.L.).

In addition to the infringements above described, an infringement is committed by anyone who knowingly sells, exhibits in public, distributes or imports (otherwise than for private and domestic use) copies unlawfully made (Section 5 of the Act). It is to be noted that in these cases proof of knowledge is essential, and, in practice, it may be difficult to establish these offences, except by giving express notice, and taking action if the offence is committed thereafter. On the other hand proof of knowledge is not necessary where a claim for conversion is made. A converter need not be an infringer; (*WEA Records Ltd.* v *Benson King (Sales) Ltd.*, 1975 1 W.L.R. 44.), but conversion cannot be claimed if there has been no infringement (*Infabrics* supra).

PERFORMANCE IN PUBLIC

It is an infringement to perform any substantial part of a literary, dramatic or musical work in public, and to permit a place of public entertainment to be used for private profit for such a performance. Whether a performance is "in public" is a question of fact in each case. It is not necessary that every member of the public shall have access, or that a charge shall be made for admission. The character of the audience is the decisive factor (see *P.R.S. Limited* v. *Harlequin Record Shops Limited* 1979 F.S.R. 233, where performance of musical records in a record shop was held to be a performance in public of the music recorded). Performances at clubs or institutes with limited membership are therefore generally in public for this purpose (see *P.R.S. Limited* v. *Rangers F.C. Supporters Club Greenock,* 1975 R.P.C. 626, held performance at such Club "in public"). In *Rank Film Production Ltd.* v. *Colin S. Dodds* (1983 New South Wales) the viewing of films on T.V. sets in guest rooms at a motel held to be in public. A place of public entertainment is defined by the Act (Section 5(6)), as including any premises which are occupied mainly for other purposes, but are from time to time made available for hire to persons desiring to hire them for purposes of public entertainment (see also "Sound Recordings", "Broadcasting and Television and Cable Programmes" *post*).

EXCEPTIONS TO LIABILITY FOR INFRINGEMENT

It cannot of course be an infringement if the consent of the owner of the copyright has been given expressly or is to be implied.

No fair dealing with literary, dramatic, musical and artistic works for purposes of research or private study is an infringement of the copyright therein. Nor is a fair dealing with such works an infringement if it is for the purposes of criticism or review of the work itself or another work, if accompanied by a sufficient acknowledgement. "Sufficient acknowledgement" is defined by the Act (Section 6 (10)). (As to the test of "fair dealing" see *post* article **Subsidiary Rights**). In *Sillitoe* v. *McGraw-Hill Book Company (U.K.) Ltd.,* 1983 F.S.R. 545, it was held that booklets for the use of students studying in copyright works ('Coles Notes') were infringements and that the exceptions of research or private study and criticism or review did not apply in the circumstances of that case.

Some other exceptions in the Act as amended (Sections 6, 9 and 14A) are: reporting current events in newspapers, etc., if accompanied by a sufficient acknowledgement, or by means of broadcasting, or in a film; reproduction for the purposes of judicial proceedings (this applies equally to films and sound and television broadcasts and cable programmes); reading or reciting in public extracts of works, if accompanied by a sufficient acknowledgement; including passages in collections intended for schools, if accompanied by a sufficient acknowledgement. Also: copying works of artistic craftsmanship and sculptures exhibited in public, copying works of architecture; including artistic works as backgrounds to films or television broadcasts; reconstructing buildings which are works of architecture. In Section 15 of the Act, making reproductions by or on behalf of librarians of the typographical arrangement of a published edition. In Section 41 of the Act, reproducing the work, or an adaptation thereof, in the course of instruction for schools, or as part of examination questions and answers. In Section 42 of the Act, making or supplying reproductions of public records.

Section 7 of the Act provides that the making or supplying of copies of articles contained in periodical publications, and of parts of published literary, dramatic, and musical works (not being such articles), and any illustrations thereof, by, or on behalf of, the librarian of a library of a class prescribed by Board of Trade Regulations, is not an infringement. (1957, S.I. No. 868).

Section 8 of the Act provides that the copyright in a musical work is not infringed by making a record of the work or of an adaptation thereof if certain conditions are complied with.

It should be observed, however, that ignorance was no defence even if reasonable in the circumstances; printers ran considerable risks in this connection since they had often no means of knowing that an infringement was being committed but they were nevertheless liable. However, now, in proceedings for conversion of infringing copies, damages cannot be recovered from an innocent defendant.

WHO IS LIABLE FOR INFRINGEMENT

In the case of an infringement by the publication of a copy, the author, publisher and printer of the infringing work are equally liable.

Where an infringement is committed by performances in public, not only the actual performers, but the firm or company by whom they are employed are liable.

Greater difficulty arises in the determination of the liability of hirers of films, owners of halls, and other persons who have not infringed either personally or by their actual servants. It is an infringement, however, to "authorise" the doing of any infringing act; see "What Constitutes Infringement" *ante*. In *Amstrad* supra held that the sale of tape to tape recorders did not amount to authorising acts of infringement by purchasers thereof. Section 5 (5) of the Act, however, provides that a person who permits a place of public entertainment to be used for a performance in public of a work, does not infringe the copyright in the work, if he was not aware, and had no reasonable grounds for suspecting, that the performance would be an infringement or, if he gave his permission gratuitously, or for a nominal consideration, or for a consideration not exceeding his estimated expenses consequential from the use of the place for the performance.

THE REMEDIES FOR INFRINGEMENT

A copyright owner whose right is infringed is, in general, entitled as of right to an injunction, i.e. an Order of the Court restraining the Defendant from repeating the infringement, and can insist upon such an Order, although offered a personal undertaking first. It is to be noted, however, that such an Order will be directed only to repetition of the actual infringement; i.e. an Order cannot normally be obtained to restrain copying of future parts of a serial story because earlier parts have been copied; but see *Independent Television Productions Ltd.*, supra.

A second remedy is damages for infringement. These are usually based upon evidence of loss suffered by the Plaintiff, i.e. that if the infringing book had not been published, he would have been able to publish more copies of his own book or that he otherwise has lost a market for his material. Damages for infringement, may, however, be increased, in effect, by way of an award of exemplary damages if the Court, having regard to the flagrancy of the infringement, and any benefit shown to have accrued to the Defendant by reason of the infringement, is satisfied that effective relief is not otherwise available to the Plaintiff (Section 17 (3) of the Act and see *Beloff* v. *Pressdram Ltd.* 1973 F.S.R. 33 and *Ravenscroft* v. *Herbert* 1980 R.P.C. 193). It is permissible, in assessing damages, to have regard to the sort of fee which would have been asked if a licence had been requested. However, if it is proved or admitted that, at the time of infringement, the Defendant was not aware, and had no reasonable grounds for suspecting, that copyright subsisted in the work, the Plaintiff cannot recover infringement damages from the Defendant (Section 17 (2) of the Act). In view of the fact that every work enjoys copyright without formality, such ignorance is difficult to establish, except in special circumstances such as where it might be reasonably thought that the work was out of copyright, or not protected in this country.

Damages, however, can also be based upon a claim for conversion, upon the principle that the infringing material is deemed, by the Act, the property of the copyright owner: Torts (*Interference with Goods*) Act 1977. Under this head, regard is had, not to the loss to the copyright owner, but to the value of the infringing work. Where only a portion of the work containing the infringement represents infringing material, it is necessary, first to assess the value of the infringing work as a whole by reference to the sale price of each copy multiplied by the number of copies disposed of, and then to assess the damages at that fraction of this figure which the infringing material bears to the whole. Where the portion of the whole which is infringing is relatively slight, e.g. in the case of an infringing article in a newspaper, this calculation is difficult. However, a plaintiff is not entitled to damages for conversion if it is proved or admitted that, at the time of conversion, either that the defendant was not aware and had no reasonable grounds for suspecting that copyright subsisted in the work, or that the defendant believed, and had reasonable grounds for believing, that the articles converted were not infringing copies (Section 18 (2) of the Act, and see "What Constitutes Infringement" *ante*). Although damages for infringement and damages for conversion are cumulative, not alternative, so that, in appropriate cases, a successful plaintiff may be able to recover both, this is subject to the principle of overlap. In *Lewis Trusts* v. *Bambers Stores Ltd.*, 1983 F.S.R. 453, the Court of Appeal, by a majority, held that overlap did occur and that, in the circumstances of that case, the plaintiff was restricted to the conversion damages only.

An alternative remedy is an account of profits. Here the claim is based, not upon the value of the infringing material, but upon the amount of profit made by the defendant in respect of the infringement, and the plaintiff is entitled to this relief even where the defendant's ignorance of the subsistence of copyright in the work is proved or admitted.

In addition to the foregoing remedies a successful plaintiff is entitled to have delivered up to him all infringing material in the defendant's possession.

The Act, unlike the Act of 1911, does not specifically provide for any period during which a copyright action may be brought, so that, presumably, the Limitation Act of 1939 (and now the Limitation Act 1980) will apply (see Section 18 (1) proviso of the Act). Therefore the period for bringing actions in respect of infringements of copyright will be six years from the infringement, and, in respect of actions for conversion of infringing copies, will be six years from the conversion whether there is only one conversion, or a succession of conversions. Under the Act of 1911 the period in each case was three years.

There are further restrictions on the remedies obtainable in the case of exclusive licensees (Section 19 of the Act) and in relation to buildings (Section 17 (4) of the Act).

Section 20 of the Act provides for various presumptions of facts in copyright actions. These deal with the subsistence of copyright in a work, the owner of the copyright, the author of the work, the originality of the work, the first publication of the work, and the maker and date and place of first publication of records. These presumptions can greatly simplify the evidence which would be required in a copyright action.

The above remedies are enforceable by civil action.

OTHER REMEDIES

In addition to the remedies above mentioned there are certain special forms of procedure open to persons whose rights are infringed.

Certain infringements of copyright constitute a criminal offence rendering the offender liable to fines or imprisonment (Section 21 of the Act as amended); as to a conspiracy to contravene Section 21 of the Act see *Scott* v. *Metropolitan Police Commissioner* 1974 3 W.L.R. 741. It should be noted, however, that proof of knowledge that an infringement is being committed is essential in all these cases.

It is breach of statutory duty, but not a criminal offence, in relation to literary, dramatic, musical and artistic works without licence: (1) to affix another person's name on a work of which that person is not the author, so as to imply that the other person is the author; (2) to publish, or sell, a work, or reproductions thereof, on which the other person's name has been affixed, knowing that person is not the author; (3) to perform in public, or broadcast, a work, as being a work of which another person is the author, knowing that other person is not the author; (4) to publish or sell an altered artistic work, or reproduction of the altered artistic work, as being the unaltered work, or a reproduction of the unaltered work, knowing that is not the case, and (5) to publish, sell, or distribute reproductions of an artistic work as reproductions made by the author, knowing that is not the case (Section 43 of the Act). Damages are recoverable where such an offence has been committed. "Name" includes initials or a monogram. The right of action under Section 43 is not limited to professional authors and, where the claim under Section 43 is linked to another cause of action, such as defamation, a separate award of damages can be given as respects Section 43 if the other cause of action does not cover the injury caused by the false attribution of authorship; *Moore* v. *News of the World Ltd.* 1972 2 W.L.R. 419.

Provision is also made (Section 22 of the Act), for the detention by the Customs authorities of infringing copies of copyright works made abroad to be imported into the United Kingdom.

THE DURATION OF COPYRIGHT PROTECTION

The normal period of copyright protection is during the life of the author and fifty years from the end of the calendar year in which he died (Sections 2 (3) and

3 (4) of the Act). In the case of a work of joint authorship, the protection, if it has not expired before the commencement of the Act (see below), extends during the life of the author who dies last and fifty years from the end of the calendar year in which he died (paragraph 2, Third Schedule to the Act).

The Act contains special provisions for determining the period of copyright in relation to works of joint authorship, which are first published under two or more names, of which one or more of the names, or all the names, are pseudonyms (paragraph 3, Third Schedule to the Act).

In the case of literary, dramatic or musical works which have not been published, performed in public, broadcast or included in a cable programme before the death of the author, the period is fifty years from the end of the calendar year which includes the earliest occasion on which one of these acts is done (Section 2 (3) of the Act as amended). In the case of engravings not published before the death of the author, the period is fifty years from the end of the calendar year in which they are first published (Section 3 (4) of the Act). For photographs, except those made before the commencement of the Act (see below), the period is fifty years from the end of the calendar year in which the photograph is first published (Section 3 (4) of the Act). For Government publications the period for literary, dramatic and musical works, if published, is until fifty years from the end of the calendar year in which it is first published, and for artistic works fifty years from the end of the calendar year in which the work was made; but, if the artistic work is an engraving or photograph, the period is fifty years from the end of the calendar year in which the engraving or photograph is first published (Section 39 (3) and (4) of the Act). (See as to duration of copyright in "Published Editions" and "Anonymous and Pseudonymous works" *ante* and see "Films", "Sound Recordings", "Broadcasting and Television and Cable Programmes" *post*).

In the case of works which were in existence before the commencement of the Act of 1911 (July 1, 1912) the terms of copyright above described apply if the work enjoyed copyright at such date (paragraph 35, Seventh Schedule to the Act). This involves an examination of the terms of copyright subsisting under the various Acts in force before 1912. In general, protection under these Acts was the life of the author and seven years, or forty-two years from publication (whichever was the longer), but different terms of copyright were given by the various Acts dealing with artistic works.

Where the copyright in a pre-Act of 1911 work has been assigned before 1912, and copyright subsists therein by virtue of any provisions of the Act, such copyright reverts to the author or his assigns at the expiration of the old term of copyright applicable to the work (paragraph 38, Seventh Schedule to the Act), but subject to various options in favour of the assignee.

In the case of records and photographs coming into existence after July 1, 1912, but before the commencement of the Act, the Seventh Schedule to the Act provides that the period of copyright under the Act of 1911 shall apply; further, copyright is not to subsist under the Act in a joint work first published after July 1, 1912, but before the commencement of the Act, if the period of copyright under the Act of 1911 in that work expired before the commencement of the Act. This is because the Act provides different periods for these works from those under the Act of 1911. (See as to assignments before 1957 under the Act of 1911 "Generally" *ante*.)

FILMS

(1) Under the Act copyright now subsists in films as such (Section 13 of the Act), but without prejudice to the copyright in any literary, dramatic, musical or artistic works from which the subject-matter is derived (Section 16 (6) of the Act). Thus, there is now copyright in the film itself, and a separate copyright in its subject-

matter, whereas under the Act of 1911, films were protected only as to their constituent parts such as photographs, and, in most cases, as dramatic works. The new film copyright is not to subsist in films made before the commencement of the Act, but the Act provides for the protection of such films if they were dramatic works, and of the photographs forming part of such films (paragraphs 14-16, Seventh Schedule to the Act).

(2) "Film" is defined by the Act (Section 13 (10)), and includes the sounds embodied in any sound track associated with the film. The definition is considered to cover video tapes. Copyright subsists in every film of which the maker was a qualified person for the whole, or a substantial part, of the period during which the film was made, or which is first published in the United Kingdom. The "maker" of a film is defined as the person by whom the arrangements necessary for the making of the film are undertaken, and he is entitled to the copyright in the film. Film copyright subsists, if the film is registrable under Part II of the Films Act, 1960, until registration, and thereafter until fifty years from the end of the calendar year in which it is so registered. If not so registrable, then until the film is published and fifty years from the end of the year in which it is first published; if copyright only subsists in such a film by virtue of its place of publication, then until fifty years from the end of the calendar year in which it was first published.

A form of infringement peculiar to film copyright is to cause the film, in so far as it consists of visual images, to be seen in public, or, in so far as it consists of sounds, to be heard in public, except in the case of newsreel films where fifty years have elapsed from the end of the calendar year in which the principal events depicted in the film occurred. Another act of infringement of the copyright in a film is to make a copy of it. In *Spelling Goldberg Productions Inc.* v. *B.P.C. Publishing Ltd.* 1981 R.P.C. 283 it was held that to make a copy of one frame of a film was to make a copy of it.

(3) It is an infringement of the copyright in a novel, or story, to convert it into a film, whether the actual language of the literary work is taken or not. But something more than a mere plot or idea must be taken; it must be proved that the film adopts a substantial part of the incidents used in the story to work out the plot.

There is no copyright in a scene in actual life, e.g. sporting events, so that the organiser has no remedy in the case of the filming of such events provided that the film can be taken without trespass, and the passer-by cannot complain if he is filmed in the street.

(4) Under the Act of 1911, the making of a film involved the creation of an artistic work, i.e. a series of photographs, and, unless it was merely a record of passing events, the creation of a dramatic work. The first owner of the artistic copyright was the owner of the negative at the time it was made, whereas the first owner of the dramatic work copyright might have been difficult to determine. In fact a commercial film used to involve the exercise of a number of separate copyrights since, at each stage of its inception, a separate copyright work might have been produced, e.g. story, screen dialogue and the film as finally cut, and the ownership of copyright would depend upon the agreements of the various parties concerned with the film company.

SOUND RECORDINGS

The Act provides that copyright subsists in every sound recording of which the maker was a qualified person at the time the recording was made, or which has been first published in the United Kingdom (Section 12 of the Act). "Sound recording" is defined by the Act as meaning the aggregate of the sounds embodied in, and capable of being produced by means of, a record of any description other than a film sound track.

The maker of the sound recording is entitled to the copyright therein, except where sound recordings are commissioned, and the "maker" is defined as the person who owns the first record at the time the recording is made. Copyright in sound recordings subsists for a period of fifty years from the end of the calendar year in which the record is first published.

Such copyright can be infringed by making a record of the recording or causing the recording to be heard in public, but it is not an infringement to allow the recording to be heard in public (i) as part of the amenities for the residents of any premises where persons reside or sleep unless a special charge for admission is made, or (ii) as part of the activities of a club or other non-profit-making organisation whose main objects are charitable unless a charge is made for admission, and any of the proceeds are not applied for the purposes of the organisation. In *Phonographic Performance Ltd.* v. *Pontins Ltd.* 1967 3 W.L.R. 1622 it was held that the holiday camp there in question constituted premises where persons reside or sleep and that, on the facts of that case, records were caused to be heard in public as part of the amenities provided exclusively or mainly for residents or inmates of that camp. If a record of music is performed in public, a licence to perform is required in respect of the record as well as in respect of the music itself. (But see below as to broadcast performances).

The Seventh Schedule to the Act contains provisions relating to the subsistence of copyright under the Act in records made before July 1, 1912.

A literary, dramatic or musical work is infringed by making a record of it or including it in the sound track of a film (Sections 2 (5)(*a*) and 48 (1) of the Act). The right to record such a work is therefore a valuable right and is quite distinct from the publishing right and performing right.

There are, however, a complicated series of provisions (Section 8 of the Act) under which, when a musical work has been once recorded with the consent of the copyright owner, it can be recorded thereafter by anyone else on payment of a fixed royalty, the payment whereof is in general secured by the issue of adhesive stamps to be attached to the record. The normal royalty is 6¼ per cent of the ordinary retail selling price of the record with the minimum of .313p for each work reproduced on a single record. In December 1976 a public enquiry was held to consider whether the royalty rates should be varied; the result is "no change". Where the retail selling price was partly cash and partly three chocolate wrappers, it was held by the House of Lords in *Chappell & Co. Ltd.* v. *The Nestle Co. Ltd.*, 1953 3 W.L.R. 168 that the section did not apply. As to the manner of calculating the royalty see *Discount etc. Ltd.* v. *Micrometro Ltd.* 1984 R.P.C. 198.

BROADCASTING AND TELEVISION AND CABLE PROGRAMMES

(1) The Act for the first time establishes copyright in television and sound broadcasts as such, if made by the B.B.C. or the I.B.A., and from a place in the United Kingdom (Section 14 of the Act). This right is therefore limited in this country to broadcasts by these two bodies and the copyright in their broadcasts vests in them. Further, copyright does not so subsist by virtue of the Act in television and sound broadcasts made before the commencement of the Act. "Television broadcast" means visual images broadcast by way of television together with any sounds broadcast for reception with those images, and "sound broadcast" means sounds broadcast otherwise than as part of a television broadcast. "Broadcasting" is defined by the Act (Section 48 (2)). By reason of 1959 S.I. No. 2215 1960 S.I. No. 847 1961 S.I. Nos. 60, 2460, 2462 and 2463 1962 S.I. Nos. 1642, 1643, 2184 and 2185 1963 S.I. Nos. 1037, 1038, 1039 and 1147 1964 S.I. No. 689 1965 S.I. Nos. 1858, 1859, 2009, 2010, and 2158, 1966 S.I. Nos. 79 and 685, 1967 S.I. No. 974, 1972 S.I. No. 1724, 1979 S.I. No. 910 and 1984 S.I. No. 541 copyright now subsists in broadcasts made in the Isle of Man,

Sarawak, Gibraltar, Fiji, Uganda, Zanzibar, Bermuda, North Borneo, Bahamas, Virgin Islands, Falkland Islands, St. Helena, Seychelles, Kenya, Mauritius, Montserrat, St. Lucia, Botswana, Cayman Islands, Grenada, British Honduras, St. Vincent, Hong Kong and the British Indian Ocean Territory. By reason of 1979 S.I. No. 1715 as amended copyright now subsists in sound broadcasts made in Austria, Barbados, Brazil, Chile, Colombia, Congo (People's Republic), Costa Rica, Czechoslovakia, Denmark, Ecuador, El Salvador, Federal Republic of Germany and Berlin (West), Fiji, Finland, Guatemala, Ireland, Italy, Luxembourg, Mexico, Niger, Norway, Panama, Paraguay, Philippines, Sweden and Uruguay, and in television broadcasts made in Austria, Barbados, Belgium, Brazil, Chile, Colombia, Congo (People's Republic), Costa Rica, Cyprus, Czechoslovakia, Denmark, Ecuador, El Salvador, Federal Republic of Germany and Berlin (West), Fiji, Finland, France, Guatemala, Ireland, Italy, Luxembourg, Mexico, Niger, Norway, Panama, Paraguay, Philippines, Spain, Sweden and Uruguay; see as to protection in Gibraltar and in Bermuda 1979 S.I. No.1715 as amended.

Copyright in television and sound broadcasts subsists until the end of fifty years from the end of the calendar year in which the broadcast is made. Such copyright is infringed *inter alia* (*a*) in the case of television broadcasts in so far as it consists of visual images, by making a film of it otherwise than for private purposes, or by causing it to be seen in public by a paying audience: in so far as it consists of sounds, by making a record of it otherwise than for private purposes, or by causing it to be heard in public by a paying audience, (*b*) in the case of a sound broadcast, by making a record of it otherwise than for private purposes and (*c*) in the case of television and sound broadcasts, including it in a cable programme in certain circumstances. Where the alleged infringement is of the visual images of a television broadcast, it is only necessary to prove that the act in question extended to a sequence of images sufficient to be seen as a moving picture. Further, the Act provides that television broadcasts are seen or heard by a paying audience, if seen or heard by persons who either (i) have been admitted for payment to the place where the broadcast is seen or heard and are not (*a*) residents of such place nor (*b*) members of a club or society where the payment is only for membership and the provision of facilities for seeing or hearing television broadcasts is only incidental to the main purposes of the club or society, or (ii) have been admitted to such place in circumstances where goods or services are supplied at prices which exceed the price usually charged at that place, and are partly attributable to the facilities afforded for seeing or hearing the broadcasts.

The Cable and Broadcasting Act 1984 for the first time establishes copyright in cable programmes included in a cable programme service provided in the United Kingdom, but not if the programme is included in the cable programme service by the reception and immediate re-transmission of a television or sound broadcast. This protection only applies to cable programmes included in a cable programme service after the 1st January 1985. Copyright in a programme exists if included in a cable programme service provided by, for instance, a United Kingdom company, and subsists (with certain restrictions) until the end of the period of 50 years from the end of the calendar year in which the programme was included in the service. The acts of infringement in relation to a cable programme are similar to those for broadcasts. The copyright belongs to the person providing the service which includes the programme.

(2) Literary, dramatic and musical works, records and films are infringed by broadcasting them and including them in a cable programme, and artistic works are infringed by including such works in a television broadcast or in a cable programme: since these rights are now additional to the right to perform in public, authors will need to consider this when drafting agreements. If broadcast performances, for instance, in the case of sound broadcasts, are played from a

loud-speaker in a public place, this in general involves a separate public performance not covered by any licence to perform given to the broadcasting body, but if the broadcast is from a record, the performance of the broadcast does not, as under the Act of 1911, infringe the copyright in the record as well (Section 40 (1) of the Act); and see Section 40A as to Cable Programmes. And, dramatising a literary work for the purposes of a broadcast would infringe the right to make adaptations thereof, unless the necessary licence had been given. In *Independent Television Companies Association Ltd.* v. *P.R.S. Ltd.,* The Times 23 November 1982, it was held that television programme contractors, as well as The Independent Broadcasting Authority, were broadcasting and one or other needed a licence to broadcast works in the P.R.S. repertoire.

PERFORMING RIGHT TRIBUNAL

The Act (Sections 23-30), (as amended by the Copyright (Amendment) Act 1971 and the Cable and Broadcasting Act 1984), for the first time establishes a Tribunal, in particular to control licence fees, but it is concerned only with disputes between licensing bodies and persons, or organisations, concerned in the public performance of works. See as to the Isle of Man 1971 S.I. No. 1848 and as to Hong Kong 1979 S.I. No. 910. By definition, licensing body excludes organisations whose objects only include negotiation or granting of individual licences each relating to a single work, or works of a single author, where such licences are to do acts with which a writer is most concerned, e.g. licences to perform in public, or broadcast, or include in a cable programme, literary, dramatic and musical works, or adaptations thereof. Writers, other than perhaps songwriters, are not likely, therefore, to be concerned with the Tribunal, and, where necessary, expert advice should be taken.

The Tribunal consists of a chairman, who can be either a barrister or solicitor, or a person who has held judicial office, and not less than two, nor more than four other members appointed by the Board of Trade. The Fourth Schedule to the Act contains provisions relative to the functions of the Tribunal. Questions of law may be referred to the High Court before, and in some circumstances after, the Tribunal has given its decision, see *AIRC Limited* v. *PPL Limited* 1983 F.S.R. 637. Rules relating to the Tribunal came into operation on 1st June 1957 (1957 S.I. No. 924 as amended) and have been revoked and replaced by other rules (1965 S.I. No. 1506 as amended by 1971 S.I. No. 636). Upon a reference to the Tribunal under Section 25 of the Act by the Scottish Ballroom Association, the Tribunal varied a 1957 fee tariff and upon an application under Section 27 of the Act by Southern Television Limited the Tribunal held that a clause in a draft licence to perform was unreasonable. During 1960 references were made to the Tribunal in respect of the *Juke Box* tariffs both of the P.R.S. for music and the P.P. Ltd. for records, in each case the tariffs were in substance confirmed. In 1965 the Tribunal determined the terms and charges on which the Isle of Man Broadcasting Company Limited could broadcast records. In 1967, and again in 1972, the Tribunal determined the terms and charges on which the BBC could broadcast music. In 1978 the Court, reversing the decision of the Tribunal, held that the jurisdiction of the Tribunal did not extend to licences to authorise public performance; *Reditune Ltd.* v. *PRS* 1981 F.S.R. 165. The main decision, in a reference before the Tribunal concerned with the broadcasting of sound recordings on independent local radio, was given in 1980, but the proceedings are not yet complete. In February 1982 the Tribunal gave its decision on a preliminary point in a reference concerned with the broadasting of music on independent television; this was appealed to the court by case stated, with the result mentioned above, reported in The Times 23 November 1982. The final decision of the Tribunal was given on the 19 October 1983.

PUBLISHING AGREEMENTS

The simplest form of publishing agreement is a mere licence to publish in a newspaper or periodical for a single payment. The terms of such agreements usually depend upon implication, or trade custom. Where an article is sent to a periodical without a covering letter, there will be implied, on the one hand a licence to publish, and on the other, an agreement to pay such remuneration as is normal and reasonable. If the article is kept, and the author is sent a proof for revision, the author is entitled to a fee, even if the work is not actually published.

Where a work is to be published on royalty terms, it is important from the point of view of the author that he does not assign his copyright, but only grants a licence. If he assigns, he will not be able to prevent the publisher from selling the rights in the work. He may be seriously prejudiced if the publisher gets into financial difficulties. Some protection is given to authors under Section 60 of the Bankruptcy Act 1914, but this is not available where the publisher is a limited company. A licence, however, is generally personal to the publisher, even if this is not expressly stated, and provision can be made to protect the author in the case of insolvency of the publisher. A difficult question concerns the extent to which works may be altered, the most important consideration being whether the author has assigned his copyright, or merely granted a licence to publish. If the former, then the assignee may freely alter, subject to possible proceedings by the author for defamation, malicious falsehood or under section 43 of the Act. If the latter, then alterations may be freely made by the publisher unless the licence expressly or implicitly forbids it, but subject to defamation and so on as before. However the courts will be very willing to imply a term limiting the right to make alterations: *Frisby* v. *BBC* 1967 2 W.L.R. 1204. There may be cases, however, where it could be established to the satisfaction of the court that custom permits reasonable alterations, at least of unsigned articles.

It is often difficult to determine whether the words used involve an assignment, or a licence, and this should be clearly expressed. However, an exclusive licensee under a written exclusive licence now has, under the Act, the same rights of action and remedies as if the licence has been an assignment (see "Licences", *ante*).

The publishing agreement, in the interests of the author, should require publication within some fixed time, should deal with the style and price of publication, the method of advertising, the number of free copies allowed, and provide for proper accounts.

Publishing agreements often provide options to the publisher to acquire other rights in a work such as rights to make adaptations, including translations and dramatisation rights and rights to broadcast and include in a cable programme (see "Broadcasting and Television and Cable Programmes", *ante*), film rights, and rights to publish abroad. From the author's point of view it is usually preferable that such rights should be granted on royalty terms rather than for a single payment. In view of the provisions of the Act as to future copyright, care should be taken when drafting an agreement (see "Assignment of Copyright", *ante*). In drafting agreements regard should also be had to the provisions of the Treaty of Rome which have been given legal effect in the United Kingdom by the European Communities Act 1972.

Apart from express agreement a publisher may be entitled to dispose of stock in hand after the licence is determined, since such stock, having been lawfully made, does not constitute infringing copies.

WORKS ORIGINATING ABROAD

The Act, except as extended by Order in Council, applies only within the United Kingdom, including Northern Ireland (Sections 31, 32 and 51 of the Act), whereas the Act of 1911, in practice, applied throughout the British Commonwealth.

Therefore, there will now be one code for the United Kingdom and other codes for other parts of the Commonwealth, unless the Act, or similar legislation, is in force there. This may not necessarily occur.

Orders in Council under the Act may direct that any of the provisions of the Act shall (*a*) extend to the Channel Islands, the Colonies and Dependencies and (*b*) apply to any other countries to which those provisions do not extend. By an Order (1957 S.I. No. 1523), which came into operation on the 27th September, 1957 (the date at which the Universal Copyright Convention came into effect between the U.K. and other members), as amended, the Act was applied to works originating in Universal Copyright or Berne Convention countries. At that time this included most of the world except the U.S.S.R. This Order for the first time protected works first published in the U.S.A. which was not a member of the Berne Union. This Order and its ancillary orders were largely revoked and replaced by a further Order (1964 S.I. No. 690), which was itself amended and revoked and replaced by another Order (1972 S.I. No. 673 as amended), which, with its amending orders, has now been revoked and replaced by another Order, 1979 S.I. No. 1715, now amended. Under this Order the Act has been applied to works originating *inter alia* in the U.S.S.R. By a further order (1985 S.I. No. 1777) the Act has been applied to works originating in Taiwan. By an Order (1959 S.I. No. 861), the Act was extended to the Isle of Man; such order was amended by 1970 S.I. No. 1437; see 1971 S.I. No. 1848. By further Orders 1959 S.I. No. 2215, 1960 S.I. No. 847 (and 1985 S.I. No. 198), 1961 S.I. Nos. 60, 2462 and 2463, 1962 S.I. Nos. 629, 1642 (and 1985 S.I. No. 1985), 2184 and 2185 (and 1985 S.I. No. 1988), 1963 S.I. Nos. 1037, 1038, 1039 and 1147, 1964 S.I. No. 689, 1965 S.I. Nos. 1858 (and 1985 S.I. No. 1987), 1859, 2009, 2010 and 2158, 1966 S.I. Nos. 79 and 685, 1967 S.I. No. 974, 1972 S.I. No. 1724, 1979 S.I. No. 910 and 1984 S.I. No. 541 the Act was extended to Sarawak, Gibraltar, Fiji, Uganda, Zanzibar, Bermuda, North Borneo, Virgin Islands, Falkland Islands, St. Helena, Seychelles, Kenya, Mauritius, Monserrat, St. Lucia, Botswana, Cayman Islands, Grenada, Guyana, British Honduras, St. Vincent, Hong Kong and the British Indian Ocean Territory, respectively. Works originating in British Colonies other than Sarawak, Gibraltar, Fiji, Uganda, Zanzibar, Bermuda, North Borneo, Virgin Islands, Falkland Islands, St. Helena, Seychelles, Kenya, Mauritius, Monserrat, St. Lucia, Botswana, Cayman Islands, Grenada, Guyana, British Honduras, St. Vincent, Hong Kong and the British Indian Ocean Teritory are still protected under the old law as no new Orders have yet been made, as are existing works of foreign origin. In those cases the place of first publication remains of substantial importance. A work is deemed first published within the United Kingdom, or in any other country, if published there within thirty days (or 14 days in the case of existing works) after first publication elsewhere (Section 49 (2)(*d*) of the Act), and a work is published if reproductions are issued to the public in such quantities as are reasonably necessary to meet the public demand.

Copyright throughout the British Empire extended, prior to the commencement of the Act, to works first published in countries of the Copyright Union, and unpublished works of authors who were nationals of, or resident at the time of the making of the work in, such countries.

HOW FAR BRITISH WORKS ARE PROTECTED ABROAD

Works first published in the United Kingdom, and unpublished works of British subjects, are protected in all Berne and Universal Copyright Convention countries though it should be noted that "first publication" in this case has not necessarily quite the same meaning in all countries. Some countries do not accept the mere issue of copies as constituting publication in a country, and require that copies shall be issued from a distributing centre in the nature of a publishing house in the country, and the simultaneous publication period which, under the Act, will be thirty days, is not universal.

As regards other foreign countries, copyright can only be secured by complying with the formalities prescribed by the law of the country. For instance, the U.S.A. copyright, prior to the 27th September 1957, was secured by registration and deposit of copies. Copyright could not be acquired unless a "Copyright Reserved" notice was affixed to all copies sold in the U.S.A. Application for registration had to be made promptly or the right to protection was lost, but ad interim protection could be obtained which enabled the position to be preserved pending publication in the U.S.A. Books, or periodicals, in the English language, could not secure permanent protection in the U.S.A. unless an edition was printed in the U.S.A. from type set up there. However, after the 27th September 1957, British authors were relieved of most of the formalities connected with obtaining U.S.A. copyright in published works, including the "Copyright Reserved" notice, registration, deposit of copies, and printing of editions from type set up in the U.S.A. The only formality required was that, from first publication, all copies of the work, whether sold in the U.S.A. or elsewhere, bore the symbol ©, together with the name of the copyright proprietor, and the year of first publication. There is now a new American Copyright Act 1976 which came into force on 1st January 1978 (see *post* **U.S. Copyright**).

THE COPYRIGHT ACTS 1956 and 1911

The Copyright Act 1956 is published by HMSO at £6.30 net. Amendments 1971 3p. net; 1982 40p. net., 1983 80p. net., 1984 (Cable and Broadcasting Act) £5.55 net; 1985 (Copyright (Computer and Software) Amendment Act) 40p. net. The Copyright Act 1911 is published by HMSO at 60p net.

Further reading:

Skone James, E. P., J. F. Mummery and J. Rayner James. *Copinger and Skone James on Copyright*. Sweet and Maxwell. 12th ed. 1980. £95.00.

McFarlane, Gavin. *Practical Introduction to Copyright Law*, McGraw Hill, 1982. £15.95. 256 pp.

McFarlane, Gavin. *Copyright through the Cases,* Waterlow Publishers Ltd., 1986. £15.00. 320 pp.

U.S. COPYRIGHT

GAVIN McFARLANE, LL.M., PH.D.
Barrister

THE SYSTEM OF INTERNATIONAL COPYRIGHT
The International Copyright Conventions

There is no general principle of international copyright which provides a uniform code for the protection of right owners throughout the world. There are however two major international copyright conventions which lay down certain minimum standards for member states, in particular requiring members to accord to right owners of other members the same protection which is granted to their own nationals. One is the higher standard Berne Convention of 1886, the most recent revision of which was signed in Paris in 1971, to which the United States does not at present adhere, although it is hoped that as a result of the new domestic American law of copyright she will feel able to join in the near future. The other is the Universal Copyright Convention signed in 1952 with lower minimum standards, and sponsored by Unesco. This also was most recently revised in Paris in 1971, jointly with the Berne Convention. To this latter Convention the United States belongs.

Summary of the Universal Copyright Convention

(1) The fundamental intent is to accord reciprocally in each member state to nationals of all other member states the same protection as that member grants to its own nationals.

(2) The minimum term of protection is the life of the author and twenty-five years after his death (by contrast with the Berne Convention which demands a term of the life of the author and a post-mortem period of fifty years).

(3) Any national requirement as a condition of copyright of such formalities as deposit, registration, notice, payment, or manufacture or publication within that state shall be satisfied for all works first published outside its territory and of which the author is not one of its nationals if all copies bear the symbol © accompanied by the name of the copyright owner and the year of first publication.

(4) Publication for the purposes of the Universal Convention means the reproduction in tangible form and the general distribution to the public of copies of a work from which it can be read or otherwise visually perceived.

(5) The effect of American ratification of the Universal Copyright Convention on 16 September 1955 was to alter completely the nature of the protection granted by the United States to copyright works originating abroad. The previous policy of American domestic law had been extremely restrictive for foreign authors, particularly those writing in the English language. But in consequence of ratification American law was amended to exempt from many of these restrictions works published in other member states, or by nationals of other member states. Recent amendments have relaxed the position even further.

Effect on British Copyright Owners

The copyright statute of the United States having been brought into line with the requirements of the Universal Copyright Convention, compliance with the formalities required by American law is all that is needed to acquire protection for the work of a British author first published outside the United States.

SUMMARY OF UNITED STATES COPYRIGHT LAW

Introduction of new Law

After many years of debate, the new Copyright Statute of the United States was passed on 19 October 1976. The greater part of its relevant provisions came into force on 1 January 1978. It has extended the range of copyright protection, and further eased the requirements whereby British authors can obtain copyright protection in America.

Works protected in American Law

Works of authorship include the following categories:
(1) literary works;
(2) musical works, including any accompanying words;
(3) dramatic works, including any accompanying music;
(4) pantomimes and choreographic works;
(5) pictorial, graphic and sculptural works;
(6) motion pictures and other audiovisual works;
(7) sound recordings, but copyright in sound recordings is not to include a right of public performance.

The rights of a copyright owner

(1) To reproduce the copyrighted work in copies or phonorecords;
(2) to prepare derivative works based upon the copyrighted work;
(3) to distribute copies or phonorecords of the copyrighted work to the public by sale or other transfer of ownership, or by rental, lease or lending;
(4) in the case of literary, musical, dramatic and choreographic works, pantomimes, and motion pictures and other audiovisual works, but NOT sound recordings, to perform the copyrighted work publicly;
(5) in the case of literary, musical, dramatic, and choreographic works, pantomimes, and pictorial, graphic, or sculptural works, including the individual images of a motion picture or other audiovisual work, to display the copyrighted work publicly.
(6) By the Record Rental Amendment Act 1984, s.109 of the Copyright Statute is amended. Now, unless authorised by the owners of copyright in the sound recording and the musical works thereon, the owner of a phonorecord may not, for direct or indirect commercial advantage, rent, lease or lend the phonorecord. A compulsory licence under s.115(c) includes the right of a maker of a phonorecord of non-dramatic musical work to distribute or authorise the distribution of the phonorecord by rental, lease, or lending, and an additional royalty is payable in respect of that.
(7) The Semiconductor Chip Protection Act 1984 adds to the Copyright Statute a new chapter on the protection of semiconductor chip products.

Manufacturing Requirements

With effect from 1 July 1982, these ceased to have effect. Prior to 1 July 1982, the importation into or public distribution in the United States of a work consisting preponderantly of non-dramatic literary material that was in the English language and protected under American law was prohibited unless the portions consisting of such material had been manufactured in the United States or Canada. This provision did not apply where, on the date when importation was sought or public distribution in the United States was made, the author of any substantial part of such material was neither a national of the United States or, if a national, had been domiciled outside the United States for a continuous period of at least one year immediately preceding that date.

Thus since 1 July 1982, there is no manufacturing requirement in respect of works of British authors, but the requirements of the copyright notice, deposit and registration must be met. Certain interested groups in the United States still lobby for the restoration of the manufacturing clause in American law. Countries such as Britain will no doubt oppose this vigorously through diplomatic channels.

Formalities: Notice, Deposit and Registration
(1) Notice of copyright.
Whenever a work protected by the American Copyright Statute is published in the United States or elsewhere by authority of the copyright owner, a notice of copyright shall be placed on all publicly distributed copies. This shall consist of (i) Either the symbol © or the word "Copyright", or the abbreviation "Copr." plus (ii) the year of first publication of the work, plus (iii) the name of the copyright owner.
(2) Deposit
Unless exempted by the Register of Copyrights, the owner of copyright or the exclusive right of publication in a work published with notice of copyright in the United States shall within three months of such publication deposit in the Copyright Office for the use or disposition of the Library of Congress two complete copies of the best edition of the work (or two records, if the work is a sound recording). Penalties are provided for failure to comply with the requirement of deposit.
(3) Registration.
While deposit is mandatory, registration for copyright in the United States is optional. However, any owner of copyright in a work first published outside the United States may register a work by making application to the Copyright Office with the appropriate fee, and by depositing one complete copy of the work. This requirement of deposit may be satisfied by using copies deposited for the Library of Congress. But it is vital to note that no action may be brought for infringement of copyright in the United States until registration of the claim to copyright has been made according to the statutory provisions.

Duration of Copyright
An important change in the new American law is that in general, copyright in a work created on or after 1 January 1978 endures for a term of the life of the author, and a period of fifty years after the author's death. This brings the United States into line with most other advanced countries, and will enable her government to ratify the higher standard Berne Convention in due course. Copyright in a work created before 1 January 1978, but not published or copyrighted before then, subsists from 1 January 1978, and lasts for the life of the author and a post-mortem period of fifty years.

Any copyright, the first term of which under the previous law was still subsisting on 1 January 1978, shall endure for twenty-eight years from the date when it was originally secured, and the copyright proprietor or his representative may apply for a further term of forty-seven years within one year prior to the expiry of the original term. In default of such application for renewal and extension, the copyright shall end at the expiration of twenty-eight years from the date copyright was originally secured.

The duration of any copyright, the renewal term of which was subsisting at any time between 31 December 1976 and 31 December 1977, or for which renewal registration was made between those dates, is extended to endure for a term of seventy-five years from the date copyright was originally secured.

These alterations are of great importance for owners of existing American copyrights.

All terms of copyright provided for by the sections referred to above run to the end of the calendar year in which they would otherwise expire.

Public Performance

Under the previous American law the provisions relating to performance in public were less generous to right owners than those existing in the copyright law of the United Kingdom. In particular, performance of a musical work was formerly only an infringement if it was "for profit". Moreover, the considerable American coin operated record playing machine industry (juke boxes), had obtained an exemption from being regarded as instruments of profit, and accordingly their owners did not have to pay royalties for the use of copyright musical works.

Now by the new law one of the exclusive rights of the copyright owner is, in the case of literary, musical, dramatic and choreographic works, pantomimes, and motion pictures and other audiovisual works, to perform the work publicly, without any requirement of such performance being "for profit". By Section 114 however, the exclusive rights of the owner of copyright in a sound recording are specifically stated not to include any right of public performance.

While coin operated record players are not brought within the net of public performance, the liability of their operators is fulfilled by obtaining a compulsory licence on application to the Copyright Office, and payment of an annual fee per machine. This royalty is subject to review by the Copyright Royalty Tribunal.

These extensions of the scope of the right of public performance should augment the royalty income of authors, composers and publishers of musical works widely performed in the United States. All such right owners should ensure that their American interests are properly taken care of.

Mechanical Right-Alteration of the rate of royalty

Where sound recordings of a nondramatic musical work have been distributed to the public in the United States with the authority of the copyright owner, any other person may, by following the provisions of the law, obtain a compulsory licence to make and distribute sound recordings of the work. This right is known in the United Kingdom as "the mechanical right". Notice must be served on the copyright owner, who is entitled to a royalty in respect of each of his works recorded of either two and three fourths cents, or one half of one cent per minute of playing time or fraction thereof, whichever amount is the larger. Failure to serve or file the required notice forecloses the possibility of a compulsory licence, and in the absence of a negotiated licence, renders the making and distribution of such records actionable as acts of infringement.

Transfer of Copyright

Under the previous American law copyright was regarded as indivisible, which meant that on the transfer of copyright, where it was intended that only film rights or some other such limited right be transferred, the entire copyright nevertheless had to be passed. This led to a cumbersome procedure whereby the author would assign the whole copyright to his publisher, who would return to the author by means of an exclusive licence those rights which it was not meant to transfer.

Now it is provided by Section 201(d) of the Copyright Statute that (1) the ownership of a copyright may be transferred in whole or in part by any means of conveyance or by operation of law, and may be bequeathed by will or pass as personal property by the applicable laws of intestate succession and (2) any of the exclusive rights comprised in a copyright (including any subdivision of any of the rights set out in Paragraph B3 above) may be transferred as provided in

(1) above and owned separately. The owner of any particular exclusive right is entitled, to the extent of that right, to all the protection and remedies accorded to the copyright owner by that Statute. This removes the difficulties which existed under the previous law, and brings the position much closer to that existing in the copyright law of the United Kingdom.

Copyright Royalty Tribunal

A feature of the new United States law is the establishment of a Copyright Royalty Tribunal, with the purpose of making adjustments of reasonable copyright royalty rates in respect of the exercise of certain rights, mainly affecting the musical interests. The Tribunal is to consist of five commissioners appointed by the President with the advice and consent of the Senate for a term of seven years each. This body will perform in the United States a function similar to the Performing Right Tribunal in the United Kingdom.

The new American law spells out the economic objectives which the Copyright Tribunal is to apply in calculating the applicable rates. These are:

(1) to maximise the availability of creative works to the public;
(2) to afford the copyright owner a fair return for his creative work and the copyright user a fair income under existing economic conditions;
(3) to reflect the relative roles of the copyright owner and the copyright user in the product made available to the public with respect to relative creative contribution, technological contribution, capital investment, cost, risk, and contribution to the opening of new markets for creative expression and media for their communication.
(4) to minimise any disruptive impact on the structure of the industries involved and on generally prevailing industry practices.

Every final determination of the Tribunal shall be published in the Federal Register. It shall state in detail the criteria that the Tribunal determined to be applicable to the particular proceeding, the various facts that it found relevant to its determination in that proceeding, and the specific reasons for its determination. Any final decision of the Tribunal in a proceeding may be appealed to the United States Court of Appeals by an aggrieved party, within thirty days after its publication in the Federal Register.

Fair Use

One of the most controversial factors which held up the introduction of the new American copyright law for at least a decade was the extent to which a balance should be struck between the desire of copyright owners to benefit from their works by extending copyright protection as far as possible, and the pressure from users of copyright to obtain access to copyright material as cheaply as possible—if not completely freely.

The new law provides by Section 107 that the fair use of a copyright work, including such use by reproduction in copies or on records, for purposes such as criticism, comment, news reporting, teaching (including multiple copies for classroom use), scholarship or research is not an infringement of copyright. In determining whether the use made of a work in any particular case is a fair use, the factors to be considered shall include:

(1) the purpose and character of the use, including whether such use is of a commercial nature or is for non-profit educational purposes;
(2) the nature of the copyrighted work;
(3) the amount and substantiality of the portion used in relation to the copyrighted work as a whole; and

(4) the effect of the use upon the potential market for or value of the copyrighted work.

It is not an infringement of copyright for a library or archive, or any of its employees acting within the scope of their employment, to reproduce or distribute no more than one copy of a work, if:

(1) the reproduction or distribution is made without any purpose of direct or indirect commercial advantage;
(2) the collections of the library or archive are either open to the public or available not only to researchers affiliated with the library or archive or with the institution of which it is a part, but also to other persons doing research in a specialised field, and
(3) the reproduction or distribution of the work includes a notice of copyright.

It is not generally an infringement of copyright if a performance or display of a work is given by instructors or pupils in the course of face to face teaching activities of a non-profit educational institution, in a classroom or similar place devoted to instruction.

Nor is it an infringement of copyright to give a performance of a non-dramatic literary or musical work or a dramatico-musical work of a religious nature in the course of services at a place of worship or other religious assembly.

It is also not an infringement of copyright to give a performance of a non-dramatic literary or musical work other than in a transmission to the public, without any purpose of direct or indirect commercial advantage and without payment of any fee for the performance to any of the performing artists, promoters or organisers if either (i) there is no direct or indirect admission charge or (ii) the proceeds, after deducting the reasonable costs of producing the performance, are used exclusively for educational, religious or charitable purposes and not for private financial gain. In this case the copyright owner has the right to serve notice of objection to the performance in a prescribed form.

Note the important decision of the Supreme Court in *Sony Corporation of America* v. *Universal City Studios*. (No. 81-1687, 52 USLW 4090.) This decided that the sale of video-recorders to the public does not amount to contributory infringement of the rights in films which are copied as a result of television broadcasts of them. (The practice known as time-switching.) Among other reasons for their decision advanced by the majority of the judges was their opinion that even unauthorised time-switching is legitimate fair use.

REMEDIES FOR COPYRIGHT OWNERS
Infringement of Copyright
Copyright is infringed by anyone who violates any of the exclusive rights referred to in B.3 above, or who imports copies or records into the United States in violation of the law. The owner of copyright is entitled to institute an action for infringement so long as that infringement is committed while he or she is the owner of the right infringed. *It is vital to note that by virtue of Section 411 of the new law, no action for infringement of copyright can be instituted until registration of the copyright claim has been made.*

Injunctions
Any court having civil jurisdiction under the copyright law may grant interim and final injunctions on such terms as it may deem reasonable to prevent or restrain infringement of copyright. Such injunction may be served anywhere in the United States on the person named. An injunction is operative throughout

the whole of the United States, and can be enforced by proceedings in contempt or otherwise by any American court which has jurisdiction over the infringer.

Impounding and disposition of infringing articles
At any time while a copyright action under American law is pending, the court may order the impounding on such terms as it considers reasonable, of all copies or records claimed to have been made or used in violation of the copyright owner's exclusive rights; it may also order the impounding of all plates, moulds, matrices, masters, tapes, film negatives or other articles by means of which infringing copies or records may be reproduced. A court may order as part of a final judgement or decree the destruction or other disposition of all copies or records found to have been made or used in violation of the copyright owner's exclusive rights. It also has the power to order the destruction of all articles by means of which infringing copies or records were reproduced.

Damages and profits
An infringer of copyright is generally liable either for the copyright owner's actual damage and any additional profits made by the infringer, or for statutory damages.
(1) The copyright owner is entitled to recover the actual damages suffered by him as a result of the infringement, and in addition any profits of the infringer which are attributed to the infringement and are not taken into account in computing the actual damages. In establishing the infringer's profits, the copyright owner is only required to present proof of the infringer's gross revenue, and it is for the infringer to prove his or her deductible expenses and the elements of profit attributable to factors other than the copyright work.
(2) Except where the copyright owner has persuaded the court that the infringement was committed wilfully, the copyright owner may elect, at any time before final judgement is given, to recover, instead of actual damages and profits, an award of statutory damages for all infringements involved in the action in respect of any one work, which may be between $250 and $10,000 according to what the court considers justified.
(3) However, where the copyright owner satisfies the court that the infringement was committed wilfully, the court has the discretion to increase the award of statutory damages to not more than $50,000. Where the infringer succeeds in proving that he was not aware that and had no reason to believe that his acts constituted an infringement of copyright, the court has the discretion to reduce the award of statutory damages to not less than $100.

Costs: Time Limits
In any civil proceedings under American copyright law, the court has the discretion to allow the recovery of full costs by or against any party except the Government of the United States. It may also award a reasonable sum in respect of an attorney's fee.
 No civil or criminal proceedings in respect of copyright law shall be permitted unless begun within three years after the claim or cause of action arose.

Criminal Proceedings in respect of Copyright
(1) Anyone who infringes a copyright wilfully and for purposes of commercial advantage and private financial gain shall be fined not more than $10,000 or imprisoned for not more than one year, or both. However, if the infringement relates to copyright in a sound recording or a film, the infringer is liable to a fine of not more than $25,000 or imprisonment for not more than one year or both

on a first offence, which can be increased to a fine of up to $50,000 or imprisonment for not more than two years or both for a subsequent offence. (2) Following a conviction for criminal infringement a court may in addition to these penalties order the forfeiture and destruction of all infringing copies and records, together with implements and equipment used in their manufacture. (3) It is also an offence knowingly and with fraudulent intent to place on any article a notice of copyright or words of the same purport, or to import or distribute such copies. A fine is provided for this offence of not more than $2,500. The fraudulent removal of a copyright notice also attracts the same maximum fine, as does the false representation of a material particular on an application for copyright representation.

Counterfeiting

By the Piracy and Counterfeiting Amendment Act 1982, pirates and counterfeiters of sound recordings and of motion pictures now face maximum penalties of up to 5 years imprisonment or fines of up to $250,000.

GENERAL OBSERVATIONS

The copyright law of the United States has been very greatly improved as a result of the new statute passed by Congress on 19 October 1976. (Title 17, United States Code.) Apart from lifting the general standards of protection for copyright owners to a much higher level than that which previously existed, it has on the whole shifted the balance of copyright protection in favour of the copyright owner and away from the copyright user in many of the areas where controversy existed. But most important for British and other non-American authors and publishers, it has gone a long way towards bringing American copyright law up to the same standards of international protection for non-national copyright proprietors which have long been offered by the United Kingdom and the other major countries, both in Europe and elsewhere in the English speaking world.

SUBSIDIARY RIGHTS

E. P. SKONE JAMES M.A.

GENERALLY

The Copyright Act 1956 ("the Act"), in Section 1(1), defines "copyright" in relation to a work as the exclusive right to do, and to authorise other persons to do, certain acts in relation to that work in the United Kingdom or in any other country to which the relevant provisions of the Act extend. Such acts in relation to a work of any description, being those acts which in the relevant provision of the Act are designated as acts restricted by the copyright in a work of that description.

The "copyright" in respect of any work therefore consists of several different "restricted acts", or rights, which are not the same in respect of all works, and each of which may be the subject of a separate licence. It follows, therefore, that great care should be taken in drafting and signing agreements concerned with copyright, that such an agreement expressly refers to the rights in respect of which a licence is intended to be granted. For instance, an agreement to print and publish would not normally vest in the publisher any other rights of the author such as film rights, nor would an agreement granting a publisher the right to convert a literary work into a dramatic work vest in the publisher the film or broadcasting rights. However, such an agreement could expressly give a publisher an option to acquire additional rights, or specify who was to exploit such other rights, and, if the publisher, then specifying whether the author was to receive a percentage of the publisher's receipts. If the author is to receive a percentage, then such percentage should vary with the different rights since some rights will be obviously more valuable than others. In drafting agreements regard should also be had to the provisions of the Treaty of Rome which have been given legal effect in the United Kingdom by the European Communities Act 1972.

It should be noted also that, since, under the Act, it is now possible to assign and licence future copyright (e.g. copyright which will, or may come into existence in respect of any future work or class of works or other subject-matter), care should be taken that any such agreement expressly excludes future copyright if so desired.

The Act contains special provisions as to libraries, permitting copying for special purposes unless the librarian knows the name and address of a person entitled to authorise the making of the copy, or could, by reasonable enquiry, ascertain the name and address of such a person. For this reason, an author should give his publisher power to grant such authorisation so that the publisher may be entitled to demand a fee, a percentage of which should be payable to the author.

It is not possible in this article to deal with all the rights restricted by copyright in a work but some of those of the greatest importance to writers and artists will be considered, either because they are rights conferred by the Act, or because they form part of such rights. Computer programs are now protected as literary works by the Copyright (Computer Software) Amendment Act 1985 which contains special provisions relating to computer programs. It has been held that a parody of a work such as a painting or a song is not an infringement if the parody amounts to an original work and does not reproduce a substantial part of the plaintiff's work; if so, no licence need be asked for or given (*Joy Music Ltd.* v. *Sunday Pictorial Newspapers (1920) Ltd.* 1960 2 W.L.R. 645, *Schweppes Ltd.* v. *Wellingtons Ltd* 1984 F.S.R. 210).

RIGHT TO REPRODUCE THE WORK BY RECORDS OR FILMS

It is a restricted act in relation to literary, dramatic, musical and artistic works (*inter alia*), to make a record or film thereof. Separate licences for each of these acts would therefore be necessary, though not in the case of a film of an artistic work if such work was included in the film only by way of background or was otherwise only incidental to the principal matters represented in the film.

Film companies will usually require to have the right to broadcast the film of the work but this is not, of course, the same as the right to broadcast the work itself using live actors, which right an author should be sure to retain.

RIGHT TO BROADCAST THE WORK

The Act for the first time makes "broadcasting" (e.g. by sound or television), a separate right in respect of literary, dramatic and musical works, and "including the work in a television broadcast" a separate right in the case of an artistic work, so that a separate licence to broadcast by sound or to broadcast by television is required, except where an artistic work is included in a television broadcast, if its inclusion therein was only by way of background, etc., as mentioned above in respect of a film. See also the Cable and Broadcasting Act 1984 as to including a work in a cable programme.

RIGHT TO MAKE ADAPTATIONS OF THE WORK

An "adaptation" is a new expression in the Act the making of which is a restricted act applicable only to literary, dramatic and musical works. An "adaptation" is defined by the Act and means (1) An arrangement or transcription of a musical work, (2) Converting a non-dramatic work into a dramatic work or vice versa, (3) Translations of literary or dramatic works. The person making a translation will acquire a copyright in his work if he had a right to translate. (4) Versions of literary or dramatic works in which the story or action is conveyed wholly or mainly by means of pictures in a form suitable for reproduction in a book or in a newspaper, magazine or similar periodical, e.g. comic strips. This is a new right granted by the Act.

The Copyright Act 1911 contained certain similar rights, but not classed under the one heading, and care should be taken to limit a licence to the particular "adaptation" intended as a licence to make "adaptations" would confer all such rights.

RIGHT TO SERIALISE

The Act does not define "serial rights" though, by reason of common usage, its meaning is well known. In the case of *Jonathan Cape Ltd.* v. *Consolidated Press Ltd.*, 1954 1 W.L.R. 1313, by Clause 1 of an Agreement between the author of an original work and the plaintiff publishers, the author agreed to grant to the publishers the exclusive right to print and publish the work "in volume form". Clause 12 of the Agreement referred, *inter alia*, to the first serial rights in the work in the terms "publication of instalments in several issues of a newspaper, magazine or periodical prior to publication in volume form", and Clause 13 referred, *inter alia*, to "all rights of serialisation subsequent to publication in volume form". It was held that Clauses 12 and 13 of the Agreement were concerned with serial rights in regard to the work, and they indicated that the transfer of rights effected by the Agreement was not to include, in the terms contained in Clause 1, the rights as regards the publication of the work in serial form. Further, looking at the Agreement, the real point was that the distinction was made between the publication of the work as a whole, which was meant by the word "volume", and the publication of the work by instalments, which was publication in a serial form, and was dealt with by the Agreement in a separate way. In that case, the defendants published a story in a single edition of a periodical, and it was held that there was an infringement of the plaintiffs' rights to publish in volume form. It would, of course, be possible to licence specifically publication in a single edition of a periodical.

It must be noted that serial rights are not limited to one serialisation since there can be first, second and third, etc., serial rights. Thus the licence should specify in respect of which serial rights it is granted.

Other matters which the licence should specify are: (1) the price to be paid; (2) the date of payment; (3) the date of publication; (4) the place of publication. The last two are most important. The date of publication is important because the article may be a topical article: therefore, in order to preserve the value of the first serial rights, these should be sold on terms that they will be published by a prescribed date. The place of publication is important, and should always be stipulated, because serial rights, like other rights, may be separately sold for publication in different countries.

RIGHT TO HAVE THE WORK, OR PART THEREOF, INCLUDED IN AN ANTHOLOGY

An anthology, strictly a collection of poems, but also extended to include collections of short passages from various authors, is itself the subject of copyright protection. This was decided in an Indian case dealing with Palgrave's *The Golden Treasury of Songs and Lyrics*. The inclusion of a work, or part of it, in an anthology would be an infringement of the author's right to reproduce the work and to publish it, if unpublished, and would require a separate licence. Such a licence would not normally be included in a licence to print and publish (see also "Quotations" below).

RIGHT TO HAVE THE WORK ABRIDGED

The usual form of abridgement, or digest, of a work consists of a statement designed to be complete and accurate of the thoughts, opinions and ideas expressed in the work by the author but set forth much more concisely in the compressed language of the abridger (per Lord Atkinson in *Macmillan & Co. Ltd.* v. *Cooper,* 1923, 40 T.L.R. 186), and is itself the subject of copyright protection. Again, to make a digest of a work would be an infringement of the author's right to reproduce the work and to publish it would also be an infringement. A digest which consisted merely of a synopsis of the plot of a work might not be an infringement of that work, (but see *Sillitoe* v. *McGraw-Hill Book Company (UK) Ltd.* 1983 F.S.R. 545, study notes for students held to be infringements). However an offence might be committed if the name of the original author was put on such digest in such a way as to imply that the original author was the author of the digest (Section 43 of the Act).

RIGHT TO HAVE THE WORK QUOTED

Quotation in the wide sense, by including part of the work in an anthology, has been referred to above, and, as a general rule, quotations from works are only permissible if licensed. But it is generally more convenient if the publisher is given a right to license quotations so that the author does not have to be sought on each occasion.

However, the Act provides exceptions to this rule. Thus, no fair dealing with the work for the purposes of research, private study, criticism or review is an infringement of the copyright therein, if, in the last two cases, the work and the author are identified. What is "fair dealing" is a matter of degree and involves a consideration of the number and extent of the quotations and extracts and of the use made of them. It applies to unpublished as well as to published works.

"Fair dealing" for the purpose of criticism covers, not only criticism of the literary style of the work, but also of the doctrine or philosophy expounded in the work; *Hubbard* v. *Vosper* 1972 2 W.L.R. 389. The publication of information known to have been "leaked" will not be a "fair dealing"; *Beloff* v. *Pressdram Ltd.* 1973 F.S.R. 33. In *Sillitoe* (*supra*) it was held that booklets for the use of students studying in copyright works ('Coles Notes') were infringements and that the exceptions of research or private study and criticism or review did not apply in the circumstances of that case.

Similarly no fair dealing with the work for the purpose of reporting current events in newspapers, etc., or by broadcasting, or in a film, is an infringement if, in respect of newspapers etc., the work and author are identified.

Further, the reading or recitation in public (other than for the purposes of broadcasting), by one person of any reasonable extract from a published, literary or dramatic work, is not an infringement if the work and author are identified. Again, in certain circumstances, the inclusion of a short passage from a published literary or dramatic work in a collection intended for the use of schools is not an infringement.

All these exceptions apply to adaptations of the work as well as to the work itself (as to the meaning of "adaptation" see above).

RIGHT TO HAVE THE WORK REPRINTED

A licence to print and publish may be expressly confined to one edition only, with a right for the author to require further editions to be published when the first edition has gone out of print. If the publisher, on receipt of a notice from the author requesting the publication of a further edition, will not do so, the author should be entitled to go to another publisher.

RIGHT TO HAVE THE WORK PRINTED BY BOOK CLUBS

Book Clubs normally produce a special edition of the work at a cheaper price, and therefore the author's licence to the publisher should contain express provisions as to whether, and on what terms, such editions may be printed.

LIBEL

JAMES EVANS and ANTONY WHITAKER

What follows is an outline of the main principles of the law of Libel, with special reference to points which appear most frequently to be misunderstood. But it is no more than that and specific legal advice should be taken when practical problems arise. The law discussed is the law of England and Wales. Scotland has its own, albeit somewhat similar, rules.

LIBEL: LIABILITY TO PAY DAMAGES

English Law draws a distinction between defamation published in permanent form and that which is not. The former is Libel, the latter Slander. "Permanent form" includes writing, printing, drawings and photographs and radio and television broadcasts. It follows that it is the law of Libel rather than Slander which most concerns writers and artists professionally, and the slightly differing rules applicable to Slander will not be mentioned in this article.

Publication of a libel can result in a civil action for damages, an injunction to prevent repetition and/or in certain cases a criminal prosecution against those responsible, who include the writer (or artist or photographer), the printers, the publishers, and the editor, if any, of the publication in which the libel appeared. Prosecutions are rare. Certain special rules apply to them and these will be explained below after a discussion of the question of civil liability, which in practice arises much more frequently.

Civil libel cases, for which legal aid is not available, are usually heard by a judge and jury, and it is the jury who decide the amount of any award. It is not necessary for the plaintiff to prove that he has actually suffered any loss, because the law presumes damage. While the main purpose of a libel claim is to compensate the plaintiff for the injury to his reputation, a jury may give additional sums either as "aggravated" damages, if it appears a defendant has behaved malevolently or spitefully; or as "exemplary", or "punitive", damages where a defendant hopes the economic advantages of publication will outweigh any sum awarded against him. Damages can also be "nominal" if the libel complained of is trivial. It is generally very difficult to forecast the amounts juries are likely to award.

In an action for damages for libel, it is for the plaintiff to establish that the matter he complains of (1) has been published by the defendant, (2) refers to himself, (3) is defamatory. If he does so, the plaintiff establishes a *prima facie* case. However, the defendant will escape liability if he can show he has a good defence. There are five defences to a libel action. They are Justification, Fair Comment, Privilege, S 4 of the Defamation Act, 1952, Apology, etc., under the Libel Acts, 1843 and 1845. A libel claim can also become barred under the Limitation Acts, as explained below. These matters must now be examined in detail.

THE PLAINTIFF'S CASE

(1) "Published" in the legal sense means communicated to a person other than the plaintiff. Thus the legal sense is wider than the lay sense but includes it. It follows that the contents of a book is published in the legal sense when the manuscript is first sent to the publishing firm just as much as it is when the book is later placed on sale to the public. Both types of publication are sufficient for

the purpose of establishing liability for libel, but the law differentiates between them, since the scope of publication can properly be taken into account by the jury in considering the actual amount of damages to award.

(2) The plaintiff must also establish that the matter complained of refers to himself. It is of course by no means necessary to mention a person's name before it is clear that he is referred to. Nicknames by which he is known or corruptions of his name are just two ways in which his identity can be indicated. There are more subtle methods. The sole question is whether the plaintiff is indicated to those who read the matter complained of. In some cases he will not be unless it is read in the light of facts known to the reader from other sources, but this is sufficient for the plaintiff's purpose. The test is purely objective and does not depend at all on whether the writer intended to refer to the plaintiff.

It is because it is impossible to establish reference to any individual that generalisations, broadly speaking, are not successfully actionable. To say boldly "All lawyers are crooks" does not give any single lawyer a cause of action, because the statement does not point a finger at any individual. However, if anyone is named in conjunction with a generalisation, then it may lose its general character and become particular from the context. Again if one says "One of the X Committee has been convicted of murder" and the X Committee consists of, say, four persons, it cannot be said that the statement is not actionable because no individual is indicated and it could be referring to any of the committee. This is precisely why it is actionable at the suit of each of them as suspicion has been cast on all.

(3) It is for the plaintiff to show that the matter complained of is defamatory. What is defamatory is decided by the jury except in the extreme cases where the judge rules that the words cannot bear a defamatory meaning. Various tests have been laid down for determining this. It is sufficient that any one test is satisfied. The basic tests are : (i) Does the matter complained of tend to lower the plaintiff in the estimation of society? (ii) Does it tend to bring him into hatred, ridicule, contempt, dislike or disesteem with society? (iii) Does it tend to make him shunned or avoided or cut off from society? The mere fact that what is published is inaccurate is not enough to involve liability, it is the adverse impact on the plaintiff's reputation that matters.

"Society" means right-thinking members of society generally. It is by reference to such people that the above tests must be applied. A libel action against a newspaper which had stated that the police had taken a statement from the plaintiff failed, notwithstanding that the plaintiff gave evidence that his apparent assistance to the police (which he denied) had brought him into grave disrepute with the underworld. It was not by their wrongheaded standards that the matter fell to be judged.

Further, it is not necessary to imply that the plaintiff is at fault in some way in order to defame him. To say of a woman that she has been raped or of someone that he is insane imputes to them no degree of blame but nonetheless both statements are defamatory.

Sometimes a defamatory meaning is conveyed by words which on the face of them have no such meaning. "But Brutus is an honourable man" is an example. If a jury finds that words are meant ironically they will consider this ironical sense when determining whether the words are defamatory. In deciding therefore whether or not the words are defamatory, the jury seek to discover what, without straining the words or putting a perverse construction on them, they will be understood to mean. In some cases this may differ substantially from their literal meaning.

Matter may also be defamatory by innuendo. Strictly so called, an innuendo is a meaning that words acquire by virtue of facts known to the reader but not stated in the passage complained of. Words, quite innocent on the face of them, may acquire a defamatory meaning when read in the light of these facts. For example, where a newspaper published a photograph of a man and a woman, with the caption that they had just announced their engagement, it was held to be defamatory of the man's wife since those who knew that she had cohabited with him were led to the belief that she had done so only as his mistress. The newspaper was unaware that the man was already married, but some of its readers were not.

DEFENCES TO A LIBEL ACTION

Justification:

English law does not protect the reputation that a person either does not or should not possess. Stating the truth therefore does not incur liability and the plea of justification namely, that what is complained of is true in substance and in fact, is a complete answer to an action for damages. However, this defence is by no means to be undertaken lightly. For instance, to prove one instance of using bad language will be insufficient to justify the allegation that a person is "foulmouthed". It would be necessary to prove several instances and the defendant is obliged in most cases to particularise in his pleadings giving details, dates and places. However, if there are two or more distinct charges against the plaintiff the defence will not fail by reason only that the truth of every charge is not proved, if the words not proved to be true do not materially injure the plaintiff's reputation having regard to the truth of the remaining charges. It is for the defendant to prove that what he has published is true, not for the plaintiff to disprove it, though if he can do so, so much the better for him.

One point requires special mention. It is insufficient for the defendant to prove that he has accurately repeated what a third person has written or said or that such statements have gone uncontradicted when made on occasions in the past. If X writes "Y told me that Z is a liar", it is no defence to an action against X merely to prove that Y did say that. X has given currency to a defamatory statement concerning Z and has so made it his own. His only defence is to prove that Z is a liar by establishing a number of instances of Z's untruthfulness. Nor is it a defence to prove that the defendant genuinely believed what he published to be true. This might well be a complete answer in an action, other than a libel action, based on a false but non-defamatory statement. For such statements do not incur liability in the absence of fraud or malice, which, in this context, means a dishonest or otherwise improper motive. Bona fide belief, however, may be relevant to the assessment of damages, even in a libel action.

Special care should be taken in relation to references to a person's convictions however accurately described. Since the Rehabilitation of Offenders Act, 1974, a person's convictions may become "spent" and thereafter it may involve liability to refer to them. Reference to the Act and orders thereunder must be made in order to determine the position in any particular case.

Fair Comment:

It is a defence to prove that what is complained of is fair comment made in good faith and without malice on a matter of public interest.

"Fair" in this context means "honest". "Fair comment" means therefore the expression of the writer's genuinely held opinion. It does not necessarily mean opinion with which the jury agree. Comment may therefore be quite extreme and still be "fair" in the legal sense. However, if it is utterly perverse the jury may be led to think that no one could have genuinely held such views. In such a case the defence would fail, for the comment could not be honest. "Malice" here includes the popular sense of personal spite, but covers any dishonest or improper motive.

The defence only applies when what is complained of is comment as distinct from a statement of fact. The line between comment and fact is notoriously difficult to draw in some cases. Comment means a statement of opinion. The facts on which comment is made must be stated together with the comment or be sufficiently indicated with it. This is merely another way of saying that it must be clear that the defamatory statement is one of opinion and not of fact, for which the only defence would be the onerous one of justification. The exact extent to which the facts commented on must be stated or referred to is a difficult question but some help may be derived in answering it by considering the purpose of the rule, which is to enable the reader to exercise his own judgement and to agree or disagree with the comment. It is quite plain that it is not necessary to state every single detail of the facts. In one case it was sufficient merely to mention the name of one of the Press lords in an article about a newspaper though not one owned by him. He was so well known that to mention his name indicated the substratum of fact commented upon, namely his control of his group of newspapers. No general rule can be laid down, save that, in general, the fuller the facts set out or referred to with the comment the better. These facts must always be true, except that in an action for libel partly in respect of allegations of fact and partly of expressions of opinion, a defence of fair comment will not fail by reason only that the truth of every allegation of fact is not proved, if the expression of opinion is fair comment, having regard to such of the facts alleged or referred to in the matter complained of as are proved.

The defence only applies where the matters commented on are of public interest, i.e. of legitimate concern to the public or a substantial section of it. Thus the conduct of national and local government, international affairs, the administration of justice, etc., are all matters of public interest, whereas other people's private affairs may very well not be, although they undoubtedly interest the public.

In addition matters of which criticism has been expressly or impliedly invited, such as publicly performed plays and published books, are a legitimate subject of comment. Criticism need not be confined merely to their artistic merit but equally may deal with the attitudes to life and the opinions therein expressed.

It is sometimes said that a man's moral character is never a proper subject of comment for the purpose of this defence. This is certainly true where it is a private individual who is concerned and some authorities say it is the same in the case of a public figure even though his character may be relevant to his public life. Again, it may in some cases be exceeding the bounds of Fair Comment to impute a dishonourable motive to a person, as is frequently done by way of inference from facts. In general, the imputation is a dangerous and potentially expensive practice.

Privilege:

In the public interest, certain occasions are privileged so that to make defamatory statements upon them does not incur liability. The following are privileged in any event: (i) Fair, accurate, and contemporaneous reports of public judicial proceedings in England published in a newspaper, (ii) Parliamentary papers published by the direction of either House, or full republications thereof. The following are privileged provided publication is made only for the reason that the privilege is given and not for some wrongful or indirect motive: (i) Fair and accurate but non-contemporaneous reports of public judicial proceedings in England, whether in a newspaper or not, (ii) Extracts of Parliamentary papers, (iii) Fair and accurate reports of Parliamentary proceedings, (iv) A fair and accurate report in a newspaper of the proceedings at any public meeting held in the United Kingdom. The meeting must be bona fide and lawfully held for a lawful purpose and for the furtherance or discussion of any matter of public concern. Admission to the meeting may be general or restricted. In the case of public meetings, the defence is not available, if it is proved that the defendant has been requested by the plaintiff to publish in the newspaper in which the original publication was made a reasonable letter or statement by way of explanation or contradiction, and has refused or neglected to do so, or has done so in a manner not adequate or not reasonable having regard to all the circumstances. This list of privileged occasions is by no means exhaustive, but they are those most commonly utilised.

S.4 of the Defamation Act, 1952:

The defence provided by the above section is only available where the defamation is "innocent". As has been seen, liability for libel is in no way dependent on the existence of an intention to defame on the part of the defendant and the absence of such an intention does not mean that the defamation is "innocent".

Defamation is innocent if the publisher did not intend to publish the matter complained of about the plaintiff and did not know of circumstances by virtue of which it might be understood to refer to him, or, if the matter published was not defamatory on the face of it, if the publisher did not know of circumstances by virtue of which it might be understood to be defamatory. Further the publisher must have exercised all reasonable care in relation to the publication. If the publisher has published matter innocently, he should make an "offer of amends" to the party aggrieved. This consists of an offer to publish a correction and apology and as far as practicable to inform others to whom the alleged libel has been distributed that the matter is said to be defamatory. If the offer of amends is accepted, it is a bar to further proceedings against the person making the offer. If rejected, the making of the offer affords a defence provided the defendant can prove that he did publish innocently and made the offer as soon as practicable after learning that the matter published was or might be defamatory. The offer must not have been withdrawn and must have been expressed to be for the purposes of the defence under S.4 and have been accompanied by an affidavit. It is vital that the offer should be made swiftly, but it is inadvisable to make it without professional advice owing to its technicality. An example of the first type of innocent publication is where a reference to a person by name has been understood to refer to another person of the same name and this could not reasonably have been foreseen.

An example of the other type of innocent publication is the case referred to earlier in this article of the man pictured with "his fiancée". The publishers did not know that he was already married and that accordingly the picture and caption could be understood to be defamatory of his wife.

In practice all the conditions for a successful defence under this section are infrequently fulfilled.

Apology under the Libel Acts, 1843 and 1845:

This defence is rarely utilised, since if any condition of it is not fulfilled, the plaintiff must succeed and the only question is the actual amount of damages. It only applies to actions in respect of libels in newspapers and periodicals. The defendant pleads that the libel was inserted without actual malice and without gross negligence and that before the action commenced or as soon afterwards as possible he inserted a full apology in the same newspaper, etc., or had offered to publish it in a newspaper, etc., of the plaintiff's choice, where the original newspaper is published at intervals greater than a week. Further a sum must be paid into court with this defence to compensate the plaintiff.

Limitation

In general, unless an action is started within three years of publication, a libel claim becomes "statute-barred" through lapse of time. But successive and subsequent publications, such as the issue of later editions of the same book, or the sale of surplus copies of an old newspaper, can give rise to fresh claims.

CRIMINAL LIABILITY IN LIBEL AND RELATED AREAS

Whereas the object of a civil action is to obtain compensation for the wrong done or to prevent repetition, the object of criminal proceedings is to punish the wrongdoer by fine or imprisonment or both. There are four main types of writing which may provoke a prosecution.

(1) Defamatory Libel:
(2) Obscene Publications
(3) Sedition and Incitement to racial hatred
(4) Blasphemous Libel

(1) The publication of defamatory matter is in certain circumstances a crime as well as a civil wrong. But whereas the principal object of civil proceedings will normally be to obtain compensation, the principal object of a criminal prosecution will be to secure punishment of the accused, for example by way of a fine. Prosecutions are not frequent but there have been signs of late of a revival of interest. There are important differences between the rules applicable to criminal libel and its civil counterpart. For example, a criminal libel may be "published" even though only communicated to the person defamed and may be found to have occurred even where the person defamed is dead, or where only a group of persons but no particular individual has been maligned. During election campaigns, it is an "illegal practice" to publish false statements about the personal character or conduct of a candidate irrespective of whether they are also defamatory.

(2) It is an offence to publish obscene matter. By the Obscene Publications Act, 1959, matter is obscene if its effect is such as to tend to deprave and corrupt persons who are likely, having regard to all relevant circumstances, to read, see or hear it. "To deprave and corrupt" is to be distinguished from "to shock and disgust". It is a defence to a prosecution to prove that publication of the matter in question is justified as being for the public good, on the ground that it is in the interests of science, literature, art or learning, or of other objects of general concern. Expert evidence may be given as to its literary, artistic, scientific or other merits. Playwrights, directors and producers should note that the Theatres Act, 1968, though designed to afford similar protection to stage productions, does not necessarily prevent prosecutions for indecency under other statutes.

(3) Writings which tend to destroy the peace of the Realm may be prosecuted as being seditious or as amounting to incitement to racial hatred. Seditious writings include those which advocate reform by unconstitutional or violent means or incite contempt or hatred for the Monarch or Parliament. These institutions may be criticised stringently, but not in a manner which is likely to lead to insurrection or civil commotion or indeed any physical force. Prosecutions are a rarity, but it should be remembered that writers of matter contemptuous of the House of Commons, though not prosecuted for seditious libel are, from time to time, punished by that House for breach of its Privileges, although, if a full apology is made, it is often an end of the matter. The Race Relations Act 1976 makes it an offence, irrespective of the author's or publisher's intention, to publish threatening, abusive or insulting matter if hatred is likely to be stirred up against any racial group in Great Britain.

(4) Blasphemous libel consists in the vilification of the Christian religion or its ceremonies. The offence lies essentially in the impact of what is said concerning,

for instance, God, Christ, the Bible, the Book of Common Prayer, etc.; it is irrelevant that the publisher does not intend to shock or arouse resentment. While temperate and sober writings on religious topics however anti-Christian in sentiment will not involve liability, if the discussion is "so scurrilous and offensive as to pass the limit of decent controversy and to outrage any Christian feeling", it will.

INCOME TAX FOR WRITERS AND ARTISTS
PETER VAINES, F.C.A., A.T.I.I.
Chartered Accountant

This article is intended to explain the impact of taxation on writers and others engaged in similar activities. Despite attempts by many Governments to simplify our taxation system, the subject has become increasingly complicated and the following is an attempt to give a broad outline of the position. At the time of writing, this year's Finance Bill is being considered by Parliament and will emerge after amendment as the Finance Act 1986. The changes proposed in the Finance Bill are reflected in this article.

HOW INCOME IS TAXED

(a) *Generally*

Authors are usually treated for tax purposes as carrying on a profession and are taxed in a similar fashion to other professional persons, i.e. as self-employed persons assessable under Schedule "D". This article is directed to self-employed persons only, because if a writer is "employed" he will be subject to the rules of Schedule "E" where different considerations apply—substantially to his disadvantage. Attempts are often made by employed persons to shake off the status of "employee" and to attain "freelance" status so as to qualify for the advantages of Schedule "D", such attempts meeting with varying degrees of success. The problems involved in making this transition are considerable and space does not permit a detailed explanation to be made here—proper advice is necessary if the difficulties are to be avoided.

Particular attention has been paid by the Inland Revenue to Fleet Street journalists and to those engaged in the TV and film industry with a view to reclassifying them as employees so that PAYE is deducted from their earnings. This blanket treatment is being extended to other areas and although it is obviously open to challenge by individual taxpayers, it is always difficult to persuade the Inland Revenue to change their views.

There is no reason why an employed person cannot carry on a freelance business in his spare time. Indeed, aspiring authors, painters, musicians, etc., often derive so little income from their craft that the financial security of an employment, perhaps in a different sphere of activity, is necessary. The existence of the employment is irrelevant to the taxation of the freelance earnings although it is most important not to confuse the income or expenditure of the employment with the income or expenditure of the self employed activity. The Inland Revenue are also aware of the advantages which could be derived by an individual having "freelance" income from an organisation of which he is also an employee. Where these circumstances are contrived, it is of course extremely difficult to convince an Inspector of Taxes that a genuine freelance activity is being carried on.

For those starting in business or commencing work on a freelance basis the Inland Revenue produce a very useful booklet entitled "Starting in Business (IR28)", which is available from any tax office.

(b) *Income*

For income to be taxable it need not be substantial, nor even the author's only source of income; earnings from casual writing are also taxable but this can be an advantage, because occasional writers do not often make a profit from their writing. The expenses incurred in connection with writing may well exceed any income receivable and the resultant loss may then be used to reclaim tax paid on other income. There may be deducted from the income certain allowable expenses and capital allowances which are set out in more detail below. The possibility of a loss being used as a basis for a tax repayment is fully appreciated by the Inland Revenue who sometimes attempt to treat casual writing as a hobby so that any losses incurred cannot be used to reclaim tax; of course by the same token any income receivable would not be chargeable to tax. This treatment may sound attractive but it should be resisted vigorously because the Inland Revenue do not hesitate to change their mind when profits begin to arise. However, in the case of exceptional or non-recurring writing, such as the autobiography of a sports personality or the memoirs of a politician, it could be better to be treated as pursuing a hobby and not as a professional author. Sales of copyright are only chargeable to capital gains tax unless the recipient is a professional author.

(c) *Royalties*

However, where the recipient is a professional author, a series of cases has laid down a clear principle that sales of copyright are taxable as income and not as capital receipts. Similarly, lump sums on account of, or in advance of royalties are also taxable as income in the year of receipt, subject to a claim for spreading relief (see below).

Copyright royalties are generally paid without deduction of Income Tax. However, if royalties are paid to a person who normally lives abroad, tax will be deducted by the payer or his agent at the time the payment is made unless arrangements are made with the Inland Revenue for payments to be made gross.

(d) *Arts Council Grants*

Persons in receipt of grants from the Arts Council or similar bodies have been concerned for some time whether or not such grants were liable to Income Tax. In 1979, the Arts Council and other interested bodies engaged in detailed discussions with the Inland Revenue which culminated in the issue of a Statement of Practice regarding the tax treatment of those awards. Grants and other receipts of a similar nature have now been divided into two categories—those which are to be treated by the Inland Revenue as chargeable to tax and those which are not. Category A awards are considered to be taxable and arise from the following:
(1) Direct or indirect musical, design or choreographic commissions and direct or indirect commission of sculpture and paintings for public sites.
(2) The Royalty Supplement Guarantee Scheme.
(3) The contract writers scheme.
(4) Jazz bursaries.
(5) Translator's grants.
(6) Photographic awards and bursaries.
(7) Film and video awards and bursaries.
(8) Performance Art Awards.
(9) Art Publishing Grants.
(10) Grants to assist with a specific project or projects (such as the writing of a book) or to meet specific professional expenses such as a contribution towards copying expenses made to a composer or to an artist's studio expenses.

Awards made under category B are not chargeable to tax and are as follows:
(1) Bursaries to trainee directors.
(2) In service bursaries for theatre directors.
(3) Bursaries for associate directors.

(4) Bursaries to people attending full time courses in arts administration (the practical training course).
(5) In service bursaries to theatre designers and bursaries to trainees on the theatre designer's scheme.
(6) In service bursaries for administrators.
(7) Bursaries for actors and actresses.
(8) Bursaries for technicians and stage managers.
(9) Bursaries made to students attending the City University Arts Administration courses.
(10) Awards, known as the Buying Time Awards, made not to assist with a specific project or professional expenses but to maintain the recipient to enable him to take time off to develop his personal talents. These at present include the awards and bursaries known as the Theatre Writing Bursaries, awards and bursaries to composers, awards and bursaries to painters, sculptures and print makers, literature awards and bursaries.

This Statement of Practice has no legal force and is used merely to ease the administration of the tax system. It is open to anyone in receipt of a grant or award to disregard the agreed statement and challenge the Inland Revenue view on the merits of their particular case. However, it must be recognised that the Inland Revenue do not issue such statements lightly and any challenge to their view would almost certainly involve a lengthy and expensive action through the Courts.

The tax position of persons in receipt of literary prizes is clearer following a recent decision by the Special Commissioners in connection with the Whitbread Literary Award. In that case it was held that the prize was not part of the author's professional income and accordingly not chargeable to tax. The decisions of the Special Commissioners are not reported until such time as an appeal is made to the High Court and the Inland Revenue have chosen not to appeal against this decision. Elsewhere in this *Yearbook* will be found details of the many literary awards which are given each year and this decision is of considerable significance to the winners of each of these prizes. It would be unwise to assume that all such awards will now be free of tax as the precise facts which were present in the case of the Whitbread award may not be repeated in another case; however it is clear that an author winning a prize has some very powerful arguments in his favour, should the Inland Revenue seek to charge tax on the award.

ALLOWABLE EXPENSES

To qualify as an allowable business expense, expenditure has to be laid out wholly and exclusively for business purposes. Strictly there must be no "duality of purpose", which means that expenditure cannot be apportioned to reflect the private and business usage, e.g. food, clothing, telephone, travelling expenses, etc. However, the Inland Revenue do not usually interpret this principle strictly and are prepared to allow all reasonable expenses (including apportioned sums) where the amounts can be commercially justified. It should be noted carefully that the expenditure does not have to be "necessary", it merely has to be incurred "wholly and exclusively" for business purposes; naturally, however, expenditure of an outrageous and wholly unnecessary character might well give rise to a presumption that it was not really for business purposes. As with all things, some expenses are unquestionably allowable and some expenses are equally unquestionably not allowable—it is the grey area in between which gives rise to all the difficulties and the outcome invariably depends on negotiation with the Inland Revenue.

Great care should be taken when claiming a deduction for items where there is a "duality of purpose" and negotiations should be conducted with more than usual care and courtesy—if provoked the Inspector of Taxes may well choose to allow nothing. An appeal is always possible although unlikely to succeed as a string of cases in the Courts has clearly demonstrated. An example is the case of *Caillebotte* v. *Quinn* where the taxpayer (who normally had lunch at home) sought to claim the excess cost of meals incurred because he was working a long way from his home. The taxpayer's arguments failed because he did not eat only in order to work, one of the reasons for him eating was in order to sustain his life; a duality of purpose therefore existed and no tax relief was due. Other cases have shown that expenditure on clothing can also be disallowed if it is the kind of clothing which is in everyday use, because clothing is worn not only to assist the pursuit of one's profession but also to accord with public decency. This duality of purpose may be sufficient to deny relief—even where the particular type of clothing is of a kind not otherwise worn by the taxpayer. In the recent case of *Mallalieu* v. *Drummond* a lady barrister failed to obtain a tax deduction for items of sombre clothing purchased specifically for wearing in Court. The House of Lords decided that a duality of purpose existed because clothing represented part of her needs as a human being.

Despite the above Inspectors of Taxes are not usually inflexible and the following expenses are among those generally allowed:

(a) Cost of all materials used up in the course of preparation of the work.

(b) Cost of typewriting and secretarial assistance, etc.; if this or other help is obtained from one's spouse then it is entirely proper for a deduction to be claimed for the amounts paid for the work. The amounts claimed must actually be paid to the spouse and should be at the market rate although some uplift can be made for unsocial hours, etc. Payments to a wife (or husband) are of course taxable in her (or his) hands and should therefore be most carefully considered. If care is not taken, liabilities to National Insurance contributions may arise which would more than outweigh the tax savings.

(c) All expenditure on normal business items such as postage, stationery, telephone, answering machine, agent's fees, accountancy charges, photography, subscriptions, periodicals, magazines, etc., may be claimed. The cost of daily papers should not be overlooked if these form part of research material. Visits to theatres, cinemas, etc., for research purposes may also be permissible (but not of course the cost relating to guests). Unfortunately expenditure on entertaining is specifically denied tax relief, other than in exceptional circumstances.

(d) If work is conducted at home, a deduction for "use of home" is usually allowed providing the amount claimed is reasonable. If the claim is based on an appropriate proportion of the total costs of rent and rates, light and heat, cleaning and maintenance, insurance, etc. then care should be taken to ensure that no single room is used "*exclusively*" for business purposes, because this may result in the Capital Gains Tax exemption on the house as an only or main residence being partially forfeited. However, it would be a strange household where one room was in fact used exclusively for business purposes and for no other purpose whatsoever (e.g. storing personal bank statements and other private papers); the usual formula is to claim a deduction on the basis that most or all of the rooms in the house are used at one time or another for business purposes, thereby avoiding any suggestion that any part was used exclusively for business purposes.

(e) The appropriate business proportion of motor running expenses may also be claimed although what is the appropriate proportion will naturally depend on the particular circumstances of each case; it should be mentioned that the well known "private motoring benefits" legislation whereby one is taxed accordingly to the size and cost of the car does not apply to self-employed persons.

(f) It has been long established that the cost of travelling to and from home to one's place of work (whether employed or self-employed) is not an allowable expense. However, if home is one's place of work then no expenditure under this heading is likely to be incurred and difficulties are unlikely to arise.

(g) Travelling and hotel expenses incurred for business purposes will normally be allowed but if any part could be construed as disguised holiday or pleasure expenditure, considerable thought would need to be given to the commercial reasons for the journey in order to justify the claim. The principle of "duality of purpose" will always be a difficult hurdle in this connection—although not insurmountable.

(h) If a separate business bank account is maintained, any overdraft interest thereon, will be an allowable expense. This is the *only* circumstance in which overdraft interest is allowed for tax purposes and care should be taken to avoid overdrafts in all other circumstances.

(i) Where capital allowances (see below) are claimed for a television, video, record or tape player, etc., used for business purposes an appropriate proportion of the costs of maintenance and repair of the equipment may also be claimed.

Clearly many other allowable items may be claimed in addition to those mentioned above. Wherever there is any reasonable busines motive for some expenditure it should be claimed as a deduction although one should avoid an excess of imagination as this would naturally cause the Inspector of Taxes to doubt the genuineness of other expenses claimed.

The question is often raised whether the whole amount of an expense may be deducted or whether the V.A.T. content must be excluded. Where V.A.T. is reclaimed from the Customs and Excise (on the quarterly returns made by a registered person), the V.A.T. element of the expense cannot be treated as an allowable deduction. Where the V.A.T. is not reclaimed, the whole expense (inclusive of V.A.T.) is allowable for Income Tax purposes.

CAPITAL ALLOWANCES

(a) *Allowances*

Where expenditure of a capital nature is incurred, it cannot be deducted from income as an expense—a separate and sometimes more valuable capital allowance being available instead. Capital allowances are given for many different types of expenditure, but authors and similar professional people are likely to claim only for "plant and machinery"; this is a very wide expression which may include motor cars, typewriters, home computers and other business machines, televisions, record and cassette players used for business purposes, books—and even a horse! Plant and machinery qualify for a 25% allowance in the year of purchase and 25% of the reducing balance in subsequent years.

The reason these allowances can be more valuable than allowable expenses is that they may be wholly or partly disclaimed in any year that full benefit cannot be obtained—ordinary business expenses cannot be similarly disclaimed. Where, for example, the income of an author does not exceed his personal allowances, he would not be liable to tax and a claim for capital allowances would be wasted. If the capital allowances were to be disclaimed their benefit would be carried forward for use in subsequent years.

Careful planning with claims for capital allowances is therefore essential if maximum benefit is to be obtained, especially where the spouse also has income chargeable to tax.

As an alternative to capital allowances claims can be made on the "renewals" basis whereby all renewals are treated as allowable deductions in the year; no allowance is obtained for the initial purchase, but the cost of replacement (excluding any improvement element) is allowed in full. This basis is no longer widely used, as it is considerably less advantageous than claiming capital allowances as described above.

Leasing is a popular method of acquiring fixed assets, and where cash is not available to enable an outright purchase to be made, assets may be leased over a period of time. Whilst leasing may have financial benefits in certain circumstances, in normal cases there is likely to be no *tax* advantage in leasing an asset where the alternative of outright purchase is available. Indeed, leasing can be a positive disadvantage in the case of motor cars with a new retail price of more than £8000. If such a car is leased, only a proportion of the leasing charges will be tax deductible.

(b) *Books*

The question of whether the cost of books is eligible for tax relief has long been a source of difficulty. The annual cost of replacing books used for the purposes of one's professional activities (e.g. the annual cost of a new *Writers and Artists Yearbook*) has always been an allowable expense; the difficulty arose because the initial cost of reference books etc. (for example when commencing one's profession) was treated as capital expenditure and no allowances were due as the books were not considered to be "plant". However, the matter has now been clarified by the case of *Munby* v. *Furlong* in which the Court of Appeal decided that the initial cost of law books purchased by a barrister was expenditure on "plant" and eligible for capital allowances. This is clearly a most important decision, particularly relevant to any person who uses expensive books in the course of exercising his profession.

PENSION CONTRIBUTIONS

(a) *Self-employed retirement annuities*

Where a self employed person pays annual premiums under an approved retirement annuity policy, tax relief may now be obtained each year for an amount up to 17½% of earnings without monetary limit.

These arrangements can be extremely advantageous in providing for a pension as premiums are usually paid when the income is high (and the tax relief is also high) and the pension (taxed as earned income when received) usually arises when the income is low and little tax is payable.

(b) *Class 4 National Insurance Contributions*

Allied to pensions is the payment of Class 4 National Insurance contributions, although no pension or other benefit is obtained by the contributions; the Class 4 contributions are designed solely to extract additional amounts from self-employed persons and are payable in addition to the normal Class 2 (self-employed) contributions. The rates are changed each year and for 1986-87 self-employed persons will be obliged to contribute 6.3% of their profits between the range £4450 − £14820 per annum, a maximum liability of £653.31 for 1986-87. This amount is collected in conjunction with the Schedule "D" Income Tax liability and appears on the same assessment; the comments below regarding assessments, appeals and postponement apply equally to Class 4 contributions although interest does not ordinarily accrue on their late payment. Tax relief is available from 6th April 1985 for one half of the Class 4 contributions.

SPREADING RELIEF

(a) *Relief for Copyright Payments*

Special provisions enable authors and similar persons who have been engaged on a literary, dramatic, musical or artistic work for a period of more than twelve months, to spread certain amounts received over two or three years depending on the time spent in preparing the work. If the author was engaged on the work for a period exceeding twelve months, the receipt may be spread backwards over two years; if the author was engaged on the work for more than 24 months, the

receipt may be spread backwards over three years. (Analogous provisions apply to sums received for the sale of a painting, sculpture or other work of art.) The relief applies to:
a. lump sums received on the assignment of copyright, in whole or in part;
b. sums received on the grant of any interest in the copyright by licence;
c. non-returnable advances on account of royalties;
d. any receipts of or on account of royalties or any periodical sums received within two years of first publication.

A claim for spreading relief has to be made within eight years from the 5th April following the date of first publication.

(b) *Relief where copyright sold after ten years*

Where copyright is assigned (or a licence in it is granted) more than ten years after the first publication of the work, then the amounts received can qualify for a different spreading relief. The assignment (or licence) must be for a period of more than two years and the receipt will be spread forward over the number of years for which the assignment (or licence) is granted—but with a maximum of six years. The relief is terminated by death, but there are provisions enabling the deceased's author's personal representatives to re-spread the amounts if it is to the beneficiaries' advantage.

The above rules are arbitrary and cumbersome, only providing a limited measure of relief in special circumstances. The provisions can sometimes be helpful to repair matters when consideration of the tax position has been neglected, but invariably a better solution is found if the likely tax implications are considered fully in advance.

COLLECTION OF TAX

(a) *Assessments*

In order to collect the tax which is due on the profits of authorship the Inland Revenue issue an assessment based on the income for the relevant period. Normally the income to be assessed will be that for the previous year (e.g. the 1986/7 assessment will be based on the accounts made up to some date in 1985/86—perhaps 31st December 1985 or 5th April 1986). However, there are complicated rules for determining the income to be assessed in the years immediately after commencement, and in the years immediately prior to the discontinuance of the profession, and if for any reason there is a change in the date to which accounts are made up.

When an assessment is received it should be examined carefully and if it is correct, the tax should be paid on the dates specified. Usually the tax is payable in two equal instalments, on 1st January in the year of assessment and on the following 1st July. If payment is delayed then interest may arise—see below.

(b) If the assessment is incorrect (for example, if it is estimated), then prompt action is required. An appeal must be lodged within thirty days of the date of issue of the assessment specifying the grounds of the appeal. An appeal form usually accompanies the notice of assessment. (If for some reason an appeal cannot be lodged within the thirty days the Inland Revenue are often prepared to accept a late appeal, but this is at their discretion and acceptance cannot be guaranteed.) If there is any tax charged on an incorrect assessment it cannot simply be forgotten, because it will become payable despite any appeal, unless an application for "postponement" is also made. (This may be done by completing the bottom half of the appeal form.) Tax can be postponed only where there are grounds for believing that too much tax has been charged, and the

Inspector of Taxes will agree to postpone tax only if these grounds are reasonable. The tax which is not postponed will usually be payable on the normal due dates. It is necessary to consider claims for postponement most carefully to ensure that approximately the correct amount of tax remains payable; otherwise an unfortunate (and expensive) charge to interest could arise. It is important to recognise that "postponement" does not mean elimination; it simply means that payment of tax may be deferred—usually for only six months. After that period has expired interest will start to run on any tax which has been postponed but which is ultimately found to be payable. As agreement of the final liability may take a long time, a large amount of interest can arise unless a reasonably accurate amount has been paid on time.

(c) *Interest*

Interest is chargeable on overdue tax at a rate of 11% per annum and does not rank for any tax relief which often makes the Inland Revenue a very expensive source of credit. Where the amount of interest is less than £30 in any year it is not usually collected but should the interest exceed £30 the full amount will be payable and it is extraordinarily difficult to persuade the Inland Revenue to withdraw a charge to interest—even where the delay is their fault.

However, the Inland Revenue can also be obliged to pay interest (known as repayment supplement) at 11% tax-free where repayments are delayed. The rules relating to repayment supplement are less beneficial and even more complicated than the rules for interest payable but they do exist and can be very welcome if a large repayment has been delayed for a long time.

(d) *Example*

Author's accounts made up to 30th April 1985 showing profits of £3,000 giving rise to tax of (say) £200.
Assessment issued in September 1986 for 1986/87 in an estimated figure of £5,000—tax charged £1,500.
Appeal must be made within 30 days of issue.

Application for postponement must also be made within 30 days to postpone £1,300 of the tax charged.
Tax therefore becomes payable thus:

1st Jan. 1987	£100
1st July 1987	£100

(if no application for postponement were to be made £750 would become payable on each of these dates. When the final liability is agreed the excess of £1,300 would be refunded but that could take some time, and repayment supplement might not apply.)

Unfortunately life is never as simple as the above illustration would suggest, but it serves to demonstrate the principle.

VALUE ADDED TAX

The activities of writers, painters, composers, etc., are all "taxable supplies" within the scope of V.A.T. and chargeable at the standard rate. (Zero rating which applies to publishers, booksellers, etc., on the supply of books does not extend to the work performed by writers; the position is less clear with regard to authors writing for foreign persons. Changes were made in the V.A.T. rules from 1st January 1978 with the effect that zero rating does not always apply. Proper advice should be sought if there is any doubt regarding the correct treatment). Accordingly, authors are obliged to register for V.A.T. if their income exceeds certain limits; the annual limit has recently been increased to £20,500 per annum with effect from 18th March 1986, but there is a quarterly limit of £7,000, which if exceeded may render the author liable to registration.

Delay in registering can be a most serious matter because if registration is not effected at the proper time, the Customs and Excise can (and invariably do) claim V.A.T. from all the income received since the date on which registration should have been made. As no V.A.T. would have been included in the amounts received during this period the amount claimed by the Customs and Excise must inevitably come straight from the pocket of the author—and he may not be able to claim reimbursement from all those whom he ought to have charged V.A.T. in the interregnum.

(This difficulty can give rise to considerable injustice and has done so on a number of occasions; the appeal tribunals concerned have often expressed sympathy for the taxpayer's predicament but have been unable to provide any relief.)

Nevertheless it is possible to regard V.A.T. registration as a privilege and not a penalty, because only V.A.T. registered persons can reclaim V.A.T. paid on such expenditure as stationery, telephone, professional fees, etc., even typewriters and other plant and machinery (excluding cars). However, many find that the administrative inconvenience, the cost of maintaining the necessary records and completing the necessary forms, more than outweighs the benefits to be gained from registration and prefer to stay outside the scope of V.A.T. for as long as possible.

OVERSEAS MATTERS

The general observation may be made that self employed persons resident and domiciled in the United Kingdom are not well treated with regard to their overseas work, being taxable on their world wide income. It is important to emphasise that if fees are earned abroad, no tax saving can be achieved merely by keeping the money outside the country. Although exchange control regulations no longer exist to require repatriation of foreign earnings, such income remains taxable in the U.K. and must be disclosed to the Inland Revenue; the same applies to interest or other income arising on any investment of these earnings overseas. Accordingly whenever foreign earnings are likely to become substantial, prompt and effective action is required to limit the impact of U.K. and foreign taxation. In the case of non resident authors it is important that arrangements concerning writing for publication in the U.K. e.g. in newspapers, are undertaken with great care. A recent case concerning the wife of one of the great train robbers who provided detailed information for a series of articles in a Sunday newspaper is most instructive. Although she was acknowledged to be resident in Canada for all the relevant years, the income from the articles was treated as arising in this country and fully chargeable to U.K. tax.

The United Kingdom has double taxation agreements with many other countries and these agreements are designed to ensure that income arising in a foreign country is taxed either in that country, or in the United Kingdom. Where a withholding tax is deducted from payments received from another country, (or where tax is paid in full in the absence of a double taxation agreement) the amount of foreign tax paid can usually be set off against the related U.K. tax liability. Many successful authors can be found living in Eire because of the complete exemption from tax which attaches to works of cultural or artistic merit by persons who are resident there. However, such a step should only be contemplated having careful regard to all the other domestic and commercial considerations and specialist advice is essential if the exemption is to be obtained and kept; a careless breach of the conditions could cause the exemption to be withdrawn with catastrophic consequences.

COMPANIES

When an author becomes successful the prospect of paying tax at alarmingly high rates often drives him to take hasty action such as the formation of companies etc., which may not always be to his advantage. Indeed some authors seeing the exodus into tax exile of their more successful colleagues even form companies in low tax areas in the naive expectation of saving large amounts of tax. Unfortunately such action is just as likely to *increase* their tax liabilities and generate other costs and should never be contemplated without expert advice; some very expensive mistakes are often made in this area which are not always able to be remedied.

To conduct one's business through the medium of a company can be a most effective method of mitigating tax liabilities, providing it is done at the right time and under the right circumstances, when very substantial advantages can be derived. However, if done without due care and attention the intended advantages will simply evaporate. At the very least it is essential to take care to ensure that the company's business is genuine and conducted properly with regard to the realities of the situation. If the author continues his activities unchanged, simply paying all the receipts from his work into a company's bank account he cannot expect to persuade the Inland Revenue that it is the company and not himself who is entitled to, and should be assessed to tax on, that income. It must be strongly emphasised that many pitfalls exist which can easily eliminate all the tax benefits expected to arise by the formation of the company. For example, company directors are employees of the company and will be liable to pay much higher National Insurance contributions; the company must also pay the employers proportion of the contribution and a total liability of nearly 20% of gross salary (up to certain limits) may arise. This compares most unfavourably with the position of a self-employed person. Moreover on the commencement of the company's business the individual's profession will cease and the Inland Revenue have the power to re-open earlier years assessments and may be able to increase the liabilities for previous years; this is always a crucial factor in determining the best moment when the changeover to a company should take place.

No mention has been made above of personal reliefs and allowances (for example the single and married persons allowances, etc.); this is because these allowances and the rates of tax are subject to constant change and are always set out in detail in the explanatory notes which accompany the Tax Return. The annual Tax Return is an important document and should not be ignored because it is crucial to one's tax position. Indeed, it should be completed promptly with extreme care because the Inland Revenue treat failures to disclose income very harshly, invariably exacting interest and penalties—sometimes of substantial amounts. If filling in the Return is a source of difficulty or anxiety, comfort may be found in the Consumer Association's publication *Money Which—Tax Saving Guide*; this is published in March of each year and includes much which is likely to be of interest and assistance.

SOCIAL SECURITY CONTRIBUTIONS

J. PHILIP HARDMAN, F.C.A., F.T.I.I.
Chartered Accountant

INTRODUCTION

In general, every person who works in Great Britain either as an employee or who is self employed is liable to pay social security contributions. The law governing this subject is complicated and the following should only be regarded as a summary of the position.

All contributions are payable in respect of years ending on the 5th April, the classes of contributions being as follows:

Class 1 These are payable by employees (primary contributions) and their employers (secondary contributions) and are based on earnings.

Class 2 These are flat rate contributions, payable weekly by the self employed.

Class 3 These are weekly flat rate contributions, payable on a voluntary basis in order to provide, or make up entitlement to, certain social security benefits.

Class 4 These are payable by the self employed in respect of their trading or professional income and are based on earnings.

EMPLOYED OR SELF EMPLOYED?

The question as to whether a person is employed under a contract *of* service and is thereby an employee liable to Class 1 contributions, or performs services (either solely or in partnership) under a contract *for* service and is thereby self employed liable to Class 2 and Class 4 contributions, often has to be decided in practice. Probably the best guide can be found in the case of *Market Investigations Limited* v. *Minister of Social Security* (1969 2 WLR 1) when Cooke J. remarked as follows:

". . . the fundamental test to be applied is this: 'Is the person who has engaged himself to perform these services performing them as a person in business on his own account?' If the answer to that question is 'yes', then the contract is a contract for services. If the answer is 'no', then the contract is a contract of service. No exhaustive list has been compiled and perhaps no exhaustive list can be compiled of the considerations which are relevant in determining that question, nor can strict rules be laid down as to the relative weight which the various considerations should carry in particular cases. The most that can be said is that control will no doubt always have to be considered, although it can no longer be regarded as the sole determining factor; and that factors which may be of importance are such matters as
—whether the man performing the services provides his own equipment,
—whether he hires his own helpers,
—what degree of financial risk he takes,
—what degree of responsibility for investment and management he has, and
—whether and how far he has an opportunity of profiting from sound management in the performance of his task."

There have been three cases in recent years, all dealing with musicians, which provide further guidance on the question as to whether an individual is employed or self-employed.

Midland Sinfonia Concert Society Ltd. v. *Secretary of State for Social Services* (The Times, 10th November 1980)

A musician, employed to play in an orchestra by separate invitation at irregular intervals and remunerated solely in respect of each occasion upon which he does play, is employed under a contract for services. He is therefore self-employed, not an employed earner, for the purposes of the Social Security Act 1975, and the orchestra which engages him is not liable to pay National Insurance contributions in respect of his earnings.

Addison v. *London Philharmonic Orchestra Limited* (The Times, 21st October 1980)

This was an appeal to determine whether certain individuals were employees for the purposes of section 11(1) of the Employment Protection (Consolidation) Act 1978.

The Employment Appeal Tribunal upheld the decision of an industrial tribunal that an associate player and three additional or extra players of the London Philharmonic Orchestra were not employees under a contract of service, but were essentially freelance musicians carrying on their own business.

The facts found by the industrial tribunal showed that, when playing for the orchestra, each appellant remained essentially a freelance musician, pursuing his or her own profession as an instrumentalist, with an individual reputation, and carrying on his or her own business, and they contributed their own skills and interpretative powers to the orchestra's performances as independent contractors.

Winfield v. *London Philharmonic Orchestra Limited* (ICR 1979, page 726)

This case dealt with the question as to whether an individual was an employee within the meaning of section 30 of the Trade Union and Labour Relations Act 1974.

The following remarks by the appeal tribunal are of interest in relation to the status of musicians:

". . . Making music is an art, and the co-operation required for a performance of Berlioz's *Requiem* is dissimilar to that required between the manufacturer of concrete and the truck driver who takes the concrete where it is needed . . . It took the view, as we think it was entitled on the material before it to do, that the company was simply machinery through which the members of the orchestra managed and controlled the orchestra's operation . . . In deciding whether you are in the presence of a contract of service or not, you look at the whole of the picture. This picture looks to us, as it looked to the industrial tribunal, like a co-operative of distinguished musicians running themselves with self and mutual discipline, and in no sense like a boss and his musician employees."

Accordingly, if a person is regarded as an employee under the above rules, he will be liable to pay contributions even if his employment is casual, part time or temporary.

Furthermore, if a person is an employee and also carries on a trade or profession either solely or in partnership, there will be a liability to more than one class of contributions (subject to certain maxima—see below).

Exceptions

There are certain exceptions to the above rules, those most relevant as regards artists and writers being:

(a) The employment of a wife by her husband, or vice versa, is disregarded for social security purposes unless it is for the purposes of a trade or profession (for example, the employment of his wife by an author would not be disregarded and would result in a liability for contributions if her salary reached the minimum levels).

(b) The employment of certain relatives in a private dwelling house in which both employee and employer reside is disregarded for social security purposes provided the employment is not for the purposes of a trade or business carried on at those premises by the employer. This would cover the employment of a relative (as defined) as a housekeeper in a private residence.

(c) In general, lecturers, teachers and instructors engaged by an educational establishment to teach on at least four days in three consecutive months are regarded as employees, although this rule does not apply to fees received by persons giving public lectures.

CLASS 1 CONTRIBUTIONS BY EMPLOYEES AND EMPLOYERS

As mentioned above, these are related to earnings, the amount payable depending upon whether the employer has applied for his employees to be "contracted-out" of the State earnings-related pension scheme; such application can be made where the employer's own pension scheme provides a requisite level of benefits for his employees and their dependents.

Up to 6th October 1985, when earnings reach the lower earnings limit primary and secondary Class 1 contributions are payable on earnings up to the upper earnings limit, although for contracted-out employments there are reduced rates of contributions in respect of earnings between the lower and upper limits.

From 6th October 1985 the upper earnings limit for secondary contributions, but not for primary contributions, is removed, and contribution rates on lower earnings reduced.

Contributions are normally collected via the PAYE tax deduction documents.

Employees liable to pay contributions

These are payable by any employee who is aged 16 years and over (even though he may still be at school) and who is paid an amount equal to, or exceeding, the lower earnings limit (see below).

Nationality is irrelevant for contribution purposes and, subject to special rules covering employees not normally resident in Great Britain, Northern Ireland or the Isle of Man, or resident in countries with which there are reciprocal social security agreements, contributions must be paid whether the employee concerned is a British subject or not provided he is gainfully employed in Great Britain.

Employees exempt from liability to pay contributions

Persons over pensionable age (65 for men and 60 for women) are exempt from liability to pay primary contributions, even if they have not retired.

However, the fact that an employee may be exempt from liability does not relieve an employer from liability to pay secondary contributions in respect of that employee.

Rate of employees' contributions

For earnings paid prior to 6th October 1985, all employees liable to pay contributions (which are calculated on gross earnings before PAYE and other deductions) pay at the standard rate of 9.00%. This rate is reduced to 6.85% on earnings above the lower and up to and including the upper earnings limit in respect of contracted-out employments. However, certain married women who made appropriate elections before the 12th May 1977 may be entitled to pay a reduced rate of 3.85%. However, these ladies will have no entitlement to benefits in respect of these contributions.

For earnings paid on or after 6th October 1985 employees are liable at rates of 5%, 7% or 9% on all their earnings up to and including the upper earnings limit depending upon the particular band into which their earnings fall (see below). It is emphasized that the rate of contributions attributable to the band into which a person's weekly, monthly, etc., earnings fall is applied to *all* those earnings (up to the upper limit) and not merely to the earnings falling into that band. The above three rates of primary contributions are reduced to 2.85%, 4.85% and 6.85% in respect of earnings above the lower and up to and including the upper earnings limits for contracted-out employments. The position for married women entitled to pay the reduced rate is unchanged.

Employers' contributions

All employers are liable to pay contributions on the gross earnings of employees. As mentioned above, an employer's liability is not reduced as a result of employees being exempted from, or being liable to pay only the (3.85%) reduced rate of, contributions.

For earnings paid prior to 6th October 1985, employers' contributions are payable at the rate of 10.45%, although in the case of contracted-out employments the rate reduces to 6.35% on earnings above the lower and up to and including the upper earnings limit.

For earnings paid on or after 6th October 1985 employers are liable at rates of 5%, 7%, 9% or 10.45% on earnings paid (without any upper earnings limit) depending upon the particular band into which the earnings fall (see below). The rate of contributions attributable to the band into which the earnings fall is applied to *all* those earnings and not merely to the earnings falling into that band. The above four rates of secondary contributions are reduced to 0.9%, 2.9%, 4.9% and 6.35% in respect of earnings above the lower earnings limit for contracted-out employments.

The employer is responsible for the payment of both employees' and employer's contributions, but is entitled to deduct the employees' contributions from the earnings on which they are calculated. Effectively, therefore, the employee suffers a deduction in respect of his social security contributions in arriving at his weekly or monthly wage or salary.

Special rules apply to company directors and persons employed through agencies.

Rates of Class 1 contributions and earnings limits from 6th April 1986

Earnings per week	Rates payable on all Earnings			
	Contracted In		Contracted Out	
	Employee	Employer	Employee	Employer
£	%	%	%	%
0.00 – 37.99	-	-	-	-
38.00 – 59.99	5.00	5.00	*5.00/2.85	5.00/0.90
60.00 – 94.99	7.00	7.00	*7.00/4.85	7.00/2.90
95.00 – 139.99	9.00	9.00	*9.00/6.85	9.00/4.90
140.00 – 285.00	9.00	10.45	*9.00/6.85	10.45/6.35
Over £285	-	10.45	-	10.45

*The first figure is the rate to the lower earnings limit and the second is to the top of the earnings or the upper earnings limit whichever is the lower.

As the employers' contributions are on all pay those employees who are over £285 per week and are contracted out will attract employers' contributions at 10.45% on all pay less 4.10% on £247 per week (£285 – £38).

Where a married woman contributes at the lower rate of 3.85% the above employer's rates apply whether contracted in or contracted out.

Those who are over 65 (60 for women) do not pay employees' contributions but their pay does attract employers' contracted-in contributions. This also applies to those who were contracted out until pensionable age and who continue to work.

Items included in, or excluded from, earnings

Contributions are calculated on the basis of a person's gross earnings from his employment. This will normally be the figure shown on the tax deduction card, except where the employee pays superannuation contributions and from 6th April 1987 charitable gifts—these must be added back for the purposes of calculating Class 1 liability.

Earnings include salary, wages, overtime pay, commissions, bonuses, holiday pay, payments made while the employee is sick or absent from work, payments to cover travel between home and office, and payments under the statutory sick pay scheme.

However, certain payments, some of which may be regarded as taxable income for income tax purposes, are ignored for social security purposes. These include gratuities paid other than by the employer, redundancy payments and payments in lieu of notice, payments in kind, reimbursement of specific expenses incurred in the carrying out of the employment, benefits given for personal reasons (e.g. wedding and birthday presents), compensation for loss of office, and meal vouchers.

Maximum contributions

There is a limit to the total liability for social security contributions payable by a person who is employed in more than one employment, or is also self employed or a partner.

For 1986/87 these are as follows:

(a) Where only Class 1, or Class 1 and Class 2 contributions are payable:
 (i) if contributions payable at standard rate—53 primary Class 1 contributions at standard rate on upper weekly earnings limit
  —if all employments not contracted-out £1359.45
  —if all employments contracted-out £1078.02
 (ii) if contributions payable at reduced rate—53 primary Class 1 contributions at reduced rate on upper weekly earnings limit £581.41

(b) Where Class 1, 2 and 4 contributions are payable, the combined annual maximum amount to be paid is £852.06 where the Class 1 earnings are £7300.67 or less. Where Class 1 earnings are more than £7300.67 the combined annual maximum increases in line with the Class 1 earnings to the limit of £1359.45. In these circumstances deferment of Class 2 and 4 contributions is available by application before the beginning of the tax year.

Company directors

Directors with comparable annual earnings, but differing earnings patterns (for example, a small regular salary topped up with an annual bonus as compared with a regular salary only) have in the past had widely differing contribution liabilities in view of the rules regarding earnings periods. In addition, a wide variety of pay practices has created many problems in assessing the correct liability.

As from the 6th April 1983 new provisions took effect specifically for company directors. These provisions should in the majority of cases reduce the potential unevenness of contribution liability hitherto experienced. In general, directors are treated as being paid annually but the provisions are complex and outside the scope of this article.

Miscellaneous rules

There are detailed rules covering a person with two or more employments; where a person receives a bonus or commission in addition to a regular wage or salary; and where a person is in receipt of holiday pay.

CLASS 2 CONTRIBUTIONS BY THE SELF EMPLOYED

Rate

Class 2 contributions are payable at the rate of £3.75 per week as from the 6th April 1986.

Exemptions from Class 2 liability

These are as follows:
(1) A man over 65 or a woman over 60.
(2) A person who has not attained the age of 16.
(3) A married woman or, in certain cases, a widow could elect prior to the 12th May 1977 not to pay Class 2 contributions.
(4) Persons with small earnings (see below).
(5) Persons not ordinarily self employed (see below).
(6) Persons in receipt of invalid care allowance.
(7) Persons in receipt of sickness, invalidity or injury benefits or unemployability supplements, or maternity allowances, or incapable of work or in prison or legal custody.

Small earnings

Any person who can show that his net self employed earnings per his profit and loss account (as opposed to taxable profits):
(1) for the year of application are expected to be less than a specified limit (£2,075 in the 1986/87 tax year); or
(2) for the year preceding the application were less than the limit specified for that year (£1,925 for 1985/86) and there has been no material change of circumstances;
may apply for a certificate of exception from Class 2 contributions. Certificates of exception must be renewed each tax year. At the Secretary of State's discretion the certificate may commence up to 13 weeks before the date on which the application is made. Despite a certificate of exception being in force, a person who is self employed is still entitled to pay Class 2 contributions if he wishes, in order to maintain entitlement to social security benefits.

Persons not ordinarily self-employed

Part-time self employed activities as a writer or artist are disregarded for contribution purposes if the person concerned is not ordinarily employed in such activities. There is no definition of "ordinarily employed" for this purpose but the D.H.S.S. regard a person who has a regular job and whose earnings from spare-time occupation are not expected to be more than £800 per annum as falling within this category. Persons qualifying for this relief do not require certificates of exception. It should be noted that many activities covered by this relief would probably also be eligible for relief under the small earnings rule (see above).

Method of payment

Class 2 contributions may be paid by purchasing stamps to be fixed to contribution cards, or alternatively application may be made to pay contributions by direct debit through a bank account or the Post Office giro system.

Overpaid contributions

If, following the payment of Class 2 contributions, it is found that the earnings are below the exception limit (e.g. the relevant accounts are prepared late), the Class 2 contributions that have been overpaid cannot be reclaimed.

CLASS 3 CONTRIBUTIONS

These are payable voluntarily, at the rate of £3.65 per week from the 6th April 1986 by persons aged 16 or over with a view to enabling them to qualify for a limited range of benefits if their contribution record is not otherwise sufficient. In general, Class 3 contributions can be paid by employees, the self employed and the non employed. A married woman who will be 60 before her husband is 65 should enquire from the DHSS whether she has at least 10 years of full contributions thus entitling her to a reduced minimum basic pension. If not, then she may be able to pay Class 3 contributions before the tax year in which she becomes 60 in order to complete that 10 years and thus obtain the minimum pension.

Broadly speaking, no more than 52 Class 3 contributions are payable for any one tax year, and contributions are not payable after the end of the tax year in which the individual concerned reaches the age of 64 (59 for women).

Class 3 contributions may be paid by purchasing stamps to be fixed to contribution cards, or by direct debit through a bank account or the Post Office giro system.

CLASS 4 CONTRIBUTIONS BY THE SELF EMPLOYED

Rate

In addition to Class 2 contributions, self employed persons are liable to pay Class 4 contributions. These are calculated at the rate of 6.30% on the amount of profits or gains chargeable to income tax under Schedule D Case I or II which exceed £4,450 per annum but which do not exceed £14,820 per annum for 1986/87. Thus the maximum Class 4 contribution is 6.30% of £10,370—i.e. £653.31 per annum.

For the tax year 1986/87, Class 4 contributions are based on the income tax assessment for 1986/87 (for example, the profits of the year ending 31st December 1985) and so on for subsequent years.

The income tax assessment on which Class 4 contributions are calculated is after deducting capital allowances and losses, but before deducting personal tax allowances.

Class 4 contributions produce no additional benefits, but were introduced to ensure that self employed persons as a whole pay a fair share of the cost of pensions and other social security benefits without the self employed who make only small profits having to pay excessively high flat rate contributions.

For 1985/86 and subsequent years, one half of the Class 4 contributions (as finally settled) is deductible in computing total income. It should be noted that this deduction is given in arriving at total income for income tax purposes and not in arriving at the profits assessable under Schedule D. Where a wife's earnings election is in force or the couple have elected to be taxed separately, it appears that the deduction is given against her income and not that of her husband. Although the legislation states that a claim is necessary, it is understood that in practice the deduction will be given automatically. This deduction is broadly equivalent to that available to employers for tax purposes in respect of their secondary contributions, and was introduced to rectify the previous anomaly in that employers, but not the self employed, were eligible for tax relief for the contributions they bore. Where deferment of Class 2 and 4 contributions has been obtained ensure that the eventually assessed Class 4, if any, is allowed for income tax purposes.

Payment of contributions

In general, contributions are calculated and collected by the Inland Revenue together with the income tax under Schedule D Case I or II, and accordingly the contributions are due and payable at the same time as the income tax liability on the relevant profits.

Persons exempt from Class 4 contributions

The following persons are exempt from Class 4 contributions:
(1) Men over 65 and women over 60 at the commencement of the year of assessment (i.e. on the 6th April).
(2) An individual not resident in the United Kingdom for income tax purposes in the year of assessment.
(3) Persons whose earnings are not "immediately derived" from carrying on a trade, profession or vocation (for example, sleeping partners and, probably, limited partners).
(4) A child under 16 on the 6th April of the year of assessment.
(5) Persons not ordinarily self employed (see above as for Class 2 contributions).

Calculation of liability for married persons and partnerships

The Class 4 liability of a husband and wife is calculated separately although the liability is that of the husband. If however a husband or wife has elected to be assessed separately for income tax purposes, or if they have jointly elected that the wife's earned income should be taxed as if she were a single person, the election will also apply for Class 4 purposes. This means that the Class 4 contributions of the wife will be assessed on, and collected from, her instead of her husband.

As regards partnerships, each partner's liability is calculated separately, and the Inland Revenue will normally collect each partner's Class 4 liability in the partnership name as is the case with the income tax liability of the partnership under Schedule D. If a partner also carries on another trade or profession, the profits of all such businesses are aggregated for the purposes of calculating his Class 4 liability; in these circumstances the Class 4 liability in respect of his share of partnership profits may be assessed separately and not in the partnership name.

When an assessment has become final and conclusive for the purposes of income tax, it is also final and conclusive for the purposes of calculating Class 4 liability.

SOURCES OF FURTHER INFORMATION

Further information can be obtained from the many booklets published by the Department of Health and Social Security, and from Accountants Digest No. 172 published by The Institute of Chartered Accountants in England and Wales. Individuals resident abroad should address their enquiries to the D.H.S.S. Overseas Branch, Newcastle-upon-Tyne, NE98 1YX.

SOCIAL SECURITY BENEFITS

K. D. BARTLETT, F.C.A.
Chartered Accountant

Social Security benefits are quite difficult to understand. There are many leaflets produced by the Department of Health and Social Security but there is no one source available to research a query.

This article is written to try to simplify some of the more usual benefits that are available under the Social Security Acts. It deliberately does not cover every aspect of the legislation but the references given should enable the relevant information to be easily traced. These references are to the leaflets issued by the Department of Health and Social Security.

It is usual for only one periodical benefit to be payable at any one time. If the contribution conditions are satisfied for more than one benefit it is the larger benefit that is payable. Benefit rates shown below are those payable from week commencing 28 July 1986.

Employed persons (Category A contributors) are covered for all benefits. Certain married women and widows (Category B contributors) who elected to pay at the reduced rate receive only attendance allowance, guardian's allowance and industrial injuries benefits. Other benefits may be available dependent on their husband's contributions.

Self-employed persons (Class 2 and Class 4 contributors) are covered for all benefits except earnings-related supplements, unemployment benefit, widow's and invalidity pensions and widowed mother's allowance.

FAMILY BENEFITS

Child Benefits (CH 1)

Child benefit was introduced to replace family allowances and is payable for all children who are either under 16 or under 19 and receiving full-time education at a recognised educational establishment. The rate is £7.10 a week per child. It is payable to the person who is responsible for the child but excludes foster parents or people exempt from United Kingdom tax. A higher benefit (£4.60 a week more) is payable for the first or only child in a one parent family.

Maternity Benefits (NI 17A)

A woman is entitled on confinement to a maternity grant of £25 provided she has been present in Great Britain for a total of at least 6 months in the period of 52 weeks immediately preceding the beginning of the week in which the baby is expected.

Maternity Allowance (NI 17A)

On giving up work a woman is entitled to a maternity allowance of £29.45 a week normally for 18 weeks commencing with the 11th week before the expected week of confinement provided that the necessary contribution conditions have been met.

Guardian's Allowance (NI 14)

This is paid at the rate of £8.05 a week to people who have taken orphans into their own family. Usually both of the child's parents must be dead and at least one of them must have satisfied a residence condition.

The allowance can only be paid to the person who is entitled to child benefit to the child (or to that person's spouse). It is not necessary to be the legal guardian. The claim should be made within three months of the date of entitlement.

BENEFITS FOR HANDICAPPED OR DISABLED PEOPLE
Mobility Allowance (NI 211)

This is a non-contributory benefit payable to persons aged between 5 and 65 who are unable to walk because of physical disablement. The allowance is £21.65 per week. It is no longer subject to tax.

Attendance Allowance (NI 205)

This is payable to persons aged 2 or over who are so severely disabled physically or mentally that they require frequent attention during the day or night or frequent attention for both day and night. A higher rate is payable (£30.95 a week) if attention is required day and night and a lower rate of £20.65 is payable if attention is only required in the day or in the night. The attendance allowance board decide whether, and for how long, a person is eligible for this allowance. Attendance allowance is not taxable.

BENEFITS FOR THE ILL OR UNEMPLOYED
Sickness Benefit (NI 16)

Since 6 April 1983 most employees have been entitled to receive statutory sick pay (SSP) from their employers for initial periods of absence from work due to sickness or disablement. SSP is payable up to 8 weeks of absence in all in a tax year. Once SSP is exhausted sickness benefit is payable but only for a maximum of 120 days, then only if certain contribution conditions have been met. The claimant may be disqualified from receiving benefit if he has delayed his own recovery or fails to attend a medical examination when asked to do so. Only employed persons who pay Class 1 contributions or self employed persons who pay Class 2 contributions qualify. Sickness benefit is not payable for the first 3 days of a period of interruption of employment.

Invalidity Benefit (NI 16A)

An invalidity pension is substituted for sickness benefit after this has been paid for 168 days of incapacity. To qualify one must be unable to work and have been entitled to sickness benefit for 168 days in a period of interruption of employment. This pension is currently £38.70 a week.

An invalidity allowance is payable with invalidity pension to those who are more than 5 years away from retirement age. The rates are as follows:

Standard rate of invalidity pension:

	£
Single person	38.70
Spouse or adult dependent	23.25
Invalidity allowance:	
(i) Higher rate	8.15
(ii) Middle rate	5.20
(iii) Lower rate	2.60

For each dependent child £8.05 is payable.

SOCIAL SECURITY BENEFITS

Severe Disablement Allowance (NI 252)

This allowance has replaced non-contributory Invalidity Pension and Housewife's non-contributory Invalidity Pension. This new allowance is similar to the old allowances and claimants on the old system will generally qualify for the new allowance. There is now no longer a "household duties test" with the result that men and women now qualify on an equal basis. This is a non-taxable benefit paid to people of working age who cannot work due to physical or mental ill-health, but who do not have N.I. contributions to qualify for sickness or invalidity benefit. The basic allowance is £23.25 a week. There are increases of £13.90 a week for adult dependents and £8.05 for each dependent child.

Invalid Care Allowance (NI 212)

This is a taxable benefit paid to people of working age who cannot take a job because they have to stay at home to look after a severely disabled person.

Unemployment Benefit (NI 12)

Unemployment benefit is payable for a maximum period of one year in any period or interruption of employment. Once this year's unemployment pay is reached a claimant cannot qualify again until he has worked as an employee for at least 13 weeks and has worked in each of these weeks for 16 hours or more.

To be eligible the claimant must be unemployed but available for work but can be disqualified from receiving benefit for a period of up to 6 weeks if he lost his employment without just cause or failed to accept suitable employment offered.

Unemployment benefit is not payable for the first three days of a period of interruption of employment in the same way as for sickness benefit.

Persons over 18 should register for work at their local Employment Office or Job Centre and should go to their local unemployment benefit office to claim benefit. Either a P45 or a note of their national insurance number should be produced. Persons under 18 should register for work at their local Youth Employment Office. From April 1981 unemployment benefit is reduced, pound for pound, for those whose pensions exceed £35 a week.

The standard rate of unemployment benefit is £30.80 for a single person and £19.00 for a wife or other adult dependent.

PENSIONS AND WIDOW'S BENEFITS (NP 23, NP 35, NP 31)

The State Pension Scheme

The Social Security Pensions Act 1975 introduced the new State Pension Scheme launched in 1978. The major effect of this scheme is that an employed person, can, on retirement, qualify for a pension in two parts—an earnings-related part, as well as the basic part—and both will be protected from the effects of inflation. Widows' pensions and invalidity pensions will also include an additional earnings-related pension.

Retirement, invalidity and widow's pensions for employees are related to the earnings on which national insurance contributions have been paid.

The self-employed are not covered for the earnings-related pension and pay a flat weekly contribution. They are also liable for an earnings-related Class IV contribution of 6.3% of their profits chargeable to Case I and Case II of Schedule D tax between £4450 and £14,280 during 1986-7, being a maximum figure of £653.31. There are exceptions to this, the main one being that it does not apply to men over 65 and women over 60 in the year of assessment following 65th (or 60th) birthday and to subsequent years. One half of the Class IV payment is allowed as a charge against the income tax liability.

The pensionable age is the 65th birthday for men and 60th birthday for women. Employees over pensionable age do not have to pay contributions after 6th April,

1978, although their employers are still liable for their own contributions (at the not-contracted-out rate in all cases).

The basic pension is £38.70 a week for a single person and an additional £23.25 for a wife where her pension is based only on the husband's contributions. Pension increases will take place each year and will be in line with the greater of the annual movement in the general level of earnings or the rise in prices.

The earnings-related pension will be 1¼% of average earnings between the lower earnings limit for contribution liability and the upper earnings limit for each year of such earnings under the scheme and will thus build up to 25% in 20 years. If the number of years exceeds 20, pension will be based on the contributors 20 best years of earnings between age 16 and pension age. Actual earnings will be revalued in terms of the earnings level current in the last complete tax year before pension age (or death or incapacity).

Widows will receive the whole or part of additional pensions earned by their husbands with their widow's pensions or widowed mother's allowances. They can add to their own retirement pensions based on their own contributions any additional pension earned by their husbands but the maximum pension they can receive is limited to the maximum payable on one person's contributions. A woman staying at home to bring up her children or look after a person who qualifies for attendance allowance, can have her basic pension rights protected without the need to pay contributions. For each year (from 1st April 1978) the number of years of contributions needed to qualify for a full basic pension will be reduced by the number of years for which the protection is given but contributions must still have been paid for at least 20 years to qualify for the full basic pension. Since 5th April 1979 married women are no longer subject to the rule that they must have paid minimum level contributions in at least half the years between their marriage and their 60th birthday in order to receive any basic contributions.

Widows' Benefits (NI 13)

Widows' Allowance

Widow's benefits are paid on the late husband's contributions. If the widow was under 60 or her husband was not drawing retirement pension when he died then she is entitled to widow's allowance for the first 26 weeks. If the husband did not pay full contributions then the full amount of benefit will not be payable. Widow's benefit cannot be paid for any period after remarriage; nor can it be paid for any period during which a widow is living with a man as his wife or while she is imprisoned or detained in legal custody.

The widow's allowance is paid at the rate of £54.20 a week. If widows receive child benefits then they receive an extra £8.05 for each child.

Widowed Mothers' Allowance

If the widow has at least one qualifying child, she can receive widowed mother's allowance when her widowed allowance ends. The rate is £38.70 a week and continues until the youngest child reaches the age of 19. The increases for children are the same as for widow's allowance.

Widow's Pension

This is payable to widows aged 40 or more when their husband dies or when the widowed mother's allowance ends. It continues to be paid until she reaches 60 and retires or 65 if she does not retire. The amount of the pension depends on the age the husband died (or when the widowed mother's allowance ended). It reaches £38.30 a week from aged 50. The rate of pension depends on the age the entitlement began and does not increase as the widow gets older.

SOCIAL SECURITY BENEFITS

Retirement Pensions (NI 15)

Retirement pension is paid to men at 65 and women at 60 provided that they have retired and paid sufficient national insurance contributions. It is paid to men at 70 and women at 65 whether or not they have given up work. A single person receives £38.70 a week and a married couple £61.95. Some graduated pension may be payable if the claimant went on working after normal retirement age. People aged 80 or over receive an additional 25 pence a week. The full pension is only payable if sufficient national insurance contributions have been paid at the full rate for most of the years since 1948.

Married women who paid reduced rate contributions do not receive a full pension of their own but may receive some graduated pension.

It is important to actually claim the pension and tell the D.H.S.S. when one is about to retire. The claim form should be completed before pension age so that the pension can be paid promptly. If the claim is delayed until after one retires the pension will not normally be backdated more than three months.

From April 1979 retirement pension is related to employee's earnings under the New State Pension Scheme.

Death Grants (NI 49)

This grant is paid when someone has died as a contribution towards the expenses of the funeral. Most people qualify. The exceptions are men born before 5th July 1883, women born before 5th July 1888 and still born babies. The grant is usually paid to the spouse but it can be paid to the person paying for the funeral. The usual grant is £30 but the grant is less to persons who die under the age of 18 or to men born before 5th July 1893 and women who were born before 5th July 1898.

FAMILY INCOME SUPPLEMENTS (FIS 1)

The main qualifying conditions for this benefit are:
> either member of the couple must be in full-time work, provided that his or her spouse (or unmarried partner) is not receiving certain other benefits for a short term period off work, and there must be at least one dependent child in the family; and the family's normal gross weekly income must be below a prescribed level.

A claim can be made by a lone parent and the self-employed. Full-time work means working for 30 hours or more a week. Those not in full-time work may be entitled instead to supplementary benefit (see leaflet SBI). All children under 16 and those over 16 who are still at school are included in the family if they live in the household.

The level of income below which family income supplement can be received depends on the number of children in the family and is the same for parents and for couples. When calculating the level of income the following benefits do not count as income:
> Child benefit, the first £4 of a war disablement pension, payments for children boarded out with families, children's income, the whole of any attendance allowance and mobility allowance, rent allowances.

The prescribed weekly amount for any family from July 1986 is between £98.60 and £100.60 for a family with one child plus increases for each additional child dependent on their ages. The weekly rate of the family income supplement will be half of the amount by which the family income falls short of the prescribed amount. The maximum payment is £26.30 for families with one child increased by amounts for each additional child dependent on their ages. The award is usually made for 52 weeks and the rate of payment is not affected by any change in circumstances, whether favourable or not.

Those who receive family income supplements are also entitled to
   Free NHS prescriptions, dental treatment and spectacles,
   Free milk and vitamins for expectant mothers and children under school age.
   Free school meals.
   Refund of hospital fares, and
   Free legal advice and assistance unless their capital exceeds prescribed limits.

SUPPLEMENTARY BENEFITS (SB1, SB2, SB9)

Supplementary benefit is a non-contributory benefit which can be paid to anyone aged 16 or over who has left school and is not in full-time work. In general the amount of benefit is the difference between the person's "resources" and his "requirements" under the scheme.

In calculating "resources" different types of income are treated as follows:
(a) Earnings—generally the first £4 of a week of part-time earnings plus the first £4 of a wife's earnings are discounted. In the case of the parent of a one-parent family £6 is ignored. However, someone who is unemployed and required to register for work has only the first £2 ignored. The earnings of children under 16 (or over 16 and in full-time secondary education) are disregarded. Earnings means the net amount received after deducting tax, national insurance and pension contributions, trade union subscriptions, travelling expenses and other expenses, connected with work.
(b) Child benefit and most national insurance benefits and maintenance payments are fully taken into account.
(c) Occupational pension or weekly payments under a redundancy scheme—the first £1 a week is disregarded.
(d) Disablement and war widow's pensions—up to £4 a week is disregarded.
(e) Other income—up to £4 a week of the total of most forms of income is disregarded. The total of income other than earnings which can be ignored is limited to £4.
(f) Savings and capital—the value of personal chattels, the first £1,500 surrender value of life assurance policies and an owner occupied house is ignored. The joint capital of a husband, his wife and his dependents under £3,000 is disregarded and so is any income that capital produces.

A person's "requirements" are made up of the appropriate scale rate(s) plus an addition for rent and any special additions to which the claimant has entitlement. Where a claimant is entitled to attendance allowance the "requirement" is increased by the amount of attendance allowance payable.

A householder will usually have his rent and rates allowed in full in addition to his basic requirement. Other outgoings such as mortgage interest are also allowable.

The benefits range from a maximum of £48.40 for a married couple to £10.20 for children under 11. The rates are increased to supplementary pensioners and also to those below pension age (other than the unemployed who are required to register for work).

GRANTS FROM LOCAL AUTHORITIES
Housing Benefit (RR1)

Housing benefit is the scheme which helps people pay their rent and/or rates. Both the local council and the DHSS are involved in running the scheme which affects about one in three households. Anyone can apply including pensioners, the unemployed or those in work. Housing Benefit can be paid to Council housing associations or private tenants, or owner occupiers. It is possible to receive Housing Benefit either by a reduction in rent or rates or by receiving a rent allowance. One should apply to the DHSS first of all which will ensure the earliest possible start to any benefit you might receive. The DHSS will then advise the Council to see if you are eligible for Supplementary Benefit, so that the Housing Department can arrange the Housing Benefit or alternatively if the claimant is not eligible for Supplementary Benefit then he should complete a Standard Housing Benefit claim form and return it to the Housing Department.

The above does not set out to cover every aspect of the Social Security Acts Legislation.

Further information can be obtained from the local office of the Department of Health and Social Security or from Accountants Digest No. 183 published by the Institute of Chartered Accountants in England and Wales. Readers resident abroad who have queries should write to the Department's Overseas Branch, Newcastle upon Tyne, NE98 1YX.

AGREEMENTS

PUBLISHERS' AGREEMENTS
Royalty Agreements

The royalty agreement is now the most usual arrangement between author and publisher, and almost invariably the most satisfactory for the author. It provides for the payment to the author of a royalty of an agreed percentage on all copies of the book which are sold. The rate of royalty varies with circumstances: for general books it is often ten per cent of the published price. Lower rates will be payable on copies sold at a high discount, for example in some export areas and to book clubs. There may be a provision for the rate to rise after the sale of a specified number of copies. Similarly, most authors can secure in their contracts provision for an advance from the publisher in anticipation and on account of the specified royalties, and the amount of this advance will depend largely upon the publisher's estimate of the book's prospect of sales.

Because many publishers' accounts are now computerised there is a trend towards paying royalties on the price received—which can easily be read from a computer printout—rather than on the published price. Appropriate adjustments are of course made to the royalty figure and the arrangement is of no intrinsic disadvantage to the author.

Most publishing houses nowadays have printed agreement forms in which blanks are left for the insertion of the proposed royalty rates, the sum payable in advance, and so on. The terms are usually agreed between author and publisher before the form is completed, but the fact that a printed form or word-processed agreement has been signed by the publisher does not mean that an author, before signing it, cannot discuss any of its clauses with the publisher. The majority of publishers value the establishment of confidence and understanding between themselves and their authors and are willing to make reasonable amendments.

It is impossible to set out in detail here the numerous provisions of publishing agreements or to comment on the differing effects of these upon different sorts of book. Every sensible author will scrutinise his agreement carefully before signing it, will not hesitate to ask the publisher to explain any point in it which is not clear, and if in any doubt will seek professional advice from a reliable literary agent, or the Society of Authors, or one of the few firms of solicitors who specialise in authors' business.

The careful author will look for a comprehensive clause setting out the contingencies in which the contract is to terminate, what happens if the publisher goes out of business or is taken over, and whether the publisher can sell his rights in the book to a third party without consulting the author.

The agreement should specify the respective responsibilities of author and publisher in the provision of illustrations, indexes, etc. Unexpected fees for reproducing illustrations can swiftly eat up an advance.

The author will examine the clauses covering the handling of overseas sales, American rights and subsidiary rights (film, serial, broadcasting, etc.) which for some books may well bring in more than the book publication rights.

Consider carefully clauses giving the publisher an option to publish future works and clauses which may restrict a specialist author's future output by preventing him or her from writing other books on the same subject. The author should also be sure that he or she understands what the contract proposes in relation to cheap editions, 'remainders', sheet sales, reprints and new editions.

Outright Sale

Outright sale of copyright for an agreed sum is rarely suggested by a publisher, and hardly ever to be recommended, though it may be justified in special cases, as when an author is commissioned to supply a small amount of text as a commentary for a book which consists primarily of illustrations. It is a survival from the days when copyright meant for all practical purposes, merely the exclusive right of publication in book form. So long as it was possible to gauge approximately a book's potential sales and the profit to be anticipated, the value of a copyright could be fairly accurately estimated. But to-day, anything from 1,000 to a million copies of a book may be sold and when the various subsidiary rights—the film rights in particular—may prove either valueless or worth thousands of pounds, any arrangement for an outright sale of copyright must be a gamble in which the author is likely to be the loser.

Profit-Sharing and Commission Agreements

Under a profit-sharing agreement the publisher bears the cost of production, but the author makes no money until the book shows a profit, at which point the profit is divided in agreed proportions between author and publisher. In theory this sounds fair, but it is rarely satisfactory in practice. Such agreements can lend themselves readily to abuse, largely because of the difficulty of defining the term 'profit'.

Under a commission agreement the author bears the cost of production and pays the publisher a commission for marketing the book. If no publisher is prepared to publish a work on the normal royalty basis, the chances are that the author who decides to finance his or her own publication will lose most, if not all, of the money outlaid. In consequence commission agreements, save in exceptional circumstances, are to be discouraged. Many good publishers refuse to handle books on commission in any circumstances whatsoever; others confine their commission publishing to authoritative books of a highly specialised or scholarly nature. The specialist author who decides that commission publishing is justified by special circumstances should make sure that the firm which offers such an arrangement is reputable and able to market his book efficiently.

No firm of standing will publish fiction or poetry on commission and publishers offering to do so should be given a wide berth. There are a few firms ready to exploit the vanity of a would-be author. Such firms ask the author for a large sum as 'a contribution towards the cost' of producing the book. Too often it more than covers the cost of bringing out a small and shoddy edition, which the 'publisher' makes no effort to distribute.

Publishing agreements are lucidly discussed at considerable length in Sir Stanley Unwin's *The Truth About Publishing* (8th edition George Allen and Unwin, Ltd. £10.95). *Publishing Agreements: A Book of Precedents*, (2nd edition edited by Charles Clark, George Allen and Unwin, Ltd. reprint £15.00), gives a detailed stock of precedents forming a base for the founding of agreements.

THE FLORENCE AGREEMENT AND ITS NAIROBI PROTOCOL

This Agreement, on the Importation of Educational, Scientific and Cultural Materials, generally known as the Florence Agreement, was adopted by the Unesco General Conference in Florence in 1950 and came into force on 21 May 1952. It is concerned with the free flow of a wide variety of articles including books and the removal of tariff and trade obstacles. The principal undertaking of the contracting states is the exemption of books and other educational, scientific and cultural imports from customs duties, and the granting of licences and foreign exchange as far as possible for their importation. Books of every sort are included in the Agreement, not exempting those printed abroad from the work of an author in the importing country. Unbound sheets do not come under the Agreement.

The following is an up-to-date list of the States parties to the Agreement: Afghanistan, Austria, Barbados, Belgium, Bolivia, Burkina-Faso, Cameroon, Congo, Cuba, Cyprus, Democratic Kampuchea, Denmark, Egypt, El Salvador, Fiji, Finland, France, Gabon, Germany (Federal Republic of), Ghana, Greece, Guatemala, Haiti, Holy See, Hungary, Iran, Iraq, Ireland, Israel, Italy, Ivory Coast, Japan, Jordan, Kenya, Lao People's Democratic Republic, Luxembourg, Madagascar, Malawi, Malaysia, Malta, Mauritius, Monaco, Morocco, Netherlands, New Zealand, Nicaragua, Niger, Nigeria, San Marino, Norway, Oman, Pakistan, Philippines, Poland, Portugal, Romania, Rwanda, San Marino, Sierra Leone, Singapore, Socialist People's Libyan Arab Jamahiriya, Spain, Sri Lanka, Sweden, Switzerland, Tanzania (United Republic of), Thailand, Tonga, Trinidad and Tobago, Tunisia, Uganda, United Kingdom, United States of America, Viet-Nam (Socialist Republic of), Yugoslavia, Zaire, Zambia.

A Protocol to the Florence Agreement or Nairobi Protocol adopted by the Unesco General Conference in Nairobi in 1976 came into force on 2 January 1982. It is open only to states which are parties to the Agreement. The Protocol broadens the scope of the Agreement by extending the benefits it offers to additional objects and by granting further benefits to a number of materials. The following States adhere to the Protocol: Barbados, Denmark, Egypt, Greece, Holy See, Iraq, Ireland, Italy, Luxembourg, Netherlands, Portugal, San Marino, United Kingdom, Yugoslavia.

NET BOOK AGREEMENT

The Net Book Agreement is an undertaking signed by all members of the Publishers Association, which represents some 95 per cent of all book publishing in the United Kingdom, by which they agree to sell their net-priced books to booksellers on the strict condition that they may not offer them to the public at less than the price fixed by the publisher. Booksellers may, under licence from the Publishers Association, supply public libraries at a ten per cent discount. There is an identical Agreement between publishers not in membership of the Publishers Association who publish at net prices, who nominate the Association as their agent.

The Agreement was referred to the Restrictive Practices Court in 1962 under the Restrictive Trade Practices Act 1956, and was successfully defended as being not contrary to the public interest, and necessary for the maintenance of a healthy book trade able to meet the public's needs. The Agreement was also vindicated in 1967 under the Resale Prices Act of 1964.

Because the vast majority of school books are bought in class sets they are published at non-net prices so that booksellers and school contractors may sell them at a discount.

THE SOCIETY OF AUTHORS

AIMS
The Society, which was founded in 1884, is an independent trade union which represents, assists and protects its 3,300 members.

The permanent staff (including a solicitor) has wide professional experience of the many problems encountered by authors. They also have immediate access to lawyers, accountants and insurance consultants, retained by the Society.

WHAT THE SOCIETY DOES FOR MEMBERS
Individually

Through its permanent staff, the Society is able to give its members a personal service unequalled by any other organisation representing writers, in the following ways:

By providing information about agents, publishers, and others concerned with the book trade, journalism and the performing arts;

By advising on negotiations (including clause-by-clause vetting of contracts) with publishers, broadcasting organisations, theatre managers, film companies, etc.;

By taking up complaints on members' behalf;

By taking legal action in respect of breach of contract, copyright infringement and claims in liquidation and bankruptcy, when the risk and cost preclude individual action by a member and issues of general concern to the profession are at stake;

By sending to all members free of charge the Society's quarterly journal, *The Author*, and, on request, free copies of *Quick Guides* on Copyright, Protection of Titles, Copyright After Your Death, Libel, Income Tax, VAT, Authors' Agents and Publishing Contracts, as well as leaflets entitled *Teachers as Authors, Sell your Writing, Guidelines for Educational Writers* and *Guidelines for Authors of Medical Books*. Members concerned with broadcasting also receive the Society's twice yearly *Broadcasting Bulletin*; similarly, translators are sent *Translators News*;

By giving members access to the Retirement Benefit Scheme, the BUPA Group and hospital cash benefit schemes, the Pension Fund and the Contingency Fund (for emergency aid);

By inviting members to meetings, seminars and social occasions.

Specially

Members may (if eligible) belong to any of the following groups within the Society at no extra cost—Translators Association, Broadcasting Group, Educational Writers Group, Children's Writers Group, Technical Writers Group and Medical Writers Group. Meetings of each group are held regularly so that issues of particular concern to a section of the membership can be resolved quickly and effectively.

The Society frequently secures improved conditions and better returns for its members. In particular it is recognised by the BBC for the purpose of negotiating rates for writers' contributions to radio drama, talks and features, as well as for the broadcasting of published material.

Generally
Through regular discussions with the following: Arts Council, Association of Authors' Agents, BBC, Booksellers Association, British Council, Broadcasting and Entertainment Trades Alliance, Equity, Independent Broadcasting Authority, Library Association, Minister for the Arts, National Union of Journalists, Publishers Association, and Writers' Guild.

Through membership of: Congress of European Writers Organisations, British Copyright Council, National Book Committee, Radio and Television Safeguards Committee, and the International Confederation of Societies of Authors and Composers (CISAC).

Through lobbying Members of Parliament, Ministers and Government Departments.

Through promoting legislation benefitting the profession, e.g. the Copyright Acts 1911 and 1956, Defamation Act 1952, and the Public Lending Right Act 1979. Concessions have been obtained under various Finance Acts, in addition to improvements gained to the Social Security Act 1973.

Through helping to set up the Authors Lending and Copyright Society (ALCS); the purpose being to collect and distribute fees from reprography and other methods whereby copyright material is exploited without payment to the originators.

Through litigating in matters of importance to authors. For example the Society backed Andrew Boyle when he won his appeal against the Inland Revenue's attempt to tax the Whitbread Award which he received in 1974. It also backed a number of its members in proceedings against the BBC and Desmond Wilcox in connection with the publication of a book *The Explorers* and in copyright infringement proceedings against *Coles Notes*.

ADDITIONAL BENEFITS OF MEMBERSHIP

The Contingency Fund, available to authors in temporary need; and the Pension Fund for elderly members, who must be at least 60 years of age and have belonged to the Society for not less than ten clear years before application.

The Retirement Benefits Scheme, which has flexible premium arrangements to suit authors with fluctuating incomes. Contributions by members now exceed £600,000.

Books and stationery at special rates

Free membership of The Authors Lending and Copyright Society

The Society has Group Insurance Schemes for general provision against the cost of illness.

The Society's copying machine is available for members' use by appointment at a moderate charge.

AWARDS ADMINISTERED BY THE SOCIETY

Three travel awards—The Somerset Maugham Awards, the Travelling Scholarships and the Betty Trask Awards.

Two poetry awards—The Eric Gregory Awards and the Cholmondeley Award.

The Tom-Gallon Award for short story writers.

The Crompton Bequest for aiding financially the publication of selected original work.

The Authors' Foundation, which is endowed with wide powers to support literary and artistic effort and research.

The Margaret Rhondda Award for women journalists.

The Scott Moncrieff Prize for translations from French.
The Schlegel-Tieck Prize for translations from German.
The John Florio Prize for translations from Italian.
The Hawthornden Prize for a work of imaginative literature by a British writer under the age of 41.
The Roger Machell Prize for a book on the performing arts.
The Francis Head Bequest for assisting authors who, through physical mishap, are temporarily unable to maintain themselves or their families.

HOW TO JOIN

There are two categories of membership (admission to each being at the discretion of the Committee of Management):

Full Membership—those authors who have had a full-length work published in the U.K. or have an established reputation in another medium.

Associate Membership—those authors who have had a full-length work accepted for publication, but not yet published; and those authors who have had a number of radio scripts broadcast, plays performed, or translations, articles, illustrations or short stories published.

Associate members pay the same annual subscription and are entitled to the same benefits as full members. The owner or administrator of a deceased author's copyrights can become a member on behalf of the author's estate.

The Annual Subscription (which is tax deductible under Schedule D) for full or associate membership of the Society is £50 (£45 by direct debit), and there are special joint membership terms for husband and wife.

Further information from The Society of Authors, 84 Drayton Gardens, London, SW10 9SB *T.* 01-373 6642.

THE WRITERS GUILD OF GREAT BRITAIN

The Writers' Guild of Great Britain is the writers' trade union, affiliated to the TUC, and representing writers' interests in film, radio, television, theatre and publishing. Formed in 1959 as the Screenwriters' Guild, the union gradually extended into all areas of freelance writing activity and copyright protection. In 1974 when book authors and stage dramatists became eligible for membership substantial numbers joined, and their interests are now strongly represented on the Executive Council. Apart from necessary dealings with Government and policies on legislative matters affecting writers, the Guild is, by constitution, non-political, has no involvement with any political party, and pays no political levy. The Guild employs a permanent secretariat and staff and is administered by an Executive Council of twenty-nine members. There are also Regional Committees representing Scotland, Wales, the North and West of England.

The Guild comprises practising professional writers in all media, united in common concern for one another and regulating the conditions under which they work.

WHAT IT DOES
The Guild gives help and advice to individual members on any aspect of their business life, including contracts, agents, publishers, television companies and fees. Also in:

Television
The Guild has national agreements with the BBC and the Commercial companies regulating minimum fees and going rates, copyright licence, credit terms and conditions for television plays, series and serials, dramatisations and adaptations. One of the most important achievements in recent years has been the establishment of pension rights for Guild members only. Both the BBC and Independent Television Companies pay an additional 7½% of the going rate on the understanding that the Guild member pays 5% of his or her fee. The Guild Pension Fund now stands at one million pounds. In 1985, a comprehensive agreement was negotiated with the BBC to cover cable sales, in addition a special agreement was negotiated to cover the very successful twice weekly serial *Eastenders*. Most children's and educational drama has been similarly protected within the above industrial agreements.

Film
On March 11th 1985, an important agreement was signed with the two producers organisations: the British Film and Television Producers Association and the Independent Programme Producers Association. For the first time, there exists an industrial agreement which covers both the independent television production and independent film production. Pension fund contributions have been negotiated for Guild members in the same way as for the BBC and the ITCA.

Radio
The Guild has fought for and obtained a standard agreement with the BBC, establishing a fee structure which is annually reviewed. The current agreement includes a Code of Practice which is important for establishing good working conditions for the writer working for the BBC. In December 1985 the BBC agreed to extend the pension scheme already established for television writers to include radio writers for the first time. It was also agreed that all radio writers would be

entitled to at least one attendance payment as of right. Again this brings the radio agreements more into line with the television agreements.

The independent radio companies do very little drama and so far no major independent radio company has signed an agreement with the Guild. Nevertheless, with the advent of a possible network things could change. More drama production in the independent field should be expected and it follows that the Guild would negotiate agreements to cover such drama.

Books

The Guild fought long, hard and successfully for the loans-based Public Lending Right to re-imburse authors for books lent in Libraries. This is now law and the Guild is constantly in touch with the Registrar of the scheme which is administered from offices in Darlington.

The Guild together with its sister union, the Society of Authors has drawn up a draft Minimum Terms Book Agreement which has been widely circulated amongst publishers. In 1984, the Unions achieved a significant break through by signing agreements with two major publishers; negotiations were also opened with other publishers. The publishing agreements will, it is hoped, improve the relationship between writer and publisher and help to clarify what the writer might reasonably expect from the exploitation of the copyright in works written by him or her.

Theatre

In 1979, the Guild with its fellow union, the Theatre Writers' Union negotiated the first ever industrial agreement for theatre. The Theatre National Agreements covers the Royal Shakespeare Company, the National Company and the English Stage Company. Negotiations with the Theatrical Managers Association have been concluded. At the time of reading this piece, it is hoped that the signed agreement will be operating for some 95 provincial theatres. Draft proposals for an agreement to cover the Independent Theatre Council membership have been presented to the ITC. It is hoped that formal negotiation will lead to an agreement in 1986 or 1987.

Miscellaneous

The Guild is in constant touch with Government and national institutions wherever and whenever the interests of the writer are in question or are being discussed. Amongst matters dealt with recently, are the Private Members' Bill proposing changes in the law on obscenity. Effectively the Bill as it stood would have been a straitjacket on the writing profession including as it did draconian measures for censoring the work of writers. The Guild has been amongst the leaders in the campaign which undoubtedly had its effect in helping to kill the Bill.

Proposals for changes in the law on copyright, published in a White Paper in 1986, have been comprehensively reviewed and important submissions have been made by the Guild on behalf of its membership.

Working with federations of other unions, that is the Federation of Film Unions, the Federation of Theatre Unions and the Federation of Broadcasting Unions, the Guild makes its views known to Government bodies and to bodies like the Arts Council of Great Britain and other national bodies. Perhaps one of the closest working relationships the Guild has is with its fellow arts unions, Equity and the Musicians Union. Closer contacts have been established with the National Union of Journalists in recent months.

Regular Craft Meetings are held by all the Guild's specialist committees. Each section (Television and Film, Radio, Theatre and Books) hold some four craft meetings each per annum. This gives Guild members the opportunity of meeting those who control, work within, or affect the sphere of writing within which they work. Opportunities are also given to younger and less experienced members to discuss problems and ideas with members who have been long established within the profession.

Internationally, the Guild plays a leading role in the International Affiliation of Writers Guilds, which includes the American Guild East and West, the Canadian Guilds (French and English) and the Australian and New Zealand Guilds. Views are exchanged at an annual conference each year. When it is possible to make common cause, then the Guilds act accordingly. In addition to the International Affiliation of Writers Guilds, the Writers' Guild of Great Britain plays a leading role in the European Writers Congress. The last Congress held in Germany in December 1986 had representatives from every Western European country. The next conference is to be held in Madrid in 1987. At that conference the Guild will be making important contributions to a major discussion on Public Lending Right.

The Guild also fights on behalf of individual members, gives advice on contracts and helps with those problems which affect the lives of its members as professional writers.

The Guild publishes a monthly Newsletter for its members giving details of current work and negotiations. The magazine also contains articles, letters and reports written by members and the General Secretary.

MEMBERSHIP

Membership is by a points system. One major piece of work (a full-length book, an hour-long television or radio play, a feature film, etc.) entitles the author to full membership; lesser work helps to accumulate enough points for full membership, while temporary membership may be enjoyed in the meantime. Importantly, a previously unpublished broadcast or performed writer can apply for membership when he receives his first contract. The Guild's advice before signature can often be vital. Affiliate membership is enjoyed by agents and publishers.

The subscription is 1% of that part of an author's income earned in the areas in which the Guild operates. There is a minimum annual subscription of £30 and a maximum of £480.

IN CONCLUSION

The writer is an isolated individual in a world in which individual voices are not always heard. A good agent can provide protection for his clients, but there are many vitally important matters which are susceptible to influence only from the position of collective strength which the Guild enjoys. The writer properly cherishes his or her individuality; it will not be lost within a union run by other writers.

The Writers' Guild of Great Britain, 430 Edgware Road, London, W2 1EH *T.* 01-723 8074. *General Secretary:* Walter J. Jeffrey.

THE AUTHORS LENDING AND COPYRIGHT SOCIETY LTD

ALCS was set up in 1977 to collect and distribute money to writers for payments which authors and other copyright holders are unable to collect individually. For instance, under Federal German law Public Lending Right payments to foreign authors can only be paid through a collecting society. And in Britain there is no way in which an author could individually collect fees due to him for the copying of his work in schools except at a cost far in excess of the fees themselves.

ALCS is a non-profit-making company limited by guarantee (i.e. not having a share capital). It is run by members through a Council of Management on which the Society of Authors and the Writers' Guild of Great Britain are represented.

ALCS is affiliated to CISAC (International Confederation of Authors' and Composers' Societies) and through it maintains constant links with continental European and overseas collecting societies. It also has reciprocal or bi-lateral agreements with many individual countries.

MEMBERSHIP

There are three groups of membership: ordinary members (any author), successor members (surviving spouses, heirs etc), corporate members (the Society of Authors and the Writers' Guild of Great Britain). Others (such as representatives of Estates) may become Associates of the Society.

ADMINISTRATION

The Council of Management has twelve members, all of whom are active writers. Four are elected by and from the Ordinary Members of ALCS, four are nominated by the Society of Authors and four by the Writers' Guild. They meet as often as business requires and are unpaid.

POWERS

On joining, members transfer to the Society the power to administer on their behalf specific rights which the member is unable to exercise as an individual. Under the Society's constitution ALCS may adminsiter (a) in the United Kingdom and the Republic of Ireland and (b) in other countries:
  the lending right (for foreign schemes)
  the reprography right in published works
  the private and off-air-recording right
  the cable TV right
(where such a right can be exercised by an individual, the Society does not intervene).

An extra right to be exercised in the UK and Republic of Ireland can be added by a Special Resolution of a General Meeting (requiring a majority of votes). An extra overseas right can be added by the Council, provided it decides that the right can only be effectively administered by collective means. Members are entitled to opt out of any right that is added after they joined.

AREAS OF CURRENT ACTIVITY
Foreign PLR

Since 1980 ALCS has distributed to its members over £400,000 from the Federal German Republic collection society, VG WORT. Further money is held in

Germany on behalf of British writers who have not yet joined ALCS. Those eligible to receive German PLR through ALCS are:
 Living British authors resident anywhere;
 Heirs of British authors through successor membership;
 Foreign writers resident in Britain, writing in English;
 British illustrators.

Reprography

In 1983 ALCS and the Publishers Licensing Society set up a joint body, the Copyright Licensing Agency (CLA), to license the copying of copyright material from books, periodicals and journals under certain licensing terms. Considerable progress has been made to license users despite the complexity of the subject and the number of conflicting interests.

Eventually monies so collected will, in the case of books, be shared equally between publishers and authors after deduction of administrative costs. The authors' portion will be distributed through ALCS.

Cable and satellite broadcasting

ALCS has agreements with Belgium and Holland, through the relevant collecting societies, for distribution of monies received for the simultaneous cabling of BBC TV programmes.

It is also monitoring the situation with regard to satellite broadcasts and will act as and when necessary on behalf of British writers.

GENERAL

ALCS serves on the British Copyright Council and the PLR Advisory Committee, set up by the Registrar of British PLR. It keeps a watchful eye on all matters affecting authors as copyright holders. Its principal aims are twofold; to press for and make practical the establishment of collecting schemes by statute or voluntary agreement; and to make sure that the writers' share is a just one.

TO JOIN

ALCS is financed at present by membership fees and a percentage handling charge for distribution. The current annual subscription is £5.00 and to join the Society, write for an application form to: The Secretary General, 7 Ridgmount Street, London WC1E 7AE *T*. 01-580-2181.

Members of The Society of Authors and The Writers' Guild now have free membership of ALCS.

PUBLIC LENDING RIGHT IN THE UK

JOHN SUMSION
Registrar of Public Lending Right

INFORMATION FOR WRITERS AND ILLUSTRATORS OF BOOKS

Outline

Under the PLR system, payment is made from public funds to authors (writers, translators and illustrators) whose books are lent out from public libraries. Payment is made once a year, in February, and the amount each author receives is proportionate to the number of times (established from a sample) that his books were lent out during the previous year (July to June).

The legislation

PLR was created, and its principles established, by the Public Lending Right Act 1979 (HMSO, 30p). The Act required the rules for the administration of PLR to be laid down by a scheme. That was done in the Public Lending Right Scheme 1982 (HMSO, £2.95), which includes details of transfer (assignment), transmission after death, renunciation, trusteeship, bankruptcy, etc. Amending orders were made in March and November 1983 and in December 1984 (S.I. 1847, £1.30).

How the system works

From the applications he receives, the Registrar of PLR compiles, to hold on his computer, a register of authors and books. A representative sample is recorded, consisting of all loans from twenty public libraries. This is then multiplied in proportion to total library lending to produce, for each book, an estimate of its total annual loans throughout the country. Each year the computer compares the register with the estimated loans to discover how many loans are credited to each registered book for the calculation of PLR payments. The computer does this using code numbers—in most cases the ISBN printed in the book.

Parliament allocates a sum each year (£2,750,000 in 1986/87) for PLR. This Fund pays the administrative costs of PLR and reimburses local authorities for recording loans in the sample libraries. The remaining money is then divided in order to work out how much can be paid for each estimated loan of a registered book.

Limits on payments

(1) *Bottom limit* If the registered interest in a book scores so few loans that it would earn less than £1 in a year, no payment is due.
(2) *Top limit* If the books of one registered author score so high that the author's PLR earnings for the year would exceed £5,000, then only £5,000 is paid. No author can earn more than £5,000 in PLR in any one year.

The bottom limit operates for each edition of a book, the top limit per author. Money that is not paid out because of these limits belongs to the Fund and increases the amounts paid that year to other authors.

The sample

The sample represents only public libraries (no academic, private or commercial ones) and only loans made over the counter (not consultations of books on library premises). The reference sections of public libraries are not included in PLR. It follows that only those books which are loaned from public libraries can earn PLR and make an application worthwhile.

The sample consists of the entire loans records for a year in twenty public libraries representatively spread through England, Scotland, Wales and Northern Ireland. Sample loans are about one per cent of the national total. In order to counteract sampling error, libraries in the sample change every two – four years. Loans are totalled every 12 months for the period 1 July to 30 June.

An author's entitlement to PLR depends, under the 1979 Act, on the loans scored by his books in the sample. This score is multiplied to produce regional and national estimated loans.

ISBNs

PLR depends on the use of code numbers to identify books lent and to correlate loans with entries on the register so that payment can be made. Chiefly the system uses the International Standard Book Number—the ISBN—which consists of ten digits and is usually printed with the publishing information on the back of the title page; it may also be on the back or back flap of the jacket or cover. Examples are: 0 10 541079 9 and 0224 01787X.

Some books—particularly those published before 1970—lack an ISBN; if the book has no ISBN, the Registrar will allocate to it another code number so that it can still score loans and earn PLR. However, where there is an ISBN, an author who applies for registration is asked to give it on his application form. Different editions (for example, 1st, 2nd, hardcover, paperback, large print) of the same book have different ISBNs.

Authorship

In the PLR system the author of a book is the writer, illustrator, translator, compiler, editor or reviser, provided that his name is on the book's title page. He is eligible for PLR as an author even if he does not own the copyright. PLR and copyright are different. Note also that:

(1) *Illustrators* include photographers, provided that the photographer is (in the words of section 48 of the Copyright Act 1956) 'the person who, at the time when the photograph is taken, is the owner of the material on which it is taken'.
(2) *Minors:* For the registration of an author who is less than 18 years old the application must be made by his parent or guardian. Upon reaching the age of 18, the author should apply for the PLR to be registered in his own name: until this is done the PLR belongs to the parent or guardian.
(3) *Compiler or Editor:* must also have written at least 10% of the book's contents or at least 10 pages of text.
(4) *Reviser:* may be regarded as an editor.

The sole writer of a book may not be its sole author because, for PLR, all the eligible contributors named on the title page are its co-authors.

Co-authorship/illustrators

In the PLR system the authors of a book are those writers, translators, editors, compilers and illustrators whose names appear on the title page. Authors must apply for registration before their books can earn PLR. Books with *no more* than three named writers (excluding translators, editors and compilers) or illustrators can be registered for PLR.

Applications from Writers and/or Illustrators

Writers and illustrators must apply for registration jointly. At least one of them must be eligible and they must jointly specify what share of PLR each will take. They must agree and sign the form even if one or two are ineligible or do not wish to register for PLR. If they are not all eligible, those who are will receive a share(s) specified in the joint application. PLR can be any whole percentage. Detailed advice is available from the PLR office.

Applications from Translators

Translators, may apply, without reference to other authors, for a 30% fixed share (to be divided equally between joint translators).

Applications from Editors, Compilers

An editor or compiler who has also made a significant written contribution to the book, and who is named on the title page, may apply, either with others or without reference to them, to register a 20% share provided he has written 10% of the book or at least 10 pages of text: this should be substantiated by photocopies of the title and contents pages. The shares of joint editors/compilers is 20% in total to be divided equally.

An application from an editor or compiler to register a greater percentage share must be accompanied by supporting documentary evidence of actual contribution. A special form is available from the PLR Office.

Dead or Missing Co-authors

Where it is impossible to include a co-author on the form because that person is dead or untraceable, then the surviving co-author or co-authors may submit an application without the dead or missing co-author, but must name the co-author and provide supporting evidence as to why that co-author has been omitted. The living co-author(s) will then be able to register a share in the book which will be 20% for the illustrator (or illustrators) and the residual percentage for writer (or writers).

If this percentage is to be divided between more than one writer or illustrator, then this will be in equal shares unless some other apportionment is requested and agreed by the Registrar.

Writers or illustrators may apply for a different percentage apportionment— and the Registrar will register different percentage shares if it is reasonable in relation to the authors' contribution to the particular book. Detailed advice and forms are available from the PLR Office.

The PLR Office keeps a file of missing authors (mostly illustrators) to help applicants locate co-authors. Help is also available from publishers, the writers' organisations, and the Association of Illustrators, 1 Colville Place, London W1.

Life and death

Authors and books can be registered for PLR only when the authors apply during their lifetime. However, once an author's books have been registered, the PLR in those books continues until 50 years after the author's death. Registered authors can assign the PLR in each or all of their registered books to other people and they can bequeath it by will.

Eligible authors

If he is (in the senses described above) the author or a co-author of a book that is eligible (as described below), then he is eligible for PLR registration provided that he is: resident in the United Kingdom or the Federal Republic of Germany. A resident in these countries (for PLR purposes) has his only home there or his principal home there. The United Kingdom does not include the Channel Islands or the Isle of Man.

Eligible books

In the PLR system each separate edition of a book is registered and treated as a separate book.

A book is eligible for PLR registration provided that:
(1) it has an eligible author (or co-author) named on its title page;
(2) it is printed and bound (paperbacks counting as bound);
(3) copies of it have been put on sale (i.e. it is not a free handout and it has already been published);
(4) it is not a newspaper, magazine, journal or periodical;
(5) it does not have more than three writers or illustrators named on the title page;
(6) the authorship is personal (i.e. not a company or association) and the book is not crown copyright;
(7) it is not wholly or mainly a musical score.

Notification and payment

Every registered author will receive from the Registrar an annual statement of estimated loans for each book and the PLR due.

SAMPLING ARRANGEMENTS

Libraries

After a survey of the 1981 situation and discussions between a lot of librarians and their computer staff, it was decided that it would be much more economical if the designation of sample libraries, and therefore the collection of loans data, was confined to those libraries which already had computerised circulation systems. In two cases PLR works in libraries which did not have an automated issue system but have taken the PLR requirement as the occasion to introduce computerisation. The supply of PLR loans data has been made by making changes behind the scenes in computer programs, rather than by going into the long-winded exercise of labelling books and installing light-pen issue terminals from scratch.

In the sample libraries every time a book is issued the light pen is passed across the bar label inside the book—and across the reader's ticket. This data is used by the library to control its circulation; but it is also used as the issue record for PLR purposes. (There are some electronic alternatives to the light pen.)

The size of the sample at 20 service points was less than the 72 and 45 originally recommended by the statisticians; this reduction was aimed to keep costs down. The Scheme specifies the seven regions within which either two or more service points have to be designated. With such a small sample, random selection would not necessarily produce a statistically more accurate result than consciously aiming for a reasonable spread—considering as many factors as possible likely to influence the result.

In July 1986 the service points, designated in close collaboration with the public libraries and local authorities involved, are at: Hinckley, Market Drayton, York, Bridgwater, Cambridge, Droitwich, East Grinstead, West Swindon, Highfield (Sheffield), Oldham, Penn (Wolverhampton), Charing Cross (Westminster), Ealing, Aberystwyth, Wrexham, Aberdeen, Larbert, Wishaw, Bangor (N.I.), Suffolk (Belfast).

Participating local authorities are reimbursed on an actual cost basis for additional expenditure incurred in providing loans data to the PLR Office. The extra PLR work mostly consists of modifications to computer programs to accumulate data already held in the local authority computer and to produce a monthly magnetic tape to be sent to the PLR Office at Stockton-on-Tees.

SUMMARY OF THE THIRD YEAR'S RESULTS
Registration: authors

When registration closed for the third year (June 30) the number of books registered was about 99,079 for 11,307 authors. This increase included 107 West German authors and 61 who registered translations only.

Library loans

The ISBN was used for 79% of the books; the remaining 21% were identified by author and title referring to the PLR database.

The sample loans are 0.9% of total issues from UK public libraries—644.5 million per annum.

Because the sampling strength is different in each region, the calculation is done in two stages. For example the loans recorded in Wales are multiplied by 40 because issues in the two Welsh sampling points represent 2.5% of borrowings from all public libraries in Wales; but in London the multiplication factor is 90 since only 1.1% of issues from all London libraries have been sampled.

Eligible loans

Of these 644.5 million estimated loans, 217 million belong to books on the PLR register. The loans credited to registered books—33.6% of all library borrowings—qualify for payment. The remaining 66.4% of loans relate to books that are ineligible for various reasons, to books written by dead or foreign authors, and to books that have simply not been applied for.

Money and payments

Operating the Scheme this year cost £289,000 and there have been payments to local authorities of £53,000. The Rate per Loan for 1985/1986 was set at 1.27 pence and calculated to distribute all the £2,408,000 available. The total of PLR distribution and costs is therefore the full £2.75 million which the Government provided in 1985/1986.

Most of the setting up and computer system was paid for in previous financial years: £372,000 in 1981/1982, £350,000 in 1982/1983 and £107,000 in 1983/84.

Within this figure some £347,000 would have gone to the most popular authors—but the maximum limit of £5,000 per author has in effect transferred this money to increase payments to other authors.

Payments to authors earning PLR this year average £250 and the numbers of authors in various payment categories are as follows:

```
                                          £
       63 payments between  4,900 – 5,000
      141 payments between  2,500 – 4,999
      345 payments between  1,000 – 2,499
      470 payments between    500 –   999
    2,425 payments between    100 –   499
    6,182 payments between      1 –    99
    ─────
    9,626 TOTAL
```

There were also 1,681 registered authors whose books earned them *nil* payment.

CRITICAL FEATURES
Book identification
A key task at registration is to record the book's ISBN. Authors can mostly supply this, but they often miss some editions. The VDU operators consult the database in order to:
(1) make sure the ISBN is correct;
(2) allocate another number if there is no ISBN;
(3) find any other editions;
(4) display features to check:
    (a) eligibility of book
    (b) joint authors/illustrators
    (c) editor/compiler/translator(s)
(5) provide a record for confirmation without having to type it afresh (and without the opportunity to type it wrongly).

This provides a very powerful computer facility to validate or query the eligibility of books and to get complete and accurate registration. The problems with inaccurate or duplicated ISBNs are mostly overcome by authors and careful bibliographic work. In anticipation of some problems the Scheme puts the onus firmly on to the author to supply the book's ISBN on his application; the Registrar's function is to raise queries.

Joint authorship
Books with more than *three* writers or illustrators are out. This rule has been useful and generally accepted.

Title page
An author can register a book only if he is named on the title page. This can produce occasional oddities, but it is definitive and, therefore, helpful.

Illustrators
Illustrators are difficult to find. When they are paid a fee rather than commission they soon disappear from publishers' records. The PLR office has now built up information to help locate missing illustrators to a useful extent.

After death
Once registered, the book stays on the register for 50 years after the author's death. The owner of the right can assign it as any other property, but it cannot be split.

Amendments to the PLR scheme
Major amendments to the PLR Scheme came into effect on January 1st 1985. The major changes were:

Additional Titles/Editions: these will now be accepted on a simple form with no second statutory declaration required – but not before date of publication.
Books under 24/32 pages: no page limit.
Dead/Missing Co-Authors: special arrangements for living co-authors to register a part share.
Nationality: foreign citizens with their home in the U.K. (or in West Germany) can now register books.
Translators: can register a fixed 30% share.
Editors and Compilers who have contributed to the text can register a 20% share under new regulations. (In cases of substantial contribution more than 20% may be allowed).

Sample Libraries were increased from 16 to 20 in July 1985.

Among the requirements which continued unchanged are:
Nobody can register a share unless named on the title page
Illustrators and writers (if alive) need to agree their percentage shares.
Books with more than three writers or illustrators named on the title page are not eligible.

Reciprocity
In 1981 – 1982 reciprocal arrangements with West Germany were demanded by the writers—fearful that they might lose the West German PLR they had enjoyed since 1974. The West German Scheme, although loan based, is very different in most other respects. There is no question of harmonisation, but simple reciprocity was included in changes brought into effect in January 1985. (Comparison of PLR schemes internationally and consideration of prospects for reciprocity are fascinating but beyond the scope of this article.)

CONCLUSION

On the question of practical feasibility—the central question has been how a writer can collect when the value of each transaction is so small that, with conventional methods, the cost of collecting the money would be far greater than its value. (There is an obvious parallel here with photocopying.)

We now have a basically satisfactory way of calculating PLR remuneration. The objections to PLR as being infeasible or impractical have been completely overcome through the use of the latest available library computing technology and an approach familiar to businessmen dealing with stock control problems.

An important result will be the provision of information on book loans and author payments so that future developments and improvements in PLR can be based on a factual review of public library lending. The analysis of PLR results has only just begun: a preliminary review is contained in the Registrar's Report to the Advisory Committee *Setting up Public Lending Right* published September 1984 and available from the PLR Office at £2.95 (including postage if pre-paid). It is certain that computer technology will not stay still; and it is likely that the 1980's will see continuing refinement and development in PLR from this base.

PLR application forms and details can be obtained from The Registrar, PLR Office, Bayheath House, Prince Regent Street, Stockton-on-Tees, Cleveland TS18 1DF *T.* (0642) 604699. The Minister's Annual Report to Parliament and the statutory accounts may be obtained from this address or from H.M.S.O.

JOURNALISTS' CALENDAR
1987

ANNIVERSARIES AND CENTENARIES

37 Tiberius, d., Caligula succeeded as Roman Emperor.
Flavius Josephus, historian, b.
287 *c.* Carausius declared "Emperor of Britain".
537 King Arthur reputedly killed at Battle of Camlan.
Rome besieged by Goths.
637 *c.* Capture of Jerusalem by Omar; Mosque of Omar begun.
937 Battle of Brunanburh; Aethelstan's victory.
1037 Castile and León united in Spain.
c. Cathedral of St. Sophia and gate at Kiev built.
1087 Constantine the African, d.
1137 *c.* Saladin, b.
See of Aberdeen created.
Mayence (Mainz) Cathedral completed.
1187 Gerard of Cremona, translator, d.
1237 *c.* Mongol invasion of Russia ("Golden Horde").
1337 Plague of locusts in Europe.
1387 Fra Angelico, artist, b.
Milan Cathedral begun.
1437 *c.* Elizabeth Woodville, consort of Edward IV, b.
Nicholas of Clémanges, theologian, d.
All Souls' College, Oxford, founded.
1487 Bernardino Ochino, reformer, b.
1537 *c.* Nicholas Hilliard, miniaturist, b.
c. Sir Alexander Fraser, founder of Fraserburgh, b.
1587 Davis strait explored.
Christians persecuted in Japan.
Endymion Porter, royalist, b.
Second Virginia settlement.
Rialto Bridge, Venice, begun.
Alfonso Ferrabosco's madrigals published.
1637 *c.* John Tradescant, senior, naturalist, b.
First opera house, Venice, built.
Russian expedition reached Pacific.
Dietrich Buxtehude, composer, b.
1687 Giuseppe Guarnerius, violin maker, b.

1737 Rudolf Raspe, original "Baron Munchausen", b.
Radcliffe Camera (library), Oxford, begun.
Göttingen University, founded.
Association formed to invite Young Pretender to Britain.
Alexander Geddes, theologian, b.
Richmond, Virginia, founded.
Francis Eginton, painter on glass, b.
1787 Association for abolition of slave trade formed in Britain.
Patrick Miller's steamboat.
Settlement of Sierra Leone.
Thomas Coke became first Methodist "bishop" in America.
George Dixon discovered Queen Charlotte Islands.
c. William Hickey, philanthropist, b.
1837 Offences for capital punishment reduced.
Durham University rechartered.
John Fawcett, actor-dramatist, d.
Gutenberg Monument, Mainz, built.
1887 Godiva procession discontinued in Coventry.
Stacy Aumonier, architectural sculptor, b.
Astronomical Society of France formed.
Esperanto invented.
Ashanti War.
Flood of Hoang-Ho River, China.
U.S. obtained use of Pearl Harbour as naval base.
Artificial silk invented.
Arthur Lucan, ("Old Mother Riley"), comedian, b.
Mont Follick, educationist, b.
L. Wolfe Gilbert, composer, b.
Thomas Dow Richardson, founder of Commonwealth Winter Games, b.
Sir Edward Robinson, numismatist, b.
1937 Golden Gate bridge, San Francisco, opened.
Aden became a Crown Colony.
Nylon patented.
First jet engine.

PUBLICATIONS (Books)

1537 *Institutions of a Christian Man:* Cranmer.
Thomas Matthews's Bible.
1587 *Worthiness of Wales:* Churchyard.
First German work on Faustus.

Whole Works: Gascoigne.
Voyages made into Florida: Hakluyt.
First Book of Cattell: Mascall.
Mirrour of Monsters (attack on theatre): Rankins.

JOURNALISTS CALENDAR

Tragical Tales: Turberville.
1637 *Discours de la Méthode:* Descartes.
Les Visionnaires: Desmarets.
The Elder Brother (printed): Fletcher.
Pleasant Dialogues and Dramas (from Lucian): Heywood.
Comus (published) and *Lycidas:* Milton.
Young Admiral: Shirley.
Aglaura and *A Sessions of the Poets:* Suckling.
1687 *Lucky Chance* and *Emperor of the Moon:* Behn.
Oraison funèbre de Condé: Bossuet.
Travels: Burnet.
Works: Cleveland.
Song for St. Cecilia's Day and *The Hind and the Panther:* Dryden.
Education des Filles: Fénelon.
The City Mouse and the Country Mouse: Prior.
Tenth Satire of Juvenal (translated): Shadwell.
The Island Princess: Tate.
1737 *The Dragon of Wantley:* Carey.
Biblical Concordance: Cruden.
The King and the Miller of Mansfield: Dodsley.
Leonidas: Glover.
Tears of the Muses: Hill.
The British Librarian: Oldys.
The Schoolmistress (first draft): Shenstone.
Divine Legation of Moses (begun): Warburton.
Collection of Psalms and Hymns: Wesley.
Josephus: Whiston.
Concilia: Wilkins.
1787 *Defence of the Constitutions:* Adams.
Vathek (in original French): Beckford.
A Defence of Usury: Bentham.
Poems chiefly in Scottish dialect: Burns.
Iphigenie auf Tauris: Goethe.
Ardinghello: Heinse.
Life of Johnson: Hawkins.
Gott: Herder.
Hermanns Tod: Klopstock.
Poems: Pye.
Don Carlos: Schiller.
Ode upon Ode: Wolcot.
Thoughts on the Education of Daughters: Wollstonecraft.
1837 *Crichton:* Ainsworth.
Ingoldsby Legends: Barham.
French Revolution: Carlyle.
Phantasmion: Sara Coleridge.
Early Recollections of Coleridge: Cottle.
Pickwick Papers: Dickens.
Venetia: Disraeli.
Twice-Told Tales: Hawthorne.
Letters: Lamb.
The Pentameron: Landor.
Life of Scott (begun): Lockhart.
Rory O'More: Lover.
Ernest Maltravers: Lytton.
Essay on Bacon: Macaulay.
Principles of Toleration: James Mill.
Lectures on the Prophetical Office of the Church: Newman.
Paper Money Lyrics: Peacock.
The Poetry of Architecture: Ruskin.
The Vicar of Wrexhill: Frances Trollope.
Poems (based mainly on the abolition of slavery): Whittier.
1887 *Life and Letters:* Darwin.
A Study in Scarlet: Doyle.
Thyrza: Gissing.
Jess, She and *Allan Quartermain:* Haggard.
The Woodlanders: Hardy.
Plain Tales from the Hills: Kipling.
Myth, Ritual and Religion: Lang.
Ballads and Poems of Tragic Life: Meredith.
Temptation of Pescara: Meyer.
Odyssey (translated): Morris.
Episodes in a Life of Adventure: Oliphant.
Imaginary Portraits: Pater.
Revolution in Tanner's Lane: Rutherford.
Elizabethan Literature: Saintsbury.
Memories and Portraits: Stevenson.
The Father: Strindberg.
Frau Sorge: Sudermann.
Locrine: Swinburne.
1937 *Letters from Iceland:* Auden and MacNeice.
An Elegy and Other Poems: Blunden.
The Mortal Storm: Bottome.
Susannah and the Elders: Bridie.
Daughters and Sons: Compton-Burnett.
The Citadel: Cronin.
Electre: Giraudoux.
To Have and Have Not: Hemingway.
The Trial: Kafka.
Three Ways Home: Kaye-Smith.
Something of Myself: Kipling.
The Four Winds of Love: Mackenzie.
Oxford Book of Greek Verse.
Time and the Conways: Priestley.
Three Comrades: Remarque.
In Divers Tones: Roberts.
Some Flowers and *Pepita:* Sackville-West.
The Zeal of Thy House and *Busman's Honeymoon:* Sayers.
Of Mice and Men: Steinbeck.
The Hobbit: Tolkein.

COPYRIGHT, TAX, SERVICES

PUBLICATIONS (Journals)

1737 *Belfast Newsletter.*
Grub Street Journal (ended).
1787 *Hull Packet.*
1837 *Forres Gazette.*
Justice of the Peace and Local Government Review.
Lancaster Guardian.
Monmouthshire Beacon.
Sussex Express.
University of Durham Calendar.
Wilts and Gloucestershire Standard.
1887 *Annals of Botany.*
Ballymena Weekly Telegraph.
Brighouse Echo.
British Baker.
British Bandsman.
Broughty Ferry Guide.
Chichester Observer.
Classical Review.
Dorking Advertiser.
Drapers' Record.
Essex Naturalist.
Financial Times Mining International Year Book.
Forward (as *Our Soldiers' Magazine*).
Guide to International Journals.
Handy Shipping Guide.
Journal of Laryngology and Otiology.
Journal of the Marine Biological Association.
Leatherhead Advertiser.
Loughton and District Advertiser (now incorporated with the *Loughton Gazette*).
Midwives' Chronicle.
Peeblesshire News and County Advertiser.
Sporting Chronicle Handicap Book (now *Raceform Handicap Book*).
Stalybridge Herald (now incorporated with *Stalybridge Reporter*).
Star (Sheffield).
Suffolk Sheep Society Flock Book.
Two Worlds.
1937 *Anglo-Soviet Journal.*
Art and Craft.
Barnoldswick and Earby Times.
Bird Research.
Built Environment.
Cine Technician (now *Film and Television Technician*).
Craven Herald and Pioneer.
Crosby Herald.
Dandy.
Evening News (Worcester).
Export.
Home Mission News.
Italian Studies.
Log.
London Bird Report.
Madam.
Modern Law Review.
School Librarian.
Scunthorpe Evening Telegraph.
Short Wave Magazine.
Tribune.
Weekly Horoscope (now incorporated with *Prediction*).
Woman.
Year Book of the General Conference of the New Church.

JANUARY

1 New Year Day customs.
Edward Topham began *The World*, 1787.
Sir Grafton Elliot Smith, anthropologist, d. 1937.
2 Mario Roatta, Italian general, b. 1887.
3 Catherine de Valois, d. 1437.
4 Louis Bernard Guyton de Morveau, French chemist, b. 1737.
5 General Courtney Hodges, commander of 1st Army, World War II, b. 1887.
Bernard Howell Leach, potter, b. 1887.
6 Epiphany. Twelfth Night. Old Christmas Day.
Thomas Cavendish passed through Magellan's Straits, 1587.
Charles Dickens, junior, b. 1837.
7 Patrick Nasmyth, artist, b. 1787.
Thomas Henry Ismay, ship-owner, b. 1837.
Polish-Danzig agreement, 1937.
8 Giotto di Bondone, artist, d. 1337.
Henry Tonks, artist, d. 1937.
11 François Gerard, artist, d. 1837.
John Field, composer, d. 1837.
Sir Stafford Henry Northcote, Earl of Iddesleigh, statesman, d. 1887.
Bismarck urged need for larger German army, 1887.
13 Albert van de Sandt Centlivres, chief justice, South Africa, b. 1887.
17 Oscar Browning, scholar, b. 1837.
18 Sir Frederick Pollock, jurist, d. 1937.
19 Mary Aikenhead, founder of Irish sisterhood, b. 1737.
Bernardin de Saint-Pierre, French writer, b. 1737.
W. W. Keen, American neurological surgeon, b. 1837.
Sir Robert Harmsworth, newspaper proprietor, d. 1937.
20 Martin Luther King Day.

Sir John Soane, architect, d. 1837.
William Gardner, inventor of Gardner gun, d. 1887.
21 Lucy Baxter, ("Leader Scott"), art writer, b. 1837.
G. B. Hunter, ship builder, d. 1937.
22 Eden Pastora Gómez, Nicaraguan guerrilla leader, b. 1937.
24 William Wake, archbishop, d. 1737.
Elizabeth Penrose, (Mrs Markham), children's writer, d. 1837.
25 Conversion of St. Paul.
Burns Night.
The Naiads, W. Sterndale Bennett, first produced, 1837.
26 Australia Day (1788).
Proclamation of the Republic of India (1950).
Michigan became an American state, 1837.
Sir Halley Stewart, businessman and philanthropist, d. 1937.
27 Joseph Knight, artist, b. 1837.
Carl Blegen, American archaeologist, b. 1887.
28 Arthur Rubenstein, pianist, b. 1887.
29 Tom Paine, b. 1737.
30 Augusta Webster, poet, b. 1837.
Vanessa Redgrave, actress, b. 1937.
Boris Spassky, chess master, b. 1937.
— Dicing for Maid's Money, Guildford, Surrey.
— Patrick Roland John, first Prime Minister of independent Dominica, b. 1937.

FEBRUARY
1 Richard Whately, archbishop of Dublin, theologian, b. 1787.
2 Candlemas. Purification.
4 Sri Lanka Independence Day (1948).
Sir Frederick Leith-Ross, expert in finance, b. 1887.
Sheila Kaye-Smith, novelist, b. 1887.
5 Dwight Moody, evangelist, b. 1837.
6 Waitangi Day, New Zealand (1840).
Joseph Cardinal Frings, Archbishop of Cologne, b. 1887.
7 John Watts, educationist and social reformer, d. 1887.
8 Mary, Queen of Scots, beheaded, 1587.
9 Philemon Holland, translator, d. 1637.
S. G. Tartakower, chess expert, b. 1887.
10 Alexander Pushkin, Russian poet, d. 1837.
Mrs Henry Wood, novelist, d. 1887.
11 John Jackson, astronomer, b. 1887.
12 Edmond Warre, headmaster, b. 1837.
13 Jan Swammerdam, Dutch naturalist, b. 1637.
Comte de Vergennes, French statesman, d. 1787.

Philip Bourke Marston, poet, d. 1887.
14 St. Valentine's Day.
15 Emperor Ferdinand II, d., Ferdinand III acceded, 1637.
H. M. Bateman, cartoonist, b. 1887.
16 Charles Cotton, poet, buried, 1687.
17 Joseph Bech, Luxembourg statesman, b. 1887.
18 Gambia Independence Day (1965).
Bishop Gilbert Foliot, d. 1187.
19 Georg Büchner, German playwright, d. 1837.
20 James I of Scotland murdered, James II acceded, 1437.
Carl Ebert, opera director, b. 1887.
Vincent Massey, Canadian diplomat, b. 1887.
Charles Gordon, 11th Marquess of Huntly, d. 1937.
21 Edward Garnett, literary critic, d. 1937.
22 Ann Thicknesse (Ford), authoress, b. 1737.
Assembly of Notables, France, opened, 1787.
23 Emma Willard, American educationist, b. 1787.
24 Algernon Mitford, Lord Redesdale, diplomat and author, b. 1837.
25 General McNaughton, Canadian commander, World War II, b. 1887.
27 Independence Day, Dominican Republic (1844).
28 Borodin, d. 1887.
William Taylor, designer (dimple golf ball), d. 1937.
Maximiliano Zomosa, ballet dancer, b. 1937.
— (or March) Joan, Princess of North Wales, d. 1237.
— (and April 2) Declarations of Indulgence by James II, 1687.

MARCH
1 St. David's Day. Welsh customs.
William Dean Howells, American writer, b. 1837.
Sir Walter Elliot, archaeologist, d. 1887.
2 Abdel-Aziz Bouteflika, Algerian minister, b. 1937.
3 Shrove Tuesday. Pancake and football customs.
Thomas Pitt, politician and connoisseur, b. 1737.
Kurt Wolff, German bookseller, b. 1887.
4 Ash Wednesday. First day of Lent.
Hugh Carter, artist, b. 1837.
Martin van Buren became President of United States, 1837.
Joseph Hocking, novelist, d. 1937.
5 Heitor Villa-Lobos, Brazilian composer, b. 1887.

Olusegun Obasanjo, Nigerian head of state, b. 1937.
6 Frank Vosper, actor, d. 1937.
Valentina Tereshkova, Russian cosmonaut, b. 1937.
8 James Buchanan Eads, American engineer, d. 1887.
Henry Ward Beecher, American preacher, d. 1887.
9 Philip Mead, cricketer, b. 1887.
10 Commonwealth Day.
William Etty, artist, b. 1787.
H. T. Colebrooke, first great European scholar in Sanskrit, d. 1837.
12 Anne Hyde, Duchess of York, b. 1637.
Alexandre Guilmant, composer, b. 1837.
John Ward, mystic, d. 1837.
13 Triple Alliance (Germany, Austria, Italy) against France and Russia, 1887.
14 Sylvia Beach, American bookshop operator, b. 1887.
15 Ides of March.
Patrick Adamson, Scottish divine, b. 1537.
16 Georg Simon Ohm, scientist, b. 1787.
Austen Chamberlain, statesman, d. 1937.
17 St. Patrick's Day. Irish customs.
Edward III's eldest son became the first English duke, 1337.
Edmund Kean, actor, b. 1787.
18 Stephen Grover Cleveland, U.S. President, b. 1837.
Edward Everett Horton, film star, b. 1887.
Charles Shannon, artist, d. 1937.
19 Kiplingcotes horse-race, South Dalton, Yorkshire.
Daniel Gookin, writer on American Indians, d. 1687.
20 St. Cuthbert, bishop of Lindisfarne, d. 687.
Baron Somers, Chief Scout, governor of Victoria, Australia, b. 1887.
Harry Vardon, golfer, d. 1937.
21 Vernal equinox.
Lajos Kassak, Hungarian writer and painter, b. 1887.
Baron Percy of Newcastle, politician and educationist, b. 1887.
Eric Mendelsohn, German architect, b. 1887.
David Keilin, biologist, b. 1887.
Fred Akuffo, Ghana head of state, b. 1937.
22 Duchess of Bedford, airwoman, d. 1937.
23 Richard Proctor, astronomer, b. 1837.
Prince Felix Yusupov, Russian nobleman, assassin of Rasputin, b. 1887.
25 Annunciation. Lady Day. Tichborne Dole.
Greek Independence Day (1821).
Sir Geoffrey Langdon Keynes, surgeon and scholar, b. 1887.
Raymond Gram Swing, American broadcaster, b. 1887.
John Drinkwater, d. 1937.
27 Mrs Fitzherbert, consort of George IV, d. 1837.
28 Sir Constantijn Huygens, Dutch poet, d. 1687.
29 Mothering Sunday.
Arthur, Duke of Brittany, b. 1187.
Joseph Fry, type-founder, d. 1787.
Billy Carter, b. 1937.
Karol Szymanowski, composer, d. 1937.
31 End of financial year.
John Constable, artist, d. 1837.
John Godfrey Saxe, American poet, d. 1887.
— Oranges and lemons ceremony, St Clement Danes, London.

APRIL
1 April Fools' Day customs.
Floyer Sydenham, translator of Plato, d. 1787.
Indian Constitution came into force, 1937.
Burma and Aden separated from India, 1937.
2 Luise Dorothea Schroeder, German politician, b. 1887.
3 John Burroughs, American poet, b. 1837.
4 First Colonial Conference, London, 1887.
5 Passion Sunday.
Income Tax year ends.
Algernon Charles Swinburne, poet, b. 1837.
8 W. H. Hadow, educationist and musician, d. 1937.
9 Alfred Ainger, writer, b. 1837.
Henri Becque, French dramatist, b. 1837.
10 Bernardo Alberto Houssay, Argentine physiologist and Nobel Prize winner, b. 1887.
Algernon Ashton, composer, d. 1937.
12 Palm Sunday.
13 Lanford Wilson, playwright, b. 1937.
15 Easter Day, Coptic Church.
Baroness Asquith, b. 1887.
16 Distribution of Maundy money.
George Villiers, Duke of Buckingham, d. 1687.
Paul Cardinal Richaud, French prelate, b. 1887.

17 Good Friday.
   John Pierpont Morgan, American financier, b. 1837.
   Hugo William Denison, Earl of Londesborough, sportsman, d. 1937.
18 John Foxe, martyrologist, d. 1587.
19 Easter Day.
   Drake's expedition to Cadiz, ("singed the King of Spain's beard"), 1587.
   Baron Conway, art collector and mountaineer, d. 1937.
20 Easter Monday customs.
   Vyell Walker, cricketer, b. 1837.
22 Jack Nicholson, actor, b. 1937.
23 St. George's Day customs.
   Shakespeare's birthday customs.
   John Ceiriog Hughes, Welsh poet, d. 1887.
25 Anzac Day.
26 Tyburn Walk, London.
   Johann Ludwig Uhland, German poet, b. 1787.
   Baron Kinnaird, philanthropist, d. 1887.
27 Edward Gibbon, b. 1737.
   Guernica destroyed by Spanish insurgents, 1937.
28 Saddam Hussein, President of Iraq, b. 1937.
29 Birthday of Emperor of Japan.
   First of Ramadan.
   General Georges Boulanger, b. 1837.
30 Hocktide customs, Hungerford, Berkshire.
   Queen's Day in the Netherlands.
— Kate Kennedy celebrations, St Andrews, Scotland.
— Melbourne, Australia, founded, 1837.

MAY

1 May Day customs.
   Sir Alan Gordon Cunningham, army officer, b. 1887.
2 Michael Bohnen, German opera singer, b. 1887.
3 Mary Ann Yates, actress, d. 1787.
   Alexandra Balashova, ballet dancer, b. 1887.
4 May Day Holiday.
   Eustace Budgell, writer, drowned, 1737.
5 Yorkist rebellion, 1487.
   Nicola Zingarelli, composer, d. 1837.
   James Grant, novelist, d. 1887.
   Sir Charles Richard Fairey, aircraft designer, b. 1887.
   Lord Fisher of Lambeth, archbishop of Canterbury, b. 1887.
6 German airship, "Hindenburg", destroyed at Lakehurst, America, 1937.
7 Samuel Cousins, mezzotint engraver, d. 1887.
8 George Conquest (Oliver), actor-manager, b. 1837.
   Alphonse Legros, artist, b. 1837.
   Thomas Stevenson, engineer, d. 1887.
9 VE Day (1945). Liberation Day, Channel Islands.
   André Pierre, French journalist, b. 1887.
10 Impeachment of Warren Hastings, 1787.
11 *Book of Good Manners* (translation), published by Caxton, 1487.
   Ion Grant Neville Keith-Falconer, Arabic scholar and cyclist, d. 1887.
12 Coronation of George VI, 1937.
14 George Macartney, 1st Earl, ambassador, b. 1737.
   Convention of states met to draw up American constitution, 1787.
15 Edwin Muir, poet and critic, b. 1887.
   Philip Snowden, socialist politician, d. 1937.
17 Norway Constitution Day (1814).
20 Lord Shelburne, Prime Minister, b. 1737.
21 Sir Philip Joubert de la Ferté, air chief marshal, b. 1887.
22 Constantine the Great, d. 337.
23 José Collins, actress, b. 1887.
   John D. Rockefeller, d. 1937.
24 Lambert Simnel crowned "king" in Dublin, 1487.
25 Spring Bank Holiday.
   Francesco Forgione, Capuchin friar, b. 1887.
26 Ba U, Burmese statesman, b. 1887.
   Egypt joined the League of Nations, 1937.
27 Frank Woolley, Kent and England cricketer, b. 1887.
28 Ascension Day.
   Baron Shaw, politician, d. 1937.
   Alfred Adler, Austrian psychologist, d. 1937.
   Stanley Baldwin resigned as Prime Minister, succeeded by Neville Chamberlain, 1937.
29 Sir Thomas Hamilton, Scottish statesman, d. 1637.
   Harry Stuart Goodhart-Rendel, architect, b. 1887.
30 Sir Ralph Sadler, diplomat, d. 1587.
   Alexander Archipenko, Ukrainian sculptor and artist, b. 1887.
   Arthur George Perkin, chemist, d. 1937.
31 Republic Day, South Africa (1961).
   Joseph Grimaldi, clown, d. 1837.
   T. S. Baynes, man of letters, encyclopaedia editor, d. 1887.
   Saint-John Perse, French poet, b. 1887.
— Louis V of France, d. 987.

— Charles I attempted to introduce Prayer Book in Scotland, 1637.
— *Strafford*, Robert Browning, first produced, 1837.

JUNE
1 Joseph Philip Knight, composer, d. 1887.
 Clive Brook, actor, b. 1887.
2 Coronation Day (1953).
 Republic Day, Italy (1946).
 Sir Francis Bigod, rebel, hanged, 1537.
3 Duke of Windsor married Mrs Wallis Simpson, 1937.
5 Constitution Day, Denmark (1849).
6 D-Day (1944).
7 Whit Sunday. Pentecost.
8 Whit Monday customs.
 Donald McMillan, U.S. Salvation Army commander, b. 1887.
10 George Henry Harlow, painter, b. 1787.
 Sir Robert Borden, Canadian statesman, d. 1937.
11 Kamehameha Day, Hawaii.
 Reginald Joseph Mitchell, aircraft designer, d. 1937.
12 Philippines Independence Day (1898).
 Ship money case of John Hampden, 1637.
13 Roman general, Agricola, b. 37.
 André François-Poncet, French diplomat, b. 1887.
14 Prynne condemned for second time, 1637.
15 Giacomo Leopardi, poet, d. 1837.
 Malvina Hoffman, American sculptor, b. 1887.
16 Defeat of rebels, Stoke-on-Trent, 1487.
 Sir Edward de Stein, merchant banker and philanthropist, b. 1887.
17 Mark Hopkins, American educationist, d. 1887.
 Dr. James Edward Welldon, headmaster and churchman, d. 1937.
19 John Kite, bishop of Carlisle, archbishop of Armagh, d. 1537.
 John Brown, preacher and Bible pedlar, d. 1787.
 Sir James Barrie, playwright, d. 1937.
20 Henry Neville, actor, d. 1837.
 William IV d., Queen Victoria acceded. Separation of Hanover from Britain, 1837.
21 Longest day. Summer solstice.
 Queen Victoria's golden jubilee, 1887.
 Baron Ismay of Wormington, British general, b. 1887.
 Zululand annexed by Britain, 1887.
22 Julian Huxley, biologist, b. 1887.
 Sir Eric Geddes, statesman, d. 1937.
24 St. John the Baptist. Midsummer Day.
 Well-dressing ceremonies (and on other dates during summer).
 Admiral Fisher, d. 1937.
25 Henry Hobhouse, politician, d. 1937.
26 Sir John Clegg, football administrator, d. 1937.
27 George Drummond, six times Provost of Edinburgh, b. 1687.
 Sir Henry Binns, Prime Minister of Natal, b. 1837.
28 Robert Aske, Robert Constable and others seized and later executed, ("Pilgrimage of Grace"), 1537.
30 John Nyren, cricket writer, d. 1837.
— Festival of Good Neighbours, Dumfries.
— Beltane Festival, Peebles.
— Braw Lads' Gathering, Galashiels.
— Lord Darcy, accused of being a rebel, beheaded, 1537.

JULY
1 Dominion Day, Canada (1867).
 Star Chamber decree against printing, 1637.
 Rowland Prothero, Baron Ernle, writer and politician, d. 1937.
2 Amelia Earhart, airwoman, d. 1937.
3 J. S. Copley, artist, b. 1737.
 Hawes Craven, scenery artist, b. 1837.
4 American Independence Day (1776).
 Crusaders defeated in Palestine, 1187.
 Spaniards captured Sluys, 1587.
6 Foundation stone of Imperial Institute laid by Queen Victoria, 1837.
7 Marc Chagall, artist, b. 1887.
9 Joan of Navarre, consort of Henry IV, d. 1437.
 Samuel Eliot Morison, historian, b. 1887.
 David Hockney, artist, b. 1937.
10 Bahamas Independence Day (1973).
11 George Gershwin, composer, d. 1937.
12 James II dissolved Parliament, 1687.
13 Henry Edward Armstrong, chemist, d. 1937.
14 Bastille Day, France (1789).
 Robert Venables, puritan soldier, d. 1687.
 Alfred Krupp, industrialist, d. 1887.
15 Carlists defeated at Valencia, 1837.
 National Library of Wales, Aberystwyth, opened, 1937.
16 Viscount Knollys of Caversham, private secretary to Edward VII, b. 1837.
17 Janet Douglas, Lady Glamis, burnt alive, Edinburgh, 1537.
 Percy Gardner, classical archaeologist, d. 1937.
18 Roald Hoffmann, Polish chemist, b. 1937.
20 Hans Sommer, composer, b. 1837.
 Marconi, d. 1937.
21 Belgium Independence Day (1831).

Thomas Bodkin, Irish art critic, b. 1887.
22 St. Mary Magdalene.
    Sir Robert Lindsay Burnett, Scottish admiral, b. 1887.
    Gustav Hertz, German scientist, b. 1887.
    Alfred George Edwards, first archbishop of Wales, d. 1937.
23 Egypt National Day (1952).
25 Henry Mayhew, journalist and social historian, d. 1887.
27 Cardinal Hugh of Evesham, d. 1287.
    John Gerard, jesuit, d. 1637.
    French Parlement exiled, 1787.
    "China incident", Japanese against China, 1937.
    Admiral Sir Somerset Arthur Gough-Calthorpe, d. 1937.
28 Tetsu Katayama, Japanese statesman, b. 1887.
    Marcel Duchamp, French artist, b. 1887.
29 Marmoru Shigemitsu, Japanese statesman, b. 1887.
    Rudi Stephan, composer, b. 1887.
—   (and August) Highland Games.
—   Hugh Capet crowned King of France, 987.
—   Bishop Thomas Ken, theologian and hymn-writer, b. 1637.
—   *Underwoods*, R. L. Stevenson, published, 1887.

AUGUST
1 Lammas.
   Louis VI d., Louis VII acceded, 1137.
   Joe O'Gorman, comedian, d. 1937.
3 Rupert Brooke, poet, b. 1887.
5 William Thomas Lewis, Baron Merthyr, industrialist, b. 1837.
6 Transfiguration.
   Hiroshima Peace Festival.
   Independence Day, Jamaica (1962).
   Ben Jonson, dramatist, d. 1637.
   Annie Horniman, theatrical manager, d. 1937.
   F. C. S. Schiller, philosopher, d. 1937.
7 A. J. Foli (Foley), Irish opera singer, b. 1837.
   Lady Maud Tree, actress, d. 1937.
8 John Lawless, ("Honest Jack"), Irish agitator, d. 1837.
   Esmé Percy, actor, b. 1887.
   Dustin Hoffman, actor, b. 1937.
9 Moment of Silence, Nagasaki.
   Henry V, b. 1387.
   André Beaumont, (Jean Conneau), aviation pioneer, d. 1937.
10 Edward King, ("Lycidas"), drowned, 1637.
   Sir David Masson, chemist, d. 1937.
   John Hodge, labour leader, d. 1937.
11 Joseph Nollekens, sculptor, b. 1737.
   Marie François Sadi Cornot, French President, b. 1837.
   Edith Wharton, American writer, d. 1937.
12 "Glorious Twelfth"; grouse shooting begins.
   Edelmiro Farrell, Argentine statesman, b. 1887.
   Erwin Schrödinger, physicist, b. 1887.
13 Walter Runciman, Baron Runciman, shipowner, d. 1937.
14 Pakistan Independence Day (1947).
   VJ Day (1945).
   Richard Jefferies, naturalist writer, d. 1887.
   Sir Thomas Bennett, architect, b. 1887.
   Cyril McNeile, ("Sapper"), novelist, d. 1937.
15 Assumption.
   India National Day.
   Sir Johann von Haast, explorer, d. 1887.
17 Isaac Taylor, author and inventor, b. 1787.
   Riots in Paris, 1787.
18 Robert Redford, actor, b. 1937.
19 James Molloy, composer, b. 1837.
20 Johann Gerhard, Lutheran theologian, d. 1637.
22 Sir Walter Citrine, trade unionist, b. 1887.
23 Alvin Harvey Hansen, American economist, b. 1887.
24 Blessing the mead, Gulval, Cornwall.
   Michael Wise, composer, d. 1687.
   James Weddell, navigator, b. 1787.
   Carlists victorious at Herrera, Spain, 1837.
   François Dubois, composer, b. 1837.
26 Baron Dalton, British statesman, b. 1887.
27 Sir Lionel Rothschild, 2nd Baron Rothschild, d. 1937.
30 Bruce McLaren, racing driver, b. 1937.
31 Conrad of Würzburg, German poet, d. 1287.
   "Bombadier" Billy Wells, boxer, b. 1887.
   Friedrich Adolf Paneth, scientist, b. 1887.
   Walter Lawry Waterhouse, agricultural scientist, b. 1887.
— Welsh Eisteddfodau.
— Coracle races, River Teifi, Cilgerran, Dyfed.
— Richard Watson, bishop of Llandaff, b. 1737.

SEPTEMBER
1 Sir Henry Brackenbury, military writer, b. 1837.

Lady Victoire Crampton, singer, b. 1837.
Brighton Devil's Dyke railway, opened, 1887.
2 Morse Code instrument demonstrated, 1837.
Sir Robert Bruce Lockhart, diplomat and writer, b. 1887.
Gustave Strauss, writer, d. 1887.
3 Ralph Copeland, astronomer, b. 1837.
Sir Irvine Masson, scientist, b. 1887.
4 Lord Ashbourne, politician, b. 1837.
Dawn Fraser, Australian swimmer, b. 1937.
5 Joseph ("Count") Boruwlaski, dwarf, d. 1837.
6 Henry Thomas Edwards, Welsh divine, b. 1837.
Claud Mullins, magistrate, b. 1887.
7 Brazil National Day (1822).
Sir Carleton Kemp, legal scholar, b. 1887.
Dame Edith Sitwell, poet, b. 1887.
8 Sir Egerton Brydges, genealogist, d. 1837.
9 Constantine II became "Augustus", 337.
William I, ("the Conqueror"), d., William II, ("Rufus"), acceded, 1087.
Luigi Galvani, physiologist, b. 1737.
10 John Jordan Crittenden, American statesman, b. 1787.
Giovanni Gronchi, Italian statesman, b. 1887.
11 Lady Isabel Hutton, Scottish doctor, b. 1887.
12 Samuel William Ryley, actor, d. 1837.
14 Pierre Vernier, French mathematician, d. 1637.
Lady Annie (Anna) Brassey, traveller and writer, d. 1887.
Karl Taylor Compton, American scientist, b. 1887.
Thomas Masaryk, d. 1937.
15 Battle of Britain Day (1940).
Independence Day in Costa Rica (1821).
Ernest Albert Whitfield, Baron Kenswood, violinist and economist, b. 1887.
Sir Bernard Paget, army officer, b. 1887.
16 Mexico Independence Day (1810).
Jean Arp, French sculptor, artist and poet, b. 1887.
Nadia Juliette Boulanger, orchestral conductor, b. 1887.
Allotments Act, 1887.
17 American constitution ratified by Convention, 1787.
Helena Wright (Lowenfeld), gynaecologist, b. 1887.
Albertine Sarrazin, French novelist, b. 1937.
18 Chile Independence Day (1810).
Samuel Johnson birthday celebrations.
19 Charles Carroll, American political leader, b. 1737.
20 Robert Sanderson, bishop of Lincoln, b. 1587.
Nathaniel Mist, printer, d. 1737.
21 Belize Independence Day (1981).
Sir Thomas Herbert Parry-Williams, Welsh poet, b. 1887.
22 D. N. Pritt, British lawyer, b. 1887.
23 Autumn equinox.
24 Seventh Council of Nicaea, regulating image worship, 787.
Marcus Hanna, American politician, b. 1837.
George Fordham, jockey, b. 1837, (d. October 12, 1887).
Lord Linlithgow, viceroy of India, b. 1887.
26 Sir Barnes Wallis, aircraft designer, b. 1887.
27 Lady Cynthia Asquith, b. 1887.
28 Birthday of Confucius.
Avery Brundage, Olympic Games president, b. 1887.
Viscount Peel, statesman, d. 1937.
29 Michaelmas Day.
Election of Lord Mayor of London.
Catharine McAuley, founder of Religious Sisters of Mercy, b. 1787.
— Cornish Gorsedd.
— Harvest and sea harvest customs.
— Hornblowing custom at Bainbridge, North Yorkshire, begins (nightly throughout winter).
— George Whetstone, author, d. 1587.

OCTOBER
1 People's Republic of China founded (1949).
Wilson Midgley, journalist, b. 1887.
Stewart Blacker, inventor and explorer, b. 1887.
2 Saladin took Jerusalem, 1187.
Thomas Price, Welsh historian, b. 1787.
3 Yom Kippur.
4 St. Francis of Assisi.
François Guizot, French historian and statesman, b. 1787.
Mary Elizabeth Braddon (Maxwell), novelist, b. 1837.
5 René Cassin, Nobel Peace Prize winner, b. 1887.
6 Jean François Lesueur, composer, d. 1837.
Maria Jeritza, opera singer, b. 1887.
Charles Edouard Le Corbusier (Jeanneret), Swiss architect, b. 1887.
8 Thanksgiving Day, Canada.

10 Spanish stronghold of Breda captured by the Dutch, 1637.
François Fourier, French socialist writer, d. 1837.
11 Samuel Wesley, musician, d. 1837.
Pierre-Jean Jouve, French poet, b. 1887.
Bobbie Charlton, footballer, b. 1937.
12 Edward VI, b. 1537.
Dinah Maria Mulock, (Mrs Craik), authoress, d. 1887.
13 William Brockedon, artist and inventor, b. 1787.
Nana Mouskouri, Greek singer, b. 1937.
16 W. S. Gosset, ("Student"), d. 1937.
17 Nathaniel Field, actor-dramatist, baptised 1587.
Gustav Robert Kirchhoff, German physicist, d. 1887.
Joseph Bruce Ismay, shipowner, d. 1937.
19 Lord Rutherford, physicist, d. 1937.
20 A. J. Beresford-Hope, politician, d. 1887.
21 Trafalgar Day customs.
Edmund Waller, poet, d. 1687.
22 Edward Thring, headmaster and educationist, d. 1887.
23 Sir Michael Hicks Beach, Earl St. Aldwyn, statesman, b. 1837.
24 United Nations Day.
Jane Seymour, d. 1537.
Eugénie Victoria, Spanish queen consort, b. 1887.
26 George Horatio, Baron Nelson of Stafford, businessman, b. 1887.
27 Dr. John Preston, puritan, b. 1587.
Whitelaw Reid, American journalist and diplomat, b. 1837.
William George Constable, art historian, b. 1887.
28 Annie Mary Rogers, protagonist of women's rights in education, d. 1937.
29 Turkey Republic Day (1923).
Don Giovanni, Mozart, first produced, 1787.
31 Hallowe'en.
Sir George Alexander Macfarren, composer, d. 1887.
Chiang Kai-shek, Chinese head of state, b. 1887.
C. W. Gordon, ("Ralph Connor"), d. 1937.
Canon H. R. L. ("Dick") Sheppard, dean of Canterbury, d. 1937.
— National Gaelic Mod.
— Mop Fairs, Stratford-on-Avon.
— Edward III claimed French crown, 1337.
— Lady Jane Grey, b. 1537.

NOVEMBER
1 All Saints' Day.
Laurence Stephen Lowry, artist, b. 1887.
2 J. E. McCullough, American actor, b. 1837.
Baron (Farrer) Herschell, lord chancellor, b. 1837.
Jenny Lind, Swedish singer, d. 1887.
Maude Valérie White, song writer, d. 1937.
3 Panama Independence Day (1903).
Truro Cathedral consecrated, 1887.
David Clarke, archaeologist, b. 1937.
4 Alfred Lee Loomis, physicist, b. 1887.
5 Guy Fawkes' Day customs.
Sir John Richardson, explorer, b. 1787.
Donald Baillie, theologian, b. 1887.
6 Sir Johnston Forbes-Robertson, actor, d. 1937.
Italy joined Anti-Comintern Pact, 1937.
7 Elijah Lovejoy, martyred abolitionist, d. 1837.
9 Alfred Holmes, violinist and composer, b. 1837.
James Ramsay MacDonald, Prime Minister, d. 1937.
10 Arnold Zweig, German-Jewish writer, b. 1887.
11 Martinmas.
Armistice Day. Veterans' Day, U.S.A.
George Wyndham, 3rd Earl Egremont, patron of the arts, d. 1837.
12 Thomas Burt, politician, b. 1837.
Sir Michael Bass, Baron Burton, b. 1837.
13 Nell Gwyn, d. 1687.
Irish "Bloody Sunday", London, 1887.
14 Cavendish captured treasure ship off California, 1587.
Bernhard Paumgartner, Austrian musicologist, b. 1887.
15 Gluck, composer, d. 1787.
R. H. Dana, American writer, b. 1787.
Marianne Craig Moore, poet, b. 1887.
16 Oscar Helmer, Austrian statesman, b. 1887.
17 Valentine Baker, ("Pasha"), army officer, d. 1887.
Field-Marshal Viscount Montgomery of Alamein, b. 1887.
Halifax-Hitler meeting, 1937.
19 Emma Lazarus, American poet, d. 1887.
20 Queen Caroline, consort of George II, d. 1737.
Samuel Thompson, free-thinker, d. 1837.
21 Bryan Procter, ("Barry Cornwall"), poet, b. 1787.
Edison announced invention of phonograph, 1887.

Sir Samuel Cunard, founder of line of steamships, b. 1787.
22 Papineau rebellion, Canada, 1837.
Philip László de Lombos, artist, d. 1937.
23 St. Athanasius released from banishment, 337.
Joseph Lyne, ("Father Ignatius"), b. 1837.
Boris Karloff, actor, b. 1887.
H. G. Moseley, atomic scientist, b. 1887.
Sir Jagadis Chunder Bose, Indian physiologist, d. 1937.
24 Erich von Manstein, German field-marshal, b. 1887.
25 Coronation of Elizabeth, consort of Henry VII, 1487.
Lilian Baylis, theatre manager, d. 1937.
27 American Thanksgiving Day.
29 Advent Sunday.
Proclamation of Republic of Yugoslavia (1945).
30 St. Andrew's Day.
Henry Smith Holden, forensic scientist, b. 1887.
— Powers of Court of Star Chamber reformed and extended, 1487.

DECEMBER

1 Walter Field, artist, b. 1837.
Ernst Philip Goldschmidt, scholar, b. 1887.
2 A. W. Ward, historian, b. 1837.
4 Lothair II, ("the Saxon"), Roman Emperor, d. 1137.
Nicholas Ferrar of Little Gidding, d. 1637.
5 Francesco Geminiani, composer, baptised, 1687.
6 Finland Independence Day (1917).
Lynne Fontanne, actress, b. 1887.
Ernest Pezet, French political writer, b. 1887.
7 Disraeli made his maiden speech in Parliament, 1837.
9 Emperor Sigismund, d. 1437.
Sir Eldred Frederick Hitchcock, industrialist, b. 1887.
10 Human Rights Day.
Thomas Gallaudet, American educationist, worker for the deaf and dumb, b. 1787.
Edward Eggleston, American author, b. 1837.

11 John Strype, ecclesiastical writer, d. 1737.
Italy left the League of Nations, 1937.
12 J. R. Green, historian, b. 1837.
Leonard Stein, British Zionist, b. 1887.
13 John McGovern, politician, b. 1887.
15 Emperor Nero, b. 37.
Charles Cowden Clarke, writer, b. 1787.
16 Sir William Petty, political economist, d. 1687.
Mary Russell Mitford, novelist, b. 1787.
Adone Zoli, Italian statesman, b. 1887.
Glyn Warren Philpot, artist, d. 1937.
17 Kenneth Bird, ("Fougasse"), cartoonist, b. 1887.
John Brande Trend, scholar, b. 1887.
18 Antonio Stradivari, violin maker, d. 1737.
19 Balfour Stewart, scientist, d. 1887.
Sir Charles Galton Darwin, physicist, b. 1887.
20 Thales Fielding, artist, d. 1837.
General Erich von Ludendorf, d. 1937.
21 Winter solstice.
Philip Bliss, antiquary, b. 1787.
Frank Billings Kellogg, (Kellogg Pact), d. 1937.
22 Shortest Day.
24 Elizabeth Haldane, liberal thinker and writer, d. 1937.
25 Christmas Day.
Conrad Nicholson Hilton, American businessman, b. 1887.
26 Boxing Day. St. Stephen.
Alexander Hay Japp, publisher, b. 1837.
27 Masons' Walk, Melrose.
Edward Andrade, scientist, b. 1887.
28 Sir John Jarvis, racehorse trainer, b. 1887.
Gertie Gitana, music hall artiste, b. 1887.
Maurice Ravel, composer, d. 1937.
29 Irish Free State renamed Eire, 1937.
30 Henry George Ley, composer, b. 1887.
K. M. Munshi, Indian politician, b. 1887.
31 Hogmanay and turn of the year customs.
— Christmas mumming plays.
— John Forbes, physician and early advocate of the use of the stethoscope, b. 1787.

BOOKS, RESEARCH AND REFERENCE SOURCES FOR WRITERS

MARGARET PAYNE, A.L.A.

Almost every writing project will involve the use of books or research at some stage, some references are quickly found, others require accumulating numerous books or information files on a specific topic and visits to specialist libraries or other relevant places or people. Although research can be an interest or pleasure in itself, it can also be time-consuming, cutting into writing or earning time. Even checking a single fact can take hours or days if you ask the wrong question or check the wrong source first. No article or book can hope to solve all problems—sometimes there are no answers, or the lack of information is itself the answer—but a few guidelines as to routines and sources may save much time and money. The following is an introduction to printed sources, for a more detailed approach, including guides to original and unpublished material, it is recommended you consult Ann Hoffmann's *Research for Writers*, 3rd ed. Black, 1986, £6.95, a most useful book which covers methods, sources, specific organisations and specialist libraries.

Suggestions for a core collection of reference books to own are given later under the *Writer's Reference Bookshelf*. The final choice of title often depends on personal preference and interests, space, the frequency with which it needs to be consulted, its cost and the proximity of your nearest public reference library. Anyone living in or near a large city has an advantage over the country dweller, and those living within easy reach of London have the best advantage of all: a choice of major reference libraries, a variety of specialist sources such as headquarters of various societies, companies and organisations, academic and other specialist libraries and the government and the national copyright British Library. The latter is the ultimate rather than the first choice, however, often a question can be answered much nearer home, but you may find the further back in time you go, or the more detailed your research, the further afield you need to travel.

CHECKING A FACT

What do you really want to know? Clarifying your question in advance can save much work for you or your researcher. If you want to check someone's date of birth and know the person is alive or very recently dead and in *Who's Who*, then ask for that book, or phrase your telephone request so that the librarian goes straight to that source. Do not start with general questions such as 'Where are the biographies?', in a branch library you may be shown sections of individual lives, on the telephone you are adding to British Telecom's profits and your telephone bill as well as wasting time. If the person is dead, did he or she die recently enough to have a newspaper obituary?—it often mentions the date of birth—or long enough ago to be in a volume of *Who Was Who* or the *Dictionary of National Biography?* Never assume that information that you know is necessarily common knowledge, it needs to be specified.

Go straight to the index. Most reference books are arranged in alphabetical order but if not they should have an index. Some indexes are inadequate, but have you used the right key word? A good index should refer you from the one not used, for example some will use carpentry and ignore woodwork as an entry, others will ignore both and go straight to the object to be made or repaired. If there is no index, turn first to the contents page, in some books the index is in the front rather than the back.

Is it important to be up to date? Most books have the date of publication on the back of the title page. Is the answer given one which may be surpassed or superceded? Despite some instant publishing, when they deal with statistics most books have a built in obsolescence, for there is a cut off date when the text goes to the printer and the up-dating must wait for the next edition. Some current events are too recent to be found in books at all, although well documented at the time in newspapers and magazines (see below).

If in doubt, re-check your answer. If the answer is of importance, try not to depend on one source. Mistakes can occur in print or in transcribing. Sometimes it is necessary to check another source for verification or to obtain another point of view, and in all cases you should . . .

Note your source. Even if you think you will remember, always note where you find your information, preferably next to the answer or in a card file or book where it can be easily found. Note the title, author, publisher and date of publication as well as the page number. Nothing is more annoying than having to undertake the same search twice.

RESEARCHING A SUBJECT

Reference has already been made to Ann Hoffmann's book for detail, but Kipling's six honest serving men can still be the basis for any subject, What? Why? When? How? Where? Who? cover aspects of most enquiries. The starting point depends on the writer's personal knowledge of the subject, but where it is unfamiliar always start from the general and go on to the particular. An article in an encyclopedia can fill in the background and often provide recommended bibliographies or other references. If the article in the *Encyclopaedia Britannica* is too detailed or too complex, try *The World Book*, the latter may be in the children's library, but because it has to appeal to a wider readership, the text and illustrations are clearer. Avoid a detailed book on the subject until you need it, it may tell your more than you want to know.

The following sources are suggestions as sources of information, but not all will be relevant to your subject.

Reference Libraries. Use the largest one in your vicinity, for encylopedias, specialised reference books, annuals and for back numbers of newspapers and periodicals. Ask for *Walford's Guide to reference material*, the three volumes list the standard reference works of subjects, most of which should be available for consultation.

Lending Libraries. Find the class number of the books you want and see what is available.

Special Libraries. *The Aslib Directory of Information sources in the United Kingdom* should be available in your reference library and give details of special libraries and also industries and organisations and societies.

Catalogues, bibliographies and subject guides. Some libraries publish their catalogues, but this is becoming less frequent. There is a series of subject catalogues to the British Library (formerly the British Museum Library) up to 1975 and the *British National Bibliography* updates this (see compiling a bibliography).

Newspapers and bibliographies. There is a monthly index to *The Times*, cumulated annually, which often provides the date of an event, the index also includes the

Times Supplements. For periodical articles, begin with the *British Humanities Index*, and check also the specialist indexes and abstracting journals such as *Current Technology Index* if necessary. Your public library can often locate runs of periodicals and magazines, and the interloan service can obtain specific periodical articles if you have the details.

COMPILING A BIBLIOGRAPHY

Checking what books are already available may reveal both the range of titles already in print and the potential market for your work. If yours is to be the tenth book on the subject published in the last two years, saturation point may be near. On the other hand, if you know the books and believe you can do better, or have evolved a different approach, you can mention this in a covering letter to a potential publisher. A quick way to evaluate what is available is by checking the shelves of a public library or bookstore, but it should be remembered that in a library, many of the best books will be on loan. This practice also makes one aware of publishers' interests.

A more comprehensive and systematic list of recent books can be compiled by consulting the *British National Bibliography*, a cumulating list based on the copyright books in the British Library, with advance notice (up to three months) of new books through the Cataloguing in Publication scheme. The arrangement is by the Dewey Decimal Classification used in all public libraries. Other subject lists are less satisfactory to consult, the British Museum (now British Library) has a series of subject indexes up to 1975, and many British books are included in the American *Cumulative Book Index* (1928 on). *British Books in Print* is predominantly an author-title list, but does index some books under the key word of a subtitle.

Facilities now exist to obtain a bibliography on any subject by using one of the computer data banks based on the British Library or the Library of Congress or commercial firms. The difficulty is expense (£25.00+ per hour) and at the time of going to press some initial teething problems. The Book Information Service of Book Trust (formerly the National Book League) will compile booklists and bibliographies at a charge currently of £6.00 an hour to members and £8.00 to non-members. The address is Book Information Service, Book Trust, Book House, 45 East Hill, London SW18 2QZ.

OBTAINING BOOKS

Books in print. In 1985 52,994 different books were published in the United Kingdom alone, joining the many thousands of other titles still in print from previous years. The number of books available means that the chances of finding a copy of what you want on your bookseller's shelf when you want it may be slim, but if it is in print it can be ordered for you, although delivery times vary with the publisher. Most large bookshops and libraries now have the monthly microfiche editions of *British Books in Print* giving details of authors, publishers, price, number of pages and international standard book numbers (ISBN), the latter is often useful for speeding the order.

Out of print books present more difficulty, and generally the older the book, the more difficult it may be to obtain. Such books are no longer available from the publishers, who retain only a file copy, all other stocks having been sold, so that unless you are lucky enough to find an unsold copy on a bookseller's shelves, it must be sought in the second hand market or through a library loan. There are many specialist second hand and antiquarian booksellers, and a number of directories listing them and their interests, the most well known being *Dealers in Books*, now published by Europa, *Cole's Register* and Peter Marcan's *Directory of Specialist Book Dealers in the United Kingdom*, copies of these should be in your local reference library. Many advertise in *Book and Magazine Collector*, a monthly magazine, which has an extensive wants column.

Public libraries should be able to obtain books for you whether or not they are in print, either from their own stock, from other libraries in the system or through the interloan scheme. This operates through the British Lending Library, but all requests must go through your library, you cannot apply direct. Your local library tickets may sometimes be used in other libraries, but different issuing systems have discouraged this in recent years.

A WRITER'S REFERENCE BOOKSHELF

However good and accessible a public library may be, there are some books required for constant or instant consultation, within easy reach of the desk or typewriter. The choice of title may vary, but the following list is offered as suggestions for a core collection.

1. *Dictionaries.* With the use of word processor packages, a dictionary is no longer quite so essential for spelling checks, although still needed to clarify definitions and meanings. A book is often easier to consult and portable, the complete *Oxford English Dictionary* is not, and although the definitive work, neither the full nor the compact edition with its magnifying glass, nor the two volume *Shorter Oxford Dictionary* are easy to handle for quick reference, so a one volume dictionary is more practical. The number of new words and meanings coming into vogue suggests a replacement every five or ten years or supplementing your choice by a good paperback edition. If you use an old copy, you will also be surprised by the improved format and readability of the new editions.

The most popular one volume dictionaries are the *Concise Oxford Dictionary* (7th ed. 1982, £11.95 – 80,000 definitions) or *Chambers' Twentieth Century* (4th ed. 1983, £11.95 – 150,000 entries), the latter particularly appeals to crossword addicts. Recommended paperback dictionaries are *Oxford Paperback Dictionary* (1983, £3.25 – 50,000 entries) or the *Penguin English Dictionary* (n.e. 1985, £2.95 – 80,000 entries). If you write for the American market, it is advisable to have an American dictionary also to check variant spellings and meanings. The equivalent of the Oxford family of dictionaries is Webster's, the most popular one volume edition being *Webster's New Collegiate Dictionary* (Merriam U.S., 1983, £18.95 – 175,000 entries).

2. *Roget's Thesaurus..* When the exact word or meaning eludes you, the thesaurus may help clear a mental block. There are many versions of Roget available both in hardback and paperback including a revision by S. M. Lloyd (Longman, 1982, £10.50), another edited by D. C. Browing (Dent, 1982, £6.95) and a paperback edition from Penguin (1970, £2.95).

3. *Grammar and English usage.* A wide choice is available but Fowler's *Modern English Usage* remains a standard work (2nd ed. revised Sir Ernest Gowers, Oxford U.P., £9.75 and £4.50 (paperback) also Omega Books, 1984, £8.90). Many prefer Sir Ernest Gowers' *Complete Plain Words* (3rd ed. 1986 revised Sidney Greenbaum and Jane Whitcut, H.M.S.O., £5.50; Penguin new edition due 1987).

4. *Encyclopaedias and annuals.* Multi-volume encyclopaedias are both expensive and space consuming, so are best left for consultation at the nearest reference library, where the most up to date versions should be available, unless your use justifies them. Of the single volumes, *Pears Cyclopaedia* contains a surprising amount of general information, a new edition is issued annually (Pelham Books, 94th ed. 1985-86). For those concerned with current affairs, the complete edition of *Whitaker's Almanack* has valuable statistics and information on government

and countries as well as many miscellaneous facts not found elsewhere. For annual replacement if constantly used.

5. *Atlases, gazetteers and road maps.* These also need replacing with updated editions from time to time, an old edition can be misleading with recent changes of placenames and metrification. The *Times Atlas of the World* is the definitive work, but it is expensive and bulky for quick reference. The *Times Concise Atlas of the World* (Times Books, 1983, £18.50) is a little more manageable but still requires special shelving, and it has the most comprehensive gazetteer-index.

With the building of the M25 and other motorways, most road atlases of Britain over three years old are out of date and need replacing. Among the most recent are *The Illustrated Road Atlas of the British Isles* (AA/Hamlyn, 1986, £9.95), *Collins Road Atlas of Great Britain and Ireland* (Collins, 1984, £9.95) and the *Ordnance Survey Atlas of Great Britain* (Newnes, 1985, £9.95).

6. *Literary companions and dictionaries.* There are many to choose from, and frequency of consultation will determine the need as to whether all or some of the following are desirable. *Brewer's Dictionary of Phrase and Fable* (13th ed., Cassell, 1981, £11.95) avoids many distractions and diversions by settling queries, as does *The Oxford Companion to English Literature* (5th ed. edited by Margaret Drabble, Oxford U.P., 1985, £17.50), the new edition complementing rather than replacing Sir Paul Harvey's earlier editions. Either can be used for checking an author's work, but the definitive and exhaustive lists are to be found in the *New Cambridge Bibliography of English Literature*, but at £95.00 per volume for the four volumes and £35.00 for the index volume it is very expensive.

7. *Books of quotations.* Once divorced from their text and unattributed, quotations are not easy to trace, which should be a warning to any writer or researcher to note author, title and page number to any item copied. Tracing quotations often needs resource to more than one collection, but the most popular anthologies are *The Oxford Dictionary of Quotations* (3rd ed., Oxford U.P., 1979, £17.50) and the *Penguin Dictionary of Quotations* (Penguin, 3rd ed. 1979, £3.95). The *Penguin Dictionary of Modern Quotations* (Penguin, 1980, £3.95) contains more recent material.

8. *Biographical dictionaries.* Pears Cyclopaedia contains a brief but useful section, but for a fuller working tool, the standard works are *Chambers' Biographical Dictionary* (Chambers, 1984, £25.00 – 15,000 entries) or the American biased *Webster's Biographical Dictionary* (Merriam U.S., 1976, £21.00 – 150,000 entries). Frequency of consultation will determine whether you need a personal copy of *Who's Who* or the *Concise Dictionary of National Biography*, which are available in most libraries.

9. *Dates and anniversaries.* A brief guide to anniversaries is included in the Journalists' Calendar section of this book (see **Index**). *The Encyclopaedia of Dates and Events*, edited by L. C. Pascoe in the Teach Yourself series (Hodder, 1979, £4.95) and *Chambers' Dictionary of Dates* (Chambers, 1983, £4.95), both paperback, are the most used works.

10. *Working directories for Writers.* A current copy of *Writers' & Artists' Yearbook* is essential, recent moves and mergers have made so many publishers' details out of date. It is useful for very much more information beside that found in the first section. Browse through or use the index in spare moments to familiarise yourself with its contents for future reference.

Frequency of consultation will determine whether you also need *Willing's Press Guide* (annual, 112th ed. 1986, Thomas Skinner Directories, £39.00) or *Benn's Media Directory*, both very comprehensive in their coverage of British and overseas newspapers, magazines and other media information. *Cassell's Directory of Publishing* complements all the above, but gives more information about publishing personnel not found elsewhere.

SOME BOOKS ABOUT WRITING AND THE BOOK TRADE

The book trade has changed considerably in the last ten years, the paperback explosion of the seventies appears to have settled down, but in turn we seem to be experiencing a bookshop chain development. In publishing, computerisation is beginning to affect many aspects and we are undergoing another period of mergers and takeovers of publishing companies large and small. Partly for that reason, much material in older books is inapplicable, although a few remain important for historical reasons. The following is a selection from recent publications.

Blond, Anthony. *The Book Book*. Cape, 1985. £9.95. The book trade from a publisher's point of view.

Bolt, David. *The Author's Handbook*. Piatkus Books, 1986. £7.95 & £3.95. Written to fill some of the gaps in the author's search for information.

Bonham-Carter, Victor. *Authors by Profession, volume 2: From the Copyright Act 1911 until the end of 1981*. Bodley Head, 1984, £12.50. Volume one published by the Society of Authors covered the history of authorship up to 1911, the present volume brings it closer to date.

Curwen, Peter. *The World Book Industry*. Euromonitor, 1986, £38.00. The only book attempting a world survey, but marred by a lack of index. To be dipped into rather than read.

Field, Michele. *The Publishing Industry: Growth prospects fade?* Comedia, 1986. £15.00. An assessment of the trade by an Australian journalist.

Legat, Michael. *An Author's Guide to Publishing*. Robert Hale, 1982. £7.95. Assumes no experience of publishing, a useful, clear introduction with a glossary.

Legat, Michael. *Writing for Pleasure and Profit*. Robert Hale, 1986. £8.95. The best of the recent introductions to writing, covering novels, non-fiction and other topics briefly, but clearly.

Mumby, F. A. *Publishing and Bookselling in the Twentieth Century*. Bell & Hyman, 6th ed. 1982. £12.95; Paperback 1984. £7.95. Revised by Ian Norrie to include events up to 1970, this is the most comprehensive modern survey.

GET CLUED UP WITH A & C BLACK

WRITING A THRILLER
André Jute

WRITING CRIME FICTION
H R F Keating

Take some expert advice on writing from two leading authorities in their field. H. R. F. Keating well known author of the Inspector Ghote novels, and André Jute an internationally successful thriller writer offer practical information and guidance on all aspects. The two books cover how to choose a theme, character creation, plot, research, writing, cutting and rewriting to finally submitting the finished manuscript for publication.

WRITING A THRILLER
André Jute

WRITING CRIME FICTION
H. R. F. Keating

£4.95 each

Word Power

A Guide to Creative Writing

£6.95 net

Julian Birkett

Many of us would like to write but find it hard to get going. **Word Power** is the answer. It gives lively and practical suggestions to help new writers give shape and substance to their ideas. A wide range of literary forms – from one-act plays to haiku – is explored as well as many aspects of imaginative writing: character creation, writing dialogue and different narrative techniques. Informal, lucid and a very good read, this is an essential handbook for all would-be writers.

A & C Black

MAKING A BOOK

PREPARATION OF TYPESCRIPT

Neatness
The first impression made on a publisher and a publisher's reader may be vital. They will try to discount the physical appearance of your typescript, but a tatty typescript covered with handwritten corrections, on different sizes of paper and with inadequate margins and spacing, will perhaps not receive benign consideration first thing on a Monday morning.

The printer
Even if you have followed the advice below, have a signed contract in your pocket, and the publisher is awaiting the final manuscript with impatience, there is another reason for neatness. The manuscript has to go to a printer for setting. The printer's compositor is basically a copy typist, working a complicated and expensive set of keyboards. He must be able to read your typescript quickly and accurately, and at the same time he must interpret a code of marks which the copy editor will make all over it.

Typing
Many publishers refuse even to consider handwritten manuscripts. No publisher will accept them as final copy. If you cannot afford to have the whole script typed before acceptance, there are ways round the problem. See below under "preliminary letter."

The paper used should be uniform in size, preferably the standard size A4, which has replaced the old foolscap and quarto sizes. Neither flimsy paper nor very thick paper should be used. If in doubt, ask the stationer for a standard A4 typewriter paper. Use one side of the paper only. It is helpful but not essential if manuscripts are typed to a width of 60 characters per line. This makes it easier for printers and publishers to calculate the extent of a work and so—using copyfitting tables—to work out the space occupied when it is printed.

For ordinary typescripts, use the black ribbon. For plays, use red for names of characters, stage directions, etc., and black for dialogue. If a two-colour ribbon is not available use capitals for character names and underline stage directions in red by hand. Keep a fairly new ribbon in the typewriter so that it is black but not splodgy. Remember that typewriter maintenance is a tax-deductible expense!

Margins
Good margins are essential, especially on the left hand side. This enables the copy editor to include instructions to the printer. On A4 paper a left hand margin of 1½ – 2 inches allows sufficient space.

Double spacing
This is necessary if you are to make any corrections to the typescript, and there are always some improvements which you will want to make; they can only be made clear to the printer if there is space available between the lines. The copy editor too needs this extra space. Double spacing means a *full* line of space between two lines of copy—not half a line of space.

Corrections to typescript
Corrections to the final typescript should be kept to a minimum. Often the publisher's editor will want to suggest a few additional changes—this happens even to the best authors—and once all or some of these are included, the typescript may have become very messy. If the publisher then feels it is not in a fit state for the printer he may well ask you to have it retyped.

Consistency
Be as consistent as possible in your choice of variant spellings, use of subheadings, etc.

Numbering
Pages (or folios as publishers prefer to call them to distinguish them from the pages of the final book) should be numbered throughout. If you need to include an extra folio after say folio 27, call it 27a, and write at the foot of folio 27: "Folio 27a follows". Then write at the foot of 27a: "Folio 28 follows". Don't do this too often or you will confuse and irritate your readers.

Binding
Printers prefer to handle each folio separately, so do not use a binder which will make this impossible. Ring binders are very acceptable. Alternatively you can use a cardboard envelope folder. In this case it will help if you can clip the pages of each chapter together, but never staple them.

Protection of typescripts
This can be achieved by placing a stiffer piece of paper at front and back. On the first folio of the typescript itself, give the title, your name and, most important of all, your address. It is worth including your address elsewhere also, just in case the first folio becomes detached.

SUBMISSION OF MANUSCRIPTS
Publishers use the word manuscript when they mean typescript, so in dealings with publishers this is the word to use.

Choosing your publisher
It will save you time and postage if you check first that you are sending your manuscript to a firm that will consider it. Publishers specialise. It is no use sending a work of romantic fiction to a firm that specialises in high-brow novels translated from obscure languages just because they are described in this book as fiction-publishers. It is still less use to send it to a firm which publishes no fiction at all.

The way to avoid the more obvious mistakes is to look in your library or bookshop for books which are in some way similar to yours, and find out who publishes them. Remember, though, that paperbacks are usually editions of books published first in cased editions. Paperback publishers will not be interested in a first novel, for instance.

Preliminary letter
This again will save you time, money and probably frustration. The letter by itself will tell the publisher very little; what he or she would in most cases prefer to see is a brief preliminary letter together with a synopsis of the book and one or two specimen chapters from it. From this material the publisher will be able to judge whether the book would perhaps fit the list, in which case you will be asked to

send the complete manuscript. This is one way of avoiding paying a typing bill until it looks as though the investment in the manuscript may be worthwhile.

There is no point whatsoever in asking for a personal interview. The publisher will prefer to consider the manuscript on its own merits, and will not want to be influenced by a personal meeting.

Postage of manuscripts

Always send postage to cover the return of your manuscript, or explain that you will arrange to pick it up from the publisher's office if you prefer. (Again, if your manuscript has been rejected the publisher will not be willing to discuss the reasons in person.)

Manuscripts are best sent by recorded delivery. Registered post is not recommended. You are unlikely to agree with the Post Office on the value of your lost manuscript, and if anyone does rob the mail, they head for the registered packets first. Recorded delivery is useful because you can check that the publisher has received the manuscript. Whether you send it first or second class depends entirely on how fast you want it to arrive. A properly packed parcel almost always arrives by either rate.

Packing is important. It is not enough to put the manuscript in an envelope. Padded bags are a good idea and are available in several sizes from many stationers.

At all costs, *Keep a duplicate*, with all the latest changes to the text included on it.

Estimating

To estimate the length or *extent* of a manuscript, calculate the average number of words per page over say eight pages. Multiply the average by the number of pages in the manuscript, making allowances for half-pages at the end of chapters, etc.

What is the publisher doing with your manuscript?

Whether or not the publisher finally accepts or rejects the manuscript, there is usually a considerable interval between submission and the publisher's decision. Most publishers acknowledge receipt of manuscript, and if you do not receive an acknowledgement it is advisable to check that the manuscript has arrived. Apart from that, it is not worth chasing the publisher for a quick decision: if pressed, the publisher will probably reject, purely because this is the safer decision.

You should hear from the publisher within about two months. During this time he will either have had the manuscript read "in the house" or will have sent it to one or more advisers whose opinions he respects. Favourable readers' reports may mean that the publisher will immediately accept the manuscript, particularly if it fits easily into his current publishing programme.

On the other hand, a reader's report may be glowing, but the publisher may still hesitate. He knows he has a good book, but he wants to be sure he will be able to sell it. He is, after all, considering an investment of at least £5000 and frequently more. He may need time to obtain further opinions, and also to obtain estimates from printers, to judge whether the book could be produced at a reasonable price. The worst delays occur when the publisher is attracted to a manuscript but cannot see how he can publish it successfully.

If you have not had a decision after two months, write either a tactful letter saying 'I don't want to rush you, but . . . . ' or alternatively request an immediate decision and be prepared to start again with another publisher.

If your book is topical you have a right to a speedy decision, but it is as well to establish this early on.

Illustrations

If illustrations form a large part of your proposed book, and you expect to provide them yourself, then they should be included with the manuscript. If you are sending specimen pages you should include also some sample illustrations. This applies largely to children's picture books and to travel and technical books. It is prudent to send duplicate photographs, photocopies of line drawings and so on so that little harm is done if illustrations go astray.

In the case of a children's book, if you intend to illustrate it yourself, then obviously one finished piece of artwork is essential plus photocopies of roughs for the rest (one must bear in mind that the final artwork may have to be drawn to a particular size and the number of illustrations fixed according to the format chosen by the publisher). If you have written a children's story, or the text for a picture book, do *not* ask a friend to provide the illustrations. The publisher who likes your story may well not like your friend's artwork: you will have considerably lengthened the odds against the story being accepted. Of course this does not apply when an artist and author work closely together to develop an idea, but in that case it is best to start by finding a publisher who likes the artist's work before submitting the story.

Travel manuscripts should be accompanied by a sketch map to show the area you are writing about. The publisher will have an atlas in his reference shelves, but it may not have sufficient detail with which to follow your manuscript. Irreplaceable material should not be sent speculatively.

Many illustrated books these days have illustrations collected by the publishers. If your proposed book is to be illustrated, it is best to establish early on who is responsible for the illustration costs: an attractive royalty offer might be less attractive if you have to gather the pictures, obtain permission for use, and foot the bills.

Quotations

It is normally the author's responsibility to obtain (and pay for) permission to quote written material which is still in copyright. Permission should always be sought from the publisher of the quoted work, not from the author. Fees for quotation vary enormously: for fashionable modern writers permission may be costly, but in other cases only a nominal fee of a few pounds is charged. There is no standard scale of fees. It is permissible to quote up to about 200 words for the purpose of criticism or review, but this does not apply to use in anthologies, nor does it apply to poetry. And it is a concession, not a right. Even though this is your area of responsibility, your publisher will be able to give you some advice.

AFTER ACCEPTANCE

There are many ways of producing books, especially with the advent of modern printing processes but they all have certain points in common from the author's point of view, and it is as well to be forewarned.

As author you will see either one or two stages of proofs. Sometimes you will be shown the finalised copy of the typescript immediately before it goes to press. If so, this is really your last chance to make changes which will not tend to sour relations with your publisher! Take the opportunity to comb through the manuscript, and if there are changes which you suspect you will want to make in proof, make them now.

Corrections to proofs

There was a time when authors could virtually rewrite their books in galley proof, and revise them again at page. Do not be seduced by biographies of Victorian writers into thinking this is the way the professional writer works!

MAKING A BOOK

Modern printing is highly mechanised, but corrections involve extensive handwork. This makes corrections far more costly than the original setting. You will probably have signed a contract undertaking to pay the cost of corrections (other than printer's errors) over say 10 per cent or 15 per cent of the cost of composition. This does not mean that you can change ten or fifteen lines in every hundred.

The cost of adding a comma at galley stage, in modern processes, may be £1.00. If you add a word in one line of a paragraph, it will probably mean resetting down to the end of the paragraph. If you add a word at page stage, and this results in the paragraph being longer, many pages may have to be adjusted by one line until the end of the chapter is reached. The cost of adding that one word could be as much as £15 in an extreme case. What to you seemed a simple improvement may take an hour's work on expensive equipment.

Stages of proofs

Increasingly often only one stage of proofs is used in book production, and there is rarely any need for the author to see more than one stage. The proofs may be in several forms. Ask your editor how many stages of proofs you will see. It could be that you will be asked to check computer print-outs which bear no resemblance to the finished book but which do contain everything that will appear in that book!

Galley proofs hold columns of text about two feet long. They may be either a rough print taken from metal type, or photographic proofs called *ozalids* if the text has been set by filmsetting.

Page proofs have been made up into pages, including page numbers, headlines, and so on. It is prohibitively expensive to make corrections at this stage, except to the printer's own errors.

Page-on-galley proofs are an intermediate stage, used mainly for books without illustrations. Corrections which result in extra lines are nearly as expensive as in full page proofs.

It is worth noting that during the production of some books which have illustrations in the text, such as children's or 'coffee table' books, the editor or designer has to do a scissors and paste job to put the whole thing together. This may require some minor modifications to the text to make the final result come together happily.

Authors who want to know more about the technicalities of preparing a manuscript for the press should consult *Copy-Editing* by Judith Butcher, Cambridge University Press, Desk edition 1983, £17.50. Much of this is outside the author's scope, but dipping into this book would make him aware of points of style and consistency, particularly with reference to the use of inverted commas, roman and arabic numerals, italic and roman, rendering of foreign words, etc.

WORD PROCESSING

A BEGINNER'S GUIDE FOR AUTHORS
LOUIS ALEXANDER

DO YOU NEED ONE?

It was recently reported in *The Times* that Patrick Moore, who for light-years has been scanning the skies for space invaders, has asked his friends to keep their eyes open for a *Woodstock 5* typewriter. He wants to cannibalize it to maintain the 1908 model he uses. This, give or take a generation of typewriters or two, sums up the attitude of most of us who are fearful of disturbing the typing routines of a life-time.

You can assess for yourself whether you need a word processor by considering the following questions: Do you demand a high standard of typing accuracy? Are you fastidious about the state of your finished manuscripts? Are you a less than proficient typist? Have you ever caught yourself letting something unsatisfactory stand in an otherwise beautifully finished page because you simply couldn't bring yourself to type it again for the *nth* time? Do you have to make use of varied layouts and tables? Do you have to make use of different typographical conventions which need to be maintained consistently throughout a particular work? Do you do a lot of re-writing? Do you write books that require constant up-dating? Do you make a lot of use of scissors and paste? Do you have spin-off publications from a single key-work? Has all your available storage space been taken up by encroaching mountains of manuscripts? Do you employ a professional typist to produce your fair copies? If you do, then are you fearful that your typist, in the process of cleaning up *your* mistakes, will make a fair number of new ones? These (together with quite a few of your own) will remain undetected until the first day of publication, when, of course, they will all suddenly burst into view. Do you always need two or three photocopies? Do secretarial services cost you a fair amount of money?

If you have answered most of these questions (but particularly the last) in the affirmative, you should be asking yourself whether you can afford to remain without a word processor any longer.

WHAT IS A WORD PROCESSOR?

As you know, computers make use of ordinary QWERTY keyboards. Allowing for a few variations, they look (and very often feel) just like typewriters. A computer adopts the identity of the program that is loaded into it. Built into every computer is a memory (known as RAM = 'Random Access Memory') through which it 'remembers' the program you load. If you load a company pay-roll program, for example, your computer will become 'dedicated' to payroll; if you then replace the payroll program by, say, a chess program, your computer will become a chess player, and so on. So, of course, if you load a word processing program, it will become a word processor. A computer can be loaded in three ways: through information carried in disc form (rapidly loaded and rapidly retrieved), or carried on magnetic tape (slow to load and slow to retrieve); or – mainly in the case of games – carried in the form of a cartridge (known as ROM = 'Read Only Memory'), which has no loading time at all: you push in the cartridge and start playing the game. Inside every computer there is an Operating System which is also usually in the form of a ROM.

A word processing program allows you (more or less) to use the keyboard as a typewriter. The words you type are displayed on a screen. You can make any changes you like to this display. For example, you can add or delete words, move blocks of text, and so on. You can instruct your computer to print the text that is on the screen at any time. Depending on the kind of printer you have, your computer can provide a page of A4 in a couple of minutes. If you're not satisfied with it, you can go on tinkering with the screen version endlessly until you get it right. You can store what you've written on a disc and recall it at any time, either to print and/or make further changes. The notion of 'top copy', that uniue typescript representing the distillation of all your efforts, is consigned with relief to oblivion. The top copy is replaced by what you've stored on disc. A printout is simply known as a 'hard copy' and you never feel reverential towards it!

Dedicated Word Processors

Word processors fall into two broad categories: 'dedicated' machines and micros. The dedicated machines are so called because they are computers which can only do word processing. This is an extremely wasteful way of using a computer because it confines its use to a single activity. Dedicated machines tend to be expensive (most of them costing between seven and twelve thousand pounds). Typical dedicated word processors are the Wang System 5, the Wordplex 80-3, the Xerox 860, the IBM Displaywriter and the CPT 8100.

These machines have three main advantages: firstly, they have many tailor-made keys for particular functions, so that for example, you can delete or insert text at a stroke; secondly, the various bits of hardware (keyboard, screen, printer, etc.) tend to be well integrated; and thirdly, the computers used are powerful, so that editing and other operations can be performed at enormous speed. The size of a computer is measured by its memory, which, in turn, is stated in 'K'. 'K' is a unit of measurement for computer storage. 'One K' is the equivalent of 1024 characters (known as 'bytes'). Dedicated machines are 128K and upwards, which makes them very powerful indeed for word processing purposes. You may often see references to 'megabytes': 'one M' or 'Mega' is 1024 x 1024 which is 1,048,576 characters. We should be aware, however, that all dedicated word processing machines are only as good as the programs created for them and virtually all these programs have been designed to meet office (not author) needs.

Micros

On the strength of what you've read so far, you may be inclined to dismiss word processing on the grounds of cost alone. Cost need not be the deciding factor if you decide to use a popular micro computer as a word processor. A system which is likely to prove acceptable to a fairly demanding author will run to anything between £1,500 and £2,500. Even cheaper systems are available, but they are unlikely to prove satisfactory for a variety of reasons which we shall see later.

As soon as you're in the market for a micro, you'll get caught up in jungle warfare and electronic crossfire – so tread carefully. This is the minimum you need to set up an acceptable system:

       A micro-computer
       A disc drive
       A printer
       An RS232C interface
       A Visual Display Unit
       A word processing program

A good instruction manual
A supply of discs
A supply of paper

Let's look at each of these in turn.

Micro-computers. We can divide these broadly into upper, upper-middle, middle and lower price-range models. At the top end of the scale is the IBM PC and the numerous (cheaper and compatible) clones it has spawned (the Olivetti M24, the Compaq and the – quite cheap – Sanyo). Broadly in the same price-range (but not compatible) is the ACT Apricot Series (offering a broad range of computers at various prices) and the Apple Macintosh and Apple IIe. In the middle range come the Sinclair QL and the BBC B. In the lowest price range come the few home computers that have somehow managed to survive the vicious price wars: e.g. the Commodore 64 and the Atari 800 XL.

The main advantage of the larger computers is that they are usually based on two widely-used operating systems, known as CP/M (Control Program/Microprocessor) and MSDOS (MicroSoft Disc Operating System). This means they will run a wide range of business software, including the word-processing program Wordstar (the copyright program of the Micropro International Corporation). Wordstar is so widely used that it has become an industry standard word processing package and is now in its third version. However, it is being rivalled by a whole range of sophisticated word-processing packages mostly in the region of £300 – £400. Some of the best known of these are: Microsoft Word, Multimate, Word Perfect and Volkswriter DeLuxe.

The Amstrad PCW-8256 is to be recommended as an amazingly cheap (£400) and effective system to start with. The price is all-inclusive: computer + built-in discdrive + screen + printer + word-processing package. But do bear in mind that it makes use of non-standard 3" discs, which may not always be easy to obtain. Amstrad promise to bring out a cheap IBM compatible computer on which it should be possible to run sophisticated word-processing packages at present only available for more expensive MSDOS and CP/M machines.

Increasingly popular among authors are highly portable machines with pop-up screens which give a (not always easy to read) liquid crystal display (LCD). These are known in the trade as 'Laptops'. They can cost as little as £399 for the Olivetti M-10 and as much as £2,577 for the Data General One (the R-R of Laptops). In between are medium-priced machines like the Epson PX-8 (£917) and the Tandy (£799). The main disadvantage of these machines is that most of them make use of 3½" discs. Which means that you can't finish off that novel you began on a desert island using your standard equipment back home with its 5.25" floppies. Also some of them have limited screen display (only eight lines in the case of the Epson) and/or no permanent form of storage (in the case of the Tandy and Olivetti). Perhaps the long-awaited IBM Laptop will set a new industrial standard and it might be worth waiting for it to appear before making a decision. (Of course, it will breed clones galore!)

When selecting a micro which is going to be used *primarily* for word processing, there are two important criteria to bear in mind: (1) the size of the memory (RAM) which should be expandable to at least 64K, and (2) the kind of keyboard. It's not even worth looking at 'touch sensitive' membrane keyboards. You want something that has the look and feel of a proper typewriter. But don't be deceived by appearances. Some apparently ordinary-looking keyboards are the very devil to type on because the keys are set too closely together. Others have correct spacing but small-sized keys. You should be able to type on a computer, just as you do on a typewriter, without making any compromises. You should also take a good look at the layout of the keyboard and note how many 'special key functions' are separated from the QWERTY layout you're familiar with. Remember that because micros are not designed to be dedicated to word processing, you're going to have to use a great many key combinations (where you are required to press more than one key at a time) which you will need to learn before you can start typing. Finally, you should allow for the possibility that you might put your micro to uses other than word processing when you've got used to it. A micro with a 64K capacity is likely to have a large range of sophisticated software available for it. You can run filing systems on it, produce colour graphics, compose music and do a hundred and one other things that are remote from word processing.

Disc-drives. Some small micros can run up to four disc-drives which will take 5¼-inch floppy discs. A disc-drive is an expensive item. Whatever the salesman tells you, you can manage with just one to start with. It is standard practice to make a 'back-up copy' of every disc you create. You can do this easily (but relatively slowly) with one drive. Later on you can add another, so that you can copy discs from one drive to another with minimum effort. If you have large-scale word processing to do and are using one of the upper range Personal Computers, you may need to consider the possibility of using a hard disc (known as a 'Winchester'). The disc is encased in a vacuum and can hold e.g. 10 megabytes of data. Of course, this option is much more expensive than an ordinary disc-drive, but extremely useful in some applications.

Printers. There are two kinds of printers that are likely to provide the quality you require: dot-matrix and daisy wheels. Dot-matrix printers use tiny needles to create the letter shapes on the page, so they don't have conventional typing heads with embossed characters. Daisy wheels use typing heads which are metal or plastic discs with letters embossed at the end of each 'petal'. Like golf balls, daisy wheels are interchangeable to give a variety of high-quality typing styles. Dot-matrix printers print relatively quickly (many are bi-directional). Some of the fastest can achieve speeds of 600 characters per second. Usual speeds for small machines are around 80 characters per second. By comparison, daisy wheels print slowly: they can be as slow as 17 characters per second, which is a real plodding pace, if you're sitting there watching and waiting!

Until recently, dot-matrix printers could not provide letter-quality print, but this situation is rapidly changing. Some of the latest machines produce excellent print with a choice of styles and right-hand margin justification. They may very well supersede daisy wheels entirely as they catch up in quality and come down in price. The chances are that the printer you buy will be dictated to you by your word processing package, which will specify which printer(s) can be operated with it. Typical cheap and effective dot-matrix printers are the Epson MX-80F/T III and the NEC8023A. These are usually referred to as '80 column printers', which simply means that they can print 80 characters to a line in a standard size typeface. Daisy-wheel printers tend to be more expensive than dot-matrix, but if you insist on letter quality, there are inexpensive daisy wheels, like the Juki which are available at around £350.

RS 232C. To operate a printer, a computer needs a device which will act as go-between (or 'interface'). A Centronics interface is fast and efficient and is widely-used. Some computers, such as the PET, use IEE-488. The most common interface, however, is something called RS232C. As it is the one factor many different computers have in common, it is important in a great many ways, for it can allow your computer to communicate with another. In fact, it is such a vital part that you should not even consider a computer which won't take this interface.

Visual display unit. Generally known as a VDU, or a monitor, this is a screen, usually with a diagonal measurement of 12 or 14 inches, on which you can see what you write. Monitors are designed for use with computers or in TV studios. They may be mono or colour, but they do not include a TV tuner as well. Many home computers are designed to plug into an ordinary TV, but TVs do not have good enough quality to use as your normal screen.

Some reasonably cheap mono screens, such as the Transtec 1200, give a very pleasant green-on-green; more expensive screens are covered with anti-glare mesh, and there are some which tilt and swivel to reduce neck strain. A4-sized screens are also becoming available, but are still very expensive because they cannot use standard television components.

Colour monitors are paradoxically more expensive than colour TVs of an equivalent size. This is because they are 'high resolution', giving you readable print on your screen (in mono or in colour). The BBC colour monitor is good value at around £300. If you're in the market for a colour monitor, you might consider buying a small colour TV, but only Grundig appear to make a set (16 inch) which has a direct video input, so that you can enjoy all the sights and sounds of your micro software without any 'white noise' in the background. There is also a Ferguson with direct RGB (Red, Green, Blue) input, designed to serve as a TV as well as run off most home computers. More TVs with direct video input are likely to become available as manufacturers respond to the widespread ownership of video recorders. However, even a small TV is fairly bulky and won't sit comfortably on top of your micro.

Word processing programs. Effectively, your purchase begins with the word processing package. Begin by defining your own needs. For example, the needs of a novelist (the creation of copy with straightforward editing requirements) are likely to be very different from the needs of a technical writer, who may have to produce elaborate page layouts, running heads, footnotes, indexes and may need to integrate with other business packages, such as Delta or DBase2, etc. A novelist might be quite adequately served by an inexpensive system like the Atariwriter, while a technical author may need to consider Wordstar or MS Word.

If a particular micro takes your fancy, the first thing to do before buying it is to find out what word processing programs are available to go with it. Sometimes you will find there are several with many price variations. This is because keen amateurs write and publish word processing discs to go with particular computers, and these are often marketed side by side with the 'official' word processor which has usually been produced by the computer manufacturer. Your word processor will simply consist of a single disc (with a back-up copy usually provided) which you have to load into the computer through your disc drive before you can do any work. (This loading process generally takes less than a minute).

Word processing packages are so varied that you will need to ask some pretty searching questions before you commit yourself. Price can provide you with a rough guide. (You may reasonably expect that a £15 processor is going to be a great deal less versatile than one costing over £100.) A general rule of thumb is that the more tasks your word processor can perform, the better, even if it means you will have to master a more complicated instruction manual.

You can only find out about a word processor by asking some pretty searching questions. Ideally, it's best to talk to someone who's already using the processor you're interested in. Failing that, have a close look at the manual. Unfortunately shop assistants can tell you very little about word processing packages. You only become aware of their strengths and limitations when you work with them, and of course few shop assistants have done this.

Here is a brief checklist of questions you might ask:

Are there easy editing facilities for deleting, adding and moving text?

Are there reliable and comprehensive page layout control codes which will enable you to indicate top/bottom and right/left margins, line-spacing, paragraph indentation, page depth and tab settings?

Are there pagination features which will divide your document into pages of the length you require as well as number them and add headings?

Can you override a page layout setting by starting or breaking a line at any point you wish?

Can you see a page before printing it?

Does your word processor allow you to type page by page if you want to, or do you have to produce a single, continuous document?

Can you use your screen as a window, so that you can examine all parts of a page? (This is called 'scrolling' and some word processors allow 'side-scrolling' as well as up and down). Alternatively, can you see on the screen the whole page you are typing?

Is there a 'search and replace' facility which will enable the computer to seek a particular word or phrase throughout a document and replace it if necessary?

Can you link different documents together? (This is called 'file merging'.)

Have you a choice of typeface styles? How do they look compared with (say) a good quality electric typewriter?

Is it possible to delete material too easily? Can you restore what you've deleted?

If you've re-written a page, does your computer keep a record of the original before you make editorial changes?

Of course, it is not necessary for a word-processing package to allow you to do *all* these things, but you never know when you might need a particular facility. Some of the most sophisticated packages for dedicated machines will even proof read by highlighting the typing mistakes you have made and then correcting them, but this kind of thing is beyond the range of most micro word processors.

Perhaps you're beginning to see why a large memory capacity in your micro is important. A serviceable word processing program will take up a lot of computer memory when you load it, leaving relatively little for you to work with. You also want your computer to perform various functions at reasonable speeds. All this requires K power!

Instruction manuals. Don't let a shop assistant sell you a word processor on the grounds that it has a short and simple manual which will be easy to master. If you want your word processor to perform a lot of functions, you can expect that each one of these will require detailed instructions. So you can expect a good manual to be fairly large. What you should be looking for is whether it is written in clear, jargon-free English. A well-written manual, designed as a step-by-step self-study guide, will allow you to master the rudiments of word processing in two or three days. (It really is *very* easy). Beware of manuals written in semi-literate computerese by people who assume you know all the jargon. Here's a sentence from an *Apple* manual which makes newspeak sound like demotic: 'This character prevents script from terminating the currently forming output line when it encounters the script command in the input stream'. (The wretched package I started out with had instructions like: 'Load your DOS', 'Format your document', which rapidly reduced me to helpless rage. It contained 'helpful information' like 'there are 4800 millidot columns per inch on your printer' – but who's counting!)

It is impossible to avoid jargon altogether. Little by little you will become familiar with bits, bytes and buffers and find them indispensable for describing computer operations. But at the outset, you want a manual written by someone with enough imagination to recall what it's like starting out with no background knowledge at all.

Discs. These come in boxes of ten produced by various manufacturers (BASF, Verbatim, Memorex, etc.) The latest ones have a clear protective seal at the centre against accidental touching. Each disc costs around £2 and is infinitely re-usable. Before you can record anything, a new disc has to be 'formatted' or 'initialised'. This is a simple electronic process you perform through your computer which makes a disc capable of receiving and storing information. I find I can store about 30 pages of A4 on a single disc, which means that the 'manuscript' of quite a large book occupies very little shelf-space – even taking into account the need for back-up copies. Discs can vary in capacity, depending on the machine on which they are used. The same 5¼-inch disc can store anything between 50K and 1200K, that is between 20 and 600 pages!

Paper. This generally comes in boxes of 2,000 sheets which are 'fan-folded' and which feed directly into your printer ('track feed'). You can also get three and even four-ply paper (with or without interleaved carbon paper, depending on what you're prepared to pay) so you can have up to four copies in a single printing session, thus dispensing with photocopying. Page sizes approximate to A4. American size is 8½" x 11"; British is 8⅛" x 12". Proper A4 (8¼" x 11⅔") is available but rare. Most printers also allow you to insert individual sheets of ordinary paper for letters, etc.

Magazines. Before embarking on any purchases, it is as well to invest in a few computer magazines to get the feel of the market. Typical magazines with reasonably accessible information are: *Which Micro?*, and *Personal Computer World*. The advertisements in these will also serve as a guide to the most competitive prices for hardware and software.

WORKING WITH A WORD PROCESSOR

The work you do on a word processor can be viewed from five different angles: writing and editing, 'formatting', 'saving', printing and 'paginating'.

Writing and editing. During this stage you create your document by manipulating what is called a 'cursor'. This is a small point of light on the screen (often taking the form of a dot or a square) which can be moved to any position. By means of the cursor you can implement any decision you make on the keyboard. You can move the cursor rapidly to any point in the text to insert, delete, etc. The first thing you have to learn is not to press carriage return. The words automatically arrange themselves and jump on to a new line (a process known as 'word wraparound') without any special action on your part. Every time you press return, you define the end of a paragraph and this is indicated by a little mark on the screen. (This technique is not universal but is very common).

Formatting: This is the process through which your computer automatically implements any layout instructions you have given it. So, for example, you might want a two-inch left-hand margin, a similar right-hand margin, single line spacing and so on. You feed in these instructions (often through a series of codes) and your document is 'formatted' accordingly. In some word processors formatting is automatically carried out while you are creating your document; in others it is a separate process.

Saving: You 'save' your text, that is, you record it on to disc via your disc drive, at regular intervals. This means you can recall what you have saved at any time to make changes. You can then save again over material that has been previously stored. This can go on indefinitely until you feel no further changes are necessary. You must always take great care never to finish a session without saving. Remember, 'saving' means that your work is transferred from computer memory on to disc. If you switch off your computer without first saving, your work will be irretrievably lost.

Paginating: Through this process you can instruct your computer to cut your text into pages of a pre-specified length, to number them and to add headings, too, if you want them. Pagination is therefore the final process necessary to produce your manuscript. Even at this stage it is not too late to make changes, so 'final' is always a relative term. Some of the better word processors have an override facility so, for example, you can prevent the computer from beginning a new chapter on the bottom line of a page.

All the processes outlined above are carried out through a series of key combinations. Many word processors give you sets of choices (called 'menus') to help you implement whatever decision you wish to make. Some even have 'help'' menus to bale you out of trouble.

SOME PUBLISHING IMPLICATIONS

Submitting disc(s) instead of manuscript is becoming increasingly common. Computer setting from disc is not as rare as it used to be. If your book is to be set in this way, make sure you negotiate a fee from your publisher for 'Reduced Keyboarding': you have earned it because you have effectively typeset your own manuscript.

IBM compatibility is becoming a de-facto standard. This means that compatibility is less of a problem than it used to be. Disc reading devices now exist that allow work created on one operating system to be transferred almost effortlessly to a completely different one. The time is not far off when it may be as unthinkable to submit a typescript as it is now to submit a manuscript in longhand.

CONCLUSION

The transition to word processing *is* an upheaval and it *is* painful at the beginning. There's no denying it. But this doesn't last long. You simply transfer the typing, editing and layout skills you already possess to an entirely new medium. You will then have at your disposal an incredibly powerful tool to help you in your work. Once you've done it, you'll soon be wondering why it took you so long to take the plunge. However, it would be foolish to under-estimate the importance of the decision because it brings with it a substantial change in the way you work.

Bear in mind that you may be committed to the system you choose for a very long time, so select your system very carefully. It's also worth noting that electronic hardware takes up a lot of desk space. You still need to reserve a corner for yourself where you can do a bit of old-fashioned scribbling.

This is an updated version of the article first published in *The Author* and reproduced here with kind permission of the Society of Authors; Mr. Alexander would like to thank the following who assisted him: Tony Friis and Paul Procter (The Book Machine), Ken Moore, David Lawrence and Michael Johnson (Longman), Derek and Julia Parker, Julia Alexander.

CORRECTING PROOFS

The following notes and table are extracted from BS 5261: Part 2: 1976 and are reproduced by permission of the British Standards Institution, 2 Park Street, London, W1A 2BS, from whom copies of the complete Standard may be obtained.

NOTES ON COPY PREPARATION AND PROOF CORRECTION

The marks to be used for marking-up copy for composition and for the correction of printers' proofs shall be as shown in table 1.

The marks in table 1 are classified in three groups as follows.
(a) Group A: general.
(b) Group B: deletion, insertion, and substitution.
(c) Group C: positioning and spacing.

Each item in table 1 is given a simple alpha-numeric serial number denoting the classification group to which it belongs and its position within the group.

The marks have been drawn keeping the shapes as simple as possible and using sizes which relate to normal practice. The shapes of the marks should be followed exactly by all who make use of them.

For each marking-up or proof correction instruction a distinct mark is to be made:
(a) in the text: to indicate the exact place to which the instruction refers;
(b) in the margin: to signify or amplify the meaning of the instruction.
It should be noted that some instructions have a combined textual and marginal mark.

Where a number of instructions occur in one line, the marginal marks are to be divided between the left and right margins where possible, the order being from left to right in both margins.

Specification details, comments, and instructions may be written on the copy or proof to complement the textual and marginal marks. Such written matter is to be clearly distinguishable from the copy and from any corrections made to the proof. Normally this is done by encircling the matter and/or by the appropriate use of colour (see below).

Proof corrections shall be made in coloured ink thus:
(a) printer's literal errors marked by the printer for correction: green;
(b) printer's literal errors marked by the customer and his agents for correction: red;
(c) alterations and instructions made by the customer and his agents: black or dark blue.

CORRECTING PROOFS

Table 1. Classified list of marks

NOTE. The letters M and P in the notes column indicate marks for marking-up copy and for correcting proofs respectively.

Group A General

Number	Instruction	Textual mark	Marginal mark	Notes
A1	Correction is concluded	None	/	P Make after each correction
A2	Leave unchanged	------- under characters to remain	✓ (encircled)	M P
A3	Remove extraneous marks	Encircle marks to be removed	✗	P e.g. film or paper edges visible between lines on bromide or diazo proofs
A3.1	Push down risen spacing material	Encircle blemish	⊥	P
A4	Refer to appropriate authority anything of doubtful accuracy	Encircle word(s) affected	(?)	P

Group B Deletion, insertion and substitution

Number	Instruction	Textual mark	Marginal mark	Notes
B1	Insert in text the matter indicated in the margin	ʎ	New matter followed by ʎ	M P Indentical to B2
B2	Insert additional matter identified by a letter in a diamond	ʎ	ʎ Followed by for example ⟨A⟩	M P The relevant section of the copy should be supplied with the corresponding encircled letter marked on it e.g. ⟨A⟩
B3	Delete	/ through character(s) or ⊢——⊣ through words to be deleted	⌿	M P
B4	Delete and close up	⌢/ through character or ⊢—⊣ through characters e.g. char*a*cter char*aa*cter	⌒⌿	M P

Table 1 *(continued)*

Number	Instruction	Textual mark	Marginal mark	Notes
B5	Substitute character or substitute part of one or more word(s)	/ through character or ⊢———⊣ through word(s)	New character or new word(s)	M P
B6	Wrong fount. Replace by character(s) of correct fount	Encircle character(s) to be changed	⊗	P
B6.1	Change damaged character(s)	Encircle character(s) to be changed	×	P This mark is identical to A3
B7	Set in or change to italic	___ under character(s) to be set or changed	⊔	M P Where space does not permit textual marks encircle the affected area instead
B8	Set in or change to capital letters	≡≡≡ under character(s) to be set or changed	≡	
B9	Set in or change to small capital letters	═══ under character(s) to be set or changed	=	
B9.1	Set in or change to capital letters for initial letters and small capital letters for the rest of the words	≡≡≡ under initial letters and ═══ under rest of the word(s)	≡=	
B10	Set in or change to bold type	∼∼∼∼ under character(s) to be set or changed	∼	
B11	Set in or change to bold italic type	∼∼∼∼ under character(s) to be set or changed	⊔∼	
B12	Change capital letters to lower case letters	Encircle character(s) to be changed	≢	P For use when B5 is inappropriate

CORRECTING PROOFS

Table 1 *(continued)*

Number	Instruction	Textual mark	Marginal mark	Notes
B12.1	Change small capital letters to lower case letters	Encircle character(s) to be changed	≠	P For use when B5 is inappropriate
B13	Change italic to upright type	Encircle character(s) to be changed	⊥⊥	P
B14	Invert type	Encircle character to be inverted	↻	P
B15	Substitute or insert character in 'superior' position	/ through character or ∧ where required	⌐ under character e.g. $\frac{2}{\ }$	P
B16	Substitute or insert character in 'inferior' position	/ through character or ∧ where required	⌐ over character e.g. $/_2$	P
B17	Substitute ligature e.g. ffh for separate letters	⊢——⊣ through characters affected	⌒ e.g. ffh	P
B17.1	Substitute separate letters for ligature	⊢——⊣	Write out separate letters	P
B18	Substitute or insert full stop or decimal point	/ through character or ∧ where required	⊙	M P
B18.1	Substitute or insert colon	/ through character or ∧ where required	⊙⊙	M P
B18.2	Substitute or insert semi-colon	/ through character or ∧ where required	;	M P

Table 1 (continued)

Number	Instruction	Textual mark	Marginal mark	Notes
B18.3	Substitute or insert comma	/ through character or ∧ where required	,	M P
B18.4	Substitute or insert apostrophe	/ through character or ∧ where required	⸜	M P
B18.5	Substitute or insert single quotation marks	/ through character or ∧ where required	⸜ and/or ⸝	M P
B18.6	Substitute or insert double quotation marks	/ through character or ∧ where required	⸜⸜ and/or ⸝⸝	M P
B19	Substitute or insert ellipsis	/ through character or ∧ where required	...	M P
B20	Substitute or insert leader dots	/ through character or ∧ where required	(...)	M P Give the measure of the leader when necessary
B21	Substitute or insert hyphen	/ through character or ∧ where required	⊢⊣	M P
B22	Substitute or insert rule	/ through character ∧ where required	⊢─⊣	M P Give the size of the rule in the marginal mark e.g. ⊢1 em⊣ ⊢4 mm⊣

Table 1 (continued)

Number	Instruction	Textual mark	Marginal mark	Notes
B23	Substitute or insert oblique	/ through character or ⋏ where required	⊘	M P

Group C Positioning and spacing

Number	Instruction	Textual mark	Marginal mark	Notes
C1	Start new paragraph	⌐⌙	⌐⌙	M P
C2	Run on (no new paragraph)	⌒⌣	⌒⌣	M P
C3	Transpose characters or words	⊔⊓ between characters or words, numbered when necessary	⊔⊓	M P
C4	Transpose a number of characters or words	3 2 1 | | |	1 2 3	M P. To be used when the sequence cannot be clearly indicated by the use of C3. The vertical strokes are made through the characters or words to be transposed and numbered in the correct sequence
C5	Transpose lines	⊐⊏	⊐⊏	M P
C6	Transpose a number of lines		——— 3 ——— 2 ——— 1	P. To be used when the sequence cannot be clearly indicated by C5. Rules extend from the margin into the text with each line to be transplanted numbered in the correct sequence
C7	Centre	[enclosing matter to be centred]	[ ]	M P
C8	Indent	⌐⌙	⌐⌙	P. Give the amount of the indent in the marginal mark

Table 1 (continued)

Number	Instruction	Textual mark	Marginal mark	Notes
C9	Cancel indent			P
C10	Set line justified to specified measure	and/or		P Give the exact dimensions when necessary
C11	Set column justified to specified measure			M P Give the exact dimensions when necessary
C12	Move matter specified distance to the right	enclosing matter to be moved to the right		P Give the exact dimensions when necessary
C13	Move matter specified distance to the left	enclosing matter to be moved to the left		P Give the exact dimensions when necessary
C14	Take over character(s), word(s) or line to next line, column or page			P The textual mark surrounds the matter to be taken over and extends into the margin
C15	Take back character(s), word(s), or line to previous line, column or page			P The textual mark surrounds the matter to be taken back and extends into the margin
C16	Raise matter	over matter to be raised / under matter to be raised		P Give the exact dimensions when necessary. (Use C28 for insertion of space between lines or paragraphs in text)
C17	Lower matter	over matter to be lowered / under matter to be lowered		P Give the exact dimensions when necessary. (Use C29 for reduction of space between lines or paragraphs in text)
C18	Move matter to position indicated	Enclose matter to be moved and indicate new position		P Give the exact dimensions when necessary

Table 1 (continued)

Number	Instruction	Textual mark	Marginal mark	Notes
C19	Correct vertical alignment	‖ ‖	‖ ‖	P
C20	Correct horizontal alignment	Single line above and below misaligned matter e.g. mi₅aligned	— —	P The marginal mark is placed level with the head and foot of the relevant line
C21	Close up. Delete space between characters or words	linking ⌒ characters	⌒	M P
C22	Insert space between characters	| between each word requiring spacing	Y	M P Give the size of the space to be inserted when necessary
C23	Insert space between words	Y between each word requiring spacing	Y	M P Give the size of the space to be inserted when necessary
C24	Reduce space between characters	| between characters affected	⋏	M P Give the amount by which the space is to be reduced when necessary
C25	Reduce space between words	⋏ between words affected	⋏	M P Give amount by which the space is to be reduced when necessary
C26	Make space appear equal between characters or words	| between characters or words affected	Ⴤ	M P
C27	Close up to normal interline spacing	(each side of column linking lines)		M P The textual marks extend into the margin

At the sign of the red pale

The Life and Work of William Caxton, by H W Larken

[An Extract]

Few people, even in the field of printing, have any clear conception of what William Caxton did or, indeed, of what he was. Much of this lack of knowledge is due to the absence of information that can be counted as factual and the consequent tendency to vague generalisation.

Though it is well known that Caxton was born in the county of Kent, there is no information as to the precise place. In his prologue to the History of Troy, William Caxton wrote "for in France I was never and was born and learned my English in Kent in the Weald where I doubt not is spoken as broad and rude English as in any place of England." During the fifteenth century there were a great number of Flemish cloth weavers in Kent; most of them had come to England at the instigation of Edward III with the object of teaching their craft to the English. So successful was this venture that the English cloth trade flourished and the agents who sold the cloth (the mercers) became very wealthy people. There have been many speculations concerning the origin of the Caxton family and much research has been carried out. It is assumed often that Caxton's family must have been connected with the wool trade in order to have secured his apprenticeship to an influential merchant.

W. Blyth Crotch (Prologues and Epilogues of William Caxton) suggests that the origin of the name Caxton (of which there are several variations in spelling) may be traced to Cambridgeshire but notes that many writers have suggested that Caxton was connected with a family at Hadlow or alternatively a family in Canterbury.

Of the Canterbury connection, a William Caxton became freeman of the City in 1431 and William Pratt, a mercer who was the printer's friend, was born there. H. R. Plomer suggests that Pratt and Caxton might possibly have been schoolboys together, perhaps at the school St. Alphege. In this parish there lived a John Caxton who used as his mark three cakes over a barrel (or tun) and who is mentioned in an inscription on a monument in the church of St. Alphege.

In 1941, Alan Keen (an authority on manuscripts) secured some documents concerning Caxton; these are now in the British Museum. Discovered in the library of Earl Winterton at Shillinglee Park by Richard Holworthy, the documents cover the period 1420 to 1467. One of Winterton's ancestors purchased the manor of West Wratting from a family named Caxton, the property being situated in the Weald of Kent.

There is also record of a property mentioning Philip Caxton and his wife Dennis who had two sons, Philip (born in 1413) and William.

Particularly interesting in these documents is one recording that Philip Caxton junior sold the manor of Little Wratting to John Christemasse of London in 1436, the deed having been witnessed by two aldermen, one of whom was Robert Large, the printer's employer. Further, in 1439, the other son, William Caxton, conveyed Wratting to John Christemasse, and an indenture of 1457 concerning this property mentions one William Caxton veyed his rights in the manor Bluntes Hall at Little alias Causton. It is an interesting coincidence to note that the lord of the manor of Little Wratting was the father of Margaret, Duchess of Burgundy.

In 1420, a Thomas Caxton of Tenterden witnessed the will of a fellow townsman; he owned property in Kent and appears to have been a person of some importance.

[1] See 'William Caxton'.

attached to Christchurch Monastery in the parish of

AT THE SIGN OF THE RED PALE

The Life and Work of William Caxton, *by H W Larken*

An Extract

FEW PEOPLE, even in the field of printing, have any clear conception of what William Caxton did or, indeed, of what he was. Much of this lack of knowledge is due to the absence of information that can be counted as factual and the consequent tendency to vague generalisation.

Though it is well known that Caxton was born in the county of Kent, there is no information as to the precise place. In his prologue to the *History of Troy*, William Caxton wrote '. . . for in France I was never and was born and learned my English in Kent in the Weald where I doubt not is spoken as broad and rude English as in any place of England.'

During the fifteenth century there were a great number of Flemish cloth weavers in Kent; most of them had come to England at the instigation of Edward III with the object of teaching their craft to the English. So successful was this venture that the English cloth trade flourished and the agents who sold the cloth (the mercers) became very wealthy people.

There have been many speculations concerning the origin of the Caxton family and much research has been carried out. It is often assumed that Caxton's family must have been connected with the wool trade in order to have secured his apprenticeship to an influential merchant.

W. Blyth Crotch (*Prologues and Epilogues of William Caxton*) suggests that the origin of the name Caxton (of which there are several variations in spelling) may be traced to Cambridgeshire but notes that many writers have suggested that Caxton was connected with a family at Hadlow or alternatively a family in Canterbury.

Of the Canterbury connection: a William Caxton became freeman of the City in 1431 and William Pratt, a mercer who was the printer's friend, was born there. H. R. Plomer[1] suggests that Pratt and Caxton might possibly have been schoolboys together, perhaps at the school attached to Christchurch Monastery in the parish of St. Alphege. In this parish there lived a John Caxton who used as his mark three cakes over a barrel (or tun) and who is mentioned in an inscription on a monument in the church of St. Alphege.

In 1941, Alan Keen (an authority on manuscripts) secured some documents concerning Caxton; these are now in the British Museum. Discovered in the library of Earl Winterton at Shillinglee Park by Richard Holworthy, the documents cover the period 1420 to 1467. One of Winterton's ancestors purchased the manor of West Wratting from a family named Caxton, the property being situated in the Weald of Kent. There is also record of a property mentioning Philip Caxton and his wife Dennis who had two sons, Philip (born in 1413) and William.

Particularly interesting in these documents is one recording that Philip Caxton junior sold the manor of Little Wratting to John Christemasse of London in 1436—the deed having been witnessed by two aldermen, one of whom was Robert Large, the printer's employer. Further, in 1439, the other son, William Caxton, conveyed his rights in the manor Bluntes Hall at Little Wratting to John Christemasse, and an indenture of 1457 concerning this property mentions one William Caxton alias Causton. It is an interesting coincidence to note that the lord of the manor of Little Wratting was the father of Margaret, Duchess of Burgundy.

In 1420, a Thomas Caxton of Tenterden witnessed the will of a fellow townsman; he owned property in Kent and appears to have been a person of some importance.

---

[1] See 'William Caxton'.

Table 1 *(continued)*

Number	Instruction	Textual mark	Marginal mark	Notes
C28	Insert space between lines or paragraphs		or	M P The marginal mark extends between the lines of text. Give the size of the space to be inserted when necessary
C29	Reduce space between lines or paragraphs		or	M P The marginal mark extends between the lines of text. Give the amount by which the space is to be reduced when necessary

EDITORIAL, LITERARY AND PRODUCTION SERVICES

The following list of specialists offer a wide variety of services to writers (both new and established), to publishers, journalists and others. Services include advice on MSS, editing and book production, indexing, translation, research, ghost writing, marketing and publicity.

Academic Projects/Research Factors (Features & Editorial Services), 56 Church Street, Norwich NR6 7DR *T*. (0603) 402673. *Editors:* Dr. Dennis Chaplin, Janey Chaplin, Paul Wilson. Features, backgrounders, research briefs for press and broadcasting. Subjects include: defence, politics, technology, medicine, economics, finance, business, marketing, PR, advertising. Also: press releases, promotorials, special feature projects, ghosted books/features, book editing, typing.

Anvil Editorial Associates (1966), Lleifior, Malltraeth, Bodorgan, Anglesey, Gwynedd, LL62 5AF. *T*. Bodorgan (0407) 840688. *Director:* H. Bernard Smith. Comprehensive editorial service, including editing, indexing, copy-editing, proof-reading, and ghost writing. Planning, preparation, writing and editing of books, house journals, company histories, reports, brochures, promotional literature, pamphlets and scripts. Full MS service using justifying and multi-pitch electronic typewriters and word processors.

Appleround Associates (1983), 1 Newburgh Street, London W1V 1LH *T*. 01-734 0881 and 01-937 6106. *Telex:* 8951182 GecomsG. *Director:* Caroline Hobhouse. General editorial services ranging from complete co-published books, through provision of camera-ready, to consultancy.

Authors' Advisory Service (1972), 21 Campden Grove, Kensington, London W8 4JG *T*. 01-937 5583. Typescripts critically evaluated and edited by long-established publishers' reader with wide experience of current literary requirements.

Authors' Research Services (1966), Ann Hoffmann, 104 Russell Court, Woburn Place, London WC1H 0LP. *T*. 01-837 3038. Offers comprehensive research service to writers, proof reading, indexing, photo-copying and secretarial assistance. Specialising in constructive advice to new writers.

Benn's Editorial Media Information Service (BEMIS), formally established 1978 in association with *Benn's Press Directory*, now re-titled *Benn's Media Directory*, Benn Business Information Services Ltd., P.O. Box 20, Sovereign Way, Tonbridge, Kent, TN9 1RQ *T*. (0732) 362666. *Telex:* 95454. *Manager:* Patricia Dunkin Wedd. Primary—but not exclusively—an updating service for subscribers to *Benn's Media Directory*. Spot enquiries by post or telephone regarding the Press or broadcasting media—either in the UK or elsewhere in the world—answered by return, normally without charge. Enquiries needing in-depth research (current or historical) individually costed before the work is undertaken.

Book Production Consultants (1973), 47 Norfolk Street, Cambridge CB1 2LE *T*. (0223) 352790. *Telex:* 817135. *Directors:* A. P. Littlechild, C. S. Walsh. Complete book production service: editing, designing, illustrating, translating, indexing, artwork; production management of printing and binding. For books, journals, manuals, reports, diaries, promotional products.

Bookwatch (1982), 7-Up, Sycamore Place, Hill Avenue, Amersham, Bucks HP6 5BG *T.* (02403) 28232. *Telex:* 837089 Harlan G. *Director:* Peter Harland. Market research, bestseller lists, syndicated reviews, features.

Bridgeman, Harriet, and Elizabeth Drury, 19 Chepstow Road, London, W2 5BP *T.* 01-229 7420. Editors; specialists in fine art book production and design.

Brooke, Michael Z. (1979), 21 Barnfield, Urnston, Manchester, M31 1EW *T.* 061-748 6768. *Proprietor:* Michael Z. Brooke, M.A., PH.D. Research, editing, ghost writing, indexing. Specialises in business, management, history, biography, social science.

Buckmaster, Mrs. D. (1966), 4 Waddon Park Avenue, Croydon, CR9 4AX *T.* 01-688 5673. General editing of MSS, specialising in traditional themes in religious, metaphysical and esoteric subjects.

Bucks Literary Services (1983), 73 Vicarage Road, Marsworth, Nr Tring, Herts HP23 4LU. *T.* Cheddington (0296) 668630. *Partners:* J. L. N. Stobbs, A. M. B. Stobbs. Authors' advisory, editorial and research service; typing.

Cave, Ronald G. and Joyce, (1984), 6 Tithe Close, Gazeley, Newmarket, Suffolk CB8 8RS *T.* (0638) 750095. Educational consultancy service to authors and publishers. General publishing policy, publicity, advisory panels, finding authors, criticism, probable markets, revision, rewriting and adjustment of language levels.

Central Office of Information, Hercules Road, London, SE1 7DU *T.* 01-928 2345. Commissions feature articles on British affairs for publication in overseas newspapers, magazines and trade press.

Chelmer Management Consultancy (1980), 26 Broomfield Road, Chelmsford, Essex, CM1 1SW *T.* (0245) 262549. *Managing Director:* M. Saeed Sheikh. Consultants to publishers; organises conferences and exhibitions. Management, business studies, word processing and computer studies books. Preliminary letter and s.a.e. requested.

Christmas Archives (1978), Wassail House, 64 Severn Road, Cardiff CF1 9EA *T.* (0222 41120). All aspects of Christmas, graphic design, folklore, custom, folk art and religious celebration; greeting cards, books, magazines, photographs.

Clarke, Joseph F. (1977), 37 Grafton Way, London, W1P 5LA. Bibliographical and literary research.

Conferences & Communications (Joan Wilkins Associates Ltd.), 54 Church Street, Tisbury, Salisbury, Wilts SP3 6NH *T.* Tisbury (0747) 870490. Comprehensive editorial (editing, sub editing, indexing, proof reading) and production (from MSS to printing and binding) of short run camera ready books and reports. Word processing. Conference services include recording, verbatim reporting and tape transcribing. Rates on application.

Coxson, Peter, Fairwinds, Hillbrow, Liss, Hampshire GU33 7NW *T.* Liss (0730) 892271. Advice given on the publishing potential of manuscripts.

EDITORIAL, LITERARY AND PRODUCTION SERVICES

Cranfield, Ingrid (1972), 16 Myddelton Gardens, Winchmore Hill, London N21 2PA *T.* 01-360 2433. Non-fiction research, advisory and editorial services for authors and media, including critical assessment, rewriting, proof reading, copy editing, writing of marketing copy, indexing. Special interests: geography, travel, exploration, adventure, language, education, youth training. Translations from German and French.

Creative Comics, Denis Gifford, 80 Silverdale, Sydenham, SE26 *T.* 01-699 7725. Specialises in strip cartoons and comics for both adults and children, custom-tailored to clients' requirements. Everything from jokes, puzzles, and single strips to serials and complete comics, books, supplements, and giveaways.

Crush, Margaret (1980), Moonfleet, Burney Road, West Humble, Dorking, Surrey, RH5 6AU. *T.* (0306) 884347. Comprehensive editorial and writing service for publishers. Specialise in illustrated books and children's books.

DD Editorial Services (1983), Office No.2, Gosford House, Gosford Road, Beccles, Suffolk, NR34 9QX. *T.* (0502) 717735. *Partners:* D. Derbyshire, J. Nicholls. Proof reading, copy editing, indexing, index repagination.

Editorial/Visual Research (1973), Angela Murphy, 14 Lonsdale Road, London, W11 2DE *T.* 01-727 4920. Comprehensive research service including historical, literary, film and picture research for writers, publishers, film and television companies. Services also include copy-editing, proof reading, and travel and feature writing.

Edwards, Dr Martin, (1985), Rose Cottage, 68 Greenhill Road, Sandford, Avon BS19 5PB *T.* (0934) 852470. Specialist editorial and research service in the medico-scientific field: including copy-editing, co-editorial/-authorship, proof reading, abstracting and conference productions. Special interest in the improvement of foreign texts.

Exonia Editorial Bureau (1981), 18 St. Michael's Close, Exeter EX2 8XH *T.* (0392) 50936. Complete advisory and editorial services for publishers and authors, with special interest in children's and educational books.

Fact & Fiction Agency Ltd. 16 Greenway Close, London, NW9 5AZ *T.* 01-205 5716. *Directors:* Roy Lomax, Vera Lomax. Booklength appraisal for publishers and authors, including rewrites and script doctoring. On contract, vetting of company copy for best P.R. Contract newspaper library research at British Museum. Over 9,000 short stories out of copyright.

Ford, Brian J., Mill Park House, 57 Westville Road, Cardiff, CF2 5DF T. Cardiff (0222) 487222. Consultant adviser to international bodies on scientific matters, author, producer/director and editor of specialist publications including film, radio and television in addition to science magazines, books and journals. Presenter of several major BBC programmes.

Freelance Press Services (1967), 5-9 Bexley Square, Manchester, M3 6DB *T.* 061-832 5079. A Market Research Department for the freelance writer and photographer. Issues a monthly Market News service the *Contributor's Bulletin*; £13.75 p.a., also *Freelance Writing and Photography* (Q.); £5.50 p.a. A good rate of pay made for news of editorial requirements. (Small amounts are credited until a worthwhile payment is reached.) Agents for the U.K. for the books of the American Writer Inc. and Writers Digest, including *The Writers Handbook*; also the American *Writers Market*. Writers' market guides for Canada and Australia.

Gay, Jean (1965), Highfields, Dinton Road, Fovant, Salisbury, Wiltshire, SP3 5JW *T.* (072270) 282. *Director:* Mrs. Jean Ayres-Gay. Copy-editing, proof reading, indexing, index-refolioing.

Geoslides, 4 Christian Fields, London, SW16 3JZ *T.* 01-764 6292. Visual aid production services: slide packs; filmstrips; colour to monochrome processing; packaging. Photo library. Commission photography. Specialist work for educational publishing. Audio tape production.

Guildford Reading Services (1978), 1 The Crescent, Guildford, Surrey, GU2 6AL *T.* 504325. *Director:* B. V. Varney. Proof reading, press revision, copy preparation, sub-editing.

Hassell, John (1973), Mayfield House, Clench, Marlborough, Wiltshire, SN8 4NT *T.* Marlborough 810 384. *Director:* John Hassell. Advisory and editorial work for authors and publishers.

Hawton, Bernard, 137 Park Road, Chandler's Ford, Hampshire SO5 1HT *T.* (04215) 67400. Proof reading.

Historical Newspaper Loan Service (1972), 8 Monks Avenue, New Barnet, Herts, EN5 1DB *T.* 01-440 3159. *Proprietor:* John Frost. Headline stories from 25,000 British and overseas newspapers reporting major events since 1850.

Holland-Ford Associates (Robert), 103 Lydyett Lane, Barnton, Northwich, Cheshire, CW8 4JT *T.* (0606) 76960. *Director:* Robert Holland-Ford. Impresarios, Concert/Lecture Agents.

Indexers, The Society of, c/o Library Association, 7 Ridgmount Street, London WC1E 7AE (see **Societies** and **Article** for further details).

Indexing Specialists (1965), Richard Raper, 84 Osborne Villas, Hove, East Sussex, BN3 2RB *T.* (0273) 720530. *Telex:* 877159 Bhvtxs G ref Raper. Indexes for books, journals, magazines on scientific and technical subjects. Consultancy; also hi-tech indexing and effective index designs.

Jackson, Ken (1985), Woodside, Hadlow Park, Hadlow, Tonbridge, Kent TN11 0HZ. *T.* (0732) 851438. Commissioning, copy-editing, proof-reading, indexing, particularly of technical or religious manuscripts.

Janes, Dr. Michael (1977), 25 St. Helens Road, Gants Hill, Ilford, Essex, IG1 3QJ. *T.* 01-518 0722. Compilation of English and French dictionaries, linguistic research, translation from French and Spanish; editing of French and Spanish texts.

Lennard Books Ltd. (1979), Mackerye End, Harpenden, Herts. AL5 5DR. *T.* (05827) 69636. *Directors:* A. K. L. Stephenson, K. A. A. Stephenson, R. H. Stephenson, D. Pocknell. Book production company originating and developing illustrated books: sport, leisure activities, entertainment. Design, editorial and general production services.

Library Research Agency (1974), Rosenthorn, Herbert Road, Salcombe, Devon TQ8 8HN. *T.* (0548 84) 2769. *Directors:* D. J. Langford, M.A., B. Langford. Research and information service for writers, journalists, artists, businessmen from libraries, archives, museums, record offices and newspapers in UK and Europe. Sources may be in English, French, German, Russian.

Low, Betty, 71 Ravenslea Road, London, SW12 8SL *T.* 01-673 3239. Editing, copy-editing, proof-reading, writing (reports, jacket blurbs, etc.) and research. Speciality: Economics and business books.

MADES (Malham Administrative, Design and Editorial Services) (1977), Sheila Malham, The Post Office, High Street, Aldeburgh, Suffolk IP15 5AA *T.* (072885) 2755. Design, print and editorial services; typing.

Manuscript Appraisals (1984), 53 Beauchamps Drive, Wickford, Essex, SS11 8LX. *T.* (0268) 734115. *Proprietor:* Raymond J. Price. *Consultants:* N. L. Price, M.B.I.M., Mary Hunt, William J. Ling. An independent appraisal of authors' MSS (fiction and non-fiction, but no poetry) with full editorial guidance and advice. Proof reading if required. Interested in the work of new writers.

Marlinoak Ltd (1984), Anbrian House, St. Mary's Street, Worcester, WR1 1HA. *T.* (0905) 24626. *Directors:* Alan L. Billing, M.B.I.M., M.I.E.D., Hazel J. Billing, B.A., Dip. Ed. Preparation of scripts, plays, books. MS service, ghostwriting, translation, proof reading, research undertaken. Full secretarial facilities.

Morley Adams, Ltd. (1917), 7th Floor, Hulton House, 161 Fleet Street, London, EC4A 2DY *T.* 01-353 7131. *Directors:* V. G. R. Lucas, T. A. H. Griffin, W. J. M. Grimshaw. Specialists in the production of crosswords and other puzzles, quizzes, etc. Experts in handling advertisers' competitions.

Murray, Elizabeth, (1975), 3 Gower Mews Mansions, Gower Mews, London, WC1E 6HR *T.* 01-636 3761. Literary, biographical, historical research for authors, radio, theatre and television.

Nash, Andrew, (1981), 46 Church Avenue, Farnborough, Hampshire, GU14 7AT. *T.* (0252) 514466. Writing, rewriting and editing including joint authorship with subject specialists. Reworking of books, leaflets, etc., in any subject to chosen reading level. Rewriting of specialist and technical material in plain English. For texts thus written or edited, preparation of artwork brief, glossary, and/or index. Also copy-editing and proof-reading. Member of the Society of Authors.

Nash, Paul (1979), Kirkton House, Abernyte, Inchture, Perthshire PH14 9SS *T.* Inchture (0828) 86474. Indexing of technical publications, copy editing, proof reading. Registered Indexer with Society of Indexers.

Niekirk, Paul H. (1976), 40 Rectory Avenue, High Wycombe, Buckinghamshire, HP13 6HW *T.* (0494) 27200. Text editing for works of reference and professional and management publications, particularly texts on law. Freelance writing. Editorial consultancy and training. Marketing consultancy and research.

Northgate Training (1978), Northgate House, Perrymead, Bath, Avon, BA2 5AX. *T.* (0225) 832103. *Directors:* M. R. Lynch, J. M. Bayley. Editorial services for education and training, including writing and design of educational resources (audio-visual aids, games, booklets) and of management games and training packs. Specialising in distance and open learning training packages.

Oriental Languages Bureau, Lakshmi Building, Sir P. Mehta Road, Fort, Bombay 400 001, India. *T.* 259258. *T.A.* Orientclip. *Partner:* Rajan K. Shah. Undertakes translations and printing in all Indian languages and a few foreign languages.

Ormrod Research Services (1982), Weeping Birch, Burwash, East Sussex, TN19 7HG. *T.* (0435) 88254. Comprehensive research service; literary, historical, academic, biographical, commercial. Critical reading with report, editing, indexing, proof reading, ghosting.

Oxprint (1974), Aristotle House, Aristotle Lane, Oxford OX2 6TR *T.* (0865) 512331. *Directors:* Per Saugman, John Webb (Managing), I. W. Goodgame, F.C.A. Editorial, design, typesetting, illustrating scientific, educational and general books. Specialists in taking complete projects from start to finish.

Pageant Publishing (1978), 5 Turners Wood, London, NW11 6TD. *T.* 01-455 3703. *Director:* Gillian Page. Consultancy on all aspects of academic publishing: publication of academic journals.

Penman Literary Service, The (1950), 175 Pall Mall, Leigh-on-Sea, Essex, SS9 1RE *T.* (0702) 74438. Preparation of authors' MSS. for submission, from typing, with any necessary attention to punctuation, spelling and general lay-out, to full revision and re-typing if requested. Charges depend upon work recommended and/or desired in the particular case. Also stencil cutting and duplicating.

Pick, Christopher, 41 Chestnut Road, London, SE27 9EZ *T.* 01-761 2585. Writer, editorial planner and consultant, editor. Author and editor of non-fiction books for all popular markets. Special interests: travel and current affairs. Non-fiction title and series planning and development projects undertaken; re-writing.

Picture Research Agency, Pat Hodgson, Jasmine Cottage, Spring Grove Road, Richmond, Surrey, TW10 6EH *T.* 01-940 5986. Illustrations found for books, films and television. Written research also undertaken particularly on historical subjects, including photographic and film history. Small picture library.

Prefis Ltd (Book Machine) (1982), 11 Amwell End, Ware, Herts SG12 9HP. *T.* (0920) 5890. *Directors:* Paul Procter B.A., Tony Friis M.TECH., M.B.C.S. Originators of a word-processing and text-preparation system (the **Book Machine**) specifically designed for the author, publisher's editor and designer, and the typesetter.

Press Editorial Syndicate (1964), 27A Arterberry Road, Wimbledon, London, SW20 8AF. *T.* 01-947 5482. *T.A.* Bakerbook, London. *Director:* W. Howard Baker. Specialist editorial services for book publishers.

Rich Research (1978), 13 Knoll House, Carlton Hill, St. John's Wood, London, NW8 9XD *T.* 01-624 7755. *Director:* Diane Rich. Professional picture research and fee negotiation. Illustrations found for books, films, television; advertising agencies; and exhibitions. Fast access to world-wide sources.

Rippon, Anton, Press Services, 45 Overdale Road, Derby, DE3 6AU *T.* (0332) 769753. Writer and researcher on historical, sociological and sporting topics. Features, programmes, brochures produced, ghost writing.

Robinson, Vernon, Editorial Services, (1973), 114 Blinco Grove, Cambridge, CB1 4TT *T.* (0223) 244414. Copy-editing and proof reading of all educational books to university level. Competitive rates. Specialise: science, maths, building/construction, economics, computer science.

Roger Smithells Ltd., Editorial Services, 6 Balfour Road, London, N5 2HB *T.* 01-226 4345. Journalistic specialists in everything relating to travel and holidays; newspaper and magazine articles; tv scripts; compilers of travel books.

Roth-Mills (1974), 22 Quarry High Street, Oxford, OX3 8JT *T.* (0865) 60088. *Directors:* Ernest Roth, Sonya Mills. Publishers' editorial service, copy-editing, anglicising, proof-reading, D.I.Y. features, non-technical translation from French, German and Italian. Word processing facilities.

Science Unit, Mill Park House, 57 Westville Road, Penylan, Cardiff, CP2 5DF *T.* Cardiff (0222) 487222. Independent scientific consultancy specialising in microscopical matters. Advises on programmes and publications in general scientific field. Activities are world-wide, with publications in many overseas and foreign-language editions.

Seager, Mrs Ellen, Flat 2, Trafalgar Mansions, York Place, Harrogate, North Yorkshire *T.* 509770. Critical assessment of fiction and non-fiction work with helpful direction, tuition and advice. Ghost writing. Publishing and market information.

Seminar Cassettes Ltd. (1973), 218 Sussex Gardens, London, W2 3UD *T.* 01-262 7357. *Directors:* Rose-Mary Sands, Sunday Wilshin. Spoken word cassettes on current affairs, psychology, metaphysics, ecology and interviews with literary and artistic figures. Widely used in English language teaching and in universities, polytechnics, school libraries and bookshops as unique and authentic source material. Sole European agent for *Psychology To-day* USA library of spoken-word cassettes and *Science in Society* audio cassettes.

Shuttleworth, Christine (1981), 12 Glazbury Road, London W14 7AS *T.* 01-603 7636. Indexing, copy preparation, sub-editing, proof reading, non-technical translation from German, French, Italian. Registered Indexer, Society of Indexers.

Songhurst, Robert and Jane (1976), 3 Yew Tree Cottages, Grange Lane, Sandling, near Maidstone, Kent, ME14 3BY *T.* Maidstone 57635. Literary consultants, authors' works advised upon, literary and historical research, feature writing, reviewing, editing.

Tasiemka, Hans, Archives (1950), 80 Temple Fortune Lane, London, NW11 7TU *T.* 01-455 2485. *Proprietor:* Mrs. Edda Tasiemka. Comprehensive newspaper cuttings library from 1850's to the present day on all subjects for writers, publishers, picture researchers, film and TV companies.

Taylor, Lyn M., 42 Slamannan Road, Falkirk, Stirlingshire FK1 3BW *T.* (0324) 37649. Comprehensive editorial service. Copy-editing and proof reading in all subjects. Specialising in scientific, medical and educational.

Taylor, Raymond J., A.C.I.S., A.I.B., F.A.A.I., (1979), Room 11, Wellington House, 14-16 Church Road, Ashford, Kent TN23 1RE *T.* (0233) 35323. Indexing, research, proof reading.

Technical Writers, (1984), Queen's Chambers, King Street, Nottingham, NG1 2BR. *T.* (0602) 505499. *Partners:* Carole Baker, B.A., Charles Mansfield. Writing and documentation specialists. Technical publications for the computer and information technology industry. Documentation for business systems, programming languages and software products. Provide on-line document storage, electronic text editing, short-run printing and production of booklets, User Guides and Operators' Manuals. Member of the Technical Writers' Group at the Society of Authors.

Technidraught (Cartography) (1984), 3 Rayleigh Road, Basingstoke, Hampshire, RG21 1TJ. *T.* (0256) 28186. *Partners:* P. J. Corcoran, Rosemary Corcoran. Cartographic design and draughting service for publishers and authors, research and editing facilities, specializing in academic, education, travel and related fields.

Tecmedia Ltd. (1972), 5 Granby Street, Loughborough, LE11 3DU *T.* (0509) 230248. *Telex:* 341995 ref. 214. *Directors:* J. G. Barker, D. J. Wakeman, M. J. Potter, J. D. Baxter. Specialists in the design, development and production of mixed media training packages.

Thomas, Hilary, (1974), 27 Grasvenor Avenue, Barnet, Herts, EN5 2BY *T.* 01-440 5662. Genealogical, literary and historical research.

3 & 5 Promotion (1985), 5 Church Street, Harston, Cambridge CB2 5NP *T.* (0223) 871028. *Proprietor:* Rosemary Dooley. Publicity services for publishers.

Towns, Elaine (1978), 72 Atlantic Way, Westward Ho, Bideford, Devon, EX39 1JG *T.* (02372) 77722. Copy-editing, proof reading, research, indexing. Natural history, cookery, social science, computer books, general fiction and non-fiction.

Unwin, Toni, 44 Walton Street, Oxford, OX2 6AD *T.* 50897. Freelance editing, rewriting, proof-reading.

Vasey, Patricia M. (1982), 78 North Parade, Belfast, BT7 2GJ. *T.* (0232) 693845. Indexing, research, proof-reading, editing. Law, socio-legal studies, management, accountancy. Member of Society of Indexers.

Vickers, John, 27 Shorrolds Road, London, SW6 7TR *T.* 01-385 5774. Archives of British Theatre photographs by John Vickers, from 1939 – 1960.

Wainwright, Gordon R., 22 Hawes Court, Sunderland, SR6 8NU *T.* 489342. Criticism, advice, revision and all other editorial work for publishers and authors, especially those concerned with educational books. Public relations and publicity. Preparation, planning, editing, writing and publication of books, pamphlets, house journals, company histories, brochures, reports, promotional literature, etc. Articles on education and training matters supplied to newspapers, journals and magazines. Training in report writing, rapid reading and non-verbal communication. Lecture service. Consultancy service in all aspects of communication. Ghost writing service. Travel writing assignments undertaken.

Worts-Power Associates (1983), 48 Kings Road, Long Ditton, Surrey KT6 5JF. *T.* 01-398 7723 and 8723. *Directors:* Kim Worts, Shelley Power. Represents freelance publishing workers; supplies book production and design, editors, copyeditors, proof readers, indexers.

Writerlink Ltd (1984), 28 Lexington Street, London W1R 3HR *T.* 01-930 0745 and 439 8427. *Directors:* Charles Dawes, John Hare, John Bennett, Sally Cartwright. Expert individual advice given to authors by a team of readers widely experienced in publishing.

EDITORIAL, LITERARY AND PRODUCTION SERVICES 489

Writers' Markets (1985), Amazing Tales Bookshop, 10 Southwell Road, Sneinton, Nottingham NG1 1DL *T.* (0602) 586083. Bi-monthly magazine giving details of new publications, literary competitions and information of interest to freelance writers. Send stamp or IRC for sample. *Subscription:* £7.00 p.a.

Yorkshire Literary Services, 11 Mill Hill, Haworth, Keighley, West Yorkshire BD22 8QH *T.* (0535) 45796. Editorial service for printers, publishers, including educational, training and children's publications. Writing, rewriting, updating, revision, copy-editing and ghost writing. Research undertaken. Book and series planning and development. Complete editorial and production service for magazines, house journals, promotional literature, etc. All aspects of communications, internal and external.

INDEXING

The Society of Indexers maintains a Register of members whose practical competence in compiling indexes has been tested and approved by its Board of Assessors. Introductions are freely available to authors, publishers, and others responsible for commissioning indexes, by contacting the Society's Registrar, Mrs. E. Wallis, 25 Leyborne Park, Kew Gardens, Surrey, TW9 3HB *T.* 01-940 4771.

In addition, there are some 200 general and specialist indexers listed in the Society's booklet *Indexers Available*, which is obtainable by sending a SAE (at least 6½ x 8½) to the *Registrar*.

For other details of the Society of Indexers, see the entry under **Societies, Associations and Clubs.**

TRANSLATION

The role of the translator in enabling literature to pass beyond its national frontiers is receiving growing recognition. In view of the general increase of activity in this field, it is not surprising that many people with literary interests and a knowledge of languages should think of adopting free-lance translating as a full- or part-time occupation. Some advice may be usefully given to such would-be translators.

The first difficulty the beginner will encounter is the unwillingness of publishers to entrust a translation to anyone who has not already established a reputation for sound work. The least the publisher will demand before commissioning a translation is a fairly lengthy specimen of the applicant's work, even if unpublished. The publisher cannot be expected to pay for a specimen sent in by a translator seeking work. If, on the other hand, a publisher specifically asks for a lengthy specimen of a commissioned book the firm will usually pay for this specimen at the current rate. Perhaps the best way the would-be translator can begin is to select some book of the type which he feels competent and anxious to translate, ascertain from the foreign author or publisher that the English-language rights are still free, translate a substantial section of the book and then submit the book and his specimen translation to an appropriate publisher. If he is extremely lucky, this may result in a commission to translate the book. More probably, however—since publishers are generally very well informed about foreign books likely to interest them and rarely open to a chance introduction—the publisher will reject the book as such. But if he is favourably impressed by the translation, he may very possibly commission some other book of a similar nature which he already has in mind.

In this connection it is important to stress that the translator should confine himself to subjects of which he possesses an expert knowledge. In the case of non-fiction, he may have to cope with technical expressions not to be found in the dictionary and disaster may ensue if he is not fully conversant with the subject. The translation of fiction, on the other hand, demands different skills (e.g. in the writing of dialogue) and the translator would be wise to ask himself whether he possesses these skills before taking steps to secure work of this nature.

Having obtained a commission to translate a book, the translator will be faced with the question of fees. These vary considerably from publisher to publisher but for the commoner European languages they range from £28.00 upwards per thousand words. Translators should be able to obtain, in addition to the initial fee, a royalty of 2½%. However, some publishers will consent to pay royalties of this nature, if at all, only on second editions and reprints. In the past it was common practice for a translator to assign his copyright to the publisher outright, but this is no longer the rule. Most reputable publishers will now sign agreements specifying the rights they require in the translation and leaving the copyright in the translator's hands. In the case of plays a proportion of the author's royalties (up to 50%) is the usual method of payment.

Advice regarding fees, copyright and other matters may be obtained from the Translators' Association of the Society of Authors (see **Societies, Associations, Clubs**).

Technical translators are catered for by the Translators' Guild Ltd., which is associated with the Institute of Linguists (see **Societies, Associations, Clubs**). Annual prizes are awarded for translations from the German, the Italian and the French languages (see **Literary Prizes and Awards**).

GOVERNMENT OFFICES AND PUBLIC SERVICES

Enquiries accompanied by a stamped addressed envelope, should be sent to the Public Relations Officer.

Agriculture, Fisheries and Food, Ministry of, Whitehall Place, London, SW1A 2HH *T.* 01-233 3000.

Ancient and Historical Monuments of Scotland, Royal Commission on, 54 Melville Street, Edinburgh, EH3 7HF *T.* 031-225 5994.

Ancient and Historical Monuments in Wales, Royal Commission on, Edleston House, Queens Road, Aberystwyth, Dyfed, SY23 2HP *T.* Aberystwyth 4381–2.

Arts Council of Great Britain, 105 Piccadilly, London, W1V 0AU *T.* 01-629 9495.

Australia, High Commissioner for Commonwealth of, Australia House, Strand, London, WC2B 4LA *T.* 01-438 8000.

Barbados High Commission, 1 Great Russell Street, London, WC1B 3NH *T.* 01-631 4975.

Bodleian Library, Oxford, OX1 3BG *T.* Oxford (0865) 244675 (from January 1987 277000).

Botswana High Commission, 6 Stratford Place, London, W1N 9AE *T.* 01-499 0031.

British Airways, Plc, Speedbird House, P.O. Box 10, London Heathrow Airport, Hounslow, Middlesex, TW6 2JA *T.* 01-759 5511.

British Broadcasting Corporation, Broadcasting House, London, W1A 1AA *T.* 01-580 4468.

British Coal, Hobart House, Grosvenor Place, London, SW1X 7AE *T.* 01-235 2020.

British Council, The, 10 Spring Gardens, London, SW1A 2BN *T.* 01-930 8466.

British Film Institute, 127 Charing Cross Road, London, WC2H 0EA *T.* 01-437 4355. *Telex:* 27624.

British Gas Corporation, Rivermill House, 152 Grosvenor Road, London, SW1V 3JL *T.* 01-821 1444. *Telex:* 938529.

British Library, The, 2 Sheraton Street, London, W1V 4BH *T.* 01-636 1544.

British Library, Document Supply Centre, Boston Spa, Wetherby, West Yorkshire, LS23 7BQ *T.* Boston Spa (0937) 843434. *Telex:* 557381. *Fax:* (0937) 845520.

British Library Newspaper Library, Colindale Avenue, London, NW9 5HE *T.* 01-200 5515.

British Museum, Great Russell Street, London, WC1B 3DG *T.* 01-636 1555.

British Railways Board, Rail House, Euston Square, P.O. Box 100, London, NW1 2DZ *T.* 01-262 3232.

British Standards Institution, *Enquiries:* Linford Wood, Milton Keynes, Bucks. MK14 6LE. *T.* (0908) 320066. *Head Office:* 2 Park Street, London W1A 2BS.

GOVERNMENT OFFICES AND PUBLIC SERVICES

British Telecommunications plc Headquarters, 81 Newgate Street, London EC1A 7AJ *T.* 01-356 5000.

British Tourist Authority/English Tourist Board, Thames Tower, Black's Road, London W6 9EL *T.* 01-846 9000.

Cadw, Welsh Historic Monuments, Brunel House, 2 Fitzalan Road, Cardiff CF2 1UY *T.* (0222) 465511.

Canadian High Commission, Cultural Affairs Division, Canada House, Trafalgar Square, London, SW1Y 5BJ *T.* 01-629 9492, ext. 246.

Central Electricity Generating Board, Sudbury House, 15 Newgate Street, London, EC1A 7AU *T.* 01-634 5111.

Central Office of Information, Hercules Road, London, SE1 7DU *T.* 01-928 2345. In the UK conducts press, television, radio and poster advertising; produces booklets, leaflets, films, radio and television material, exhibitions, photographs and other visual material. For the Foreign and Commonwealth Office supplies British information posts overseas with press, radio and television material, publications, reference services, films, exhibitions, photographs, and display and reading-room material.

College of Arms or Heralds' College, Queen Victoria Street, London, EC4V 4BT *T.* 01-248 2762.

Commonwealth Institute, Kensington High Street, London, W8 6NQ *T.* 01-603 4535. Recorded information: 01-602 3257. Information about the Commonwealth. Exhibition galleries, Arts Centre (including theatre, cinema, art galleries), licensed restaurant, bookshop, etc. Contemporary reference library for use by general public, of books and periodicals. Compix photo library of the contemporary Commonwealth.

Copyright Receipt Office, The, The British Library, 2 Sheraton Street, London, W1V 4BH *T.* 01-636 1544.

Countryside Commission, John Dower House, Crescent Place, Cheltenham, Gloucestershire, GL50 3RA *T.* (0242) 521381.

Countryside Commission for Scotland, Battleby, Redgorton, Perth, PH1 3EW *T.* (0738) 27921, ext. 265.

Court of the Lord Lyon, HM New Register House, Edinburgh EH1 3YT *T.* 031-556 7255.

Cyprus High Commission, 93 Park Street, London, W1Y 4ET *T.* 01-499 8272.

Data Protection Registrar, Office of the Data Protection Registrar, Springfield House, Water Lane, Wilmslow, Cheshire SK9 5AX *T. Enquiries:* (0625) 535777; *Administration:* (0625) 535711.

Defence, Ministry of, (Press and P.R. Depts.) (General, Navy, Army and Air Force Departments), Main Building, Whitehall, London, SW1A 2HB *T.* 01-218 9000.

Design Council, The, 28 Haymarket, London, SW1Y 4SU *T.* 01-839 8000.

Education and Science, Department of, Elizabeth House, York Road, London, SE1 7PH *T.* 01-934 9000.

Electricity Council, 30 Millbank, London, SW1P 4RD *T.* 01-834 2333.

Employment, Department of, Information Division, Caxton House, Tothill Street, London, SW1H 9NF *T.* 01-213 3000. *Public enquiries:* 01-213 5551.

Energy, Department of, Thames House South, Millbank, London, SW1P 4QJ *T.* 01-211 3000. *Telex:* 918777.

Environment, Department of the, 2 Marsham Street, London, SW1P 3EB *T.* 01-212 3434.

Foreign and Commonwealth Office, Downing Street, London, SW1A 2AL *T.* 01-233 3000. *Telex:* 297711 (a/b Prodrome London).

Forestry Commission, 231 Corstorphine Road, Edinburgh, EH12 7AT *T.* 031-334 0303.

Gambia High Commission, 57 Kensington Court, London, W8 5DG *T.* 01-937 6316.

General Register Office, now part of the **Office of Population Censuses and Surveys,** *q.v.*

Ghana, High Commission for, 13 Belgrave Square, London, SW1X 8PR *T.* 01-235 4142 – 5.

Guyana High Commission, 3 Palace Court, Bayswater Road, London, W2 4LP *T.* 01-229 7684 – 8.

Hayward Gallery (Arts Council), South Bank, Belvedere Road, London, SE1 8XZ *T.* 01-928 3144.

Health and Social Security, Department of, Alexander Fleming House, Elephant and Castle, London, SE1 6BY *T.* 01-407 5522. *Overseas Branch:* Newcastle-upon-Tyne, NE98 1YX *T.* (091) 2857111.

Historic Buildings and Monuments Commission for England, 25 Savile Row, London W1X 2BT *T.* 01-734 6010, ext. 675.

Historic Buildings & Monuments Directorate, 25 Drumsheugh Gardens, Edinburgh, EH3 7RN *T.* 031-226 3611.

Historical Manuscripts, Royal Commission on, Quality House, Quality Court, Chancery Lane, London, WC2A 1HP *T.* 01-242 1198.

Historical Monuments (England), Royal Commission on, Fortress House, 23 Savile Row, London, W1X 1AB *T.* 01-734 6010.

Home Office, Queen Anne's Gate, London, SW1H 9AT *T.* 01-213 3000. *Public Relations Branch:* Director of Information Services: B. L. Mower.

Independent Broadcasting Authority, 70 Brompton Road, London, SW3 1EY *T.* 01-584 7011.

India, Press & Information Wing, India House, Aldwych, London, WC2B 4NA *T.* 01-836 8484, ext. 144, 138.

Inland Revenue, Board of, Somerset House, London, WC2R 1LB *Press Office: T.* 01-438 6692.

Ireland, Embassy of, 17 Grosvenor Place, London, SW1X 7HR *T.* 01-235 2171.

Jamaican High Commission, 50 St. James's Street, London, SW1A 1JS *T.* 01-499 8600.

Kenya High Commissioner, 45 Portland Place, London, W1N 4AS *T.* 01-636 2371.

Lesotho, High Commission of the Kingdom of, 10 Collingham Road, London, SW5 0NR *T.* 01-373 8581-2.

London Museum—see **Museum of London.**

GOVERNMENT OFFICES AND PUBLIC SERVICES

London Records Office, Corporation of City of, Guildhall, London, EC2P 2EJ *T.* 01-606 3030.

London Regional Transport, 55 Broadway, SW1H 0BD *T.* 01-222 5600.

Malawi High Commission, 33 Grosvenor Street, London, W1X 0DE *T.* 01-491 4172 – 7.

Malaysian High Commission, 45 Belgrave Square, London, SW1X 8QT *T.* 01-235 8033. *Tourism:* 17 Curzon Street, London, W1Y 7FE *T.* 01-499 7388. *Trade:* 57 Trafalgar Square, London WC2N 5DU *T.* 01-930 7932.

Malta High Commission, 16 Kensington Square, London, W8 5HH. *T.* 01-938 1712-6.

Mauritius High Commission, 32 – 3 Elvaston Place, London, SW7 5NW *T.* 01-581 0294.

Museum of London, London Wall, EC2Y 5HN *T.* 01-600 3699. Amalgamating the collections of the London Museum and the Guildhall Museum.

Museum of Mankind (Ethnography Department of the British Museum), 6 Burlington Gardens, London, W1X 2EX *T.* 01-437 2224 – 8.

National Economic Development Office, Millbank Tower, Millbank, London, SW1P 4QX *T.* 01-211 3100.

National Maritime Museum, Greenwich, London, SE10 9NF, including the Old Royal Observatory *T.* 01-858 4422.

National Savings, Department for, Marketing and Information Division, Charles House, 375 Kensington High Street, London, W14 8SD *T.* 01-605 9432, 9436.

National Trust for Scotland, The, 5 Charlotte Square, Edinburgh, EH2 4DU *T.* 031-226 5922.

Natural Environment Research Council, Polaris House, North Star Avenue, Swindon, SN2 1EU *T.* Swindon (0793) 40101.

New Zealand, High Commissioner for, New Zealand House, Haymarket, London, SW1Y 4TQ *T.* 01-930 8422. *Telex:* 24368.

Nigeria High Commission, Nigeria House, 9 Northumberland Avenue, London, WC2N 5BX *T.* 01-839 1244.

Northern Ireland Tourist Board, River House, 48 High Street, Belfast, BT1 2DS *T.* Belfast (0232) 231221. *Telex:* 748087. Press only: (0232) 235906.

Office of Population Censuses and Surveys, St. Catherine's House, 10 Kingsway, London, WC2B 6JP *T.* 01-242 0262.

Patent Office (Department of Trade), State House, 66-71 High Holborn, London, WC1R 4TP *T.* 01-831 2525. *Sale Branch* (for information retrieval services), Patent Office, Block C, Station Square House, St. Mary Cray, Orpington, Kent, BR5 3RD *T.* Orpington 32111.

PLR Office, Bayheath House, Prince Regent Street, Stockton-on-Tees, Cleveland TS18 1DF *T.* (0642) 604699. Address enquiries to The Registrar.

Post Office Headquarters, 33 Grosvenor Place, London SW1X 1PX *T.* 01-235 8000.

Public Record Office, *Modern Departmental Records:* Ruskin Avenue, Kew, Richmond, Surrey, TW9 4DU *T.* 01-876 3444. *Medieval, Early Modern and Legal Records* and the *Census Returns:* Chancery Lane, London, WC2A 1LR *T.* 01-405 0741.

Public Trust Office, Stewart House, 24 Kingsway, London, WC2B 6JX *T.* 01-405 4300.

Racial Equality, Commission for, Elliot House, 10–12 Allington Street, London, SW1E 5EH *T.* 01-828 7022.

Regional Arts Associations, Council of, (CORAA), Litton Lodge, 13A Clifton Road, Winchester, Hants. SO22 5BP *T.* (0962) 51063.

Royal Mint, Llantrisant, Pontyclun, Mid-Glamorgan, CF7 8YT *T.* Llantrisant 222111 and 7 Grosvenor Gardens, London, SW1W 0BH *T.* 01-828 8724 – 8.

Science and Engineering Research Council, Polaris House, North Star Avenue, Swindon, SN2 1ET *T.* (0793) 26222.

Science Museum, South Kensington, London, SW7 2DD *T.* 01-589 3456. Enquiries to Information Office. Ext. 653 and 632.

Scotland, National Library of, George IV Bridge, Edinburgh, EH1 1EW *T.* 031-226 4531. *Telex:* 72638 Nlsedi G.

Scottish Information Office, New St. Andrew's House, Edinburgh, EH1 3TD *T.* 031-556 8400, ext. 5123 and Dover House, Whitehall, London, SW1A 2AU *T.* 01-233 8520 and 3688.

Scottish Record Office, HM General Register House, Edinburgh, EH1 3YY *T.* 031-556 6585.

Scottish Tourist Board, 23 Ravelston Terrace, Edinburgh, EH4 3EU *T.* 031-332 2433.

Serpentine Gallery (Arts Council), Kensington Gardens, London, W2 3XA *T.* 01-402 6075. *Recorded information:* 01-723 9072.

Sierra Leone, High Commissioner for, 33 Portland Place, London, W1N 3AG *T.* 01-636 6483-5.

Singapore High Commission, 2 Wilton Crescent, London, SW1X 8RN *T.* 01-235 8315.

South Africa, Republic of, South African Embassy, Trafalgar Square, London, WC2N 5DP *T.* 01-930 4488.

Sri Lanka, High Commission for the Democratic Socialist Republic of, 13 Hyde Park Gardens, London, W2 2LU *T.* 01-262 1841.

Stationery Office, Her Majesty's, St. Crispins, Duke Street, Norwich, NR3 1PD. *T.* (0603) 622211.

Swaziland High Commission, 58 Pont Street, London, SW1X 0AE *T.* 01-581 4976.

Tanzania High Commission, 43 Hertford Street, London, W1Y 8DB *T.* 01-499 8951.

Trade and Industry, Department of, 1-19 Victoria Street, London, SW1H 0ET *T.* 01-215 4751. *Telex:* 8811074.

Transport, Department of, 2 Marsham Street, London, SW1P 3EB *T.* 01-212 3434.

Treasury, HM, Treasury Chambers, Parliament Street, London, SW1P 3AG *T.* 01-233 3000.

Trinidad and Tobago High Commission, 42 Belgrave Square, London, SW1X 8NT *T.* 01-245 9351.

GOVERNMENT OFFICES AND PUBLIC SERVICES 497

Trinity House, London, Tower Hill, London, EC3N 4DH *T.* 01-480 6601. The General Lighthouse Authority for England, Wales, the Channel Islands and Gibraltar, the principal Pilotage Authority in the United Kingdom, and a Charitable Organisation for the relief of Mariners.

United Kingdom Atomic Energy Authority, 11 Charles II Street, London, SW1Y 4QP *T.* 01-930 5454.

Victoria and Albert Museum, South Kensington, London, SW7 2RL *T.* 01-589 6371. Closed on Fridays.

Wales, The National Library of, Aberystwyth, Dyfed, SY23 3BU *T.* (0970) 3816. *Telex:* 35165.

Wales Tourist Board, Brunel House, 2 Fitzalan Road, Cardiff, CF2 1UY *T.* Cardiff 499909. *Telex:* 497269.

Wellington Museum, Apsley House, 149 Piccadilly, Hyde Park Corner, London, W1V 9FA *T.* 01-499 5676. Closed Mondays and Fridays.

Welsh Office, Gwydyr House, Whitehall, London, SW1A 2ER *Enquiries: T.* 01-210 6724 and 6729 and Cathays Park, Cardiff, CF1 3NQ *T.* (0222) 825111.

West India Committee (The West Indies, Belize, British Virgin Islands, Turks and Caicos Islands), 48 Albemarle Street, London, W1X 4AR *T.* 01-629 6353.

Zambia High Commission, 2 Palace Gate, Kensington, London, W8 5NF *T.* 01-589 6655.

In *Whitaker's Almanack* will be found names and addresses of many other public bodies.

RECENT JOURNAL CHANGES

The following changes of title, mergers, and terminations of publication of periodicals listed in the *Yearbook* have recently taken place.

Because of the proliferation of technical journals, and the limited market in most of these for freelance contributions, a considerable number of the most specialist of such publications which were previously listed in the *Yearbook* now no longer appear.

CHANGES OF NAME AND MERGERS

Camera and Creative Photography now Creative Photography
Climber and Rambler now Climber
Daily Star now The Star
GC & HTJ now Horticulture Week
Gems and Mineral Realm now Gemmological Newsletter
Incorporated Linguist now The Linguist
The Mirror now Daily Mirror
Motorist now Practical Motorist
Nursing Mirror merged with Nursing Times
Practical Camper now Camper
Scale Models now Scale Models International
Sporting Cars now Sporting Cars International
Sports Car Mechanics now Sports Car Monthly

MAGAZINES CEASED PUBLICATION

Animal Ways
Buckingham and Berkshire Town and Countryside Magazine
Canoeing
Champ
Computing To-day
Etcetra
Farm Business
Honey
Kudos
Morning Telegraph
Movie Maker
Music Teacher
Nutty
Scottish Review

CLASSIFIED INDEX OF JOURNALS AND MAGAZINES

*Commonwealth, Irish and South African Journals

This index is necessarily only a broad classification. It should be regarded as only a pointer to possible markets, and should be used with discrimination.

SHORT STORIES

This list does not include all the women's journals requiring short stories, *see also under* FEMININE

Ambit
Anglo-Welsh Review
*Atlantic Advocate (Can.)
*(Bombay) Illustrated Weekly (In.)
Christian Herald
Company
Encounter
*Fiddlehead (Can.)
Good Housekeeping
*Ireland's Own
Iron
*Johannesburg) Sunday Times (S.A.)
*Landfall (N.Z.)
Literary Review
London Magazine
Loving
*Malahat Review (Can.)
*Personality (S.A.)
*Reality (Ire.)
Red Letter
Stand
Sunday Post
Sunday Sun
Telegraph Sunday Magazine
True Romances

LONG COMPLETE STORIES
From 8000 words upwards (See also under FEMININE)

Annabel
*Landfall (N.Z.)
My Weekly Story Library
Red Letter

SERIALS
(See also entries under FEMININE)

*(Bombay) Illustrated Weekly (In.)
*Ireland's Own
People's Friend
Red Letter
Secrets
Weekly News

CARTOONS
(See also FOR YOUNG PEOPLE: HUMOROUS AND PICTURE PAPERS)

Accountancy
Annabel
Back Street Heroes
Busy Bees' News
Catholic Gazette
Catholic Pictorial
Celebrity
*Cleo (Aus.)
Clocks
Countryman
Coventry Evening Telegraph
Daily Star
Everywoman
Fiction Magazine
Fitness
Gay Times
Guiding
Hi-Fi News
Insurance Brokers Monthly
*In Dublin (Ire.)
*Ireland's Own
Just Seventeen
Kent Life
Language Monthly
Local Government Chronicle
Morning Star
New Health
New Statesman
Parks & Sports Grounds
Private Eye
Punch
Radio Control Models
Red Tape
Scouting
She
*Southern Cross (S.A.)
Sunday Post
Teacher
Today's Guide
Traveller
Tribune
Weekend
Woman and Home
Yorkshire Post
Young Soldier, The

HUMOUR

Annabel
Custom Car
Dundee Evening Telegraph and Post
Good Housekeeping
Hi-Fi News
*Ireland's Own
Jewish Telegraph
Kent Life
Private Eye
Punch
*Reality (Ire.)
Signature
Sunday Post
Weekend

FEMININE
Fiction, Home, Fashions, Children, Beauty Culture

Annabel
*Australian Women's Weekly
*(Bombay) Eve's Weekly (In.)
Celebrity
*Chatelaine (Can.)
Cosmopolitan
Country Living
*Darling (S.A.)
Edinburgh Evening News
Elle (UK)
Everywoman
Family Circle
*Femina (SA)
Girl About Town
Good Housekeeping
Harpers and Queen
Home and Country
Home Words
Homes and Gardens
*Image (Ire.)
Just Seventeen
Lady
Living Magazine
*Living and Loving (S.A.)
Look Now
Mother
My Weekly
*New Idea (Aus.)
*New Zealand Woman's Weekly
Nursery World
Over 21
People's Friend
Red Letter
Scottish Home and Country
Secrets
She
Spare Rib
Sunday Post
Townswoman
Vogue
Weekend
Woman
Woman and Home
*Woman's Day (Aus.)
Woman's Journal
Woman's Own
Woman's Realm
Woman's Story Magazine
*Woman's Way (Ire.)
Woman's Weekly
Woman's World
Working Woman
World's Children

MEN
(See also AVIATION, SPORT, etc.)

Mayfair
Men Only

Penthouse

Signature

LETTERS TO THE EDITOR

A la Carte
Annabel
Art and Craft
*Australian Home Beautiful
*Australian Woman's Weekly
Autocar
Banking World
British Deaf News
Camper
*Commercial Transport (Ire.)
Countryman
Devon Life
Do It Yourself
Family Circle
Freelance Writing & Photography
*Furrow, The (Ire.)
Garden News
Good Housekeeping
Ideal Home
Jewish Telegraph
Living Magazine
*Living and Loving (S.A.)
Mother
19
Over 21
Photoplay
Practical Gardening
Practical Householder
Practical Model Railways
Practical Photography
Red Letter
She
Singles Magazine
*Songwriter (Ire.)
Stamps
Street Machine
Sunday Mail
True Story
Woman
Woman's Own
Woman's Realm
*Woman's Way (Ire.)
Woman's Weekly

GOSSIP PARAGRAPHS

Aberdeen Press and Journal
Angler's Mail
Angling Times
Architectural Review
Art & Design
*Aspect Magazine (Ire.)
*Auckland Star (N.Z.)
Baptist Times
Birmingham Evening Mail
Bristol Evening Post
British Deaf News
British Weekly & Christian Record
CTN
Campaign
*(Cape Town) Cape Times (S.A.)
Catholic Herald
Catholic Pictorial
Cheshire Life
Church of England Newspaper
Coin Monthly
*Commercial Transport (Ire.)
Computing
Cosmetic World News
Countryman
Coventry Evening Telegraph
Creative Photography
Cricketer International
Daily Mail

CLASSIFIED INDEX OF JOURNALS AND MAGAZINES 501

Devon Life
Diver
Do It Yourself
Drapers' Record
Early Music
Eastern Evening News
Edinburgh Evening News
Education and Training
Engineering
Entertainment & Arts
  Management
Evening Chronicle
Face, The
Fashion Weekly
Field
Financial Weekly
Fitness
*Fortnight (Ire.)
Freelance Writing &
  Photography
Garden News
Gas World
Gay News
Gemmological Newsletter
Golf Monthly
Guiding
Hi-Fi News and Record
  Review
Horse & Pony
*In Dublin (Ire.)

Insurance Brokers' Monthly
*Irish Business
Jewish Telegraph
Just Seventeen
Justice of the Peace
Lancashire Evening
  Telegraph
Language Monthly
Literary Review
Making Better Movies
Melody Maker
*Melbourne Australasian
  Post
Mirror, The
Model Boats
Mother
Over 21
PR Week
Parents
Penthouse
Popular Crafts
Poultry World
Power Farming
Printing World
Private Eye
Radio Times
Scottish Field
*Songwriter (Ire.)
*Southern Cross (S.A.)

Sport and Leisure
Stage and Television Today
Standard
Studio International
Sunday Express
Sunday Times
*(Sydney) Bulletin
Teacher
*Timaru Herald (N.Z.)
Times
Times Educational
  Supplement
Times Educational
  Supplement Scotland
Times Higher Education
  Supplement
Treasure Hunting
Universe
West Africa
Western Mail
Western Morning News
Woman's Realm
*Woman's Way (Ire.)
Working Woman
World Bowls
Writers' Monthly
Yachts and Yachting
Yorkshire Life
Yorkshire Post

BRIEF FILLER PARAGRAPHS

Aberdeen Press and Journal
Aeroplane Monthly
African Business
Air Pictorial
Angler's Mail
Angling Times
Annabel
Architectural Design
Architectural Review
Art & Design
Art Magazine
*Auckland Star (N.Z.)
Australian Home Beautiful
Autocar
Balance
Baptist Times
Birmingham Evening Mail
British Deaf News
British Weekly & Christian
  Record
Budgerigar World
Building
Busy Bees News
CTN
*(Cape Town) Cape Times
  (S.A.)
Catholic Herald
Catholic Pictorial
Cheshire Life

Church of England
  Newspaper
Classical Music
Coin Monthly
*Commercial Transport
  (Ire.)
Cosmetic World News
Countryman
Cricketer International
Cue
Daily Star
Daily Telegraph
Dairy Industries
  International
Devon Life
Do It Yourself
Drapers' Record
Early Music
Eastern Evening News
Edinburgh Evening News
Education and Training
Electrical Review
*Electronics Australia
Engineering
Face, The
*Farmer's Weekly (S.A.)
Fashion Forecast
Fashion Weekly
Fitness

Freelance Writing &
  Photography
*Furrow, The (Ire.)
Garden News
Gas World
Gay News
Gay Times
Gemmological Newsletter
Golf Illustrated
Golf Monthly
Guiding
Hi-Fi News and Record
  Review
Homes and Gardens
Horticulture Week
*Hotel and Catering Review
  (Ire.)
*Image (Ire.)
*In Dublin (Ire.)
*Irish Business
Jewish Telegraph
Just Seventeen
Lancashire Evening
  Telegraph
Language Monthly
Literary Review
Liverpool Echo
Local Government
  Chronicle

W.A.Y.B.—26

COPYRIGHT, TAX, SERVICES

Making Better Movies
Manx Life
Masonic Square
Melody Maker
Model Boats
Model Engineer
Motor Boat & Yachting
Nautical Magazine
New Musical Express
*New Zealand Gardener
Over 21
Penthouse
Pilot
Pony
Popular Crafts
Poultry World
Practical Fishkeeping
Printing World
Private Eye
Radio Times
Reader's Digest
Safety Education
She
Ship and Boat International
Singles Magazine
Snooker Scene
*Songwriter (Ire.)
*Southern Cross (S.A.)
Spare Rib
Sport and Leisure
Standard
*Sudanow (Sudan)
Sunday Express
Sunday Sun
Sunday Times
*(Sydney) Bulletin
Teacher
Tennis World
*Theatre Ireland Magazine
*Timaru Herald (N.Z.)
Times Educational
 Supplement
Times Educational
 Supplement Scotland
Times Higher Education
 Supplement
Town and Country
 Planning
Treasure Hunting
Universe
Waterways World
Woman's Realm
Working Woman
World Bowls
World Fishing
Writers' Monthly
Yachting Monthly
Yachts and Yachting
Yorkshire Post

FOR YOUNG PEOPLE
PERIODICALS

Beezer
Blue Jeans
Brownie
Bunty
Bunty Library
Busy Bees News
Commando
Jackie
Junior Bookshelf
Patches
Pepper Street
Pippin
Pony
Scouting
Star Love Stories
Today's Guide
Topper
Victor

HUMOROUS AND PICTURE PAPERS

Beano, The
Beano Library
Beezer
Bunty
Buster
Commando
Dandy, The
Dandy Library
Debbie Library
Football Picture Library
Girl
Hoot
Judy
Mandy
Mandy Library
Nikki
Star Love Stories
Starblazer Library
Suzy
Today's Guide
Twinkle
Warlord

SOME JOURNALS WHICH CONTAIN A CHILDREN'S PAGE OR COLUMN

Birmingham Evening Mail
Church Times
Coventry Evening
 Telegraph
*Ireland's Own
Jewish Chronicle
*Melbourne Age (Aus.)
Morning Telegraph
Nursery World
People's Friend
Sunday Post
Woman

SUBJECT ARTICLES
ADMINISTRATION AND LAW

Administrator
Banking World
Contemporary Review
Country
Criminologist
Education
Family Law
Hospitality
Insurance Brokers Monthly
Justice of the Peace
Land & Liberty
Local Council Review
Local Government
 Chronicle
Local Government Review
*Management (N.Z.)
Millennium
Municipal Review
New Society
Personnel Management
Police Journal
Political Quarterly
Post
Sociological Review
Solicitors' Journal
Voluntary Action
Work Study

CLASSIFIED INDEX OF JOURNALS AND MAGAZINES

ADVERTISING AND SALESMANSHIP

Campaign
Design

Insurance Brokers Monthly

Selling Today

AGRICULTURE AND GARDENING

Amateur Gardening
Country
Country Life
Countryman
*Countryman (Aus.)
Country-side
Dairy Farmer
*Farmer, The (Zimbabwe)

Farmer's Weekly
*Farmer's Weekly (S.A.)
Farming News
Field
Fruit Trades' Journal
*Garden and Home (S.A.)
Garden News
Grower
Horticulture Week

*New Zealand Farmer
*New Zealand Gardener
Pig Farming
Power Farming
Practical Gardening
Scottish Farmer
Town and Country
  Planning

ANIMALS, ETC

Animal World
BBC Wildlife Magazine
Cage and Aviary Birds
Cat World
Countryman
Country Quest
Country-side

Dog & Country
Entomologist's Monthly
  Magazine
European Racehorse
Heredity
Horse and Hound
Horse and Pony

Horse and Rider
Pig Farming
Pony
Poultry World
Practical Fishkeeping
Shooting Times and
  Country Magazine

ARCHITECTURE AND BUILDING

Architects' Journal
Architectural Design
Architectural Review
Building
Building Societies' Gazette
Built Environment
Burlington Magazine
Contemporary Review
Design

Designers' Journal
Education
Homes and Gardens
House & Garden
House Builder
Ideal Home
International Construction
Local Historian

Middle East Construction
Municipal Review
Museums Journal
National Builder
Retail Attraction
Studio International
Town and Country
  Planning

ART AND COLLECTING

Antique Collector
Antique Dealer and
  Collectors Guide
Antiques
Apollo
Art & Artists
Art Book Review
Art & Design
Art Magazine
Artist

Arts Review
Burlington Magazine
Coin & Medal News
Coin Monthly
Contemporary Review
Country Life
Creative Camera
Design
Fine Art Trade Guild

Journal
Gemmological Newsletter
Illustrated London News
Leisure Painter
Museums Journal
Numismatic Chronicle
Stamp Magazine
Studio International
Treasure Hunting
Tribune

AVIATION

Aeromodeller
Aeroplane Monthly
Air Pictorial
*Australian Flying

*Canadian Aviation (Can.)
Flight International
Pilot
Spaceflight

Town and Country
  Planning
World Airnews (S.A.)

BLIND AND DEAF-BLIND
Published by the Royal National Institute for the Blind, see **United Kingdom Publishers**)

Braille Chess Magazine
Braille Digest

Braille Journal of
  Physiotherapy

Braille Music Magazine
Braille News Summary

Braille Radio Times
Braille Rainbow
Braille TV Times
Channels of Blessing
Crusade Messenger
Daily Bread
Diane
Fleur de Lys
Gleanings
"Law Notes" Extracts
Light of the Moon
Monthly Announcements
Moon Magazine
Moon Messenger
Moon Newspaper
Moon Rainbow
National Braille Mail
New Beacon (in Braille and letterpress)
Nuggets
Physiotherapists' Quarterly
Piano Tuners' Quarterly
Portland Magazine
Progress
Roundabout
School Magazine
Scripture Union Daily Notes
Tape Record
Theological Times
Torch
Trefoil Trail

CINEMA AND FILMS

Campaign
Films & Filming
International Broadcast Engineer
Making Better Movies
New Statesman
Photoplay
Screen International
Sight and Sound
Speech and Drama
Stand
Studio Sound
Tribune
*What's on Video (Aus.)

COMPUTERS

Computing
Personal Computer World
Practical Computing
Which Computer?
Your Computer

ECONOMICS, ACCOUNTANCY AND FINANCE

Accountancy
Accountant's Magazine
Administrative Accountant
African Business
*Aspect Magazine (Ire.)
*Australian Financial Review (Aus.)
Banker
Banking World
Building Societies Gazette
Business Credit
Business Scotland
*(Calcutta) Capital (In.)
Certified Accountant
Commerce International
*Commerce (In.)
Contemporary Review
Dairy Industries
Economic Journal
Economica
Economist
Financial Times
Financial Weekly
Grower
Insurance Brokers Monthly
*Investors Chronicle
*Irish Business
Local Government Chronicle
New Statesman
*Studies (Ire.)
Tribune
West Africa

EDUCATION

Amateur Stage
Art & Craft
British Esperantist
British Journal of Special Education
Child Education
Education
Education and Training
Guiding
Health Education Journal
Industrial Society
Junior Bookshelf
Junior Education
Local Historian
Modern Language Review
Modern Languages
Month
Mother
Municipal Review
Museums Journal
New Blackfriars
New Statesman
Nursery World
Parents Voice
Preparatory Schools Review
*Reality (Ire.)
Report
Safety Education
School Librarian
Scottish Educational Journal
Speech and Drama
Spoken English
Teacher
Theology
Times Educational Supplement
Times Educational Supplement Scotland
Times Higher Education Supplement
Together
Tribune
Unesco Courier
Universities Quarterly
Uses of English
WES Journal
World's Children

CLASSIFIED INDEX OF JOURNALS AND MAGAZINES

ENGINEERING AND MECHANICS
(See also under AGRICULTURE, ARCHITECTURE, AVIATION, MOTORING, NAUTICAL, RADIO, SCIENCE, TRADE AND COMMERCE)

*Australian Mining
Buses
Car Mechanics
Civil Engineering
Clocks
Control and Instrumentation
Design
Electrical Review
Electrical Times
Engineer
Engineering
Engineering Materials and Design
Everyday Electronics
Gas World
International Construction
Model Engineer
Model Railway Constructor
*N.Z. Engineering
Practical Woodworking
Railway Gazette
Railway Magazine
Railway World
Spaceflight

HEALTH, MEDICINE AND NURSING

Balance
British Deaf News
British Medical Journal
*Caritas (Ire.)
Community Care
Fitness
Handicapped Living
Health & Efficiency
Health Education Journal
Here's Health
Hospitality
*Irish Journal of Medical Science
*Irish Medical Times
Lancet
Mother
New Health
New Statesman
Nursery World
Nursing Times
Parents
Pharmaceutical Journal
Physiotherapy
Practitioner, The
Pulse
Quarterly Journal of Medicine
Running
Slimmer Magazine
Vegetarian

HISTORY AND ARCHAEOLOGY

Albion
Antiquity
Bedfordshire Magazine
Coin & Medal News
Contemporary Review
Country Quest
English Historical Review
Geographical Magazine
Heythrop Journal
History
History Today
Illustrated London News
In Britain
Lancashire Life
Local Historian
Museums Journal
New Blackfriars
Scottish Historical Review
*Studies (Ire.)

HOME
(See also FEMININE)

A la Carte
*Australian Home Beautiful (Aus.)
*Caritas (Ire.)
Design
DIY Today
Do It Yourself
Embroidery
*Garden and Home (S.A.)
Home Science
Homes and Gardens
House & Garden
Ideal Home
Jewish Telegraph
Modus
Mother
Parents
Practical Householder
Safety Education
*Your Family (S.A.)

LITERARY

Anglo-Welsh Review
Argo
Author
Book Collector
Books & Bookmen
*Books Ireland
Bookseller
*Canadian Author (Can.)
*Canadian Forum
*Canadian Literature
Cencrastus
*Chandrabhaga (Ind.)
Chapman
Contemporary Review
Critical Quarterly
*Dalhousie Review (Can.)
Dickensian
Edinburgh Review
Encounter
Fiction Magazine
Freelance Writer & Photography
Granta
Illustrated London News
Index on Censorship
Indexer
Information & Library Manager
*Islands (N.Z.)
Journalist
Junior Bookshelf
*Landfall (N.Z.)
Language Monthly

Library
Library Review
Literary Review
Llais Llyfrau
London Magazine
London Review of Books
*Malahat Review (Can.)
New Library World
New Society
New Statesman
Orbis
Outposts Poetry Quarterly
Powys Review
Present Tense
Publishing News
*Quill & Quire (Can.)
*Reality (Ire.)
Signal
Spectator
Stand
*Studies (Ire.)
Times Literary Supplement
Tribune
Use of English
Woman Journalist
Women's Review
Writers' Monthly
Writing
Writing Women

MOTORING

Autocar
Back Street Heroes
Car
Car Mechanics
Caravan Magazine
Commercial Motor
*Commercial Transport (Ire.)
Custom Car
Dirt Bike Rider
Mobile & Holiday Homes
Motor
Motor Cycle News
Motorcaravan and Motorhome Monthly
Performance Car
Popular Caravan
Practical Motorist
*Racing Car (Aus.)
Scootering
Sporting Cars International
Street Machine
Thoroughbred and Classic Car

MUSIC AND RECORDING

Classical Music
Early Music
Entertainment & Arts Management
Gramophone
Hi-Fi News
Jazz Journal International
Melody Maker
Music and Letters
Music & Musicians
Music Review
Music Week
Musical Opinion
Musical Times
New Hi-Fi Sound
New Musical Express
Organ
*Songwriter (Ire.)
Studio Sound
Tempo

NATURAL HISTORY

Aquarist and Pondkeeper
BBC Wildlife Magazine
Budgerigar World
Butterfly News
Cage and Aviary Birds
Country Life
Countryman
Country Quest
Country-side
Dalesman
Dog & Country
Ecologist
Entomologist's Magazine
Essex Countryside
Geological Magazine
Grower
Guiding
Lancashire Life
Museums Journal
Natural World
Naturalist
Nature
Practical Fishkeeping
Scottish Field
Shooting Times
*Swara (Africa)

NAUTICAL OR MARINE

Diver
*Modern Boating (Aus.)
Motor Boat & Yachting
Nautical Magazine
Navy International
Port of London
Practical Boat Owner
Sea Breezes
Ship & Boat International
Ships Monthly
Yachting Monthly
Yachting World
Yachts and Yachting

PHILATELY

Stamp Lover
Stamp Magazine
Stamp Monthly
Stamp News
Stamps and Foreign Stamps

PHOTOGRAPHY

Amateur Photographer
British Journal of Photography
Creative Camera
Creative Photography
Forensic Photography
Practical Photography
Studio International
35mm Photography

CLASSIFIED INDEX OF JOURNALS AND MAGAZINES

POLITICS

*Australian Quarterly
Candour
China Quarterly
Contemporary Review
*Current Affairs Bulletin (Aus.)
*Fortnight (Ire.)
Illustrated London News
International Affairs
Justice of the Peace
Labour Weekly
Liberal News
*National Times (Aus.)
New Blackfriars
New Society
New Statesman
Peace News
Political Quarterly
Round Table
Scorpion
South
*Studies (Ire.)
Town and Country Planning
Tribune
Unesco Courier
Voice of the Arab World
West Africa
*Winnipeg Free Press (Can.)
World Development
World Today

RADIO AND TELEVISION

Broadcast
Campaign
Celebrity
Gramophone
Hi-Fi News
InterMedia
International Broadcast Engineer
Listener
Media Reporter
New Statesman
Practical Wireless
Radio Times
Short-Wave Magazine
Stage and Television Today
Studio Sound
Television
Tribune
TVTimes
Video Week

RELIGION AND PHILOSOPHY

*Aryan Path (In.)
Baptist Times
British Weekly & Christian Record
Catholic Gazette
Catholic Herald
Catholic Pictorial
*Catholic Weekly (Aus.)
Christian Herald
Church News
Church of England Newspaper
*Church of Ireland Gazette
Church Times
Clergy Review
Contemporary Review
Day by Day
Downside Review
Evangelical Quarterly
Faith and Freedom
Friend
*Furrow, The (Ire.)
Heythrop Journal
Home Words
Inquirer
Jewish Telegraph
Life and Work
Methodist Recorder
Mind
Modern Churchman
Month
New Blackfriars
*Quaker Monthly
*Reality (Ire.)
Reform
Sign
*Southern Cross (S.A.)
Spiritualists Gazette
*Studies (Ire.)
Studies in Comparative Religion
Tablet
Theology
Third Way
Today
Together
Universe
War Cry
West Africa
*Word (Ire.)
World Outlook
Young Soldier

SCIENCE

(See also under AGRICULTURE, AVIATION, CINEMA, ENGINEERING, HEALTH, HISTORY, MOTORING, NATURAL HISTORY, NAUTICAL, PHOTOGRAPHY, RADIO, SPORTS, TRAVEL)

Contemporary Review
Criminologist
Data Processing
Design
Geological Magazine
Heredity
Illustrated London News
Impact of Science on Society
*Irish Press
Mind
Nature
New Blackfriars
New Scientist
Practical Electronics
Science Progress
Sociological Review
West Africa

SERVICES: NAVAL, MILITARY, AIR, AND CIVIL

Air Pictorial
Legion
Red Tape
Round Table
RUSI Journal

SPORTS, GAMES, HOBBIES AND PASTIMES

(*See also under* AGRICULTURE, ANIMALS, ART, AVIATION, CINEMA, FEMININE, HOME, MEN, MOTORING, MUSIC, PHILATELY, PHOTOGRAPHY, RADIO, THEATRE, TRAVEL)

Aeromodeller
Anglers' Mail
Angling Times
*Australasian Dirt Bike
*Australasian Sporting Shooter
*Australian Angler's Fishing World
*Australian Outdoors
Boards
Bridge International
British Chess Magazine
Camper
Camping & Trailer
Climber
Club Secretary
Cricketer International
Cycling
Darts World
Dog & Country
Edinburgh Evening News
European Racehorse
Field, The
Gemmological Newsletter

Golf Illustrated
Golf Monthly
Golf World
Great Outdoors
Guiding
Horse and Hound
Horse and Rider
In Britain
Karate
Leisure Manager
Military Modelling
Model Boats
Model Engineer
Model Railway Constructor
Parks & Sports Grounds
Popular Crafts
Practical Model Railways
Proteus
*Racing Car (Aus.)
Radio Control Models
Railway World
Running Magazine
Scale Models International

Scottish Field
Scouting
Sea Angler
Shooting Times
Ski Magazine
Snooker Scene
*South African Yachting, Power Waterski & Sail
Sport and Leisure
Sporting Life
Sports Car Monthly
Tennis
Tennis World
Trout and Salmon
Wisden Cricket Monthly
Woodworker
*Word (Ire.)
World Bowls
World Fishing
Yachting Monthly
Yachting World
Yachts and Yachting
Your Model Railway

THEATRE, DRAMA AND DANCING

(*See also under* CINEMA, MUSIC)

Amateur Stage
Ballroom Dancing Times
Celebrity
Contemporary Review
Cue
Dance & Dancers
Dancing Times
Drama
Entertainment & Arts

Management
Gambit
Illustrated London News
In Britain
Karate
*Landfall (N.Z.)
New Statesman
New Theatre Quarterly
*Performing Arts in Canada

Plays & Players
Radio Times
*Reality (Ire.)
Speech and Drama
Stage and Television Today
*Theatre Ireland Magazine
Tribune
TVTimes

TOPOGRAPHY

Bedfordshire Magazine
Cheshire Life
Country Life
Country Quest
Coventry Evening Telegraph
Cumbria
Dalesman
Derbyshire Life and Countryside
Devon Life
Dorset
Eastern Daily Press

Essex Countryside
Gloucestershire and Avon Life
Hampshire
Hertfordshire Countryside
In Britain
Inverness Courier
Kent
Kent Life
Lancashire Evening Post
Lancashire Life
Lancashire Magazine

Local Historian
Manx Life
Scottish Field
Surrey Life
Sussex Life
This England
Town and Country Planning
Warwickshire and Worcestershire Life
Yorkshire Life
Yorkshire Riding

CLASSIFIED INDEX OF JOURNALS AND MAGAZINES

TRADE AND COMMERCE
(*See also under* ARCHITECTURE, ADVERTISING, AGRICULTURE, CINEMA, ECONOMICS, ENGINEERING, MOTORING)

- Achievement
- Bookseller
- Brewing & Distilling International
- British Printer
- Business Credit
- CTN
- Cosmetic World News
- Data Processing
- Draper's Record
- European Plastics News
- Fashion Forecast
- Fashion Weekly
- Gifts International
- Grocer
- Hospitality
- *Hotel and Catering Review (Ire.)
- Industrial Participation
- Industrial Society
- PR Week
- Printing World
- Purchasing
- Retail Attraction
- Toy Trader
- Woodworker
- World Development

TRAVEL AND GEOGRAPHY

- British Esperantist
- British-Soviet Friendship
- Bulletin of Hispanic Studies
- Caravan Magazine
- Contemporary Review
- *Geo (Aus.)
- Geographical Journal
- Geographical Magazine
- Illustrated London News
- In Britain
- *Ireland of the Welcomes
- Local Historian
- London Traveletter
- *Natal Witness (S.A.)
- Railway World
- Town and Country Planning
- Traveller

UNITED KINGDOM PRESS-CUTTING AGENCIES

In the following section it should be noted that no agency can check every periodical, local paper, etc., and that some agencies cover more than others. Special attention should be given to the time limit specified by certain agencies.

International Press-Cutting Bureau (1920), 224-236 Walworth Road, London, SE17 1JE *T.* 01-708 2113. *T.A.* Adverburo, London, SE1. *Subscription rates:* On application. *Representatives:* Brussels, Copenhagen, Geneva, Madrid, Milan, Paris, Lisbon, Stockholm, Berlin, Helsinki, The Hague.

Newsclip (incorporating **Apcut Ltd.**), 52-53 Fetter Lane, London, EC4A 1BL *T.* 01-353 7191. *Subscription rates:* On application.

Press Information (Scotland), Ltd., Virginia House, 62 Virginia Street, Glasgow, G1 1TX *T.* 041-552 6767. Comprehensive Scottish cuttings service. *Subscription rates:* On application.

OVERSEAS PRESS-CUTTING AGENCIES

AUSTRALIA

Australian Press Cuttings Agency Reg., Stalbridge Chambers, 443 Little Collins Street, Melbourne, Victoria, 3000. *T.* 67-5133. $40 to $45 per 100 cuttings.

CANADA

Canadian Press Clipping Services, 4601 Yonge Street, North York, Ontario M2N 5L9 *T.* 416-221-1660.

INDIA

International Clipping Service, Lakshmi Building, Sir P. Mehta Road, Fort, Bombay, 1. *T.* 259258. *T.A.* Orientclip. *Partner:* Rajan K. Shah. Supplies Press Cuttings of news, editorials, articles, advertisements, press releases, etc., from all India and Goa papers. Undertakes compilation of statistical reports on competitive Press advertising pertaining to all products.

NEW ZEALAND

Chong Services: Press Cutting Bureau, P.O. Box 68 – 143, Newton, Auckland. All New Zealand newspapers and most magazines covered, any selected topic, $15 per week plus 50c. per clipping.

SOUTH AFRICA

S.A. Press Cutting Agency, 2nd Floor, Lionel House, Pickering Street, Durban, Natal. *T.* 370403. *T.A.* Newscut, Durban. English and Afrikaans newspapers and trade journals from Zambia to the Cape. *Minimum rates:* R.45.00 per 100 cuttings.

UNITED STATES

Burrelle's Press Clipping Service (1888), 75 East Northfield Avenue, Livingston, New Jersey 07039. *T.* 201-992-6600.

Luce Press Clippings, Inc., 420 Lexington Avenue, New York, N.Y., 10017.

New England Newsclip Agency, Inc., 5 Auburn Street, P.O. Box 91 2F, Framingham, Mass., 01701-9128. *T.* 617-879 4460.

Reviews on File, Walton, N.Y., 13856. *T.* 607-865-4226. *Owner:* Dorothy M. Brandt. Back clippings on authors.

index

African Journals, 87-9
  Publishers, 186-88
  South, Journals, 105-8
  South Publishers, 188-90
Agencies, News, 109-15
  Photographic, 278-91
  Press, 109-15
  Press-Cutting, 510-11
Agents, Art, 267, 271-3
  Film, Play, Radio and Television, 263
  Literary, 241-63
Agreement, Florence, 421-2
  Net Book, 422
Agreements, Commission, 421
  Outright Sale, 421
  Profit-sharing, 421
  Publishers, 420-2
  Publishing, 373
  Royalty, 420-1
Anniversaries of interest
  to Writers, 438-48
Anonymous and Pseudonymous Works, 361-2
Art Agents, 267, 271-3
  Studios, Commercial, 271-3
Artists and Designers, Code of
    Professional Conduct, 269-70
  Clubs and Societies, 326-55
  Designers and Photographers, 265-97
  and Income Tax, 395-404
  Markets for, 271-4
  Opportunities for Freelance, 265-8
Arts Associations, Regional, 348-9
Asian Publishers, 186-8
Associations, 326-55
Australian, Broadcasting, 237
  Commercial Broadcasting, 237
  Journals, 89-95
  Literary Agents, 259
  Press-Cutting Agency, 510
  Publishers, 173-6
Authors, Clubs and Societies, 326-55
  Lending and Copyright Society Ltd, 429-30
  Society of, 423-5
Awards, Literary, 306-55

Book Clubs, 203-4, 387
  Packagers, 199-202
Books for Writers, 449-56
  Writing, 122-207
British Broadcasting Corporation, 226-31
British Copyright, 357-75

Broadcasting, 226-40
  Addresses, 228-40
  Copyright, 370-2
  Rights and Terms, 227-8

Cable Programmes, 370-2, 430
Calendar, Journalists, 438-48
Calendars, Photographs for, 275-6
Canadian, Broadcasting, 238
  Journals, 95-7
  Press-Cutting Agency, 510
  Publishers, 176-8
Changes of names of Magazines, 498
Character Merchandising, 264
Classified Index of Journals and
    Magazines, 499-509
Clubs, Book, 203-4, 387
  Societies, etc., 326-55
Code of Professional Conduct, 269-70
Commercial Art Studios, 271-3
Commission Agreements, 421
Commonwealth and South African
    Journals, 87-108
  Publishers, 173-88
Copyright, 357-83
  Acts, 375
  Assignment of, 362
  British, 357-75
  Cable programmes, 370-2, 430
  Duration of, 367-8
  Infringement of, 363-7
  Music, 298
  Protection, 361, 374-5
  Protection Society, Ltd, Mechanical, 304
  Sound Recording, 369-70
  U.S., 376-83
Correcting Proofs, 470-80
Criminal Libel, 393-4

Design, 266
Designers and Artists, Code, 269-70
Designs for Cards, 273-4
Drawings for Cards, 273-4

Editorial Services, 481-9
European Literary Agents, 260-2
Exhibitions, Photographic, 296

Fees, Artists', 267
Film Agents, 263

Films, Copyright, 368-9
　Screenplays for, 220-2
　Writing for, 218-9
Fine Art, 265
Florence Agreement, 421-2
Folio, 266
Freelance, Artists, 265-8
　Photographer, 277

Galley Proofs, 461
Ghana, Publishers, 186
Ghost Writing, 481
Government Offices and Public Services, 492-7
Grants and Income Tax, 396-7
Graphic Designers, 268
Greetings Cards, Drawings for, 273-4
　Photographs for, 275-6

Hong Kong Publishers, 186-7

Illustrations and Design, 266
Illustrations, 292, 460
Illustrators, *see* Artists
Income Tax, 395-404
　Arts Council Grants, 396-7
　Royalties, 396
Independent Broadcasting, 232-6
　Radio, 234-6
　Television, 232-4
Index, Classified, of Journals, 499-509
Indexing, 490
India, Broadcasting, 238
　Commercial Radio, 238
　Journals, 97-9
　Press-Cutting Agency, 510
　Publishers, 178-82
Insurance, The Writer and National, *see* Social Security
International Reply Coupons, 13
International Standard Book Numbering, 205-6, 432
Irish Broadcasting, 238-9
　Journals, 99-103
　Music Publisher, 302
　Publishers, 182-4

Joint Authors, 362, 432, 433
Journalists' Calendar, 438-48
　Clubs, 326-55
Journals, *see* individual countries

Kenya, Journals, 87-8
　Publishers, 187

Lending and Copyright Society Ltd, Authors, 429-30
Lending Right, Public, 431-7
Libel, 388-99
　Criminal, 393-4

Libraries, 450-1, 452
　Picture, 278-91
　see Government Offices
Light Entertainment, Radio, 226-7
Literary Agents, 241-63
　Foreign, 259-62
　United Kingdom, 241-54
　United States, 254-9
Literary Prizes and Awards, 306-25
Literary Services, 481-9
Local Radio, B.B.C., 230-1
　Independent, 234-6
London Theatres, 212-3

Magazines, *see* individual countries
　Ceased Publication, 498
　Changes, Mergers, 498
　Classified Index, 499-509
　Publishers, United Kingdom, 85-7
　Writing for, 11-121
Malaysia, Publishers, 187
Manuscripts, After acceptance of, 460
　Submission of, 458-60
Marketing a Play, 208-11
Markets for Plays, 212-7
　for Screenplays, 218-9
　for Poetry, 116-121
　see Classified Index, 499-509
Mechanical-Copyright Protection Society Ltd., 304
Merchandising, Character, 264
Music for Radio, 226
Music Publishers, 298-304
　Ireland, 302
　New Zealand, 302
　United Kingdom, 298-302
　United States, 302-4
Musicians, Clubs and Societies, 326-55

Net Book Agreement, 422
New Zealand, Broadcasting, 239
　Journals, 103-5
　Literary Agents, 261-2
　Music Publisher, 302
　Press-Cutting Agency, 510
　Publishers, 184-6
News Agencies, 109-115
Newspapers, 11-121
　Writing for, 11-121
Nigeria Journal, 88
　Publishers, 187

Outright Sale, 421
Overseas Journals, Writing for, 12-13
　Postage, *see* International Reply Coupons
　Press-Cutting Agencies, 510-11

Packagers, Book, 199-202
Page-on-galley Proofs, 461
Page Proofs, 461

Performing Right Society Ltd., 304-5
Performing Right Tribunal, 372
Photographer, Freelance, 277
Photographers, Markets for, 275-6
Photographic, Agencies and Picture Libraries, 278-91
  Exhibitions, 296
Picture Libraries, 278-91
Picture Research, 292-7
Play Agents, 263
  Manuscript Preparation, 220-2
  Marketing, 208-11
  Publishers, 217
Plays, Markets for, 212-7
  Radio, 226
Poetry, Market for, 116-121
Poetry Prizes, *see* Literary Prizes and Awards
Preparation of Typescript, 457-61
Press Agencies, 109-115
Press-Cutting Agencies, 510-11
  Foreign, 510-11
  United Kingdom, 510
  United States, 511
Presses, Small, 117-8
Prizes and Awards, Literary, 306-25
Production Services, 481-9
Profit Sharing, 421
Proof Correcting, 470-80
Proofs, Stages of, 461
Provincial Theatres, 214-6
Pseudonyms and Titles, 360
Public Lending Right, 431-7
  Authorship, 432
  Illustrators, 432, 433, 436
  Payments, 431, 435
  Sampling, 434-5
Public Services Government Offices and, 492-7
Publishers, *see* individual countries
  Agreement, 420-2
  Association, 347
  Music, 298-304
Publishing, Poetry, 116-121
  Vanity, 119, 207

Radio, 226-7, 228
  Agents, 263
  B.B.C. Local, 230-1
  Independent, 234-6
  Plays for, 226
  Talks for, 228
  Writing for, 226-40
Reference Sources for Writers, 449-54
Regional Arts Associations, 348-9
Reprography, 430
Research for writers, 449-54
Rights and Terms in Broadcasting, 227-8
  Serial, 385-6
  Subsidiary, 384-7

Royalties and Income Tax, 396
Royalty Agreements, 420-1

Screenplays for Films, 220-2
  Markets for, 218-9
Serial Rights, 385-6
Services, Editorial, Literary and Production, 481-9
Short Stories, Radio, 226
  and see Classified Index
Signs Used for Correcting Proofs, 470-80
Singapore Publishers, 187-8
Small Presses, 117-8
Social Security, 405-19
  Benefits, 413-9
  Contributions, 405-12
Societies and Clubs, 326-55
Society of Authors, 423-5
Sound Recordings, Copyright, 369-70
South Africa, Broadcasting, 239-40
  Journals, 105-8
  Literary Agents, 262
  Press-Cutting Agency, 510
  Publishers, 188-90
Submission of Manuscripts, 458-60
Subsidiary Rights, 384-7
Sudan Journal, 88
Syndicates, News and Press Agencies, 109-115

Talks for Radio, 228
  for Television, 228
Tanzania, Journals, 88
  Publishers, 188
Television, 226, 228, 232-4
  Agents, 263
  Independent, 232-4
  Writing for, 223-5
Theatre, Writing for, 208-17
Theatres, London, 212-3
  Provincial, 214-6
Titles and Pseudonyms, 360
Touring Companies, 216-7
Translation, 490-1
Typescript, Preparation and Submission, 457-61

Uganda, Journals, 88
  Publisher, 188
United Kingdom, Journals, 13-85
  Literary Agents, 241-54
  Magazine Publishers, 85-7
  Music Publishers, 298-302
  Press-Cutting Agencies, 510
  Publishers, 122
United States Broadcasting, 240
  Copyright, 376-83
  Journals, 108
  Literary Agents, 254-9
  Music Publishers, 302-4
  Press-Cutting Agencies, 511
  Publishers, 190-8

Vanity Publishing, 119, 207
Verse, Markets for, *see* Markets for Poetry
Verses for Cards, 273-4

Word Processing, 462-9
 Discs, 468
 Microcomputers, 464-5
 Printer, 465
 Programs, 466-7
 Visual display unit, 466
Writer, and Income Tax, 395-404
Writer, and Social Security, 405-19
 Books for, 449-56

Writers, Research and Reference
 Sources for, 449-54
Writers' Guild of Great Britain, 426-8
Writing Books, 122-207
 for Newspapers, Magazines, etc.,
  11-121
 for Overseas Markets, 12-3
 for Television, 223-5
 Theatre, Films, Radio and Television,
  208-40

Zambia Publisher, 188
Zimbabwe Journals, 88-9
 Publishers, 188